INTERNATIONAL MACROECONOMICS

As the title suggests, a study of international macroeconomics, covers an enormous range of issues. Given such a broad area much of the literature has tended to focus on sub-divisions or has been in the form of edited volumes. In *International Macroeconomics: Theory and Policy*, Victor Argy has drawn the issues together to present a phenomenal, up-to-date and comprehensive coverage of the entire subject.

The book has four principal objectives. The first is to describe the evolution of and experience with global exchange rate regimes. This includes a detailed description of and evaluation of the gold standard regimes, the IMF system, the float and the EMS. The second objective is to introduce the reader to a detailed and rigorous analysis of open economy models. The coverage is extensive, including the Mundell–Fleming model and its many variants. The variants include the well known Dornbusch and Branson models, models with flexible wages and prices, portfolio balance models, disequilibrium models, two and three country models and models with traded and non-traded goods. There are also chapters on the New Classical contributions and an extensive review of exchange rate models. The third aim is to apply the model framework to address key policy issues, such as desirable macro targets, how to assign instruments to targets, how to choose an exchange rate regime, the advantages and disadvantages of macro policy co-ordination and how to evaluate the global macro performance. The fourth objective is to review some country experiences of macro policy, notably those of Thatcherism, Reaganomics, Japan, Australia and New Zealand. The style is clear, persuasive and to the point. Although the presentation is rigorous and mathematics are used extensively, they are kept as simple as possible. *International Macroeconomics: Theory and Policy* presents a balanced assessment of the key issues, post-Maastricht, in international open economy macroeconomics and international monetary economics.

Professor Victor Argy, late Professor of Economics at Macquarie University, Sydney, Australia, had an outstanding reputation in the field of international macroeconomics. He served as Chief of the Financial Studies division at the IMF, as a consultant to both the IMF and at the OECD and as a visiting scholar to the Bank of Japan and to Japan's Ministry of Finance, and from 1983 he had been a regular Visiting Professor at the Sorbonne.

INTERNATIONAL MACROECONOMICS

THEORY AND POLICY

VICTOR ARGY

LONDON AND NEW YORK

First published 1994
by Routledge
11 New Fetter Lane, London EC4P 4EE

Simultaneously published in the USA and Canada
by Routledge
29 West 35th Street, New York, NY 10001

Typeset in Compugraphic Times by
Mathematical Composition Setters Ltd, Salisbury, Wiltshire

Printed and bound in Great Britain by
T.J. Press Ltd, Padstow, Cornwall

British Library Cataloguing in Publication Data

A catalogue record for this book is available from the British Library

Library of Congress Cataloging in Publication Data

Argy, Victor E.
Internationl macroeconomics : theory and policy /
Victor Argy.
    p. cm.
Includes bibliographical references and index.
ISBN 0-415-09822-X.—ISBN 0-415-09823-8
1. Macroeconomics. 2. Foreign exchange—
Econometric models.
I. Title.
HB172.5.A73 1994   93-4621
339—dc20   CIP

ISBN 0-415-09822-X
ISBN 0-415-09823-8 (pbk)

Contents

Figures

Tables

Acknowledgements

I am indebted to many people for help and encouragement in the production of this work. In particular, I would like to acknowledge helpful comments from Dr Percy Ip, Dr Costas Karfakis, Mr Marc Lombard, Mr Graham Madden, Professor Mitsuaki Okabe, Professor Leslie Stein, Dr Graeme Wells and some anonymous referees. I have tried versions of chapters of the book on some postgraduate classes both at Macquarie University and at the University of Paris 1 (Sorbonne) over the last three years. Students' reactions have been very helpful to me.

I also owe a special debt to Professors A.D. Browlie and C. Simkin who first impressed on me the importance of dealing with economic issues rigorously.

Mr Alan Jarvis, Economics Editor, and Alison Kirk, Assistant Economics Editor, of Routledge have provided very helpful guidance on the structure of the book and on editorial aspects.

I acknowledge a very special debt to my secretary, Ms Debbie Jeffery, who was completely responsible for the preparation of the text from the start and who worked long tedious hours with great skill, accuracy and patience at several drafts of the book. Debbie provided much more than secretarial assistance; she also had administrative responsibility, attending to all the correspondence, organisation, presentation and questions associated with the preparation of the book.

Finally, I would like to thank my wife, Renate, my daughter, Jacqueline and my son, Frederick, for their continued support in writing this book. Their patience, help in tracking references in the library and their willingness to forego long periods of my company is very much appreciated.

General introduction

MARKET FOR THE BOOK

The book assumes that the reader has completed an intermediate course in macroeconomics which includes some international macroeconomics. It is thus intended as a senior undergraduate and graduate text.

Although mathematics is extensively used, the level required is very simple. The reader is expected to be familiar with elementary calculus and some straightforward algebra, particularly the latter. It is assumed that the reader would be able to solve a set of n equations for n variables. This is a minimal demand. The more mathematical reader could use matrix algebra to arrive at the solutions found in the text. The less mathematical can solve by simple successive substitution.

Some chapters are more difficult than others. Part I is deliberately drafted for the more general reader. The more difficult chapters in the book are 13–17, 21, 22, 24, Part V, 39 and 45. It is envisaged that a selection of the easier chapters or parts of them could, in combination, offer a package which could be the base text for a senior undergraduate or a senior business management course in international macroeconomics. The larger package could be used for a master's or PhD course programme.

STRUCTURE OF THE BOOK

The basic intention of the book is

a) to introduce the reader to a rigorous analysis of open economy models of the kind one finds in the literature;

b) to apply the framework to a very wide range of macro policy issues;

c) to review some country experiences of macro policy (notably those of Thatcherism, Reaganomics, Japan and Australia–New Zealand).

Part I is intended to be a purely descriptive review of the evolution of and experiences with exchange rate regimes over the last 110 years or so. It provides an important background, and a historical perspective, to the chapters which follow, easing the transition to more technical analysis. Chapters 1–4 evaluate respectively the experiences of the gold standard regime (1880–1914, 1925–31), the IMF system (1946–73), the float (1973 to date) and the European Monetary System (EMS) (1979 to date and still in the process of evolution). The chapter on the EMS also reviews and interprets the exchange crises which occurred in late 1992. It provides detailed references to the various parts in the text which deal with the EMS and its variants. The last chapter in Part I describes the evolution of financial interdependence amongst the industrial countries.

Part II is essentially a survey of open economy models found in the literature. The methodology employed is that of comparative statics. We analyse the end result of a policy change, without reference to the dynamic path of adjustment.

Chapter 6 presents in some detail the best known open economy model, that first developed in the early 1960s by Mundell and Fleming (the so-called MF model). Because of the importance of this model, Chapter 7 explains in detail its strengths and limitations. The model predicts fairly well outcomes over a year or so but is deficient for the analysis of shorter periods (in part because of the presence of J curves) as well as for longer periods (because now we need to accommodate price–wage adjustments and stock–wealth effects).

The chapters which follow in Part II (8–17) are extensions and modifications of the base MF model, with which results are frequently compared. The MF model thus becomes a reference point for the chapters which follow. The methodology employed is to introduce one major modification at a time and show how that alters outcomes, primarily of the effects of monetary and fiscal policies for fixed and flexible rate regimes. This methodology is important for teaching purposes. First it avoids too many complexities all at once at this early stage. Second, more importantly, it allows the reader to understand how a single change affects the working of the adjustment mechanism.

Chapter 8 accommodates wage and price adjustment. Chapter 9 focuses on simple models of product market disequilibrium. Chapter 10 is a general introduction to the portfolio balance model of the monetary sector, and Chapter 11 accommodates the portfolio balance model with wealth in a simple open economy framework. Chapter 12 is an introduction to the micro-elasticities approach to a devaluation. Chapters 13–15 deal with the large-country case. Chapter 16 extends the large-country case to a world which comprises three countries: two giants and one smaller. This three-country framework is applied to the case of the EMS.

Part III introduces simple dynamics. It opens with two very well known dynamic models of the impacts under flexible rates of a monetary expansion: those of

Dornbusch and Branson. Chapter 20 examines the dynamic adjustment to a fiscal deficit, the emphasis being on highlighting differences between short- and longer-run effects. Chapter 21 accommodates J curves in an MF–Dornbusch type model. Chapter 22 examines the important question of the output loss over time from a restrictive money growth policy. The emphasis here is on the determinants of the output loss.

Part IV is a general treatment of New Classical themes. Chapter 23 summarises the policy-impotence hypothesis. Chapter 24 extends the analysis to the open economies, focusing on the dynamic effects of anticipated monetary and fiscal policies under flexible rates. Chapter 25 is an evaluation of the literature which argues that discretionary monetary policy will deliver the worst of all worlds: more inflation and no change in unemployment. The emphasis in the chapter is on the role and importance, in theory and practice, of central bank independence. Chapter 26 is a general treatment of the Ricardian equivalence hypothesis.

Part V is important. It tries to bring together, in a much larger model, the elements introduced as original extensions of the MF model. Chapter 27 focuses on modelling the goods and money markets. Chapter 28 is essentially a survey of the literature on supply-side modelling. Chapter 29 raises fundamental methodological questions about how to undertake medium- to long-run analysis. The models presented are extremely difficult to solve. Chapter 30 uses a simpler, but nevertheless now broader, model and it is shown how such a model is solvable. It is shown that because of the complexities here the solutions can sometimes be perverse, often ambiguous.

Part VI surveys the theoretical and empirical literature on (a) reduced form models of exchange rates, (b) foreign exchange market efficiency and (c) financial integration.

Part VII addresses policy issues. How should monetary and fiscal policy be designed? How do we go about choosing an exchange rate regime? Policy questions necessarily can only be addressed after the analytical treatments in Parts I–V have been completed. We cannot, for example, deal with the question of how monetary and fiscal policy can be used or combined until we know how such policies impact on the economy in the short, medium and longer runs.

Chapter 34 looks more closely at the question of how to rationalise the targets of macro policy. Chapter 35 defines different types of policy regimes and provides a framework to evaluate macro performance. Chapter 36 addresses the question of the criteria to apply in choosing an exchange rate regime. These criteria are then applied to a variety of exchange rate regimes, including an EMS-type system. The theme is developed further in subsequent chapters.

Chapter 37 looks at the historical evolution of the debate over policy rules versus discretion. Chapter 38 reviews the most recent literature on how monetary fiscal policies ought to be combined to achieve internal and external balance. It also looks at how fiscal and exchange rate policy might be combined, in an adjustable peg regime, to achieve the same two objectives.

Chapter 39 uses a two-country model, developed in earlier chapters, to evaluate

Part I

GLOBAL EXCHANGE RATE REGIMES

In the last hundred years or so the industrial world has seen four principal types of international monetary regimes: first, the gold standard regime, which operated between 1880 and 1914 and again between 1925 and 1931; second, the managed float regime, which operated between 1918 and 1925 and again from 1973 to date; third, the IMF (Bretton Woods) type regime which functioned between 1946 and 1973; fourth, a collective exchange rate arrangement such as that embodied in the European Monetary System (EMS), which came into operation in 1979.

These four regimes are distinguishable, principally, by their differing prescriptions on exchange rates and the adjustment mechanism. At one extreme, in the gold standard regime exchange rates are permanently fixed and adjustment occurs by allowing deficits/surpluses to act on the volume of money. At the other extreme – the managed float regime – exchange rates are principally determined by market forces; in turn these changes in exchange rates serve to equilibrate the demand and supply for foreign exchange. The IMF regime represents, in intention, the intermediate case. It allows exchange rate flexibility in the long term to correct fundamental disequilibria but, at the same time, there is an obligation on participant countries to maintain the exchange rate fixed within a narrow band in the short term. The EMS is also an intermediate regime; amongst participating countries, the exchange rate principles parallel those of the IMF; at the same time member currencies jointly float *vis-à-vis* the main currencies outside the EMS.

These four regimes are described in some detail in the first four chapters of the book.

Part II will develop, in detail, the theme that the effects of monetary and fiscal policies depend not only on the exchange rate regime in operation but also, critically, on the degree of capital mobility. It is important, therefore, before we embark on such analyses to describe the evolution in the degree of financial interdependence amongst industrial countries. Chapter 5 in Part I addresses this theme. We show how, beginning in the late 1950s, there has been a gradual progress in the direction of greater financial integration. In today's world, with very few exceptions, there are few remaining barriers to the movement of capital.

1

The gold standard regime

INTRODUCTION

Although it is now over sixty years since the gold standard regime has been in operation it continues to appeal to and to cast a spell over many economists, some very distinguished, and policy-makers.

As noted in the introduction a gold standard regime was in place on two occasions: between 1880 and 1914 and again between 1925 and 1931.

In this chapter we propose to spell out the general principles underlying the gold standard, to explain briefly its workings on the two occasions and to outline why it ultimately broke down in 1931. (For general references see Meade (1951), Yeager (1976), Ford (1962), Moggridge (1972), Brown (1940), Hawtrey (1931) and Kindleberger (1973).)

GOLD STANDARD RULES

The gold standard regime has conventionally been associated with three rules of the game. The first rule is that in each participating country the price of the domestic currency must be fixed in terms of gold. The second rule is that there must be a free import and export of gold. The third rule is that the surplus country, which is gaining gold, should allow its volume of money to increase while the deficit country, which is losing gold, should allow its volume of money to fall.

The first two rules together ensure that exchange rates between participating countries are fixed within fairly narrow limits. With the price of any two currencies fixed in terms of gold the implied exchange rate between the two currencies is also fixed and any significant deviation from this fixed rate will be rapidly eliminated by arbitrage operations.

Suppose, for example, that the two currencies concerned are the US dollar and the franc and suppose that $40 exchange for an ounce of gold in the USA while 160 francs exchange for an ounce of gold in France. This fixes the bilateral exchange rate at 4 francs to $1. Suppose, too, to begin with, that arbitrage (i.e. the converting and shipping of gold) is costless. Now consider the case where France is running a deficit. The excess demand for the dollar cannot produce an exchange rate such that more than 4 francs would sell for $1. At that rate no one would want to sell francs because it would be cheaper to sell francs for gold, ship the gold to the USA and convert the gold there into US dollars. In other words, traders could get more US dollars per franc by transacting in gold than by selling francs for dollars in the foreign exchange market. By the same token if France were in surplus the exchange rate could not be such that fewer than 4 francs would sell for $1; for, in that case, no one would want to sell US dollars at that rate since it would be cheaper to convert US dollars into gold, ship the gold to France and convert it into francs at the official rate.

In reality, of course, there are costs associated with the buying and shipping of gold (e.g. a service charge by the central authority, a shipping charge, insurance costs and a loss of interest during transit). This means that deviations from the implicit exchange rate are quite possible so long as these deviations are equal to or less than the costs of transacting in gold. Suppose that these costs amount, roughly, to 5 per cent; then the exchange rate could fluctuate within the range of, say, $1 for 3.8–4.2 francs (the so-called gold points) without any shipment of gold. The rate of $1 for 3.8 francs is, from the point of view of France, its gold import point while the rate of $1 for 4.2 francs is its gold export point. In other words, if the French franc is weak and the exchange rate is being pushed beyond 4.2 francs to the dollar, France will lose gold to the USA, while if the US dollar is weak and the exchange rate is being pressed below 3.8 francs to the dollar the USA will lose gold to France.

The third rule, requiring the volume of money to be linked in each participating country to balance of payments developments, provided an 'automatic' mechanism of adjustment which ensured that, ultimately, any balance of payments disequilibria would be corrected. There are several potential mechanisms by which changes in the money supply serve to correct the disequilibria. One mechanism is through the variations in the interest rate which induce corrective movements of capital; for example, the surplus country would lower its interest rate while the deficit country would raise its interest rate and capital would flow from the former to the latter. Another mechanism, through the goods markets, operates more slowly. Deflation and inflation of the money supplies will lead to relative changes in prices and/or real output that will correct the imbalances. The adjustment through prices is associated with the classical price–specie flow mechanism while the adjustment through output is associated with (later) Keynesian thinking.

The precise operation of the three rules will vary depending on the institutional arrangements. Consider, first, a primitive monetary system represented by a gold specie standard, where money is made up only of gold coins with a fixed gold content and the national mint will always supply gold by melting down gold coins or coin gold supplied to it by the public. In these conditions adjustment is simple and automatic. The exchange rate cannot move outside the gold points; gold will flow out (after being melted down) at the gold export point and will flow in at the gold import point.

Next consider the simplest gold bullion standard where money is made up of notes only, which are themselves backed 100 per cent by gold. In this case the outcomes and method of adjustment are effectively the same. For example, instead of melting coins for payment notes are presented for conversion into gold. Suppose, however, that notes in circulation are not backed 100 per cent by gold but, initially, by, say, only 50 per cent gold and there is no legal reserve requirement. The balance of the backing is assumed to be in loans to the private sector (commercial banks are assumed, at this point, to be non-existent). The central bank balance sheet in its simplest form would now have the note issue in its liabilities (say 100 units) and half of that (50 units) as loans and the other half (50 units) as gold in its assets. Now suppose that a payment of 5 units needs to be made overseas. Notes and gold will now both drop by 5 units and so gold reserves will have fallen by 10 per cent while the volume of money will have fallen by only 5 per cent. Partial backing, therefore, may weaken the corrective mechanism of the gold standard and threaten the reserve position. The smaller this backing the greater the danger that the corrective mechanism might not work before reserves are severely depleted. By contrast, with 100 per cent backing the corrective process cannot fail since the volume of money cannot be reduced 100 per cent.

Suppose, now, that a legal reserve ratio of the order of 40 per cent is imposed while the central bank, *de facto*, holds 50 per cent. (It is necessary to hold excess reserves if the strict letter of the law is not going to be broken since with notes and gold falling by equal amounts the reserve ratio falls.) Clearly, to restore the reserve ratio of 50 per cent a reduction in gold of 10 per cent must be associated with a reduction in notes of 10 per cent as well and hence loans, in our example, must also fall by 10 per cent. The reduction in gold will then also be associated with a reduction in the domestic assets of the central bank. How much of this process is automatic and how much is discretionary depends, of course, on the legal reserve requirement and the margin of excess reserves.

Now consider the case where commercial banks exist and suppose that money is made up of notes as well as bank deposits. (To place this in historical perspective, in Britain the proportion of money held in the form of demand deposits had increased from some 35 per cent in 1885 to some 60 per cent in 1913.) The non-bank private sector now holds notes as well as deposits while the banks hold, say, a proportion of their deposit liabilities as deposits with the central bank. In turn the central bank has domestic assets as well as gold. Now central bank reserve ratios may apply only to the note liability or may extend as well to the deposit liabilities or may be different for the two forms of liabilities. Clearly, in this more complicated system the possible slippages are greater; how the total volume of money will respond to a change in gold reserves will clearly depend not only on central bank legal reserve requirements but also on cash/deposit and notes/deposit conventions by commercial banks and the private sector respectively. The adjustment will now be automatic, proportionate and predictable only so long as the relevant ratios (of the commercial banks, central banks and private sectors) are all rigidly defined and exactly observed.

Suppose, finally, that the system in force is a gold exchange standard, where one country's currency (the reserve currency) is held as 'reserves' by the rest of the world while the reserve currency itself is backed by gold. To take the simplest case, if central banks hold their foreign exchange as deposits with the commercial banks in the reserve currency country, settlement of disequilibria may be effected by changes in the ownership of deposits with the commercial banks without any change in the total volume of their deposits or in their cash reserves. For example, if sterling were the reserve currency, a British deficit might be financed by the switch in the ownership of a deposit from, say, a British resident to a foreign central bank. In this case there would be no automatic adjustment. There would also be an asymmetry in that the full burden of adjustment would now fall on the rest of the world. The automaticity of a gold standard regime in this case (with a reserve currency) would be further weakened. (See on this also Chapter 13.)

THE FIRST GOLD STANDARD PERIOD 1880–1914

Although by 1819–21 Britain was already on a full-fledged gold standard, it was not until about 1880 that most of the industrial world joined Britain in meeting the conditions of the gold standard. This regime was to endure until the outbreak of the First World War.

How is it possible to account for the survival of the gold standard fixed rate regime over a thirty-five-year period? Several reasons may be advanced. First, the world economy was relatively stable: there were no major wars or disturbances; governments and their budgets were relatively small and hence were not a volatile element in the economy; monetary conditions and the financial environment tended to be relatively stable; the period was distinguished by powerful long-term expansionist influences while, more important, output growth was relatively steady. Second, economic cycles of participating countries were highly synchronised, thus averting the emergence of large disequilibria. Third, it is likely, as Triffin (1964) has argued, that substantial discrepancies in cost competitiveness were not allowed to surface because participating countries exercised *ex ante* constraint in the conduct of their monetary policies.

Fourth, sterling's dominant role at the centre of the world financial scene considerably facilitated the workings of the gold standard system. For almost every year in the thirty-five years of the gold standard Britain had a current account surplus. Indeed her basic economic strength is evidenced by the fact that these surpluses actually grew over the time period. This surplus tended to fluctuate by only small margins over economic cycles and this meant that Britain's task became essentially one of tailoring her lending overseas to the fluctuations in her current account; this she managed with considerable success. This is so despite the fact that Britain had relatively meagre international reserves. For example, if we take the ratio of reserves to imports as a very rough measure of a country's reserve adequacy, Bloomfield (1959) found that the UK's ratio was very low in a sample of ten countries. Also, although Britain's sterling liabilities to foreigners exceeded her gold holdings (by 1913 they were over twice as much) sterling was never under speculative attack in those years.

Fifth, the adjustment mechanism appeared to have worked relatively painlessly and without undue strain on the system. In general, an outflow (inflow) of gold tended to be associated with an increase (decrease) in the central bank discount rate. In turn, these variations in the discount rate acted to correct the external position. For the UK at least, the central bank rate mechanism worked so quickly and effectively that any changes did not have to be sustained for too long. Much of the evidence now suggests that the adjustment came about largely through changes in the flow of capital which was particularly sensitive to changes in the UK bank rate (Bloomfield 1959; Ford 1962). Economic activity and employment, it appears, were only marginally affected by the bank rate. The effects on relative prices, to the extent that they occurred, would have been considerably delayed and, with early reversals of policies, dispersed over time. Indeed the evidence suggests that movements in price levels were predominantly in the same rather than in the opposite direction in participating countries.

Sixth, and finally, over the period as a whole the supplies of gold accruing to central authorities were adequate to meet the needs of the regime. Ford (1962), in summarising the role of monetary gold stocks in this period, asserts: 'the main role of the increasing gold supplies was to facilitate the workings of the international payments system, so that as trade and payment flows expanded the system was never permanently braked by sharply rising interest rates through shortage of cash ...' (pp. 24–7).

THE SECOND GOLD STANDARD PERIOD 1925–1931

Background

The dislocation of the war had made it impossible to return immediately to the gold standard. Its enormous success, however, in the pre-war years and the absence of clearly defined alternatives left no doubt in the minds of policy-makers and the financial community about the desirability of a return to the gold standard as soon as conditions rendered it appropriate. This attitude is most clearly reflected in the views of the UK's Cunliffe Committee set up in January 1918 to examine currency issues in the years after the war. Its report presented a glowing picture of the workings of the pre-war gold standard and concluded that the objective of policy was to restore the gold standard along traditional lines at pre-war parity as soon as feasible.

In the years immediately following the war exchange rates for the major currencies were allowed to move more or less in line with market forces. Indeed, in the period 1920–4 the sterling–dollar exchange rate fluctuated with very little official intervention. Its pre-war parity had been $4.86, but by early 1920 it had dropped to a low $3.18, 35 per cent below par. Intent on restoring pre-war parity and strengthening the currency, the British authorities responded by implementing severe deflationary policies in 1920–1. This led to a sharp drop in wages and prices (the latter falling by as much as 50–60 per cent from their peak levels in 1920); at the same time unemployment rose substantially. In the event, the exchange rate rose to about $4.2 by early 1922. Policy reversals in 1922–3, which now gave greater priority to domestic over external considerations, were successful in bringing down the rate of unemployment. Prices, however, remained relatively stable in the two years between March 1922 and March 1924. The exchange rate moved roughly in line with relative prices in the UK and USA, strengthening as US prices rose between 1922 and 1923 and then weakening as US prices fell again in the year to 1924. Then, in the year that followed, US prices rose more rapidly than British prices and, at the same time, foreign exchange markets began to anticipate a return to gold at parity. The combination of influences forced the rate up to $4.78 by early 1925, only $1\frac{1}{2}$ per cent below parity.

The Chamberlain–Bradbury Committee, set up in June 1924 to take up once again the issues originally raised by the Cunliffe Committee, was now sufficiently impressed by the strength of sterling to recommend an immediate return to gold at parity. Winston Churchill, who was then Chancellor of the Exchequer, announced in his Budget Speech in April 1925 that Britain would immediately return to gold. Most countries followed and by 1927 the gold standard had, in fact, been restored. This time, however, it did not have the endurance of the pre-war phase. After a few turbulent years, including the world collapse into the Great Depression after 1929, Britain left the gold standard in September 1931. She was subsequently followed by other countries, notably the USA in 1933 and the French Bloc in 1936.

Reasons for collapse

We now turn to an examination of the changing environment under which the postwar gold standard operated, and the fundamental reasons for its disintegration.

First, it is almost certain that sterling was overvalued at its pre-war par rate when Britain returned to gold in 1925. The war had transformed Britain's current account adversely in a number of ways. There was some decline in her export markets, due to increased competitiveness, at the same time as there was an increase in her import needs. There was also a loss of property income, an increased war indebtedness and some loss of earnings from the switch in financial services from London to New York as well as from her merchant shipping losses. In addition, the structure of her trade had changed significantly, creating greater uncertainty in her trade position. Finally, purchasing power parity calculations suggested a probable overvaluation of sterling by something of the order of 10 per cent.

Second, a widely held view was that the adjustment mechanism worked unsatisfactorily during the restored gold standard. One argument supporting this view was that the stock of monetary gold was poorly distributed among participating countries. Concern centred on the excessive gold holdings in the USA and France and the inadequate gold stocks in the UK. On the one hand, the USA and France came under criticism for allegedly failing to adjust by allowing credit to expand in line with their accrual of gold; on the other hand, the UK came under criticism for continuing to expand credit even in the face of stable or declining gold stocks.

Another widely held view was that the adjustment mechanism in the postwar gold standard had become costlier because wages and prices had become more rigid, and hence the burden of adjustment would be more likely to fall on employment than on prices. This was sometimes combined with the view that in the postwar environment, with a deteriorating employment position and increased domestic political pressures, priorities by governments had shifted away from external towards domestic targets. Triffin (1964) is one of the few to question the view that wages had become more rigid. He points to the fact that in the fifty years or so preceding the First World War there were very few instances of actual declines in money wages and these declines in any case were moderate, while, on the other hand, there were very sharp drops in wages in the 1920–2 recession and some (less severe) wage cuts in the first years of the Depression. As against this, however, it could be asserted that the employment situation was considerably less favourable in the postwar period, and hence that wages should have shown even greater flexibility. For example, in the UK the unemployment rate averaged 10.5 per cent in the interwar period as against 4.5 per cent in the pre-war period. Moggridge (1972) has also argued that 'The General Strike (1926) removed the possibility of widespread reductions in money wages and costs, if only because attempts at reductions were too expensive socially and economically' (p. 235).

Third, the political and economic environment had become much more hostile towards the efficient functioning of the gold standard. The postwar years saw cycles less synchronised. Economic conditions, in general, deteriorated and the structure of external payments was radically transformed. There was, too, a possible intensification of hot money flows as capital markets may have become more united. Reparations and war debts not only dramatically altered the current account positions of a number of individual countries (for instance, Germany as a donor and France as a recipient) but also contaminated the political environment, making cooperation more difficult.

Fourth, the gold exchange standard system in operation in the restored gold standard exposed the reserve currencies to risks of speculative attack. The Genoa Conference of 1922 had in fact recommended the increased holding of foreign exchange in reserves as a means of economising on gold, which was then thought to be in short supply. Whether in fact foreign exchange had increased in relative importance during the restored gold standard remains a matter for debate. Lindert (1969) asserts that, whereas in 1924–5 foreign exchange represented some 17 per cent of reserves, in

1913 the roughly comparable figure was some 16 per cent. Lindert also asserts that Britain's vulnerability (as measured by the ratio of her liquid liabilities to her reserves) may have been no worse on the eve of the 1931 crisis than it had been in, say, 1913. There are several points, however, that make this argument somewhat unconvincing. There is little doubt about Britain's basic payments weakness in the postwar years, and with the more volatile political and economic environment in those years her need for reserves was surely greater. Moreover, the sharp fluctuations in foreign exchange holdings in those years added to the vulnerability of the reserve currencies. For example, Yeager (1976) reports that Germany's foreign exchange ratio fell from 63 per cent in December 1924 to 18 per cent in December 1928. France's conversions or threats of conversions posed a continuing danger to the system.

Fifth, another major development in the postwar environment, unfavourable to the gold standard, was the weakened position of London as the financial centre of the industrial world. New York and, to a lesser extent, Paris were now vying with London as a financial centre. This not only rendered the system less efficient (in so far as international clearing operations had now become more complex) but also exposed it to more 'hot money' flows between centres. Also the USA was ill-equipped to assume the dominant role that Britain had played in the management of the international financial system: reasons for this included parochialism, isolationism, immaturity, some hostility to US foreign investment, which was less dependable, and a central banking structure too decentralised and complex.

Finally, all the difficulties associated with the restored gold standard were further accentuated by the onset of the Great Depression in 1930. Britain's earnings from overseas investments began to fall promptly. American lending abroad declined drastically; the Smoot–Hawley Tariff of 1930 in the USA added to the uncertainties of trade. The immediate reasons for the collapse of the gold standard and Britain's withdrawal were a succession of crises beginning with the weakness of the powerful Austrian Credit-Anstalt Bank in May 1931. This frightened foreign creditors and led to withdrawals from Austrian banks. These economic difficulties, as well as the (earlier) political tensions created by Austria's proposal for an economic union with Germany, began to shake confidence across the Continent. In Germany, whose official financial standing was, in any case, weak (her short-term foreign liabilities being about twice her short-term assets), a run on German banks ensued, while her official reserves fell by about a third in June. Despite official help extended to both Austria and Germany, confidence did not return.

It was now Britain's turn to be in difficulties. Britain had been liberal in her advances to German banks and industry, and when the collapse occurred in Germany and the Berlin banks closed, her German assets were frozen. Britain's own financial weaknesses were now exposed and there was a run on sterling. Between July and September her reserve losses were huge and in September 1931 the Bank of England finally announced that it would no longer support the gold standard.

The aftermath

The years that followed were marked by rising protectionism and by a succession of competitive exchange rate adjustments. Britain's devaluation of 1931 put pressure on the USA which then in 1933 also left the gold standard and herself devalued. The US devaluation in turn put pressure on the French gold bloc which itself devalued in 1936. In that year, too, France withdrew from the gold standard. Interestingly, the end result of all these competitive devaluations was more or less to restore the 1930 relationships.

The dissatisfaction with the workings of the exchange rate regime led once again to a reaction. This came in 1936 with the signing of the Tripartite Agreement (between the USA, the UK and France), which endorsed moves in the direction of stabilising exchange rates.

2

The International Monetary Fund system

INTRODUCTION

Already by 1941 plans were being prepared in both the UK and the USA to set up a new postwar international monetary order. In the UK it was Keynes, as advisor to the Treasurer, who was assigned the task of formulating the outlines of a new monetary system, while in the USA it was Harry Dexter White, from the US Treasury, who was given responsibility in the area. In 1942 the original Keynes and White Plans surfaced, setting in motion a series of bilateral talks between the two countries based on these plans.

The British and American negotiations began with some common ground. Both sides were opposed to a system of freely fluctuating exchange rates, which they judged to have had adverse effects on the world economies in the years immediately after the First World War but also again in the 1930s. At the same time, the unfavourable experience during the restored gold standard argued against absolutely fixed exchange rates. There was, in addition, a measure of consensus that unregulated and competitive restrictions on trade for balance of payments purposes (as practised during the 1930s) were not in the best interest of the international community. By contrast, both countries also agreed, in principle, that countries should be relatively free to control certain capital transfers, particularly those at the short end.

At the same time, there were differences in the attitudes of the two negotiating parties. The UK was very internationally minded and dedicated to the resolution of world divisions through international institutions and cooperation. The USA for its part was still somewhat isolationist and retained some suspicion about international organisations. (It had, in fact, refused to join the interwar League of Nations.) The USA was at the time anti-imperialist in its pronouncements, opposing the formation of economic blocks, preferential trade agreements and direct control over trade, while emphasising multilateralism. The British, on the other hand, were anxious to retain Commonwealth economic and financial ties, arguing, too, that British relaxation of exchange controls and restrictions on trade would only be feasible if US aid and credit were very liberal.

Britain had, virtually, a 'fixation' about full employment and was determined to avoid repeating her experience during the restored gold standard when her overvalued currency had proved costly in terms of output and employment. Keynes insisted that there should be the least possible interference with internal national policies and that governments should be left relatively free to determine their desired levels of employment, while the exchange rate should be set so as to make possible those levels of employment. As Keynes put it, the external value of sterling should be altered 'to conform to whatever *de facto* internal value results from domestic policies which themselves shall be immune from criticism' (Gardner 1975: 207). So Keynes's emphasis was on the ability to change the exchange rate. The USA, on the other hand (whose experience with the gold standard had not been nearly as unfortunate as Britain's), tended to emphasise the stability of exchange rates and wanted them changed only in circumstances that they visualised as occurring quite infrequently (e.g. to meet a fundamental disequilibrium). Britain, too, felt that adjustment to correct balance of payments disequilibria was required by both surplus and deficit countries, while the USA took the view that the burden of adjustment should fall largely on the deficit countries.

If Britain was particularly concerned with the risks of unemployment attendant on an inappropriate exchange rate regime, the USA was somewhat more concerned with the possible risks of inflation which it felt attached to Britain's proposals. Again, if Britain was anxious to avoid political interference the USA appeared to have few reservations about this.

Britain also wanted to retain some role for sterling as a reserve currency in the postwar years, while the USA did not envisage a major reserve currency role for the dollar. Britain, as a potential debtor, whose financial needs were expected to be enormous after the war, visualised an institution providing relatively generous credit to member countries while the USA, the potential creditor, had in mind a more modest scale of financing. Britain's approach to an international institution was somewhat radical while the USA was more conservative, emphasising sound 'banking principles' in the lending operations. Finally, Britain was quite firm on the need to allow countries to assert control over their capital movements, while the USA seemed anxious to define more explicitly the circumstances in which countries should be allowed this right (e.g. in the face of disequilibrating short-term capital as against the movement of productive capital which should not be restricted).

In the event, what finally emerged was (not surprisingly, given the dominance of the USA at the time) much closer to the US plan than to the Keynes Plan (see later), although the USA did, at several points in the negotiations, make a number of concessions to British objections.

THE IMF SYSTEM – PRINCIPLES AND REGULATIONS

The original Articles of Agreement of the IMF spell out the purposes of the IMF, the obligations and responsibilities of its members and the administrative duties as well as the organisational structure of the institution.

The principal functions of the IMF, from our perspective, fall conveniently into two categories: one, most importantly, relating to provisions on the adjustment mechanism; the other relating to provisions bearing on the supply of credit to member countries. Articles IV, VII, VIII and XIV carry the principal provisions bearing on the adjustment mechanism to correct balance of payments disequilibria.

Article IV requires each member country to establish a par value for its currency to be expressed in terms of gold as a common denominator or in terms of the US dollar of the weight and fineness in effect on 1 July 1974. Maximum and minimum rates for exchange transactions between currencies of members are not to differ from parity by more than 1 per cent. At the same time, these par values may be changed but only to correct a fundamental disequilibrium in the balance of payments. (The term fundamental disequilibrium is not defined in the Articles.) Section 4, however, makes it clear that in general these changes would be expected to be relatively infrequent and that a country has an obligation 'to promote exchange stability, to maintain orderly exchange arrangements with other members'. Article IV also allows the Fund to propose uniform percentage changes in par values of all member countries, thus revaluing gold in terms of all currencies.

To hold the exchange rate within the narrow limits defined by the IMF, central banks were required to intervene by buying foreign currencies (generally the US dollar) as the exchange rate approached the upper limit or by selling these currencies as the exchange rate approached the lower limit. Short-term deficits would then be financed by (temporarily) running down international reserves, by borrowing from the IMF or other central banks, while countries with short-term surpluses would be temporarily building up their international reserves. The USA in the main played a passive role in exchange markets since its rate was determined by the intervention of all other countries and by its own obligations to undertake to convert officially held dollar holdings into gold at a fixed dollar–gold price.

Article VIII barred member countries from imposing, without approval of the Fund, restrictions on the making of payments and transfers for current international transactions. Members were to avoid discriminatory currency practices and their currencies were to be freely convertible into one another at official rates. In deference, however, to the abnormal conditions expected to prevail in the years immediately after the war, Article XIV did recognise a transition period of five years during which countries would be given the opportunity gradually to dismantle their controls over current transactions. The Articles did not prohibit resort to controls over capital movements; indeed 'in the face of a large or sustained outflow of capital the Fund may request a member to exercise (such) controls'.

One issue that divided Britain and the USA, as we have seen, had to do with the relative obligations of deficit and surplus countries in the adjustment process. Article VII (on scarce currencies) made some concession to the principle of symmetry in adjustment by permitting various kinds of discrimination against payments to a country whose currency had been so much in demand that it would be declared 'scarce'. Thus the objective of multilateral free trade was compromised in this case, but the intention of the provision was to put pressure on the surplus country to undertake some adjustment.

To sum up the key exchange rate provision, in the longer run exchange rates would be directed at securing external balance while in the shorter run reserves or official borrowings would bear the brunt of the adjustment. At the same time, the presumption was that independent monetary and fiscal policies, freed from any external constraint, would be directed at the domestic economy. (This also sums up the essential spirit of what Keynes wanted.)

A member could obtain access to Fund resources by supplying its own currency in exchange for the currency of a member country whose reserve position was relatively strong. A member enjoyed automatic access to borrowings up to 25 per cent of its quota (originally the gold tranche). Beyond that a member had drawing rights equal to its quota. These additional drawing rights were referred to as credit tranches, which were divided into four equal parts, each representing again a quarter of its quota. The first credit tranche was made available relatively easily but borrowings beyond the first credit tranche were subject to increasingly restrictive conditions. These had to 'support a program aimed at establishing or maintaining the enduring stability of the member's currency at a realistic rate of exchange'. For these borrowings the Fund negotiated a 'stabilization program' with the member country aimed at ultimately correcting its deficit. The Fund imposed an interest and service charge on its sales of foreign exchange; this charge increased with the member's scale of borrowing.

Each member's quota, which determined its borrowing capacity, was calculated largely on the basis of a formula that took account of the country's national income, its trade and its international reserves.

THE KEYNES PLAN

Reference was made earlier to a Keynes Plan, Britain's alternative to the White Plan, the latter ultimately providing the basis for the IMF Agreement. It is interesting, from this distance, to look again at the principal ways in which Keynes's plan differed from the IMF Agreement. (Keynes's plan is reproduced in Horsefield (1969).)

Keynes called his international institution a Clearing Union. Members would hold deposits (a new international currency which he called Bancor) with the Union. These deposits could only be used for transfers to the accounts of other central banks and could be obtained in exchange for gold, but gold could not be obtained in exchange for Bancors. The price of Bancors would be fixed (although alterable) in terms of gold, while par values would be fixed (although again alterable) in terms of Bancors.

Each member of the Union would be assigned a quota that determined the limits of its drawings (overdraft) from the Union. The quota was to be determined by the sum of a country's exports and imports, on average, over the previous three to five years. Periodic revisions to the quotas would be made as foreign trade increased. A country suffering a deficit in excess of its credit balance could draw on its overdraft facility to make payment. There was to be a charge of 1 per cent per annum if the debit balance exceeded one-quarter of its quota, and an additional 1 per cent on balances exceeding one-half of the quota. Keynes limited the rights to accumulate a debit balance in any one year to one-quarter of the quota. Creditors were also required to pay charges of 1 per cent if their credit balance exceeded one-quarter of their quota, and an additional 1 per cent on balances over one-half of the quota.

Keynes laid down detailed actions that would be required in the event that debit or credit balances exceeded one-half of the quota. For deficit countries the Union would have powers to require members (a) to devalue, (b) to control outward capital transactions and (c) to surrender a suitable proportion of any separate gold or other liquid reserves in reduction of its debit balance. For surplus countries measures included (a) the expansion of domestic credit and demand, (b) appreciation, (c) the reduction in tariffs or other barriers against imports and (d) development loans.

An interesting and important feature of the scheme is that members could escape the charges by recycling funds to one another. In other words, debtors could borrow directly from creditors after consulting with the Union.

How different was this Keynes Plan in essentials from the IMF Agreement, as finally ratified? First, the Keynes Plan, while in some ways somewhat more radical, had the advantage of simplicity in its administration. The creation of a single international currency would have replaced the complicated schemes of transactions in multiple currencies. Second, the Keynes Plan was considerably more generous than the IMF scheme. The latter provided some $8–$9 billion, while Keynes had in mind some $26 billion. As Gardner (1975) has noted, had the USA negotiated on the basis of the Keynes Plan it might have accumulated a very large credit balance in the earlier postwar years which it could have used in later years to finance its own deficits; at the same time, it might have reduced the volume of aid it eventually provided by way of the Marshall Plan.

Third, Keynes clearly had in mind not only a more flexible exchange rate regime but also provided in some detail for the possible triggering of exchange rate changes for both deficit and surplus countries. In this respect, it is reminiscent of proposals made in the 1960s for presumptive indicators to trigger exchange rate changes (Argy 1981). Fourth, Keynes was explicit about the need for symmetry in the treatment of deficit and surplus countries, providing a mechanism by which penalties for non-adjustment would fall on surplus as well as deficit countries. In the Articles of Agreement, only the scarce currency provision deals explicitly with this. Fifth, Keynes did play down the role of gold in his scheme; Bancors, not gold, were at the centre of it and his numeraire was Bancors, not gold, although the price of the Bancor itself was determined by gold. Sixth, his scheme to permit the recycling of funds among members was novel and interesting and indeed is reminiscent of some features of the Eurodollar market in today's world.

Seventh, neither scheme really provided for the secular growth of international reserves, as we shall see shortly in respect of the IMF. Perhaps surprisingly in retrospect the question of providing for the future growth of reserves did not assume any importance in the minds of the negotiators at the time. In Keynes's scheme new international reserves are created by the exercise of a member's overdraft facilities. If country A overdraws the volume of Bancors in the world increases. With quotas revised upwards as the volume of foreign trade increases it is likely that the stock of international reserves will increase over time; but the counterpart of the increase will be an increased volume of debit balances, which presumably will have a somewhat depressing influence on world trade. Thus the stock of owned reserves will not be increasing over time. This failing, so to speak, in the Keynes Plan is perhaps all the more surprising when one recalls the third of the so-called objects of his plan. To quote Keynes:

> We need a quantum of international currency which is neither determined in an unpredictable and irrelevant manner as, for example, by the technical progress of the gold industry nor subject to large variations depending on the gold reserve policies of individual countries; but is governed by the actual current requirements of world commerce and is also capable of deliberate expansion and contraction to offset deflationary and inflationary tendencies in effective world demand.
>
> (Horsefield 1969: vol. 3, p. 20)

It is worth noting, in this connection, that his Union was entitled also to reduce the quotas of members if it was necessary to correct an excess of world purchasing power.

THE BREAKDOWN OF THE IMF SYSTEM

It is convenient to identify five basic reasons why the system broke down, although, as we shall see, the reasons are closely interrelated.

Failure to provide for the secular growth in reserves

The Bretton Woods system, as originally conceived, had not provided for systematic long-term growth in international reserves. In general, it was felt that IMF lending and an increased supply of gold would probably, in combination, meet the world's needs; there was, as well, one provision that could have been invoked to raise world liquidity: the section in Article IV which allowed the IMF to recommend uniform changes in par values (i.e. to raise the price of gold). As it happened, however, these potential sources proved inadequate or were deemed unsatisfactory.

In the event the US dollar stepped into the breach and the subsequent growth of reserves was *ad hoc* and unplanned (Table 2.1).

Table 2.1 International reserves, 1950–72 (billions of SDRs)

End of year	Gold	SDRs[a]	Reserve positions in Fund[b]	Foreign exchange[c]		Total reserves	Change in total reserves (%)
1950	33.4	–	1.6	13.3	(4.9)	48.3	–
1951	33.6	–	1.7	13.5	(4.2)	48.5	0.4
1952	33.5	–	1.8	14.4	(5.6)	49.3	1.6
1953	33.9	–	1.9	15.4	(6.5)	51.2	3.8
1954	34.6	–	1.8	16.5	(7.5)	52.9	3.3
1955	35.0	–	1.9	16.8	(8.3)	53.7	1.5
1956	35.7	–	2.3	17.8	(9.2)	55.8	3.9
1957	36.9	–	2.3	17.1	(9.1)	56.3	0.9
1958	37.6	–	2.6	17.1	(9.7)	57.3	1.8
1959	37.6	–	3.3	16.1	(10.1)	57.0	– 0.5
1960	37.7	–	3.6	18.5	(11.1)	59.8	4.9
1961	38.5	–	4.2	19.2	(11.8)	61.9	3.5
1962	38.9	–	3.8	19.9	(12.9)	62.6	1.1
1963	39.9	–	3.9	22.7	(14.4)	66.5	6.2
1964	40.5	–	4.2	24.2	(15.8)	68.9	3.6
1965	41.5	–	5.4	24.0	(15.8)	70.9	2.9
1966	40.7	–	6.3	25.7	(14.9)	72.7	2.5
1967	39.4	–	5.7	29.3	(18.2)	74.4	2.3
1968	38.7	–	6.5	32.5	(17.3)	77.8	4.6
1969	38.9	–	6.7	33.0	(16.0)	78.7	1.2
1970	37.0	3.1	7.7	45.4	(23.8)	93.2	18.4
1971	35.9	5.9	6.4	75.1	(45.5)	123.2	32.2
1972	35.6	8.7	6.3	96.2	(48.8)	146.8	19.2

Source: IMF, *International Financial Statistics*
Notes: [a] Special Drawing Rights; see the text.
[b] Contribution of IMF lending to international reserves. See Argy (1981) on the way in which IMF lending creates international reserves.
[c] Foreign exchange comprised mostly sterling and dollar official claims.
Items in parentheses are dollar claims.

The years 1950–9 saw almost continuous US deficits; these deficits were, in substantial part, financed by the creation of official liabilities against the US government. The official liabilities were themselves convertible into gold at the fixed price of \$35 an ounce (the par value for the US dollar under the Bretton Woods Agreement).

The continuing US deficits and the growth in official liabilities in those years, however, were not viewed with alarm. On the contrary, they were seen as accommodating the need for additional reserves on the part of the rest of the world and as a means of restoring balance in the distribution of world reserves. Moreover, in those years the USA had more than enough gold to meet any claims from official holders of US dollars.

The next decade is best viewed as the decade of the 'Triffin awakening'. In an important and influential book in 1960, Triffin had warned that the emerging gold exchange standard was unstable. His reasoning was as follows. In the longer run a reserve currency (i.e. a currency such as the US dollar which is included in other countries' reserves) can continue to provide for the secular growth in reserves, through sustained deficits, only at the cost of a rise in the ratio of its official liabilities to its gold supplies. A point would then clearly be reached when confidence in the viability of the reserve currency would be shaken. This would provoke shifts from the reserve currency into gold. These shifts would maintain intact the rest of the world's reserves but would lower the reserves of the reserve currency country, forcing the reserve country to take measures to correct its position, measures that could be harmful to world trade and employment. If confidence in the reserve currency was restored by the elimination of the deficits, world reserves would cease to rise and this would again have adverse effects on world trade and growth. Ultimately, therefore, Triffin argued, the system, as it operated, was doomed since either the reserve currency (the dollar) continued to provide the needed reserves, in which case the system was exposed to increasing crises of confidence, or it ceased to be the source of reserves, in which case the system would be imperilled by a shortage of reserves.

Many signs of the Triffin dilemma surfaced in the course of the decade. The US deficits continued, albeit on a smaller scale, to 1966. By that time the USA had just enough gold reserves to meet all of its official liabilities. Also by then, the USA, concerned over the situation, had begun to take measures designed to discourage official convertibility. In 1963 and 1964 there were sales of Roosa Bonds to foreign central banks; these were medium-term US government bonds denominated in foreign currencies and designed to 'freeze' some of the official dollar liabilities. In the same spirit, during the 1960s the USA also appealed to allied countries to exercise restraint in converting official dollars into gold, an appeal that was largely heeded by most countries.

The situation was transformed in 1966 and again in 1968–9 when there were overall surpluses in the US balance of payments. In 1968–9 these were substantial, raising alarms at the time about how the needed future growth of reserves was in fact to be met.

The obvious difficulties with the gold exchange standard also led, from the start of the decade, to discussions to reform the system. Much of the emphasis in these discussions was on how to create a new reserve asset which might replace the dollar and at the same time allow some management of the growth in liquidity. These discussions culminated in 1968 with the decision to create the Special Drawing Right (SDR). In the three years 1970–2 a total of $9.5 billion in SDRs was to be allocated to member countries (Argy 1981).

The decision to create the SDR was a landmark. Its original very modest aim was to supplement what was thought at the time to be a shortage of reserves. Its longer-term aim was to make the SDR the principal reserve asset in the system.

SDRs are a 'paper' asset created by the IMF in 1970. Participation in the scheme was voluntary but, in fact, nearly all member countries opted to participate. The SDR, which has no backing, was originally fixed in value in terms of gold, one SDR being equal to 1/35th of an ounce of gold (which equalled US$1). Through the intermediary of the IMF, SDRs are given up by deficit countries in return for foreign exchange while SDRs are absorbed by surplus countries who in turn give up some foreign exchange. There are rules governing the uses of SDRs to meet deficits and some limits on obligations with respect to the holdings of SDRs by surplus countries. Countries earn (pay) interest only on the excess (deficiency) of holdings over original allocations.

The IMF made careful calculations of the amount of SDRs that needed to be created over the three years 1970–2. In the first place it had to calculate what reserve needs were for the world as a whole. In the second place it had to make a guess as to how much of this would be provided from other sources (e.g. by US deficits).

The Fund concluded that reserves needed for the world as a whole were of the order of $4–$5 billion a year. At the same time, they judged that other reserve growth would amount to $1–1.5 billion a year (made up of central bank accruals of dollars arising from US deficits of $0.5–$1 billion and another $0.5 billion from gold and reserve positions (automatic borrowing rights in the Fund)). This suggested a figure of $3–$3.5 billion a year to meet reserve needs by the creation of SDRs. The final proposal, which was accepted and implemented, was to distribute $3.5 billion in 1970 and $3 billion in each of the following two years.

These IMF calculations proved to be disastrously wide of the mark. The huge unanticipated US deficits (nearly $10 billion in 1970 and $30 billion in 1971) swelled world reserves, which increased by about 18 per cent and 32 per cent in 1970 and 1971 respectively.[1] These reserves came on top of the SDRs created. Largely because of this unfortunate initial experience with SDRs no new allocation was made in 1973 when one would have been due. However, small further allocations were made in later years.

After 1 July 1974 the SDR link with gold was cut and it was valued in terms of a weighted basket of sixteen currencies. Subsequently there were small changes in the weights assigned to individual countries but in 1980 the decision was taken to simplify the valuation of the SDR (which was complex) and base it on the currencies of six key countries only (the USA, Germany, the UK, France, Japan and the Netherlands). Also since 1978 the rules for the use and designation of SDRs have been made more flexible. Finally, whereas the interest rate originally paid on SDRs was only 1.5 per cent it has since been linked more directly to interest rates in the major industrial countries.

Inflexible exchange rate system

Another reason for the collapse of the IMF system was that in the years between 1949 and 1967 the exchange rate system had become very inflexible. Between 1958 and 1967, for example, the only change in the exchange rate made by an industrial country was in 1961 when West Germany and the Netherlands made small revaluations to their currencies. Yet during these years major imbalances were developing, placing great strains on the system. The major sources of imbalances were Japan (in the later

1960s) and Germany on the one hand with strong currencies and the UK and the USA on the other with weak currencies.

Japan and West Germany, with strong entrenched interests in their export sectors and a belief in the 'virtuous circle' of export-led growth, hesitated to force a structural readjustment away from their export and import-competing sectors by a revaluation and were content to allow their international reserves to rise.

The USA and the UK hesitated to devalue for reasons which were far more complex. One, probably relatively unimportant, consideration was national pride. A more important consideration had to do with the unique problems associated with a devaluation of a reserve currency such as the dollar and sterling, the latter also at the time serving as a reserve currency. Since reserves held in the devalued currency will fall in value, countries might become more hesitant about holding reserves in that currency, prompting shifts out of the reserve currencies, which can be destabilising. Inflicting losses on holders of reserve currencies was also felt to be unethical. Additionally, a US devaluation effectively meant an increase in the official price of gold, which would have favoured the countries hoarding it, the gold producers (South Africa and the USSR) and the private speculators.

A further consideration in the case of the USA was the fact, as we saw, that its deficits were being financed in large part by the creation of new official dollar liabilities. In other words, surplus countries were accumulating US dollars in their reserves, which was equivalent to the USA borrowing from these countries on a short-term basis. With little pressure on its gold stocks, the USA was largely free from the discipline imposed on a deficit country to take corrective measures. Finally, in the case of the UK, an additional factor was that massive financial assistance was being provided not only by the IMF but also by the USA and the central banks. In retrospect it can be seen that the international community virtually conspired to hold the UK exchange rate by being overgenerous with financial aid.

The UK and West Germany illustrate the kinds of strains that developed. Determined to defend an exchange rate which had become inappropriate, the UK was periodically forced to resort to import restrictions and to deflationary measures which on occasions created stagnating conditions and growing unemployment (reminiscent of the second gold standard experience).

In contrast, West Germany, anxious to keep its own rate of inflation below the rate prevailing in the rest of the industrial world, and at the same time determined to hold the exchange rate, was intermittently threatened with imported inflation.

Freeing of capital movement

Alongside this rigidity in exchange rates was the gradual freeing of capital movements among the industrial countries, especially after 1958 (see Chapter 5). Barriers to the free movement of capital were relaxed. Furthermore, the growth of the multinationals and the Eurodollar markets meant that huge sums were available to move from country to country in search of profit. This had important consequences. On the one hand, any suggestion that a currency was overvalued (undervalued) tended to trigger the movement of huge sums out of (into) that currency. These 'speculative flows' made it increasingly difficult for central banks to hold the line on exchange rates. On the other hand, it also made it increasingly difficult for industrial countries to maintain relatively independent monetary policies. For example, an attempt to set interest rates above (below) world levels would tend to result in the movement of capital into (out of) the country.

Many developed countries experienced difficulties of this kind in 1969–71. In 1969, when interest rates were very high in the USA, the huge outflows of capital from Europe made it difficult for these countries to hold their interest rates down. In 1970–1, when US interest rates were very low and European interest rates were relatively high, capital or 'hot money' flooded into these countries, expanding their money supplies and frustrating, in varying degree, their attempts to implement relatively restrictive policies. Despite growing resort in those years to restrictions on capital movements, as a means of attaining greater independence for monetary policy, it proved extremely difficult to regulate the flow of funds across nations.

The asymmetries of the IMF system

Less important, but emerging as irritants, were a number of asymmetries in the IMF system. First, there were the asymmetries associated with the scope, and initiative, for exchange rate changes and with the maintenance of exchange margins. With the US dollar as the principal intervention currency and intervention points determined in relation to the dollar, the maximum possible change in the dollar *vis-à-vis* another currency was effectively half the change possible between any two non-dollar currencies. Also, while most of the rest of the world met their obligations on exchange rate margins by buying and selling their intervention currency (notably the dollar) in the foreign exchange markets the USA met its obligation (until 1971) by buying and selling gold in exchange for dollar reserves. In effect, then, the USA played a predominantly passive role in securing the exchange margins for the US dollar *vis-à-vis* other currencies.

Second, there tended to be more pressure, potentially, on deficit countries than on surplus countries to initiate exchange rate changes and, with the US dollar at the centre of the system, this could create a devaluation bias against the US dollar.

Third, with the failure of the exchange rate adjustment mechanism, more of the adjustment burden fell on demand management policies and direct import controls. The charge was made that with deficit countries having to do most of the adjusting a 'deflationary bias' would be injected into the world economy while the use of direct import controls would have an adverse effect on the allocation of world resources.

Fourth, there was the asymmetry associated with the reserve currency role of the dollar. The principal charge here was that the USA was in a privileged position in that it could extract benefits, from the official use of the US dollar, in the form of seignorage. This seignorage accrues to the issuer of a currency when the resources obtained by the issuer exceed the cost of producing the currency.

The benefits are represented, basically, by the difference between the rate of interest that the reserve country pays on its obligations and the long rate it can earn by investing overseas. In other words, the seignorage accruing to the USA stems essentially from its role as a financial intermediary in the transmission of funds. However, it could be argued that in a highly competitive market these net benefits would be very small, since they would effectively be arbitraged away, with the differential covering operating costs only. (For a fuller discussion of this, see Argy (1981: Ch. 9).)

Global instability

Finally, it is possible to argue that, apart from inherent deficiencies in the system, it had come under increasing stress because of increased divergence in economic conditions as well as increased global instability. Interest differentials rose sharply in the late 1960s and early 1970s; there were huge reversals in reserve movements; reserve growth was very large and unprecedented in the early 1970s; wage explosions erupted in several countries in the late 1960s and early 1970s; the upsurge in inflation in these years added to the difficulties; the commodity price boom in 1972–3 and, most important of all, the oil price shock in 1973–4 dealt the final blows to the system (Chapter 42).

Exchange rate crises and the collapse of the system

As we noted above, until 1967 exchange rates tended to be relatively rigid. After that a succession of crises and exchange rate adjustments, extending over several years, led ultimately to the collapse of the IMF system.

Continuing difficulties over many years finally forced the UK to devalue in November 1967. The French franc came under severe attack in the spring of 1968, but it was not until August 1969 that the franc was devalued. Strong speculative inflows into Germany then forced the deutschmark to float temporarily, and later that year the exchange rate for the deutschmark was fixed at a higher level. In 1970, after strong inflows into Canada, the Canadian dollar floated. Massive US deficits and some gold losses finally forced the USA in August 1971 to take the dramatic step of suspending the convertibility of the US dollar into gold, and at the same time implement a number of measures designed to improve her balance of payments position. This touched off several months of great uncertainty during which the major currencies floated. Finally, in December 1971, the Smithsonian Agreement was reached. This embodied major realignments in exchange rates, including, most importantly, and for the first time since the war, a US devaluation against gold amounting to nearly 8 per cent. The Smithsonian Agreement also permitted a wider band of 2.25 per cent (against 1 per cent under the Bretton Woods Agreement) on either side of the official exchange rate.

The hopes of the participants in the Agreement, however, were soon shattered. In June 1972 sterling floated after coming under severe speculative attack. Continuing weakness of the US dollar forced a second devaluation of the dollar in February 1973, this time by 10 per cent, and not long after the major currencies began to float against the US dollar. The IMF system then effectively collapsed, establishing the regime which now prevails.

THE SECOND AMENDMENT TO THE IMF ARTICLES OF AGREEMENT

In March 1978 the Second Amendment to the IMF Articles of Agreement came into effect. These amendments effectively legitimised the new exchange rate arrangements.

Under the new provisions, members may follow any one of several exchange rate arrangements. They may float, for example, or they may maintain the value of their currency in terms of the SDR or some other denominator, but not in terms of gold which was now dethroned. Members, too, have an obligation to promote stable exchange rates by fostering orderly underlying economic, financial and monetary conditions. There is also a provision to restore a par value system, if endorsed by an 85 per cent weighted majority.

The most interesting innovations deal with IMF surveillance and exchange rate policies. The new Article 10 provides that the IMF shall 'exercise firm surveillance over the exchange rate policies of members and shall adopt specific principles for the guidance of all members with respect to these policies'. Following extended deliberations, a document setting out the Principles and Procedures for Surveillance was approved in April 1977 and came into effect in March 1978. This replaced the older guidelines for floating.

Members have an obligation to provide the IMF with information required for surveillance and to consult with the IMF on exchange rate policies. There are three principles for the guidance of members. Principle A provides that 'a member shall avoid manipulating exchange rates or the international monetary system in order to prevent effective balance of payments adjustment or to gain an unfair competitive advantage over other members'. Principle B provides that 'a member should intervene in the exchange market if necessary to counter disorderly conditions which may be characterised *inter alia* by disruptive short-term movements in the exchange value of its currency'. Principle C provides that, in their intervention policies, members 'should take into account' the interests of other members.

There are also principles for the guidance of the IMF in its evaluation of a member's exchange rate policies. Five indicators are put forward as possible pointers 'to an inappropriate exchange rate policy: protracted intervention in one direction in the exchange market, undue official or quasi-official borrowing, restrictions on, or incentives for, current and capital transactions, the use of monetary/financial policies to stimulate or discourage capital flows, exchange rate behaviour that appears to be unrelated to underlying economic and financial conditions including factors affecting competitiveness and long-term capital movements'.

3

The float

INTRODUCTION

The generalised float effectively came into being in February 1973, so it has now been in operation for some twenty years.

It is fair to say that there has been considerable disenchantment with the workings of the flexible rate regime. The original hopes and expectations of its advocates have not been realised. This explains why in recent years there have been numerous proposals for the reform of the exchange rate regime (see Chapter 36).

Subsequent chapters will deal in some detail with the way in which flexible exchange rates work. The technical details are held over to those chapters. This chapter presents a simple and broad picture of the experience to date with flexible rates, addressing in particular three questions. First, what were the original expectations about the flexible rate regime? Second, what has been the reality since 1973 and what are the reasons why the expectations were not realised? Third, smaller countries could choose from a variety of potential exchange rate regimes, so what decisions did they make?

THE ORIGINAL EXPECTATIONS ABOUT THE FLEXIBLE RATE REGIME

Beginning in the late 1950s and continuing into the 1960s some economists were unhappy over the workings of the IMF system; this in turn provoked a lively debate over the potential alternatives (see on this Argy 1981). Many began to advocate the adoption of flexible exchange rates. What we shall try and do here is summarise the claims made and the expectations held at the time by these advocates for flexible rates. We concede that there is an element of oversimplification in our presentation of their views, but we do capture the essential spirit of the debate at the time.

One expectation was that under a flexible rate regime nominal rates would tend to move in line with relative prices and with other changes in 'fundamentals' and that any deviation from these trends would be quickly eliminated by stabilising speculation. Thus changes in real exchange rates (i.e. exchange rates adjusted for relative prices) would be small and would reflect changes in fundamentals (other than relative prices). In this perspective, persistent current account imbalances, unmatched by long-term capital movements, would be rapidly eliminated by changes in real exchange rates. In such a world there would be no fundamental disequilibrium or real exchange rate misalignments of the kind which had recurrently beset the Bretton Woods system. Without these misalignments too, resources would be more efficiently allocated.

Friedman had the classic answer to those who argued that speculation might be destabilising to exchange rates:

> People who argue that speculation is generally destabilising seldom realise that this is largely equivalent to saying that speculators lose money, since speculation can be destabilising in general only if speculators on the average sell when the currency is low in price and buy when it is high.
>
> (1953a: 175)

A second expectation was that flexible rates would provide macroeconomic independence. There were in fact several aspects of this which were highlighted.

One took as a starting point that there was a long-run Phillips curve trade-off for each country between the rate of inflation and the rate of unemployment, i.e. the higher the rate of inflation the lower will tend to be the rate of unemployment. Different countries, it was acknowledged, had different preferences with respect to unemployment and inflation. Moreover, for a variety of reasons the position of countries' Phillips curves tended to be different. In a fixed rate world of the Bretton Woods variety, countries would be forced to operate with a common world rate of inflation. Thus, for example, the Germanys of the world would be exposed to unwanted imported inflation, while the United Kingdoms of this world would be forced to operate at a lower than preferred inflation and hence a potentially higher unemployment rate.

Flexible exchange rates allowed countries to choose their own combinations of inflation and unemployment. Countries, it was argued, would have to be better off since they were being allowed to exercise more choice.

Another aspect of the claim of greater macroeconomic independence was that the money stock would be easier to control and that a given dose of monetary and fiscal policies would be more effective in controlling the level of aggregate demand. Thus fine tuning would be improved (Chapter 6). At the same time, free of the external constraint, monetary and fiscal policies could now be directed at achieving domestic objectives. This had proved difficult to do under the IMF system, although, as we noted, it had been its original intention.

Yet another aspect of the claim of greater macroeconomic independence was that flexible exchange rates would shelter the economy from policies and disturbances abroad. Thus, specifically, the USA would no longer be able to transmit her inflation, as she did in the late 1960s following the Vietnam War, nor her monetary policies, as she did in a dramatic form between 1969 and 1972 (Chapters 2 and 42).

Finally, in this same context, flexible exchange rates were supposed to be 'morally' superior. On the one hand, stable economies would enjoy the fruits and reap their rewards, free from interference from overseas. On the other hand, unstable economies would pay the price for their own profligacy and would not be able to export their instability. (In other words, the effects of their instability would be contained within their economies.)

The third expectation was that flexible rates would do away with the need for reserves; hence it would instantly remove from the scene all problems associated with the provision of international reserves, e.g. SDR creation (as noted in Chapter 2). Those countries which had positive net reserves would be able to improve their real incomes at the expense of those economies which had negative net reserves, i.e. those which had been net short-term official borrowers such as the UK and the USA.

The fourth expectation was the claim that flexible rates would reduce protectionist tendencies. This was thought to be the case because flexible rates would reduce misalignments and also because protection under flexible rates neither increased aggregate demand nor improved the trade balance (Dunn 1983).

THE REALITY SINCE 1973

From today's perspective, twenty years on, none of the above expectations proved realistic.

First, real exchange rates have been much more volatile than originally supposed. It could also be argued (but with caution) that far from removing misalignments and fundamental disequilibria flexible exchange rates have aggravated these. Compare, for example, the huge overvaluation of sterling in early 1981 (anything between 30 and 60 per cent) with the overvaluation of sterling in late 1967 which led to a 'mere' 14 per cent devaluation of sterling. Compare, too, the heated debate in 1984–5 over the overvaluation of the US dollar (of perhaps 25–30 per cent) with the equally heated debate in the second half of 1971 over the then overvaluation of the US dollar (believed by the USA to be about 15 per cent) which led, in the Smithsonian Agreement, to an effective devaluation of less than 8 per cent. Compare, also, the magnitude of large-country current account imbalances in recent years with the more modest imbalances of the late 1960s, early 1970s.

Second, the idea that flexible exchange rates will buy you macroeconomic policy independence has not been borne out by recent experience. Between 1968 and 1972, when the par value system prevailed, Europe felt acutely, and complained bitterly about, the effects of swings in US monetary policy, as we saw in the previous chapter. The abandonment of Bretton Woods was, partly at least, motivated by a wish to enjoy an independent monetary policy. Between 1979 and 1984, however, with flexible rates Europe continued to feel the impacts of US financial policies and criticism of US policies was equally fierce.

Third, we know that international reserves have continued to play a crucial role in the international monetary system. Indeed, the need for reserves is as great today as in the fixed rate period.

Fourth, we have in recent years witnessed an increase in protectionist devices. This is now well documented (Bhagwati 1989). Witness the conflicts that have erupted recently between Japan and the USA over trade and the US moves to protect its economy from imports.

EXPLAINING THE REALITY

Why has the experience not quite matched the expectations?

Exchange rate volatility and misalignment

Why have exchange rates been so volatile and how can one explain the persistent misalignments (large current account imbalances) even under flexible rates?

The literature on exchange rate overshooting (i.e. overshooting its long-run equilibrium rate) is now very large and will be reviewed in more detail in the chapters that follow. The phenomenon can arise for several distinctive reasons.

First, financial markets (interest rates, exchange rates) tend to adjust instantly, while prices, output and the current account adjust more slowly. When that happens a monetary change is likely to produce an overadjustment in the exchange rate. This is a feature of the models in Dornbusch (1976) and Branson (1977) (see Chapters 18 and 19).

Second, there are long lags in the adjustment of the trade balance to a change in the exchange rate. For a while at least exchange rate changes can have perverse (J curve) effects on the trade balance. When that happens the exchange rate can overreact at first to a disturbance (see Chapters 7 and 21).

Third, speculation in foreign exchange markets may not be stabilising, as Friedman suggested. Indeed, as we shall see, there is now very convincing evidence that, at least over the short run, speculation can be destabilising (see Chapter 33). This *reinforces* exchange rate trends, pulling the exchange rate away from equilibrium over extended periods.

Fourth, one of the themes of this book is that the longer-run effects of policy changes (i.e. after wages–prices have fully adjusted and wealth effects are accounted for) are often dramatically different from short-run effects. Often the ultimate direction of change in the real exchange rate is the reverse of that in the short run (see

Chapters 20 and 30). This again introduces an element of inherent instability in the exchange rate, notably in response to a sustained disturbance.

Fifth, wage indexation creates the potential for generating vicious circles of exchange rate depreciation (appreciation) inflation (deflation). Wage indexation was widely used in wage contracts, particularly in Europe, at least to the mid-1980s. If real wages are fixed, changes in real exchange rates may be difficult to realise and so current account imbalances will be difficult to correct (Chapter 8).

Sixth, when markets are highly integrated financially, as they now are, real exchange rates respond more to real interest rates but less so to cumulative current account imbalances. Thus it now takes substantially *longer* for real exchange rates to return ultimately to their equilibrium levels (see Blundell-Wignall and Browne 1991).

Seventh, we have in the last twenty years lived in a very unstable world. At the time of the switch to flexible exchange rates industrial countries were in the throes of an explosion in money growth; subsequently, we had two major oil price shocks and, in the first half of the 1980s, we had the massive fiscal policy asymmetries, primarily between the USA on the one hand and the other industrial countries on the other. The disequilibria, divergences and uncertainties that these developments created would have played havoc with any conceivable exchange rate regime (Chapter 42).

Finally, let us ask, in what sense has exchange rate volatility been excessive?

It is true that exchange rates have been more volatile than prices, but the more appropriate comparison is with other asset prices (e.g. share prices, interest rates) and there is evidence that shows that exchange rates have fluctuated by less than share prices or interest rates (Bergstrand 1983; Frenkel and Goldstein 1988).

It is also true that real exchange rates have fluctuated by some two and a half times as much again as in the fixed rate period but this may not be an entirely appropriate basis for comparison since macro conditions were far more stable then.

On the other hand, it is probably also true that exchange rate volatility has been excessive relative to what one might have had if we had not seen bandwagon effects or if expectations had been based on 'longer-run' fundamentals.

Macroeconomic independence

Why did flexible exchange rates not deliver macro independence?

First, and most important, already by the late 1960s economists had come to reject the notion of a trade-off between inflation and unemployment. With no trade-off countries can no longer determine their own independent unemployment rate; they can only choose their own independent inflation rate which, depending on how macro discretion is used, may or may not be a good thing (see Chapter 25).

Second, the 'conventional wisdom' about the way in which monetary and fiscal policies impacted on the economy under flexible rates was embodied in the so-called Mundell–Fleming model (Chapter 6). Over time, however, this model was shown to have numerous deficiencies, particularly so for relatively short time horizons (of say up to nine months, when J curves are likely to operate) and for longer time horizons (beyond say two years) (Chapter 7). In the Mundell–Fleming model, when capital mobility is low and wages and prices are relatively sticky, both monetary and fiscal policies tend to have powerful effects on economic activity and in principle can be used for stabilisation purposes. In more refined models the effects are more complicated and less certain (Chapter 30).

Third, when capital mobility is very low it is true that, in general, a country is largely sheltered under flexible rates from foreign policies and disturbances. However, when capital is very mobile a country feels powerfully the effects of disturbances from abroad, so the country is no longer protected by flexible rates (Chapters 13 and 14). As Dornbusch (1983) put it, 'flexible rates leave us with as much interdependence, or even more, as there is under a fixed rate regime' (p. 4).

Exchange rate management

The original advocates had envisaged that the float would be a pure one, in the sense that monetary authorities would not try to 'manage' exchange rates, allowing these to be determined by market forces alone. In reality, for a variety of reasons, monetary authorities did intervene in foreign exchange markets. Such intervention can be unilateral (i.e. it is undertaken by individual central banks) or coordinated (it is undertaken jointly by a number of the large economies). Both forms of intervention have taken place. (See Chapters 36 and 45).

Exchange rate management takes three principal forms (Argy 1982). First, the monetary authorities may intervene by buying and selling currencies in the foreign exchange market. The intervention in turn may or may not be sterilised (a sterilisation operation is one which neutralises the effects of intervention on the base money).

To undertake intervention of this kind the monetary authorities need to hold an adequate stock of international reserves. Given that central banks chose to intervene in this form on an extensive scale the need for reserves did not decline significantly under the float.

Second, the authorities may use interest rate policy to stabilise the exchange rate without, in principle, using reserves.

The difference between unsterilised intervention and the use of interest rate policy may be illustrated with a simple example. Suppose the foreign interest rate rises; there will be an immediate outflow of capital. If the monetary authorities intervene by selling reserves (in exchange for domestic currency) domestic base money will fall and this will put upward pressure on the home interest rate. Alternatively, the authorities, by an appropriate open market sale, can raise the home interest rate to foreign levels; in this case there will be a drop in the supply of base money but reserves need not have changed.

Third, the authorities may use capital controls as a means of alleviating pressures on the exchange rate.

Capital controls may be used to serve three distinct purposes. First, on a continuing basis, they may be used to shelter the economy from potentially destabilising inflows or outflows of capital. This effectively limits the overall degree of capital mobility.

Second, they may be used to offset longer-term weaknesses or strengths in the current account, by biasing the controls against outflows in the case of a weak currency (as in the UK until 1979) or by biasing the controls against inflows in the case of a strong currency (as in Germany until the early 1970s).

Third, they may be used to offset short-term exchange market pressures in either direction, i.e. when the currency is under pressure tighten controls over outflows and ease controls over inflows, and when the currency is strong tighten controls over inflows and ease controls over outflows. This is in essence what Australia and Japan did until the end of the 1970s (Argy 1987).

Less important methods of managing exchange rates include the use of fiscal policy, of administrative controls over imports and exports and of special inducements to foreign banks to hold reserves in a particular currency.

Protection

We can be very brief on this. We have shown how misalignments have persisted under flexible exchange rates. It is this in turn which has provoked new protectionist tendencies.

Conclusions

The above survey of the experience of a flexible exchange rate system in the last twenty years has shown that a combination of (a) flaws in the original underlying model, (b) theoretical refinements developed since, (c) institutional changes (increased financial integration, the widespread use of wage indexation) and (d) unstable economic conditions made flexible rates work in ways which were clearly not foreseen at the time.

EXCHANGE RATE PRACTICES IN THE SMALLER OECD COUNTRIES

As noted in the previous chapter, smaller countries (defined as those outside the big three) were free to choose the exchange rate regime that they felt best suited them. Many European countries entered into collective exchange rate arrangements (Chapter 4). Some have floated: Canada (since 1970) and Switzerland (since 1973). The Nordic countries (Sweden, Finland and Norway) have had an adjustable peg regime (not unlike the old IMF system) with the central rate pegged to a basket of currencies (the basket itself evolving over the years). By 1991 all three were pegged to the European Currency Unit (ECU) (Chapter 4). By the end of 1992 all three were floating.

Sweden's experience is worth highlighting here. For a while, in the early to mid-1970s, Sweden joined a European collective exchange rate arrangement known as the Snake (see the next chapter). In August 1977 Sweden withdrew from the Snake and pegged the krona unilaterally to a trade-weighted currency basket. In November 1981 and again in October 1982 the krona was devalued. In June 1985 Sweden officially adopted a band of ±1.5 per cent around the central rate; prior to that there was an 'unofficial' band of ±2.25 per cent. In May 1991 the krona was pegged to the ECU without any realignment put into place. The band continued as previously. In November 1992 the krona, under strong speculative pressures, was allowed to float.

The UK floated in 1972; in the earlier Thatcher years (from 1979) there was very little management; later, exchange rates were increasingly managed. In 1990 the UK joined the EMS exchange rate arrangements. In September 1992 sterling withdrew from the exchange rate arrangements and was floating independently. Australia and New Zealand adopted variations on the adjustable peg regime, the first until 1983, the second until 1985. Since those dates, both countries have been floating (Chapter 48). Italy also joined the ranks of the floaters in September 1992.

4

The European Monetary System

INTRODUCTION

The establishment of the European Monetary System (EMS) and its progress to date together constitute one of the most important developments in the international economy in the postwar years. It deserves, therefore, a brief chapter all to itself. At least until August 1992 it was widely perceived as having been a success. This success encouraged members to take further steps to consolidate and reform the system over the next few years.

We deal here with the following: first we review the historical background to the creation of the EMS, and we look at its key features; we then look at how it has evolved to end 1992–early 1993. Next, we briefly evaluate the performance to date. The literature on this topic is extensive and the reader is referred to it for further details (see Artis 1987; Gros and Thygesen 1988; Guitian 1988; Russo and Tullio 1988; Schinasi 1989; Eichengreen 1990; Giovannini 1990; Goodhart 1990; Ungerer *et al*. 1990; Bovenberg *et al*. 1991; Emerson and Huhne 1991; Frenkel and Goldstein 1991; Hildebrandt 1991; Masson and Taylor 1992).

BACKGROUND

In December 1969 the European Economic Community (EEC) Heads of State decided that steps should be taken to proceed with the formation of a monetary union. A committee headed by Werner was assigned the task of investigating the viability of proceeding with a union. The committee's report, which appeared in October 1970, made several recommendations. It envisaged a ten-year horizon, over which there would be a gradual advance towards complete monetary unification, which it judged to be attainable by 1980. It proposed a progression towards this aim in three stages. The first stage, which was spelt out in some detail, was to last three years to the end of 1973. Initially, attention was to centre on limiting exchange rate fluctuations among member countries, on extending facilities for short- and medium-term credit, on relaxing intra-EEC exchange controls and on greater cooperation in economic policies. In the later stages, exchange rates would become permanently fixed, capital markets would be progressively unified, reserves would be pooled and policies would become fully coordinated.

In March 1971 the EEC Council of Ministers endorsed the Werner Report, in substance, and decided to implement some modest steps in the direction of a union, including the provision of medium-term credit facilities and, from June 1971, a reduction in the maximum spread for intra-EEC exchange rate margins from the prevailing 1.5 to 1.2 percentage points. In the event, exchange markets became very unstable from May 1971 and the exchange rate provision was never implemented.

A more important step was taken in April 1972, when it was decided that from July 1972 the maximum spread was to be 2.25 per cent, half the new Smithsonian allowable spread of 4.5 per cent. This was the origin of what came to be labelled the Snake in the tunnel (the tunnel being the larger spread allowable with outside currencies). The participants in the agreement were Germany, France, Italy, the Benelux countries, the UK, Ireland, Norway and Denmark (the last four being then prospective EEC members), but by June 1972 with sterling under attack the UK and Ireland left the Snake. Italy left in February 1973 and by March 1973 there was effectively no tunnel and the remaining members then floated against outside currencies. Sweden joined in March 1973 but France left the Snake in January 1974, returning in July 1975 but leaving again in March 1976. Sweden left in 1977. By 1978 the only members left were Germany, the Benelux countries, Denmark and Norway.

This initial experiment with monetary unification must be judged to have been largely a failure. A report in 1975, prepared by a study group headed by Marjolin, concluded that monetary and economic policies had become even more divergent and that 'Europe is no nearer to European Monetary Unification than in 1969. In fact, if there has been any movement it has been backward.' It reaffirmed the key importance of close economic coordination and asserted that in its absence there was no point in trying to pursue monetary unification further.

The early attempt at monetary unification may be said to have failed for several reasons, including, principally, the upheavals in the international monetary system, the oil crisis and the very weak efforts at macro coordination.

In late 1977 Roy Jenkins, the President of the Commission, revived the idea of a monetary union, recommended new initiatives in that direction and supported the concept of a common European currency. The proposal fell on receptive ears. As it happened, several factors during 1978 appeared to be conspiring to strengthen the case for a union: dissatisfaction with the ways in which exchange markets were functioning, the alarm over the collapse of the US dollar in the second half of 1978, the growing view that the uncertainties associated with exchange rate instability were having an adverse effect on employment, trade and investment and the specific concern over the inflationary effects of currency devaluations, and finally some convergence during 1978 in inflation and monetary performances.

PRINCIPAL FEATURES

The original members which adopted the exchange rate mechanism (ERM) (i.e. the exchange rate rules) of the EMS were Belgium, Luxembourg, Denmark, France, Germany, Ireland, Italy and the Netherlands. The UK joined the EMS but at the time did not adopt its exchange rate rules.

The ERM is at the heart of the EMS. Members of the ERM have certain well-defined exchange rate obligations. Each currency in the scheme is given a central rate which is expressed in terms of ECUs; the ECU in turn is a basket of given amounts of currencies of members of the EMS.

Members have the option of adopting a narrower (± 2.25 per cent) or wider (± 6 per cent) margin of fluctuation around the central rate. Italy opted for the wider margin, all other members the narrower margin. Members therefore have an obligation to intervene in the foreign exchange market to ensure that bilateral exchange rates are maintained within the boundaries. Changes in the central rate may be made by mutual agreement.

An interesting innovation is the adoption of a 'divergence indicator'. A complicated formula serves to flash a signal that the currency is approaching its outward limits. At this point a presumption is created that some corrective measures need to be taken. These corrective measures may take many forms, including appropriate domestic monetary policies and/or changes in central rates. Central rates will be altered when fundamental conditions (e.g. rates of increase in costs and prices) in one country have drifted away from those in the other members.

On joining the EMS members are to deposit 20 per cent of their gold holdings and 20 per cent of their gross reserves in US dollars in exchange for ECUs. Interest is paid (earned) by participants when their holdings fall below (are in excess of) the amounts received against their deposits. Extensive short-term as well as medium-term financial assistance is also available when needed.

In the time that the EMS has operated the ECU has in fact served primarily as a unit of account and not, as originally hoped, either as a reserve asset or as a means of settlement of debts.

At the outset members were allowed to maintain exchange controls. France, Italy and Ireland exercised this right.

Altogether since the EMS was created and until the crisis in the second half of 1992, there were twelve realignments of central rates, some of these being quite insignificant, involving only one or two currencies, and others being much more significant.

It is evident from the above that the EMS resembles the old IMF system in many important respects, but on a smaller scale, e.g. its exchange rate provisions, the parallels between the ECU and the SDR and the financing facilities. This is no doubt true. There are, nonetheless, some technical differences. It was not launched as a gold or US dollar based system; the decision-making mechanism for changes in central rates is different; and most important of all one ultimate objective of the EMS, in sharp contrast to the IMF, is economic and political coordination.

In October 1990 the UK joined the ERM scheme, thus accepting its exchange rate obligations, but opted for the wider (6 per cent) band. In June 1989 Spain also joined the ERM, also adopting the wider band. In April 1992 Portugal joined the ERM, again with the wider bands. Greece (1981) joined the European Community (EC) and the EMS but not the ERM. In January 1990 Italy took the important step of switching from the wider to the narrower band.

THE EVOLUTION OF THE EUROPEAN MONETARY SYSTEM

It is convenient to break down the period of existence of the EMS into four sub-periods: March 1979 to March 1983, March 1983 to January 1987, January 1987 to August 1992 and September 1992 to February 1993 (see Goodhart 1990; Ungerer *et al*. 1990). This section focuses on the first three sub-periods.

March 1979 to January 1987

The first period was one of 'trial and orientation.' Several realignments (seven altogether) took place to offset differences in cost movements and other fundamentals. There was very little policy coordination and it seemed that domestic macro policies continued to be largely independent. The system thus behaved in ways similar to a discretionary crawling peg and possibly not much better than the Snake.

Nineteen eighty-one to 1983 were the 'early' years of the new French Socialist government headed by Mitterand. Those years were marked by a radical shift towards Keynesian-style macro policies; these policies, predictably, manifested themselves in cost differences and a substantial current account deficit. Not surprisingly, therefore, the period saw a succession of realignments *vis-à-vis* the deutschmark (15 per cent in October 1981, 10 per cent in June 1982) culminating in the March 1983 realignment of some 8 per cent. These were intended to correct for fundamental divergences either *ex ante* or *ex post*.

March 1983 is probably a turning point in the evolution of the EMS and marks the end of the first period. All the currencies of the EMS were involved in the realignment. At the same time France now decided to reverse its macro policy stance, implement more conservative policies and try and maintain a stronger currency within the EMS. The Italians too, in the meantime, had adopted more conformist policies.

The second period could be characterised as one of introspection, consolidation and self-evaluation. There were some minor speculative bursts and fewer realignments (four now); in these respects it was a calmer period. During this period, too, it seems that the deutschmark came to be accepted as the key anchor currency of the system.

A very important step was taken in June 1985 when the EC Commission set a timetable for the ultimate removal, by the end of 1992, of existing barriers to trade and finance and for the formation of a single internal market in Europe.

January 1987 to August 1992

The third period was important in that, other than the single Italian realignment to mark its adoption of narrower bands, there were no other realignments. There was very little serious speculation in the period and more coordination in economic policy.

In September 1987 members agreed on measures to liberalise the financing of intra-marginal interventions and on the more flexible use of interest rates and fluctuation margins in the event of exchange market pressure (the Basle/Nyborg Agreement). In June 1988 a very important further step was taken when members of the EC adopted a directive to liberalise capital movements completely by July 1990. Special extensions beyond that date, however, were granted to Portugal, Spain, Greece and Ireland. Also in that month a committee headed by Jacques Delors was established to look at concrete steps that might be taken towards greater economic and monetary union (EMU). The Delors Report was released in April 1989.

Ahead of schedule, in January 1990, France abolished its remaining restrictions on capital movements; Italy too abolished its restrictions in May 1990.

The Maastricht Agreement

The agreement reached in December 1991 in Maastricht by the EC Heads of State built on the earlier Delors Report. The treaty defines progress to be made towards full monetary unification. It now (end 1992) requires ratification by the member states.

Beginning 1 January 1994, a European Monetary Institute (EMI) will be established to take over the current responsibilities of the Committee of Governors of the EC Central Banks. Coordination of monetary policies will be tightened but national authorities will continue to have primary responsibility for their monetary policy. There is to be a progressive narrowing of exchange rate margins; at the same time, realignments will only be condoned in emergencies.

The next important stage of monetary unification is to begin no later than 1 January 1999. Exchange rates between member countries will now be permanently fixed. At the same time a European Central Bank (ECB) and a European System of Central Banks (ESCB) will assume full responsibility for monetary policy in the participating countries. A single currency, the ECU, will replace national currencies. The ESCB will also hold and manage members' foreign exchange reserves.

To be eligible to participate in this last stage, a number of criteria are laid down (the so-called convergence criteria). Public sector deficits ought not to exceed 3 per cent of gross domestic product (GDP) and the ratio of government debt to GDP should not exceed 60 per cent (some exceptions are allowed). The treaty demands steady progression towards these fiscal targets. The rate of inflation is not to exceed by more than $1\frac{1}{2}$ percentage points the average of those of the three member states with the lowest inflation. Interest rates on long-term government bonds must not exceed by more than 2 percentage points the average of those of the three low-inflation countries. There is to have been no realignment initiated by the member state for a period of two years.

THE EVENTS FROM SEPTEMBER 1992 AND THEIR AFTERMATH

Beginning in September 1992 exchange markets in Europe were shaken by a succession of crises. A number of European currencies became the object of speculative attacks; in all these cases there were massive shifts of funds out of these currencies and into the deutschmark. As particular currencies fell to the speculators, attention shifted to other vulnerable currencies.

In September sterling and the lira came under attack; resistance ultimately broke down and both currencies withdrew from the ERM and began to float independently. In the same month the Spanish peseta was devalued by 5 per cent. In the subsequent weeks there were strong attacks on the French franc, the Irish punt and the Danish krone. At the end of January 1993 the Irish punt was devalued by 10 per cent.

European currencies outside the EMS also came under attack. The Swedish krona, the Norwegian krone and the Finnish markka had been pegged to the ECU; these currencies had aspired at some stage to join the exchange rate arrangements of the EMS. Under attack all three currencies ultimately succumbed. Before the end of 1992 all three were floating. The Swedish krona put up a vigorous and determined fight against the speculation, pushing up its own interest rates to exorbitant levels to discourage the flight of capital, but in the event it all proved to be of no avail.

Key factors underlying the crisis

Why did the crisis erupt when it did?

a) In the wake of Germany's reunification, the public sector deficit had been allowed to rise sharply. At the same time, inflation by 1991–2 had reached some 4–5 per cent, a level which was considered unacceptable. This combination of circumstances produced interest rates which were particularly high relative to those prevailing in the USA, Japan and, most importantly, other EMS countries. Several EMS countries were forced to raise their own interest rates at a time when their economies were showing signs of considerable weakness. This generated a good deal of tension within the EMS.

b) Many felt that sterling had joined the ERM at an overvalued exchange rate. The exchange rate was intended to be a compromise between, on the one hand, achieving competitiveness and, on the other, enjoying inflation discipline. In the event it was probably tilted too strongly in the direction of the latter. Inevitably, too, parallels were made between the entry into the ERM and Britain's re-entry into the gold standard in 1923, as described in Chapter 1 (Miller and Sutherland 1992).

c) With inflation rates diverging, exchange rate stability had in fact been achieved at the expense of cumulative gains and losses in competitive positions amongst participating countries. Sterling had appreciated in real terms by some 10 per cent against the mark since it joined the ERM. The lira had appreciated in real terms by some 18 per cent against the mark since its last realignment in 1987. Similar stories could be told about the Spanish peseta and the Portuguese escudo. Projections of labour costs and inflation in the years ahead also suggested further erosion of competitiveness for several ERM currencies (IMF 1993). This build-up in fundamental imbalances had produced some loss of credibility with respect to existing exchange rates.

d) Doubts were also beginning to emerge about the feasibility of achieving the convergence criteria, at least in the time envisaged. Table 4.1 presents a progress report in 1991–2 on the convergence indicators. What is striking about the table is that many of the countries were still a long way from meeting the criteria. Again, projections suggested that such deviations were likely to persist into the future, making realisation problematical. There were also concerns expressed about the impacts on the real economies, which were in recession, of serious attempts to accelerate progress towards the fiscal targets.

e) Fundamental factors to one side, there was a degree of self-fulfilling prophecy attached to the outcomes. Speculators picked out currencies which they decided were potentially vulnerable, drawing on massive reserves of funds (exceeding in many cases those ultimately available to central banks to defend their currencies).

The case of the French franc was particularly revealing. Everyone agreed that the fundamentals were all 'sound' in France. Inflation was relatively low, the current account was in surplus and France met all the convergence criteria without difficulty. This, however, did not stop the speculators from attacking the franc on several occasions. Why was this?

To begin with, a determined speculative attack, deserved or otherwise, can always succeed in principle if the central bank exhausts its reserves (or its borrowing capacity) or is obliged to raise interest rates to unacceptable levels in its efforts to defend the currency. The Bank of France did exhaust a large portion of its foreign currency reserves; it also raised its interest rates at a time when its own economy was in recession.

There were other factors at work. The Maastricht Treaty had been ratified in a referendum in France but only by a tiny majority (51–49). France was in severe recession and was desperately looking for a way out, including an easier monetary policy. Some were casting envious eyes at the British. There was a respectable body of opinion amongst academics and politicians in favour of a French float. Finally, as

Table 4.1 European countries: convergence indicators for 1991 and 1992

	Consumer price inflation 1991	1992	General government balance–GDP 1991	1992	Gross government debt–GDP[a] 1991	1992	Long-term interest rates 1991	1992
EC countries								
France	3.1	2.8	−2.1	−2.9	47.1	47.7	9.2	8.7
Germany	4.8	5.0	−3.2	−3.2	41.7	42.5	8.5	7.8
Italy[b]	6.3	5.5	−10.2	−10.4	103.5	108.5	13.0	13.5
UK[b]	5.9	3.7	−2.7	−6.3	34.4	35.9	9.9	9.0
Largest four countries[c]	4.9	4.3	−4.4	−5.4	55.2	56.9	10.0	9.6
Belgium	3.2	2.4	−7.6	−6.8	134.4	133.4	9.3	8.8
Denmark[d]	2.4	2.1	−2.3	−2.3	66.7	71.3	9.6	8.9
Greece	19.5	16.0	−17.4	−13.8	115.5	114.8	23.3	21.5
Ireland	3.2	3.3	−2.8	−1.8	98.0	100.0	9.2	10.0
Luxembourg	3.1	2.8	1.5	1.0	6.2	5.8	8.2	7.8
Netherlands	3.9	3.3	−3.9	−4.0	79.6	80.0	8.7	8.0
Portugal	11.4	9.2	−6.7	−5.7	65.3	69.5	18.5	16.5
Spain	5.9	5.9	−4.9	−5.1	44.7	46.0	12.6	12.6
Smallest eight countries[c]	5.5	5.0	−5.5	−5.2	75.5	77.4	11.6	11.1
All EC[c]	5.1	4.5	−4.6	−5.3	59.4	61.3	10.3	9.9
Maastricht convergence criteria[f]	4.4	4.0	−3.0	−3.0	60.0	60.0	11.0	10.7
Non-EC countries								
Austria	3.3	3.8	−2.2	−1.9	56.5	55.8	8.6	7.9
Finland	4.2	2.7	−6.0	−8.8	21.7	33.0	12.2	12.8
Norway	3.2	2.3	−1.1	−4.3	43.3	50.0	9.9	9.6
Sweden	9.3	2.2	−1.5	−6.4	44.8	50.0	10.7	10.3
Switzerland	5.9	4.0	−1.7	−1.7	32.1	34.3	6.4	6.6
Five non-EC countries	5.7	3.1	−2.4	−4.4	38.6	43.7	9.3	9.1

Source: IMF 1993.
Notes: [a] Debt data are from national sources. They relate to the general government but may not be consistent with the definition agreed at Maastricht.
[b] Debt on fiscal year basis.
[c] Average weighted by 1991 GDP shares.
[d] The debt–GDP ratio would be below 60 per cent if it was adjusted in line with the definition agreed at Maastricht.
[e] Long-term interest rate is the twelve-month treasury bill rate.
[f] Unweighted averages.

many other currencies were devaluing, France's competitive position was eroding; France, too, one should add, has always been acutely conscious of its competitive strength.

The aftermath

The exchange crises provoked a lively debate about the future of the EMS, the timetable for reform and the exchange rate policy options open to governments.

Many commentators diagnosing the events argued that had *orderly* realignments been allowed in 1991–2 or even earlier the crises would not have erupted.

Doubts were raised about whether the target for EMU was now viable. Several options were debated. One was to return, for a while at least, to a system of frequent but small realignments. Another was to allow wider bands. Yet another was to reimpose capital controls as a means of resisting speculative attacks. There was also serious talk of a two-speed convergence to EMU, with France, Germany and the Benelux countries accelerating progress towards EMU and others joining them at some point in the future. The large differences in the degree to which the convergence criteria were being met pointed in that direction. More generally, there was some support for postponing the timetable for reform or at least applying softer criteria. At the other extreme, there was some support for the idea of abandoning the EMS, allowing each member to choose its own independent regime. Some might choose to stay with the mark, some might float, some might go off in yet another direction. Whatever, each decided it would no longer be a grand coordinated exchange rate arrangement.

The UK float provoked mixed reactions, some highly unsympathetic (charging Britain with having deserted the cause), some supportive. Freed of the exchange rate constraint flexible rates had allowed the UK to drop her interest rates substantially in a succession of steps. By late February 1993 sterling had devalued by some 20 per cent relative to its September 1992 central rate with the mark. Not everyone, however, agreed that this was a wise move; as we shall see in our theoretical analysis in the chapters which follow, there was anxiety over the inflationary effects, the initial perverse effects on both output and the current account. By early 1993 the official line in the UK was that the UK had no intention of returning to the ERM before the end of 1993.

Germany did make some interest rate cuts but these only came after the crisis had already been under way and, in any event, the cuts were too small to provide any real relief to other European economies.

PERFORMANCE OF THE EUROPEAN MONETARY SYSTEM

How are we to evaluate the performance of the EMS or a system similar to the EMS or its variant the EMU? This is a very difficult task; nor is it a task we can attack without first being properly equipped with an analytical framework. So the task will be undertaken in steps over the whole book as the analytical underpinnings are presented. At this point all we can do is make a few brief comments about the treatment in the literature of the performance to August 1992. The reader is warned that, in the light of events since, the comments will need now to be strongly qualified.

At the simplest level we might ask first whether it succeeded in its principal avowed objective of stabilising nominal and real bilateral exchange rates. In this respect there is little doubt of its success. However, on exchange rate stabilisation in general, there are doubts at two levels. Goodhart (1990) questions whether the EMS reduced medium- to long-run real exchange rate misalignments. Also between 1975–8 and 1978–89 there was a fall in the variability of the real effective rate in five of the seven member countries, but in most cases the fall was not so dramatic. Moreover in many countries outside the ERM this variability also fell.

Did the EMS succeed in exercising inflation discipline? Most commentators have assumed that Germany is the anchor of the system, providing the inflation discipline. Accepting this, has the disinflationary process proceeded more rapidly inside than outside the EMS or is it true that members disinflated faster than they otherwise would have? The answers to these questions may well be a subdued yes. However, a dissenting voice is that of Collins (1988) who in fact concludes that 'there is little or no evidence of any special shift (in inflation behaviour) between 1979 and 1985 among EMS members.' This view is probably too strong and may not hold for the period extended beyond 1985.

One might also want to look at the unemployment performance of the EMS. It is not difficult to find a theoretical link between the constraints imposed by the EMS and unemployment. Inflation discipline exercised by Germany may come at a cost in terms of unemployment (Chapter 22).

There may also be a link between external imbalances and the EMS constraints. Differential rates of inflation combined with relatively rigid exchange rates within the EMS could be associated with changes in relative competitive positions which, in turn, could manifest themselves in changes in external balance. This link, however, is much more difficult to establish empirically.

In this same context, Walters has been critical of the way in which the EMS has been functioning. His criticism has come to be called the 'Walters critique'. In his own words:

> The EMS forces countries to have the same nominal interest rates. If, however, Italy is inflating at a rate of 7 per cent and Germany at a rate of 2 per cent (both over the relevant period of [exchange rate] fixing) then there is a problem of perversity. With the same interest rate at say 5 per cent, the *real* interest rate for Italy is *minus* 2 per cent and for Germany plus 3 per cent. Thus Italy will have an expansionary monetary policy, while Germany will pursue one of restraint. But this will exacerbate inflation in Italy and yet restrain further the already low inflation in Germany. This is the opposite of 'convergence', namely it induces divergence.
>
> (1990: 79–80)

On the face of it this critique appears powerful. However, as Walters himself conceded, it would not hold completely in countries such as France and Italy which (at least until 1990) maintained controls over capital movements which then allowed them to have interest rates which diverged from those of other member countries. Moreover, much hinges on how credible the system is. If a country's rate of inflation is persistently high, there is a good chance that it will be associated with an ultimate devaluation of the currency. In this case the home interest rate can be higher at home to offset the expected devaluation (see Miller and Sutherland 1991).

The proper framework to apply here is one of asking how each and every one of the ERM countries would have performed if it had not entered the EMS. This calls for defining very complicated alternative scenarios which, in principle, might be simulated by econometric models (see also Chapter 36).

Much of the debate over the economic costs and benefits to a member of the union is perhaps beside the point. The truth is that, whatever the net gain or loss, the real driving force behind the union is political rather than economic.

EMS–EMU performance and this book

To help the reader who is trying to understand how a system such as the EMS or an EMU might function and its strong and weak points we provide here a brief guideline to the chapters which bear most directly on these themes.

Chapter 16 is highly pertinent. It presents a model of a three-country world which comprises two giant economies (Germany or Japan and the USA) and a third one, which could be large or small. This third country can, for example, peg to one of the giants (as France, for example, effectively pegs to the mark) or it can float *vis-à-vis* the giants (as the UK is currently doing). The framework allows us to analyse the effects of monetary and fiscal policies in the third country and, more importantly, the impacts of monetary and fiscal policies in one or other of the giants on the third country. This provides the analytical underpinning for a review of recent developments.

Chapter 14 analyses the case of asymmetrical exchange market intervention in a two-country framework, where one country has an independent monetary policy and the second has to conform to the other country's monetary policy. This corresponds roughly to the case of Germany and the other members of the EMS.

Chapter 36 is a most important chapter in this context. The EMS is both an adjustable peg and a target zone type of system. These systems are analysed in the chapter. The chapter also analyses the pros and cons of an EMU system, contrasting this with the US case.

Chapter 21 also bears on any analysis of the short-term effects of the recent UK float. The UK started out with a current account deficit, a modest inflation and considerable unemployment. The chapter shows that in the short run of some nine months or so a monetary expansion might have 'perverse' effects on the current account, on inflation and on unemployment.

Finally, we note that a rationale for fiscal convergence rules is provided in Chapter 34.

5

The increased financial interdependence in the world economy

INTRODUCTION

In this chapter we consider developments in the world economy in recent decades which have had a bearing on the degree of financial integration.

TRADE, MULTINATIONALS AND FINANCIAL INTEGRATION

In the wake of lower trade barriers and reduced costs of transportation there has been a dramatic increase in trade amongst developed economies: for the OECD as a whole, for example, exports represented some 11.6 per cent of gross national product (GNP) in 1960; by 1975 this share had grown to 17.4 per cent; in 1980 it was 20 per cent; since then it has fallen marginally.

Increased trade produces closer financial links for a number of reasons. It increases the scope for interest rate arbitrage and leads and lags amongst traders; it increases the demand for foreign currency assets; financial enterprises are also likely to follow their trading customers and set up facilities abroad. In general trade enhances exposure to and awareness of financial markets in countries with which one trades (Bryant 1987). Thus for any given set of restrictions on the movement of capital one would expect a greater responsiveness to interest rate or speculative incentives (unless effective countermeasures are implemented).

The increased presence of multinational business also increases financial links and has very similar effects to the increase in trade. The existence of foreign-controlled resident companies or resident companies with affiliations abroad facilitates the transfer of funds between national economies (e.g. by altering the timing of the repatriation of profits or of payments for transactions, by transfer pricing).

The rapidly expanding presence of foreign banking entities in national markets is also a factor making for increasing financial integration. Several countries in recent years have permitted foreign banks to operate or have liberalised their activities. A study by the Bank for International Settlements (1986) documents these developments, noting that 'foreign establishments as a rule carry out a higher proportion of their business in foreign currency with non residents or multi-national companies than do domestically-owned banks'.

TECHNOLOGY, EURO-CURRENCY MARKETS AND INTEGRATION

Technological developments in communication, transportation and information gathering may also have contributed to the integration of national financial markets. The lower costs of international transactions, the rapidity with which international transactions can now be effected, the breadth of information available and the speed at which such information becomes available through computer technology have facilitated the transmission of capital across frontiers.

The rapid growth of the Euro-currency markets, particularly in the 1970s, and the internationalisation of banking, by acting as a channel for the transmission of capital, are also widely held to have increased financial integration. Bryant (1987) shows that international banking has expanded even more rapidly than trade.

OFFICIAL DISMANTLING OF CAPITAL CONTROLS

Over the last thirty years or so there has been a dramatic lowering of official barriers to the movement of capital. This progress has not, however, been uninterrupted. At the same time official as well as academic attitudes to capital controls have swung full circle.

Immediately after the Second World War, at the time when the IMF was set up, there was considerable opposition in both official and academic circles to the free movement of capital, which was judged to be dis-equilibrating. The IMF Articles reflected these views, as we have seen, permitting controls over such movements. In the decade or so which followed countries retained considerable barriers to capital flows.

The first wave of liberalisation came in 1958 when current account convertibility was re-established. Between 1960 and 1968 there was some further reduction in the barriers, particularly on outflows, in several European economies. A notable exception to this trend, however, was the USA which introduced new restrictions on outflows.[1]

As we saw in Chapter 2, in the years 1968–72 barriers were reimposed in response to the huge swings in US monetary policy. In 1968–9 the tight monetary policy in the USA led to huge outflows from the rest of the world; one response was to tighten controls over outflows. In sharp contrast, in 1970–1 US interest rates tumbled; the rest of the world now put up barriers to the inflow of capital.

A second big wave of liberalisation came in 1973–4 in the wake of the switch to flexible exchange rates. Several countries, notably the USA and Germany, reduced their barriers.

Some liberalisation continued in the subsequent years but from 1979 there was a third big wave of liberalisation. In 1979 the UK dismantled its exchange controls; in 1980 Japan took a major step forward in liberalising her capital movements; Germany further liberalised her international capital markets in 1981; Australia abandoned her capital controls in 1983; New Zealand followed Australia in 1984; Denmark liberalised her controls over capital movements between 1983 and 1985.

There was yet another wave of liberalisation in 1989–90. Sweden abandoned most of her controls in the course of 1989 and 1990; Norway and Finland relaxed most controls in 1989–90. In 1990 France and Italy also abandoned their remaining controls. By mid-1991 very few OECD member countries retained significant controls.

Reasons for dismantling of capital controls

Why this dramatic shift in official and indeed academic opinion towards capital controls? Amongst the more important reasons were the following: some disillusionment over their effectiveness, the switch to flexible exchange rates, the large current account and budget deficits in the wake of the two oil price shocks, liberalisation in domestic capital markets, international pressures and perhaps, too, a marked swing towards conservative convictions that markets should be freed.

Controls tend to proliferate to close emerging loopholes in earlier controls. Germany's and Australia's experience, to mention only two, illustrate this. Baumgartner reviewing Germany's experience concluded that:

> in order to reduce capital inflows caused by the relatively higher degree of monetary tightness in the domestic economy, Germany first introduced discriminatory minimum reserve requirements against the growth (and subsequently also against the level) of banks' liabilities to non-residents, of money market paper and for 'en pension' transactions regarding domestic fixed-interest securities for money market investment. Soon these measures had to be supplemented by a cash deposit for non-bank borrowing abroad (tightened in several stages) in an effort to close loopholes that were widely used for evading the regulations. Finally, borrowing by non-bank residents from non-residents, certain inward direct investment, and the cession of claims to non-residents were restricted administratively, and banks were requested not to sell to non-residents their portfolio holdings of deutsche mark bonds of foreign issuers. These measures aimed at containing capital imports, whether induced by differing monetary conditions or exchange rate expectations, and were complemented in this respect by the restriction of approvals for the payment of interest on bank deposits of non-residents.

(1977: 39)

Australia also found that important loopholes in the application of capital controls came from the activities of multinationals and from traders, so in due course the authorities moved to regulate the timing of payments by traders and to increase surveillance over multinational accounts (Argy 1987).

There has also been some disillusionment in countries which typically have tried to use capital controls to buy monetary independence under a managed exchange rate regime. There is a considerable body of opinion, for example, that Sweden at least in recent years has not been able to achieve much monetary independence (see Horngren and Viotti 1985; OECD 1985).

Scepticism over the continued effectiveness of controls is also expressed in a GATT study, which the IMF summarised in the following terms: 'For capital controls to be effective [GATT argues], restrictions would have to directly cover every aspect of a country's international transactions – a proposition that is highly unlikely to succeed in a market economy' (IMF 1980).

With fixed exchange rates capital controls are thought to be needed to buy monetary independence. When monetary independence was severely threatened in 1968–71, barriers to the flow of capital were further raised. A major motivation in the switch to flexible exchange rates was the conviction that with flexible exchange rates would come monetary independence. In this context capital controls were not only unnecessary but indeed served to weaken the effectiveness of monetary policy (albeit strengthening the effectiveness of fiscal policy) (Chapter 6). There was here then what looked like a solid theoretical rationale for liberalising capital flows.

In the aftermath of the first oil price shock in 1974 large current account and budget deficits surfaced. To finance these many developed economies liberalised their policies towards capital inflows. In the wake of the second oil shock again the large current account deficits encouraged further liberalisation of inflows.

Many developed economies from the mid-1970s moved to deregulate their domestic capital markets. Liberalising on the external front was seen as a logical extension of this, although sometimes reverse pressure (from international to domestic liberalisation) may have been at play.

International pressures have also been of some importance over the years. Both the OECD and the EC uphold the principle that international markets should be progressively freed. The 1961 OECD Code of Liberalisation of Capital Movements, to which member countries subscribe, imposes an obligation to 'progressively abolish between one another . . . restrictions on movements of capital to the extent necessary for effective economic cooperation'. Japan has also come under considerable pressure, notably from the USA, to liberalise its own international markets (Frankel 1984).

OTHER DEVELOPMENTS AND CONCLUSIONS

It is difficult to evaluate the effects of domestic financial deregulation and of financial innovations on financial integration. The creation of new financial instruments may have served to attract more foreign capital. A host of international innovations have also reinforced the integration process (for detailed documentation see Bank for International Settlements 1986).

Finally the Bank for International Settlements (1986) also notes that 'a growing number of institutionally managed funds ... have actively pursued a policy of diversifying their portfolios internationally' (p. 155).

All the influences noted so far, if anything, serve to increase asset substitution. We note here, however, one potentially important influence pushing in the other direction. The switch to flexible rates by increasing exchange rate volatility has probably increased the risk premium and so reduced asset substitution. At the same time transactions costs have increased, with the same outcome.

There is now very convincing evidence that after individual countries dismantled their exchange controls covered interest rate parity tended to hold, and so capital mobility was effectively perfect (Argy 1987). Prominent illustrations are Germany (after 1973), the UK (after 1979), Japan (after 1980), Australia (after 1984) and France and Italy (from 1990). This does suggest, importantly, that a dominant influence on asset substitution was capital controls and that many of the other influences reviewed (risk premium apart) could only have played a secondary role.

Part II

OPEN ECONOMY MODELS –
COMPARATIVE STATICS ANALYSIS

Part II introduces the reader to open economy models. The analysis undertaken in these chapters is comparative statics, in the sense that we concentrate only on the final outcomes for each model without paying any serious attention to dynamics.

Part II opens with the best known of the open economy models, the one first developed by R. Mundell and M. Fleming, the so-called Mundell–Fleming (MF) model. The chapters that follow are variations on this basic theme.

Chapter 7 outlines the strengths and limitations of the MF model. The model is extended or modified in subsequent chapters in a number of directions. Chapter 8 allows wages and prices to adjust. Chapter 9 introduces the reader to disequilibrium models, long popular on the European continent. Chapter 10 presents the portfolio balance model of the monetary sector. The model is an important alternative to conventional Keynesian approaches to the monetary sector; it also allows us to introduce wealth in the asset demand equations. With this as background, we turn in Chapter 11 to a model where wealth appears not only in the monetary sector but also in the real demand for goods.

Chapter 12 introduces the reader to the elasticities approach to a devaluation, focusing here exclusively on partial micro analysis.

Chapter 13 extends the MF model to the large-country case. This chapter assumes that the world comprises only two countries; the model is used to analyse the macroeconomic interactions between the two countries. In Chapter 14 we extend this to the case where wages and prices are flexible in one or both of the two countries. Chapter 15 reviews the econometric evidence which bears on the macroeconomic interactions between two large countries. Chapter 16 extends the two-country model to a three-country world, introducing a small country facing two economic giants.

Finally, Chapter 17 introduces the reader to a model of a small economy with two sectors, a traded goods sector and a non-traded goods sector. This model is contrasted with MF-type models.

6

The Mundell–Fleming model

INTRODUCTION

It is appropriate to begin this part of the book with a presentation of the Mundell–Fleming (MF) model which is easily the best known and most widely used model of the open macro economy. It is fair to say that, over time, it has assumed the role of a reference point against which other models have been compared. The basics of this model are now taught in most universities in first- and second-year macroeconomics courses; it should therefore be familiar to students who have advanced to that point (see Fleming 1962; Mundell 1963a).

The MF model is a model of a small open economy oriented primarily towards adjustment over a period roughly of a year or so. Consistently with its short-run orientation it assumes that wages and prices are fixed; the model is thus Keynesian in spirit. In such a model aggregate supply is perfectly elastic, with aggregate demand determining the actual level of output.

The model is essentially an extension to the open economy of an IS–LM framework, now very familiar to any first-year student of macroeconomics. The model is modified to accommodate the determination of the balance of payments; this last comprises a trade balance[1] and a capital account. In the MF model the trade balance is explained by the level of output at home in relation to output abroad and by the exchange rate. The capital account is explained by the level of output at home in relation to output abroad and by the exchange rate. The capital account is explained by the level of the home interest rate in relation to the interest rate abroad. The sensitivity of the capital account to the interest rate differential is a measure of the degree of capital mobility (asset substitution). The degree of capital mobility plays a key role in the MF model.

The model can readily be manipulated to analyse the effects of monetary, fiscal policies at home, and as well the effects of a variety of disturbances (expenditure, monetary or supply) originating at home or abroad, on such variables as output, the interest rate and the exchange rate, for different exchange rate regimes and for different assumptions about the degree of capital mobility. Typically, three types of exchange rate regime are distinguished: a fixed exchange rate regime with sterilised intervention (where the monetary authorities are assumed to have control over the money stock) (regime 1, MR), a fixed exchange rate regime which allows the money supply to respond to the balance of payments (the case of unsterilised foreign exchange intervention) (regime 2, GR) and a pure float (regime 3, FR).

These three regimes correspond roughly to the three regimes discussed in more detail in Chapters 1–3 in Part I. Regime 2 corresponds to the gold standard regime of Chapter 1. Regime 1 in essence corresponds to the IMF-type system of Chapter 2. It will be recalled that the original intention of the regime was that it should allow both monetary and fiscal independence. Regime 3 corresponds to the float (without here any management).

Under a pure float the balance of payments is always equal to zero (meaning that any surplus in the current account must be exactly matched by a deficit on the capital account). This is because by definition there is no foreign exchange intervention. In regime 2 there is unsterilised intervention to maintain the fixed exchange rate; a gold standard mechanism of adjustment thus comes into play. This adjustment proceeds until the balance of payments is also restored to zero, but now only after the lapse of some time. In regime 1, however, because of the operation of sterilisation operations, there are no endogenous forces at work to restore equilibrium to the balance of payments which now need not converge towards zero.

THE MODEL

We first present the model in mathematical form; in the next section we present the model in graphical form; we then demonstrate outcomes in this form. The outcomes are later confirmed by a more rigorous mathematical treatment. Appendix 1 explains the derivation of the model in logarithmic form.

The goods market

$$yr = \alpha_1 e + \alpha_3 gr - \alpha_4 r_d + \alpha_8 yr^* \tag{1}$$

The money market

$$mo_d = \alpha_5 yr - \alpha_{10} r_d \tag{2}$$

$$mo_s = \overline{mo} - \pi_1(e - \bar{e}) \tag{3}$$

$$mo_d = mo_s \tag{4}$$

The foreign exchange market

$$\frac{B}{X_0} = \alpha_{13}e - \text{yr} + \text{yr}^* + \alpha_{14}(r_d - r^*)$$

$$\alpha_{13} > \alpha_1 \tag{5}$$

Notation

All variables are in logarithms (except for the interest rate r_d and B/X_0).

yr domestic output
r_d domestic interest rate
e exchange rate (units of domestic currency per unit of foreign currency)
gr real government expenditure (the fiscal policy instrument)
mo stock of money
$\overline{\text{mo}}$ the exogenous component of the money stock (the monetary policy instrument)
B/X_0 overall balance of payments over initial exports
$\bar{e}$ target exchange rate
r^* foreign interest rate
yr^* foreign level of output

Equation (1) says that the real demand for goods is a positive function of the exchange rate, of real government expenditure (the fiscal policy variable) and of the foreign level of output (assumed fixed) and a negative function of the interest rate. The positive coefficient on the exchange rate assumes that the Marshall–Lerner condition holds (see Appendix 1). The foreign level of output appears in the equation because that determines the small country's level of exports which in turn are a component of the domestic demand for goods (see again Appendix 1).

Equation (2) is a conventional money demand equation. Money balances are a positive function of output and a negative function of the interest rate.

Equation (3) is the monetary policy reaction function. There are two components to the money supply process, one of which is exogenous ($\overline{\text{mo}}$), the other endogenous. The exogenous component by definition is the component of the money supply which is controlled by the monetary authorities; a change in the stance of monetary policy would be represented by a change in $\overline{\text{mo}}$.

The other component is assumed to respond to the difference between the market exchange rate and a target exchange rate ($\bar{e}$). It says that the monetary authorities will increase (decrease) the money stock in some degree when the market exchange rate is below (above) the target exchange rate.

To illustrate how this equation functions, suppose the monetary authorities implemented an easier monetary policy by buying government securities from the public.[2] In this case $\overline{mo}$ would increase. This would show up in the central bank's balance sheet as an increase in both its cash liabilities and its domestic assets. Domestic assets represent the monetary policy control instrument. If the exchange rate is floating the monetary authorities do not buy or sell foreign exchange and so the *change* in its foreign assets (i.e. the overall balance of payments) is always zero. In this case the change in the money stock (more precisely high-powered money) is equal to the change in the domestic assets of the central bank. The money stock is thus assumed to be completely controlled by the authorities.

Suppose now a balance of payments deficit emerges. If the authorities want to maintain the exchange rate at its original level they will sell foreign currency from the stock of international reserves. This will reduce both the cash base and the foreign assets of the central bank balance sheet. At this point the authorities may either sterilise the effects of the deficit on the cash base or leave things as they are (in which case we have unsterilised intervention). If they decide to sterilise they will again buy government securities, restoring the original cash base. The end result of the sale of foreign assets and the sterilisation operation, in combination, on the central bank balance sheet is that foreign assets will fall and domestic assets will increase by an equivalent amount. In this case, too, the monetary authorities control the cash base and the money stock.

There is an intermediate case. The authorities may allow the deficit to fall partly on the exchange rate (there will be some devaluation) and partly on the cash base (there will be some sales of foreign assets). This is a policy of 'leaning against the wind'. Again, the sales of foreign assets might or might not be sterilised. This intermediate case is in fact only of academic interest in this chapter since we deal only with fixed and flexible rate regimes.

Equation (3) accommodates all these possibilities. If $\pi_1 = 0$ we have an exogenous money stock which is consistent with either a flexible rate regime or a fixed rate regime with perfect sterilisation. If $\pi_1 \rightarrow \infty$ we have a fixed rate regime with monetary management, i.e. monetary policy is used to restore the target exchange rate. If $\pi_1 < \infty > 0$ we have a managed float (the intermediate case) with π_1 representing the degree to which monetary policy is used to 'lean against the wind'.

Equation (5) explains the overall balance of payments (B/X_0). The overall balance of payments is composed of a trade balance and a capital account. The trade balance is determined by the exchange rate and the level of output at home in relation to output abroad (assumed fixed). The capital account is determined by the home interest rate in relation to the interest rate abroad (assumed fixed). α_{14} therefore represents the degree of capital mobility.

In this chapter we are interested in the effects of monetary and fiscal expansion under different exchange rate regimes and for different assumptions about the degree of capital mobility.

THE GRAPHICAL REPRESENTATION

In the MF model there are three key markets each of which can be represented graphically: a goods market (IS), a money market (LM) and a foreign exchange market (B). These are all shown in Figure 6.1.

IS traces the combinations of the interest rate and the level of output which will maintain equilibrium in the goods market. This is derived from (1). Dropping yr^* and rearranging we have

$$r_d = -\frac{1}{\alpha_4} \, yr + \frac{\alpha_1}{\alpha_4} \, e + \frac{\alpha_3}{\alpha_4} \, gr \tag{6}$$

This is shown in Figure 6.1. The shift variables are e and gr. A devaluation (appreciation) or an increase (decrease) in government expenditure will shift the schedule to the right (left).

LM traces the combinations of r_d and yr which will maintain equilibrium in the money market. From (2), setting $mo_d = mo_s$,

$$r_d = \frac{\alpha_5}{\alpha_{10}} \, yr - \frac{1}{\alpha_{10}} \, mo \tag{7}$$

An increase (decrease) in the money stock will shift the LM schedule to the right (left).

We can represent the foreign exchange market by the use of a B schedule which traces now the combinations of r_d and yr which will preserve equilibrium in the overall balance of payments. From (5) setting $B/X_0 = 0$ we have

$$r_d = r^* + \frac{1}{\alpha_{14}} \, (yr - yr^*) - \frac{\alpha_{13}}{\alpha_{14}} \, e \tag{8}$$

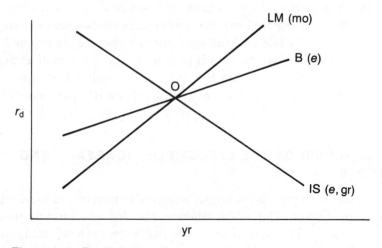

Figure 6.1 Equilibrium in the goods, money and foreign exchange markets

The schedule is positively sloped because as income increases and the current account deteriorates a rise in the interest rate, which induces an inflow of capital, is required to restore equilibrium to the overall balance of payments. The slope $1/\alpha_{14}$ of this schedule reflects the degree of capital mobility. When capital is completely immobile (i.e. insensitive to interest rate changes so that $\alpha_{14} = 0$), the B schedule is vertical. At the other extreme, when the degree of capital mobility is infinite (i.e. when the domestic interest rate cannot diverge from the foreign interest rate and $\alpha_{14} \to \infty$), the schedule is horizontal. Hence, as B moves in a clockwise direction the slope decreases and the degree of capital mobility increases, requiring a progressively smaller rise in the interest rate to offset a given current account deficit.

This B schedule will shift to the right (left) if foreign output increases (decreases) or if the foreign interest rate falls (rises). These are not shown because they will be held fixed in our analysis. Again, the schedule will shift to the right (left) if there is a devaluation (revaluation), provided, in all these cases, that the Marshall–Lerner condition holds. To see why it shifts with a devaluation, recall that a devaluation improves the current account, and so to restore equilibrium what is required is, given the interest rate, a higher level of output or, given output, a lower interest rate.

The area to the right (left) of the B schedule will represent an overall deficit (surplus) in the balance of payments because, in that area, the level of output is too high (low) and/or the interest rate is too low (high) relative to the levels of output and the interest rate required to secure overall balance of payments equilibrium.

It is also worth noting that the horizontal distance from the point of intersection of the IS–LM schedules and the B schedule represents the *overall* balance of payments disequilibrium. If the intersection is to the right (left) of the B schedule this will correspond to an overall balance of payments deficit (surplus).

Figure 6.1 represents a situation where there is equilibrium in all three markets at point O.

For regimes 2 and 3 full equilibrium always requires that all markets be in equilibrium, so for any disturbance a new equilibrium will be located at the intersection of all three schedules. In regime 2 any disequilibrium in the balance of payments will force shifts in the LM schedule until full equilibrium is restored. In regime 3 any disequilibrium in the balance of payments will be removed by appropriate exchange rate changes which shift, now, the IS and B schedules. For regime 1 equilibrium is located at the intersection of LM and IS but not necessarily on B, and so equilibrium is consistent with a surplus or deficit in the overall balance of payments.

GRAPHICAL ANALYSIS OF THE EFFECTS OF MONETARY AND FISCAL POLICIES

Our primary focus here is on the relative output effects of monetary and fiscal expansion under the three regimes. This is the criterion Mundell and Fleming used to evaluate the three regimes. The more effective the policy the more advantageous is the regime, other things being equal.

The relative effectiveness of monetary policy

Consider, first, the effects of an exogenous open market purchase under the three regimes (MR, GR and FR) and assume, initially, that capital is completely immobile, so that the B schedule is vertical (see Figure 6.2).

Suppose that at the start of our analysis all markets are in equilibrium at yr_0. Now an increase in the volume of money will shift the LM schedule to the right to LM_1, raising the level of income to yr_1.

At yr_1 there will be a current account deficit represented by ab. If the monetary authorities sterilise the monetary effects of this deficit, say by additional open market purchases, the level of output can be sustained, in the short term, at yr_1, which then represents the solution for the MR regime. With this solution the goods and money markets are in equilibrium but the foreign exchange market remains in disequilibrium.

If there is no sterilisation, as in the GR regime, the volume of money is allowed to shrink in line with the deficit, and this continues until the original level of output yr_0 is restored. At this point, all three markets return to equilibrium at the original intersection of the three schedules. Monetary policy will have been completely unsuccessful while, at the same time, there will be a loss of reserves from the current account deficit exactly equal to the original open market purchase.

To see this, imagine that output had fallen back but was still higher than its initial

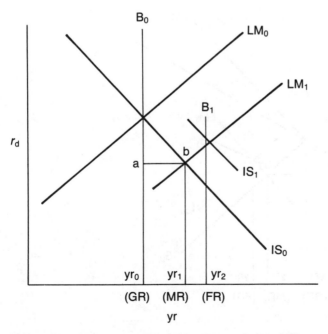

Figure 6.2 Monetary policy with zero capital mobility

level because the loss in reserves had not fully offset the initial injection of money into the economy. At this point, there will be a current account deficit, albeit a smaller one, a loss of reserves and the money stock will continue to fall.

With flexible exchange rates (FR) the deficit cannot influence the money supply since there is no central bank intervention, but now the exchange rate devalues. Assuming the Marshall–Lerner condition holds, this shifts the IS schedule to the right, lifting further the level of income. As a result of the devaluation the B schedule also shifts to B_1. In the end all markets are again in equilibrium and the final solution must be a point at which all three schedules intersect, as at yr_2.

With zero capital mobility, then, monetary policy is most effective for FR, has some effectiveness for MR and is completely ineffective for GR.

Now consider the case where there is some capital mobility (Figure 6.3). An expansionary monetary policy will again raise the level of income to yr_1; now, however, the deficit (ab) will be larger than previously (cb) because with lower interest rates there are also outflows of capital. In the MR regime the economy will settle at yr_1 and the monetary authorities will now have to undertake larger sterilisation operations (e.g. by making larger purchases of government securities) so as to preserve the new higher volume of money. It is perhaps intuitive that the higher the degree of capital mobility is, the larger is the reserve loss associated with a given change in the money stock.

In the GR regime the volume of money will be allowed to fall and again equilibrium can only be restored at the original level of output. Monetary policy will again be

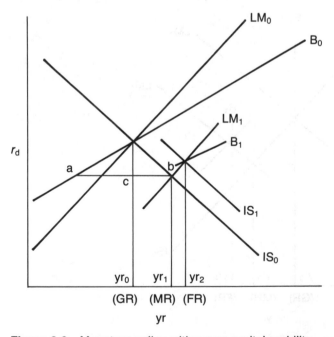

Figure 6.3 Monetary policy with some capital mobility

completely ineffective, the only difference being that with the larger initial deficit the movement to equilibrium will be accelerated and final solution will be reached sooner.

In the FR regime the larger deficit will lead to a larger devaluation and hence to a larger stimulus to domestic income. The IS schedule will now shift still further to the right. The final solution for income for FR is therefore at a higher level than in the case where the degree of capital mobility is zero.

An important result here is that monetary expansion will *improve* the trade balance (and the current account), with outflows now offsetting the current account surplus. In other words, the devaluation has to proceed to the point where there is a current account surplus sufficient to keep the balance of payments at zero and match the outflows.

Finally, consider the case where capital mobility is perfect (Figure 6.4). Suppose again that you have an open market purchase. So long as the cash base exceeds its original level there will be some downward pressure on the home interest rate. This, however, is not sustainable. There will be immediate outflows of capital equal to the original injection of cash, leaving the cash base unchanged. If the monetary authorities persist in their objective of easing monetary policy, they will repeat the exercise but with the same outcome (an equivalent outflow). All this happens very quickly and in the meantime such policies will be associated with huge losses in reserves (triggering now speculative outflows in anticipation of a devaluation, thus compounding the problem further).

What this says is that with fixed rates monetary policy is completely ineffective. Sterilisation is no longer a viable policy and it is no longer feasible to distinguish regimes 1 and 2 (see Appendix 2).

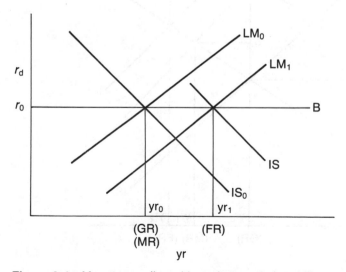

Figure 6.4 Monetary policy with perfect capital mobility

By contrast, with FR, monetary policy is now very powerful. The reason for this is the following. The lower interest rate raises income; so long as the interest rate is below the foreign interest rate, the exchange rate devalues and income increases, pushing up the demand for money and interest rates until interest rates return to their original level. Output, at that point, must have increased in the same proportion as the volume of money, replicating, in effect, 'quantity theory' results. With capital mobility perfect the current account surplus and hence the capital outflows are at their maximum.

This last case poses what appears to be a puzzle. How can there be capital outflows if at the limit the home interest rate is equal to the foreign interest rate? There are two points to make here. Since for reasons already explained the current account surplus and the outflows get progressively larger as capital mobility increases, it should not be surprising that these reach a maximum when mobility is perfect. A more direct answer is the following. Suppose interest rates were exactly equal and there were no outflows. Then we would be left with a current account surplus which in turn would appreciate the currency but the moment this happens the IS schedule starts shifting back, lowering output and the interest rate. It takes an 'infinitely small' drop in the interest rate to produce the matching outflows.

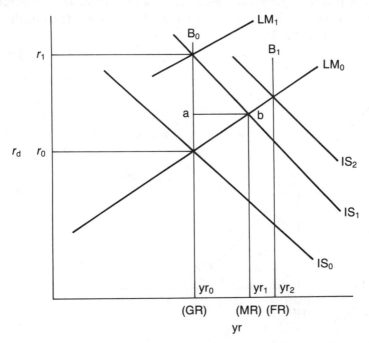

Figure 6.5 Fiscal policy with zero capital mobility

The relative effectiveness of fiscal policy

Consider, now, the effects of an increase in government expenditure and assume again that initially capital is completely immobile (see Figure 6.5).

The increase in expenditure will shift the IS schedule to the right and raise the level of income to yr_1, which now represents the solution for the MR regime. At yr_1 the monetary authorities will sterilise the effects of the current account deficit, represented by ab, on the volume of money.

In the GR regime the deficit will reduce the money supply, and so the LM schedule will shift to the left. This must continue until the deficit has been eliminated and income reverts to its original level. At this point, all the expansionary effects of the increased government expenditure will have been completely offset by reduced private expenditure, induced, in this case, by the rise in the interest rate from r_0 to r_1.

In the FR regime the deficit will induce a devaluation of the exchange rate, shift IS further to the right (to IS_2) and lift the level of income to yr_2. The devaluation will also shift the B schedule to the right to meet the IS and LM schedules.

Consider, now, what happens as capital mobility increases. It is most important here to distinguish between a relatively 'low' degree of capital mobility, defined as a situation where the B schedule is to the left of the LM schedule in the upper range (as, for example, B_1 in Figure 6.6), and a relatively 'high' degree of capital mobility, where the B schedule has moved beyond LM (to the right of LM) (as, for example, at B_2). So long as the degree of capital mobility is relatively low, fiscal expansion will

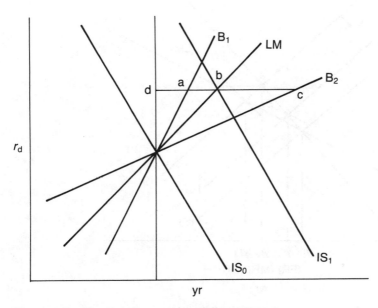

Figure 6.6 Fiscal policy and capital mobility

open up an overall deficit in the balance of payments (equal to ab in Figure 6.6). The reason is that, although there is now some capital inflow in response to the higher interest rate, these inflows are not sufficient to offset the current account deficit associated with the higher level of income. In the figure db represents the current account deficit and ad the inflow of capital. When B coincides with LM the overall balance of payments is in equilibrium, the surplus in the capital account now exactly offsetting the deficit in the current account. Beyond LM (at B_2) fiscal expansion actually improves the balance of payments (opening up a surplus equal to bc). Now the associated inflow of capital more than offsets the current account deficit. In the figure db is again the current account deficit and dc the inflow of capital.

With low capital mobility (as defined) the rankings for the three regimes are similar to the case where capital mobility is zero. The relative effectiveness of fiscal policy, however, is changed. Fiscal policy now has some effectiveness in the GR regime because the current account deficit associated with the increase in output can be offset by some capital inflow. By contrast, fiscal policy is less effective with FR because the deficit is smaller and hence the devaluation will be weaker. At the same time, in regime 1, the effectiveness of fiscal policy remains the same.

What happens when the degree of capital mobility is relatively high (i.e. when the B schedule has shifted beyond LM)? (See Figure 6.7.) In the MR regime the solution will be at yr_2, with the surplus (ab) sterilised by, say, open market sales. In the GR

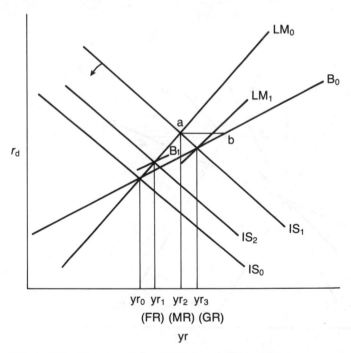

Figure 6.7   Fiscal policy with high capital mobility

regime the surplus will add to the domestic money supply, shift the LM schedule to the right (to, say, LM_1) and raise the level of income to yr_3. With FR the exchange rate will revalue, B will shift to the left to B_1, the IS schedule will shift to the left to IS_2 and the level of income will now drop to yr_1. Fiscal policy is, then, most effective for GR and least effective for FR, with MR in the intermediate position.

Finally, if capital mobility is perfect, fiscal policy becomes very potent under fixed rates (for both MR and GR) (Figure 6.8). Fiscal expansion now opens up a surplus, increasing the volume of money to accommodate the increase in output (to yr_1) at a fixed interest rate. By contrast, fiscal policy is completely ineffective under FR. So long as income and the interest rate are above their original levels, the currency will continue to appreciate until the original income and interest rate are restored. In this case, the deficit in the trade balance will have completely offset the increase in government expenditure. In other words, with money supply fixed, by definition, and interest rates unchanged, income cannot change in this model.

One very important result here is that under flexible exchange rates and perfect capital mobility, *a fiscal deficit produces an equivalent current account deficit*, so we have here a twin deficit result.

This is easily demonstrated as follows:

$$Y = C + I + G + (X - M) \tag{9}$$

Suppose that $C + I$ is a positive function of output and a negative function of the interest rate and suppose, too, that taxes are some proportion of output.

With output and the interest rate both fixed, $C + I$ and taxes will all be unchanged. This means that the budget deficit is equal to the increase in government expenditure.

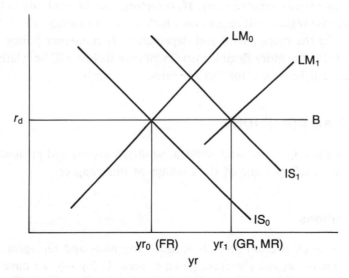

Figure 6.8 Fiscal policy with perfect capital mobility

So we have

$$\Delta(X - M) = -\Delta G \tag{10}$$

SUMMARY AND CONCLUSIONS

In the model that we have used monetary policy is always more effective with flexible exchange rates than with fixed rates and the advantage of flexible exchange rates increases the higher the degree of capital mobility. Monetary policy is always completely ineffective with fixed rates if there is no sterilisation, whatever the degree of capital mobility. If capital mobility is perfect sterilisation is no longer feasible and monetary policy is then completely ineffective under fixed rates. On the other hand, with perfect capital mobility monetary policy is very effective under flexible exchange rates.

With low capital mobility fiscal policy is most effective under flexible exchange rates and least effective under fixed rates without sterilisation. With high capital mobility the rankings are reversed, fiscal policy being most effective with fixed rates without sterilisation and least effective with flexible rates. With perfect capital mobility fiscal policy is completely ineffective with flexible exchange rates and very effective with fixed rates.

With low capital mobility, then, both monetary and fiscal policies are most effective under flexible exchange rates. From the standpoint of macro policy, therefore, it would appear that a flexible rate system is to be preferred in these conditions. However, with high capital mobility there is a trade-off: flexible rates will improve the performance of monetary policy but weaken the performance of fiscal policy. With perfect capital mobility monetary policy is not usable under fixed rates and fiscal policy is not usable under flexible rates. If, therefore, capital mobility is high the choice of exchange rate regime will depend on which macro instrument (monetary or fiscal) is judged to be the more useful and dependable. If monetary policy, for example, is viewed as being the more flexible instrument then its loss will be relatively more severe and there will be a case for flexible rates.

THE MATHEMATICAL SOLUTIONS

In this section we first show how the mathematical solutions are arrived at; next we show how the solutions confirm some of the findings of this chapter.

How to find the solutions

In regime 1 the money stock is controlled. It is thus exogenous and represents the monetary policy instrument. π_1 can therefore be set at zero. Using (4), we have one equation to represent the money market. Combining (2) (setting $mo_d = mo_s$) and (1) allows us to solve for output and the interest rate for a monetary policy change (Δmo) and a fiscal policy change (Δgr).

Having solved for both output and the interest rate we can then use (5) to solve for the overall balance of payments, which of course need not be zero.

Consider now regime 2. In this case the monetary policy instrument is $\overline{mo}$, with the money stock endogenous.

In this regime in equilibrium $B/X_0 = 0$. With e fixed we can use (1) and (5) to solve directly for yr and r_d. We can then use the solution to solve for the money stock from (2) (setting $mo_d = mo_s$). $\overline{mo}$ does not appear in the solution but gr does.

Now, consider regime 3. B/X_0 is again zero. Now also $\pi_1 = 0$, but the exchange rate is endogenous. We can use (1), (2) (setting $mo_d = mo_s$) and (5) (setting $B/X_0 = 0$) to solve for yr, e and r_d.

An important technical point is that if capital mobility is perfect in regimes 2 and 3 r_d is *exogenous* in the sense that it is predetermined by the foreign interest rate r^*. Since there is now one less variable to solve, one equation becomes redundant. The redundant equation is (5). In this extreme case capital flows are *residual*, with the balance of payments equal to zero and the *current account* determined endogenously. Capital flows are simply the negative of the current account balance.

Finally, we can also use the more general model to solve for intermediate regimes as well as end points. First, set $mo_d = mo_s$. We are left with four equations (1), (2), (3) and (5) (with $B/X_0 = 0$) to solve for four variables (with $\bar{e}$ fixed) yr, r_d, mo and e in terms of $\Delta\overline{mo}$ and Δgr. We can then find the solutions for the special cases represented by regimes 2 and 3. Regime 2 is the case where $\pi_1 \to \infty$; regime 3 is the case where $\pi_1 = 0$.

Interpreting the solutions

Table 6.1 sets out the mathematical solutions to the model. Each of the conclusions reached in the text can be verified by mathematical analysis. It is easy to verify the following.

a) Under flexible rates monetary policy is more powerful the higher is the degree of capital mobility. As α_{14} increases the solution for flexible rates becomes progressively larger. At the limit, for example, when capital mobility is perfect the solution reduces to $1/\alpha_5$.

b) Monetary policy is always more powerful under flexible than under fixed rates. This is readily seen by comparing the solutions for output for regime 3 with regime 1.

c) Fiscal policy weakens under flexible rates as capital mobility increases. As α_{14} increases the multiplier becomes progressively smaller; when $\alpha_{14} \to \infty$ the multiplier becomes zero.

d) In regime 2 fiscal policy becomes more powerful the higher the degree of capital mobility; when $\alpha_{14} = 0$ the multiplier is zero; it reaches its maximum when $\alpha_{14} \to \infty$.

Table 6.1 Solutions for three regimes (Mundell–Fleming model)

	Regime 1	Regime 2	Regime 3
Monetary expansion			
yr	$\dfrac{\alpha_4}{d_2}$	0	$\dfrac{\alpha_1\alpha_{14} + \alpha_4\alpha_{13}}{d_5}$
r_d	$-\dfrac{1}{d_2}$	0	$-\dfrac{\alpha_{13} - \alpha_1}{d_5}$
e	0	0	$\dfrac{\alpha_{14} + \alpha_4}{d_5}$
Fiscal expansion			
yr	$\dfrac{\alpha_3\alpha_{10}}{d_2}$	$\dfrac{\alpha_3\alpha_{14}}{d_4}$	$\dfrac{\alpha_3\alpha_{13}\alpha_{10}}{d_5}$
r_d	$\dfrac{\alpha_3\alpha_5}{d_2}$	$\dfrac{\alpha_3}{\alpha_4}$	$\dfrac{\alpha_3\alpha_{13}\alpha_5}{d_5}$
e	0	0	$\dfrac{\alpha_3(\alpha_{10} - \alpha_{14}\alpha_5)}{d_5}$

$d_1 = \alpha_9\alpha_{10}(1 - \alpha_{15}) + \alpha_1\alpha_{10} + \alpha_4[1 + \alpha_5\alpha_9(1 - \alpha_{15})]$
$d_2 = \alpha_4\alpha_5 + \alpha_{10}$
$d_3 = \alpha_{14}\alpha_9(1 - \alpha_{15}) + \alpha_1\alpha_{14} + \alpha_4[\alpha_{13} + \alpha_9(1 - \alpha_{15})]$
$d_4 = \alpha_4 + \alpha_{14}$
$d_5 = \alpha_{10}(\alpha_{13} - \alpha_1) + \alpha_4\alpha_5\alpha_{13} + \alpha_1\alpha_{14}\alpha_5$

e) The relative effectiveness of fiscal policy under fixed and flexible rates depends on the degree of capital mobility. If α_{14} is set equal to zero (infinity) fiscal policy is most (least) effective under flexible rates.

APPENDIX 1   DERIVATION OF EQUATIONS IN LOGARITHMIC FORM

We show here how equations (1) and (5) can be written in logarithmic form. We begin with the definition of national product.

$$Yr P_d = CP + IP + Gr P + XP_d - MP^*E \tag{A1}$$

where

Yr is the real level of national output,
C is real consumption,
I is real investment,
Gr is the real value of government expenditure,
X is the volume of exports,
M is the volume of imports,

P^* is the foreign price level,

P_d is the price of domestic production,

P is the general price level appropriate to consumption, investment and government expenditure,

E is the exchange rate and,

P $P_d{}^{\alpha_{15}}P^*E^{1-\alpha_{15}}$ (this says that the overall price level is a weighted average of home and import prices).

We start by expressing (A1) in terms of differentials. All initial prices (P, E, P_d and P^*) are assumed to be equal to unity.

$$\Delta Yr + Yr_0\, \Delta P_d = \Delta C + C_0\, \Delta P + \Delta I + I_0\, \Delta P + \Delta Gr + Gr_0\, \Delta P + \Delta X$$

$$+ X_0\, \Delta P_d - \Delta M - M_0\Delta E - M_0\, \Delta P^* \tag{A2}$$

In the MF model $\Delta P_d = 0$. Also, we assume foreign prices are fixed so that $\Delta P^* = 0$, and so some of the expressions can be disregarded.

We now write the underlying behavioural equations.

$$\Delta C = c\, \Delta Yr \tag{A3}$$

$$\frac{\Delta I}{I_0} = -b\, \Delta r_d \tag{A4}$$

$$\Delta M = m\, \Delta Yr - a_1\, \Delta E \tag{A5}$$

$$\Delta X = x\, \Delta Yr^* + a_2\, \Delta E \tag{A6}$$

$$a_1 = \left| \frac{\partial M}{\partial E} \right| \qquad a_2 = \left| \frac{\partial X}{\partial E} \right|$$

We also know that

$$\mathrm{edm} = \frac{1}{M_0} \frac{\partial M}{\partial E}$$

and

$$\mathrm{edx} = \frac{1}{X_0} \frac{\partial X}{\partial E}$$

where edm and edx are respectively the elasticity of demand for imports and the elasticity of demand for exports.

So we can now write

$$a_1 = \mathrm{edm}M_0 \qquad a_2 = \mathrm{edx}X_0$$

We also assume that the original trade balance is zero. This allows us to set $X_0 = M_0$.

We can now rewrite (A2) as

$$\Delta Yr = c\, \Delta Yr - bI_0\, \Delta r_d + (C_0 + I_0 + G_0)\, \Delta P + x\, \Delta Yr^* + \mathrm{edx}X_0\, \Delta E - m\, \Delta Yr$$

$$+ \mathrm{edm}X_0\, \Delta E - X_0\, \Delta E + \Delta Gr \tag{A7}$$

Collecting terms and dividing through by Yr_0, the original level of output, allows us to rewrite (A7) in percentage change form. We also note that $C_0 + I_0 + G_0 = Yr_0$ (because the original trade balance is zero).

$$\frac{\Delta Yr}{Yr_0} = -\frac{bI_0}{(1-c+m)Yr_0}\Delta r_d + \frac{1}{1-c+m}\Delta P + \frac{xYr_0^*}{(1-c+m)Yr_0}$$

$$\frac{\Delta Yr^*}{Yr_0^*} + \frac{X_0}{Yr_0}\frac{edx+edm-1}{1-c+m}\Delta E + \frac{Gr_0}{Yr_0(1-c+m)}\frac{\Delta Gr}{Gr_0} \tag{A8}$$

where $edx + edm - 1$ is the Marshall–Lerner condition (see Chapter 12).

If we disregard ΔP (which will be influenced only by the exchange rate in this model), noting that the percentage change in a variable is the change in the logarithm of that variable and assuming the coefficients are constants, we can rewrite (A8) in level logarithmic form as

$$yr = -\frac{bI_0}{(1-c+m)Yr_0}r_d + \frac{xYr_0^*}{(1-c+m)Yr_0}yr^* + \frac{X_0(edx+edm-1)}{Yr_0(1-c+m)}e$$

$$+ \frac{Gr_0}{Yr_0(1-c+m)}gr + k_1 \tag{A9}$$

where k_1 is a constant. This confirms (1) in the text where the coefficients in (1) correspond to the coefficients in (A9).

We turn now to the trade balance (TB) equation:

$$TB = XP_d - MP^*E \tag{A10}$$

Differentiating as previously and now dividing through by X_0, the original volume of exports, will give us

$$\frac{\Delta TB}{X_0} = x\frac{Yr_0^*}{X_0}\frac{\Delta Yr^*}{Yr_0^*} + (edx+edm-1)\,\Delta E - \frac{Yr_0 m}{X_0}\frac{\Delta Yr}{Yr_0} \tag{A11}$$

Since $x = \partial X/\partial Yr^*$ and if we assume that average and marginal propensities to import are the same, the expression $xYr^*/X_0 = 1$. By similar reasoning we can show that $Yr_0 m/X_0 = 1$. This allows us to simplify and write (A11) as

$$\frac{\Delta TB}{X_0} = \Delta yr^* - \Delta yr + \alpha_{13}\Delta e \tag{A12}$$

or, to simplify,

$$\frac{TB}{X_0} = (yr^* - yr) + \alpha_{13}e + k_2 \tag{A13}$$

where α_{13} is the constant Marshall–Lerner condition and k_2 is a constant.

We have shown that

$$\alpha_1 = \frac{X_0(edx + edm - 1)}{Yr_0(1 - c + m)}$$

It is readily shown that, since $X_0/[Yr_0(1 - c + m)] < 1$, $\alpha_{13} > \alpha_1$.

We also simplified by assuming

$$\frac{\Delta TB}{X_0} = \Delta \left(\frac{TB}{X_0}\right)$$

The latter is

$$\frac{\Delta TB}{X_0} + \frac{TB}{X_0}\frac{\Delta X}{X_0}$$

We can dismiss the last expression as being of the second order of importance. X_0 is an initial value which is given before any changes occur.

A similar manipulation for the capital flow equation will yield (5) in the text where

$$\frac{B}{X_0} = \frac{TB}{X_0} + \frac{K}{X_0}$$

where K represents net capital inflows.

APPENDIX 2   STERILISATION AND CAPITAL MOBILITY

To illustrate what is meant by sterilisation policies, we present the following highly simplified system of equations (see Argy and Kouri 1974):

$$\Delta H = \Delta NFA + \Delta NDA \tag{B1}$$

$$\Delta NFA = A - a\Delta NDA \tag{B2}$$

$$\Delta NDA = Z - b\Delta NFA \tag{B3}$$

$$\Delta H = \frac{1 - b}{1 - ab}A + \frac{1 - a}{1 - ab}Z \tag{B4}$$

$$\Delta NFA = \frac{1}{1 - ab}A - \frac{a}{1 - ab}Z \tag{B5}$$

$$\Delta NDA = \frac{1}{1 - ab}Z - \frac{b}{1 - ab}A \tag{B6}$$

NFA is net foreign assets of the central bank
NDA is net domestic assets of the central bank
H is base money
Z is the autonomous component of the change in net domestic assets
A is the autonomous component of the change in net foreign assets.

In equation (B1) the change in base money is broken down into its external (ΔNFA) and its domestic (ΔNDA) components. In equation (B2) the change in net foreign assets is explained by the change in domestic assets and by a number of other variables represented by A. In this equation, a is the offset coefficient, i.e. it represents the extent to which the effect on base money of a change in net domestic assets is counteracted by concurrent movements in the balance of payments. Equation (B3) may be viewed, in part, as a reaction function of the monetary authorities, where the change in domestic assets (the policy instrument) is explained by the current change in foreign assets and by other targets which are represented by the symbol Z.

The coefficient b in equation (B4) is a measure of the degree to which the monetary authorities attempt to sterilise, within the same period, the balance of payments effects on liquidity. Where $b = 0$, there is no attempt to sterilise, and base money is allowed to respond to current developments in the balance of payments (A) as well as to other targets (Z). On the other hand, where $b = 1$, sterilisation is complete, and base money is then oriented solely to targets other than current developments in the balance of payments.

Equations (B4) and (B5) illustrate the effects of sterilisation policies under different conditions with respect to the degree of financial integration. The coefficient a might be taken as indicative of the degree of money market integration. It is clear from equations (B4) and (B5) that the higher the degree of financial integration, given the degree of sterilisation b, the weaker are the effects of independent monetary policies on base money and the stronger the effects on reserves. At the same time, the larger the sterilisation coefficient, given a, the larger the effects of independent monetary policies on base money and the larger the effects on reserves. Where capital mobility is perfect ($a = 1$) the authorities lose control over base money (the coefficient of Z in equation (B4) is zero), and any attempt to sterilise destabilises reserves (the coefficient of Z approaches infinity in equation (B5)).

In equation (B6) the coefficient for Z shows by how much domestic assets ultimately change, given some sterilisation, for any given exogenous change in domestic assets. For example, suppose the offset coefficient a is 0.5 and the authorities completely sterilise so that $b = 1$; then if the authorities wish to bring about an increase in base money of 10 units, the ultimate increase in domestic assets, after full sterilisation of the foreign leakage, must be 20.

7

The Mundell–Fleming model –
its strengths and limitations

INTRODUCTION

Chapter 6 presented in some detail the MF model, which, it is worth repeating, is the starting point of all open economy model building and, today, familiar to most intermediate–senior undergraduates.

What we want to do in this chapter, before we extend and build on this important model in the chapters that follow, is to present in a very explicit way its principal strengths and its limitations. The limitations derive in large part from potential weaknesses in the behavioural relations underlying the model, its method of analysis and some general omissions. Subsequent chapters will deal in detail with these limitations.

ITS STRENGTHS

The model is readily understood and its behavioural equations are simple; it has immediate appeal and is recognisable as a model which captures observable features of the real world.

Its overriding strength is that it offers some insights into the behaviour of an economy, in the wake of a disturbance, policy or otherwise, over a time horizon of something like a year or so. In other words, if after a shock, and all other things being equal, we were to take a snapshot of the economy about a year later, we would recognise many, indeed most, of the outcomes predicted by the model, as these were summarised in Chapter 6.

Tables 7.1 and 7.2 report various simulations of the effects, after one year, of a 10 per cent increase in the money stock and of a fiscal expansion, taking the form of an increase in government spending by 5 per cent of GNP. The models simulated

Table 7.1   Flexible rates: effect of a monetary expansion of 10 per cent – year 1

	Australia		Canada	UK
	MSG2	NIF	MultiMod	MultiMod
yr	+5.2	+3.6	+3.5	+2.1
e	−14.7	−8.4	−13.3	−13.5
p	+3.5	+2.6	+1.0	+0.5
r_d	−1.9	−2.0	−2.6	−2.3
CAB (or TB) as percentage of GNP	+0.9	+1.2	−2.2	−4.0

Sources: MSG2, McKibbin 1988a; NIF, Simes 1991; MultiMod, Masson et al. 1990
Notes: Percentage deviations from control with perfect asset substitution.
    yr, output; e, exchange rate; p, price level; r_d, interest rate; CAB, current account; TB, trade balance.

are the McKibbin–Sachs global model (MSG2), the MultiMod (IMF), the MCM (Federal Reserve Board) and the Amps (Murphy) model (for Australia). (See the original sources for a description of the models. See also Chapter 15.)

All these models assume perfect asset substitution. As we shall see when we deal with expectations in later chapters, risk-free perfect arbitrage requires that the excess (shortfall) of the home interest rate over the foreign interest rate reflect, for the relevant time horizon, an expected devaluation (appreciation) of the currency. What this means, importantly, is that with perfect asset substitution one should not expect, at

Table 7.2   Flexible rates: effect of a fiscal expansion[a] – year 1 (perfect asset substitution)

	Australia		Canada		UK	
	Amps (Murphy)	MSG2	MultiMod	MCM	MultiMod	MCM
yr	+0.6	+0.67 (+2.41)	+1.2	+6.0	+2.7	+3.0
e	+12.2	+2.29 (0)	+4.0	+1.5	+4.7	+1.2
p	+0.35	−0.58 (+0.08)	+0.1	+1.0	+0.5	−0.5
r_d (short)	+3.0	+0.22	−0.4	+2.0	−0.2	+0.5
(long)		(+0.02)	0.0	−	+0.5	−
CAB as percentage of GNP	−1.5	−0.54 (−0.79)	−2.1	−5.5	−0.7	−10.5

Sources: Amps, Martin et al. 1987; MSG2, McKibbin 1988a, Argy et al. 1989; MCM, Edison et al. 1986; MultiMod, Masson et al. 1990.
Notes: [a]Increase of government spending by 5 per cent of GNP.
    Results for fixed rates (Australian dollar tied to the US dollar) are given in parentheses.

least over shorter horizons, the home interest rate to be predetermined by the foreign interest rate. This needs to be kept in mind when interpreting the tables.

What do these tables reveal? A monetary expansion under flexible rates leads to a devaluation, some increase in output, only a 'modest' increase in prices and some fall in the interest rate. A fiscal expansion under flexible rates leads to some appreciation of the currency, some increase in output, some rise in the interest rate (except surprisingly in MultiMod where there is a fall in the short-term interest rate) and a deterioration in the current account.

These outcomes largely confirm the MF predictions. There is one major reservation to be noted, however. The reservation is that a monetary expansion does not necessarily open up a current account surplus, as predicted by the MF model. Indeed, in two of the models there is a current account deficit. At this point, we note that one reason for the ambiguity in a modified MF model is that a monetary expansion *increases* domestic expenditure, which has a negative effect on the current account, but devalues the currency, which has a positive effect on the current account (Boughton 1989).

To test for the effects of a fiscal expansion under fixed rates, we report in Table 7.3 simulations for France and Italy and, as well, one for Australia in Table 7.2 (which allows us to compare outcomes *directly* with those for flexible rates). These appear to confirm that fiscal policy is more effective under fixed than under flexible rates. (Compare for example the effects on output for France and Italy under fixed rates with the effects in Canada and the UK for the same model.) The price effects are again weak, the interest rate rises marginally and there is, predictably, a current account deficit.

ITS LIMITATIONS – SOME GENERAL PRINCIPLES

We intend later in this chapter to present what we consider to be the key assumptions of the MF model, assumptions which will be systematically relaxed in later chapters.

Table 7.3 MultiMod simulations: fiscal expansion[a] for France and Italy under narrow exchange rate bands

	France	Italy
yr	+ 3.4	+ 3.6
e	+ 0.1	+ 0.1
p	+ 1.0	+ 1.1
r_d	+ 0.1	+ 0.1
CAB as percentage of GNP	− 2.4	− 2.2

Source: MultiMod, Masson *et al*. 1990
Notes: [a] As in Table 7.2.
Perfect asset substitution; monetary policy is completely ineffective.

As we shall see, as these assumptions are relaxed, so the conclusions reached in Chapter 6 will correspondingly also need to be modified.

Before we do this, however, we will illustrate this general proposition by making two 'minor' variations to the MF model and show how even minor variations can make a significant difference to the outcome. This is admittedly 'nitpicking', but it does, early in this book, serve to demonstrate, in a dramatic form, the general truth of the proposition.

The two variations we will make, each independently, are first to modify very slightly the money demand equation used in the MF model and second to extend the capital flow equation by adding one more variable to it.

A variation on the money demand equation

It will be recalled that in the MF model prices do not appear in the money demand equation. If the price level which is relevant to the demand for money balances is the price of home produced goods, such a procedure is legitimate since this price level is assumed fixed in the MF model. If, however, more realistically, the relevant price level is the *consumer* price index, which also includes the price of *imported* goods, then some variation to the model is needed.

Suppose the consumer price index p is a weighted average of the price of home produced goods (p_d) and the price of imported goods in home currency ($p^* + e$), i.e. the foreign price level p^* adjusted by the exchange rate (see Chapter 8). With p_d and p^* both fixed, we can write the equation for the consumer price as

$$p = (1 - \alpha_{15})e \tag{1}$$

where $1 - \alpha_{15}$ represents the weight attaching to imports in the consumer price index. This clearly assumes that the price of imported goods adjusts more rapidly than the price of home goods, a not unreasonable assumption.

We now modify the MF model, for the flexible rate case, to accommodate an extended money demand equation.

$$mo = (1 - \alpha_{15})e + \alpha_5 yr - \alpha_{10}\bar{r}_d \tag{2}$$

Since we are only interested in making one particular point we need only limit ourselves to the case of perfect capital mobility where r_d is exogenously given by the foreign interest rate. It should be noted that the presence of e means that e is now also a *shift* variable in the money demand equation.

Only one additional equation is needed to complete the model here – the demand for goods.

$$yr = \alpha_1 e - \alpha_4 \bar{r}_d + \alpha_3 gr \tag{3}$$

Equations (2) and (3) now determine e and yr jointly for a monetary (mo) and fiscal (gr) expansion.

The solutions are simple:

$$\frac{yr}{mo} = \frac{\alpha_1}{k_1} \tag{4}$$

$$\frac{e}{mo} = \frac{1}{k_1} \tag{5}$$

$$\frac{yr}{gr} = \frac{\alpha_3(1 - \alpha_{15})}{k_1} \tag{6}$$

$$\frac{e}{gr} = -\frac{\alpha_3\alpha_5}{k_1} \tag{7}$$

where $k_1 = \alpha_1\alpha_5 + (1 - \alpha_{15})$. These solutions bear comparison with the MF solutions for the special case where $\alpha_{14} = \infty$ (see Table 6.1). The reader can readily demonstrate that the MF results can be reached by setting $\alpha_{15} = 1$.

The real multiplier is smaller for monetary policy and so is the exchange rate effect (i.e. there is now a *smaller* devaluation).

Why is this so? Consider the MF solution which is one where output increases substantially and the currency devalues. At this point now, in this new context, there is an increase in money demand (because the consumer price index will have increased). This is equivalent to a *fall* in the money stock, which in turn at once moderates the increase in output and the devaluation.

The case of a fiscal expansion is more interesting. It will be recalled that in the MF model fiscal policy is completely impotent. (Equation (6) shows that this is the case if $\alpha_{15} = 1$.) Now, it turns out, with the small modification we have made, that fiscal policy has some effectiveness. At the same time, the appreciation is weakened (see equation (7)). Why?

We recall again that in the MF model in equilibrium there is an appreciation of the currency. With both the interest rate and the money stock fixed, output cannot change (see equation (2) with $\alpha_{15} = 1$). Now, however, the appreciation will *reduce* money demand (shift the LM schedule to the right); this is equivalent to an *increase* in the money stock which at once increases output and weakens the appreciation. It is readily seen from (2) that with mo and r_d both fixed yr can increase if e falls.

Extending the capital flow equation

A second modification we might make is to allow the level of real income to influence capital flows, so we now write the capital flow equation as

$$\frac{K}{X_0} = \alpha_{14}(r_d - r^*) + \alpha_{20}yr \tag{8}$$

There are several ways to rationalise the presence of output in the capital flow equation (one of these appears in Chapter 10 where it is also shown that the coefficient is strictly ambiguous). At this point and for our purposes, we simply note that it might also capture the positive effect of increased domestic activity on capital flows (reflecting the improved prospects for the economy) (see Helliwell 1969).

We will proceed to show that this small change can also have quite dramatic effects on the outcomes.

For a start it is now no longer evident that the slope of the B schedule is positive. Recalling the equation for the trade balance we have

$$\frac{B}{X_0} = \alpha_{13}e - yr + \alpha_{14}(r_d - r^*) + \alpha_{20}yr \qquad (9)$$

and the slope (with $B/X_0 = 0$) is now

$$\frac{1 - \alpha_{20}}{\alpha_{14}}$$

which may be positive or negative. It will be negative if $\alpha_{20} > 1$. How is it possible for the slope to be negative?

Consider an increase in output. This now has two opposing effects on the balance of payments. On the one hand there is the conventional negative effect on the trade balance (as in the MF model); on the other hand the increased output is assumed to attract an inflow of capital. If the latter effect dominates then a *fall* in the interest rate is required to restore equilibrium to the balance of payments, implying a negatively sloped B schedule. This particular case is pursued further below. (If the slope is positive the presence of output simply *reduces* the slope.)

Since the slope of the IS schedule is also negative a critical question is the relative slopes of the two schedules. The slope of the IS schedule is $-1/\alpha_4$. The two possibilities are shown in Figure 7.1 as B_1 and B_2.

It needs to be noted that now if the economy were located on the right (left) of the B schedule the balance of payments would be in surplus (deficit), the opposite of the MF case. The reason is that at any given level of the interest rate, if output is above (below) the level required to equilibrate the balance of payments, this must now correspond to an overall surplus (deficit). At the same time, now, if there were a devaluation (appreciation), the B schedule would shift to the *left* (*right*).

To underline the difference between cases B_1 and B_2 we consider rightward shifts in LM and IS. Suppose first that B_1 is the relevant schedule. A shift in LM will now generate an overall surplus (because the income effect on inflows dominates over the continued interest rate and trade effects). If the exchange rate is fixed and there is no sterilisation, the money supply will continue to increase. This in turn will only make matters worse, increasing the surplus further. Clearly the situation is unstable. If the exchange rate is flexible the surplus will provoke an *appreciation* of the currency, a bizarre result for a monetary expansion.

If the IS schedule shifts there is again an overall surplus. Allowing the money supply to increase will again generate instability. With flexible rates there is an unambiguous appreciation, whatever the degree of capital mobility.

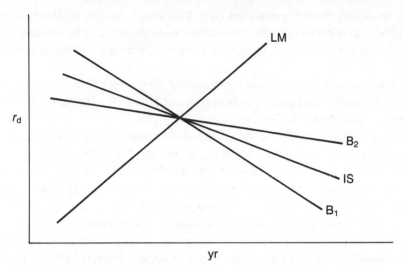

Figure 7.1 The B schedule with output in the capital flow equation

We turn now to the case where the B schedule is positioned as in B_2. This is the more realistic case, particularly if capital mobility is high.

Now the results are more recognisable. A monetary expansion opens up a deficit (the interest rate effect dominating over the positive output effect) while a shift in IS produces a surplus. This case is stable. If the exchange rate floats the presence of an output term in the capital flow equation *weakens* the exchange rate and output effects for a monetary expansion; for a fiscal expansion the currency will appreciate further while the output effect will be weakened.

ITS KEY LIMITATIONS

We turn now to the key limitations of the model.

1 If we are concerned with the medium-term effects of a permanent disturbance, it is clearly no longer appropriate to assume that wages and prices are fixed. The MF model was in due course extended to accommodate wage and price flexibility. Chapter 8 addresses this issue. It takes the MF model, as is, and adds to it a wage–price sector. This allows us to focus exclusively on the question of how wage–price adjustment modifies outcomes.

2 The theory underlying capital flows is too simple. In time, the theory was progressively refined. Exchange rate expectations were assigned a role in the capital flow equation. The MF model had implicitly assumed that the expected exchange rate was equal to the current spot rate, thus abstracting from expectations. Argy and Porter (1972) assumed that exchange rate expectations were stationary (i.e. the expected exchange rate was given); this allowed the current spot rate, which was market

determined, to depart from the expected rate. This small change, by itself, changes the MF results. Later, exchange rate expectations were assumed to be formed rationally (i.e. the impacts on exchange rates were known) (Dornbusch 1976; Branson and Buiter 1983).

A still more dramatic change came when capital flows were recast in the context of a portfolio balance framework (see Branson and Hill 1971; Hodjera 1973). This is developed in some detail in Chapter 10.

It is rewarding, at this point, to take the simplest representation of a portfolio model and to draw out some of its implications for the MF type model.

Our equation (5) in the previous chapter asserted that, if the domestic interest rate increased to a new higher level, there would be a permanently higher *flow* of capital into the economy. The alternative (portfolio) representation of capital movements argues, by contrast, that there would be a portfolio readjustment by domestic and foreign residents leading to an inflow of capital in the initial period; at the same time, however, provided wealth is growing, the higher domestic interest rate will provoke a continuing inflow of capital in subsequent periods, but at a much more modest rate.

To illustrate this, suppose domestic residents held foreign assets (but, for simplicity, foreigners did not hold domestic assets). Suppose FA represents the value of foreign assets in foreign currency held by residents, while We represents domestic wealth. Then, in its very simplest form, we have

$$\frac{EFA}{We} = \alpha_{12}(r^* - r_d) \tag{10}$$

This asserts that the proportion of wealth held in the form of foreign assets (denominated in domestic currency) increases as the foreign interest rate increases relative to the domestic interest rate. Differentiating this equation yields

$$\Delta FA = -K = \alpha_{12}We(\Delta r^* - \Delta r_d) + \alpha_{12}\Delta We(r^* - r_d) - FA\Delta E \tag{11}$$

The capital inflow following an increase in the domestic interest rate is represented by $\alpha_{12}We$; this inflow, however, is not sustained since Δr_d becomes zero in subsequent periods. The continuing flow is represented by $\alpha_{12}\Delta We$ which says that so long as home wealth is growing a larger share of the increased wealth will be absorbed in domestic, as against foreign, assets. The sustained flow is therefore $\alpha_{12}\Delta We$, while the initial stock adjustment, by contrast, is $\alpha_{12}We$. The ratio of the flow to the stock adjustment is $\Delta We/We$, which is the rate of growth of wealth. In other words, if wealth grows at 5 per cent the (sustained) flow effect will be 5 per cent of the (initial) stock effect.

For relatively short-term analysis we may disregard the change in wealth, and so $\Delta We = 0$; if we also disregard valuation effects ($FA\Delta E$), this reduces the new capital flow equation to

$$K = \alpha_{12}We(\Delta r_d - \Delta r^*) \tag{12}$$

The implications of this are radical. If we were to use (12) as the capital flow equation the B schedule becomes vertical after the economy has settled down, *as if capital mobility were zero*. This is because the *level* of the home interest rate no longer has the capacity to generate *permanent* flows.

The portfolio model, as we shall note in Chapter 10, is elegant and may be better founded in theory and in practice. It is too easy, however, to exaggerate the differences. For *short-term* analysis, there is very little difference. Beyond that, as we have seen, with wealth growing there is a *lasting* flow effect. Moreover, if stock adjustment occurs with a lag the flow effects are *extended*. Finally, perhaps oddly, if capital mobility is perfect the two models have identical implications.

3 The analysis is of a relatively small country. It assumes that the country has no significant impact on the rest of the world and hence that feedback effects from the rest of the world can be disregarded. This holds for the vast majority of economies, including many officially called large by international bodies. The exceptions are the G3 countries: the USA, Japan and Germany.

Mundell himself extended his own model to the large-country case (Mundell 1964). Typically, the large-country case is treated in the context of a world assumed to be composed of two large countries only; interdependence and interactions are then identified and analysed. Chapter 13 deals with the large-country case.

In this context the small-country case can be represented as a special case of the two-country framework. In this case the world comprises a huge closed economy entity and a small economy. The small economy cannot impact on the rest of the world but the rest of the world does impact on the small economy (Argy 1990b).

In a world where many smaller economies tie their currencies to one larger economy which in turn floats *vis-à-vis* another larger economy the two-country framework is restrictive. A more flexible and richer framework is one which assumes that the world comprises three countries, two giants and one relatively small. Such an analysis is undertaken in Chapter 16.

4 In the money market in the MF model there is a demand for a money *stock*, the only asset explicitly identified in the model. Yet the public is assumed implicitly to hold other assets. Bonds are implicitly in the model since there is an interest rate on *domestic* bonds. There are also transactions in *foreign* bonds since capital flows are also in the model, so *foreign* assets are also held. There is no *unified* system of asset demand within a portfolio, however, which explicitly identifies the assets held by the private sector.

One can take this further. Following up on comments made under (2) above, we can say that in the MF model there appears to be an inconsistency between the money market and the foreign exchange market. If there is a *stock* demand for money, there ought, with consistency, to be a *stock* not a *flow* demand for foreign bonds as part of a unified portfolio. The portfolio balance model of the monetary sector which corrects such deficiencies is presented in detail in Chapter 10.

5 There is no analysis of stock formation. Nor is any role assigned to wealth either in the demand for money or in the real demand for goods. Interest receipts on debt and net foreign assets are also neglected.

In essence, the MF equilibrium is a *flow* not a *stock* equilibrium. The analysis is incomplete in that in true *stock* equilibrium, in a stationary state, the private sector cannot be accumulating new stocks.

This difficult question is addressed in detail in Chapter 29. To anticipate, we conclude that, in a stationary state, stock equilibrium requires that *both* the budget and the current account be zero. We need thus to impose these as *conditions* of longer-run equilibrium.

There is no doubt that this puts a finger on an important deficiency in the MF model but one which is serious only when medium- to longer-run analysis is being undertaken. In the shorter run of a year or so these considerations are of lesser importance and thus again the MF model is essentially upheld.

6 The methodology employed in the MF model is one of comparative statics, i.e. a disturbance is assumed to occur and the new equilibrium is analysed without paying any attention to the dynamics of adjustment.

There were several developments on this front. For a monetary disturbance under flexible rates an important distinction was made between an initial adjustment phase during which only monetary variables – interest rates and exchange rates – adjust and a later adjustment phase during which the real sector (prices, the current account) adjust. The two 'classic' models that fall in this general category are those of Dornbusch (1976) and Branson (1977). These models are presented in Chapters 18 and 19.

Subsequently, the adjustment phases were refined. A distinction is made between a short-run MF type adjustment phase and a medium run during which portfolio balance is restored (Frenkel and Razin 1987). In some of these models prices continue to be fixed throughout and only output adjusts, so the only modification made here to the MF model is to accommodate portfolio balance and wealth. Such models are reviewed in Chapter 11.

The models were further refined when prices were also allowed to adjust. Now there is, first, a Keynesian phase, during which more refined variations on the MF model are assumed to hold, and second, a more classical medium-run adjustment phase during which prices adjust (with output now returning to its full employment level) and as well portfolio balance constraints are all observed. These models are analysed in Chapters 29 and 30.

7 The MF model assumes away possible J curve effects, supposing a devaluation (appreciation) will improve (worsen) the current account. Perverse exchange rate effects were introduced into an MF framework by Niehans (1975).

As an illustration, we saw that in the MF model under flexible exchange rates with some capital mobility a monetary expansion must provoke a devaluation and a trade surplus sufficient to absorb the net outflow of capital. If a devaluation has perverse effects, an initial deficit on the trade balance is made worse by the devaluation. Thus to restore equilibrium to the balance of payments an *inflow* of capital is needed to offset the deficit in the trade balance, an outcome which is virtually impossible within an MF framework. Moreover, in the presence of a J curve a devaluation now may have deflationary effects on the economy; it also produces more short-run inflation. It is therefore evident that a J curve has the capacity radically to transform MF results. These questions are addressed in Chapter 21.

It is easy, however, to exaggerate the difficulties here for the MF model. Evidence is presented in Chapter 12 that J curve effects are most likely to occur in the first nine months after an exchange rate adjustment, but that they tend to disappear beyond that period. Thus, if we reckon the MF model to be relevant for a short run of a year or so, one could argue that this takes us outside the 'contentious' phase. Nevertheless, a radically different approach is needed for analysis over a shorter phase of say up to the first nine months. This is of course a special case of 'dynamic' adjustment, noted earlier.

8 Exchange rate and price expectations are ignored in the MF analysis. These again introduce an element of dynamic analysis.

The New Classical economists were the first to make the important distinction between a disturbance, policy or otherwise, which was anticipated and one which was not. Most of this analysis was conducted in the context of a closed economy. Using relatively simple models, they were led to conclude that any macro policy which was anticipated would be ineffective. They went further and argued that if the authorities followed a predictable stabilisation rule sooner or later the rule would be learned and anticipated and stabilisation policy would thus be ineffective. This in turn led them to propose simple monetary fiscal rules. This particular debate is reviewed in Chapter 23.

The New Classical economists took this analysis a step further. Again using a relatively simple framework, they tried to show that if the monetary authorities were allowed discretion in the implementation of monetary policy they would end up with the worst of all possible worlds: more inflation and a return to the natural rate of unemployment. This further reinforced the case for monetary rules. This debate is reviewed in Chapter 25.

Chapter 24 introduces an open economy model which explicitly incorporates expected prices as well as exchange rates. It is shown that the analysis of an anticipated policy change can be very complicated. A monetary policy which is anticipated can produce a wage adjustment in the period in which the policy is anticipated to change which can go some way towards nullifying the real effects of such policies. An anticipated change in the currency or in the price level could also produce effects ahead of the anticipated policy change. For example, an anticipated fiscal expansion will create an anticipation of an appreciation of the currency; this in turn affects the current exchange rate and thus may have real effects ahead of the implementation of the fiscal expansion.

Also in the spirit of New Classical economics is the belief in the Ricardian equivalence hypothesis. According to this hypothesis, debt and tax finance are equivalent in their real effects on the economy, because the public will anticipate future tax liabilities if debt finance is undertaken and this will alter their real consumption behaviour in the present. This thesis has radical implications for the workings of fiscal policy. It is discussed in Chapter 26.

9 Yet another potential limitation of the MF model is that it assumes that a 'single' base good is produced in the small economy, which good is, in turn, imperfectly competitive with a good produced abroad. An alternative framework assumes that there are two types of goods produced: a traded good (which is perfectly competitive with the good produced abroad) and a non-traded good (e.g. services) which is completely sheltered from competition abroad. (Such a model is presented in Chapter 17.) A further extension accommodates two traded goods, an import good and an export good, plus a non-traded good.

10 Finally, in the MF model all imports are implicitly assumed to be of consumer goods. Allowing for imports of raw materials and intermediate goods could also modify some of the MF results. (See very briefly on this Chapter 28).

8

The Mundell–Fleming model with wage and price adjustment

INTRODUCTION

Chapter 6 presented the MF model. As we noted then and again in Chapter 7, one of the weaknesses of the model is that it assumes wages and prices are fixed; it is therefore a model which has a greater bearing and relevance to the shorter run or for the analysis of temporary short-term disturbances. For a more sustained policy change, it is clearly inappropriate to disregard wages and prices. In this chapter, we extend the MF model in one respect only retaining all the other features of the model we now accommodate wage and price adjustment. Whereas in the MF model we identified three markets – a goods market, a money market and a foreign exchange market – we now extend the model to accommodate a labour market. Again we use comparative statics analysis.

The chapter draws on Casas (1977), Argy and Salop (1979), Sachs (1980), Marston (1982, 1985) and Dornbusch (1983).

THE MODEL

To facilitate comparison with the MF model of Chapter 6 the presentation of the extended model is very similar except for the addition of a fourth market, the labour market, and the incorporation of the price level at home in the other equations.

The goods market

$$yr_d = \alpha_1(e - p_d) + \alpha_3 gr - \alpha_4 r_d \tag{1}$$

The money market

$$mo_d = p_d + \alpha_5 yr - \alpha_{10} r_d \tag{2}$$

$$mo_s = \overline{mo} - \pi_1(e - \bar{e}) \tag{3}$$

The foreign exchange market

$$\frac{B}{X_0} = \alpha_{13}(e - p_d) - yr + \alpha_{14} r_d$$

$$\alpha_{13} > \alpha_1 \tag{4}$$

The labour market

$$yr_s = -\alpha_9(w - p_d) \tag{5}$$

$$w = \pi_2 p \tag{6}$$

$$p = \alpha_{15} p_d + (1 - \alpha_{15})e \tag{7}$$

$$yr_s = \alpha_9(1 - \pi_2 \alpha_{15})p_d - \alpha_9 \pi_2(1 - \alpha_{15})e \tag{8}$$

$$yr_s = -\alpha_9(1 - \alpha_{15})(e - p_d) \text{ for } \pi_2 = 1 \tag{9}$$

Equilibrium conditions

$$yr_d = yr_s \tag{10}$$

$$mo_d = mo_s \tag{11}$$

Notation

All variables are in logarithms (except for the interest rate r_d and B/X_0).

yr	domestic output
yr_d	real aggregate demand for goods
yr_s	real aggregate supply of goods
r_d	domestic interest rate
p_d	domestic price
e	exchange rate (units of domestic currency per unit of foreign currency)
gr	real government expenditure (fiscal policy)
p	consumer price index
w	wage rate
mo	stock of money
B/X_0	overall balance of payments over initial exports

$\bar{e}$ target exchange rate
$e - p_d$ real exchange rate

Equation (1) says that the real demand for goods is a positive function of the real exchange rate $e - p_d$ and of real government expenditure (the fiscal policy variable) and a negative function of the interest rate.

Equation (2) is a conventional money demand equation. Real money balances $mo - p_d$ are a positive function of output and a negative function of the interest rate.

Equation (3) is the monetary policy reaction function. The equation was explained in some detail in Chapter 6, to which the reader is again referred.

Equation (4) explains the overall balance of payments B/X_0. The overall balance of payments is composed of a current account and a capital account. The current account is determined by the real exchange rate and the level of output at home in relation to output abroad (assumed fixed and not shown). The capital account, as in the MF model, is determined by the home interest rate in relation to the interest rate abroad (assumed fixed and also not shown). α_{14} again represents the degree of capital mobility.

Equations (5)–(9) represent the aggregate supply side of the economy. This is the major innovation of the model.

Equation (5) says that, given the stock of capital and the level of technology, the producers' willingness to supply output is a negative function of the real wage rate. From a given base, a rise (fall) in the real wage rate will induce producers to produce less (more) output. The real wage rate is defined, importantly, as the nominal wage rate deflated by the price of home goods. (See Chapter 28 for a more careful derivation of this equation from a production function and a labour demand function.)

Equation (6) explains the wage rate as a function of consumer prices. π_2 represents the degree of wage indexation in the system. Equation (7) defines the consumer price index as a weighted average of the price of home goods and the price of imported goods. The latter, as we noted in the previous chapter, is strictly $p^* + e$ where p^* is the foreign price of imports. However, with p^* given, the price of imported goods will vary with the exchange rate.

Equations (5)–(7) can be combined to arrive at (8) which is the aggregate supply equation of the model. If $\pi_2 = 1$, there is full wage indexation, and (8) can be reduced to (9).

Equation (9) is a very important equation. It says that, when wage indexation is perfect, the level of output is determined solely by the real exchange rate. According to (9), if the real exchange rate rises (i.e. there is a real devaluation), output must fall. If the real exchange rate falls, output must rise. Finally, if the real exchange rate is unchanged, output cannot change either. Why is this?

Recall first that output can only change when the real wage rate alters (equation (5)). We therefore have the relationship from (5) and (9)

$$w - p_d = (1 - \alpha_{15})(e - p_d)$$

A real devaluation (appreciation) must correspond to an increase (fall) in the real wage rate. If there is no change in the real exchange rate, the level of the real wage rate cannot change either.

Suppose, by way of explanation, that home prices rise by say 5 per cent while import prices rise by only 1 per cent, i.e. there is a real appreciation. According to (9), the level of output ought to rise. The reason is that from (7) consumer prices and hence wages (which by definition are fully indexed) will rise by something between 5 and 1 per cent depending on the weights in (7). With home prices rising by 5 per cent and wages rising by less, the real wage rate will fall and this allows producers to increase their production.

If import prices had risen by 5 per cent and home prices by only 1 per cent, the wage rate (and consumer prices) would have risen by more than 1 per cent but less than 5 per cent. In this case, with a real devaluation, the real wage rate rises and output falls.

Finally, if both import and home prices rise by 5 per cent the wage rate (and consumer prices) will also rise by 5 per cent. In this case, neither the real exchange rate nor the real wage rate will change, and so the level of output will also be unchanged.

Equations (10) and (11) are the equilibrium conditions for output and money.

The general model above incorporates:

a) the degree of exchange rate flexibility (represented by the coefficient π_1);
b) the degree of capital mobility (represented by α_{14}); and
c) the degree of wage indexation (π_2).

Since the extreme case of fixed wages and prices has already been dealt with, we focus in this chapter on the other polar extreme where wages and prices are perfectly flexible and indexation is perfect. So in what follows we assume $\pi_2 = 1$ and use only equation (9), not (8), of the model.

TECHNICAL FEATURES OF THE MODEL

As in Chapter 6, the monetary policy instrument, whatever the exchange rate regime, is represented by $\overline{mo}$. A change in $\overline{mo}$ therefore represents a monetary policy change.

The fiscal policy instrument, again whatever the regime, is represented by gr. A change in gr represents a change in fiscal policy.

As in the MF model, we are interested in the effects on a number of endogenous variables of a change in monetary and fiscal policy for different exchange rate regimes.

We now identify a number of potential exchange rate regimes and indicate how the solution for the endogenous variables may be obtained for monetary and fiscal policy. The equilibrium conditions are imposed throughout.

A fixed rate regime with complete sterilisation (regime 1)

In this case e is fixed, $\pi_1 = 0$, and so (3) can be readily substituted into (2). Equations (1), (2) (modified) and (9) in combination solve for yr, p_d and r_d in terms of $\overline{mo}$ and gr. Having solved for p_d, yr and r_d, this then allows us to solve for B/X_0 which in this case need not be zero.

A fixed rate regime with monetary adjustment (unsterilised) intervention (regime 2)

In this regime the balance of payments converges towards zero in equilibrium, so we can set $B/X_0 = 0$. We can now combine (1), (4) (with $B/X_0 = 0$) and (9) to determine yr, p_d and r_d. Since the money stock is endogenous we can then use the solutions for these three variables to solve for the money stock in (2).

A flexible rate regime (regime 3)

Again in equilibrium $B/X_0 = 0$ but now the money stock is exogenous and $\pi_1 = 0$. Again substituting (3) into (2) we have (1), (2), (4) and (9) to determine in combination yr, p_d, e and r_d.

The generalised system

A more general system would comprise equations (1), (2), (3) ($mo_d = mo_s$), (4) ($B/X_0 = 0$) and (8), five equations which solve for mo, e, yr, r_d and p_d in terms of $\overline{mo}$ and gr. Because we have used (8) not (9) the solutions allow us to figure out the effects of

a) changing the degree of exchange rate flexibility (π_1);
b) changing the degree of capital mobility (α_{14}); and
c) changing the degree of wage indexation (π_2).

When a solution is reached outcomes should of course be consistent with equilibrium in all markets; any other outcome would not equilibrate all markets. This will be demonstrated as we proceed.

Is it possible to replicate the MF results as a special case of this model? In the MF model $\pi_2 = 0$ and so we can readily impose that condition on (8). At the same time p_d does not change. Imposing $\pi_2 = 0$ on (8) reduces the equation to yr $= \alpha_9 p_d$. If we further assume $\alpha_9 \to \infty$ this ensures that prices also will not change.

THE GRAPHICAL REPRESENTATION OF THE MODEL

In principle, we can employ the same graphical apparatus as in the MF model. We can once again represent the goods market by the IS schedule, the money market by the LM schedule and the foreign exchange market by the B schedule. The important difference is that whereas in the MF model we could focus only on nominal variables, what matters now in this larger model is the real variables.

The IS schedule is easily derived from (1). Rearranging and setting $yr_d = yr$, we have

$$r_d = -\frac{1}{\alpha_4}\,yr + \frac{\alpha_1}{\alpha_4}\,(e - p_d) + \frac{\alpha_3}{\alpha_4}\,gr \tag{12}$$

It is readily seen that the negative slope of the IS schedule is $1/\alpha_4$ with the real exchange rate $e - p_d$ and real government expenditure as the shift variables. A real devaluation (appreciation) will shift the schedule to the right (left) while a fiscal expansion (contraction) will also shift it to the right (left). (See Figure 8.1.)

The LM schedule is again easily derived from (2), setting $mo_d = mo$. Rearranging we have

$$r_d = -\frac{1}{\alpha_{10}}\,(mo - p_d) + \frac{\alpha_5}{\alpha_{10}}\,yr \tag{13}$$

The positive slope of the LM schedule is now α_5/α_{10}, with real money balances $mo - p_d$ as the shift variable. An increase (decrease) in real money balances will shift the schedule to the right (left) (Figure 8.1).

Finally, the B schedule can be readily derived from (4). Setting $B/X_0 = 0$ and rearranging we have

$$r_d = -\frac{\alpha_{13}}{\alpha_{14}}\,(e - p_d) + \frac{1}{\alpha_{14}}\,yr \tag{14}$$

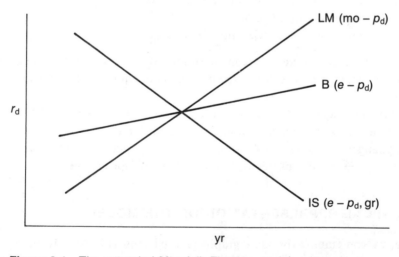

Figure 8.1   The extended Mundell–Fleming model

The positive slope is now $1/\alpha_{14}$ with the real exchange rate the shift variable. A real devaluation (appreciation) will shift the schedule to the right (left).

This completes the formal presentation of the model. As with the MF model we will focus attention on only three regimes: fixed rates with sterilisation (regime 1), fixed rates without sterilisation (regime 2) and flexible rates (regime 3).

REGIME 1

Table 8.1 shows the solutions for the three endogenous variables. The table also repeats the solutions for the MF model to facilitate comparison.

We focus primarily on output effects. Consider first the case of a monetary expansion. It can be readily demonstrated that the effects on output are weaker in the extended model.

The extended MF solution can be rewritten as

$$\frac{\alpha_4}{\alpha_4\alpha_5 + \alpha_{10} + \{[\alpha_4 + \alpha_1\alpha_{10}]/[\alpha_9(1 - \alpha_{15})]\}}$$

The denominator is now larger by the bracketed expression.

A similar result can also be demonstrated for a fiscal expansion. The extended

Table 8.1 Regime 1

	MF solutions	Extended MF solutions
Monetary expansion		
yr	$\dfrac{\alpha_4}{d_2}$	$\dfrac{\alpha_4\alpha_9(1 - \alpha_{15})}{d_1}$
p_d	0	$\dfrac{\alpha_4}{d_1}$
r_d	$-\dfrac{1}{d_2}$	$-\left\|\dfrac{\alpha_1 + \alpha_9(1 - \alpha_{15})}{d_1}\right\|$
Fiscal expansion		
yr	$\dfrac{\alpha_3\alpha_{10}}{d_2}$	$\dfrac{\alpha_3\alpha_9\alpha_{10}(1 - \alpha_{15})}{d_1}$
p_d	0	$\dfrac{\alpha_3\alpha_{10}}{d_1}$
r_d	$\dfrac{\alpha_3\alpha_5}{d_2}$	$\dfrac{\alpha_3[1 + \alpha_5\alpha_9(1 - \alpha_{15})]}{d_1}$

$d_1 = \alpha_9\alpha_{10}(1 - \alpha_{15}) + \alpha_1\alpha_{10} + \alpha_4[1 + \alpha_5\alpha_9(1 - \alpha_{15})]$
$d_2 = \alpha_4\alpha_5 + \alpha_{10}$

MF solution is now

$$\frac{\alpha_3\alpha_{10}}{\alpha_4\alpha_5 + \alpha_{10} + \{[\alpha_4 + \alpha_1\alpha_{10}]/[\alpha_9(1-\alpha_{15})]\}}$$

where again the denominator is larger by the bracketed expression.

Why are the real effects now weaker?

To understand the adjustment process, it is convenient to take the MF result as a starting point. Consider the case of a monetary expansion. In the MF model output rises, the interest rate falls but prices do not change.

Now visualise a hypothetical dynamic adjustment occurring in two stages: first, a price adjustment; second, a wage adjustment. Figure 8.2 tries to illustrate the adjustment mechanism, using conventional aggregate demand (AD) and aggregate supply (AS) schedules. The AD schedule is derived by combining (1) and (2) (with $mo_d = mo_s$); the AS schedule is derived from (5). mo and gr are shift variables in AD; w is a shift variable in AS. The exchange rate is fixed.

With a monetary expansion the AD schedule shifts to the right. In the MF model the AS schedule is horizontal (because prices are fixed); equilibrium is located at yr_1.

Starting with the MF result, suppose producers now raise the home price level to the point where the real wage rate has fallen sufficiently to make the MF equilibrium output profitable. This price level is shown as Q in Figure 8.2. With the home price

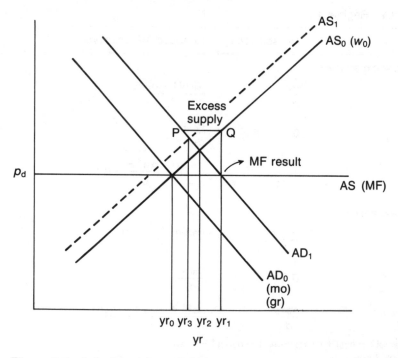

Figure 8.2   Adjustment in regime 1

level higher demand will now fall for two reasons. First, the higher price level reduces real money balances, pushing up the interest rate; this in turn reduces real demand. Second, with prices higher than abroad there is also a substitution effect in favour of imports (equation (1)). This further reduces real demand. These two negative effects on output are represented by the bracketed expression of the denominator explained above.

With production unchanged at the MF level, there is now an excess supply of goods (PQ in Figure 8.2), so the price level must start falling back; in turn this will mitigate the fall in real demand. There is now some domestic price level higher than the original level (i.e. before the monetary change) which reduces the real wage rate and allows an expansion in output exactly sufficient to match the higher real level of demand. This, of course, will be below the MF level, which is not sustainable, but above the original level of output before the monetary change (yr$_2$ in the figure).

This, however, is still not the end of the story. With the home price level up, the wage rate will also rise but by less than the increase in home prices (equation (7)). There is now, so to speak, a wage shock imposed on the system, and so the AS schedule starts shifting to the left. Faced with higher wages, the producers will now want to produce less and to do so they will need to raise their home price level further. In turn there will be another wage round; it is readily seen, however, that these adjustments become progressively smaller until the economy converges to a new equilibrium.

A new equilibrium is finally reached where there is some increase in both output and prices and the interest rate falls (Table 8.1). The new equilibrium is yr$_3$ in Figure 8.2 which shows only the final shift in the AS schedule, not the successive shifts. These outcomes are consistent with the restoration of equilibrium in the markets for goods, money and labour. From (1) we can see that the positive effect of the fall in the interest rate will dominate the negative effect of the rise in home prices (given gr). At the same time the money market is also in equilibrium with the expansion in the money stock, manifesting itself partly in an increase in output and home prices and partly in a fall in the interest rate. Finally, the supply side of the economy is also in equilibrium; with home prices rising more than wages the real wage rate ultimately falls to producers (but not of course in terms of the consumer price index), thus allowing some expansion in output.

The reader can readily confirm that no other combination of results will be consistent with equilibrium in all markets. If home prices rise, output must also rise, and so the interest rate must fall to equilibrate the goods market.

As already noted, having solved for output, home prices and the interest rate, we can now use equation (4) to solve for the overall balance of payments. It is readily seen that both the current and the capital accounts will be in deficit, so there must be an overall deficit, which in turn is not allowed to impact on the money supply because of sterilisation operations.

These adjustments are shown in Figure 8.3(a). The MF solution is shown at the intersection of LM and IS. With home prices now rising and given the new money

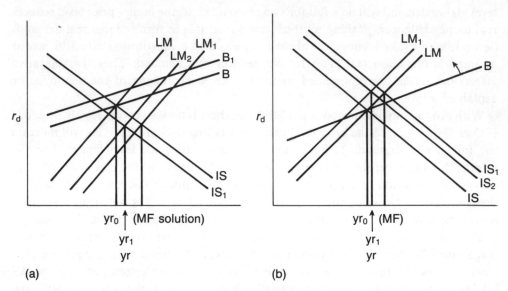

Figure 8.3 Effects of (a) monetary policies and (b) fiscal policies in regime 1

stock the IS and LM schedules both shift to the left; so does the B schedule. The final result is yr_1 which is higher than the original solution at yr_0.

The case of a fiscal expansion can be analysed along similar lines. As Table 8.1 shows prices and output both rise but now the interest rate also rises. In the goods market the fiscal expansion (increase in gr) dominates over the deflationary effects of a higher interest rate and higher domestic prices. In the money market, with the money stock fixed, equilibrium requires that the increase in output and home prices be associated with a rise in the interest rate. Finally, the outcome is associated with a fall in the real wage rate and hence an increase in output. Again, no other combination of outcomes will equilibrate all markets.

The adjustment mechanism parallels the analysis of a monetary expansion. The solution for fiscal expansion is shown in Figure 8.3(b), which is self-explanatory.

These results are important. They demonstrate that even with the consumption real wage rate fixed monetary and fiscal policy retains some capacity to be effective. This is because with the exchange rate fixed this allows the real wage rate to fall to *producers* while remaining unchanged to *consumers*.

REGIME 2

Monetary policy is ineffective, as in the MF model, despite the allowance now made for wage and price adjustment. An independent monetary policy will leave output, interest rates and prices all unchanged. The exogenous open market operation, sooner or later (depending on the degree of asset substitution), will be offset by an opposite movement in international reserves.

This is easily seen by inspection of equations (1), (4) (with $B/X_0 = 0$) and (9). Substituting for p_d from (9) into (1) and into (4) we have the following result. From (1) with gr fixed output can only increase if the interest rate falls; from (4), however, output can only increase if the interest rate rises (to offset the current account deficit). To equilibrate both the goods and the foreign exchange markets none of the variables can change.

Consider now the case of fiscal policy. If asset substitution is zero ($\alpha_{14} = 0$) fiscal policy will be completely impotent, a result which is identical with that for the MF model (see Table 8.2). This is easily seen from (4) and (9) in combination. According to (9) if output increases the price level must also rise. According to (4) if output and the price level both rise the trade balance and equivalently the overall balance of payments (given that asset substitution is zero) will also be in deficit; this cannot be an equilibrium outcome. (The money stock will fall, pushing down both output and prices.) This solution is shown in Figure 8.4.

The IS schedule shifts to the right. The increase in output and prices opens up a current account deficit which in turn reduces the money stock (shifts LM to the left) until the original level of output and prices is restored, but now at a higher interest rate. Fiscal expansion will be completely crowded out (see equation (1)). The money market is also in equilibrium, the rise in the interest rate now being consistent with the fall in the money stock.

So long as there is some asset substitution fiscal policy will have some effectiveness. In Table 8.2 we can readily demonstrate that as α_{14} increases the effect on output increases. Output and prices can both rise, equilibrating the labour market, but now the interest rate can also rise, inducing capital inflows to offset the trade deficit. The higher the capital mobility the larger the trade deficit that can be offset by capital

Table 8.2 Regime 2

	MF solutions	Extended MF solutions
Monetary expansion		
yr	0	0
p_d	0	0
r_d	0	0
Fiscal expansion		
yr	$\dfrac{\alpha_3\alpha_{14}}{d_4}$	$\dfrac{\alpha_3\alpha_{14}\alpha_9(1 - \alpha_{15})}{d_3}$
p_d	0	$\dfrac{\alpha_3\alpha_{14}}{d_3}$
r_d	$\dfrac{\alpha_3}{d_4}$	$\dfrac{\alpha_3[\alpha_{13} + \alpha_9(1 - \alpha_{15})]}{d_3}$

$d_3 = \alpha_{14}\alpha_9(1 - \alpha_{15}) + \alpha_1\alpha_{14} + \alpha_4[\alpha_{13} + \alpha_9(1 - \alpha_{15})]$
$d_4 = \alpha_4 + \alpha_{14}$

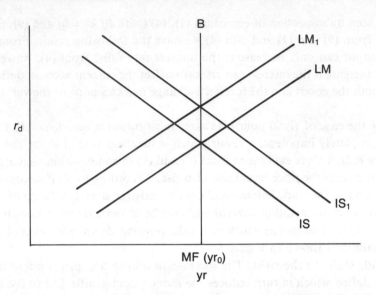

Figure 8.4 Fiscal expansion with zero capital mobility (regime 2)

inflows and hence the higher the level of output. When asset substitution is perfect fiscal policy is most effective. The solution is now

$$\frac{\alpha_3\alpha_9(1-\alpha_{15})}{\alpha_1+\alpha_9(1-\alpha_{15})}$$

We note again that, provided there is some capital mobility, fiscal policy is weakened relative to the MF model. The presence of wage–price adjustment thus serves again to render fiscal policy less potent. This is readily shown by comparing the two solutions in Table 8.2.

The case where asset substitution is perfect is illustrated in Figure 8.5. Starting with the MF solution as shown the price level will start to rise, as already demonstrated earlier, and this shifts both the IS and LM schedules to the left, meeting now at a lower level of output but at the same interest rate.

REGIME 3

The solution in this case is readily derived from the following three equations:

$$yr = \alpha_1 er + \alpha_3 gr - \alpha_4 r_d \tag{15}$$

$$0 = \alpha_{13} er - yr + \alpha_{14} r_d \tag{16}$$

$$yr = -\alpha_9(1-\alpha_{15})er \tag{17}$$

where $er = e - p_d$ (the real exchange rate). These three equations can be solved for three variables: er, r_d and yr.

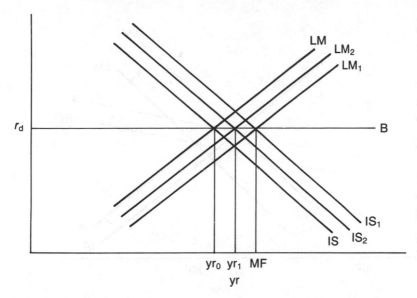

Figure 8.5 Fiscal expansion with perfect capital mobility in regime 2

Since monetary policy does not appear in any of these equations, the level of output, the interest rate and the real exchange rate are all independent of monetary policy. From (2) in the model, with yr and r_d given, the price level must rise proportionately. With the real exchange rate unchanged the currency must also devalue proportionately.

This is an important result. Monetary policy under flexible rates with perfect wage indexation cannot change the real variables; it can only change the nominal variables (prices, the exchange rate). This result is completely independent of the degree of capital mobility.

The general case is illustrated in Figure 8.6. In the MF model monetary expansion shifts the LM schedule to the right; the associated balance of payments deficit forces a devaluation which in turn shifts both the IS and B schedules to the right. The devaluation reinforces the effect on output, which is larger the higher the degree of capital mobility.

In the extended model prices start to rise. Producers raise their prices in relation to wages. Wages in turn rise because of the rise in home prices but also because of the devaluation. The real devaluation is weakened and the IS and B schedules shift to the left again. With home prices rising too, LM also shifts to the left. In the end all the schedules return to their original positions. With the real exchange rate and real money balances unchanged, none of the schedules will move.

It is easily shown that these outcomes are consistent with equilibrium in all markets. In the goods market, with the real exchange rate and the interest rate both fixed, output cannot change. The money market is also in equilibrium, the expression $mo - p_d$ remaining unchanged. The current account and the capital account will also

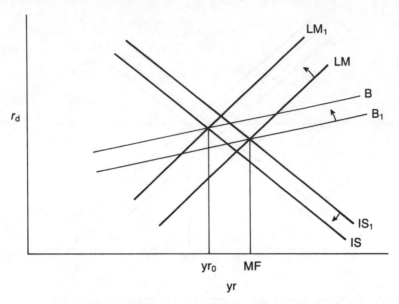

Figure 8.6 Monetary expansion – flexible rates

be in balance. Finally, with the real exchange rate unchanged the labour market can only be in equilibrium if output does not change.

It is also readily shown that any other result cannot equilibrate all markets. Suppose, for example, that we had a result that output and prices increased, the currency devalued in real terms and the interest rate fell. Such a result is consistent with equilibrium in the goods, foreign exchange and money markets but not in the labour market.

Consider now the case of a fiscal expansion. Table 8.3 shows that when capital mobility is zero ($\alpha_{14} = 0$) fiscal policy is completely impotent. This is in sharp contrast to the MF model where fiscal policy retains some effectiveness. It is also readily seen that as capital mobility increases fiscal policy becomes increasingly more potent. This is the exact opposite of the MF model where increasing capital mobility weakened the real effects of fiscal policy. With perfect capital mobility fiscal policy is completely impotent in the MF model while in the extended model it attains a maximum of effectiveness.

Suppose capital mobility were zero. Equilibrium in the labour market requires that there be a real appreciation if output is to increase, but such an outcome could not equilibrate the foreign exchange market (because on both counts the current account would be in deficit). To equilibrate all markets output cannot change, the interest rate must rise, home prices also rise and the currency devalues in proportion. The goods market is in equilibrium because the rise in the interest rate neutralises the effects on demand of the fiscal expansion. The money market is also in equilibrium because with the money stock and output fixed the rise in the price level is associated with

Table 8.3 Regime 3

	MF solutions	Extended MF solutions
Monetary expansion		
yr	$\dfrac{\alpha_1\alpha_{14}+\alpha_4\alpha_{13}}{d_5}$	0
p_d	0	1
r_d	$-\dfrac{\alpha_{13}-\alpha_1}{d_5}$	0
e	$\dfrac{\alpha_{14}+\alpha_4}{d_5}$	1
Fiscal expansion		
yr	$\dfrac{\alpha_3\alpha_{13}\alpha_{10}}{d_5}$	$\dfrac{\alpha_3\alpha_{14}\alpha_9(1-\alpha_{15})}{d_3}$
p_d	0	$\dfrac{\alpha_3\alpha_{10}[\alpha_{13}+\alpha_9(1-\alpha_{15})]-\alpha_5\alpha_3\alpha_{14}\alpha_9(1-\alpha_{15})}{d_3}$
r_d	$\dfrac{\alpha_3\alpha_{13}\alpha_5}{d_5}$	$\dfrac{\alpha_3[\alpha_{13}+\alpha_9(1-\alpha_{15})]}{d_3}$
e	$\dfrac{\alpha_3(\alpha_{10}-\alpha_{14}\alpha_5)}{d_5}$	$\dfrac{-\alpha_3\alpha_{14}-\alpha_5\alpha_3\alpha_{14}\alpha_9(1-\alpha_{15})+\alpha_3\alpha_{10}[\alpha_{13}+\alpha_9(1-\alpha_{15})]}{d_3}$

$d_3 = \alpha_{14}\alpha_9(1-\alpha_{15})+\alpha_1\alpha_{14}+\alpha_4[\alpha_{13}+\alpha_9(1-\alpha_{15})]$
$d_5 = \alpha_{10}(\alpha_{13}-\alpha_1)+\alpha_4\alpha_5\alpha_{13}+\alpha_1\alpha_{14}\alpha_5$

the rise in the interest rate. The foreign exchange market is in equilibrium; the current account must be zero; at the same time the higher interest rate has no effect on capital movements. Finally, the labour market is in equilibrium because neither output nor the real exchange rate change. This case is shown in Figure 8.7(a).

Capital mobility makes it possible for output to increase and at the same time for equilibrium to be maintained in all markets. With some capital mobility there will be a real appreciation, the interest rate will rise, output will increase while the effect on the price level is ambiguous. These outcomes are consistent with equilibrium in all markets. In particular, it is seen that it is now possible to reconcile the foreign exchange and labour markets. The real appreciation is consistent with the increase in output in the labour market; at the same time, there is now a current account deficit but this can be offset by an inflow of capital. The higher the capital mobility, the larger the current account deficit and hence the greater is the real appreciation and the increase in output.

The case where capital mobility is perfect is of particular interest. There will be a real (and nominal) appreciation, the price level will unambiguously fall, output will increase while the interest rate will be unchanged. The real appreciation is more than

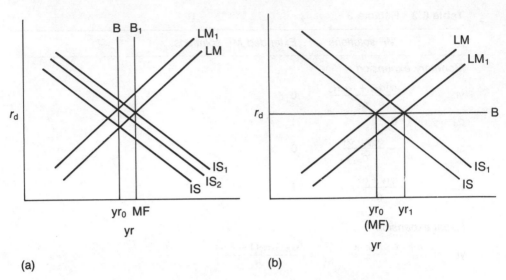

Figure 8.7   Fiscal expansion – flexible rates: (a) zero capital mobility; (b) perfect capital mobility

offset by the increase in government expenditure, allowing some increase in the demand for goods. With money supply and interest rates fixed the increase in output requires a fall in domestic prices to equilibrate the money market. Finally, the real appreciation plus the increase in output serve to worsen the current account but this is now offset by an inflow of capital.

How is it that the price level will fall with fiscal expansion when capital mobility is perfect? Recall that in this case the interest rate is fixed and so is the money stock. As capital mobility increases the devaluation weakens (the appreciation strengthens); this in turn mitigates the price level effect. When there is an appreciation the price of imported goods falls; with wages adjusting downwards producers will have an *increasing* incentive to produce more output. Suppose with capital mobility perfect output is higher but the domestic price level is unchanged or higher. There will now be upward pressure on the interest rate which in turn will force a further appreciation and further downward adjustment in wages and prices. Equilibrium can only be restored to the money market when the price level has fallen sufficiently and output has increased sufficiently to keep the interest rate unchanged.

The case of perfect capital mobility is illustrated in Figure 8.7(b).

SUMMARY AND CONCLUSIONS

So what does full wage indexation do?

Consider first monetary policy. In regime 1 monetary policy retains some effectiveness, albeit weaker, because it retains the capacity to change the real exchange rate. In regime 2, as in the MF model, monetary policy is totally ineffective. In regime 3 it is also totally ineffective whatever the degree of capital mobility. Now monetary policy simply changes prices and the exchange rate proportionately.

In general then we can sum up by saying that monetary policy is very considerably weakened, in so far as real effects are concerned, by the presence of full wage indexation.

What about fiscal policy? This is more complicated. In regime 1 again fiscal policy effectiveness is weakened by wage indexation. The same holds for regime 2. Regime 3 is different, however. With zero asset substitution fiscal policy is ineffective, in sharp contrast to the MF model where fiscal policy is effective. As asset substitution increases, however, fiscal policy effectiveness weakens in the MF model but is enhanced by wage indexation. When asset substitution is perfect fiscal policy is ineffective with the MF model but has some effectiveness in the presence of full wage indexation.

One very important result, when wage indexation is perfect, is worth highlighting. A casual examination of the results in Tables 8.2 and 8.3 reveals that the solutions for all real variables (output, the real exchange rate and the real interest rate, i.e. the nominal interest rate less the 'exogenous' rate of inflation) are identical for regimes 2 and 3. This is so, it needs to be emphasised, whatever the degree of capital mobility.

The underlying reason is straightforward. Take regime 3 as the starting point. Whatever the outcome, suppose monetary policy is used to stabilise the nominal exchange rate. If monetary policy is neutral, as it is with full wage indexation, then only nominal variables will be affected, not real variables.

An exact illustration will make this clearer. Suppose asset substitution is perfect and there is a fiscal expansion under flexible rates. The currency appreciates in real terms, output increases and the interest rate does not change. The price also falls and there is a nominal appreciation. To neutralise this nominal appreciation the money stock is allowed to increase. This leaves output, the real appreciation and the nominal interest unchanged but lowers the value of the currency (so as to keep it fixed) and raises the price level. The only difference is that the currency will return to its original level while the price level will rise, but the same real appreciation will emerge.

THE EFFECTS OF AN EXOGENOUS DEVALUATION IN THE EXTENDED MUNDELL–FLEMING MODEL

In this section we treat the exchange rate as an exogenous control instrument and enquire how a devaluation impacts on the economy. Again, we contrast the MF model with the extended version.

We analyse two cases. First, we look at the case where in the wake of a devaluation the authorities allow the money stock to respond to balance of payments developments. This corresponds to regime 2. Second, we examine the case where the money stock is exogenous (there is a money stock target). This corresponds to regime 1.

Regime 2

To find the solution to this case we use (1), (4) (setting $B/X_0 = 0$) and (9). Table 8.4 reports the results, including the result for the current account (CA/X_0).

The results are interesting. If wages are fully indexed and, moreover, if balance of payments developments are not sterilised (or as an alternative there is full monetary accommodation in the sense that the interest rate is held fixed) a nominal devaluation will

a) increase home prices proportionately leaving the real exchange rate unchanged;
b) leave the level of output and the interest rate all unchanged;
c) also leave the current account unchanged.

Finally, we can readily show that with output and the interest rate unchanged the money stock will increase proportionately (equation (2)), leaving real money balances unchanged. Table 8.4 compares these outcomes with those from an MF model.

These outcomes will equilibrate all markets. With the real exchange rate and the interest rate unchanged, the level of output cannot change. The money market is also in equilibrium as noted above. With the current account unchanged and the interest

Table 8.4 Effect of an exogenous devaluation

	MF solutions	Extended MF solutions
Regime 2		
yr	$\dfrac{\alpha_1\alpha_{14} + \alpha_4\alpha_{13}}{\alpha_4 + \alpha_{14}}$	0
p_d	0	1
r_d	$-\dfrac{\alpha_{13} - \alpha_1}{\alpha_4 + \alpha_{14}}$	0
CA/X_0	$\dfrac{\alpha_{14}(\alpha_{13} - \alpha_1)}{\alpha_4 + \alpha_{14}}$	0
Regime 1		
yr	$\dfrac{\alpha_1\alpha_{10}}{\alpha_{10} + \alpha_4\alpha_5}$	$-\dfrac{\alpha_4\alpha_9(1 - \alpha_{15})}{d_6}$
p_d	0	$\dfrac{d_6 - \alpha_4}{d_6}$
r_d	$\dfrac{\alpha_1\alpha_5}{\alpha_{10} + \alpha_4\alpha_5}$	$\dfrac{\alpha_9(1 - \alpha_{15}) + \alpha_1}{d_6}$
CA/X_0	$\dfrac{\alpha_{10}(\alpha_{13} - \alpha_1) + \alpha_{13}\alpha_4\alpha_9}{\alpha_{10} + \alpha_4\alpha_5}$	$\dfrac{\alpha_{13}\alpha_1\alpha_4 + \alpha_4\alpha_9(1 - \alpha_{15})}{d_6}$

$d_6 = \alpha_9\alpha_{10}(1 - \alpha_{15}) + \alpha_1\alpha_{10} + \alpha_4 + \alpha_4\alpha_5\alpha_9(1 - \alpha_{15})$

rate restored to its original level, the balance of payments must be zero. Finally, the labour market is in equilibrium; with the real exchange rate fixed, output cannot change.

It needs to be emphasised that this is a medium-run result. In the transition to this result a nominal devaluation will have effects on output, the current account and the real exchange rate. How long it will take for the economy to converge towards these ultimate results depends on the rigidities in the system, e.g. J curves, the frequency of wage and price adjustment. All of these considerations are abstracted from here.

Figure 8.8(b) demonstrates these results for the MF model and the extended model. The solution for the extended model is at yr_0. With the real exchange rate and real money balances unchanged, none of the three schedules shifts ultimately. In sharp contrast, in the MF model there are real effects. The IS and B schedules shift to the right (following the devaluation); there are accumulated surpluses which attract money into the economy, shifting the LM schedule to the right. In equilibrium the interest rate falls (the outflow being exactly offset by the current account surplus) and output increases.

Regime 1

This case is different. Consider first the extended MF model. The devaluation raises output and prices. Wages now adjust, pushing domestic prices up further. With the money stock fixed, real money balances fall, pushing up interest rates and exerting a deflationary effect on the economy.

In the end, output must fall, the interest rate rises and so do prices; at the same time there is a real devaluation (home prices rising by less than the devaluation). With

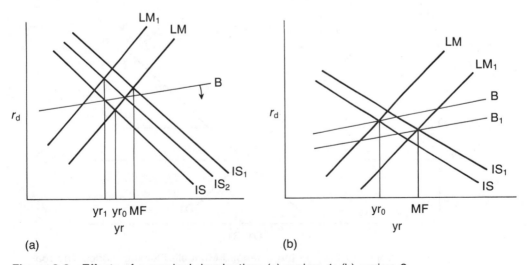

Figure 8.8 Effects of a nominal devaluation: (a) regime 1; (b) regime 2

a real devaluation and output falling the current account must improve. These outcomes are consistent with equilibrium in all markets. The real devaluation increases
the demand for goods but this is more than offset by the higher interest rate. Real
money balances fall and this is consistent with the combined fall in output and the
rise in the interest rate. Both the current and capital accounts will be in surplus, which
in turn is sterilised by the authorities. Finally, in the labour market, the real devaluation is consistent with the fall in output. This case is shown in Figure 8.8(a).

These results are in sharp contrast with the MF model, also shown in Figure 8.8(a).
In the MF model output and the interest rate both rise.

UNEMPLOYMENT IN THE EXTENDED MUNDELL–FLEMING MODEL

Although we have an explicit labour market in the extended model, nothing has been
said so far about unemployment as such. So how does involuntary unemployment
surface in the model?

Implicit in the aggregate supply equation (5) is a demand for labour equation,
which explains the real demand for labour (D1) as a negative function of the real wage
rate (see Chapter 28). *Unemployment is represented by the excess of the supply of
labour over the demand for labour.* Suppose that the supply of labour (S1) is a positive function of the consumer price index as defined by (7). We can then draw labour
demand (D1) and labour supply (S1) schedules as in Figure 8.9 and each as a function
of the real wage rate $w - p_d$. Note that the real exchange rate will be a shift variable
for the S1 function.[1] The economy is assumed to be placed, in equilibrium, at or
above wr_0, i.e. where there is full employment or an excess supply of labour.

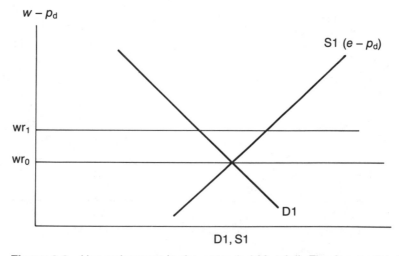

Figure 8.9 Unemployment in the extended Mundell–Fleming model. The real
wage rate $wr = w - p_d$

By definition the economy is always placed, in equilibrium, on its demand for labour function, corresponding to an equilibrium supply of output. But this need not produce full employment as at wr_0. The economy may end up at wr_1, where there is some unemployment (see again Chapter 28). The solutions obtained for the extended MF model correspond to positions on the D1 function above wr_0.

9

Disequilibrium models of product and labour markets

INTRODUCTION

In the chapters to this point we assumed that the goods market was always in equilibrium, in the sense that the desired aggregate demand for goods was always equal to the desired aggregate supply of goods. In the models presented so far, however, the labour market was not necessarily in equilibrium. In general we allowed the desired real supply of labour to exceed the desired real demand for labour, thus accommodating some involuntary unemployment. In these models then the goods market 'cleared', but not so the labour market.

In this chapter we extend our analysis of general disequilibrium by now accommodating the possibility that the goods and labour markets may both simultaneously be in disequilibrium. This allows us to deal with *combinations* of generalised disequilibrium in the two markets.

With this objective in mind the analysis begins by assuming, consistently with the spirit of this literature, that both product prices and nominal wages are rigid. Later in the chapter we try to rationalise, albeit somewhat unconvincingly, as we shall see, such nominal rigidities. This in turn draws on various strands of the so-called New Keynesian literature which aims at providing a micro foundation for macro price–wage rigidities.

Models of general product and labour market disequilibrium, taking nominal rigidities as a starting point, have their origins in a famous paper by Barro and Grossman (1971). The subsequent literature, however, was totally dominated by Europeans (see in particular Malinvaud (1977) who in turn made seminal contributions to disequilibrium models; see also Muellbauer and Portes (1978) and Sinclair (1987)). As

Gordon notes:

> Research on general disequilibrium or fixed price models appears to have become a specialised European activity in macroeconomics, with near-total invisibility in a recent survey I conducted of first-year graduate macro reading lists at the top ten American economics departments.
>
> (1990: 1138)

Models of the kind reviewed in this chapter need to be carefully distinguished from models which recognise *temporary* disequilibrium in the goods market as in Dornbusch's model of Chapter 18. *Ultimately*, however, in these models goods market equilibrium is restored.

A VERY SIMPLE DISEQUILIBRIUM MODEL WITH NOMINAL RIGIDITIES

Perhaps one of the most frustrating aspects of this literature is the fact that it is virtually entirely confined to the closed economy case and it is not apparent how the extension might be made to the open economy. (We take this up later).

We, too, will work with a model of the closed economy. This is desirable for two reasons: it is consistent with the literature but, more important, it allows us to see the essentials of the analysis. Simplicity, here, does serve to illuminate the issues.

The model can be represented by four equations:

$$yr_d = -\alpha_1 r_d + \alpha_2 yr + \alpha_3 u_1 \tag{1}$$

$$mo = \bar{p}_d + \alpha_5 yr - \alpha_{10} r_d \tag{2}$$

$$yr_s = -\alpha_9(\bar{w} - \bar{p}_d) \tag{3}$$

$$yr_d \neq yr_s \tag{4}$$

Notation

All variables are in logarithms except for the interest rate.

yr_d 'notional' aggregate demand for goods
yr actual level of national production
r_d the home interest rate
u_1 a disturbance term to aggregate demand
p_d the price level
w the wage rate
yr_s 'notional' aggregate supply of goods
mo the money stock

The model is extremely simple. Equations (1) and (2) are now familiar. In (1) real aggregate demand is a function of the actual level of output, of a disturbance term represented by u_1 and of the interest rate. Combining them yields the real aggregate demand for goods.

$$yr_d = \frac{\alpha_1}{\alpha_{10}} \, mo + \left(\alpha_2 - \frac{\alpha_1 \alpha_5}{\alpha_{10}} \right) yr - \frac{\alpha_1}{\alpha_{10}} \, p_d + \alpha_3 u_1 \tag{5}$$

This is displayed as the AD schedule in Figure 9.1 with mo, u_1 and yr as the shift variables.

Equation (3) is also a very familiar equation. This is displayed in Figure 9.1 as the AS schedule with now w as the shift variable.

Equation (4) represents the essence of disequilibrium analysis, asserting that real aggregate demand need not be equal to real aggregate supply.

In this model both w and p_d are exogenous. Throughout our analysis we will not allow p_d to change, but we will accommodate an exogenous wage shock.

The very simple model will now be put to work to illustrate four basic types of disequilibria: (a) pure classical unemployment; (b) pure Keynesian unemployment; (c) mixed classical and Keynesian unemployment; (d) repressed inflation.

The starting point for our analysis will be one where *both* the product and labour markets are in equilibrium. There is thus full equilibrium in the two key markets. AD = AS, and, as well, implicitly the aggregate demand for labour is equal to the aggregate supply, corresponding to a full employment level of output (y_f). This is represented by Q in Figure 9.1 at y^* and p_{d0}.

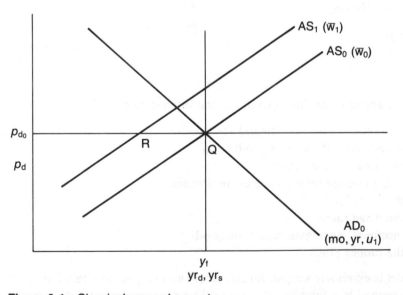

Figure 9.1 Classical unemployment

DISEQUILIBRIUM ANALYSIS

Classical unemployment

Classical unemployment is characterised by (a) an excess demand for goods and (b) an excess supply of labour.

Starting from Q we now allow $\bar{w}$ to increase but at the same time maintain the domestic price level at p_{d0}. The level of output thus *falls* from Q to R. Producers now are only willing to produce at R, output being determined on the supply side.

What happens to aggregate *demand*, as distinct from aggregate supply? We make the very simple assumption here that monetary policy is judiciously used to maintain aggregate demand at its original level (see (5)), so, by assumption, the AD schedule does not shift.

We end up with unemployment corresponding to RQ. There is now an excess supply of labour and an excess demand for goods. Unemployment of this kind cannot be cured by Keynesian demand policies. There is already an excess demand; pump priming would only *reinforce* the excess demand without delivering any reduction in unemployment. The cure in this case is the classical remedy of reducing the real wage rate, in other words *reversing* the real wage shock.

Pertinent questions to ask about this case would be the following. What happens to the excess demand? Several possibilities come to mind, none satisfactory in itself. The excess demand is rationed; the excess demand is met by a run down in inventories. It is perhaps evident that if the excess demand is *persistent* none of these can be serious solutions. In the end the excess demand is likely to be removed by some price adjustment. Moreover, in an open economy one would expect the excess domestic demand to be accommodated by imports.

Keynesian unemployment

Keynesian unemployment is characterised by an excess supply of goods and an excess supply of labour. Starting from Q now in Figure 9.2 we impose a net downward shock to aggregate demand (u_1 in (5) falls). At p_{d0}, the fixed price, there is now an excess *supply* of goods represented by AB. Although producers would like to produce at B (the *notional* supply) they will be constrained by the level of effective demand and effective production will be at A.[1]

This case is Keynesian. Unemployment of this kind can be cured by a Keynesian expansionary demand policy, i.e. implement a counter-cyclical monetary or fiscal policy to restore full employment at B.

Mixed classical and Keynesian unemployment

This case is characterised by a mix of classical and Keynesian unemployment. There is now an excess supply of labour combined with an excess demand for goods. We

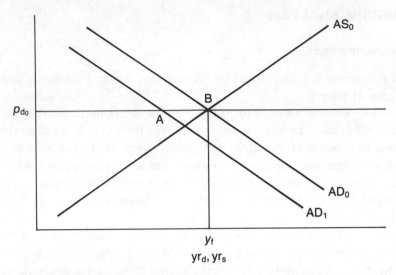

Figure 9.2 Keynesian unemployment

combine the two previous cases, supposing at once an autonomous wage shock and a net real downward demand shock. In Figure 9.3 the economy is placed at D, where there is an excess demand for goods of DE and an excess supply of labour of DF.

To remove all disequilibria a mixed strategy is required: one which increases real demand and reduces the real wage rate.

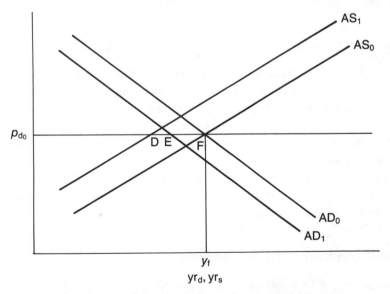

Figure 9.3   Mixed classical and Keynesian unemployment

Repressed inflation

This case was first analysed by Hansen (1951). It is characterised by an excess demand for both goods and labour.

Figure 9.4 illustrates this case. Starting from G, the initial solution, we have a fall in the real wage rate shifting the AS schedule to the right to AS_1; at the same time we imagine the AD schedule shifting to the right to AD_1.

Notional production is at H, notional demand is at K. Effective production is at the full employment level G. There is a potential excess demand for labour GH (producers would like, at the new real wage rate, to produce at H but cannot find labour), and an effective excess demand for goods GK.

Appropriate policies here would combine some (Keynesian) reduction in demand and some supply-side policies aimed at increasing the availability of labour resources.

Potential extensions to the open economy

As already indicated the vast bulk of the literature has tended to use closed economy models, as we in fact also did. This allowed us to highlight in a very simple way the different combinations of disequilibria.

There are, however, some attempts to extend disequilibrium analysis to the open economy. An extensive treatment is to be found in Cuddington *et al.* (1984) who also review the closed economy literature. One of the authors, Cuddington (1980), published a paper which shows how the different forms of disequilibria identified above may surface, in the short run, in an open economy.

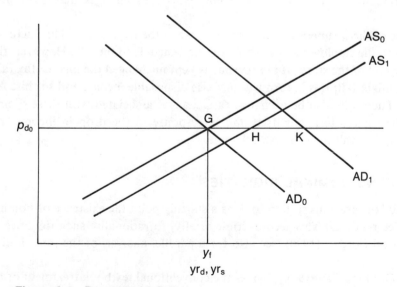

Figure 9.4   Repressed inflation

His economy has two sectors, one for the production of importables and one for the production of exportables. The exchange rate is fixed. The market for importables is always in equilibrium in the sense that the local demand for importables is always equal to its total available supply; he assumes, however, that in the market for exportables goods market disequilibrium may arise. At the same time, the labour market can be in excess supply or in excess demand. So the applications conventionally made for closed economies are now made to the open economy.

A more useful framework for the analysis of 'Keynesian' and 'classical' types of unemployment is to use an extended version of the model of Chapter 8.

Along the AS schedule the real consumption wage rate is always fixed; the exchange rate is now a shift variable (Chapter 8, equation (9)). The AD schedule will have monetary and fiscal policies and the exchange rate all as shift variables. (We solve equation (2) in Chapter 8 for rd and substitute into (1).) In the model the goods market is in equilibrium but the labour market need not be. It is therefore evident that in this kind of model either a shift in demand or a shift in supply could produce full employment. In this case the distinction between classical and Keynesian unemployment is blurred. In one sense the unemployment is classical because a fall in the real wage rate is a necessary condition for restoring full employment, but on the other hand demand expansion alone is sufficient to restore full employment. This in turn will have to be associated with a fall in the real wage rate to the producer (i.e. the so-called product real wage).

Thus to make some sense of the distinction in the case where the goods market is in equilibrium (but not so the labour market) we might have to say that exogenous shifts in aggregate supply indicate that, in broad terms, classical forces are at work, while exogenous shifts in aggregate demand indicate that Keynesian forces are at work. One reservation to note is that some exogenous changes may shift both schedules.

To be more explicit, suppose there is an increase in the payroll tax. This increases the wage cost to the employer and so shifts the AS schedule to the left. However, this cannot be the end of the story. If tax revenue is kept unchanged the income tax rate, for example, might fall; this in turn will increase disposable income and so shift AD to the right. There will also be exchange rate changes associated with these events. Moreover, the wage rate might itself *fall* in response to the drop in income tax, shifting perhaps as will now the AS schedule.

RATIONALISING NOMINAL RIGIDITIES

The analysis of the previous section took as a starting point the existence of nominal wage and price rigidities. This section tries, briefly, to rationalise such rigidities. It draws in part on Gordon (1990) (see also for a parallel analysis of the topic Ball *et al*. 1988).

Following Gordon, Figure 9.5 provides the conventional textbook treatment of the price–output strategy of a monopolist facing linear demand curves and a horizontal

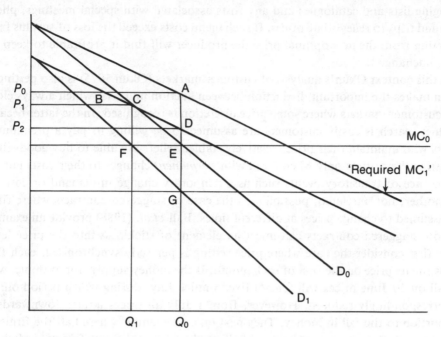

Figure 9.5 The monopolist's output–pricing strategy

marginal cost curve. (These last assumptions are readily relaxed without major change to the conclusions).

When demand is located at D_0 profit-maximising output is at Q_0 and price is at P_0. If demand falls to D_1, and if the MC function falls proportionately to MC_1 (labelled 'Required MC_1'), the optimal level of production remains at Q_0 while the price falls from P_0 to P_2.

Gordon uses these reference points as a basis for organising his thinking about potential cost and price rigidities that might arise. Rigidities fall into two distinct categories: first, what he calls 'direct barriers to price adjustment, independent of the behaviour of marginal cost, which cause the price to deviate from the price that would be set by a profit maximising monopolist who has no costs of adjustment to consider'; second, any stickiness in marginal cost, both in prices of purchased materials and in wages. Combining these two elements, Gordon summarises: 'A menu cost of wage adjustment will make marginal cost sticky and indirectly create a source of nominal price stickiness, even if costs of adjusting prices are completely absent.'

Product price rigidity

In the first category Gordon, drawing on the New Keynesian micro literature, considers two possibilities. One possibility is that there are lumpy transactions (so-called menu costs) incurred in changing prices. Such menu costs include the costs of changing lists and catalogues and any costs associated with special meetings, phone calls and trips to renegotiate prices. If such menu costs exceed the loss of surplus from deviating from the new optimal price the producer will find it profitable to keep the price unchanged.

In this context Okun's analysis of customer markets (Okun 1975) is also pertinent. Okun makes the important distinction between auction markets (which always clear) and customer markets where some price discretion is recognised. In the latter because product search is costly customers are assumed to be willing to pay a premium to sellers who maintain their prices relatively stable. Sellers are able to buy goodwill by adjusting their prices only when faced with *permanent* changes to their costs but not in the face of transitory events such as a temporary change in demand or cost.

Another, not unrelated, possibility is the case of staggered contracts where firms are assumed to change prices at different times. Ball *et al.* (1988) provide an example of how staggered contracts can inject an element of stickiness into the price level. They first consider the case where price setting is perfectly synchronised, each firm adjusting its price on the first of each month. If the money supply, for example, were to fall on 10 June prices will remain fixed until 1 July, during which period output is correspondingly reduced. However, from 1 July all prices adjust downwards in proportion to the fall in money. They next take an example where half the firms set prices on the first of each month and half on the fifteenth. Some five days after the fall in the money supply half the firms could in principle adjust their prices. However, Ball *et al.* argue that in reality they may make very little change because with the other half of prices fixed they may not want to implement changes in *relative* prices. In turn on 1 July the other half of the firms may act in a parallel fashion. This injects an element of rigidity into the price level.

The two cases complement one another. As Ball *et al.* note:

> The literature on staggered price setting complements that on nominal rigidities arising from menu costs. The degree of rigidity in the aggregate price level depends on both the frequency and the timing of individual price changes. Menu costs cause prices to adjust infrequently. For a given frequency of individual adjustment, staggering shows the adjustment of the price level. Large aggregate rigidities can thus be explained by a combination of staggering and nominal frictions: the former magnifies the rigidities arising from the latter.
>
> (1988: 12)

These two cases can be illustrated graphically in terms of Figure 9.5. Suppose again that there is a downward demand shock and suppose too, to take the extreme case, that marginal costs fall proportionately to the 'Required MC_1'. As already noted, the new optimal price level, without adjustment costs, is P_2. However, the firm may 'rationally' choose to leave its price at P_0.

How important are these two elements likely to be in generating product price rigidity, independently of the behaviour of marginal costs? It is difficult to be convinced that the two elements in combination can rationalise nominal rigidity for any extended period of time. In the face of perceived *permanent* changes in demand, menu costs will tend to be overwhelmed by the current and future discounted losses from a non-optimal pricing strategy. Moreover, as Gordon notes, the menu cost approach considers only costs of price adjustment and 'totally ignores costs of output adjustment'.

Theories of nominal wage rigidity

We review here a variety of theories which attempt to explain some nominal wage stickiness particularly in a downward direction. The principal ones are efficiency wages, the insider—outsider framework, union activity, staggered wage contracts and implicit contracts.

The key idea underlying efficiency wages is that worker productivity depends positively on the real wage rate offered by the employer. As Lindbeck and Snower (1987) note, this association has been rationalised in many different ways. First, if the wage offer should fall the most able workers may leave the firm, thus reducing overall efficiency. Second, shirking on the job intensifies (falls) the lower (higher) the real wage rate on offer. Third, on-the-job search activity is likely to increase (diminish) the lower (higher) the wage rate on offer. In turn, intensified search activity tends to be associated with lower average productivity of the work force. Fourth, an increased propensity to quit is also likely to be associated with a lower wage. The increased turnover in turn reduces efficiency by increasing the costs of retraining new staff.

The efficiency wage theory is invoked to explain why firms refuse to lower their wage offer when the economy is recessed. A lower wage offer may reduce productivity for all the reasons mentioned above and so may turn out on balance to be unprofitable. Thus the going wage rate may be an 'equilibrium' one, despite the fact that there may be an excess supply of labour. In this framework it is the firm which sets the wage rate, offering an equilibrium wage rate which is optimal in the sense of maximising its own profits.

The insider—outsider theory postulates that insiders (the employed) are able to exercise a certain degree of market power over the wage rate that gives them an ascendancy over outsiders (the unemployed). According to the theory insiders earn a rent (a margin of advantage) over outsiders; the rent is based on

a) the costs of hiring and firing;
b) the cost of refusing cooperation with entrants;
c) the adverse effect of labour turnover on work, effort and morale.

The considerations identified here are similar in spirit to those invoked by wage efficiency theories. The primary difference has to do with which party ultimately has the initiative: the employers or the employees. Wage efficiency theories give firms the discretion on wages, which are set optimally; insider—outsider theories give insiders the ultimate control. As Lindbeck and Snower put it:

> Both theories deal with employees who capture economic rent from being employed but whose wages are not underbid by the involuntarily unemployed workers. However, in the efficiency wage theory underbidding does not occur because lower wages don't appeal to the firms; whereas in the insider–outsider theory the insiders use their market power to prevent wages from falling.
>
> (1987: 407–8)

The idea that unions may exercise some degree of monopoly power over nominal wages is appealing. The flexing of union muscle is an event widely observed in industrial countries. There is as well evidence that wages in unionised sectors tend to have a margin of advantage over wages in non-unionised sectors. In addition there is now a large literature that attempts to model union behaviour in the sense that it is treated as an institution with well-defined objective functions. Lindbeck (1991), however, has noted that 'an obvious weakness of union models is that they do not really explain where the market power of unions comes from and hence why unions are able to push through and sustain non-market clearing wages' (a gap to some extent filled by insider–outsider theory, which complements it).

The theories reviewed so far are capable of explaining a certain degree of *nominal* wage stickiness, particularly in a downward direction, but are primarily theories of real wage rather than nominal wage rigidity. The next theory we turn to – that of staggered wage contracts – does aim at explaining nominal wage rigidity in an upward or downward direction but, as we shall see, is of very limited application.

Staggered wage contract theory was first developed in the USA by Fischer (1977a) and Taylor (1980). The key features of such models are

a) that wage contracts are assumed to extend over two to three years;
b) that the contracts across different sectors are not synchronised in the sense that they do not all come up for renewal at the same time.

Thus, in any one year, some contracts will be renegotiated; others, however, will be bound by the terms of the original contract. This injects an element of stickiness into nominal wage determination.

The modelling of staggered wage contracts reflects the institutional fact that in the USA in the large unionised sectors contracts are frequently negotiated for periods of up to three years.

The framework, however, is of limited applicability. In the first place, even in the USA only a small proportion of wage settlements are negotiated for contracts extending over two to three years. In the second place, often these contracts offer an indexation clause, allowing wages to adjust partially or fully in the course of the contract to any *ex post* inflation which exceeds the original expectations about inflation embedded in the original contract. In the third place, most Western countries tend to have wage contracts which last only for a year; many of these would also have some indexation provision. In the fourth place, whilst it is certainly true that contracts do inject some element of nominal rigidity, the rigidity does eventually disappear when contracts are renegotiated.

Finally, implicit contract theory also provides a rationale for wage rigidity (Azariadis 1975). Implicit contract theory takes as a starting point that workers are more risk averse than employers. The theory demonstrates that in these circumstances the employer will assume the risk of potential wage variation, paying a fixed wage rate whatever the demand conditions.

To conclude this section it seems that neither New Classical assumptions of very flexible wages and prices (see Chapter 23) nor disequilibrium models which assume *protracted* stickiness are a true reflection of reality. It is an observable fact that whilst adjustment may be slow there is some convergence ultimately towards equilibrium in the goods market. This is what is missing from disequilibrium analysis. This, of course, is not to dismiss it but to recognise it as essentially a temporary phenomenon.

REAL WAGE RIGIDITY, KEYNESIAN AND CLASSICAL UNEMPLOYMENT

In Chapter 8 we showed how unemployment arose in a model where the real wage rate was rigid. We can readily extend that framework and the one above to distinguish between Keynesian, classical and the natural unemployment rates.

Figure 9.6 shows a schedule representing the real demand for labour as a negative

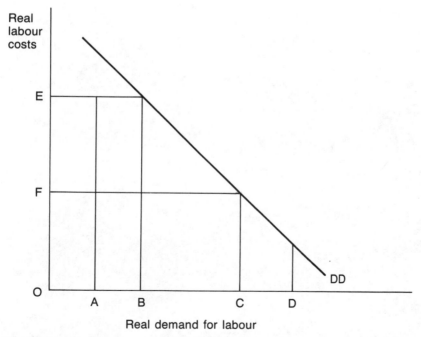

Figure 9.6 Keynesian, classical and the natural rate of unemployment

function of real labour costs. OD is the supply of labour. OC is the 'effective' supply of labour and so CD represents structural unemployment. AC is other unemployment. Suppose actual employment is at A, off the labour demand schedule. At given real labour costs E employment can increase to B, reducing the unemployment by AB. This unemployment is Keynesian. To reduce the unemployment by BC to achieve effective full employment real labour costs must fall from E to F. Thus BC represents classical unemployment.

We can thus divide unemployment, as proportions of the labour force, into three components:

$$\frac{AB}{OD} + \frac{BC}{OD} + \frac{CD}{OD}$$

These represent respectively Keynesian, classical and the natural rate of unemployment.

10

The portfolio balance model of the monetary sector

INTRODUCTION

So far in Chapters 6–8 we have represented the monetary sector in a very conventional (Keynesian) manner. In this chapter we introduce the reader to an *alternative* method of representing that sector.

Previously, we wrote down a *stock* demand for money; at the same time, with the domestic and foreign interest rates playing a key role in the adjustment process, there were demands for domestic bonds and for foreign bonds. The demand for domestic bonds was never made explicit but was in fact implicit in the analysis. We did, however, write down a demand for foreign bonds (the capital flow equation) but, as noted in Chapter 7, its consistency with the stock demand for money was called into question.

The very big advantage of a portfolio approach to the monetary sector is that it brings out into the open all these questions. The number of assets in a portfolio is explicitly defined; the determinants of each asset demand is identified and, most important, portfolio constraints are carefully imposed on the analysis. In other words, given the total of wealth, comprising a number of financial assets, an increase in the demand for any *one* of the assets must necessarily be associated with an equivalent net decline in the sum of the other assets in the portfolio. The portfolio balance approach to macroeconomic modelling was first developed in a closed economy context by Metzler (1951) and Tobin (1969) and extended to the open economy by Kouri and Porter (1974), Kouri (1976) and Branson (1977).

Unfortunately, the admittedly greater elegance of the portfolio balance model is achieved at the expense of considerably greater complexity in the analysis of, say, monetary–fiscal policy changes. These issues will be taken up in more detail in subsequent chapters.

This chapter focuses entirely on the specification of asset demands in an open economy and undertakes an analysis of the effects of a variety of *monetary* changes which throw the portfolio out of equilibrium; we then examine how adjustment in the portfolio occurs to restore equilibrium to asset demands. In this analysis the real sector is assumed to be given.

For a more detailed and technical analysis of the portfolio balance framework, the reader is referred to Branson and Henderson (1985) and the bibliography contained therein.

THE MODEL

In our economy, there are only three financial assets: domestic base money on which no interest is paid (Mo), domestic bonds (B) and foreign bonds (FA). Total financial wealth is defined as the sum of these three assets denominated in the home currency. Foreigners are assumed to hold no assets in the domestic economy. Residents do not hold foreign money. (An extension to the four-asset case, where the fourth asset is equities, is made in Argy and Murray (1985).)

We now write down the respective asset demands for each of the three assets:

$$\frac{\text{Mo}}{P} = b_1 Y - b_2 r_\text{d} - b_3 \left(r^* + \frac{E_\text{e} - E}{E} \right) + b_{14} \frac{\text{We}}{P} \tag{1}$$

$$\frac{B}{P} = -b_6 Y + b_7 r_\text{d} - b_8 \left(r^* + \frac{E_\text{e} - E}{E} \right) + b_{15} \frac{\text{We}}{P} \tag{2}$$

$$\frac{EFA}{P} = -b_{11} Y - b_{12} r_\text{d} + b_{13} \left(r^* + \frac{E_\text{e} - E}{E} \right) + b_{19} \frac{\text{We}}{P} \tag{3}$$

$$\text{We} = \text{Mo} + B + EFA \tag{4}$$

P	is the relevant price deflator
E	is the exchange rate (units of domestic currency per unit of the foreign currency)
Y	is output
FA	is the stock of foreign bonds held (denominated in foreign currency)
r_d	is the domestic interest rate
r^*	is the foreign interest rate
$(E_\text{e} - E)/E$	is the expected devaluation of the home currency
We	is financial wealth

Each asset demand in real terms is a function of relative returns, output and real wealth. The following constraints must apply:

$$b_1 = b_6 + b_{11} \qquad b_7 = b_2 + b_{12}$$

$$b_{13} = b_3 + b_8 \qquad b_{14} + b_{15} + b_{19} = 1$$

It is assumed that, as output increases, the demand for both domestic and foreign bonds decreases and the demand for domestic money increases. (For a similar assumption, see Backus (1984).) This is captured by the constraint $b_1 = b_6 + b_{11}$. If the domestic interest rate increases, the demand for domestic bonds increases at the expense of domestic money and foreign bonds ($b_7 = b_2 + b_{12}$). If the return on foreign bonds increases (either because the interest rate rises or because there is an expected devaluation of the home currency) the demand for foreign bonds increases now at the expense of both domestic money and bonds ($b_{13} = b_3 + b_8$). Finally, if real wealth increases, the increase is allocated amongst the three assets ($b_{14} + b_{15} + b_{19} = 1$). b_7, b_8, b_{12} and b_{13} are a measure of bond asset substitution. If these were all infinity, asset substitution would be perfect and expected returns would be equalised (i.e. $r_d = r^* + (E_e - E/E)$).

Equation (4) is the definition of financial wealth, which comprises the three financial assets. Assuming that FA is positive the value of this wealth could increase (decrease) either because the component stocks increase (decrease) or, given the stocks, because of a devaluation (appreciation) (which increases (decreases) the valuation of foreign asset holdings). It is important to note that FA may, in principle, be negative or positive depending on whether a country is a net creditor (FA positive) or a net debtor (FA negative) *vis-à-vis* the rest of the world. Germany and Japan would be examples of a net creditor country; Australia and the USA (in recent years) would be examples of a net debtor country. If a country were a net debtor a devaluation will reduce wealth because it will increase the indebtedness abroad denominated in domestic currency.

In Chapter 7 we noted that a portfolio theory of capital movements (as distinct from a flow theory) carried radically different implications for the analysis of policy changes. More formally, now, from (3) we can derive a capital flow equation which bears comparison with the MF capital flow equation.

$$K = \text{FA } \Delta E + b_{11} \, \Delta Y + b_{12} \, \Delta r_d - b_{13} \, \Delta \left(r^* + \frac{E_e - E}{E} \right) - b_{19} \, \Delta \text{We}$$

$$+ (b_{19}\text{We} - \text{FA}) \, \Delta P \tag{5}$$

where $K = -\Delta \text{FA}$.
In the MF model we had

$$K = \alpha_{17}(r_d - r^*) \tag{6}$$

where α_{17} was the degree of capital mobility.

Several points of difference between (5) and (6) are worth highlighting.

a) In the MF model capital flows were a function of the differences in the levels of the interest rates. In (5) they are a function of *changes* in the levels. This point was made in Chapter 7.
b) The coefficients on the domestic and foreign returns are not necessarily the same (i.e. b_{12} is not necessarily equal to b_{13}).
c) Exchange rate expectations also enter into the new equation (5). These are disregarded in the MF model.
d) There are, as well, other variables such as wealth, output, prices which enter the new equation, but which were absent in the MF model.

The implications of the new capital flow equation for the adjustment process will be pursued further in subsequent chapters.

A special case of the model in (1)–(3) assumes that the elasticity of demand for each asset *vis-à-vis* wealth is unity (as in Allen and Kenen (1980) for example). This allows us to write each asset demand as a proportion of wealth.

$$\frac{\text{Mo}}{\text{We}} = b_1 Y - b_2 r_\text{d} - b_3 \left(r^* + \frac{E_\text{e} - E}{E} \right) \tag{1a}$$

$$\frac{B}{\text{We}} = -b_6 Y + b_7 r_\text{d} - b_8 \left(r^* - \frac{E_\text{e} - E}{E} \right) \tag{2a}$$

$$\frac{EFA}{\text{We}} = -b_{11} Y - b_{12} r_\text{d} + b_{13} \left(r^* + \frac{E_\text{e} - E}{E} \right) \tag{3a}$$

Equations (1a) and (3a) are very widely used to represent the monetary sector of a macro model (Turnovsky 1976; Allen and Kenen 1980). This representation, however, suffers from one weakness: prices do not appear in the monetary sector. The reasoning underlying this is the following. Consider the money demand equation. Suppose prices increase by 10 per cent; then money demand increases by 10 per cent; at the same time the real value of wealth falls by 10 per cent reducing the nominal demand for money by 10 per cent. The net demand for money will not change.[1] This point is pursued further in Chapter 19.

In what follows, we use the set of equations (1a)–(3a) to undertake some monetary–portfolio analysis, first for flexible exchange rates and then for fixed exchange rates. We abstract altogether from real impacts, leaving these for later chapters. Although this procedure is a little artificial, focusing *solely* on portfolio adjustments does allow us to understand the adjustment mechanisms at work.

Throughout this chapter we assume that the small country concerned is a net creditor *vis-à-vis* the rest of the world. The reader should be able to figure out the solutions for the case where the country is a net debtor, i.e. where FA is initially negative; but we do not pursue this case. Obviously, this is not entirely satisfactory since, by definition, there are plenty of net debtor countries around. We do this for several reasons, however. The first is that this is almost universally the practice in the literature. The second is that a negative net foreign asset position can be a source of dynamic instability (Boyer 1977). The third is that ambiguities abound when net foreign asset positions are negative and this complicates the task of interpretation.

ADJUSTMENT UNDER FLEXIBLE EXCHANGE RATES

Our ultimate objective here is to examine the effects on the portfolio and on the endogenous variables of a number of 'monetary' disturbances to the economy.

The first step is to use equations (1a)–(3a) to find solutions for the endogenous variables of the system. We can differentiate all three equations as follows (assuming the initial exchange rate is unity):

$$\frac{1}{We} \Delta Mo = \frac{Mo}{We^2} \Delta We + b_1 \Delta Y - b_2 \Delta r_d - b_3 \Delta \left(r^* + \frac{E_e - E}{E} \right) \tag{7}$$

$$\frac{1}{We} \Delta B = \frac{B}{We^2} \Delta We - b_6 \Delta Y + b_7 \Delta r_d - b_8 \Delta \left(r^* + \frac{E_e - E}{E} \right) \tag{8}$$

$$\frac{FA}{We} \Delta E + \frac{1}{We} \Delta FA = \frac{FA}{We^2} \Delta We - b_{11} \Delta Y - b_{12} \Delta r_d$$

$$+ b_{13} \Delta \left(r^* + \frac{E_e - E}{E} \right) \tag{9}$$

Given the wealth constraint, one of the three asset demands is redundant. It is simplest, here, to disregard (9) and focus on (7) and (8). Substituting the definition of wealth in (4) into (7) and (8), we arrive at two equations:

$$\Delta r_d = \frac{b_1}{b_2} \Delta Y + \frac{b_3 We^2 + MoFA}{b_2 We^2} \Delta E - \frac{We - Mo}{b_2 We^2} \Delta Mo$$

$$- \frac{b_3}{b_2} (\Delta r^* + \Delta E_e) + \frac{Mo}{b_2 We^2} \Delta B + \frac{Mo}{b_2 We^2} \Delta FA \tag{10}$$

$$\Delta r_d = \frac{b_6}{b_7} \Delta Y + \frac{We - B}{b_7 We^2} \Delta B - \frac{B}{b_7 We^2} \Delta Mo + \frac{b_8}{b_7} (\Delta r^* + \Delta E_e)$$

$$- \left(\frac{b_8}{b_7} + \frac{BFA}{b_7 We^2} \right) \Delta E - \frac{B}{b_7 We^2} \Delta FA \tag{11}$$

Equation (10) represents money market equilibrium while (11) represents bond market equilibrium. These two equations can be used to solve jointly for the exchange rate and the domestic interest rate in terms of all the exogenous variables in the model: Y, Mo, $r^* + E_e$, B, FA.

The solution for the exchange rate is

$$\Delta E = \frac{(b_7 - b_2)B + b_7 FA}{k_1 b_7 b_2 We^2} \Delta Mo + \frac{b_8/b_7 + b_3/b_2}{k_1} (\Delta r^* + \Delta E_e)$$

$$- \frac{b_7 Mo + b_2 B}{k_1 b_7 b_2 We^2} \Delta FA - \frac{b_7 Mo - b_2 (We - B)}{k_1 b_7 b_2 We^2} \Delta B$$

$$- \frac{b_1/b_2 - b_6/b_7}{k_1} \Delta Y \tag{12}$$

$$k_1 = \frac{b_3}{b_2} + \frac{b_8}{b_7} + \frac{BFA}{b_7 We^2} + \frac{MoFA}{b_2 We^2}$$

$$b_1 > b_6 \qquad b_2 < b_7$$

and for the interest rate

$$\Delta r_d = - \frac{b_7 (k_1 - k_2)(We - Mo) + k_2 b_2 B}{k_1 b_7 b_2 We^2} \Delta Mo$$

$$+ \frac{b_7 (k_1 - k_2) Mo + k_2 b_2 (We - B)}{k_1 b_7 b_2 We^2} \Delta B$$

$$+ \left[\frac{k_2}{k_1} \left(\frac{b_8}{b_7} + \frac{b_3}{b_2} \right) - \frac{b_3}{b_2} \right] (\Delta r^* - \Delta E_e)$$

$$+ \frac{Mo b_7 (k_1 - k_2) - k_2 b_2 B}{k_1 b_7 b_2 We^2} \Delta FA + \left[\frac{b_1}{b_2} \left(1 - \frac{k_2}{k_1} \right) + \frac{k_2}{k_1} \frac{b_6}{b_7} \right] \Delta Y \tag{13}$$

$$k_2 = \frac{b_3}{b_2} + \frac{MoFA}{b_2 We^2} < k_1$$

We now proceed to introduce a simpler model for the rest of the world.

The rest of the world

$$\frac{Mo^*}{We^*} = b_{24} Y^* - b_{25} r^* \tag{14}$$

$$\frac{B^*}{We^*} = -b_{16} Y^* + b_{17} r^* \tag{15}$$

$$We^* = Mo^* + B^* \tag{16}$$

Equations (14)–(16) represent the rest of the world which is assumed to be very large relative to our home economy. Demand for the small country's bonds can thus be ignored.

For the rest of the world the solution for the interest rate is

$$\Delta r^* = \frac{b_{24}}{b_{25}} \Delta Y^* - \frac{We^* - Mo^*}{b_{25}We^{*2}} \Delta Mo^* + \frac{Mo^*}{b_{25}We^{*2}} \Delta B^* \tag{17}$$

An increase in foreign output or an increase in the foreign budget deficit (financed by an accumulation of foreign bonds) will increase the foreign interest rate while an increase in the money supply abroad will lower the interest rate.

We now use (17) to eliminate the foreign interest rate from the exchange rate equation (12) for the home economy. To simplify, we rewrite (12) as

$$\Delta E = a_1 \Delta Mo + a_2(\Delta r^* + \Delta E_e) - a_3 \Delta FA \pm a_4 \Delta B - a_5 \Delta Y \tag{18}$$

where a_4 has the only ambiguous sign. We now substitute (17) into (18):

$$\Delta E = a_1 \Delta Mo + a_2 \Delta E_e - a_3 \Delta FA \pm a_4 \Delta B - a_5 \Delta Y + a_6 \Delta Y^*$$

$$- a_7 \Delta Mo^* + a_8 \Delta B^* \tag{19}$$

where

$$a_6 = \frac{a_2 b_{24}}{b_{25}}$$

$$a_7 = \frac{a_2(We^* - Mo^*)}{b_{25}We^{*2}}$$

$$a_8 = \frac{a_2 Mo^*}{b_{25}We^{*2}}$$

Equation (19) brings out more explicitly the role of relative supplies of assets in determining the exchange rate. If domestic money increases, the currency devalues; if foreign money increases, the currency appreciates, because the foreign interest rate falls. If there is a current account surplus (holdings of foreign assets increase), there is an appreciation but this has no effect on the economy of the rest of the world. If there is a domestic deficit and the supply of domestic bonds increases, the effect on the currency is ambiguous, although it is easily shown that if domestic and foreign bonds are close substitutes the currency will appreciate.[2] If there is a foreign budget deficit and the supply of foreign bonds increases, the rise in the foreign interest rate will lead to an outflow of capital and hence to a devaluation of the home currency.

Finally, domestic and foreign output also enter into the equation. An increase in domestic output leads to an appreciation because there is an increase in money demand which in turn means that residents sell both domestic and foreign bonds; these sales will generate a potential inflow which strengthens the currency. An increase in foreign output, given the foreign money supply, increases foreign interest rates which in turn forces down the currency.

A parallel equation can readily be derived for the domestic interest rate using now

Table 10.1 Effect of an exogenous change

Exogenous change	Effect on r_d	e
1 Home open market operation ($\Delta Mo = -\Delta B$)	–	+
2 Foreign open market operation ($\Delta Mo^* = -\Delta B^*$)	?	–
3 Home budget deficit financed by money creation (ΔMo)	–	+
4 Foreign budget deficit financed by money creation (ΔMo^*)	?	–
5 Home deficit financed by bonds (ΔB)	+	?
6 Foreign deficit financed by bonds (ΔB^*)	?	+
7 Increase in home output (ΔY)	+	–
8 Increase in foreign output (ΔY^*)	?	+
9 A current account surplus (ΔFA)	?	–
10 An expected devaluation (ΔEe)	?	+
11 Sterilised intervention in foreign exchange market ($\Delta FA = -\Delta B$)	–	–

(17) and (13). Equation (13) can be rewritten as

$$\Delta r_d = -a_9 \Delta Mo + a_{10} \Delta B \pm a_{11}(\Delta r^* + \Delta E_e) \pm a_{12} \Delta FA + a_{13} \Delta Y \tag{20}$$

and now using (17)

$$\Delta r_d = -a_9 \Delta Mo + a_{10} \Delta B \pm a_{11} \Delta E_e \pm a_{12} \Delta FA + a_{13} \Delta Y \pm a_{14} \Delta Y$$

$$\pm a_{14} \Delta Mo^* \pm a_{15} \Delta B^* \tag{21}$$

The effects of a number of disturbances, in the context of this model, on the exchange rate and the interest rate are shown in Table 10.1.

FIXED EXCHANGE RATES – STERILISED INTERVENTION

We consider first the case where the money stock is exogenous, implying that the monetary authorities undertake complete sterilisation. Bearing in mind now that $\Delta E = 0$ (so $(E_e - E)E = 0$), we can manipulate (7)–(9) for a number of monetary disturbances.

An ongoing budget deficit financed by the creation of bonds

In each period the deficit creates an equivalent amount of bonds, which add to wealth and which the public have to absorb in their portfolio. The stock of money is fixed by definition; at the same time, any change in the demand for foreign assets is by definition sterilised by the monetary authorities. So, for example, if the public wanted to hold fewer foreign assets, they would initially sell their foreign assets to the authorities and acquire an equivalent amount of cash ($\Delta Mo = -\Delta FA$). Subsequently, the authorities *sell* bonds to sterilise and so the end result from the operation is $\Delta B = -\Delta FA$. These operations in themselves do not change the stock of wealth.

Thus the stock of bonds in the hands of the public changes for two reasons: to finance the ongoing budget deficit (DEF) and to sterilise changes in foreign assets.

We can read off one solution directly from (7) noting that $\Delta We = DEF$ and $\Delta Mo = 0$.

$$\frac{\Delta r_\mathrm{d}}{DEF} = \frac{Mo}{b_2 We^2} \tag{22}$$

Having already solved for the interest rate in (22), we can use this solution to solve for ΔB and ΔFA, both of which are endogenous.

$$\frac{\Delta B}{DEF} = \frac{B}{We} + \frac{b_7 Mo}{b_2 We} \tag{23}$$

and

$$\frac{\Delta FA}{DEF} = \frac{FA}{We} - \frac{b_{12} Mo}{b_2 We} \tag{24}$$

Note that implicit in these solutions is the equation

$$\Delta B = DEF - \Delta FA \tag{25}$$

which makes explicit the two sources of changes in bond holdings.

To absorb more bonds in each period, the interest rate must *keep rising*; at the same time, the rise in the domestic interest rate will in itself induce an inflow of capital (a reduction in foreign bonds). These inflows are then sterilised. However, the increase in wealth also *increases* the demand for foreign bonds, leading to an outflow. The net effect on foreign bond holding is ambiguous (equation (24)).

These results are consistent with equilibrium in all three markets. In the money market the ratio of money to wealth falls, so the interest rate has to rise. In the bond market the ratio of bonds to wealth rises and this requires a rise in the interest rate. Finally, in the foreign bond market the ratio of foreign bonds to wealth falls and again this requires that the interest rate rise.

An ongoing current account surplus

The reader can verify that the analysis of this case is identical to the previous case, the only difference being that the current account surplus CA now replaces DEF. The solutions are the same.

Initially the current account surplus manifests itself in an increase in the cash base. This is then sterilised, so at this point in time the public find themselves holding more bonds. At the same time, wealth has increased. These first-round effects exactly parallel the case of the deficit.

A rise in the foreign interest rate

We now have $\Delta Mo = \Delta We = 0$ and $\Delta B = -\Delta FA$. We can read the solution directly from (7).

$$\frac{\Delta r_d}{\Delta r^*} = -\frac{b_3}{b_2} \tag{26}$$

This is a surprising result. A rise in the foreign interest rate in the assumed conditions leads to a fall in the domestic interest rate. The reason is that the outflow is sterilised by purchases of domestic bonds and this forces down the domestic interest rate. The ratio of money to wealth is unchanged, the effects of the higher foreign interest rate offsetting the effects of the lower domestic interest rate. The ratio of bonds to wealth falls: this is consistent with the combined effects of the fall in the domestic rate and the rise in the foreign rate. Finally, the ratio of foreign bonds to wealth rises: this again is consistent with the combined effects of the fall in the domestic rate and the rise in the foreign rate.

An open market purchase

In this case $\Delta We = 0$ and $\Delta B = -\Delta Mo - \Delta FA$. ΔMo is now exogenous and so we have

$$\frac{\Delta r_d}{\Delta Mo} = -\frac{1}{b_2 We} \tag{27}$$

The open market purchase forces down the interest rate. At the same time, the lower interest rate provokes an outflow. The outflow is sterilised by further purchases of bonds.

The ratio of money to wealth increases, the ratio of foreign assets to wealth increases while finally the ratio of bonds to wealth falls (because of the initial open market purchase and also because the outflow will be sterilised). In the end, the reduction in domestic bonds is matched by an increase in money and foreign bonds.

Official intervention in the foreign exchange market

Suppose the monetary authorities buy foreign assets from the private sector and then sterilise the monetary effects of the exercise.

In this case $\Delta Mo = \Delta We = 0$. From (7) it is seen that the interest rate cannot change. How is this, when the private sector have run down their foreign assets and acquired more bonds (through the sterilisation operation)?

The answer is that the swap initially leads to a rise in the interest rate on bonds; however, this is not the end of the story. With the interest rate on bonds up the money market is now in disequilibrium. There is now a switch out of money into bonds which puts downward pressure on the interest rate; the outflow forces a reversal of the sterilisation operation. In the end, all asset holdings are at their initial levels. This result is surprising.

FIXED EXCHANGE RATES – UNSTERILISED INTERVENTION

We consider some parallel monetary shocks, now assuming that outflows–inflows are not sterilised.

A rise in the foreign interest rate

We now have $\Delta\text{We} = 0$, $\Delta B = 0$ and $\Delta\text{Mo} = -\Delta\text{FA}$. We can now use (8) to arrive at our solution:

$$\frac{\Delta r_d}{\Delta r^*} = \frac{b_8}{b_7} \tag{28}$$

The domestic interest rate now rises. At the same time, the money supply falls. There is a reduction in money and an equivalent increase in foreign bonds. The ratio of money to wealth falls: this is consistent with the rise in domestic and foreign interest rates. The ratio of bonds to wealth is unchanged: the effects of the rise in the domestic rate (pushing up the ratio) are exactly offset by the effects of the rise in the foreign rate (pushing down the ratio). The ratio of foreign bonds to wealth rises and this is also consistent with the rise in the two interest rates. In this last case we can show from (9) that

$$\frac{\Delta\text{FA}}{\Delta r^*} = \frac{(b_7 b_{13} - b_8 b_{12})\text{We}}{b_7} > 0 \tag{29}$$

A budget deficit financed by money creation

In this case again $\Delta\text{We} = \text{DEF}$ but now $\Delta B = 0$ with the money stock endogenous. We can arrive at the solution for the domestic interest rate directly from (8):

$$\frac{\Delta r_d}{\text{DEF}} = -\frac{B}{b_7 \text{We}^2} \tag{30}$$

We also now have

$$\Delta\text{Mo} = \text{DEF} - \Delta\text{FA} \tag{31}$$

There is initially an increase in money, which constitutes wealth. Only some of the increase in wealth goes into money, so there is an excess supply of money relative to domestic and foreign bonds. The interest rate on bonds falls and there is an unambiguous outflow of capital which, because of the assumption of unsterilised intervention, is allowed to reduce money, offsetting, in part at least, the original money creation. The ratio of money to wealth goes up; the ratio of bonds to wealth declines; the ratio of foreign bonds to wealth goes up.

11

The Mundell–Fleming model with wealth

INTRODUCTION

In this chapter we extend the MF model in yet another direction, this time by incorporating wealth into the model in a relatively simple way. Wealth is now allowed to influence both expenditure and the demand for money. In Chapter 10, where we introduced the portfolio balance model, we showed how wealth appeared in the monetary sector. This chapter adopts the portfolio balance of Chapter 10, now incorporating it into a larger model. *This also serves to correct one important deficiency of the MF model noted in Chapter 7: in the MF model, it will be recalled, asset demands are not explicitly modelled*; moreover, there is an underlying inconsistency between the stock money demand and the flow demand for foreign assets. Bonds were only implicitly represented in the model.

Because we now want to highlight the role of wealth in an open economy framework, we also now revert to the assumption of fixed wages and prices. To allow wages and prices to adjust as well would have complicated the model substantially and made it more difficult to identify the wealth-adjustment process.

Except for the occasional reference to potential dynamics and stability, the method of analysis used, as in the MF model, is that of comparative statics. We again investigate how the economy responds, now over a 'medium run', to a monetary and a fiscal disturbance, limiting our analysis to the flexible rate case. This end result is compared with MF outcomes.

The analysis underlying this chapter draws on a wide ranging literature. In essence, it represents an extension, to the open economy, of a well-known paper by Blinder and Solow (1973) for the closed economy. Parallel but not identical treatments of the open economy are to be found in Oates (1966), Artis (1984), Whitman (1970), Scarth

(1975), McKinnon and Oates (1966), McKinnon (1969), Penati (1983), Frenkel and Razin (1987), Rodriguez (1979) and Dornbusch and Fischer (1980).

The entire analysis is confined to the flexible rate case.

WEALTH, PRIVATE SECTOR SAVINGS AND STOCK ACCUMULATION

We begin with the familiar definition on the expenditure side of the gross domestic product Y.

$$Y = C + I + G + X - M \tag{1}$$

where C is consumption, I is investment, G is government expenditure and $X - M$ represents the trade balance (exports less imports).

We now write the equation for private sector disposable income Y_D, which is

$$Y_D = Y + r^* E \text{FA} + r_d B - T \tag{2}$$

where r^* is the foreign interest rate, FA stands for foreign assets denominated in foreign currency, E is the exchange rate, r_d is the home interest rate, B represents holdings of public sector bonds and T is taxation.

Equation (2) says that disposable income is the domestic product augmented by earnings on foreign assets (converted into domestic currency) and on public sector bonds, less tax liabilities.

Private sector disposable income is in turn absorbed by savings (Sp) and consumption (C).

$$Y + r^* E \text{FA} + r_d B - T = \text{Sp} + C \tag{3}$$

Combining (1) and (3) we have

$$\text{Sp} + (T - G - r_d B) = I + (X - M + r^* E \text{FA}) \tag{4}$$

Equation (4) says that *national* savings, made up of private sector savings plus the budget surplus, is equal to national investment plus the current account surplus.

Finally, we note that private sector savings is equal to the change in private sector wealth, which we denote by ΔWe:[1]

$$\text{Sp} = \Delta \text{We} \tag{5}$$

We turn now to the implications for *stock accumulation* of these relations. Consider, first, a simplified balance sheet of the central bank in first difference form:

$$\Delta H + \Delta \text{GD} = \Delta \text{DA} + \Delta \text{FACB} \tag{6}$$

Changes in high powered money (ΔH) plus changes in government deposits held in the central bank (ΔGD) are equal to the sum of changes in domestic (ΔDA) and foreign (ΔFACB) assets. (We ignore revaluation effects on the latter.)

The government's balance sheet is

$$G + r_dB - T = -\Delta GD + \Delta B \tag{7}$$

This says that the government deficit may be financed by some combination of money creation (running down deposits in the central bank) and direct sales of bonds to the private sector.

We can solve (7) for ΔGD and substitute in (6) to yield a 'public sector' balance sheet.

$$\Delta H + (T - G - r_dB) + \Delta B = \Delta DA + \Delta FACB \tag{8}$$

The change in foreign assets of the central bank is the change in official holdings of international reserves (the overall balance of payments) and so we can write

$$\Delta FACB = (X - M + r^*EFA) - \Delta(EFA) \tag{9}$$

The overall balance of payments is the sum of the current account and net private sector *inflows* of capital (equivalent to a reduction in stock holdings of foreign assets as we saw in Chapter 10).

Substituting (9) into (8) and rearranging gives

$$(X - M + r^*EFA) + (G + r_dB - T) = \Delta H + (\Delta B - \Delta DA) + \Delta(EFA) \tag{10}$$

Using (4) and (5) we have

$$Sp = \Delta We = I + \Delta H + (\Delta B - \Delta DA) + \Delta(EFA) \tag{11}$$

On the asset accumulation side this says that private sector saving is equal to the sum of capital accumulation (I), total acquisition of domestic bonds ($\Delta B - \Delta DA$) (where ΔDA is equivalent to central bank open market purchases), domestic money (ΔH) and foreign assets ($\Delta(EFA)$).

THE EXTENDED MODEL WITH WEALTH

In the simple model we present here, drawing on some of the literature cited above, we make three simplifying assumptions. First, there is no investment in the economy, so $I = 0$. Second, we disregard altogether all *interest* payments either on government debt or on assets held abroad. Third, related to the first, there is no real growth in the economy. These assumptions are relaxed in Chapters 27–30 and partially at the end of this chapter.

The goods market

Dropping investment we have

$$Y = C + G + X - M \tag{1a}$$

We now write down a consumption function which is an extension of the MF model.

$$C = \alpha_1 Y_D + \alpha_3 We - \alpha_2 r_d \tag{12}$$

This says that consumption is determined by disposable income Y_D and wealth. Such an equation is rationalised in most macro textbooks in terms of life-cycle models, so we are on fairly firm theoretical ground here (see for example Dornbusch and Fischer 1990).

The inclusion in (12) of the interest rate with a negative sign, however, is more controversial. It is well known that a rise in the interest rate has an income effect and a substitution effect which pull in opposite directions. The income effect *reduces* saving because less saving is now needed to achieve a target level of savings; the substitution effect *increases* saving because now the return is higher. On *purely theoretical* grounds, therefore, the outcome is ambiguous and indeed, whilst some significant net positive effects on saving have been found in some empirical work, much of this work suggests a weak and uncertain effect. Nevertheless, we include it with a negative effect on consumption (positive on savings) for three reasons: first, because there is a strong neoclassical and policy tradition that assumes that the effect on saving is positive; second, as we shall see, if α_2 were say zero the model is trivialised and if $\alpha_2 < 0$ there will be perverse effects; third, we are interested in the adjustment process with wealth and, as we shall see, adjustment is more interesting and richer if the interest rate is included.

We can now add two equations, one which defines Y_D and the other which explains net exports, along now familiar lines:

$$Y_D = Y - tY = (1 - t)Y \tag{13}$$

and

$$X - M = \alpha_{30}E - mY \tag{14}$$

Substituting (12), (13) and (14) into (1a) yields the goods market equation:

$$Y = \frac{1}{k_1} G + \frac{\alpha_{30}}{k_1} E + \frac{\alpha_3}{k_1} We - \frac{\alpha_2}{k_1} r_d \tag{15}$$

$$k_1 = 1 - \alpha_1(1 - t) + m$$

The money market

The equations comprising this market are in two parts. First, we write down our asset demands, drawn from the portfolio balance model of Chapter 10. Second, we say something about the creation (supply) of these assets.

$$Mo_d = \alpha_4 Y - \alpha_5 r_d + \alpha_6 We \tag{16}$$

$$B_d = -\alpha_{20}Y + \alpha_{12}r_d + \alpha_{16}We \tag{17}$$

$$(EFA)_d = -\alpha_{28}Y - \alpha_{14}r_d + \alpha_{18}We \tag{18}$$

$$We = Mo + B + EFA$$

$$\alpha_4 = \alpha_{20} + \alpha_{28} \qquad \alpha_{12} = \alpha_5 + \alpha_{14} \qquad \alpha_6 + \alpha_{16} + \alpha_{18} = 1 \tag{19}$$

In what follows, we will treat the demand for bonds as the residual equation. We also assume, in the spirit of the portfolio balance model, that asset substitution is imperfect (so α_{14} and α_{12} are both less than infinity).

There are three assets in the model. At the same time we are interested in the impacts of two policy changes: an open market purchase and an increase in government expenditure. So we need to ask how such policy changes impact on the *supply* of these three assets.

We need to distinguish two cases: (a) where any periodic budget imbalances are financed by the issue of new bonds – this is the case of *bond finance*; (b) where the periodic budget imbalance is financed by the creation of money – this is the case of *money finance*.

$$B_s = \overline{Bo} + \sum_{t}^{t+n} (G - T) \qquad \text{(bond finance)} \tag{20}$$

$$Mo_s = \overline{Mo} + \sum_{t}^{t+n} (G - T) \qquad \text{(money finance)} \tag{21}$$

$$(EFA)_s = \sum_{t}^{t+n} (X - M) \tag{22}$$

If there is *bond* finance the supply of bonds has an exogenous component Bo and a component which represents the cumulative sum of the public sector deficits. t is the period when the policy is changed; $t + n$ is the end (equilibrium) period. In this case, an open market purchase would be represented by $\Delta \overline{Mo} = -\Delta \overline{Bo}$ and the money stock would be entirely exogenous while the stock supply of bonds would be endogenous. If there is a bond-financed increase in government expenditure $\Delta \overline{Bo} = \Delta \overline{Mo} = 0$ while the stock of bonds is endogenous.

If there is *money* finance the money stock is endogenous and the stock of bonds exogenous. An open market purchase is again represented by $\Delta \overline{Mo} = \Delta \overline{Bo}$ but now there are no further changes in the supply of bonds. So the stock of bonds is exogenous but money is endogenous. If there is a money-financed increase in government expenditure, again $\Delta B = \Delta \overline{Mo} = 0$ while now the stock of money is endogenous.

Equation (22) simply says that the change in the stock of foreign assets is equal to the sum of the current account surpluses.

To complete the model we have the equilibrium conditions in asset markets. Each asset demand is equal to the supply of each asset.

$$Mo_d = Mo_s \tag{16a}$$

$$B_d = B_s \tag{17a}$$

$$(EFA)_d = (EFA)_s \tag{18a}$$

The medium-run constraints

In this model stock–flow equilibrium requires that the stock of wealth be stationary. In other words in equilibrium ΔWe $= 0$. From (5) above this requires that private sector savings be zero. From (4), too, without investment and interest payments this requires that the following condition hold:

$$M - X = G - T \tag{23}$$

The current account deficit (surplus) must be equal in equilibrium to the budget deficit (surplus) (a twin deficit outcome). This is sometimes referred to in the literature as the McKinnon–Oates condition for medium-run equilibrium (McKinnon and Oates 1966).

Equation (23) implies that *both* the trade balance and the budget balance may be non-zero. Is this possible?

In a flexible rate world the trade surplus (deficit) must be equal to the capital outflow (inflow). So is it possible in equilibrium to have persistent outflows or inflows of capital? Equation (18) is a key equation in addressing this question.

As we already noted in Chapters 7 and 10 the *flow* of capital is a function of the *changes* in the independent variables. In equilibrium the level of output and the stock of wealth are both stationary. Therefore, for *flows* to persist the interest rate must keep changing, e.g. for an inflow to persist the domestic interest rate must keep rising. This is evidently not viable; so in equilibrium the interest rate must also be stationary. It follows from all this that in equilibrium, and given the assumptions made about real growth, *capital flows and hence the trade balance must be zero*. It also follows from (23) that in equilibrium, too, the budget balance must be zero.

We can now, therefore, impose the following constraints on the model.

$$M - X = mY - \alpha_{30}E = 0 \tag{24}$$

$$G - T = G - tY = 0 \tag{25}$$

The presentation of the model is now complete. The static model as a whole comprises equations (15)–(19), (24) and (25). One of these, (17) say, is redundant. This leaves six equations which allow us to solve (say for debt finance) for Y, E, r_d, FA, B and We in terms of (a) an open market purchase and (b) a fiscal expansion. For money finance, Mo replaces B as the endogenous variable to be solved.

A MONETARY EXPANSION

We first present the technical analysis and the solutions. Later, we try to illuminate the adjustment process graphically and to contrast these results with those familiar in the MF model.

The technical analysis

Suppose, to begin, that we had debt finance of budget imbalances. From (25), given G, we can read the outcome for output directly. We know that $\Delta Y = 0$. From (24), too, with $\Delta Y = 0$, $\Delta E = 0$.

Imposing these results on (15), we have

$$\Delta r_{\mathrm{d}} = \frac{\alpha_3}{\alpha_2} \Delta \mathrm{We} \tag{26}$$

Inserting this solution into the money market equation, we have

$$\frac{\Delta \mathrm{We}}{\Delta \mathrm{Mo}} = -\frac{\alpha_2}{\alpha_3 \alpha_5 - \alpha_2 \alpha_6} \tag{27}$$

$\alpha_3 \alpha_5 > \alpha_2 \alpha_6$ is the stability condition which we assume holds.[2] Now, inserting (27) into (26) we have

$$\frac{\Delta r_{\mathrm{d}}}{\Delta \mathrm{Mo}} = -\frac{\alpha_3}{\alpha_3 \alpha_5 - \alpha_2 \alpha_6} \tag{28}$$

An increase in the money stock reduces the stock of wealth, lowers the interest rate, but leaves output and the exchange rate both unchanged.

We can now also use this information to figure out what happens in equilibrium to the stock of foreign and domestic bonds. We can get the solution for FA directly from (18) after substituting solutions for r_{d} and We above. Finally, we can arrive at the equilibrium stock of bonds, using (17).

We now have

$$\frac{\Delta \mathrm{FA}}{\Delta \mathrm{Mo}} = \frac{\alpha_3 \alpha_{14} - \alpha_2 \alpha_{18}}{\alpha_3 \alpha_5 - \alpha_2 \alpha_6} \tag{29}$$

Using now (17), we also have

$$\frac{\Delta B}{\Delta \mathrm{Mo}} = -\frac{\alpha_2 \alpha_{16} + \alpha_3 \alpha_{12}}{\alpha_3 \alpha_5 - \alpha_2 \alpha_6} > 1 \qquad \alpha_{12} > \alpha_5 \tag{30}$$

What happens to the stock holdings of foreign bonds is strictly ambiguous. $\alpha_3 \alpha_{14}$ captures a substitution effect, $\alpha_2 \alpha_{18}$ captures a wealth effect. The wealth effect reduces the demand for foreign assets, the fall in the interest rate increases the demand for foreign assets. This last substitution effect is likely to dominate. Since the change in the stock of foreign assets corresponds to the cumulative current account balances, an increase in the stock would correspond to cumulative current account surpluses. On the other hand, there is an unambiguous fall in the holdings of bonds which *exceeds* the initial expansion in the money stock. (The fall in bonds additional to the open market purchase comes from the budget surplus associated with the initial upward pressure on output.)

Graphical analysis and economic meaning

The model can readily be represented graphically (Figure 11.1). Equation (15) represents the new IS schedule. An increase (decrease) in wealth will now also displace the IS schedule to the right (left). Equation (16) represents the LM schedule (with $Mo_d = Mo_s$). It too will now be displaced to the right (left) if wealth falls (increases). Equation (16) shows that, when wealth increases, the demand for money increases at given levels of output and interest rate and so the whole schedule shifts to the left.

A balance of payments (B) schedule can also be represented graphically. Since our analysis is comparative static and since in equilibrium capital flows are zero the B schedule will be *vertical* (Figure 11.1). Given the exchange rate there is only one level of output consistent with full equilibrium. This is readily seen in (24). If the economy found itself to the right (left) of the schedule the trade balance would be in deficit (surplus) which in turn means that there are *transitional* flows of capital and transitional changes in wealth (see equations (4) and (5)).

We now also need to introduce a fourth schedule which represents our government budget constraint (equation (25)). Gr_0 in Figure 11.1 represents a given level of government expenditure corresponding to which there is a unique equilibrium level of output which will establish public sector balance. If the economy found itself to the right (left) of the schedule, the budget would be in surplus (deficit) which in turn (for debt finance) means the government is repaying (accumulating) debt.

In full equilibrium the economy must find itself on all four schedules (two schedules, Gr_0 and B, are vertical).

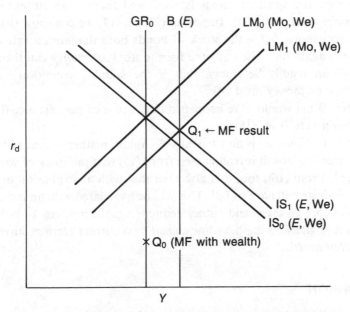

Figure 11.1 Monetary expansion in a Mundell–Fleming model with wealth

Consider now what happens when there is a monetary expansion. In the MF model the IS and LM schedules shift to the right. With capital mobility in MF terms effectively zero the vertical B schedule would also shift to the right to meet the new IS–LM at Q_1. Output increases, the interest rate drops and the currency devalues. However, in the context of this new model Q_1 cannot be an equilibrium. Why?

Capital outflows will cease, as already noted.[3] The currency must devalue sufficiently to neutralise the effects of a higher level of output on the current account. However, on the fiscal front with output higher there will be a fiscal surplus. This will be associated with a reduction in the stock of bonds held. Thus wealth will fall; the IS schedule shifts to the left while LM shifts to the right. Stability, as noted earlier, requires that the former dominate over the latter. (It is readily seen that if stability did not hold the intersection point of the IS–LM schedules would shift further and further to the right away from equilibrium on Gr_0.) The shifts now proceed until the economy finds itself at Q_0, the new result. As the level of output converges towards its initial level, the exchange rate will also appreciate (the devaluation will be reversed) until it too returns to its original level. The B schedule shifts to the left until it effectively coincides with the Gr_0 schedule.

What if the budget surplus had been financed by a *reduction* in the money stock? We do not develop this case in any detail. We note, however, that the solutions for both output and the exchange rate are the same: neither will change.

The principal difference arises as follows. Equation (26), being derived from (15), continues to hold. However, instead of using the money market equation we now need to use the equation for bonds (17). What is happening here is that we have an initial exogenous fall in bonds associated with an increase in the stock of money. From then on, however, the stock of bonds is fixed and there is an endogenous adjustment in the money stock as in (21). Imposing (26) on (17) we can show that in equilibrium with an exogenous *fall* in the stock of bonds both the interest rate and the stock of wealth will again fall. The outcome for the stock of *money* can then be solved from (16). It can readily be shown that if the stability condition holds ($\alpha_3\alpha_5 > \alpha_2\alpha_6$) the stock of money must rise.

One final point here. What would have happened in the case of debt finance if we had dropped the interest rate from (15)?

As already anticipated, the model is now trivialised. Again, neither output nor the exchange rate will change but now it is readily seen from (15) that the stock of wealth will also be unchanged. From (16), too, it is also seen that with an expansion in the money stock the interest rate will have to fall. This will be associated with an increase in the stock holdings of foreign assets and a stock reduction in the holdings of bonds. The stock increase in foreign assets implies some *transitional* current account surplus, which is *ultimately eliminated*.

A FISCAL EXPANSION

We can proceed as we did with a monetary expansion for debt financing.

The technical analysis

The solution for output can be obtained directly from (25).

$$\frac{\Delta Y}{\Delta G} = \frac{1}{t} \tag{31}$$

Output must increase sufficiently to raise revenue by enough to rebalance the budget. We can then solve for the exchange rate from (24):

$$\frac{\Delta E}{\Delta G} = \frac{m}{\alpha_{30} t} \tag{32}$$

The increase in output requires a devaluation to re-establish equilibrium to the trade balance.

We can now use (15) and (16) to solve for r_d and We.

$$\frac{\Delta We}{\Delta G} = \frac{\alpha_5 (1 - t)(1 - \alpha_1) + \alpha_2 \alpha_4}{t(\alpha_3 \alpha_5 - \alpha_2 \alpha_6)} \tag{33}$$

$$\frac{\Delta r_d}{\Delta G} = \frac{\alpha_3 \alpha_4 + \alpha_6 (1 - t)(1 - \alpha_1)}{t(\alpha_3 \alpha_5 - \alpha_2 \alpha_6)} \tag{34}$$

Not surprisingly, the stock of wealth increases and the interest rate rises.

Finally, we can use the same procedures as previously to solve for ΔFA and ΔB (noting that $\Delta Mo = 0$).

In principle, we can differentiate (18) and solve for ΔFA:

$$\Delta FA = -FA\, \Delta E - \alpha_{28}\, \Delta Y - \alpha_{14}\, \Delta r_d + \alpha_{18}\, \Delta We \tag{35}$$

The solution is cumbersome and is not reported here. Equation (35) indicates the elements that enter into the solution. The currency devalues; all other things being equal, there will be an excess holding of foreign assets denominated in domestic currency, so residents will reduce their demand for foreign assets. An increase in output is also (by assumption) going to reduce the demand for foreign assets and so will an increase in the home interest rate. Finally, the increase in wealth will *increase* the demand for foreign assets. All in all, the first three effects are almost certain to dominate, so the holding of foreign assets will decrease. Since this represents the *cumulative* current account in foreign currency, we can conclude that the current account will be in deficit.

What about the equilibrium stock holding of bonds?

$$\Delta B = \Delta We - \Delta(EFA) \tag{36}$$

It can readily be shown that this expression is positive, meaning that the stock of bonds will *increase*.

Graphical analysis and economic meaning

What is happening here? To make the comparison with the MF model we again note that the case dealt with is, in MF terms, equivalent to zero capital mobility. In the MF model in equilibrium the current account is in any event equal to zero. Not so, however, for the budget. In the MF model it is easily shown that the budget will be in deficit in this case.[4] Thus the stock of bonds and wealth will both increase shifting the IS schedule to the right and LM to the left. Assuming stability holds, this will elevate the equilibrium level of output beyond that for the MF model.

This case is shown in Figure 11.2. The Gr_0 schedule will shift to the right to its new equilibrium output level determined, as shown, at the point where the budget is in balance again, i.e. where tax revenue has increased sufficiently to match the increase in government expenditure. The MF solution is again shown at Q_1 with output at Y_1. The schedules will have to shift, as previously, until equilibrium is reached at Q_1 with output at Y_2.

The analysis of fiscal expansion assumed that the money stock was fixed and allowed bonds to adjust endogenously. As an alternative, we could have treated the level of *bonds* as given and solved for the money stock. This would have implied money financing of cumulative fiscal deficits. This, however, is not pursued here.

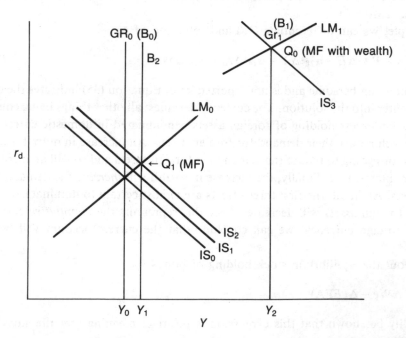

Figure 11.2   Fiscal expansion in a Mundell–Fleming model with wealth

ACCOMMODATING INVESTMENT

The reader may be concerned about the fact that in the model there is no investment. The assumption is very widely adopted in this literature as a simplification.

However, we may want very briefly to ask what might happen if we added investment to the model. To begin, one could have some exogenous net private saving and investment, which in turn allows for some exogenous growth (see also Chapter 27). This in itself poses no problem. The problem arises because the *capital stock* may change if the interest rate changes and the capital stock is also one component of private sector wealth, in addition to the financial assets (see (4) and (5)). (See also on this Tobin and Buiter (1976) and Karakitsos (1989).)

To illuminate this, consider again a monetary expansion, as above. In the 'equilibrium' reached the interest rate will have fallen. If we also had investment *the stock of real capital will now have gone up* (investment, in due course, returning to its original trend path – see Chapter 27). This increases real wealth which in turn increases the level of output, but this is not sustainable and so will require a reduction in the stock of bonds which ultimately will return us to our original equilibrium.

What this suggests is that the solution for both the exchange rate and the level of output is independent of what happens to the stock of capital. However, if there is stock accumulation, the *composition* of wealth will change. In our example the public will hold more capital and fewer bonds.

CONCLUSIONS

The conclusions are striking. In the model used in this chapter, with imperfect asset substitution and bond finance, there is a very sharp contrast between the workings of monetary and fiscal policies. Monetary policy is completely ineffective in terms of both output and the exchange rate; it does, however, alter the level of the interest rate and of wealth. Fiscal policy is very powerful, impacting on output, the exchange rate, the interest rate and the stock of wealth. Fiscal expansion provokes an unambiguous *devaluation* of the currency, without the ambiguities found in the MF model. The reason, of course, is that in a stock–portfolio model of the kind used (without growth), imposing the constraint that the current account must be zero is equivalent to assuming zero capital mobility in the MF model (extended to accommodate a wealth effect). All these outcomes are conditional on stability conditions holding.

12

The classical elasticities approach to a devaluation

INTRODUCTION

The classical elasticities approach to devaluation focuses on the effects on the value of imports and exports of changes in domestic relative to foreign prices. It is micro oriented, disregarding all macro effects such as effects on wages, prices, economic activity. Such effects are implicitly assumed to be neutralised by policy. These macro effects were analysed in Chapter 8.

THE MODEL

The basic elasticities model can be represented by the following equations:

$$\text{BT} = XP_x - MP_m E \tag{1}$$

$$X_d = -\alpha_1 \frac{P_x}{E} \tag{2}$$

$$M_d = -\alpha_2 P_m E \tag{3}$$

$$X_s = \alpha_3 P_x \tag{4}$$

$$M_s = \alpha_4 P_m \tag{5}$$

$$X_d = X_s \tag{6}$$

$$M_d = M_s \tag{7}$$

Notation

BT   balance of trade in domestic currency
E exchange rate – units of domestic currency per unit of foreign currency
edm elasticity of demand for imports
edx elasticity of demand for exports
esm elasticity of supply of imports
esx elasticity of supply of exports
M volume of imports
P_m price of imports in foreign currency
P_x price of exports in domestic currency
s, d supply and demand respectively
X volume of exports

Equation (1) is the definition of the balance of trade in domestic currency. Equations (2) and (3) assert that the demand for real exports and for real imports are functions respectively of the price of exports (in foreign currency) and the price of imports (in domestic currency). Equations (4) and (5) say that the supply of exports and of imports in turn are functions of the prices of exports and the prices of imports respectively, both denominated in the currency of the country producing the goods. Finally, equations (6) and (7) are the equilibrium conditions, stipulating that the demand and supply of both exports and imports must be equated.

Differentiating the model and noting that $\alpha_1 = \text{edx} X$, $\alpha_2 = \text{edm} M$, $\alpha_3 = \text{esx} X$, $\alpha_4 = \text{esm} M$ (see Chapter 6, Appendix), we obtain a solution[1] for the balance of trade in relation to the exchange rate:

$$\frac{\Delta BT}{\Delta E} = X \frac{\text{edx}(1 + \text{esx})}{\text{esx} + \text{edx}} + M \frac{\text{esm}(\text{edm} - 1)}{\text{esm} + \text{edm}} \tag{8}$$

This result, the Robinson–Bickerdike–Metzler solution for the balance of trade in domestic currency,[2] can be simplified if we assume that the balance of trade is initially in equilibrium ($X = M$). Then

$$\frac{\Delta BT}{X/\Delta E} = \frac{\text{edx}(1 + \text{esx})}{\text{esx} + \text{edx}} + \frac{\text{esm}(\text{edm} - 1)}{\text{esm} + \text{edm}} \tag{9}$$

This expression shows the effects of a unit percentage change in the exchange rate on the percentage change in the balance of trade, with exports as a base. These effects will depend on the magnitudes of the elasticities of supply and demand.

It is useful to take two special cases. The first is the case where the two supply elasticities are infinite (i.e. the foreign price of imports as well as the domestic price of exports are both fixed). This is the Marshall–Lerner case. The second is the 'small-country' case, where the foreign supply of imports and the demand for the home country's exports are both infinite (i.e. the foreign price of imports is fixed but now the foreign price of exports is also fixed).

THE MARSHALL–LERNER CONDITION

The two supply elasticities are assumed to be infinite, so we have esx = esm = ∞. The solution reduces to

$$\frac{\Delta \mathrm{BT}/X}{\Delta E} = \mathrm{edx} + \frac{M}{X}\,(\mathrm{edm} - 1) \tag{10}$$

The trade balance will improve if [3]

$$\mathrm{edx} + \mathrm{edm}\,\frac{M}{X} > \frac{M}{X} \tag{10a}$$

and, in the special case where there is initial equilibrium $(X = M)$, the trade balance will improve if

$$\mathrm{edx} + \mathrm{edm} > 1 \tag{10b}$$

This is the well-known Marshall–Lerner condition which says that a devaluation will improve (worsen) the balance of trade if the sum of the two demand elasticities exceeds (is less than) unity. It needs to be emphasised again that the condition assumes infinite supply elasticities as well as initial trade balance equilibrium.

An example will make clear the rationale for the Marshall–Lerner condition. Suppose edx = 0, edm = 1 and the exchange rate is devalued by 10 per cent. Consider first the effect on exports. With infinite supply elasticities the price of exports in domestic currency terms remains unchanged. This means that the price of exports in foreign currency will drop by 10 per cent; with a zero demand elasticity the volume of exports sold will be unchanged. Therefore the value of exports in domestic currency will be constant. Now consider the effect on imports. With an infinite import supply elasticity the price of imports in foreign currency will be constant and in domestic currency it will rise by 10 per cent. With a 10 per cent increase in the domestic price of imports and an import elasticity of unity the volume of imports demanded will drop by 10 per cent; hence the value of imports will also remain unchanged. When, then, the sum of the demand elasticities equals unity the balance of trade remains unchanged.

Continuing with this example, if the elasticity of demand for exports were greater than zero it is clear that there would be some increase in the volume of exports demanded and hence with a fixed domestic price of exports the value of exports would increase. In this case with the value of imports assumed unchanged the balance of trade in domestic currency would be improved.

Suppose the import demand elasticity were less than unity, while the export demand elasticity was zero. In this case the price of imports would again rise by 10 per cent but the volume demanded would fall by less than 10 per cent; hence the value of imports would now rise and with the value of exports unchanged the balance of trade would have worsened.

If the values of the elasticities were reversed with edm = 0 and edx = 1, it is easily demonstrated that in this case the value of exports would increase by 10 per cent, while the value of imports would increase by 10 per cent, leaving the balance of trade unchanged; or if edm = 0.5, edx = 0.5 the value of both imports and exports would increase by 5 per cent.

It should be noted that the terms of trade in this case have worsened by the extent of the devaluation. In domestic currency the price of imports has increased by 10 per cent while the price of exports is unchanged.

Table 12.1 provides a sample of estimates of import and export demand elasticities for the seven largest industrial countries. The table highlights the important fact that these elasticities are higher in the longer run than in the shorter run. In the short run in each case there is a perverse J curve effect, i.e. the sum of the two demand elasticities is less than unity.

THE SMALL-COUNTRY CASE

A small country cannot influence the foreign price of its imports since by definition it is a negligible buyer in the overseas market. At the same time it is assumed that

Table 12.1 IMF world trade model: price elasticities of demand for imports and exports of manufactures

	Imports			Exports		
Country	Impact elasticity	Short-run elasticity	Long-run elasticity	Impact elasticity	Short-run elasticity	Long-run elasticity
Canada	−0.72 (0.17)	−0.72	−0.72 (0.17)	−0.08 (0.22)	−0.40	−0.71 (0.26)
France	−	−0.49	−0.60 (0.18)	−0.20 (0.18)	−0.48	−1.25 (0.33)
Germany, Federal Republic of	−0.57 (0.20)	−0.77	−0.77 (0.11)	−	−	−1.41 (0.44)
Italy	−0.94 (0.23)	−0.94	−0.94 (0.23)	−	−0.56	−0.64 (0.79)
Japan	−0.16 (0.22)	−0.72	−0.97 (0.27)	−0.59 (0.16)	−1.01	−1.61 (0.25)
UK	−0.60 (0.27)	−0.75	−0.75 (0.21)	−	−	−0.31 (0.20)
USA	−	−1.06	−1.06 (0.36)	−0.18 (0.18)	−0.48	−1.67 (0.21)

Source: Artus and Knight 1984
Note: The table gives, for each country, the price elasticities of domestic demand for imports and of the foreign demand for its exports. The relative prices are defined such that these elasticities are expected to be negative. The impact elasticity gives the response in the current semester; the short-run elasticity gives the response after two semesters (one year); and the long-run elasticity gives the total response. Standard errors are given in parentheses.

it can sell any volume of its exports overseas at a given foreign price of exports. It therefore faces an infinitely elastic demand for its exports.

We now set esm = ∞ and edx = ∞. Equation (8) reduces to

$$\frac{\Delta \text{BT}}{X \Delta E} = (\text{esx} + 1) + (\text{edm} - 1) \frac{M}{X} \tag{11}$$

For the trade balance to improve

$$\text{esx} + \text{edm} \frac{M}{X} > \frac{M - X}{X} \tag{12}$$

If trade is initially in balance ($X = M$) this reduces to

$$\text{esx} + \text{edm} > 0 \tag{13}$$

The interesting point about this result is that it is unambiguously positive, implying that for the small country the perverse case (where a devaluation might *worsen* the balance of trade) is not possible when trade is initially balanced. The worse that could happen is that a devaluation will leave the balance of trade unchanged. This would be the case if both the supply elasticity of exports and the demand elasticity of imports were zero.

Suppose esx > 0, edm = 0 and again we have a devaluation of 10 per cent. On the import side the price in domestic currency will rise by 10 per cent and with a demand elasticity of zero the value of imports will rise by 10 per cent. On the export side the price of exports will now rise by 10 per cent in domestic currency terms. The reason is that the price in foreign currency cannot change (the small country accepts the given foreign price) and therefore the price in domestic currency will need to rise by the full extent of the devaluation. With an export supply elasticity exceeding zero the volume of exports sold overseas will now increase. With the price increasing by 10 per cent and the volume increasing, the value of exports must rise by more than 10 per cent. With imports rising by exactly 10 per cent the balance of trade will improve. It is easy to see that if the supply elasticity of exports had been zero the value of exports would have increased by exactly 10 per cent and the balance of trade would have remained unchanged.

It should be noted that in this case the terms of trade have remained unchanged. The price of imports in domestic currency rose by 10 per cent but so did the price of exports and so the ratio of import to export prices in a common currency remains constant.

It is important to extend the model to allow for the fact that the trade balance might be in deficit to begin with, i.e. imports exceed exports. Suppose initially that $M = 1.15X$. So we have

$$\frac{M - X}{X} = 0.15$$

In equation (12) we can now substitute for M/X (1.15) and $(M - X)/X$ (0.15). The condition for improvement in the trade balance is

$$esx + edm(1.15) > 0.15$$

Suppose now that esx = edm = 0. Previously this left the balance of trade unchanged. Now it is obvious that the balance of trade will deteriorate. So it is possible to have a J curve even for a small country with fixed terms of trade if the trade balance is initially in deficit.

The reason is the following. If esx = edm = 0, with a devaluation of 10 per cent the import bill in domestic currency goes up by 10 per cent and export receipts also rise by 10 per cent. Since imports exceed exports initially the absolute deficit increases.

This may of course be partly or more than offset by some import response and some export supply response.

APPLICATION OF THE SMALL-COUNTRY CASE TO AUSTRALIA

It may be useful to consider an application of the small-country framework to a country such as Australia.

Suppose we begin with equation (12). To figure out the effects of a devaluation on the trade balance (abstracting altogether from macro effects) we need to know

a) by how much imports initially exceed exports;
b) the import demand elasticity; and
c) the export supply elasticity.

Australia has tended to have a trade balance deficit. We assume as a very rough approximation that this corresponds to a ratio of imports to exports of something like 1:1.

A review of studies of the import demand elasticity suggests an average short-run elasticity of some 0.3 and an average long-run elasticity of about unity (Gordon, J. 1991).

We also need a measure of the export supply elasticity;[4] this, however, is very much harder to obtain. One reason is that Australia's exports fall into three distinct groups: manufacturing (20 per cent), rural (40 per cent) and minerals (40 per cent). But even this division is quite inadequate. For both rural and mineral exports we really need to disaggregate a lot more, e.g. minerals into coal, iron ore, bauxite etc., rural into wheat, wool, meat, sugar etc. Each of these has its own distinct supply elasticity (Gordon, J. 1991).

Some measures for individual commodities are available but aggregation is largely guesswork. For rural and mineral exports supply elasticities are very low in the short run, as one might expect. We can make a stab here and assume an aggregate supply elasticity of the order of 0.2 (at most).

In the short run we have, then, using (11)

$$(0.2 + 1) - (0.7)1.1 > 0 \tag{14}$$

and so it seems that there is no perverse effect.

Equation (12) assumed that the elasticity of demand for exports is infinite, i.e. that Australia is a small producer of a homogeneous product in world markets for her exports. The reality is not quite so simple. Australia is a substantial producer of some rural and mineral exports; also some one-fifth of her exports are manufacturing differentiated products. An equation such as (8) provides a more satisfactory framework for such an analysis. Using (8) we need only impose the realistic condition that esm → ∞. We then need edx, esx and edm for the short and long runs. Not all this information is available, however.

ABSORPTION, SAVINGS–INVESTMENT APPROACH TO A DEVALUATION

As already noted, the elasticities approach focuses on the 'substitution' (micro) effects of a devaluation. A devaluation, however, is also likely to have macro effects on domestic prices, domestic activity (employment) etc. as we saw in Chapter 8. We note here the conditions for a successful devaluation at the macro level.

We have

$$Y = A + (X - M) \qquad \text{or} \qquad (X - M) = Y - A \tag{15}$$

where Y is the national product, A is the sum of all expenditure on consumption, investment and government expenditure, and $X - M$ is the trade balance.

We also know that from the National Accounts we can arrive at the equation (Chapter 11)

$$X - M = \text{PSS} + (\text{Sp} - \text{Ip}) \tag{16}$$

PSS is the public sector surplus and Sp – Ip is the excess of private savings over private investment.

These two equations correspond to two ways of looking at the conditions for a successful devaluation. Equation (15) represents the absorption approach to a devaluation. It says that for a devaluation to improve the current account balance it is necessary for output to increase by more than absorption. Equation (16) represents the savings–investment approach to devaluation. It says that for a devaluation to improve the current account it is necessary for domestic savings to increase by more than domestic investment.

These two approaches indicate the conditions which need to be met if devaluation is to succeed in improving the current account. *Neither approach provides any analysis of whether or not these conditions are likely to be met.*

It is worth noting in this context that the New Cambridge School in the UK once argued that (a) Sp − Ip as a proportion of GNP is small and relatively constant over time and (b) the PSS is exogenous. It follows (from equation (16)) that a devaluation is unlikely to be effective in improving the current account balance unless it is associated with an increase in government savings (Rowan 1976). Contention (a), however, is not supported by the evidence.

13

A two-country Mundell–Fleming type model

INTRODUCTION

Up to now we have assumed that we are dealing with a relatively small economy whose impact on the rest of the world is minimal. Feedback effects from the rest of the world could thus be disregarded.

It is now time to take a larger perspective and assume we are dealing with a much larger economy, e.g. the USA. At this point it is convenient to assume that the world is actually made up of only two very large economies, e.g. the USA on the one hand and the rest of the industrial world on the other. We label these two countries A and B. In Chapter 16 we extend the model to a three-country world, comprising two very large countries and one small one.

The model below is a straightforward extension of the MF model presented in Chapter 6. Each country is modelled along MF lines, but now particular care has to be taken to ensure that relationships are consistent, e.g. country A's imports equal country B's exports and B's imports equal A's exports, A's balance of payments outcome is always the opposite of B's balance of payments outcome. Having placed the MF model in the context of a two-country world, it follows that the small-country MF world ought to emerge as a special case of the large-country situation. The special small-country result will be shown to be equivalent to conventional MF results. (On the large-country case see Mundell (1964), Mussa (1979a), Swoboda and Dornbusch (1973) and Argy and Salop (1983).)

To maintain consistency with some earlier chapters, we again analyse the effects of a monetary or fiscal expansion, principally originating in one of the two countries, for the same three potential exchange rate regimes: fixed rates with sterilised intervention (regime 1), fixed rates without sterilisation (regime 2) and flexible rates (regime 3). However, we now also extend the analysis to accommodate the case of mixed regimes, e.g. the case where say one country sterilises and the other does not.

In each case we look closely at the macro effects on the country where the change in macro policy originated and on the second country, noting particularly the feedback effects.

THE MODEL

The model is a two-country extension of the MF model in Chapter 6. As in Chapter 6 an appendix shows how the goods market equations are arrived at.

The real demand for goods

$$y_A = \alpha_1 e + \alpha_2 y_B + \alpha_3 g_A - \alpha_4 r_A \qquad \alpha_2 < 1 \tag{1}$$

$$y_B = -b_1 e + b_2 y_A + b_3 g_B - b_4 r_B \qquad b_2 < 1 \tag{2}$$

where y_A, y_B are respectively output in A and B, r_A, r_B are respectively the interest rate in A and B, e is the exchange rate defined as units of A's currency per unit of B's currency, and g_A, g_B represent respectively the level of government expenditure in A and B (the fiscal policy variable). All variables are in logarithms except for the interest rate.

Equation (1) says that the real demand for goods (which, as in the MF model, equals supply) is a positive function of the exchange rate, B's output and A's government expenditure and a negative function of its own interest rate. B's output now appears in the equation because an increase (fall) in B's output means that B increases (decreases) its own imports (A's exports) and hence increases (decreases) the demand for goods in A. A parallel equation applies to B.

It should be noted that, given the way the exchange rate is defined, an increase in e represents a devaluation of A's currency and an appreciation of B's currency. Thus, the effects on output are opposite in the two economies. Note too that (1) and (2) are written in a general form, accommodating the possibility that the structural coefficients in the two economies might differ.

As shown in the Appendix, if A were the small country, $b_1 = b_2 = 0$. This is intuitive. The small country cannot impact on output in B; moreover, e would now stand for A's exchange rate *vis-à-vis the whole of the rest of the world*, which, by definition, would have virtually no effects on B.

The monetary sector

We first write down the two equations for the demand for money. For convenience we assume that the coefficients in A and B are identical.

$$mo_A = \alpha_5 y_A - \alpha_{10} r_A \tag{3}$$

$$mo_B = \alpha_5 y_B - \alpha_{10} r_B \tag{4}$$

where mo_A, mo_B are respectively the logarithms of the money stock in A and B.

We turn now to the equations explaining the money supply in each economy. We use a procedure similar to that of Chapters 6 and 8.

$$mo_{As} = \overline{mo}_A - \pi_{10}(e - \bar{e}) \tag{5}$$

$$mo_{Bs} = \overline{mo}_B + \pi_{12}(e - \bar{e}) \tag{6}$$

where $\overline{mo}_A$, $\overline{mo}_B$ represent the exogenous components of the money stock in the two economies and π_{10} and π_{12} represent the degree of exchange rate stabilisation in the two economies. In equilibrium,

$$mo_A = mo_{As} \tag{7}$$

$$mo_B = mo_{Bs} \tag{8}$$

As in earlier chapters, equations (5) and (6), written in a fairly general form, allow us to distinguish a number of alternative exchange rate regimes.

Suppose, first we had a flexible rate regime. Then $\pi_{10} = \pi_{12} = 0$. Using (7) and (8) leaves us with essentially the two equations (3) and (4) with the money stock exogenous in the two economies.

Suppose next we were in regime 1, i.e. fixed rates with sterilised intervention. Then, again, $\pi_{10} = \pi_{12} = 0$ and again the money stocks are exogenous.

Suppose, finally, we were in regime 2. We consider here three possibilities. *First*, we examine the case where the two economies are of equal size and there is *symmetrical* intervention, in the sense that the two central banks intervene to keep the exchange rate fixed, without sterilisation. In this case we have $\pi_{10} = \pi_{12}$. Adding (5) and (6) we have

$$mo_{As} + mo_{Bs} = \overline{mo}_A + \overline{mo}_B \tag{9}$$

Second, we consider the case where the two economies are again of equal size but there is now *asymmetrical* intervention, in the sense that one of the two countries sterilises but the other does not. If A sterilised we would have $\pi_{10} = 0$ and $\pi_{12} \rightarrow \infty$.

Third, for the case where A is the small economy, together with the other conditions noted earlier we now also have $\pi_{12} = 0$ and $\pi_{10} \rightarrow \infty$. We are now back to the MF small-country case with fixed exchange rates without sterilisation.

The foreign exchange market

Finally, we need to represent the foreign exchange market. Since $B_A = -B_B$ we need write only one of the equations for A.

$$\frac{B_A}{X_0} = \alpha_{13}e + y_B - y_A + \alpha_{14}(r_A - r_B) \tag{10}$$

where B_A is A's overall balance of payments deflated by initial exports. We note that

$$\alpha_{13} = edx + edm - 1 \qquad \alpha_{13} > \alpha_1 \text{ and } \alpha_{13} > b_1$$

Also we note that $\alpha_2\alpha_{13} = \alpha_1$ and $b_2\alpha_{13} = b_1$ (see the Appendix).

As in the previous analysis B_A/X_0 will be set at zero for flexible rates and for the fixed rate regime with monetary management. It will find its own level for fixed rates with sterilised intervention.

Table 13.1 Two-country model, regime 1

Monetary expansion in A	
y_A	$\dfrac{\alpha_4(\alpha_{10} + b_4\alpha_5)}{d_7}$
y_B	$\dfrac{b_2\alpha_{10}\alpha_4}{d_7}$
r_A	$-\dfrac{\alpha_{10}(1 - \alpha_2 b_2) + b_4\alpha_5}{d_7}$
r_B	$\dfrac{\alpha_5 b_2\alpha_4}{d_7}$
$y_A + y_B = y_w{}^a$	$\dfrac{\alpha_4}{\alpha_4\alpha_5 + \alpha_{10}(1 - \alpha_2)}$
Fiscal expansion in A	
y_A	$\dfrac{\alpha_3\alpha_{10}(\alpha_{10} + b_4\alpha_5)}{d_7}$
y_B	$\dfrac{b_2\alpha_{10}{}^2\alpha_3}{d_7}$
r_A	$\dfrac{\alpha_3\alpha_5(\alpha_{10} + b_4\alpha_5)}{d_7}$
r_B	$\dfrac{\alpha_5 b_2\alpha_3\alpha_{10}}{d_7}$
$y_A + y_B = y_w{}^a$	$\dfrac{\alpha_3\alpha_{10}}{\alpha_4\alpha_5 + \alpha_{10}(1 - \alpha_2)}$

$d_7 = \alpha_{10}(\alpha_{10} + b_4\alpha_5) + \alpha_4\alpha_5(\alpha_{10} + b_4\alpha_5) - \alpha_2 b_2\alpha_{10}{}^2 > 0$

Note: [a] $\alpha_4 = b_4$; $\alpha_2 = b_2$.

ADJUSTMENT IN REGIME 1

This case is fairly straightforward. We can use the four equations (1), (2), (3) and (4) to solve for y_A, y_B, r_A and r_B. $B_A / X_0 \neq 0$ and so we can solve for the balance of payments after insertion of these solutions in (10). The solutions for the four key variables are shown in Table 13.1.

Fiscal expansion in A lifts output in both A and B. The proportionate increase in A's output is greater than that in B. Interest rates will rise in A and B. From (10) we can also readily see that, depending on the degree of asset substitution, the sign of the effect on the balance of payments is ambiguous.

Monetary expansion in A also lifts output in both A and B. The interest rate falls in A but rises in B. A's balance of payments unambiguously deteriorates.

These results are intuitive. An expansionary macro policy in A will lead to some increase in output in A, along conventional lines, but now A will also import more from B; the expansion in B's exports will also serve to increase B's output which in turn will lead to some increase in B's imports (A's exports). With the money stock fixed in B the interest rate in B must rise to equilibrate the money market.

These cases are shown in Figures 13.1 and 13.2. The IS schedules are derived from equations (1) and (2). The LM schedules are derived from (3) and (4). We assume for

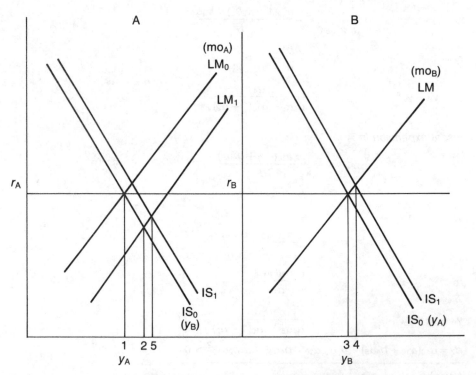

Figure 13.1   Two-country model, regime 1: monetary expansion in A

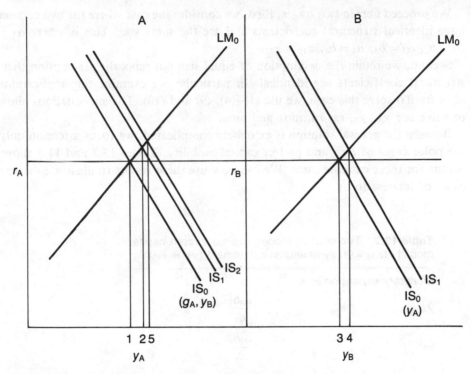

Figure 13.2   Two-country model, regime 1: fiscal expansion in A

simplicity that the interest rate is the same in the two economies to begin with. For a monetary expansion in A (shown in Figure 13.1) output increases in A from 1 to 5 (the shift in IS comes from the increase in output in B) and the interest rate drops. In B the IS schedule shifts to the right because A's output has increased. Output in B increases from 3 to 4 while the interest rate now rises.

For a fiscal expansion in A (shown in Figure 13.2) the IS schedule shifts twice in A (once for the increase in government expenditure and a second time because of the increase in output in B) while the LM schedule stays put. Output increases from 1 to 5 while the interest rate rises. In B the IS schedule shifts to the right; output increases from 3 to 4 and the interest rate rises.

If A is a small country ($b_2 = 0$), B's output is unaffected. At the same time, with feedback effects omitted the multiplier in A becomes smaller. Another way of putting this is that the larger A is, the bigger the effect on its own output from its own macro policies because of feedback effects from B. (This is readily verified by reference to Table 13.1.)

REGIME 2: SYMMETRICAL ADJUSTMENT

This is the case where neither country sterilises, so we can impose the condition that B_A/X_0 in (10) is zero.

We proceed here in two stages. First, we consider the case where the two economies have identical structural coefficients and are the same size. This is where $\alpha_1 = b_1$, $\alpha_2 = b_2$, $\alpha_3 = b_3$, $\alpha_4 = b_4$, $\pi_{10} = \pi_{12}$.

Second, we retain the assumption of equal size but relax the assumption that the structural coefficients are identical. In particular we examine the implications of $\alpha_4 \neq b_4$. To solve this case, we use (1)–(4), (9) and (10). The six equations allow us to solve for y_A, y_B, r_A, r_B, mo_A and mo_B.

Because the general solution is extremely complicated, we focus attention only on the polar cases of zero and perfect capital mobility. Tables 13.2 and 13.3 show the results for these extreme cases. We can now use these results to illustrate the special cases of interest to us.

Table 13.2   Two-country model, regime 2: zero capital mobility ($\alpha_{14} = 0$), symmetrical adjustment ($\pi_{10} = \pi_{12}$)

Monetary expansion in A

y_A $\qquad\qquad\qquad\qquad\qquad \dfrac{\alpha_4 b_4}{d_8}$

y_B $\qquad\qquad\qquad\qquad\qquad \dfrac{\alpha_4 b_4}{d_8}$

r_A $\qquad\qquad\qquad\qquad\qquad -\dfrac{b_4(1 - \alpha_2)}{d_8}$

r_B $\qquad\qquad\qquad\qquad\qquad -\dfrac{\alpha_4(1 - b_2)}{d_8}$

$y_A + y_B = y_w{}^a$ $\qquad\qquad \dfrac{\alpha_4}{\alpha_4 \alpha_5 + \alpha_{10}(1 - \alpha_2)}$

Fiscal expansion in A

y_A $\qquad\qquad\qquad\qquad\qquad \dfrac{\alpha_3 \alpha_{10} b_4}{d_8}$

y_B $\qquad\qquad\qquad\qquad\qquad \dfrac{\alpha_3 \alpha_{10} b_4}{d_8}$

r_A $\qquad\qquad\qquad\qquad\qquad \dfrac{2\alpha_3 \alpha_5 b_4 + \alpha_3 \alpha_{10}(1 - b_2)}{d_8}$

r_B $\qquad\qquad\qquad\qquad\qquad -\dfrac{(1 - b_2)\alpha_3 \alpha_{10}}{d_8}$

$y_A + y_B = y_w{}^a$ $\qquad\qquad \dfrac{\alpha_3 \alpha_{10}}{\alpha_4 \alpha_5 + \alpha_{10}(1 - \alpha_2)}$

$d_8 = 2\alpha_4 \alpha_5 b_4 + \alpha_4 \alpha_{10}(1 - b_2) + b_4 \alpha_{10}(1 - \alpha_2)$

Note: [a] $\alpha_2 = b_2$, $\alpha_4 = b_4$.

Table 13.3 Two-country model, regime 2: perfect capital mobility ($\alpha_{14} \to \infty$), symmetrical adjustment

Monetary expansion in A

$$y_A \qquad \frac{\alpha_4 + \alpha_2 b_4}{d_9}$$

$$y_B \qquad \frac{b_4(1 - \alpha_2 b_2) + b_2(\alpha_4 + \alpha_2 b_4)}{d_9}$$

$$r_w \qquad -\frac{1 - \alpha_2 b_2}{d_9}$$

$$y_w{}^a \qquad \frac{\alpha_4}{\alpha_4 \alpha_5 + \alpha_{10}(1 - \alpha_2)}$$

Fiscal expansion in A

$$y_A \qquad \frac{\alpha_3(\alpha_5 b_4 + 2\alpha_{10})}{d_9}$$

$$y_B \qquad -\frac{\alpha_3(\alpha_5 b_4 - 2\alpha_{10} b_2)}{d_9}$$

$$r_w \qquad \frac{\alpha_3 \alpha_5(1 + b_2)}{d_9}$$

$$y_w{}^a \qquad \frac{\alpha_3 \alpha_{10}}{\alpha_4 \alpha_5 + \alpha_{10}(1 - \alpha_2)}$$

$$d_9 = b_4 \alpha_5(1 + \alpha_2) + 2\alpha_{10}(1 - \alpha_2 b_2) + \alpha_4 \alpha_5(1 + b_2)$$

Note: [a] $\alpha_4 = b_4$, $\alpha_2 = b_2$

Zero capital mobility – same size and structural coefficients

Consider first the case of a monetary expansion in A (an increase in $\overline{mo}_A$ with $\overline{mo}_B = 0$). If capital mobility is zero, ($\alpha_{14} = 0$) we can readily see from (10) that, with $B_A/X_0 = 0$, $y_A = y_B$. In equilibrium, therefore, the level of output will increase equivalently in A and B; this is the condition for a zero current account. From (1) and (2) we can also readily see that with the same structural coefficients $r_A = r_B$. Finally, from (3) and (4) we can see that the increase in the money stock will be identical in A and B.

In A the monetary expansion leads to a fall in the interest rate, to an increase in output and to a current account deficit. In regime 2 this is not sustainable and there will now be a gold standard corrective mechanism at work. The money stock will fall in A and rise in B. So long as A appropriates a larger share of the increase in the world money stock, A's output will be relatively higher and its interest rate lower. The adjustment proceeds until output increases in B by the same amount as in A and its interest rate falls equally. At this point no further adjustment occurs. The current account is now in balance. It is worth noting that, because the *world* money stock has increased, *world* output must increase while the *world* interest rate must fall as shown in Table 13.2. Equation (9) shows that with $\overline{mo}_A$ up and $\Delta mo_A = \Delta mo_B$, this exogenous increase in the world money stock is equally shared by A and B.

Consider now the case of a fiscal expansion originating in A. A parallel adjustment mechanism occurs here. Output and the interest rate will both rise in A. The associated current account deficit in A will lead to a fall in the money stock in A and a parallel increase in the money stock in B. The interest rate falls in B and output increases in B. The adjustment continues until B's output increases by the same amount as in A. In equilibrium output will have increased (equally) in both A and B but whereas the interest rate rises in A it falls in B. The money stock falls in A while it increases equivalently in B. World output and the world interest rate both increase.

Zero capital mobility – different structural coefficients

What happens if the structural coefficients are different? Suppose, to take an extreme case, that $\alpha_4 = 0$ but $b_4 > 0$. Consider a monetary expansion in A; A's interest rate falls but there is no effect on A's output. There is thus no current account deficit and no loss of money to B. Output will be unchanged in A and B; B's interest rate will also be unchanged. The increase in the money stock is absorbed in A.

If $b_4 = 0$ and $\alpha_4 > 0$ the whole of the increase in the money stock will find its way into B from A, again leaving output in A and B unchanged.

For fiscal expansion the reader can figure out why it is that when $b_4 = 0$ and $\alpha_4 > 0$ output will not change in either A or B, but on the other hand in the reverse case when $\alpha_4 = 0$ and $b_4 > 0$ output does increase in A and B.

Perfect capital mobility – same size and structural coefficients

We turn now to the case of perfect capital mobility. This is the case where there is a single common world interest rate which prevails in A and B.

With identical structural coefficients the result, for a monetary expansion originating in A, is identical to the previous case. (We can thus generalise the result whatever the degree of capital mobility.) This is readily seen again from (1) and (2) setting $r_A = r_B = r_w$, r_w being the world interest rate. Monetary expansion in A will instantly provoke a leakage; the leakage, however, is not complete. Adjustment again proceeds to the point where the increase in the money stock is equally divided between the two economies.

What about fiscal expansion? With fiscal expansion in A, so long as capital mobility is low, there is an overall deficit and A's money supply will again fall and B's money supply will increase. If, however, capital mobility is high, A will enjoy an overall surplus, now attracting money from B. When B's money supply falls the effects on B's output are ambiguous. On the one hand, A's expansion lifts B's output; on the other hand, the capital outflow from B, which restricts the money supply, serves to reduce B's output. (See Table 13.3.)

When we have fiscal expansion, the *world* money stock is unchanged, but $\Delta mo_A = -\Delta mo_B$. For example, when there is perfect capital mobility it is readily seen from (3) and (4) that

$$\alpha_5 y_A - \alpha_{10} r_w = -\alpha_5 y_B + \alpha_{10} r_w$$

or

$$\alpha_5(y_A + y_B) = 2\alpha_{10} r_w$$

It can be shown (from Table 13.3) that, if we insert the solution for $y_w = y_A + y_B$ and the solution for r_w, the two expressions will be the same.

The general case for a monetary expansion in A in regime 2 is shown in Figure 13.3. In the new equilibrium there is a new lower common interest rate; at the same time the level of output and the money stock increase equally in A and B.

The case of a fiscal expansion in A in regime 2 for perfect capital mobility is shown in Figure 13.4. There is a new higher common world interest rate. Output increases in A but the effect on B is ambiguous. On the one hand the LM schedule shifts to the left, on the other the IS shifts to the right. B moves from p to q (but the position of q is strictly ambiguous). Only the net shift in IS is shown for A.

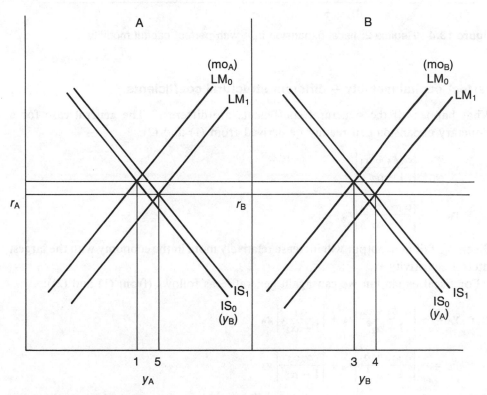

Figure 13.3 Regime 2: monetary expansion in A

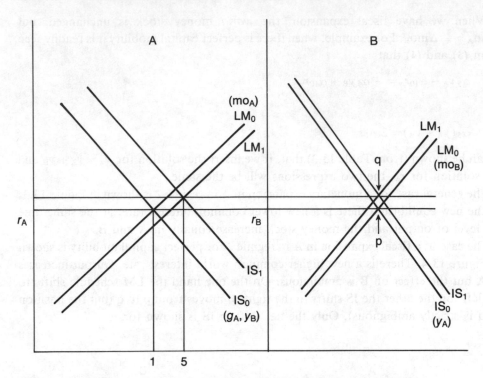

Figure 13.4   Regime 2: fiscal expansion in A with perfect capital mobility

Perfect capital mobility – different structural coefficients

What happens if the structural coefficients are different? The general case for a monetary expansion can readily be derived from (1) and (2).

$$y_A = - \left| \frac{\alpha_2 b_4 + \alpha_4}{1 - \alpha_2^2} \right| r_w$$

$$y_B = - \left| \frac{\alpha_2 \alpha_4 + b_4}{1 - \alpha_2^2} \right| r_w$$

Given the fall in r_w output will increase relatively more in the economy with the largest interest sensitivity.

For fiscal expansion we can again generalise as follows (from (1) and (2)):

$$y_A = - \left| \frac{\alpha_2 b_4 + \alpha_4}{1 - \alpha_2^2} \right| r_w + \left| \frac{\alpha_3}{1 - \alpha_2^2} \right| g_A$$

$$y_B = - \left| \frac{\alpha_2 \alpha_4 + b_4}{1 - \alpha_2^2} \right| r_w + \left| \frac{\alpha_2 \alpha_3}{1 - \alpha_2^2} \right| g_A$$

If the coefficients are the same it is readily seen that output must increase by more in A than in B. The ambiguity for y_B is also readily observed. An interesting result is that, if $b_4 \rightarrow 0$, the monetary squeeze in B disappears and output unambiguously increases in B. (This is evident if one substitutes the solution for r_w from Table 13.3 in the above.)

THE SMALL-COUNTRY CASE

Zero capital mobility

When A is the small country, we should be able to replicate the MF results. A no longer has the capability of changing output or the interest rate in B. In A, too, a monetary expansion is dissipated abroad leaving output and the interest rate unchanged.

Similarly fiscal expansion in A will now leave output unchanged. As already seen, the reduction in the money stock will push up the interest rate sufficiently to crowd out the effects of fiscal expansion. [1]

Perfect capital mobility

The small-country case is also relatively straightforward to analyse. Monetary expansion in A will be instantly ineffective. With fiscal expansion, we can readily demonstrate that now, whilst foreign variables do not change, home output will increase while the home interest rate will be unchanged. The reader can verify that the solution for y_A can readily be shown to reduce to the MF solution in Chapter 6 ($= \alpha_3$).

REGIME 2: ASYMMETRICAL ADJUSTMENT

It is interesting to consider what happens when one of the countries sterilises while the other does not. The exercise is not just of academic interest; it has real-world applications to the case of the USA *vis-à-vis* the rest of the world, particularly in the years of Bretton Woods, and to the case of Germany *vis-à-vis* other members of the European Monetary system (EMS). (On asymmetrical adjustment, see Swoboda (1978).)

Official dollar reserves may be held in three forms: as deposits with the US Federal Reserve System, as deposits with the US commercial banks and in short-term government securities. One can readily demonstrate that

a) in the first case, the cash base in the USA will change in line with developments in the balance of payments (a deficit (surplus) reducing (increasing) the cash base);
b) in the second case, the cash base will not change but the ownership of deposits will normally switch from US residents to foreign central banks (so the money supply changes only by the amount of the change in the balance of payments without any money multiplier effects);

c) finally, in the third case, there is no change in the money supply or in the cash base.

Most of these reserves are in fact held in the form of securities, so whereas there is virtually automatic sterilisation in the USA, in the rest of the world an explicit policy decision has to be taken on whether or not to sterilise.

Also, taking the EMS system as self-contained, we have on the one hand the dominant economy Germany which dictates monetary policy, effectively itself sterilising, and on the other EMS partners acting passively (without sterilising).

In what follows we suppose that it is economy A which sterilises while B does not. As we shall see, it now makes a difference whether the macro policy originates in A or in B. Our analysis will focus solely the case where A and B are of equal size and their structural coefficients are the same.

Tables 13.4 and 13.5 present the solutions for the cases of zero and perfect capital mobility respectively. *It is important to note in this context that so long as one of the two countries does not sterilise the balance of payments of the two countries must be zero.*

Table 13.4 Two-country model, regime 2: zero capital mobility, asymmetrical adjustment

	Monetary expansion in A	Fiscal expansion in A
y_A	$\dfrac{\alpha_4}{d_{10}}$	$\dfrac{\alpha_3\alpha_{10}}{d_{10}}$
y_B	$\dfrac{\alpha_4}{d_{10}}$	$\dfrac{\alpha_3\alpha_{10}}{d_{10}}$
r_A	$-\dfrac{1-\alpha_2}{d_{10}}$	$\dfrac{\alpha_3\alpha_5}{d_{10}}$
r_B	$-\dfrac{1-\alpha_2}{d_{10}}$	$-\dfrac{\alpha_3\alpha_{10}(1-\alpha_2)}{\alpha_4 d_{10}}$
y_W	$\dfrac{2\alpha_4}{d_{10}}$	$\dfrac{2\alpha_3\alpha_{10}}{d_{10}}$

	Monetary expansion in B	Fiscal expansion in B
y_A	0	0
y_B	0	0
r_A	0	0
r_B	0	$\dfrac{\alpha_3}{\alpha_4}$
y_W	0	0

$d_{10} = \alpha_4\alpha_5 + \alpha_{10}(1-\alpha_2)$

Note: A sterilises, B does not (identical coefficients and size).

Table 13.5 Two-country model, regime 2: perfect capital mobility, asymmetrical adjustment

	Monetary expansion in A	Fiscal expansion in A
y_A	$\dfrac{\alpha_4}{d_{10}}$	$\dfrac{\alpha_3\alpha_{10}}{d_{11}}$
y_B	$\dfrac{\alpha_4}{d_{10}}$	$\dfrac{\alpha_3(\alpha_2\alpha_{10} - \alpha_4\alpha_5)}{d_{11}}$
r_w	$-\dfrac{1 - \alpha_2}{d_{10}}$	$\dfrac{\alpha_3\alpha_5}{d_{11}}$
y_w	$\dfrac{2\alpha_4}{d_{10}}$	$\dfrac{\alpha_3[\alpha_{10}(1 + \alpha_2) - \alpha_4\alpha_5]}{d_{11}}$
	Monetary expansion in B	Fiscal expansion in B
y_A	0	$\dfrac{\alpha_2\alpha_3\alpha_{10}}{d_{11}}$
y_B	0	$\dfrac{\alpha_3(\alpha_{10} + \alpha_4\alpha_5)}{d_{11}}$
r_w	0	$\dfrac{\alpha_2\alpha_3\alpha_5}{d_{11}}$
y_w	0	$\dfrac{\alpha_3[\alpha_{10}(1 + \alpha_2) + \alpha_4\alpha_5]}{d_{11}}$

$$d_{10} = \alpha_4\alpha_5 + \alpha_{10}(1 - \alpha_2)$$
$$d_{11} = \alpha_{10}(1 - \alpha_2^2) + \alpha_4\alpha_5(1 + \alpha_2)$$

Note: A sterilises, B does not (identical coefficients and size).

The solutions are obtained as follows. Since A sterilises its money stock is fixed. At the same time, $B_A / X_0 = 0$. We can then use (1)–(3) and (10) to solve for y_A, y_B, r_A, and r_B. Equation (4) then determines B's money stock. If capital mobility is perfect, we can drop (10) and use (1), (2) and (3) to solve for y_A, y_B and r_w.

Suppose the monetary expansion originates in A. Whatever the degree of capital mobility the end result is the same: output and the interest rate are equalised in A and B. A noteworthy result here is that the increase in world output and the fall in the interest rate are *twice* those of the case where *neither* country sterilises. Why is this?

A's money stock increases at first. Either instantly (if capital mobility is perfect) or after some increase in output in A (if capital mobility is low) some of the money stock leaks to B, which does not sterilise. In A any loss abroad will need to be sterilised, so the authorities will engage in *additional* open market purchases. All leakages are sterilised until the system reaches equilibrium. In equilibrium the world money stock will be twice as large. This is why a monetary expansion in A, the country which sterilises, now has a more powerful effect than in the case where neither sterilises.

It is also worth noting that, in contrast to the small-country case, even with fixed exchange rates and perfect capital mobility a large country such as A can now sterilise.

The analysis is entirely different if the monetary expansion originated in B. Suppose capital mobility is zero. B's interest rate falls and its output increases. Some of the additional money stock will start leaking abroad. A, however, does not allow its money stock to increase; it implements a restrictive open market sale to sterilise the inflow. The leakage thus continues until the world money stock returns to its original level. B's original open market purchase is ultimately exactly offset by A's open market sales. Output returns to its original levels in A and B. B is thus incapable of making any impact on the world money supply or output, even though it is a large country. B is being frustrated by A's sterilisation efforts.

A parallel reasoning applies to the case of perfect capital mobility, where now, interestingly, the small-country case applies.

We turn now to the case of fiscal expansion. Suppose capital mobility is zero and the fiscal expansion originates in A. There is a current account deficit in A, so money leaks to B. A sterilises the leakage by engaging in an open market purchase. This reinforces the world monetary effects. A's money stock is unchanged but B's is allowed to increase. Output increases equally in A and B; the output effect is magnified by the increase in the world money stock. (The effect is twice as large – compare Table 13.4 with Table 13.2.)

In this instance, the small-country case cannot be derived directly from the general solutions in Tables 13.2 and 13.3. For identical coefficients, the more general system can be represented as follows:

$$y_A(1 - \alpha_2) = \alpha_3 g_A - \alpha_4 r_A$$

$$y_A(1 - \alpha_2) = -\alpha_4 r_B \qquad (y_A = y_B)$$

$$mo_A = \alpha_5 y_A - \alpha_{10} r_A$$

$$mo_B = \alpha_5 y_A - \alpha_{10} r_B$$

$$mo_A + \pi mo_B = \overline{mo}_A$$

where π represents the ratio of B's money stock to A's. If $\pi \to 0$ the system reduces to the small-country case.[2]

The five equations above jointly determine y_A, r_A, r_B, mo_A and mo_B for changes in $\overline{mo}_A$ and g_A. As indicated, the small-country solution is the special case where $\pi \to \infty$.

The opposite happens if the fiscal expansion originates in B. B's money stock falls but A's money stock is not allowed to increase. The world money stock thus falls, crowding out output in both A and B. At the same time, the world interest rate rises on two counts: the world fiscal expansion and the decline in the world money stock.

What if capital mobility were perfect? Suppose there is a fiscal expansion in A. A's money stock now potentially increases because of a surplus in A but this is sterilised by a restrictive monetary policy. B's money stock, however, falls. Thus the world money stock falls, weakening the global effects relative to the case where *neither* country sterilised. In the end output increases in A but the effect on B's output and the world output is now ambiguous. The associated current account deficit in A is matched by an inflow of capital.

Suppose the fiscal expansion had originated in B. The reader can readily verify that in this case the world money stock will rise, increasing in B and staying unchanged in A. This reinforces the global effects both relative to the immediately preceding case and relative to the case where neither country sterilises. Output will now increase by more in B than in A with capital flows moving from A to B. The world interest rate will rise by less.

REGIME 3: FLEXIBLE EXCHANGE RATES

The solutions for this case are set out in Table 13.6. Again, we focus on polar cases of capital mobility.

We now use five equations of the model ((1)–(4), (10)) to solve for the five variables y_A, y_B, r_A, r_B and e. We note again that B_A/X_0 has to be set at zero.

We focus primarily on the case where the two countries are of equal size and have identical structural coefficients. (The reader can readily figure out what the outcomes might be if the structural coefficients were not identical.)

Consider first the case of a monetary expansion in A with zero capital mobility. The current account must be zero in A and B. Output increases in A, opening up a potential current account deficit in A, which, in turn, provokes a devaluation in A's currency to keep the current account in balance. B's currency appreciates; the deflationary effects of the appreciation exactly offset the expansionary effects of the increase in A's output. All variables in B except the exchange rate are unchanged; B is thus completely sheltered from the effects of A's monetary expansion. In other words, all the effects are now contained within A. It should come as no surprise, therefore, that A's result replicates exactly the small-country MF result. (Compare the solution for A in Table 13.6 with that of Table 6.1.)

Figure 13.5 illustrates this case. All the effects are contained in A. There is a shift to the right in B of the IS schedule because A's output increases but it shifts right back because of the appreciation.

Taking this initial result as a starting point, we can now analyse the effects of increasing capital mobility.

As capital mobility increases A experiences not only a current account deficit but as well a progressively larger capital outflow. A's currency thus devalues more; at the same time the effect on A's output is reinforced. The progressively larger outflow in A must be matched by a progressively larger current account surplus. In B, on the other hand, capital mobility opens up a matching current account deficit, which in turn now serves to *reduce* B's output.

Why is this? When capital mobility was zero, B's output was unchanged. We now allow progressively larger inflows and hence a progressively larger appreciation. This is the mirror image of the progressively larger devaluation in A which progressively *reinforces* output in A but has the opposite effect on B.

This is an important result: with some capital mobility a monetary expansion in A lifts output in A but lowers it in B. World output, however, must increase since,

Table 13.6 Two-country model, regime 3: flexible exchange rates

	$\alpha_{14} = 0$	$\alpha_{14} = \infty$
Monetary expansion in A		
y_A	$\dfrac{\alpha_4\alpha_{13}}{\alpha_{10}(\alpha_{13} - \alpha_1) + \alpha_4\alpha_5\alpha_{13}}$	$\dfrac{\alpha_{10}\alpha_1 + b_4\alpha_5\alpha_1 - b_1(\alpha_2\alpha_{10} - \alpha_4\alpha_5)}{\alpha_5 d_{12}}$
y_B	0	$-\dfrac{\alpha_{10}(b_1 - \alpha_1 b_2)}{\alpha_5 d_{12}}$
r_A	$-\dfrac{\alpha_{13} - \alpha_1}{\alpha_{10}(\alpha_{13} - \alpha_1) + \alpha_4\alpha_5\alpha_{13}}$	$-\dfrac{b_1 - \alpha_1 b_2}{d_{12}}$
r_B	0	$-\dfrac{b_1 - \alpha_1 b_2}{d_{12}}$
$y_w{}^a$	$\dfrac{\alpha_4}{\alpha_{10}(1 - \alpha_2) + \alpha_4\alpha_5}$	$\dfrac{\alpha_4}{\alpha_{10}(1 - \alpha_2) + \alpha_4\alpha_5}$
e	$\dfrac{\alpha_4}{\alpha_{10}(\alpha_{13} - \alpha_1) + \alpha_4\alpha_5\alpha_{13}}$	Not reported [b]
Fiscal expansion in A		
y_A	$\dfrac{\alpha_3\alpha_{13}\alpha_{10}}{\alpha_{10}(\alpha_{13} - \alpha_1) + \alpha_4\alpha_5\alpha_{13}}$	$\dfrac{\alpha_3\alpha_{10}b_1}{d_{12}}$
y_B	0	$\dfrac{\alpha_3\alpha_{10}b_1}{d_{12}}$
r_A	$\dfrac{\alpha_3\alpha_{13}\alpha_5}{\alpha_{10}(\alpha_{13} - \alpha_1) + \alpha_4\alpha_5\alpha_{13}}$	$\dfrac{\alpha_5\alpha_3 b_1}{d_{12}}$
r_B	0	$\dfrac{\alpha_5\alpha_3 b_1}{d_{12}}$
$y_w{}^a$	$\dfrac{\alpha_3\alpha_{13}\alpha_{10}}{\alpha_{10}(\alpha_{13} - \alpha_1) + \alpha_4\alpha_5\alpha_{13}}$	$\dfrac{\alpha_3\alpha_{10}}{\alpha_4\alpha_5 + \alpha_{10}(1 - \alpha_2)}$
e	$\dfrac{\alpha_3\alpha_{10}}{\alpha_{10}(\alpha_{13} - \alpha_1) + \alpha_4\alpha_5\alpha_{13}}$	$-\dfrac{\alpha_3[\alpha_{10}(1 - b_2) + b_4\alpha_5]}{d_{12}}$

$d_{12} = \alpha_1\alpha_{10}(1 + b_2) + b_1[\alpha_{10}(1 - \alpha_2) + \alpha_4\alpha_5] + b_4\alpha_5\alpha_1$

Notes: [a] $\alpha_1 = b_1$, $\alpha_2 = b_2$ and $\alpha_4 = b_4$.
[b] Expression very complicated.

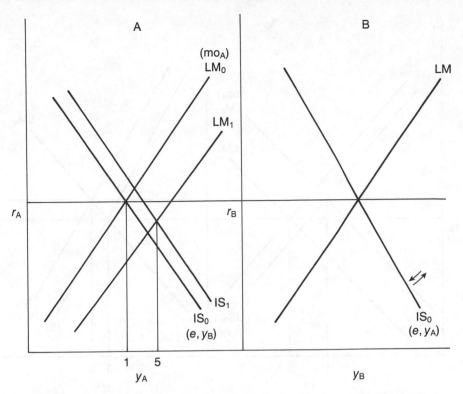

Figure 13.5 Regime 3: monetary expansion in A with zero capital mobility

globally, the world money stock has increased. The progressive fall in B's output as capital mobility increases gradually pulls back B's interest rate until it is brought into equality with A's, whose own interest rate *rises* as its own output increases.

When capital mobility is perfect interest rates are equalised. A's output increases, B's falls, while the common world interest rate falls.

The reader can verify the following from Table 13.6, when capital mobility is perfect. When the structural coefficients are identical in A and B (and the two economies are of equal size) the expansion in A's output is

$$\frac{\alpha_{10}(1 - \alpha_2) + 2\alpha_4\alpha_5}{2\alpha_5[\alpha_{10}(1 - \alpha_2) + \alpha_4\alpha_5]}$$

and B's is

$$-\frac{\alpha_{10}(1 - \alpha_2)}{2\alpha_5[\alpha_{10}(1 - \alpha_2) + \alpha_4\alpha_5]}$$

It is readily seen that the increase in A's output exceeds the fall in B's output.

Figure 13.6 illustrates the case of a monetary expansion in A with perfect capital mobility. In A both IS and LM shift to the right. In B, however, only IS now shifts to the left. Output rises in A from 1 to 5; output falls (by less) in B from 2 to 3.

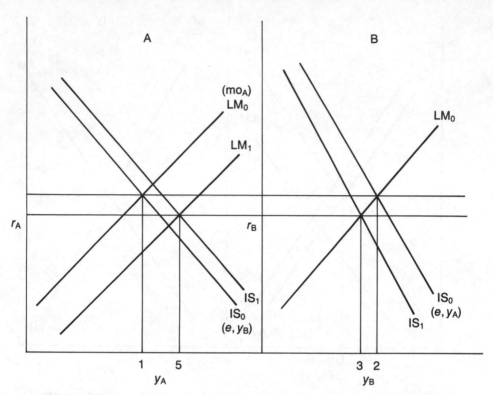

Figure 13.6 Regime 3: monetary expansion in A with perfect capital mobility

If A is the small economy, $(b_1 = 0, b_2 = 0)$ the increase in output in A is $1/\alpha_5$ which corresponds to the MF solution. Also, in this case the devaluation in A is equal to α_{10}.

Consider now the case of fiscal expansion originating in A. When capital mobility is zero the potential current account deficit in A provokes a devaluation sufficient to keep the current account in balance; at the same time there will be some increase in output in A. B is again totally sheltered from A's fiscal expansion, the appreciation suppressing any potential current account surplus. This is the same result as in the MF model.

As capital mobility increases, as in the MF model, A's devaluation is initially weakened; with capital mobility relatively high, A's currency appreciates because capital inflows from B now exceed the current account deficit. As the currency progressively strengthens in A the increase in A's output is dampened; at the same time B's output progressively increases. B's currency, on the other hand, progressively weakens, while its current account surplus increases. A's current account deficit and B's current account surplus are matched by capital outflows from B into A.

Ultimately, when capital mobility is perfect, B's output will have increased sufficiently and A's output fallen back sufficiently to the point where the levels of output in A and B will be equalised. To see why this must be so, consider the two money demand equations. The money stock is fixed in both A and B and so we have

$$\Delta y_A = \alpha_{10} \, \Delta r_w$$

$$\Delta y_B = \alpha_{10} \, \Delta r_w$$

where r_w is the common world interest rate. If the coefficients are the same, output levels must be equalised.

Suppose, for example, that A's output level was higher than B's. Then A's interest rate would have to be potentially higher than B's. This provokes a further appreciation (devaluation) of A's (B's) currency which in turn reduces A's output and increases B's. This continues until output is equalised.

Figure 13.7 illustrates the case of a fiscal expansion in A with perfect capital mobility. The LM schedules stay put but the two IS schedules shift to the right equally in A and B. The increase in output is the same in A and B and there is a new higher common world interest rate.

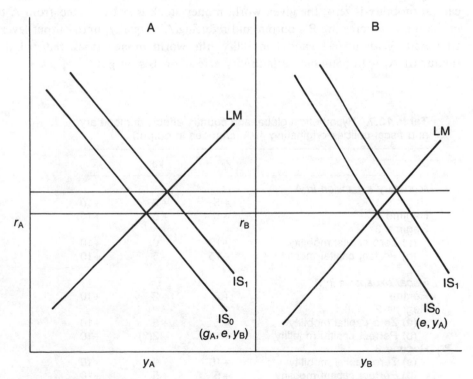

Figure 13.7 Regime 3: fiscal expansion in A with perfect capital mobility

GLOBAL EFFECTS AND THE EXCHANGE RATE REGIME

We now present an important conclusion for the special case where the countries are of equal size, their structural coefficients are the same and there is symmetry in adjustment.

It turns out that global effects are identical whatever the exchange rate regime and whatever the degree of capital mobility. The exchange rate regime and the degree of capital mobility serve only to determine *the distribution* of the global effect. This result is perhaps intuitively evident but is nevertheless worth illustrating further.

Table 13.7 presents some hypothetical outcomes for output for the different regimes and for different assumptions about capital mobility. The table assumes that the increase in world output is 10 units for both monetary and fiscal expansion. The reader can confirm that world effects are identical for symmetrical regimes.

Consider first a monetary expansion. As we have seen, in regime 1, the lion's share of the increase in output is appropriated by A (8 against 2). When A and B both do not sterilise, output falls back in A and rises equally in B until output levels are equalised. In regime 3 with zero capital mobility the whole of the increase in output is appropriated by A. As capital mobility increases, however, and A's currency progressively weakens, output increases further in A and falls equally in B.

For fiscal expansion we have a parallel result for regime 1, with the lion's share of the increase in output appropriated by A. When sterilisation is abandoned and capital mobility is zero, the given world money stock is redistributed from A to B, in the process increasing B's output and reducing A's equally, until output levels are equalised. With perfect capital mobility, the world money stock redistributes in favour of A, with potential deflationary effects on B's output.

Table 13.7 Hypothetical global and country effects of monetary and fiscal policies originating in A (changes in output)

	y_A	y_B	y_w
Monetary expansion in A			
Regime 1	+8	+2	+10
Regime 2	+5	+5	+10
Regime 3			
(a) Zero capital mobility	+10	0	+10
(b) Perfect capital mobility	+15	−5	+10
Fiscal expansion in A			
Regime 1	+8	+2	+10
Regime 2			
(a) Zero capital mobility	+5	+5	+10
(b) Perfect capital mobility	+12	−2(?)	+10
Regime 3			
(a) Zero capital mobility	+10	0	+10
(b) Perfect capital mobility	+5	+5	+10

Finally, in regime 3 with zero capital mobility, the whole of the increase in world output is appropriated by A. As A's currency progressively strengthens, output falls back in A and rises equally in B until output levels are equalised.

THE TRANSMISSION OF FOREIGN DISTURBANCES TO A SMALL COUNTRY

In this simple model, how do policy changes in B, the large country, impact on the small country? We limit ourselves to a few very brief observations which derive from the model in this chapter.

If B is the large country, there is no feedback from A to B. B is now effectively self-contained. In principle, we can solve independently for the effects on B of B's macro policies and then, taking the model for A, figure out how changes in B impact on A.

In this simpler model, there are two routes by which B's policies will transmit to A: through changes in B's output and through changes in B's interest rate. B's output appears in A's real demand for goods (equation (1)) and in A's trade balance (equation (10)) while B's interest rate appears in A's balance of payments equation.

We briefly illustrate these points for a peg and a float in the face of an expansion in the money supply abroad and an easier fiscal policy. In each case, we assume perfect capital mobility, i.e. the small country A has to accept B's interest rate.

It is readily seen from (2) and (4) that the following will hold:

$$y_B = \pi_{12} mo_B \qquad r_B = -\pi_{14} mo_B$$

$$y_B = \pi_{16} gr_B \qquad r_B = \pi_{18} gr_B$$

where the coefficients $\pi_{12}-\pi_{18}$ correspond to the solutions to the two-equation system.

In A for fixed rates, we can read off the solution directly from (1):

$$y_A = \alpha_2 y_B - \alpha_4 r_B$$

Using the solutions for y_B and r_B, it is readily seen that (a) for a monetary expansion abroad, output in A must increase; (b) for a fiscal expansion abroad, the effect on A's output is ambiguous.

In A, for flexible rates, we can read off the solution directly from (3). With mo_A fixed, we have

$$y_A = \frac{\alpha_{10}}{\alpha_5} r_B$$

We now have (a) for a monetary expansion abroad, output will fall in A; (b) for a fiscal expansion, output must increase.

Table 13.8 shows that these results are confirmed for a simulation, using the MSG2 model, of the impacts of a monetary and fiscal expansion in the USA on output in a small country such as Australia.

Table 13.8   Impact of US macro policy on Australian output

	1% expansion in US money stock	Increase by 1% of GNP in US government expenditure
A$ pegged to US$	+0.20	−1.54
A$ floats	−0.15	+0.20

Source: Argy et al. 1989.
Note: MSG2 model, perfect asset substitution; first-year impacts on output.

APPENDIX

Notation

Y_i real output
G_i real government expenditure
R_i interest rate
P_i overall price level
P_{di} price of domestic goods
E exchange rate (units of A's currency per unit of B's)
A_{ri} real absorption
X volume of A's exports
M volume of A's imports
I real investment
edx   elasticity of demand for A's exports
edm   elasticity of demand for A's imports
er_i semi interest elasticity of investment
k_i multiplier to be defined below

The subscript i can take on the value for A or B.

The real demand for goods (= real supply)

Country A

$$Y_A P_{dA} = A_{rA} P_A + X P_{dA} - M P_{dB} E \tag{A1}$$

$$A_{rA} = \beta_{10} \frac{Y_A P_{dA}}{P_A} - \beta_{13} R_A + G_A \tag{A2}$$

$$X = \beta_8 \frac{P_{dB} E}{P_{dA}} + \beta_{12} Y_B \tag{A3}$$

$$P_A = P_{dA}{}^{\alpha_{15}} P_{dB} E^{1-\alpha_{15}} \tag{A4}$$

Country B

$$Y_B P_{dB} = A_{rB} P_B + M P_{dB} - \frac{X P_{dA}}{E} \tag{A5}$$

$$A_{rB} = \beta_{20} \frac{Y_B P_{dB}}{P_B} - \beta_{30} R_B \tag{A6}$$

$$M = \beta_9 Y_A + \beta_{11} \frac{P_{dA}}{P_{dB} E} \tag{A7}$$

$$P_B = P_{dB}{}^{\beta_{14}} \frac{P_{dA}}{E} (1 - \beta_{14}) \tag{A8}$$

We have two countries labelled A and B. A's exports in (A1) in domestic currency $X P_{dA}$ must be equal to B's imports, as shown in (A5). These imports are then revalued in B's currency. E is the exchange rate between A and B. B's exports in B's currency $M P_{dB}$ are equal to A's imports, now converted into A's currency as in (A1). Exports and imports in the two economies are a function of relative prices. A's exports X are also a function of B's output (A3), which is now explained by the model. Similarly B's exports (= A's imports) are explained in part by A's output (A7) which is also explained by the model. The overall price level in each country is a weighted average of own home prices and own import prices.

The next step is to differentiate the equations for each country, so as to derive a single real aggregate demand for goods for A and B. The reader will be spared all the details (see Chapter 6, Appendix 1). The summary equations in logarithmic form (except for the interest rate) are

$$y_A = \alpha_1 e + \alpha_2 y_B + \alpha_3 g_A - \alpha_4 r_A \tag{A9}$$

$$y_B = -b_1 e + b_2 y_A - b_4 r_B + b_3 g_B \tag{A10}$$

Prices have been dropped from the equations. All terms of trade effects are disregarded. The initial current account is assumed to be zero. All initial prices, including the exchange rate, are set at unity. Marginal and average propensities to import are assumed to be the same.

The following can readily be shown to hold:

$$\alpha_1 = k_A \frac{X}{Y_A} (edx + edm - 1)$$

$$\alpha_2 = k_A \frac{X}{Y_A} \quad (<1)$$

$$\alpha_3 = k_A \frac{G_A}{Y_A}$$

$$\alpha_4 = k_A \frac{I_A}{Y_A} \, \mathrm{erA}$$

$$k_A = \frac{1}{1 - \beta_{10} + \beta_9}$$

where $\beta_9 = X/Y_A$.

$$b_1 = k_B \frac{X}{Y_B} \, (\mathrm{edx} + \mathrm{edm} - 1)$$

$$b_2 = k_B \frac{X}{Y_B} \qquad (<1)$$

$$b_4 = k_B \frac{I_B}{Y_B} \, \mathrm{erB}$$

$$k_B = \frac{1}{1 - \beta_{20} + \beta_{12}}$$

where $\beta_{12} = X/Y_B$.

The small-country case is a special case of the above. It is readily seen that in the small country $X/Y_B \to 0$ and hence $b_1 = b_2 = 0$.

14

The two-country model with flexible wages and prices

INTRODUCTION

We now extend the two-country model of the previous chapter to accommodate flexible wages and prices. The model we will present is a more general one, allowing us also to say something about differences in the way in which labour markets work in our two economies. In addition we assume that asset substitution is perfect and limit our analysis to the flexible rate case.

We will proceed as follows. First, we present the more general model. Second, we look at the special case where real wages are fixed in the two economies. This has its counterpart in the small-country case of Chapter 8. Third, we examine in more detail a special case of asymmetry, where there is full wage indexation in *one* of the two countries and *zero* indexation in the other.

THE MODEL

Goods markets

$$y_A = \alpha_1(e + p_{dB} - p_{dA}) - \alpha_4[r_A - ({}_tE_{p_At+1} - p_A)] + \alpha_2 y_B + \alpha_3 \text{gr}_A \tag{1}$$

$$y_B = \alpha_1(e + p_{dB} - p_{dA}) - \alpha_4[r_B - ({}_tE_{p_Bt+1} - p_B)] + \alpha_2 y_A + \alpha_3 \text{gr}_B \tag{2}$$

Money markets

$$\text{mo}_A = \alpha_5 y_A + p_{dA} - \alpha_{10}r_A \tag{3}$$

$$\text{mo}_B = \alpha_5 y_B + p_{dB} - \alpha_{10}r_B \tag{4}$$

$$r_A - r_B = {}_tE_{et+1} - e \tag{5}$$

Labour markets/production

$$y_A = -\alpha_9(w_A - p_{dA}) \tag{6}$$

$$y_B = -\alpha_9(w_B - p_{dB}) \tag{7}$$

$$w_A = (1 - \lambda)(_{t-1}E_{p_A t}) + \lambda(_{t-2}E_{p_A t}) + \pi_1[p_A - (1 - \lambda)_{t-1}E_{p_A t} - \lambda(_{t-2}E_{p_A t})] + \pi_3 y_{A-1} \tag{8}$$

$$w_B = (1 - \beta)(_{t-1}E_{p_B t}) + \beta(_{t-2}E_{p_B t}) + \pi_2[p_B - (1 - \beta)_{t-1}E_{p_B t} - \beta(_{t-2}E_{p_B t})] + \pi_4 y_{B-1} \tag{9}$$

$$p_A = \alpha_{15}p_{dA} + (1 - \alpha_{15})(e + p_{dB}) \tag{10}$$

$$p_B = \alpha_{15}p_{dB} + (1 - \alpha_{15})(p_{dA} - e) \tag{11}$$

The trade balance

$$CA/X_0 = \alpha_{13}(e + p_{dB} - p_{dA}) - (y_A - y_B) \qquad (\alpha_{13} > \alpha_1) \tag{12}$$

Notation

Subscripts A and B stand for countries A and B, respectively. All variables are in logarithms except for the interest rate and the trade balance.

Y	output
r	interest rate
p_d	home price
p	consumer price
e	exchange rate (units of A's currency per unit of B's currency)
gr	real government expenditure
m	money stock
w	wage rate
$_tE_{xt+1}$	expectations about x formed in period t for $t + 1$
α_6	share of wages to profits in the private sector
CA/X_0	A's trade balance deflated by initial exports

Equations (1) and (2) represent the real demand for goods in A and B. Real demand is a function of the real exchange rate, the real interest rate and the other country's level of output. Equations (3)–(6) describe the money markets. Equations (3) and (4) are conventional money demand equations used previously. Equation (5) embodies the assumption of perfect asset substitution. Arbitrage ensures that the return on domestic investment (rd) must equal the return on foreign investment after adjustment is made for the expected change in the exchange rate ($r^* + (_tE_{et+1} - e)$).

Equations (6)–(11) describe the production side of the economy. Output in A and B is a negative function of the real wage rate; (8) and (9) are generalised wage equations which accommodate a number of possibilities.

In A (B) a proportion $1 - 2\lambda$ $(1 - 2\beta)$ of wage contracts last one period while a proportion 2λ (2β) last two periods, evenly distributed over these two periods. If contracts are for one period only $\lambda = \beta = 0$. If all contracts are for two periods $\lambda = \beta = \frac{1}{2}$. Contracts are negotiated in advance and are based on the expected consumer price index over the life of the contract. At the same time there may be an indexation provision in the contract, which allows partial or full correction for any gap between the actual and expected price level. If indexation is perfect $\pi_1 = \pi_2 = 1$. We also allow the level of output to influence the market wage rate. π_3 and π_4 are a measure of *real wage flexibility*.

We note that if indexation is perfect the two wage equations reduce to

$$w_A - p_A = \pi_3 y_{A-1} \tag{13}$$

$$w_B - p_B = \pi_4 y_{B-1} \tag{14}$$

which simply say that the real wage rate responds to the level of activity.

Equations (10) and (11) define the consumer price index in each economy as a weighted average of domestic and import prices.

Equation (12) explains A's trade balance in terms of the real exchange rate and the difference in the levels of output.

The model accommodates potential differences in the behaviour of labour markets in our two economies. In terms of the model there could be differences in (a) the length of the contract, (b) the indexation provision in the contract and (c) the degree of real wage flexibility. (These points are taken up again in several subsequent chapters).

These differences, notably the length of the contract and the degree of real wage flexibility, carry important implications for the adjustment to policy shocks. Longer, but not fully indexed, contracts *prolong* the real adjustment process; on the other hand, a high degree of real wage flexibility accelerates adjustment to a disturbance.

We proceed now to manipulate this model for two special cases: the case where there is full indexation in the two economies and the case where there is full indexation in one but zero in the other.

REAL WAGES FIXED IN A AND B

To make the model manageable, we now impose the following conditions:

$$\pi_3 = \pi_4 = 0 \qquad \pi_1 = \pi_2 = 1$$

$$_tE_{et+1} = e \qquad _tE_{p_A+1} = p_A \qquad _tE_{p_B+1} = p_B$$

We also have a single interest rate which is common to the two economies.

Using the production–labour markets block, as in Chapter 8, we can express each country's supply of output as a function of its own real exchange rate. This gives us two equations on the supply side and with a common interest rate four other equations in the system ((1)–(4)). The six equations solve for y_A, y_B, r_w, e, p_{dA}, p_{dB}. All structural coefficients are identical.

The results, for a monetary expansion in A, are similar to the small-country case. There are no real effects in either A or B. Prices increase proportionately in A and A's currency also devalues in the same proportion. The interest rate is unaffected, as is the current account.

Whereas in the fixed price model output in B falls, output in B now remains unchanged. The higher imported prices in B (A's inflation) are exactly neutralised by B's appreciation. B's prices are unchanged as is B's interest rate. The effects of a monetary expansion in A are thus contained within A; B is completely sheltered from monetary policies in A.

It is easy to see that all markets in the model, as summed up above, are equilibrated. In (1) the real exchange rate, y_B, gr_A and r_w are all unchanged, so output in A cannot change. In (2) all independent variables again are unchanged. In (3) real money balances ($mo_A - p_{dA}$) are unchanged with the right-hand variables also unchanged. In (4) nothing changes. With the real exchange rate unchanged output cannot change in either country. Finally, with the real exchange rate and output unchanged the current account cannot change.

The case of a fiscal expansion in A is more complicated. It can be shown that output will expand in A but at B's expense; output in B will fall. The common interest rate will rise; prices in B must rise but in A the effect on prices is ambiguous. Also, A's current account must deteriorate (and B's of course improves); in equilibrium there will be a matching outflow of capital from B into A. Finally there is a real appreciation in A and a real depreciation in B. A's nominal currency appreciates, B's depreciates.

We can show that these results equilibrate all three markets. Consider first the real demand for goods ((1) and (2)).On the one hand the real appreciation, the fall in output in B and the higher interest rate combine to reduce real demand in A. On the other hand the increase in government expenditure increases real demand. This last is the dominant influence. In B the dominant influence is the higher interest rate, only partly neutralised by the expansion in output in A and the real devaluation in B.

We turn now to the monetary sector ((3) and (4)). mo_A is fixed. The effect on p_{dA} is ambiguous because the increase in output reduces the price level but the increase in the interest rate allows some increase in A's price level. In B because output falls and the interest rate rises, given mo_B, the price level must rise.

Finally, the aggregate supply equations are the easiest to deal with. The real appreciation in A and the real devaluation in B are consistent with the increase in output in A and the equal fall in output in B. Fiscal expansion in A thus turns out to be a 'beggar thy neighbour' type policy.

These results, for a fiscal expansion, appear to have major implications for macroeconomic coordination and the interdependence of policy (see also Chapter 45).

From (3) and (4) with money stocks fixed

$$p_{dA} + p_{dB} = -\alpha_5 y_A - \alpha_5 y_B + 2\alpha_{10} r_w$$

With $y_A = -y_B$, $r_w > 0$ and the world price level will rise from a fiscal expansion.

Suppose now A had some 'excess' unemployment; B's unemployment rate was about right. A uses fiscal policy to reduce its own unemployment but now B's unemployment goes up. B now retaliates by implementing an easier fiscal policy restoring the original unemployment rates in A and B; now, however, the *world* price level is higher. Both A and B are worse off.

A INDEXES BUT B DOES NOT

We turn now to the case where $\pi_1 = 1$, $\pi_2 = 0$. We also continue to assume that $\pi_3 = \pi_4 = 0$, and expectations are static. Our analysis is limited to the one-period outcome, with wages in B fixed during this period.

The merit of the analysis of this section is that in reality different countries have different institutional arrangements *vis-à-vis* wage indexation and this will have a bearing on outcomes of policies. For example, it is frequently said that European economies have a greater degree of real wage rigidity than the USA. (For analysis of the effects of differences across countries in the degree to which wages are indexed, see Argy and Salop (1983), Oudiz and Sachs (1984) and Branson and Rotemberg (1980).)

The solutions in general for this case are very complicated and will not be reported. Table 14.1, however, reports the direction of changes in the principal variables for a monetary and a fiscal expansion originating in A or B.

Consider first the case where there is a monetary expansion in A. As it happens, this replicates the result of the previous section and the small-country case of Chapter 8. Notwithstanding the fact that B is unindexed, A's being indexed is sufficient to produce neutral outcomes. On the other hand, if the monetary expansion had originated in B the results would be quite different. Output now increases in both A *and* B (unlike the MF result where output in B falls); prices also rise in A and B.

Table 14.1 Monetary and fiscal expansion in A and B – direction of change in variables

	y_A	p_{dA}	y_B	p_{dB}	r_w	e
Monetary expansion in A	0	↑	0	0	0	↑
Monetary expansion in B	↑	↑	↑	↑	↓	↓
Fiscal expansion in A	↑	?	↑	↑	↑	↓
Fiscal expansion in B	?	?	↑	↑	↑	↑

Note: A, indexed; B, unindexed.

Consider now the case of a fiscal expansion in A. Output now rises in both A and B, as in the MF model but unlike the case where real wages are fixed in A and B. *B being unindexed allows it to avoid a drop in output (as in the previous section).* Finally, if the fiscal expansion originates in B, output not surprisingly increases in B, but the effect on A's output is ambiguous. *A's indexing weakens the spillover effects of B's fiscal expansion.*

15

Econometric evidence –
the large-country case

INTRODUCTION

So far we have limited ourselves to modelling the impacts of monetary and fiscal policies in a two-country framework. These models have left us with a number of theoretical expectations about the impacts; in this chapter we try to review the econometric
evidence on impacts to see whether the theoretical predictions are confirmed or otherwise. The chapters to date have drawn attention to the complexities associated with
modelling the open economy; the results of our theoretical models are, inevitably,
drawn from models which are admittedly relatively simple, so we should not expect
a perfect correspondence between theoretical expectations and econometric results.
Nevertheless, we can at least hope that the models are able to provide some insights
into the actual transmission of policies across large countries.

In what follows, we shall focus almost exclusively on applications to the USA–
Japan economic interactions. Our two-country world will be represented by the USA
and Japan and we shall ask what econometric evidence has to say about own-country
as well as spillover effects originating in one or the other country.

We make the important distinction between *short-run* and *medium-run* impacts.
The short run is an MF horizon which we expect to be roughly one year. The medium
run would run over three to four years and roughly corresponds to the case where
wages and prices are allowed to adjust fully.

We proceed in two steps. In Section 1 we try to summarise in a table the impacts
of a change in monetary and fiscal policy on the two countries, drawing on results
of the previous two chapters. In Section 2 we present the econometric evidence on
USA–Japan economic interactions.

EXPECTED OUTCOMES – OWN COUNTRY AND SPILLOVER EFFECTS

Table 15.1 conveniently summarises outcomes already largely reported in the two previous chapters. These results assume that expectations are static. The case of rational expectations (i.e. where the public know the outcomes) is dealt with in future chapters.

The only minor change introduced here is to allow some adjustment in domestic prices in the short run in A and B. This extension, however, is trivial: in each country with the wage rate fixed prices will be positively associated with the levels of output.

In the short run, monetary expansion in A lowers the world interest rate, increases output and prices in A but *lowers* output and prices in B (with world output increasing). At the same time, A's currency devalues while, in the model at any rate, A's current account *improves*.

In the medium run, as in the last chapter, the model yields classical neutrality results. Monetary expansion in A devalues the currency and increases prices proportionately. Output, the interest rate and current accounts are unchanged. B's currency appreciates but otherwise B is completely sheltered from A's monetary expansion.

In the short run, following a fiscal expansion in A output and prices increase *equally* in A and B (but only so of course for identical structures and countries of equal size). The spillover effect is thus positive here. A's currency appreciates while the world interest rate increases. A's trade balance deteriorates.

In the medium run we have again a quite different result. Output rises in A but falls equally in B. The spillover effect is now negative. In B there is also more inflation. A's currency also appreciates (in nominal and real terms) and the world interest rate increases.

Table 15.1 Transmission of monetary and fiscal policies in a two-country world – static expectations and identical structural coefficients[a]

	y_A	y_B	r_w	e^b	p_{dA}	p_{dB}	CA_A
Monetary expansion in A							
Short run	↑	↓	↓	↑	↑	↓	↑
Medium run	0	0	0	↑	↑	0	0
Fiscal expansion in A							
Short run	↑[c]	↑[c]	↑	↓	↑[c]	↑[c]	↓
Medium run	↑[d]	↓[d]	↑	↓	?	↑	↓

Notes: [a] With expectations static $r_A = r_B = r_w$ and there is a single world interest rate.
[b] e↑ means a devaluation of A's currency (an appreciation of B's).
[c] Equal increases in A and B.
[d] Equal and opposite in sign.

MONETARY AND FISCAL EXPANSION IN THE USA AND JAPAN – ECONOMETRIC EVIDENCE

Tables 15.2 and 15.3 present the results of simulations of monetary and fiscal policies, originating in the USA and Japan, using three well-known econometric models: the US Federal Reserve MCM model (see Edison *et al.* 1986), the IMF's MultiMod (see Masson *et al.* 1990) and the McKibbin–Sachs MSG2 model (see McKibbin and Sachs 1991; McKibbin 1989). The simulations are for one year and four years. All the models assume perfect asset substitution.

The tables are self-explanatory. A brief summary of the outcomes should suffice.

Fiscal expansion

All the models agree on certain 'own-country' patterns. There is initially a strong positive output effect. By year 4, however, crowding out is in evidence. The associated rise in the interest rate combined with the appreciation serve to dampen the real outcomes substantially. Price effects are also positive but initially very weak, building up to more substantial effects by year 4. The trade balance worsens and this persists into the fourth year. There is also evidence by year 4 of some exchange rate reversal.

Spillover effects are positive, consistent with theory for the short-run adjustment.

Having said this, there is nevertheless also very considerable divergence in the results. For example, initial impacts on own (US) output vary from 2.8 to 10 per cent; four-year outcomes vary from -2.2 to $+4.0$. Very similar points may be made about impacts on exchange rates and prices.

Monetary expansion

All the models agree on 'own' patterns. Initial output effects are positive but by year 4 these become much weaker. The price effects are very weak at first but tend to dominate by year 4 (close to classical neutrality is achieved, as in theory). The own trade balance effect is weak and conflicting. Interest rates fall and the currency devalues.

The spillover effects on output are negative in the two models (as predicted by our theory).

In general, it appears that the differences appear to be less serious than for fiscal expansion.

Summary

Conveniently Bryant (1988), in a recent paper, has tried to summarise what six econometric models have to say about macro policy interactions between the USA and Japan. The six models he uses are the EPA, the Global Economic Model of the

Table 15.2 US and Japanese fiscal shocks[a]

	USA[b]						Japan[c]					
	Year 1			Year 4			Year 1			Year 4		
	MultiMod	MSG2	MCM	MultiMod	MSG2	MCM	MultiMod	MSG2	MCM	MultiMod	MSG2	MCM
y_A	+3.7	2.8	+10.0	-2.2	+0.9	+4.0	+0.1	-0.05	+0.5	-0.1	-0.7	+0.0
p_{dA}	+0.6	-0.6	+1.0	+3.4	+0.8	+8.0	+0.0	+1.0	+0.0	+0.2	+3.3	+0.5
r_{dA}	+0.2	+5.8	+8.5	+2.0	+5.7	+11.0	+0.1	+0.5	+0.5	+0.2	+2.5	+1.0
e_A	+5.0	–	+11.0	+3.7	–	+15.5	-1.4	–	-1.5	-1.2	–	+1.5
CA_A	-0.5	-2.0	-51.0	-0.7	-1.6	-141.0	+0.1	+0.5	+9.0	+0.1	+0.4	+7.0
y_B	+0.5	+0.9	+3.5	+0.3	-0.2	+6.0	+3.2	+1.7	+6.5	-1.6	-0.3	+6.0
p_{dB}	+0.1	+1.3	+0.5	+0.3	+4.5	+3.0	+0.7	-1.1	+1.0	+3.5	+0.0	+5.0
r_{dB}	+0.2	+2.2	+1.0	+0.5	+5.5	+2.0	+0.2	+4.1	+3.5	+2.1	+3.2	+2.5
e_B	-2.5	-25.0	-15.5	-2.0	-20.0	-18.0	+8.5	+33.2	+6.5	+6.4	+26.1	-2.0
CA_B	+0.4	+2.0	+10.0	+0.5	+1.1	+36.0	-0.9	-4.4	-14.5	-0.7	-3.3	-22.5

Sources: See text

Notes: [a] Increase of government spending by 5 per cent of GNP (standardised across models).
[b] Fiscal shock originating in the USA.
[c] Fiscal shock originating in Japan.

e_A, MCM and MultiMod, trade weighted; MSG2, yen–US$.
e_B, MCM and MSG2, US$–yen; MultiMod, trade weighted.
CA, MCM, billion US dollars; MultiMod and MSG2, as percentage of GNP.

A, USA; B, Japan.

Table 15.3 Monetary expansion[a]

| | USA[b] | | | | Japan[c] | | | |
| | Year 1 | | Year 4 | | Year 1 | | Year 4 | |
	MultiMod	MSG2	MultiMod	MSG2	MultiMod	MSG2	MultiMod	MSG2
y_A	+4.5	+4.2	+2.2	+0.7	+0.0	+0.0	−0.2	−0.1
p_{dA}	+1.0	+3.2	+8.9	+8.8	+0.0	−0.3	+0.2	+0.1
r_{dA}	−3.2	−4.6	−0.7	−0.8	−0.1	−0.2	+0.1	+0.0
e	−12.6	−	−4.0	−	+2.9	−	+1.0	−
CA_A	−0.7	+0.3	+0.5	+0.0	+0.1	+0.0	−0.1	+0.0
y_B	−0.3	−0.5	−0.9	+0.0	+4.3	+4.2	+1.0	+0.1
p_{dB}	+0.2	−0.6	+0.7	−0.2	+1.2	+3.2	+9.1	+10%
r_{dB}	−0.1	−1.2	+0.5	−0.6	−3.3	−5.4	−0.5	+0.0
e	+6.7	+15.0	+1.6	+10.0	−13.0	−15.5	−4.2	−10.0
CA_B	+0.1	−0.5	−0.3	+0.1	+0.0	+1.4	+0.0	+0.0

Sources: See text.
Notes: [a] Increase in money stock by 10 per cent.
[b] Originating in USA.
[c] Originating in Japan.

NIESR in the UK, the US Fed MCM, the IMF MultiMod, the OECD Interlink model and Taylor's model. (For a very brief description of these models, see Bryant (1988).)

In general, not surprisingly, he reports similar tendencies to those reported above. In reporting the effects of fiscal expansion on the exchange rate, Bryant notes that in five out of the six models there is initially an appreciation of the currency as predicted by most theory. In one, however (the OECD Interlink), there is a devaluation which he explains in terms of an *expected* ultimate devaluation. (See on this Chapter 30.)

16

A three-country model and the European Monetary System

INTRODUCTION

The two-country model presented in previous chapters is useful in illuminating inter-actions between large countries, e.g. the USA, Germany and Japan, or between one very large country, such as the USA and the rest of the world. The vast majority of member countries of the OECD, however, are not large. If we are interested in analysing the ways in which large countries impact on smaller countries, a broader three-country framework is needed, one in which the world is composed of two very large economies and, as well, a smaller one which is linked by trade and finance to the two larger economies. As we shall see, such a framework is much more flexible and indeed allows us to deal in a much more realistic way, in today's world, with the macro impacts of very large economies on smaller economies (see Argy *et al.* 1989).

As already noted, we will examine a world which is composed of three economies: C is the smaller economy; A and B are, as previously, the larger economies (to be defined). We also assume again, as previously, that A's and B's currencies float *vis-à-vis* one another. This more or less reflects the real-world situation today. At the same time, within this framework, C could adopt any one of a whole range of potential exchange rate regimes.

First C may peg its currency to A. This is the case, for example, of Austria, whose currency has been pegged to the deutschmark for some fifteen years at least. It is also largely true of most EMS member countries, outside Germany, which are effectively also pegged to the deutschmark. In these instances, A would represent Germany while B appropriately would be the USA. C could be any one of these smaller economies.

Second, C could float (with or without some exchange rate management). In today's world (end 1992), there are several smaller OECD member countries that fall into this category: Australia, New Zealand, Switzerland, Canada, Sweden, Norway and Finland. The UK and Italy have now also joined this group (Chapter 4).

Third, C could peg to a 'basket' of the two currencies A and B. Until late 1992 the Nordic countries fell into this general classification.

Throughout this chapter, we again adopt the assumption that there is perfect asset substitution. We simplify further by assuming that there is a single *world* interest rate, determined by the macro policies of the two larger economies (as we saw in Chapters 13–15) and that the smaller economy A has to absorb this world interest rate determined abroad.

In dealing with the small country, we again distinguish short- and medium-run adjustment and focus on only two potential exchange rate regimes: a peg to a single currency and a float. This covers most smaller OECD member countries.

THE MODEL

We call the third country C and model country C as follows.

Demand for goods

$$y_C = b_1\phi_1 y_A + b_1\phi_2 y_B - b_3 r_w - b_1 b_4(\phi_1 + \phi_2)\,[\,p_{dC} - \beta_2(e^C_A + p_{dA})$$
$$- (1 - \beta_2)(p_{dB} + e^C_B)\,] \tag{1}$$

Money market

$$m_C = b_5 y_C - b_6 r_w + p_{dC} \tag{2}$$

Labour markets/production

$$y_C = -b_7(w_C - p_{dC}) \tag{3}$$
$$w_C = p_C \tag{4}$$
$$p_C = b_{15} p_{dC} + (1 - b_{15})p^* \tag{5}$$
$$p^* = \beta_2(p_{dA} + e^C_A) + (1 - \beta_2)(p_{dB} + e^C_B) \tag{6}$$

Exchange rate definition

$$e^C_B = e^C_A + e^A_B \tag{7}$$

Additional notation

e^C_A C's exchange rate relative to A's (units of C per unit of A)

e^C_B C's exchange rate relative to B's (units of C per unit of B)

e^A_B A's exchange rate relative to B's (units of A per unit of B)

p^* import price facing C in C's currency

b_1 $1/(1 - \pi_6 + \pi_7)$

b_{15} $1 - \phi_1 - \phi_2$

β_2 C's exports to A as a share of total exports

β_4 Marshall–Lerner condition

ϕ_1 C's exports to A as a share of GNP

ϕ_2 C's exports to B as a share of GNP

π_6 marginal propensity to spend out of output

π_7 marginal propensity to import

p_C consumer price index in C

p_{dC} the price of home goods in C

This small-country model now needs to be integrated with the model of the two large economies presented in the previous chapters. We have a world comprising three economies, two large (A and B) and one small (C).

The real demand for goods is a function of output in each of the two larger economies (with trade weights attaching to each), of the world interest rate (which is determined abroad but given to the hypothetical third country) and of the real trade-weighted exchange rate. Money and labour markets are modelled as in the larger economies.

We want now to analyse the effects of policy disturbances, primarily originating abroad (in A or B), on C's economy. We again distinguish a short-run from a medium-run adjustment horizon. The short run is defined along MF lines with wages and prices assumed fixed in *all three economies*, the medium run as one where wages and prices are fully flexible, with wages now fully indexed to the consumer price index, *again in all three economies*.

If a policy disturbance originates abroad, in A or B, we already have the solutions for A and B from earlier chapters for the short and medium runs. The solutions can be used independently of C since C is too small to impact on A or B. We are thus able to follow a two-stage procedure: first, figure out what happens abroad (with outcomes already familiar), and second, use these outcomes to figure out how C is affected. As we shall see, how C is affected will depend critically on the exchange rate regime which C has adopted.

For a domestic policy disturbance, the analysis of the small-country case parallels previous analyses. The outcomes are as in Chapters 6 and 8 corresponding to what we defined as short- and medium-run horizons.

For an external policy disturbance originating in A or B, with flexible rates prevailing between A and B, we can solve the model for the short run for the two countries as previously. This will give us familiar solutions for e^A_B, y_A, y_B, r_w (the world interest rate), noting again that all wages and prices are fixed. For the medium run, we can solve for e^A_B, y_A, y_B, r_w, p_{dA}, p_{dB}.

To figure out how C is affected by policies originating in A or B, we need to define

(a) the origin of the policy change abroad and (b) the exchange rate regime in C. As already indicated, C could be floating or could be pegged to A.

Suppose C is pegged to A   Then y_A, y_B, r_w and e^A_B are predetermined abroad. e^C_A is also fixed. With e^C_A fixed and e^A_B predetermined, we can use (7) to solve for e^C_B ($=e^A_B$). Equation (1) can then be used to solve for y_C and equation (2) can be used to solve for m_C, which is now endogenous.

In the medium run, p_{dA} and p_{dB} are *also* predetermined. We can then use (1) and (3)–(6) to solve for y_A and p_{dA}; (2) again solves for m_C.

Suppose C floats *vis-à-vis* A and B   Variables in A and B are again predetermined. In the short run, we can use (1), (2) and (7) to solve for y_A, e^C_B and e^C_A. In the medium run, we add (3)–(6) to solve, additionally, for p_{dA}.

SOME RESULTS

Domestic macro policies

Suppose C were to shift from a flexible to a partially fixed rate (pegging to A). The shift produces the following, now familiar, results. *First*, C loses its capacity to conduct an independent monetary policy in the short or medium run. This means, in the short run, that it cannot use monetary policy for stabilisation; in the medium run it loses its capacity to have an independent *inflation* target.

Second, fiscal policy becomes *more powerful* in the short run. There is thus a trade-off: the loss of monetary policy for stabilisation is 'compensated' by the gain in fiscal policy for stabilisation. (Exchange rate crowding out disappears.) In the medium run, it is not quite so obvious that it can 'go it alone' on the fiscal front (e.g. because of current account effects).

Macro policies originating in one of the two large countries

C pegs to A

C's pegging to A carries two important implications. First, it is likely that the trade weights will change in favour of A. Second, by pegging its currency to A, C's currency in relation to B becomes A's mirror image.

It matters a great deal here where the macro policy originates, and whether adjustment is in the short or medium run.

We are interested in four potential disturbances: a monetary expansion originating in either A or B and a fiscal expansion originating in either A or B. We first deal with the case where wages and prices are fixed in all three economies.

Consider first a monetary expansion which originates in A. We know, from previous analysis, that A's currency will devalue (B's appreciating), A's output will rise, and B's will fall but by less than the increase in A; at the same time the world interest rate will fall.

Focusing on (1), r_w will fall, y_A will rise and y_B will fall. All prices are fixed and the variation in e^C_A is zero, so A's currency devalues in trade-weighted terms, devaluing relative to B.

Unless C's trade with B is overwhelmingly dominant, an extremely improbable case, the impulses are on balance expansionary. C's output will be stimulated by the net increase in output abroad, its trade-weighted devaluation and the fall in the world interest rate.

We can also readily see from (2) that with y_C increasing and r_w falling the money stock in C will rise.

What if the monetary expansion had originated in B? We now have the outcomes in reverse: output increases in B but falls in A (by less), B's currency now devalues (A's appreciating) while the world interest rate again falls.

Now the outcome in C is less clear-cut. World output has risen on balance; how A is affected by this depends on its trade links with A and B. If C is very strongly linked by trade with A and only very weakly with B it is conceivable that the net impact will be deflationary. There is also a second unambiguously deflationary impact from the fact that C's currency now appreciates in trade-weighted terms. On the other hand, the fall in the world interest rate will have positive effects on C's output. So, on balance, the impact on C's output is ambiguous; it is unambiguously *less* expansionary than in the first case, however.

Now suppose A engages in fiscal expansion. We know that A's currency will appreciate, B's devalue, output in A and B will increase (indeed equally in our simple framework) while the world interest rate will rise.

Focusing on the effects on C's output, it is evident that there are now some positive impulses (the increase in output in A and B) and some negative impulses (the trade-weighted appreciation and the rise in the world interest rate), with ambiguous net outcomes.

If B had undertaken the fiscal expansion, B's currency would have appreciated, A's devalued, output would increase (again equally) in A and B and the world interest rate would rise. The principal difference is that there are now two positive impulses (the increase in world output and the trade-weighted devaluation) and one negative impulse (the increase in the world interest rate), with a stronger possibility of a positive outcome on A's output.

In the medium run, with wages and prices fully flexible, the outcomes are much more straightforward. If the monetary expansion originates in A, we have the familiar result that prices increase proportionately in A; A's currency also devalues proportionately relative to B. Output in A and B as well as the world interest rate are all unchanged. C, not surprisingly, imports A's inflation, devaluing proportionately relative to B.

If the monetary expansion originates in B, C is now fully protected, as is A, from B's inflation.

Suppose we had a fiscal expansion originating in A. This case is slightly more complicated. To understand what might happen here, suppose $\Delta y_A = -\Delta y_B$ (the result from Chapter 14) and $\phi_1 = \phi_2$ (the trade weights are the same). From (1) we then have

$$y_C = -b_3 r_w - \pi_{10}\text{ertw} \tag{8}$$

where ertw is the real trade-weighted exchange rate (a rise implying a real appreciation) and

$$\pi_{10} = b_1 \beta_4 (\phi_1 + \phi_2)$$

We also know from (3)–(6) that

$$y_C = b_7(1 - b_{15})\text{ertw} \tag{9}$$

Combining (8) and (9) it follows that, if a fiscal expansion raises the world interest rate, output in C must fall; at the same time there must be a real trade-weighted devaluation of C's currency.

These real outcomes are particularly interesting because they are both (a) independent of the exchange rate regime and (b) independent of the *source* of the fiscal shock.

C floats

This is essentially the position the UK was placed in at the end of 1992.

We can find the solution for output in the short run in C for any shock abroad directly from (2). With both m_C and p_{dC} fixed the world interest rate determines what happens to C's output. If the world interest rate rises (falls) A's output necessarily must rise (fall).

So for a monetary expansion abroad from whatever source output in C must fall; on the other hand for a fiscal expansion abroad output in C must rise.

To understand what is happening here we can now return to equation (1). With fixed prices we have

$$y_C = b_1\phi_1 y_A + b_1\phi_2 y_B - \beta_3 r_w + b_1\beta_4(\phi_1 + \phi_2)[\beta_2 e^C{}_A + (1 - \beta_2)e^C{}_B] \tag{1a}$$

where the last expression is C's trade-weighted exchange rate.

Suppose, to simplify, that $\phi_1 = \phi_2$. If there is a monetary expansion abroad, we know that output in C must fall. Output abroad rises and the world interest rate falls and so on these two counts, according to equation (1a), output should rise; it follows that there must be a trade-weighted appreciation sufficient to offset these influences and push output down. With interest rates down abroad there is now a large inflow of capital which, in turn, provokes the appreciation and it is this which ultimately reduces C's output.

We have also seen that a fiscal expansion abroad must raise output in C. We can again use equation (1a) to figure out the effects on the trade-weighted exchange rate. The reader can readily verify that the effect is strictly ambiguous (y_C rises, y_A, y_B rise, r_w rises) although it is likely that there will be a trade-weighted devaluation of C's currency.

Consider now the medium run when all wages and prices are flexible. C is now totally protected from a monetary expansion originating in either A or B. If, for example, there is a monetary expansion in A, A's currency devalues proportionately relative to B and A's prices also rise proportionately. A's interest rate and output are unchanged as are also B's. B's currency appreciates proportionately. C is placed in a position similar to B. Its currency appreciates in relation to B to offset B's higher inflation.

For a fiscal expansion in A or B, as already noted, we have *real* outcomes which are identical to the case where C is pegged to A.

APPLICATION OF THE THREE-COUNTRY FRAMEWORK

In principle, the framework could be applied to two cases: first, the case of a regime change, such as that adopted by members of the EMS; second, the case of a hypothetical regime change, e.g. if Australia and New Zealand, who currently float independently, joined a regional trade–monetary bloc dominated by Japan.

We limit our discussion to the first. On the second, see Argy *et al*. (1989).

The European Monetary System

Domestic policies

Theory says that on joining the EMS countries lose their monetary independence but gain greater fiscal independence.

The loss of monetary independence for EMS countries outside Germany is now a self-evident truth. In early 1992, for example, when the UK and French economies were in recession and the monetary authorities' hands were tied, there were loud calls from various circles in both countries that *increased* reliance should therefore be placed on fiscal policy not only because of the loss of monetary policy but because, too, fiscal policy was more powerful (see for example Brittan 1992).

Some rough evidence that fiscal policy is more effective under fixed than under flexible rates comes from the IMF MultiMod simulations, e.g. fiscal policy is more powerful in France and Italy than it is (was) in the UK (when she had flexible rates) (Masson *et al*. 1990).

External policies

Consider again what happened at the end of 1991 and early 1992 to monetary policy.

At the time, as noted, France and the UK were in substantial recession. Both, as members of the EMS, were tied to the deutschmark, sterling having at the time a wider band of exchange rate flexibility.

The USA was also in recession and implemented an easy monetary policy, lowering its own official rates on a number of occasions. Germany, on the other hand, was very concerned about its own inflation rate (of some 4 per cent); it was also very concerned about excessive wage claims which were in the pipeline. Germany's economy, whilst slowing down, was not in recession. Germany's independent central bank decided to raise its interest rates. This understandably upset its EMS partners who mostly followed suit, raising their own rates in line with Germany's. (The UK did not raise its rates but would have liked to *lower* them. France did raise hers.)

To focus on France, it was subjected to opposing influences. Germany's tight monetary policy had a deflationary effect on the French economy. The easier monetary policy in the USA would have had ambiguous effects on France, as we saw.

Consider in this context some short-run MultiMod simulations (Masson *et al.* 1990). An expansion in the German money supply has strong positive effects on output in France. According to our model, if the country *floated* its output ought to fall. (In fact, however, the UK (which was and currently is again floating) experiences a *small* increase in output.)

We also would predict that an expansion in the US money supply would have a negative effect on German output, which is confirmed, but an ambiguous effect on France (where there is a very small increase in output).

Our framework would also predict that a large German fiscal expansion would have positive effects on German output, which it does, but ambiguous effects on France's output (in France there is a very small drop in output). Output should also, and indeed does, drop in the UK (which, to repeat, was floating).

A US fiscal expansion ought to raise output in Germany but has ambiguous effects in France (on balance output should drop by less or rise by more). In fact, output rises in Germany and in France.

17

A two-sector model of a small economy with flexible exchange rates

INTRODUCTION

As we noted in Chapter 7 the MF model assumes that a single type of good is produced in the economy, which in turn is competitive with a similar good produced abroad. An alternative approach, also widely used in the literature, is to take as a starting point that the economy produces two types of goods, not one: a traded good and a non-traded good. Traded goods are assumed to be perfectly competitive with similar goods produced overseas and hence *sell at the same price when expressed in a common currency* (the so-called 'law of one price'). By contrast, non-traded goods, such as services, housing, are sheltered from overseas competition and their price is assumed to be determined by demand and supply. (Two-sector models are to be found in Prachowny (1984), Dornbusch (1975), Corden (1977) and Montiel (1987).)

The MF model of one good and the two-sector model represent polar cases. Neither case exactly replicates real small economies. The two-sector model makes the important distinction between two types of goods; evidence that the distinction is an important one in reality comes from the fact that prices of the two types of goods do diverge (Prachowny 1984). The MF model, on the other hand, dictates that the price of the single good is the same.

The assumption of the law of one price, however, is too extreme; small economies do not simply produce a traded good which is homogeneous and of which at the same time they are a very small producer in world markets. They tend to produce a differentiated product for which the law of one price would be inappropriate; moreover, even when they produce a homogeneous product they are often a substantial producer in world markets.

The two-sector model also assumes that there is a *single* traded good which is both importable and exportable. This is clearly unrealistic. Some models assume that in addition to a non-traded good there are two traded goods produced or available for consumption: one an importable, another an exportable. See Allen and Kenen (1983) and Khan and Montiel (1987). In Allen and Kenen a foreign good is supplied to the small economy at a constant foreign currency price; there are also two domestic goods, one, the export good, is also sold to foreigners while the other, the non-traded good, sells only at home.

Our own framework throughout the book leans heavily on the MF-type assumption of a single good but, because of the large literature on the alternative, it was felt appropriate to expose the reader to such models. There are also important new insights provided by the model (e.g. the distinction made between government expenditure on traded and on non-traded goods). Analysis is again based on comparative statics.

THE MODEL

The goods market

$$yr = \alpha_{15}yr_n + (1 - \alpha_{15})yr_t \tag{1}$$

$$yr_{nD} = -a_1 r_d + a_2 yr + a_3 gr_n + \frac{a_4}{\alpha_{15}}(e - p_n) \tag{2}$$

$$yr_{tD} = -a_5 r_d + a_6 yr + a_7 gr_t - \frac{a_4}{1 - \alpha_{15}}(e - p_n) a_2 < 1 \qquad a_6 < 1 \tag{3}$$

The money market

$$mo = p + \alpha_5 yr - \alpha_{10} r_d \tag{4}$$

$$p = \alpha_{15}p_n + (1 - \alpha_{15})e \tag{5}$$

Production–labour markets

$$yr_n = a_8(p_n - w) \tag{6}$$

$$yr_t = a_{10}(e - w) \tag{7}$$

$$w = \bar{w} \tag{8}$$

$$w = p \tag{8a}$$

Equilibrium condition

$$yr_n = yr_{nD} \tag{9}$$

The balance of payments

$$\frac{B}{\text{yr}_{t0}} = 0 = \alpha_{14}(r_d - r^*) + (\text{yr}_t - \text{yr}_{tD}) \tag{10}$$

Notation

All variables are in logarithms except r_d, r^* and B/yr_{t0}.

yr	national production
yr_n	production of the non-traded good
yr_t	production of the traded good
yr_{nD}	real demand for the non-traded good
yr_{tD}	real demand for the traded good
mo	money stock
p	general price index
r_d	domestic interest rate
r^*	interest rate abroad
e	exchange rate (price of traded good)
p_n	price of non-traded good
B/yr_{t0}	balance of payments as a proportion of the initial production of the traded good
w	wage rate

The model presented above is a fairly general one which in principle accommodates different assumptions about wage flexibility and the degree of capital mobility.

The goods market is represented by equations (1)–(3). Equation (1) says that domestic production is a weighted average of the production of the non-traded and the traded good. The demand for each good in turn is a function of output, of government expenditure on the good, of the interest rate and of the relative price of the two goods. A devaluation, other things being equal, will increase the relative price of the traded good, reducing the demand for the traded good and increasing the demand for the non-traded good. The substitution leaves the level of aggregate real demand unchanged. (A special case is the one where $a_2 = a_6$ and $a_1 = a_5$.)

Equations (4) and (5) represent the money market. Equation (4) is a conventional money market. Equation (5) defines the general price level as a weighted average of the non-traded and the traded good.

Equations (6)–(8a) represent the production side of the economy. The supply of each good is a function of the own price relative to a (common) wage rate. The capital stock is assumed to be fixed whilst a homogeneous labour is assumed to be perfectly mobile between the two sectors. The wage rate is assumed to be either fixed (8) or indexed to the general price level (8a).

If the structural coefficients in the model are the same in the two sectors we have

$$\frac{a_1\alpha_{15}}{1-\alpha_{15}} = a_5 \qquad \frac{a_2\alpha_{15}}{1-\alpha_{15}} = a_6 \qquad \frac{a_8\alpha_{15}}{1-\alpha_{15}} = a_{10}$$

Equation (9) is the equilibrium condition. The demand for non-traded goods is always equal to the supply. p_n, the price of the non-traded good, is endogenous and clears the market. As we shall see in a moment, the demand for the traded good is not necessarily equal to its supply.

Equation (10) defines the balance of payments. Since we shall largely limit ourselves to the flexible rate case, we can impose the condition that the balance of payments is zero.

In these models the trade balance is equal to the excess of the nominal production of traded goods over the nominal demand for traded goods. Why is this?

$$Y = E\mathrm{Yr_t} + \mathrm{Yr_n}P_n \tag{11}$$

National product is the sum of the traded and the non-traded goods. National expenditure A is

$$A = \mathrm{Yr_{tD}}E + \mathrm{Yr_{nD}}P_n \tag{12}$$

Since the market for non-traded goods always clears, we have

$$\mathrm{Yr_n}P_n = \mathrm{Yr_{nD}}P_n \tag{13}$$

Also, the trade balance TB is

$$\mathrm{TB} = Y - A = E(\mathrm{Yr_t} - \mathrm{Yr_{tD}}) \tag{14}$$

The trade balance is the excess of the supply over the demand for traded goods. Equation (10) can then be arrived at by a procedure similar to that in Chapter 6, Appendix 1.

The complete model can, in principle, be reduced to four equations which solve for four endogenous variables p_n, yr, e and r_d in terms of mo, $\mathrm{gr_t}$ and $\mathrm{gr_n}$. The model is not easy to solve so we choose to simplify by assuming that asset substitution is perfect ($r_d = r^*$). (The more general case is left to the reader to solve.) This reduces the system to three equations only in yr, e and p_n, as follows.

The market for non-traded goods

$$a_8(p_n - w) = a_2\mathrm{yr} + a_3\mathrm{gr_n} + \frac{a_4}{\alpha_{15}}(e - p_n) \tag{15}$$

The money market

$$\mathrm{mo} = \alpha_{15}p_n + (1 - \alpha_{15})e + a_5\mathrm{yr} \tag{16}$$

National production

$$yr = \alpha_{15}a_8(p_n - w) + (1 - \alpha_{15})a_{10}(e - w) \tag{17}$$

w is either exogenous or endogenous, i.e. it solves as a weighted average of p_n and e. The policy variables are mo, gr_n and gr_t (the last absent from the system of equations – to be explained below).

The solutions are all shown in Table 17.1. We make here two further simplifications: the structural coefficients are the same and the two sectors are of equal weight, i.e. $1 - \alpha_{15} = \alpha_{15}$. This effectively means assuming that $a_1 = a_5$, $a_2 = a_6$, $a_8 = a_{10}$.

MONETARY AND FISCAL POLICY WITH FIXED WAGES

We consider here the effects of a monetary expansion, an increase in the government demand for traded goods and an increase in the government demand for non-traded goods. The solutions are all shown in Table 17.1.

A monetary expansion

A monetary expansion will increase national output, increase the price of the non-traded good and devalue the currency. With $a_{10} = a_8$ the devaluation will exceed the increase in the price of the non-traded good and the trade balance will be in surplus (as in the MF model).

What is the economic reasoning underlying this result?

Monetary expansion potentially lowers the domestic interest rate, provoking outflows of capital and a devaluation of the currency. The devaluation increases the price of the traded good. This in turn induces an increase in the production of the traded good; with the wage rate fixed the production of the traded good becomes more profitable. What happens in the market for non-traded goods? On the demand side there will be a substitution effect in favour of the non-traded good. The excess demand for the non-traded good will push up the price of the non-traded good and make its production more profitable. The higher national production increases the demand for both goods. In the end the price of the traded good will rise relative to

Table 17.1 The effects of monetary fiscal policies in a two-sector model (w fixed)

	yr	e	p_n
Monetary expansion	$\dfrac{\alpha_{15}\alpha_{10}(\alpha_{15}\alpha_{10} + 2a_4)}{k_2}$	$\dfrac{a_4 + a_{10}\alpha_{15}(1 - \alpha_{15}a_2)}{k_2}$	$\dfrac{a_4 + a_{10}\alpha_{15}^2 a_2}{k_2}$
gr_n	0	$-\dfrac{a_3\alpha_{15}^2(a_5 a_{10} + 1)}{k_2}$	$\dfrac{a_3\alpha_{15}^2(1 + a_{10}\alpha_5)}{k_2}$

Note: $k_2 = \alpha_{15}(1 + a_{10}\alpha_5)(\alpha_{15}a_{10} + 2a_4)$.

the price of the non-traded good and there will be some increased production of the two goods. At the same time, there will tend to be an excess supply of traded goods, i.e. a trade balance surplus.

Referring to (15)–(17) it is readily seen that the solutions will equilibrate the three markets. The monetary expansion is absorbed by the increase in the general price level and the increase in output (16). The increase in output is made up of some increase in the production of the non-traded and the traded good. Finally, we can rewrite (15) as

$$\frac{a_{10}\alpha_{15} + a_4}{\alpha_{15}}\, p_n = a_2 \text{yr} + a_3 \text{gr}_n + \frac{a_4}{\alpha_{15}}\, e \tag{18}$$

With both e and yr up and gr_n fixed it is seen that p_n must also increase.

An increase in government expenditure on traded goods

gr_{tD} does not appear in the system of equations (15)–(17). An increase in gr_{tD} will leave all the endogenous variables yr, e and p_n unchanged. It will, however, worsen the trade balance.

What happens here is very straightforward. With e fixed, the production of the traded good will be unchanged. Nor will there be any substitution effect on the demand side. With the production of the traded goods fixed, an increase in government expenditure on traded goods will manifest itself in an excess demand for traded goods which will spill over into an equivalent reduction in exports (or an increase in imports).

An increase in government expenditure on non-traded goods

If we make the assumption that $a_8 = a_{10}$ an increase in government expenditure will leave national production unchanged but there will be an appreciation of the domestic currency and an increase in the price of the non-traded good.

It is readily seen from the money market equation (16) that with mo and yr both fixed

$$p_n = -e \tag{19}$$

This is confirmed in Table 17.1.

There will now only be a substitution effect in production. The production of the non-traded good will increase at the expense of the traded good. At the same time there will be a substitution effect on the demand side in favour of the traded good. There is also an increase in government expenditure on the non-traded good; on balance there is some excess demand for the non-traded good which pushes up its price. The increased demand is matched by some increase in supply. There is also an excess demand for the traded good (the substitution effect on the demand side combined with a fall in the production of the traded good); this will manifest itself in a deficit in the trade balance.

All in all these results are consistent with the MF model. Fiscal expansion with perfect asset substitution has no real output effects. Fiscal expansion (on non-traded goods) leads to an appreciation of the currency. Monetary expansion has output effects and leads to a devaluation.

MONETARY AND FISCAL POLICY WITH FLEXIBLE WAGES

Inspection of equations (15), (16) and (17) reveals that if wages are fully indexed we shall have a result for a monetary expansion which exactly parallels the extended MF model with flexible wages and prices. The general price level increases proportionately, the currency devalues proportionately, and the price differential and the level of output are both unchanged. The trade balance will also be unchanged.

Substituting the equation for the wage rate into (17) will readily demonstrate that if $a_8 = a_{10}$ the level of production cannot change. From (16) then we can see that the general price level will rise proportionately. Equation (15) establishes that the real exchange rate will not change.

What happens if there is an increase in government expenditure on non-traded goods? Substituting again for w in (17) establishes that if $a_8 = a_{10}$ the level of output will not change. We also have from (16) $e = -p_n$, and from (15) (after substituting for w)

$$p_n = -\frac{a_3\alpha_{15}}{a_{10}\alpha_{15} + 2a_4} \, \mathrm{gr}_n \tag{20}$$

There will be an appreciation of the currency and the price of non-traded goods will rise.

Before we complete this chapter we might note two more points. If the exchange rate were fixed we could use (15) and (17) to solve for p_n and gr (for fixed and flexible wages). Equation (16) would then solve for the money stock, which is endogenous.

Suppose the exchange rate were a policy instrument and suppose too that the wage rate was fully indexed. We would now replicate the result of Chapter 8. The level of output and the real exchange rate would be unchanged, and the home price level and the money stock all increase proportionately. Thus despite the change in the model the result of Chapter 8 is confirmed.

Part III

OPEN ECONOMY MODELS –
DYNAMIC ANALYSIS

Part II was a review of open economy models found in the literature. The analysis undertaken then was comparative statics. Part III introduces the reader to some dynamic analysis, albeit at a relatively simple level. Part V will develop the dynamic analysis further, in the context of models which are more complex.

There are five chapters in Part III. Chapters 18 and 19 summarise two of the best known dynamic models of an open economy: those of Dornbusch and of Branson. These two models address the same question – the dynamic effects of a monetary expansion under flexible rates – but use quite different models. Chapter 20 presents a simple dynamic model of the effects of an expansion in the fiscal deficit.

Chapter 21, again in the context of a model, looks at the implications of accommodating J curves into an extended MF type model. The dynamics here are confined to the short run and the long run only. Finally, Chapter 22 looks at the effects of a disinflationary monetary policy on the path of inflation and unemployment.

18

Dynamic effects of a monetary expansion under flexible rates – the Dornbusch 1976 model

INTRODUCTION

Dornbusch published a seminal paper in 1976 which has since, deservedly, been very widely cited. Dornbusch's model of a small economy provides an excellent illustration of the dynamic effects of an unanticipated change in the money supply on prices, exchange rates and interest rates, assuming expectations are rationally formed. We propose in this chapter to present its key features, highlighting particularly the long-run results, the instantaneous results and the time path of adjustment towards the longer run.

Dornbusch's model has had wide appeal for a number of reasons. First, it is a model which is at once simple, readily understood and elegant. Second, in analysing the dynamic effects of a monetary expansion, an important distinction is made between an initial phase during which only financial variables adjust and a later phase during which the real economy begins to adjust. In Dornbusch a monetary expansion instantly adjusts interest rates and exchange rates; later the price level begins to respond to the monetary expansion. This appears to conform to one's own observations of the real world.

Third, Dornbusch also assumes that the public's expectations about exchange rates are fully rationally formed. In Dornbusch this implies that, having observed an increase in the money stock, they know the *end* result; they also know the time path of adjustment of the economy towards this end point. (In short, they have perfect foresight.)

Fourth, in the interests of simplicity, Dornbusch, in the body of the paper, assumes throughout that output is fixed at its full employment level; he also disregards any stock accumulation flowing from any changes to the current account. So, in fact, the only 'real' adjustment that occurs in the later stages is the price adjustment.

Fifth, Dornbusch shows, given his basic framework, that the exchange rate must initially overshoot its long-run level. This 'exchange rate overshoot' result is one of the best known and most widely cited features of his model. It is also, again, an appealing result since it appears to conform to the real world, where we frequently observe what looks like excessive exchange rate movement.

Sixth, Dornbusch assumes that prices are sticky in the short run but ultimately adjust fully to the increase in the money stock. Dornbusch's long-run results, that prices will increase in proportion, that interest rates will return to their original levels and that the currency will also devalue in proportion, are identical to our own results in Chapter 3. They are also in essence classical.

DORNBUSCH'S MODEL

$$yr_d = -\alpha_4 r_d + \alpha_1 (e - p_d) \tag{1}$$

$$mo - p_d = \alpha_5 yr - \alpha_{10} r_d \tag{2}$$

$$r_d - r^* = {}_t E_{et+1} - e \tag{3}$$

$${}_t E_{et+1} - e = \alpha_{30} (\bar{e} - e) \tag{4}$$

$$p_{d+1} - p_d = \pi_{12} (yr_d - \overline{yr}) \tag{5}$$

Notation

All variables are in logarithms except the interest rate.

yr_d	real demand for goods
$\overline{yr}$	full employment level of output
mo	money
p_d	domestic price level
yr	level of output (fixed)
r^*	foreign interest rate
r_d	domestic interest rate
${}_t E_{et+1}$	exchange rate expected in the next period corresponding to the maturity of the interest rate
$\bar{e}$	long-run rate
e	spot rate

Equations (1) and (2) have been used previously (Chapter 8): (1) represents the real demand for goods; (2) is the money market equation. Equation (3) embodies the assumption of perfect asset substitution as in Chapter 14. Equation (4) says that the rate expected in the next period is the current rate plus some proportion of the gap between the long-run rate (assumed to be rationally arrived at) and the current spot rate. α_{30} represents the rate at which the exchange rate converges towards its equilibrium rate. The smaller α_{30} is, the slower the adjustment. For example, if $\alpha_{30} = 1$ ($_tE_{et+1} = \bar{e}$) adjustment occurs within one period; if $\alpha_{30} < 1$ only some of the gap will be closed within one period.

Equation (5) represents the supply side of the economy: the rate at which prices change is a function of the gap between the real demand and the full employment output. Prices are assumed to respond with a one-period lag to the excess demand. π_{12} is a measure of the speed of adjustment of prices to the excess demand. The smaller π_{12} is, the slower the adjustment.

We now proceed as follows. We first find the long-run solution for an unanticipated change in the stock of money. We then use this solution to arrive at the instantaneous effects of a change in the stock of money (i.e. during our financial adjustment phase). Finally, we ask how the economy behaves after the financial adjustment phase until the long-run solution is reached.

THE LONG-RUN RESULT

We consider here the long-run effects of a permanent increase in the stock of money.

In the long run $_tE_{et+1} = e$ and $\mathrm{yr_d} = \overline{\mathrm{yr}}$. At the same time, the rate of inflation in (5) becomes zero and the interest rate levels with the foreign interest rate (which is given). With $\mathrm{yr_d}$ and r_d fixed it follows from (1) that $\Delta e = \Delta p$. From (2) also with yr and r_d fixed $\Delta p = \Delta$mo. In the long run, therefore, an increase in the stock of money increases prices proportionately, devalues the currency in the same proportion (thus leaving the real exchange rate unchanged) and also leaves the interest rate unchanged. By assumption output does not change. So to sum up we have

$$\Delta\bar{p} = \Delta\bar{e} = \Delta\mathrm{mo} \qquad \text{and} \qquad \Delta r_d = 0 \tag{6}$$

This is of course exactly the same result we reached in Chapter 8.

In dealing with instantaneous effects in the next section we assume that this long-run result is known (i.e. that expectations are rationally held).

INSTANTANEOUS EFFECTS

Immediately after the increase in the stock of money only financial variables change. The two financial variables in this model are the interest rate and the exchange rate. So we focus in this section on how the interest rate and the exchange rate respond to the increase in the money stock.

We are particularly interested in what happens to the exchange rate and in whether or not it will overshoot its long-run level as in (6) above.

To arrive at our result we use only the financial sector of the model: equations (2), (3) and (4). At this point, we repeat, prices are fixed, while output is fixed throughout the analysis. We substitute (4) into (3) and then into (2). Rearranging and recalling that with rational expectations $\Delta \bar{e} = \Delta \text{mo}$ we obtain

$$\frac{\Delta e}{\Delta \text{mo}} = \frac{1 + \alpha_{10}\alpha_{30}}{\alpha_{10}\alpha_{30}} > 1 \tag{7}$$

$$\left| \frac{\Delta r_d}{\Delta \text{mo}} \right| = -\frac{1}{\alpha_{10}} \tag{8}$$

The currency will devalue, overshooting its long-run level. At the same time from (8) we can see that the interest rate will fall. Why is this?

The expansion in the money supply lowers the interest rate; at the same time the public, having now observed the increase in the money supply, form an immediate rational expectation that ultimately the currency will devalue proportionately. So on both counts there will be a potential flight of capital; this in turn puts downward pressure on the currency. The potential flight can only cease when the devaluation overshoots its long-run mark; at this point there is an expected appreciation which should exactly offset the interest rate differential favouring overseas investment. (To appreciate this, imagine that the immediate devaluation equalled the long-run devaluation. There is now no expected devaluation but the interest rate is still lower than abroad and so capital outflows and the downward pressure on the currency will continue.)

Rearranging (7) we have

$$\frac{1/\alpha_{10}\alpha_{30} + 1}{1}$$

We can readily see that the degree of overshoot is a negative function of both α_{10} and α_{30}.

α_{10} is the interest sensitivity of money demand. From (8) we can see that the smaller α_{10} is, the larger is the initial fall in the home interest rate. The larger the fall in the home interest rate the larger the gap between the home and the given foreign interest rate; the larger the gap the greater must be the expected appreciation of the currency. Another way of putting this is that the bigger the fall in the home interest rate the larger will be the potential outflow and hence the initial devaluation relative to the ultimate devaluation.

Also the smaller α_{30} is, the greater the exchange rate overshoot. To understand this, note that the interest rate differential reflects the expected appreciation *over the next period* (equation (3)). The smaller α_{30} is, the longer the expected adjustment as in (4), and so the *ultimate* expected appreciation is correspondingly larger.

THE DYNAMICS OF ADJUSTMENT

It may be useful here to proceed first with what is essentially a verbal presentation of the dynamics of adjustment and second with a more technical explanation.

Verbal explanation

In the wake of the initial money stock adjustment the interest rate falls and there is a (strong) real devaluation. From (1) we can see that real demand increases. From (5) this starts putting upward pressure on the price level. In turn, given the new money stock, and given the level of output, from (2) the rising price level now puts upward pressure on the home interest rate; in turn, this begins to narrow the gap between the domestic and the foreign interest rate. Clearly so long as the price level has not caught up with the devaluation and the interest rate is below its initial level there is some excess demand and prices continue to rise. This persists until the real devaluation is zero and the original interest rate is restored.

Figure 18.1 summarises these findings. All variables start at q_0. In the initial period the exchange rate has overshot, the price level is unchanged while the interest rate has dropped. After that the exchange rate appreciates and the price level and the interest rate rise. At q_4 all variables have reached their equilibrium levels. The interest rate returns to its original level, the price level rises and the currency devalues proportionately. The exchange rate and the price level reach equilibrium at q_1.

It is worth noting that the interest rate climbs back because prices are now rising. At the same time as the interest rate rises the gap *vis-à-vis* the foreign rate falls, requiring a smaller expected appreciation. This is exactly what happens because the currency gradually appreciates, reducing the expected appreciation.

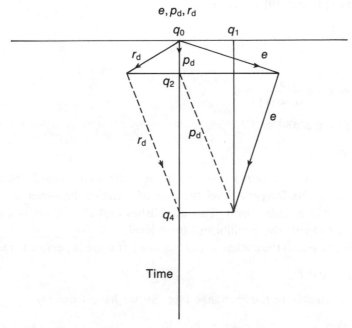

Figure 18.1 Paths of adjustment of prices, exchange rates and interest rates following an expansion in the money supply

It is also worth noting an unusual feature of the model dynamics which is that as prices rise the currency will actually be progressively *appreciating*.

Technical analysis

To understand the dynamics of adjustment, we proceed as follows. To begin, substitute (1) into (5) dropping $\overline{yr}$ which is given.

$$\dot{p}_d = -\alpha_4 \pi_{12} r_d + \alpha_1 \pi_{12} e - \alpha_1 \pi_{12} p_d \tag{9}$$

where $\dot{p}_d$ is the *rate* of inflation. The next step is to eliminaste r_d and e. From (2)–(4) (dropping r^*) we have

$$r_d = -\frac{1}{\alpha_{10}} \, \text{mo} + \frac{1}{\alpha_{10}} \, p_d \tag{10}$$

and again setting $\bar{e} = \text{mo}$

$$e = \text{mo} - \frac{1}{\alpha_{30}} r_d \tag{11}$$

or

$$e = \left| \frac{1 + \alpha_{10}\alpha_{30}}{\alpha_{10}\alpha_{30}} \right| \text{mo} - \frac{1}{\alpha_{10}\alpha_{30}} p_d \tag{12}$$

Substituting (10) and (12) into (9) we have

$$\dot{p}_d = k_1 (\text{mo} - p_d) \tag{13}$$

where

$$k_1 = \left| \frac{\alpha_4 \pi_{12}}{\alpha_{10}} + \alpha_1 \pi_{12} + \frac{\alpha_1 \pi_{12}}{\alpha_{10}\alpha_{30}} \right| > 0$$

We recall too that $\bar{p}_d = \text{mo}$ and so

$$\dot{p}_d = -k_1 (p - \bar{p}_d) \tag{14}$$

This is a differential equation with a negative coefficient. This means that if the price level exceeds (falls below) its long-run level the rate of inflation becomes negative (positive), i.e. the price level falls (rises). This establishes that the system is stable, ultimately converging towards the equilibrium price level.

What about the rate at which the exchange rate adjusts? If there is perfect foresight

$$_t E_{et+1} - e = e_{+1} - e = \dot{e}$$

where $\dot{e}$ is the rate of change in the exchange rate. So we have from (4)

$$\dot{e} = -\alpha_{30}(e - \bar{e}) \tag{15}$$

Equation (15) says that, if the currency is above its equilibrium level (meaning that the currency is too 'devalued'), its rate of change is negative, i.e. the currency will appreciate towards its long-run rate.

Consistency requires that $\alpha_{30} = k_1$. α_{30} and k_1 correspond to the rates at which the exchange rate and the price level respectively converge towards equilibrium. It is perhaps intuitively evident that the speeds of adjustment must be identical.[1] (Although the *rate* at which the gap is closed is the same the initial *gap* (i.e. after the financial adjustment phase) is not the same.)

From (2) (setting again mo $= \bar{p}_d$), (3) and (4) we also have

$$\bar{p}_d - p_d = -\alpha_{10}\alpha_{30}(\bar{e} - e) \tag{16}$$

which in turn using (14) and (15) we can write as

$$\dot{e} = -\frac{1}{\alpha_{10}k_1}\,\dot{p}_d \tag{17}$$

Finally, we turn to the interest rate. We have from (3), again assuming rational expectations,

$$r_d - r^* = \dot{e} \tag{18}$$

This also indicates the rate at which the domestic interest rate converges towards the foreign interest rate. In equilibrium, of course, when $\dot{e} = 0$, $r_d = r^*$.

THE FRENKEL–RODRIGUEZ MODIFICATION

Frenkel and Rodriguez (1982) relax Dornbusch's assumption of perfect asset substitution and demonstrate that if asset substitution is relatively weak there may be an exchange rate undershoot in the initial period. In all other respects the model is very similar to Dornbusch's. Output is fixed throughout and rational expectations are assumed. Wealth effects are also disregarded.

$$yr_d = -\alpha_4 r_d + \alpha_1(e - p_d) \tag{19}$$

$$mo - p_d = \alpha_5\overline{yr} - \alpha_{10}r_d \tag{20}$$

$$p_{d+1} - p_d = \pi_{12}(yr_d - \overline{yr}) \tag{21}$$

$$[\alpha_{13}(e - p_d) - \overline{yr}] + \alpha_{14}[r_d - (_tE_{et+1} - e)] = 0 \tag{22}$$

$$_tE_{et+1} - e = \bar{\alpha}_{30}(\bar{e} - e) \tag{23}$$

Equations (19)–(21) are similar to the Dornbusch model.[2] Equations (22) and (23) introduce the possibility of imperfect asset substitution. The second part of the left-hand side of (22) represents a conventional capital flow equation. Frenkel and Rodriguez interpret α_{14} as the speed of adjustment of capital flows to a change in expected relative returns. If $\alpha_{14} \to \infty$ the speed of adjustment is infinite and we have the case of perfect asset substitution. Frenkel and Rodriguez assume that in the long run α_{14} does approach infinity, so over longer periods there is perfect asset substitution.

Given this framework, it is readily seen that the 'long-run' solution is the same as Dornbusch's. r_d is exogenously given ($=r^*$) and so from (20) $\Delta \text{mo} = \Delta p$ and from (19) $\Delta e = \Delta p$.

It is the 'instantaneous' outcome that is different in Frenkel and Rodriguez and this comes entirely from their more general assumption about asset substitution.

Substituting (23) into (22), using (20) and (22) and recalling that prices are initially sticky, we have, again setting $\Delta \text{mo} = \Delta \bar{e}$,

$$\frac{\Delta e}{\Delta \text{mo}} = \frac{\alpha_{14} + \alpha_{10}\alpha_{14}\alpha_{30}}{\alpha_{10}\alpha_{13} + \alpha_{10}\alpha_{14}\alpha_{30}} \tag{24}$$

It is evident from (24) that overshooting will occur only if $\alpha_{14} > \alpha_{10}\alpha_{13}$. What does this condition mean?

Consider an expansion in the money supply. Domestic prices are initially fixed. The devaluation unambiguously improves the trade balance. Thus to secure equilibrium in the balance of payments there must be a matching outflow of capital. The fall in the domestic interest rate itself generates some outflow; at this point what happens to the spot rate itself, given the expected devaluation, depends on the degree of asset substitution. If it is relatively high the exchange rate has to overshoot because this creates an expected appreciation which partially offsets the lower domestic interest rate. At the limit if there is perfect asset substitution, $\alpha_{14} \to \infty$, we return to Dornbusch's result. If, however, asset substitution is low and say α_{13} high we may need an expected devaluation to reinforce the effects of a lower domestic interest rate. Thus the exchange rate may undershoot or overshoot.

One surprising feature of the Frenkel–Rodriguez model is that the initial real devaluation is allowed to affect the trade balance, virtually instantly, yet output remains fixed and the excess demand does not flow over into prices until the next period.

SOME BRIEF COMMENTS ON DORNBUSCH'S MODEL

We consider here only four questions briefly.

How is the excess demand removed in Dornbusch's model? Prices adjust gradually; at the same time, in the body of Dornbusch's paper, there is no change in production. In this particular model we have to suppose that any excess demand is accommodated by inventories or imports. Are they ever reinstated?

Again nothing whatsoever is said about the current account. Assume the current account is a negative function of output and a positive function of the real exchange rate. Observation of Figure 18.1 reveals that, for a while, there is a real devaluation. With output fixed the current account must improve. By definition this is offset by outflows of capital. In the longer run current account balance is restored. In the meantime, however, the stock of wealth will have increased and there will be higher interest receipts on the higher net stock of assets held abroad. These aspects are neglected in the model. (See also Chapters 19, 27 and 30.)

Dornbusch only analyses the case of unanticipated changes in money. What about the impacts of an anticipated change in the money supply? If a devaluation is expected in the next period, because monetary policy is expected to be easy, a devaluation will occur in advance of the change in the money supply. There may also be potential price effects in advance of the change in money. This case is analysed in detail in Chapter 24.

One 'nice' feature of Dornbusch's model is that the dynamics are extremely simple. Moving from the very short run to the longer run all three variables 'converge' gradually towards an equilibrium point. This is extremely unlikely to occur in reality. Empirical testing of a model similar to Dornbusch's suggests that the dynamics will be much more complicated (see Driskill 1981).

19

Branson's portfolio balance model – monetary expansion under flexible rates

INTRODUCTION

This chapter introduces the reader to the model in Branson (1977).

The model represents an application of the portfolio balance model presented in Chapter 10. It also provides an excellent illustration of how, using such a model, an economy adjusts dynamically to a monetary shock. In this respect it bears detailed comparison with Dornbusch's model. Branson and Dornbusch address the same question in their respective papers: how does an economy adjust over time to an exogenous increase in the money stock? However, the models they use are quite different and so, not surprisingly, they reach rather different results, although there are also many parallels between the two. Branson's model may be perceived as a complement to Dornbusch's: it fills gaps which are missing in Dornbusch but, on the other hand, it has weaknesses of its own, so in some other respects some issues are dealt with more elegantly in Dornbusch.

Because of its importance, we propose to present Branson's model in some detail. At the end, we shall make a comprehensive comparison of the Dornbusch and Branson models.

BRANSON'S PORTFOLIO BALANCE MODEL

Branson's portfolio balance model is a special case of the model presented in Chapter 10. There are three assets and the demand for each asset is determined by wealth and relative returns. The additional simplification introduced by Branson to the model is to eliminate the role of exchange rate expectations, by effectively assuming, as in the Mundell–Fleming (MF) model, that $Ee = E$. Also, since he is primarily interested in the effects of a domestic open market operation, the foreign interest rate does not change and hence can be dropped from the analysis. Output is also fixed in Branson (as in Dornbusch), so it too can be dropped. This leaves us with the truncated model as follows:

$$\frac{\text{Mo}}{\text{We}} = -b_2 r_d \tag{1}$$

$$\frac{B}{\text{We}} = b_7 r_d \tag{2}$$

$$\frac{EFA}{\text{We}} = -b_{12} r_d \tag{3}$$

where Mo is the money stock, B is the stock of bonds, FA is the bonds held abroad denominated in foreign currency, r_d is the home interest rate, E is the exchange rate, We is the stock of financial wealth and again We = Mo + B + EFA and $b_7 = b_2 + b_{12}$.

Branson also assumes, along with nearly all the literature in this area, that the country is a net creditor, and so the initial net foreign asset position is positive.

We note again here that wealth can change because of stock changes in its component parts and also, given stocks, because of a revaluation of net foreign asset holdings. Because the country is assumed to be a net creditor, a devaluation (appreciation) will unambiguously increase (reduce) the value of wealth.

Branson's concern is with the effects over time of an open market purchase, i.e. ΔMo = $-\Delta B$. The public absorb more money in their portfolio and give up an equivalent amount in bonds.

As in Dornbusch, there are two stages of adjustment. Initially, only financial markets adjust; the portfolio is thrown out of equilibrium by the open market purchase and exchange rates and interest rates have to adjust to restore equilibrium to the portfolio. In due course, the real sector will also adjust. In Branson the 'real' sector is represented by price level adjustment and by the adjustment to the current account. In sharp contrast to Dornbusch, current account adjustment is now an integral part of the adjustment process towards long-run equilibrium.

While the portfolio balance component of the adjustment process is well developed in Branson, the 'real' side of the economy is not formalised and indeed is presented in a somewhat *ad hoc* fashion, unlike in Dornbusch, who has a complete model, including an explicit real sector.

INSTANTANEOUS FINANCIAL ADJUSTMENT

We now analyse in somewhat more detail than we did in Chapter 10 the instantaneous financial effects of an open market purchase, using both mathematics and graphical analysis.

To begin, we differentiate totally all three equations of the model (taking initial values of the exchange rate as equal to unity):

$$\frac{1}{We} \Delta Mo - \frac{Mo}{We^2} \Delta We = -b_2 \Delta r_d \tag{4}$$

$$\frac{1}{We} \Delta B - \frac{B}{We^2} \Delta We = b_7 \Delta r_d \tag{5}$$

$$\frac{FA}{We} \Delta E + \frac{1}{We} \Delta FA - \frac{FA}{We^2} \Delta We = -b_{12} \Delta r_d \tag{6}$$

We can now substitute the individual components of wealth into each of the equations, i.e. $\Delta We = \Delta Mo + \Delta B + \Delta FA + FA_0 \Delta E$. Collecting terms this gives us

$$\frac{We - Mo}{We^2} \Delta Mo - \frac{Mo}{We^2} (\Delta B + \Delta FA + FA_0 \Delta E) = -b_2 \Delta r_d \tag{7}$$

$$\frac{We - B}{We^2} \Delta B - \frac{B}{We^2} (\Delta Mo + \Delta FA + FA_0 \Delta E) = b_7 \Delta r_d \tag{8}$$

$$\frac{We - FA}{We^2} \Delta FA + \frac{FA}{We}\left(1 - \frac{FA}{We}\right) \Delta E - \frac{FA}{We^2} (\Delta Mo + \Delta B) = -b_{12} \Delta r_d \tag{9}$$

We have three equations (7)–(9), only two of which (any two) allow us to solve for the two endogenous variables E and r_d. Equation (7) is the money market equation, (8) is the bond market equation and (9) is the foreign asset equation.

At this point we are only interested in the instantaneous effects of a money–bond swap. To solve mathematically we focus, as in Branson, on the bond and foreign asset markets, treating the money market as the residual equation.

Using (8) and (9) we have $\Delta Mo = -\Delta B$ and $\Delta FA = 0$. The equations simplify to

$$\frac{1}{We} \Delta B - \frac{B}{We^2} FA_0 \Delta E = b_7 \Delta r_d \tag{10}$$

$$\frac{FA}{We}\left(1 - \frac{FA}{We}\right) \Delta E = -b_{12} \Delta r_d \tag{11}$$

The solutions for E and r_d for a fall in the holdings of B are

$$\frac{\Delta r_d}{\Delta B} = \frac{We - FA}{We[b_7(We - FA) - b_{12}B]} > 0 \tag{12}$$

$$\frac{\Delta E}{\Delta B} = -\frac{b_{12}(We - FA)}{We(FA/We - FA^2/We^2)[b_7(We - FA) - b_{12}B]} \tag{13}$$

This says that an open market purchase will at once lower the interest rate and devalue the home currency. This result is similar to Dornbusch's.

Why is this? The public will find themselves with excess holdings of money and a shortage of bonds. The swap in itself leaves the *stock* of wealth unchanged. To restore balance the home interest rate will fall; at the same time there is a potential outflow of capital which now also depresses the currency. The devaluation has the effect of raising the domestic currency value of the stock of foreign assets.

These adjustments restore equilibrium to all three markets. Refer again to equations (1)–(3). The ratio of money to wealth will rise and this is consistent with the fall in the interest rate. The percentage increase in money has to be greater than the percentage increase in wealth (which comes from the revaluation of foreign assets). The ratio of bonds (whose volume has fallen) to wealth (which is revalued upwards) falls and this is again consistent with the fall in the interest rate and bond market equilibrium. Finally, the ratio of foreign asset holdings to wealth rises and this is also consistent with the fall in the bond rate. The rise in the ratio comes about because the initial ratio is less than unity and both the numerator and the denominator now rise by the same absolute amount (the revaluation of foreign assets); this means that the *proportionate* rise in the numerator exceeds the *proportionate* rise in the denominator.

These results can also usefully be illustrated graphically. We can represent the money market equation (7) across an $E-r_d$ space (Figure 19.1) (MM). It is readily seen that the positive slope of the schedule is

$$\frac{b_2 \mathrm{W}e^2}{\mathrm{MoFA}}$$

Given the existing stock of assets, as r_d increases the ratio of money to wealth needs to fall and this in turn requires a devaluation of the currency to raise the valuation of wealth.

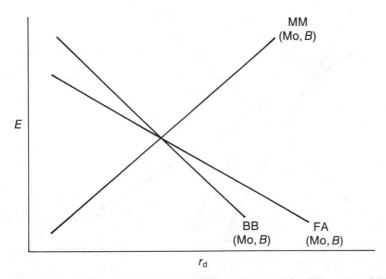

Figure 19.1 Equilibrium in the bond, money and foreign asset markets

With FA fixed in this initial period the shift variables are Mo and B. The bond market schedule BB represented by (8) has a negative slope of

$$\frac{b_7 we^2}{BFA}$$

A rise in the interest rate now requires an appreciation to increase the ratio of bonds to wealth, given the stock of all assets. Mo, B will again be the shift variables.

Finally, the foreign asset market schedule FA, derived from (9), has a negative slope of

$$\frac{b_{12}}{(FA/We)\,(1 - FA/We)}$$

It is readily shown that the slope of the BB schedule is larger (negative) than the slope of the foreign asset schedule (as shown in Figure 19.1).[1]

How will these schedules respond to an open market purchase? Consider the BB and FA schedules. From (8) it is seen that the BB schedule will shift to the left (with the stock of wealth unchanged, only the fall in bond holdings shifts the schedule). Why is this? Suppose E were unchanged; then the home interest rate has to *fall* to restore equilibrium in the bond market, with *smaller* bond holdings. Suppose, at the other extreme, that r_d is unchanged; then the currency must appreciate sufficiently to lower the value of foreign assets such that the ratio of the (lower) stock of bonds to wealth is unchanged.

Inspection of the foreign asset market equation reveals that the schedule will not

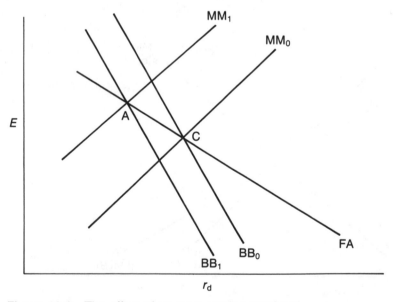

Figure 19.2 The effect of an open market purchase

shift (ΔMo $= -\Delta B$, ΔFA $= 0$). With BB$_0$ shifting to BB$_1$, the solution is found at A where the currency has devalued and the interest rate has fallen (Figure 19.2).

The reader can confirm that the (now residual) money market schedule will shift to the left to meet the other two schedules at A.

REAL ADJUSTMENT

We have completed the first stage of the analysis and can now move on to the second (and longer) phase. Throughout the analysis we note, again, that output is held fixed.

With the currency devalued and, at this point, prices unchanged, there is also now a real devaluation. This real devaluation in turn will open up a current account surplus. The current account surplus in turn means that households are accumulating foreign assets (FA) in their portfolios.

This again throws the portfolios out of equilibrium. The portfolio must absorb the given larger stock of foreign assets and we need to ask how this is going to impact on the exchange rate and the interest rate.

We can thus again use the portfolio balance model to figure out the adjustment to an increase in foreign asset holdings. Equations (7)–(9) can be used to analyse the effects of an increase in FA.

Using again (8) and (9) the solution for this special case is

$$\frac{\Delta r_d}{\Delta \text{FA}} = 0 \tag{14}$$

$$\frac{\Delta E}{\Delta \text{FA}} = -\frac{1}{\text{FA}} \tag{15}$$

The currency will appreciate proportionately to the increase in foreign asset holdings leaving the valuation of foreign assets unchanged; at the same time the interest rate will not change.

These adjustments will serve to equilibrate all three markets. With the money stock and wealth both unchanged the interest rate cannot change. Again with the stock of bonds and wealth unchanged the interest rate cannot change. Finally, the value of foreign asset holdings and wealth will not change, and so the interest rate cannot change.

The graphical representation is shown in Figure 19.3. The foreign asset market schedule FA will shift to the left. To see this imagine the exchange rate to be fixed. Then with foreign assets accumulating (numerator and denominator increasing by the same absolute amount) the ratio of foreign assets to wealth increases, requiring a drop in the home interest rate. Or at the other extreme, imagine that the interest rate is fixed. In this case the ratio of foreign assets to wealth cannot change and this requires that the currency appreciates sufficiently to restore the original value of foreign assets.

At the same time the bond market schedule BB will also shift to the left. Why is

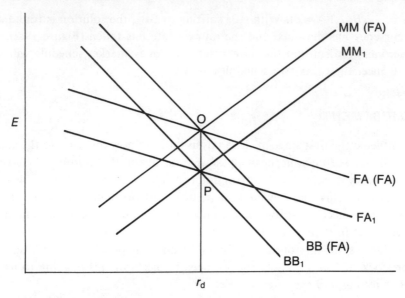

Figure 19.3   The effect of a current account surplus

this? If E were fixed this requires a fall in the interest rate to accommodate the fall in the ratio of bonds (which are unchanged) to wealth (which now rises). At the other extreme, if the interest rate is fixed, the currency must again appreciate to keep the value of foreign assets unchanged; this keeps the ratio of bonds to wealth unchanged.

The solution is shown in Figure 19.3. The economy moves from O to P. The reader can also verify that the money market schedule will shift to the right to meet the intersection of the new FA, BB schedules at P. At P the interest rate is unchanged but the currency appreciates.

What is the mechanism by which this result occurs? In the wake of the current account surplus households are holding an 'excess' supply of foreign assets in their portfolio. Because the stock of wealth has increased, only some proportion of this additional wealth will be held abroad, the balance being 'excessive'. Households will thus initiate potential sales of foreign assets in an effort to acquire, now, money and domestic bonds. This potential inflow will force an appreciation of the currency until the value of foreign assets is restored to the original level, at which point households will no longer hold an excess of foreign assets.

A very important point to make here is that in this period the currency begins to *reverse itself*. After the initial devaluation the currency begins to appreciate. Thus, as in Dornbusch, we observe an exchange rate overshoot. The reasons are quite different here, however. In Dornbusch the overshoot occurs because in the course of the initial money market adjustment the interest rate must fall below the foreign level; this in turn requires that there be an expected appreciation of the currency. Since the currency is expected ultimately to devalue in proportion to the increase in the money stock, the expected appreciation requires that the currency devalue by more than its ultimate devaluation. In Branson there is neither rational expectations nor perfect asset substitution. Branson's exchange rate overshoot comes from the fact that the initial devaluation opens up a current account surplus, which in turn will start reversing the movement in the currency.

In the meantime, while this adjustment is occurring, Branson tells us that the increase in the money stock will start pushing prices up.

LONGER-RUN ADJUSTMENT

In order to understand the adjustment from here on, we write down an equation for the current account, defined in foreign currency terms (which corresponds of course to the accumulation of foreign assets denominated in foreign currency).

$$\Delta \text{FA} = \pi_1 \left(\frac{E}{p_d} \right)_{-1} + (r^* \text{FA}_0)_{-1} \tag{16}$$

There are two components to the current account: the trade balance and the net investment earnings. The latter is equal to the interest rate on foreign assets (which is given) multiplied by the stock of net foreign assets held at the end of the previous period. Interest on foreign assets is thus assumed to be paid with a one-period lag.

The first component, the trade balance, is assumed to be a function of the real exchange rate (i.e. the nominal exchange rate adjusted by the home price level) lagged one period. This relationship was already implied in the analysis of the previous section: there we showed that the devaluation which occurs in the period of financial adjustment will open up a current account surplus in the next period. π_1 represents the trade elasticities.

We now take up the story where we left off in the previous section. We saw that in the first period of the second adjustment phase the emerging current account surplus will generate an appreciation of the currency (leaving at the same time the interest rate unchanged). In the next period again, drawing on (16) above, we can see that there will be two opposing forces acting on the current account: on the one hand the appreciation (in combination, as we shall see shortly, with the rising price level) will serve to *reduce* the current account surplus, provided of course that the Marshall–Lerner condition holds; on the other hand, the accumulation of foreign assets in the previous period will generate an *improvement* in net investment earnings abroad. The current account could thus go either way now. Stability requires that the former effect dominates, so the surplus is actually reduced. This is what will be assumed from here on.

In this next period, then, the current account surplus will be *smaller*: how much smaller depends on the trade elasticities and the foreign interest rate. The, now smaller, accumulation of foreign assets again needs to be absorbed by the portfolio; this in turn has results already analysed: a proportional appreciation, which again leaves both the value of wealth unchanged and an unchanged interest rate.

In the next period again a similar adjustment process takes place. The previous real appreciation will *further*, on balance, reduce the current account surplus, which again has to be absorbed by the portfolio.

It is now perhaps evident where this is leading us. Successive real appreciations continue to reduce the current account surplus. However, so long as a current account surplus exists *the portfolio is out of equilibrium*, requiring a further exchange rate adjustment. *This continues until the current account surplus is entirely eliminated. In equilibrium the current account will be zero.*

Imposing this condition on (16) above, we have

$$\pi_1 \frac{E}{P_d} = -r^* FA_0 \tag{17}$$

Since the investment earnings account will ultimately have improved, a zero current account requires that the trade balance be in deficit. Thus, ultimately, the exchange rate must appreciate in real terms sufficiently to open up a trade balance deficit which will *exactly* match the improvement in the earnings account. Monetary expansion ultimately *appreciates* the currency in real terms although, as we shall see in a moment, it devalues the currency in nominal terms.

Branson presents a potential scenario graphically and this is reproduced in Figure 19.4. The starting position is at $t(0)$ where $e^* = p^* = 1$. There is an instantaneous devaluation of the currency to e_1. At this point prices have not changed. The

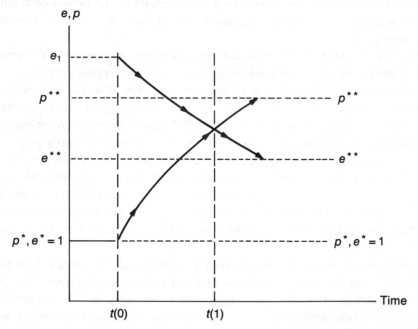

Figure 19.4   Branson: convergence to equilibrium following an open market purchase

currency now starts appreciating and prices also start rising. Suppose we reach point $t(1)$ where the nominal devaluation is exactly equal to the inflation, i.e. the real exchange rate is unchanged. (This is of course Dornbusch's result.) This cannot be an equilibrium because, although the trade balance is back to its original level, there is a surplus on the investment account and hence also on the current account. The currency thus continues to appreciate until the real appreciation is sufficient to offset the surplus on the investment account.

As already noted, a very important result here is that, as in Dornbusch, the currency initially overshoots, converging back towards a smaller ultimate devaluation.

Branson makes no further reference to the interest rate beyond the initial period, when the interest rate falls. What will happen to the interest rate? We saw earlier that a current account surplus will appreciate the currency but leave the interest rate unchanged. So it seems that the interest rate will stay at this lower level indefinitely.

One might question the result that the interest rate no longer changes beyond the initial point and stays indefinitely at its lower level, despite the fact that in the meantime prices have risen. The reason why Branson has this result is that prices, as we have already noted in Chapter 10, do not enter into the asset demands. This is a weakness to which attention has already been drawn. It also produces the unsatisfactory result that an increase in the stock of money can permanently lower the interest rate.

At the end of the day, what is the standing of the portfolio?

It turns out that the initial solution holds to the end. The money stock will have increased while the value of wealth will have increased only by the *initial* devaluation, the subsequent increases in the stock of foreign assets being neutralised by the progressive appreciations. This outcome is consistent with the ultimate drop in the interest rate. The stock of bonds falls while wealth increases, so the ratio of bonds to wealth falls, consistently with the fall in the interest rate. Finally, the ratio of foreign assets to wealth rises and this is also consistent with the drop in the interest rate.

WEAKNESSES AND STRENGTHS IN BRANSON

The model presented above has both strengths and weaknesses. Its simplistic elegance is attractive but this hides some weaknesses.

Branson's model is our first important exposure to a dynamic model which explicitly incorporates wealth. Its great strength is to show that stock adjustment underlying the current account developments requires that ultimately, in this context at any rate, the current account be zero. It also defines asset demands consistently, with the requirement that the sum of all financial asset holdings be equal to financial wealth. Also, and very importantly, it accommodates earnings on foreign assets in the adjustment process. Finally, Branson exploits the important distinction between asset adjustment, which is immediate, and longer-run real adjustment, which is driven by the requirement that the current account be zero.

On the other side of the balance sheet are some weaknesses. The real sector is not formally modelled; we are simply told that the price level comes under pressure but neither the demand nor the supply of goods is formalised, making it difficult to understand what is going on outside the monetary sector. The assumption that output is fixed is also restrictive. If wealth drives the monetary–portfolio sector, why does it not also drive the real sector? We have noted too the problem with the interest rate. The absence of prices in the simplified monetary–portfolio sector is a major weakness. Exchange rate expectations are assumed to be static, thus eliminating any role for expectations.

BRANSON AND DORNBUSCH COMPARED

We first consider parallels, next differences.

To repeat, Branson and Dornbusch address an identical question: the dynamic adjustment of the open economy to an increase in the money stock. Both distinguish an asset adjustment phase from a subsequent real phase. In both papers the immediate response to a money stock increase is a devaluation and a fall in the interest rate. In both papers, too, the currency initially overshoots, but as we noted the reasons underlying the reversal are different. In both papers output is assumed to be exogenously given (but Dornbusch does relax that assumption towards the end).

Beyond these parallels there are a number of very important differences:

a) Branson's model assumes imperfect asset substitution; Dornbusch assumes perfect asset substitution. Thus Dornbusch's model might be perceived as a special case of Branson's.

b) Dornbusch assumes perfect foresight and rationality; Branson disregards exchange rate expectations. In Dornbusch the end result plays some role in the asset adjustment phase but not so in Branson.

c) Dornbusch totally disregards any potential wealth effects; these last, however, play an integral role in Branson.

d) The end result in Dornbusch is the classical neutrality of money, prices rising and the currency devaluing proportionately. Thus the real exchange rate in the end is independent of the money stock. This is not so, however, in Branson where the real exchange rate appreciates. Thus we have the, superficially strange, result in Branson that a monetary expansion will ultimately appreciate the currency in real terms.

e) In both Dornbusch and Branson the current account is zero in long-run equilibrium. In Dornbusch this is implicit but is readily demonstrated from the fact that the real exchange rate is unchanged and output is exogenously given. In Branson the same result is necessitated by portfolio equilibrium.

f) The most important difference comes from the real adjustment. In Branson prices and the current account drive the real adjustment. As already noted, however, this

is not formalised in Branson. Dornbusch is explicit in this regard and the adjustment process is readily identifiable.

g) In Dornbusch as prices rise the interest rate creeps back, ultimately returning to
   its original level. This, however, does not occur in Branson. Despite the rising
   price level there is no feedback to the monetary sector.

20

The dynamic adjustment to a fiscal deficit – a simple framework

INTRODUCTION

How does an economy adjust over time to a fiscal expansion which takes the form of a *sustained* fiscal deficit? This chapter addresses this question, using a model which is simple but which nevertheless is capable of providing useful insights into what might happen in the real world.

Branson (1985) presents a model of a fiscal expansion under flexible rates, tracing its impact over time on exchange rates and the current account. The model is of particular interest for three reasons: first, it introduces an explicit risk premium into the dynamic analysis; second, it explicitly allows for interest payments on any cumulated external debt (as in the other Branson model of Chapter 19); third, it appears to provide a particularly useful framework which helps to explain the sharp real appreciation of the US dollar between 1982 and 1985, the subsequent even sharper real devaluation and the large and persistent current account deficit. (See also on this Sachs and Wyplosz (1984).)

BRANSON'S MODEL

The model is one which assumes that output is fixed. Moreover, in this particular paper all analysis is undertaken in real terms which allows Branson to disregard nominal and price adjustments (see, however, Branson 1988). As in Branson, the economy in question will be assumed to be that of the USA. Our actual presentation differs in several respects from Branson's but captures its essential spirit.

The goods market

As in Chapter 11, we start with the National Accounts definition:

$$(G - T) = (S - I) + \text{CAD} \tag{1}$$

where G is real government expenditure, T is real tax revenue, $S - I$ is real savings less real domestic investment and CAD is the real current account deficit. We are interested in the effects of an expansion in the budget deficit (i.e. the first bracketed expression) which is treated as exogenous in the analysis.

With output fixed, savings an increasing function of the home real interest rate, and investment a decreasing function of the interest rate, the excess of private savings over private investment is a positive function of the real interest rate (rr).

At the same time the current account deficit is a negative function of the real exchange rate (er) and a positive function of the cost of servicing borrowings from abroad (rrB, where B is the stock of debt to foreigners in domestic currency). The debt is assumed to be denominated in the home currency. So we can rewrite (1) as

$$G - T = \pi_1 \text{rr} - \pi_2 \text{er} + \text{rr}B \tag{2}$$

The financial sector

A key feature of Branson's model is to allow for a risk premium, which is an increasing function of foreign lending to the home economy, i.e. in his model foreigners' holdings of bonds in the home economy. At the same time, there is perfect capital mobility in the sense that capital is free to move into and out of the economy. However, the presence of a risk premium means that the model is one of *imperfect* asset substitution.

We can thus write

$$r_\text{d} - r^* = (_tE_{et+1} - e) + \delta B \tag{3}$$

The interest rate differential is equal to the expected rate of change in the exchange rate, adjusted now by the risk premium represented by the expression δB. This risk premium is an increasing function of the supply of dollar bonds to the rest of the world. It is now readily seen that in equilibrium with $_tE_{et+1} = e$ the domestic interest rate will exceed the foreign interest rate by a factor which depends on the supply of new bonds issued. Equation (3) can be rewritten in real terms:

$$(r_\text{d} - \dot{p}_\text{e}) - (r^* - \dot{p}_\text{e}^*) = (_tE_{et+1} - e) - (\dot{p}_\text{e} - \dot{p}_\text{e}^*) + \delta B \tag{4}$$

where $\dot{p}_\text{e}$ and $\dot{p}_\text{e}^*$ are, respectively, the domestic and foreign expected rates of inflation, both of which are exogenously given in the model. The first two bracketed expressions are real interest rates, the last two together the expected percentage change in the real exchange rate.

We can now rewrite (4) as

$$rr - rr^* = e\dot{e}r + \delta B \tag{5}$$

where $e\dot{e}r$ is the expected percentage change in the real exchange rate.

Using an equation for $e\dot{e}r$ which closely parallels Dornbusch's equation in Chapter 18 we have

$$e\dot{e}r = \phi(\overline{er} - er) \tag{6}$$

where $\overline{er}$ is the real long-run equilibrium exchange rate. Substituting (6) into (5) yields

$$rr - rr^* = -\phi er + \phi\overline{er} + \delta B \tag{7}$$

Graphical representation

This simple model, which nevertheless has considerable potential, can now be represented graphically. We show the combinations of rr (on the vertical axis) and er (on the horizontal axis) which will achieve equilibrium in the goods and financial markets (Figure 20.1).

Equation (2) represents the goods market equation. It is evident from (2) that given $G - T$ and B there is a positive relationship between rr and er. We can differentiate (2) to arrive at

$$\Delta rr = \frac{1}{\pi_1 + B_0} \Delta(G - T) + \frac{\pi_2}{\pi_1 + B_0} \Delta er - \frac{rr_0}{\pi_1 + B_0} \Delta B \tag{8}$$

where $\pi_2/(\pi_1 + B_0)$ is the slope of the goods market schedule labelled IX and $G - T$ and B are shift variables.

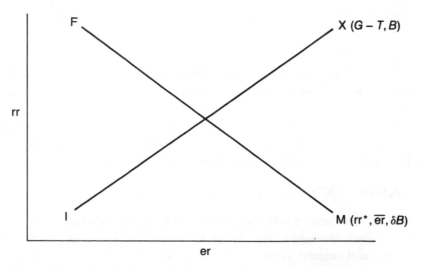

Figure 20.1 Equilibrium in the goods and financial markets

Suppose B and $G - T$ are given. A rise in rr increases the excess of $S - I$; at the same time, it worsens the servicing of the existing foreign debt (B_0). A real devaluation is therefore needed to restore equilibrium to the goods market.

Suppose the deficit increases. The IX schedule would now shift to the left. To see why this is so, suppose the real interest rate is fixed, so that $S - I$ is also fixed. This requires a real appreciation, which in turn is associated with a current account deficit (in this case, we have a twin deficit outcome). Suppose the real exchange rate is fixed; this means that the trade balance is unchanged. The real interest rate must now rise sufficiently to raise $S - I$; at the same time, there will also be some spillover into a current account deficit.

It is also readily shown by similar reasoning that an increased indebtedness abroad (an increase in B) will shift the IX schedule to the right. For example, for a given real interest rate the currency must devalue in real terms (to offset the increased servicing of the foreign debt).

To represent the financial sector, we differentiate (7) and solve for the real interest rate.

$$\Delta rr = \Delta rr^* + \phi\ \Delta\overline{er} - \phi\ \Delta er + \Delta\ \delta B \tag{9}$$

FM in Figure 20.1 shows the combinations of rr and er, given $\overline{er}$, rr^* and δB, which will equilibrate the financial market. There is now a negative relationship.

If er increases, a fall in the real interest rate is required to restore equilibrium. The reason is that if er increases and given $\overline{er}$ there is now an expected appreciation of the currency and this requires that the real interest rate fall below the foreign interest rate.

An increase in $\overline{er}$ will shift FM to the right. At the same time, as the risk premium increases (the supply of bonds increases) the FM schedule will also shift to the right requiring a higher domestic real interest rate (to offset the risk premium) and/or a devaluation (implying an expected real appreciation to offset the risk premium).

DYNAMIC ADJUSTMENT TO A FISCAL EXPANSION

Consider now what happens in the wake of a permanent fiscal expansion (an increase in $G - T$).

In the short run, with $\overline{er}$ and δB given, the IX schedule will shift to the left to $I_1 X_1$ (Figure 20.2). The economy will find itself at O, at which point the interest rate will have risen and the currency will have appreciated, all in real terms.

The increased public sector deficit is now partly absorbed by an increase in $S - I$ and partly by a current account deficit. The budget deficit is financed by the supply of new bonds, some of which are absorbed domestically by the increase in $S - I$, some of which are absorbed abroad by the current account deficit (which is of course less than the budget deficit).

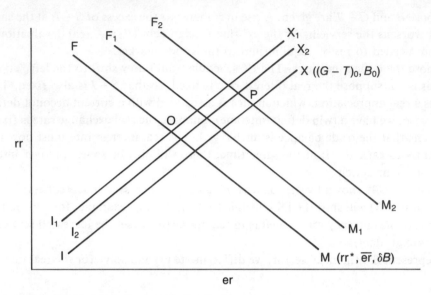

Figure 20.2 The effects of a fiscal expansion

As foreigners accumulate domestic bonds a risk premium emerges, so the FM schedule begins to shift to the right (to say F_1M_1). Also with increased foreign indebtedness the IX schedule will begin to shift to the right. At this point the currency goes into reverse (a real devaluation occurs) and the real interest rate rises further. The question now is: at what point do we return to full equilibrium?

It is perhaps evident that, so long as there is a current account deficit, bonds will continue to accrue to foreigners, the risk premium will grow and the FM schedule will continue to shift to the right while the IX schedule will shift to the right.

In equilibrium, therefore, the current account balance has to be zero. This is similar to Branson's portfolio balance model of Chapter 19, where the current account also had to converge to zero. However, the driving force here is different. In Chapter 19 it was the accumulation of foreign assets – the creation of wealth – which was the driving force; here it is the risk premium.

In Chapter 19 the improvement over time in the investment account (from the investment abroad) meant that the trade balance had to go into deficit. Now the deterioration in the investment account means that the trade balance must be in surplus. In turn, this necessitates a real devaluation of the currency. So, *ultimately*, there needs to be a net devaluation to absorb the deteriorating investment account. The final equilibrium is shown at P where the current account is in balance and the real interest rate is now higher still. There is also a net devaluation. Note that now, if the budget deficit persists, it is financed by the issue of new bonds but these are absorbed fully by an increase in $S - I$.

Table 20.1 US evolution of key domestic variables, 1981–8

	1981	1982	1983	1984	1985	1986	1987	1988
1 General government financial balance as percentage of GNP	−1.0	−3.5	−3.8	−2.8	−3.3	−3.4	−2.4	−2.0
2 Cyclic adjustment balance as percentage of GNP	1.6	0.3	−0.2	−0.5	−1.3	−1.3	−0.7	−0.7
3 Current account balance as percentage of GNP	0.2	−0.2	−1.2	−2.6	−3.0	−3.4	−3.6	−2.6
4 Net international investment income (billion $)	33.5	29.5	24.8	18.8	25.2	21.6	22.3	2.2
5 Real interest rate[a]	3.6	6.8	7.9	8.2	7.0	5.8	4.6	4.8
6 Real exchange rate (relative normalised unit labour costs) 1985 = 100 (IMF)	77.1	87.2	89.6	96.3	100.0	81.0	70.7	66.5
7 Net international investment position of USA (net foreign asset position) (billion $)	140.9	136.7	89.0	−2.2	−117.2	−273.7	−378.1	−531.1

Sources: OECD, Economic Outlooks; US Federal Reserve Bulletins; IMF, International Financial Statistics
Note: [a] Long rate less the rate of inflation.

APPLICATION OF THE MODEL TO THE USA, 1981–8

Table 20.1 shows the evolution between 1981 and 1988 of

a) the budget deficit, actual and cyclically adjusted;
b) the current account deficit;
c) the net investment income account;
d) the real interest rate;
e) the real exchange rate; and
f) the net international investment position.

Between 1982, when the fiscal deficit escalated, and 1985 the US dollar real exchange rate appreciated on average, according to the measure, by over 20 per cent. In the subsequent two years, all this gain and more was reversed. The current account moved into deficit and the investment income account sharply deteriorated. In due course, too, the USA became a net debtor country.

These developments and their timing conform well to the predictions of the Branson model. Moreover, there is plenty of evidence to suggest that a substantial part of the broad trends can be attributable to the fiscal expansion.

Econometric simulations of changes in the US fiscal deficit also confirm the general predictions of the model. (See Chapter 15.)

21

An extended Mundell–Fleming model with J curves

INTRODUCTION

So far we have assumed that exchange rate changes have 'normal' effects on the trade balance, i.e. a devaluation (appreciation) improves (worsens) the trade balance. The possibility that such effects might be perverse (there may be J curves in operation) has been ignored.

As we saw, however (in Chapter 12), there is considerable evidence that, over the short run of say six to nine months, exchange rate effects might well be perverse. It is therefore of considerable interest to examine how some of our short-run results might be affected by the presence of J curves. We deal with this as we have dealt with 'wealth' and 'wage–price effects' earlier; again, we take a relatively simple model and now simply accommodate the possibility of a J curve. This allows us to focus our attention on just this change instead of trying to deal with too many refinements at the same time.

The presence of a J curve adds many new dimensions to the analysis of the effects of monetary and fiscal policies. First, there is now the additional problem, not encountered previously, of potential foreign exchange instability. Consider, for example, a monetary expansion which potentially leads to an overall deficit in the balance of payments, made up partly of capital outflows and partly of a trade deficit. With flexible rates this will provoke a devaluation which now worsens the trade deficit. Equilibrium can only be restored, if at all, if sufficient *inflows* of capital are attracted to offset the now larger trade deficit. This, however, is not possible within an MF straitjacket. We deal with this question of stability in some detail below.

Second, there is the question of the exchange rate overshoot. Dornbusch and Branson, as we saw in Chapters 18 and 19, offered two alternative hypotheses to account for an exchange rate overshoot. The J curve, as we shall demonstrate below, now offers a third, at least as plausible, hypothesis.

Third, the initial effects on the price–output nexus are also likely to be different. Niehans (1975) was one of the first to note, in the context of a macro model, that monetary expansion in a flexible rate world and in the face of a J curve might lead in the short run to a fall in output. Dornbusch and Krugman also note:

> The central message of the empirical results is that prices rise promptly in response to a monetary expansion, but that the real effects may even be depressed or perverse. The J curve in the short run implies that a depreciation may actually lower the real demand for domestic output. In these circumstances, monetary expansion may actually lead to more inflation and more unemployment.
>
> (1976: 573)

Fourth in the MF model under flexible rates a monetary expansion unambiguously produced a current account surplus, matched by an outflow of capital. In the presence of a J curve these roles are reversed. As noted earlier, we now must have a current account deficit matched by an inflow of capital.

The remainder of this chapter is an extended analysis of the effects of a monetary and a fiscal expansion in a flexible rate world, in the presence of J curves, with particular attention being paid to (1) stability conditions, (2) the exchange rate overshoot, (3) the potential for the generation of 'stagflation', notably from monetary expansion, and (4) the current account outcome. We focus only on the short run and the longer run and assume rational expectations.

Considering the importance of this question, there is surprisingly little literature which accommodates J curves or related dynamics into a broader macro framework. The reader may find the following useful: Niehans (1975), Bhandari (1981, 1983) and Ueda (1983).

THE MODEL

The first question we need to confront is the model to be used in undertaking the analysis. Needless to say, as is evident from our analysis so far, there would be many different ways to represent the short run over which the J curve is assumed to operate.

We choose to use a special case of our model of Chapter 8 with one or two important borrowings from the Dornbusch 1976 model.

a) The short run is defined now as one during which *output* is allowed to adjust. *Home* prices and wages, on the other hand, are assumed to be fixed in this period. This assumption is in the spirit of the MF model but unlike the Dornbusch 'instantaneous' first phase when the real economy is invariant.

b) Because we also want to address the question of the effects of a J curve on inflation, we focus on the *consumer price index* which, as in previous chapters, we take to be a weighted average of home prices, which are fixed, and the exchange rate.

At the same time we also now assume that money balances are deflated by the consumer price index, not the price of home goods. These assumptions, it will be recalled, are borrowed from Chapter 7.

c) The MF assumption that capital inflows are *only* a function of the interest rate differential does not, in this context, serve us well. We therefore extend the capital flow equation to accommodate the expected change in the exchange rate, as in the modified Dornbusch model of Frenkel and Rodriguez in Chapter 18.

d) Having introduced exchange rate expectations, we need to explain these. Here, we adopt the Dornbusch (and Frenkel–Rodriguez) device of assuming rational expectations. Since we are not interested in the *time path* of adjustment from the short run to the long run, rationality here carries only the assumption that the *long-run* result is known.

e) The assumption that the Marshall–Lerner condition holds, as in the MF model, must also now be relaxed. This means that the coefficient on the exchange rate in the real demand for goods and in the trade balance equation *will be assumed to be negative* in the short run.

f) After our 'short' period we assume that the J curve is reversed, wages and prices adjust and ultimately we arrive at a long-run result.

The real demand for goods

$$\text{yr} = \alpha_1(e - p_\text{d}) - \alpha_4 r_\text{d} + \alpha_3 \text{gr} \tag{1}$$

The money market

$$\text{mo} - p = \alpha_5 \text{yr} - \alpha_{10} r_\text{d} \tag{2}$$

The foreign exchange market

$$B/X_0 = 0 = \alpha_{13}(e - p_\text{d}) - \text{yr} + \alpha_{14}[r_\text{d} - r^* - ({}_t E_{et+1} - e)] \tag{3}$$

$${}_t E_{et+1} - e = \alpha_{30}(\bar{e} - e) \tag{4}$$

The production–labour market

$$\text{yr} = -\alpha_9(w - p_\text{d}) \tag{5a}$$

$$w = \pi_2 p \tag{5b}$$

$$p = \alpha_{15} p_\text{d} + (1 - \alpha_{15})e \tag{5c}$$

Notation

All variables are in logarithms except for the interest rate and B/X_0.

yr	output
e	exchange rate
$\bar{e}$	equilibrium exchange rate
p_d	home prices
r_d	home interest rate
r^*	foreign interest rate
p	consumer price index
$_tE_{et+1}$	exchange rate expected in the next period
B/X_0	overall balance of payments divided by initial exports
w	wage rate

In the long run $\bar{e} = {_tE_{et+1}} = e$, $\pi_2 = 1$. We *define* the short run as one where $\pi_2 = 0$, $\alpha_9 \to \infty$ (both wages and *home* prices are fixed), $\alpha_1 < 0$,[1] $\alpha_{13} < 0$, $\alpha_{13} > \alpha_1$ (in absolute values) and $\bar{e}$ is the long-run solution to the exchange rate. Also, output adjusts while the consumer price index is allowed to respond during this period only to the exchange rate (as in (5c)).

If we substitute (4) into (3) and recall all the assumptions made, we have a short-run model comprising four equations (1)–(3), (5c) which in turn solve for yr, r_d, e and p for a monetary and a fiscal expansion. In the sections that follow we focus primarily on a monetary expansion; Section 4 deals briefly with the case of a fiscal expansion.

THE RESULTS FOR A MONETARY EXPANSION

The long-run solution in this case is identical to the one in Chapter 8 (despite the slight modification made to the money demand equation). In the long run we have $\Delta e = \Delta \bar{e} = \Delta p = \Delta p_d = \Delta$mo and Δyr $= \Delta r_d = 0$.

Table 21.1 gives the solutions for the four endogenous variables for the short run. It is evident that, at least for the general case, the solutions are very complicated and difficult to interpret. As it happens, fortunately, we can make some headway with verbal analysis without having to look too closely at the mathematical solutions.

Consider first the question of foreign exchange stability. Equation (3) is the key to understanding the mechanics of adjustment here. A monetary expansion we know will, initially, lower the interest rate, increase the level of output and also create an expectation of a proportionate devaluation some time in the future. *On all three counts the overall balance of payments will be in deficit*. This will trigger a devaluation. At this point the analysis becomes very complicated. *The condition for stability, as we will show below, is that, as the exchange rate devalues, the overall balance of payments must improve*. How might this happen?

The devaluation will now *worsen* the trade deficit. On the other hand, given now

Table 21.1 Short-run solutions[a] for yr, r_d, e and p for a monetary expansion with a J curve[b]

	General model	Special case where $\alpha_{14} \to \infty$
yr	$\dfrac{\alpha_4[k_2 - \alpha_{14}(1-\alpha_{15})(1+\alpha_{10}\alpha_{30})] - \alpha_{10}\alpha_1\alpha_{14}(1+\alpha_{10}\alpha_{30})}{\alpha_{10}k_2 + \alpha_1\alpha_{10}(\alpha_{10} - \alpha_{14}\alpha_5) + \alpha_4[\alpha_5 k_2 + (1-\alpha_{15})(\alpha_{10} - \alpha_{14}\alpha_5)]}$	$\dfrac{\alpha_4\alpha_{30}\alpha_{15} - \alpha_1(1+\alpha_{10}\alpha_{30})}{\alpha_{10}\alpha_{30} + (1-\alpha_{15}) + \alpha_5(\alpha_4\alpha_{30} - \alpha_1)}$
r_d	$-\dfrac{k_2 - \alpha_{14}(1-\alpha_{15})(1+\alpha_{10}\alpha_{30})}{\alpha_{10}k_2}\,mo + \dfrac{\alpha_5 k_2 + (1-\alpha_{15})(\alpha_{10} - \alpha_{14}\alpha_5)}{\alpha_{10}k_2}\,yr$	$-\dfrac{\alpha_1\alpha_{30}}{\alpha_4\alpha_{30} - \alpha_1}\,mo + \dfrac{\alpha_{30}}{\alpha_4\alpha_{30} - \alpha_1}\,yr$
e	$\dfrac{\alpha_{10} - \alpha_{14}\alpha_5}{k_2}\,yr + \dfrac{\alpha_{14}(1+\alpha_{10}\alpha_{30})}{k_2}\,mo$	$\dfrac{\alpha_4\alpha_{30}}{\alpha_4\alpha_{30} - \alpha_1}\,mo - \dfrac{1}{\alpha_4\alpha_{30} - \alpha_1}\,yr$
p	$(1-\alpha_{15})e$	$(1-\alpha_{15})e$

Notes: [a] Solutions assume α_1 and α_{13} are negative to begin with.
[b] The *complete* solutions for r_d, e and p are not given.
$k_2 = \alpha_{10}\alpha_{14}\alpha_{30} - \alpha_{13}\alpha_{10} + \alpha_{14}(1 - \alpha_{15})$.

the (fixed point) expected devaluation, we can see from (3) that the speculative component of the outflow diminishes. The currency will almost certainly need to devalue sufficiently to create an expectation of an appreciation. This in turn provokes an inflow. As the currency devalues, however, the trade balance gets progressively worse.

As well, both the level of output and the interest rate will respond to the devaluation.

To see what is happening here we combine (1) and (2):

$$\text{yr} = -\frac{\alpha_1\alpha_{10} + \alpha_4(1 - \alpha_{15})}{\alpha_{10} + \alpha_4\alpha_5} e \tag{6}$$

$$r_\text{d} = \frac{(1 - \alpha_{15}) - \alpha_1\alpha_5}{\alpha_{10} + \alpha_4\alpha_5} e \tag{7}$$

As the currency goes into a free fall, the level of output will be driven *down* from its initial point (see below) while the interest rate will be subject to two opposing influences: the fall in output drags down the interest rate but the rise in the consumer price index pulls it up.

We can now begin to put some of the pieces together. 'Initially', there is a large overall deficit which, if stability is to be restored, needs to be eliminated. First, the expected appreciation attracts inflows. Second, the fall in output *from its initial point* improves the trade balance. Third, the effect of the change in the domestic interest rate could go either way, encouraging or discouraging inflows. Fourth, to repeat the devaluation worsens the trade balance.

For argument's sake and to simplify, suppose the interest rate remains at its initially lower level (the two forces exactly offsetting each other). How is the overall deficit to be eliminated? *The combined positive effects of the reversal in output and the expected appreciation must dominate over the negative effects of the devaluation on the trade balance.* Ultimately, there will need to be a net inflow of capital (the expected appreciation dominating over the fall in the interest rate) sufficient to match the (assumed) current account deficit which comes from the devaluation itself and which may be reinforced or weakened by the net ultimate effect on the level of output (see below). If, in the end, the level of output is higher (lower) the current account deficit will be reinforced (weakened).

The *formal* condition for stability can be arrived at as follows. Drawing on (3) and substituting (6) and (7), we have (recalling that $\alpha_{30}\alpha_{14}\text{mo}$ is a fixed point)

$$\frac{B}{X_0} = -\alpha_{13}e + \frac{\alpha_1\alpha_{10} + \alpha_4(1 - \alpha_{15})}{\alpha_{10} + \alpha_4\alpha_5} e + \frac{\alpha_{14}[(1 - \alpha_{15}) - \alpha_1\alpha_5]}{\alpha_{10} + \alpha_4\alpha_5} e + \alpha_{14}e \tag{8}$$

The condition for stability is that

$$\alpha_{14}(\alpha_{10} + \alpha_4\alpha_5) + \alpha_{14}[(1 - \alpha_{15}) - \alpha_1\alpha_5] + \alpha_1\alpha_{10}$$
$$+ \alpha_4(1 - \alpha_{15}) - \alpha_{13}(\alpha_{10} + \alpha_4\alpha_5) > 0$$

This condition is almost certain to hold.[2] Moreover, when capital mobility is perfect $(\alpha_{14} \to \infty)$ $r_{\mathrm{d}} - r^* = {}_tE_{et+1} - e$ and the problem of instability no longer arises. As in Dornbusch, the currency devalues sufficiently to create an expected appreciation to offset the interest rate differential.

Will there be an overshoot? The discussion above has implied that an overshoot is virtually assured. The reason of course is that in the first period there is almost certain to be an expected appreciation sufficient to generate an inflow of capital and this implies an overshoot. (Conceivably, though, if the effect of the fall in output dominates over the J curve effect on the trade balance, the trade balance could go into surplus, requiring a net *outflow* of capital. This case, however, appears very unlikely.)

We have also confirmed that a monetary expansion will almost certainly produce a trade *deficit*, in sharp contrast to the MF result.

Finally, what will happen to output and the price level?

The general as well as the special solutions reveal that the outcome for output is ambiguous. To understand this, we again combine (1) and (2) and solve for output, using (6) and (7):

$$\mathrm{yr} = -\frac{\alpha_1\alpha_{10} + \alpha_4(1 - \alpha_{15})}{\alpha_{10} + \alpha_4\alpha_5} \, e + \left| \frac{\alpha_4}{\alpha_{10} + \alpha_4\alpha_5} \, \mathrm{mo} \right| \tag{9}$$

There is a *positive* effect on output which comes from the monetary expansion (the drop in the interest rate) and a *negative* effect which comes from the devaluation. The net outcome is thus ambiguous.

In our model, however, there is no ambiguity about the *positive* effect of the devaluation on the consumer price index. Thus, if output should fall, as well, a monetary expansion with flexible rates and a J curve may initially, at any rate, give us the worst of all worlds (a result noted by Dornbusch and Krugman in the Introduction).

A GRAPHICAL REPRESENTATION OF THE RESULT

In this section we represent these results graphically.

It is readily seen from (1) that, while the IS schedule retains its negative slope, a devaluation (appreciation) will now shift the schedule to the left (right). The reason is that, given the interest rate, a devaluation now requires a *fall* in output to restore equilibrium to the goods market.

After substituting (5c) into (2), (2) represents the LM schedule which now shifts to the left (right) as the currency devalues.

The most radical change occurs in the B schedule. We rewrite (3) as

$$r_{\mathrm{d}} = r^* + {}_tE_{et+1} + \frac{1}{\alpha_{14}} \, \mathrm{yr} - \frac{\alpha_{14} - \alpha_{13}}{\alpha_{14}} \, e \tag{3a}$$

Given r^* an expected devaluation shifts the B schedule upwards to the left. A devaluation has two opposing effects (already noted in the verbal presentation above): the

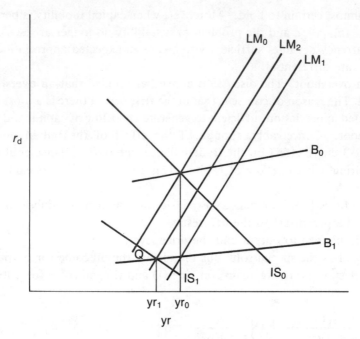

Figure 21.1   Monetary expansion under flexible rates with a J curve

J curve effect shifts the schedule to the left; speculation about the exchange rate shifts it to the right.

Figure 21.1 illustrates the results. LM first shifts to the right (to LM_1), and then shifts back (in part) in response to the devaluation (to LM_2). The IS schedule shifts to the *left* (to IS_1). It is *assumed* that output on balance falls (from yr_0 to yr_1). The B schedule shifts to the left because of '$_tE_{et+1}$' and the J curve, but to the right because of the actual devaluation. Stability requires that all three schedules ultimately meet at Q.

THE CASE OF A FISCAL EXPANSION

It is also of some interest to deal briefly with the case of a fiscal expansion in the presence of a J curve. The presentation here highlights a few important results with very little technical analysis. The reader should be able independently to undertake such analysis.

We first need to recall what happens in the MF model. Suppose capital mobility is relatively high but not perfect; then we know that a fiscal expansion will at the outset produce a net surplus in the overall balance of payments. In the MF model this provokes an appreciation of the currency which in turn will *increase* the deficit in the trade balance sufficiently to match the net inflow of capital.

In the presence of a J curve, the appreciation will now *improve* the trade balance.

What will happen to capital flows? This case is somewhat complicated because we need again some reference point for the future, i.e. the expected long-run equilibrium exchange rate. This question is taken up again in a later chapter; for the moment, however, let us suppose that there is an expectation of an ultimate appreciation which corresponds to the solution for the exchange rate in our model. Then, if the trade balance should move into surplus, this will require a net *outflow* of capital which in turn means that an expected *devaluation* is needed (the appreciation must overshoot its long-run level); to generate a *net* outflow sufficient to offset the trade surplus, the outflow from the expected devaluation must *exceed* the potential inflow from the fact that the domestic interest rate is higher.

If there is perfect capital mobility, the following can readily be shown. The level of output must rise; the interest rate is also almost certain to rise while the currency unambiguously appreciates. The appreciation, combined with the increase in government expenditure, dominates over the effect of the interest rate in (1) and this allows output to rise.

Equation (2) can be rewritten as

$$r_d = \frac{1 - \alpha_{15}}{\alpha_{10}} e + \frac{\alpha_5}{\alpha_{10}} \text{yr} \tag{2a}$$

The appreciation will tend to push down, the increase in output to push up, the interest rate. The latter is almost certain to dominate. Finally, with perfect capital mobility we have

$$r_d - r^* = \alpha_{30} (\bar{e} - e) \tag{3a}$$

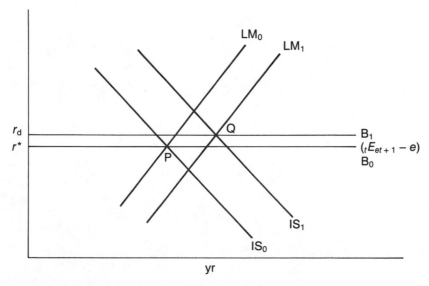

Figure 21.2   Fiscal expansion with a J curve

where $\bar{e}$ is the equilibrium appreciation (the 'long-run' solution to the model). With $r_d > r^*$, the current appreciation must *overshoot* its long-run level, producing an expected *devaluation*.

These results are represented graphically in Figure 21.2 for the case of perfect asset substitution. The IS schedule shifts to the right for two reasons: the fiscal expansion and the appreciation. The LM schedule shifts to the right because of the appreciation. Finally, the B schedule shifts upwards because of the expected devaluation, allowing the home interest rate to exceed the foreign interest rate. (See equation (3a) with $\alpha_{14} \to \infty$.) Equilibrium shifts from P to Q.

22

Effects of a restrictive money growth policy on the path of inflation and unemployment

INTRODUCTION

In this chapter we address an important question: what are the output costs (the so-called sacrifice ratio) of a deceleration in the money growth rate under flexible exchange rates? More particularly, we are interested in the factors *underlying* these output costs, i.e. what determines whether these will be large or small. *Identifying these factors also allows us to explain why the sacrifice ratio*, defined as the ratio of the percentage of GNP lost to the reduction in the inflation rate, *is different across different countries*. Later in the chapter we also look at the output costs of disinflating by pegging to a low-inflation country.

In the body of this chapter we draw very heavily on Fischer (1988a) who presents a model which allows us to address these questions more rigorously.

THE MODEL

The model below mostly reproduces the one in Fischer (1988a), with one small extension to accommodate the possibility of *ex post* wage indexation and other minor changes in presentation.

$$yr_d = \alpha_1(e - p_d) - \alpha_4[r_d - (_tE_{pt+1} - p)] \tag{1}$$

$$mo = p + yr - \alpha_{10}r_d \tag{2}$$

$$r_d - r^* = {}_tE_{et+1} - e \tag{3}$$

$$yr_s = -\alpha_9(w^* - p_d) - \pi_5\alpha_9(e - p_d) \tag{4}$$

$$w^* = \theta_{t-1}w_t + (1 - \theta)_{t-2}w_t \tag{5}$$

$$t_{-1}w_t = t_{-1}E_{pt} + h_{t-1}E_{yrt} \tag{6}$$

$$t_{-2}w_t = t_{-2}E_{pt} + h_{t-2}E_{yrt} \tag{7}$$

$$w^* = p_t \tag{5a}$$

$$p_t = \alpha_{15}p_d + (1 - \alpha_{15})e \tag{8}$$

Notation

All variables are in logarithms except for the interest rate.

yr_d	real demand for goods
yr_s	supply of output
r_d	domestic interest rate
r^*	foreign interest rate
$t_{-1}E_{qt}$	expectation formed in $t - 1$ for period t about q
mo	money stock
p	consumer price index
e	exchange rate
w^*	aggregate wage rate
$t_{-1}w_t$	wage rate negotiated in $t - 1$ for t
$t_{-2}wt$	wage rate negotiated in $t - 2$ for t
θ	proportion of wages set one period earlier

Most of the model is by now very familiar but there are some new features which will need to be highlighted. Equation (1) says that the real demand for goods is a positive function of the real exchange rate and a negative function of the real interest rate. Equation (2) is the money market equation. Note that here we follow Fischer in using the consumer price index as the deflator. Equation (3) assumes perfect asset substitution. Equation (4) is the aggregate supply equation, amended to accommodate imported inputs. α_9, as in other chapters, represents the share of wages to profits. π_5 is the ratio of imported inputs to value added. If there are no imported inputs (e.g. as in the model of Chapter 8) $\pi_5 = 0$. (See also Chapter 28, Appendix, for a more rigorous derivation.)

Equation (5) says that the wage outcome in period t is a weighted average of the wage rate negotiated in $t - 1$ and $t - 2$. Contracts are for either one period or two periods. Two-period contracts are spread evenly over the two years. In $t - 1$, therefore, all one-year contracts are renegotiated, plus half of the two-year contracts. If all contracts are for one year, $\theta = 1$; if all contracts are for two years, $\theta = 0.5$. If half the contracts are for one year and half for two years, $\theta = 0.75$. (See also Chapter 14.)

Equations (6) and (7) say that wages are negotiated for t on the basis of the expected consumer price index in t and the expected output gap in t. In other words, the *expected* real wage rate is itself now assumed to be positively related to the level of activity. h is a measure of the degree of real wage flexibility.

Equation (5a) is an alternative equation explaining the wage outcome. It simply says that the wage rate *ex post* is perfectly indexed to the consumer price index.

Equation (8) is the familiar definition of the consumer price index. The goods market is assumed to be in equilibrium.

MONETARY DISINFLATION WITH CREDIBILITY

We now want to put this model to work. We assume that the monetary authorities decide to reduce money growth by 1 per cent each year to reduce the rate of inflation in the same degree. The money stock in other words will grow by 1 per cent less each year.

We assume that in the initial period (zero) when money growth is reduced by 1 per cent the policy was not anticipated. However, once the new policy is implemented it becomes entirely credible, influencing now, from period 0, expectations about variables in the next period (1). We also assume that expectations are formed rationally.

It is perhaps intuitive in this model that the steady state solution will be reached by period 2. In period 0, by definition, because the reduction in money growth was unanticipated, the wage rate is given. However, new *expectations* now formed about future variables – the consumer price index and the exchange rate – will affect outcomes in period 0. In period 0 some contracts will be renegotiated for period 1 based on the expected consumer price index and the expected level of output in period 1. By period 1 all wage contracts will have been renegotiated so when we enter period 2 full adjustment will have taken place. *Any real changes that occur will therefore be entirely contained within periods 0 and 1.*

Before we try to identify the output costs in this model of a monetary disinflation, it is convenient first to spell out the longer-run characteristics of the model after full adjustment has occurred (i.e. in period 2). To simplify, we assume that initially the foreign and home rates of inflation were equal.

The steady state rate of inflation will have fallen in line with the reduction in money growth. At the same time, given the foreign rate of inflation, there will be a steady state rate of appreciation equal to the reduction in money growth. Output, the real exchange rate and the real interest rate all also now revert to their original levels.

A steady state appreciation has to be associated with a *drop* in the domestic interest rate relative to that abroad (equation (3)). At the same time a lower nominal interest rate, given output, means that in equilibrium there is an increase in the demand for real money balances (equation (2)). When adjustment is complete, therefore, and a lower rate of inflation is achieved there will have been a *one-off* increase in demand for real money balance; this is the so-called re-entry problem; in turn this will reduce the *price level and appreciate the level of the currency*. This result is important and indeed has been widely commented on.

We can represent this result as follows. To begin, what we have is $\Delta\text{mo}(0) = -1$, $\Delta\text{mo}(1) = -2$, $\Delta\text{mo}(2) = -3$ and so on. In other words, in period 0 the money stock will be 1 per cent lower than its base level; in period 1 2 per cent lower.

In equilibrium

$$\Delta p = \Delta p_d = \Delta e = -(j + 1 + \alpha_{10}) \qquad j \geqslant 2$$

If $j = 2$, the price level will be 3 per cent lower than its base level *minus a further adjustment represented by α_{10} which is the interest sensitivity of money demand.* α_{10} captures the *one-shot* further downward adjustment to the price *level*. In *rate of change* terms the deceleration in the rate of increase in prices and the rate of appreciation will both be equal to the deceleration in money growth. Over time the one-off effect assumes less and less significance: α_{10} will tend to be dominated by $j + 1$. (To get some idea of the orders of magnitude α_{10} could vary between 0.25 and 1.0.)

Also, in equilibrium, with the rate of inflation down and the nominal interest rate down to the same degree the real interest rate will return to its base level $\Delta [r_d - ({}_tE_{pt+1} - p)] = 0$, as will the real exchange rate.

OUTPUT LOSSES IN PERIODS 0 AND 1

We first write the definition of the sacrifice ratio (SR):

$$SR = -[\Delta yr(0) + \Delta yr(1)] \tag{9}$$

The sacrifice ratio is the sum of the output losses (i.e. relative to an initial full employment level) in periods 0 and 1 (for one-unit reduction in inflation).

The next step is to obtain solutions for $\Delta yr(0)$ and $\Delta yr(1)$. Unfortunately, these turn out to be extremely complicated; they will therefore not be presented here. The reader is referred to the appendix in Fischer for the detailed solutions.

As it happens, we are primarily interested in the factors which determine the output losses and those, as we shall see, are fairly intuitive, so we will be able to identify them without reference to the detailed solutions. Fischer also takes plausible values of the coefficients in the model and is thus able to arrive at a rough order of magnitude of the effects on the sacrifice ratio of variations in the values of these coefficients.

Before we look more closely at these underlying factors, there is one additional result we need for the alternative case where wages are *ex post* fully indexed.

Despite the fact that the deceleration in money growth in period zero is unanticipated adjustment will be complete in the same period. This corresponds to the results of period 2 for the case where wages are contractually determined. The sacrifice ratio is thus zero when wages are fully indexed, a result which at this point should not surprise. We return to this result in a moment. We will refer to this case as one where wage determination is *backward* looking, and the earlier case as one where wage determination is *forward* looking.

We will now proceed to show that the sacrifice ratio is increasing in α_{10}, α_9, α_4, α_1, α_{15} and decreasing in π_5, θ and in the degree to which wages are backward looking.

α_{10} represents the drop in velocity which occurs when the inflation rate is reduced. Any drop in velocity in the transitional period will have adverse effects on output and hence increase SR.

α_9 denotes the adverse effect of a change in the real wage rate on the supply of output. With the nominal wage rate relatively sticky in the first two periods and the price level adjusting downwards, the real wage rate will rise. Other things being equal, the larger α_9 the bigger the associated drop in output.

α_4 captures the negative effects on output of a rise in the real interest rate. In the transitional period the real interest rate will rise; the adverse effects on output will be larger the larger α_4.

α_1 captures the negative effects on output of a real appreciation which will also occur in the transitional period. These negative effects will again be larger the larger α_1.

α_{15} enters the model in several places: in the money market and in the definition of the real interest rate. The larger α_{15} the *weaker* is the *downward* push on the price level of an appreciation (equation (8)). This at once mitigates the increase in real money balances and increases the real interest rate. On both counts SR is increased.

π_5 is a measure of the ratio of imported inputs to value added. The higher π_5 is the larger is the impact of an appreciation on the cost of imported inputs. A fall in the cost of imported inputs will be reflected in some expansion in output.

θ represents the relative importance of one-period contracts. The larger θ is the greater the relative importance of one-period contracts; this *accelerates* adjustment and reduces SR. To see this, consider the case where all contracts are for one year ($\theta = 1$). Then the economy returns to equilibrium by year 1. There is no output loss in year 1.

Finally, we have already demonstrated that when wages are backward looking they are fully indexed to the consumer price index. Adjustment will be 'immediate', at least in the context of this model. Complete wage indexation is an improvement over one-period contracts; in the latter case wages are sticky for one period alone, in the former they adjust in the same period. (Of course, immediate adjustment is unrealistic and so we are really talking about *approximations*. If wages respond with a considerable lag to prior inflation, the advantage is less obvious.)

In a very similar vein *price* adjustment may be delayed (for reasons which we discussed in Chapter 9) and this is also an element which further slows down adjustment.

The above analysis assumed that the disinflationary monetary policy was entirely credible once it was put into place. However, this may be an unrealistic assumption. A more realistic extension is to allow for the possibility that the policy might become less credible with time and that this might serve to increase SR.

Another point is that monetary disinflation may be associated with an increase in net borrowing abroad, which, presumably, ultimately will need to be repaid, at some further potential cost to the community. This point is not pursued further here.

DISINFLATING BY PEGGING TO A LOW-INFLATION COUNTRY

In the previous sections we examined the output costs of a monetary disinflation under flexible exchange rates. In this section we address the following question. Suppose a country is running a relatively high rate of inflation and suppose too that it has made a decision to disinflate. Is the sacrifice ratio less or more if the country chooses to peg its currency to a low-inflation country instead of floating?

The question is far from academic. We have instances of disinflating with flexible rates and disinflating by pegging. Examples of the former would be Canada, Australia, New Zealand (all in the second half of the 1980s) and the UK (in the early 1980s). Examples of the latter would be countries in the European Monetary System (EMS) that imported inflation discipline from Germany. The best examples here are Denmark, France and Ireland. By way of background we note that in 1979 at the inception of the EMS Germany's inflation rate over the previous three years had been some 3.2 per cent. By contrast, France's and Denmark's inflation rate was around 10 per cent, Ireland's was around 12 per cent. By 1991 Germany's inflation rate was 3.6 per cent, France's 3.1 per cent, Ireland's 3.1 per cent and Denmark's 2.5 per cent (all three ironically outshining the master!). (See Andersen (1992) for a description of the experiences of these three countries. See also Dornbusch (1989a) and Kremers (1990) for an analysis of the Irish experience.)

One way to proceed is to assume that credibility is the same in the two regimes and then take a model like the one used earlier and do a parallel analysis of the sacrifice ratio under a peg. One could now look at the effects on the real economy of an unanticipated announcement that the exchange rate would henceforth be permanently pegged. Fortunately for us Fischer (1986) has taken the same model and applied it to the peg. He also tries to compare the two sacrifice ratios but in the end finds that it depends very much on the parameter values. So at this level, at any rate, nothing very conclusive can be said.

An equally pertinent question is whether there will be a difference between the two strategies in terms of *credibility*. The regime with the greater credibility, other things being equal, will endure a smaller loss in output. There is here, perhaps, a slight (but only slight) presumption that pegging the currency involves a stronger commitment than disinflating under flexible rates. But it does depend on the circumstances. The commitment may be stronger and the credibility greater if a country were to join a collective exchange rate arrangement such as the EMS. (UK's and Italy's withdrawal from the system in September 1992 however, does, raise doubts even about this.)

In addition to the potential gain in credibility, there are two other technical advantages claimed for a peg as against a money target. (Chadha *et al.* 1991). The first is the so-called re-entry problem noted above: the one-off increase in the money demand that comes from the fact that the rate of inflation and the nominal interest rate will have fallen. This problem is automatically taken care of under a peg since the money stock is now endogenous. With a money target discretion needs to be exercised.

A second technical advantage is that with a peg the exchange rate is immediately and directly observable, whereas with a money target information on the money stock is only available with a lag and then sometimes subsequently revised.

In the end, then, these issues can only be resolved by detailed country studies and by statistical–econometric analysis. Consider again the cases of Ireland, France and Denmark. Ireland's inflation rate peaked at nearly 20 per cent in 1981; it has since come down dramatically to German levels. The unemployment rate, however, surged, rising from some 8.9 per cent in 1980–1 to peak at some 17.5 per cent in 1987; in 1991 it was still nearly 16 per cent. France's unemployment rate also rose during the disinflation from some 6 per cent to 9–10 per cent. Finally, Denmark's disinflation was associated with a surge in unemployment from some 7 per cent to 10 per cent. These are very crude figures but they do suggest, at this very superficial level, that a potential lack of credibility combined with sluggish wage adjustment have together imposed substantial and protracted unemployment costs.

We still, however, need to address the question of *relative* costs under the two regimes. A recent paper by Egebo and Englander concluded, on the question of credibility in exchange rate mechanism (ERM) countries, that:

> Policy credibility in ERM countries has not significantly reduced the costs of disinflation ... the evidence presented, as well as the review of the earlier work, finds little basis for concluding that adhering to the ERM bands alters the trade-off between inflation and unemployment. Hence, either inflation expectations have not responded to the greater credibility of inflation policy or labour market institutions and rigidities have prevented lowered expectations from translating into lower inflation.
>
> (1992: 45, 51)

This appears to reaffirm our own very tentative conclusion.

The study also compares the sacrifice ratios of the ERM countries endured in the 1980s with those in earlier episodes of disinflation, but find if anything that the sacrifice ratio may actually have crept up in the 1980s for nearly all the countries. The same comparison between the 1980s and earlier episodes is made for countries outside the ERM, finding now that there are fewer countries whose sacrifice ratios actually increased in the 1980s. Andersen (1992) also concludes that 'the exchange rate commitment did not help to reduce the transitory costs'.

Another way to address this question is to undertake an econometric simulation of an economy for the two alternative strategies and then observe the differences in the adjustment paths. Chadha *et al.* (1991) do just this for the UK using the IMF Multimod. However, they find that the output losses are in fact considerably less for a peg than for a money target.

Part IV

NEW CLASSICAL THEMES

Part IV contains four chapters which deal with the New Classical contributions to macroeconomic theory and policy.

Chapter 23 focuses on the New Classical idea that only unanticipated policy will have any real effectiveness while macro policy which is fully anticipated will be ineffective. The model used to demonstrate these hypotheses is one of a simple closed economy.

The model is extended to the open economy in Chapter 24. This chapter focuses on the effects of temporary or permanent anticipated macro policy changes at home. The central concern is with the dynamics of adjustment, in particular how the economy is affected by an anticipated policy change in the period *prior* to the implementation of policy.

Chapter 25 reviews literature concerned with the potential implications, for the equilibrium rate of inflation, of allowing governments discretion with respect to the use of monetary policy. This literature contends that with discretion governments will end up delivering excessive inflation without altering the rate of unemployment.

Chapter 26 deals with yet another New Classical contribution: the Ricardian equivalence hypothesis. According to this hypothesis, households fully discount to the present all future taxes expected to be levied to meet interest payments on existing government debt.

23

Macro policy impotence and the New Classical paradigm

INTRODUCTION

A very influential body of thinking, known as the New Classical school, has attempted to revive old classical ideas. Its leading exponents are, in the USA, T. Sargent, N. Wallace, R. Barro, R. Lucas, and in the UK, P. Minford. (See on all this Sargent and Wallace (1976), Begg (1982), Minford and Peel (1983), Attfield *et al.* (1985), *Journal of Money, Credit and Banking* (1980).)

Although there are differences in detail in the way in which different protagonists of the New Classical school propound their ideas, there are nevertheless a number of features which are, so to speak, common property of the school.

In this chapter, we focus on one contribution they made to the macro policy debate, notably the idea they share that only unanticipated policy will have any real effectiveness while macro policy which is fully anticipated will only be reflected in changes in prices.

It is possible to sum up their system in terms of four key propositions.

a) There is considerable wage and price flexibility in the economy. In some extreme models, this is taken to mean that both product prices and the price of labour are determined in essentially competitive markets by the laws of supply and demand. In less extreme models, some reaction lag may be allowed; nevertheless adjustment tends to be speedy. In one scenario (the one we present below) prices adjust almost continuously but wages are predetermined by, say, a one-period contract; however, this would be a short contract of say at most one year.
b) The reaction speed of the public authorities is at least as long as the reaction speed of the private sector participants.

c) Expectations are formed rationally in the sense that all currently available information is fully exploited in forming expectations.

d) Governments are assumed not to be privileged in their access to information, sharing a common set of information with other private participants.

It will be shown that a failure to meet these key assumptions will discredit their conclusions.

We proceed, therefore, to outline the basic model, show how their conclusions follow from the model and then demonstrate how changes to the underlying assumptions will weaken the policy conclusions they draw.

A NEW CLASSICAL MODEL

The base model we use here is one of a closed economy very much in the spirit of the American contributions. In the next chapter we extend the model and analysis to the open economy, focusing particularly on potential impacts on the economy of anticipated policies in the period *before* such policies are implemented.

A 'typical' New Classical model would take the following form

$$yr_d = \alpha_1 mo - \alpha_1 p_d + \alpha_3 gr + \alpha_3 u_1 \tag{1}$$

$$yr_s = \overline{yr} + \alpha_2 (p_d - {}_{t-1}E_{p_d t}) + \alpha_5 (yr_{-1} - \overline{yr}) + u_2 \tag{2}$$

$$yr_d = yr_s \tag{3}$$

$$mo = \overline{mo} - \alpha_4 (yr_{-1} - \overline{yr}) + u_3 \tag{4}$$

$$gr = \overline{gr} - \alpha_6 (yr_{-1} - \overline{yr}) + u_4 \tag{5}$$

Notation

All variables are in logarithms except for the interest rate.

$\overline{yr}$ full employment output
yr_d real demand for goods
yr_s real supply of goods
mo money stock
p_d price level
gr real government expenditure
u_1 serially uncorrelated expenditure disturbance with zero mean
${}_{t-1}E_{xt}$ expectation formed in $t - 1$ about variable x for period t
u_2 serially uncorrelated supply disturbance with zero mean
u_3, u_4 disturbances to money stock and government expenditure

Equation (1) is the aggregate demand equation. It can be viewed as a reduced form equation derived from a real aggregate demand and a money demand equation.[1] Equation (2) is the aggregate supply equation. For our purposes it is best to interpret the expected price variable as a proxy for wages which are contracted in the 'preceding' period, assumed to be short. α_5 represents a 'persistence' effect, i.e. a change in the real wage rate has effects which persist into the next period. u_1 and u_2 are disturbance terms to aggregate demand and supply with a mean of zero. The coefficient on u_2 is assumed to be unity, for simplicity.

Equations (4) and (5) are alternative monetary and fiscal policy stabilisation rules. When the previous period's level of output exceeds (falls short of) full capacity output monetary and fiscal policies are tightened (eased).

Workers set their wages for the next period on the basis of information about next period's expected price level formed this period; prices, however, are flexible. At the same time, the authorities stabilise today on the strength of information about output in the previous period. In other words, stabilisation policy is undertaken with a lag and this lag is the same as that operative to wage determination (e.g. when the level of output today is known the authorities plan their next period's policy).

Proposition (c) in the Introduction states that in forming expectations about future prices all currently available information is exploited. If this model were the correct one, this amounts to saying that the model structure (i.e. price formation in the model) becomes the basis for the price forecast.

From (2) it is easily seen that, in equilibrium, with $yr_s = yr_d = yr_{-1}$, $u_2 = 0$ and $p_d = {}_{t-1}E_{p_dt}$, $yr = \overline{yr}$, output cannot change in the longer run. With output fixed, neither monetary nor fiscal policy can have any longer-run potency. Also from (1) with $u_1 = 0$,

$$\frac{p_d}{mo} = 1 \qquad \text{and} \qquad \frac{p_d}{gr} = \frac{\alpha_3}{\alpha_1}$$

So much then for the longer-run results, which are of course classical. What we are concerned with is the conditions under which this long-run result might hold *in the short run*. In what conditions then would we have short-run policy ineffectiveness?

A first step is to use (1)–(3) and eliminate yr, to obtain, after rearranging,

$$p_d = \frac{\alpha_1}{\alpha_1 + \alpha_2}\, mo + \frac{\alpha_3}{\alpha_1 + \alpha_2}\,(gr + u_1) + \frac{\alpha_2}{\alpha_1 + \alpha_2}\,{}_{t-1}E_{p_dt}$$

$$- \frac{\alpha_5}{\alpha_1 + \alpha_2}\, yr_{-1} - \frac{1}{\alpha_1 + \alpha_2}\, u_2 - \frac{1 - \alpha_5}{\alpha_1 + \alpha_2}\, \overline{yr} \qquad (6)$$

This is the solution for prices in the model. Prices will be determined in the current period by monetary–fiscal policies, disturbances (u_1 and u_2), the previous level of output and, most importantly, by the price this period expected the previous period (because the latter determines wages which in turn influence the real wage rate and hence the level of current output and prices).

If expectations are rationally formed and if (6) is the correct model of price formation, then it will also be the basis for price expectations, and so we can write (6) as

$$
{}_{t-1}E_{p_{dt}} = \frac{\alpha_1}{\alpha_1 + \alpha_2}{}_{t-1}E_{mot} + \frac{\alpha_3}{\alpha_1 + \alpha_2}{}_{t-1}E_{grt} + \frac{\alpha_2}{\alpha_1 + \alpha_2}{}_{t-1}E_{p_{dt}}
$$

$$
- \frac{\alpha_5}{\alpha_1 + \alpha_2}\,\mathrm{yr}_{-1} - \frac{1-\alpha_5}{\alpha_1 + \alpha_2}\,\overline{\mathrm{yr}} \tag{7}
$$

Since the mean of the disturbance terms u_1, u_2 is zero, the expected value of the disturbance term is also zero, so they drop out of (7). Also, in the previous period when expectations are formed, the level of output yr_{-1} is assumed to be known.

Equation (7) allows us to solve for ${}_{t-1}E_{p_{dt}}$.

$$
{}_{t-1}E_{p_{dt}} = {}_{t-1}E_{mot} + \frac{\alpha_3}{\alpha_1}{}_{t-1}E_{grt} - \frac{\alpha_5}{\alpha_1}\,\mathrm{yr}_{-1} - \frac{1-\alpha_5}{\alpha_1}\,\overline{\mathrm{yr}} \tag{8}
$$

Equation (8) can now be substituted into (6) to obtain

$$
p_d = \frac{\alpha_1}{\alpha_1 + \alpha_2}\,\mathrm{mo} + \frac{\alpha_3}{\alpha_1 + \alpha_2}\,(\mathrm{gr} + u_1) + \frac{\alpha_2}{\alpha_1 + \alpha_2}{}_{t-1}E_{mot}
$$

$$
+ \frac{\alpha_2\alpha_3}{\alpha_1(\alpha_1 + \alpha_2)}{}_{t-1}E_{grt} - \frac{\alpha_5}{\alpha_1}\,\mathrm{yr}_{-1} - \frac{1}{\alpha_1 + \alpha_2}\,u_2 - \frac{1-\alpha_5}{\alpha_1}\,\overline{\mathrm{yr}} \tag{9}
$$

This is the equation which explains how prices are determined.

THE NEW CLASSICAL RESULTS

A solution for output is now obtained by substituting (9) and (8) into (2):

$$
\mathrm{yr} = \frac{\alpha_1\alpha_2}{\alpha_1 + \alpha_2}\,(\mathrm{mo} - {}_{t-1}E_{mot}) + \frac{\alpha_2\alpha_3}{\alpha_1 + \alpha_2}\,(\mathrm{gr} - {}_{t-1}E_{grt})
$$

$$
+ \frac{\alpha_1}{\alpha_1 + \alpha_2}\,u_2 + \frac{\alpha_2\alpha_3}{\alpha_1 + \alpha_2}\,u_1 + \alpha_5\mathrm{yr}_{-1} + (1-\alpha_5)\overline{\mathrm{yr}} \tag{10}
$$

Equations (10) and (9) together demonstrate the following. A fully anticipated change in monetary or fiscal policy has no real effect, even in the short run, while the price effects can be read off from (9) (these are the same as the long-run results). This is readily seen by setting $\mathrm{mo} = {}_{t-1}E_{mot}$ and $\mathrm{gr} = {}_{t-1}E_{grt}$. However, an unanticipated change in policy will have real effects at the same time as some, but weaker, price effects. In this case *expected* policies are unchanged but *actual* policies are allowed to change.

Thus policy which is fully anticipated cannot be stabilising even in the short run.

It is one thing, however, to show that fully anticipated policies will be impotent; it is another to establish that macro policies to stabilise the economy will themselves be anticipated. Will they be?

The contention of the New Classical School is that, if anticipations are rationally formed, macro policy stabilisation rules will also be anticipated. Therefore macro policy stabilisation will ultimately fail.

To understand the result, we can concentrate on monetary policy and replace $_{t-1}E_{\text{mo}t}$ with

$$_{t-1}E_{\text{mo}t} = \overline{\text{mo}} - \alpha_4 \text{yr}_{-1} + \alpha_4 \overline{\text{yr}} \tag{11}$$

We then have

$$\text{mo} - {}_{t-1}E_{\text{mo}t} = \overline{\text{mo}} - \alpha_4 \text{yr}_{-1} + \alpha_4 \overline{\text{yr}} + u_3 - \overline{\text{mo}}$$

$$\text{mo} - {}_{t-1}E_{\text{mo}t} + \alpha_4 \text{yr}_{-1} - \alpha_4 \overline{\text{yr}} = u_3 \tag{12}$$

The error in forecasting monetary policy is a random term u_3. Since α_4, the stabilisation term, drops out of the result stabilisation policy is ineffective.

Why is this? Consider an expenditure disturbance u_1 in period t. By definition, it is unanticipated. The authorities can do nothing to counter it in period t. Wages in t are also predetermined. It is seen from (10) and (9) that both output and prices will increase.

The authorities observe the current increase in output. Because, importantly, there is a persistent effect into the next period, the authorities can in principle alter their monetary policy so as to counter this lagged effect in the next period. Suppose for a moment that this change in monetary policy is unanticipated. An optimal monetary policy in these circumstances is one which will now neutralise the secondary effect.

So far, the story is straightforward enough. The contribution of the New Classical economists is to argue as follows. The private sector, notably the 'workers' in this case, will also observe the increase in current output. They will also, with time and effort, have figured out the monetary policy rule as in (4). They will therefore reason that in the next period monetary policy will be tighter. From (8) they will conclude that prices will be lower; they will set their contract wages proportionately less. With the real wage rate unchanged in the next period, output cannot be reduced to offset the persistence effect. So monetary stabilisation policy will fail. It will fail to stabilise output but it will also destabilise prices (from (9)).

It is a clever story; it is also an important contribution to macro policy. However, in its extreme form presented above, it is not very credible since it relies for its conclusion on several key assumptions, each of which may be shown to be untenable.

THE CRITIQUE OF THE NEW CLASSICAL SCHOOL

There is now a vast literature concerned with criticising some of the assumptions of the model. There is also a large empirical literature concerned with testing the New Classical propositions. In this section we examine the theoretical critique.

Consider first the assumption that expectations are formed rationally. There are two potential criticisms of this. The public may not know the structure of the model or they may not know the policy rule.

There is disagreement amongst economists about the appropriate model. Is it sensible to suppose that there is in fact an agreed model on which expectations are based and, moreover, that the true values of the underlying coefficients are known? Even if there is a known structural model, some of the underlying coefficients will change in value over time, necessitating a gradual, time-consuming, learning process to master the new structure.

It is also difficult to believe that the private sector would know a monetary policy rule of the type represented by (4). Changes in governments produce changes in policy reaction functions; the coefficients are bound to change over time. Even if a simple policy rule is sustained over many years, it will take time for the public to know this rule; in the meantime, policy will be effective.

For these reasons, we can conclude that the assumption that expectations are rationally formed in the sense above is probably not very realistic.

We turn now to more fundamental criticisms. Suppose that expectations are rationally formed but suppose here too that the key assumption, that the stabilisation policy lag is no shorter than that operative to say wage (or price) determination, does not hold. Suppose that monetary policy is a sufficiently flexible instrument so it can actually squeeze in, so to speak, between the private sector decision-making period. To be more precise, suppose monetary policy reacts almost instantly so that $\alpha_4 yr$ replaces $\alpha_4 yr_{-1}$ in (4). Then it is obvious that the 'rigidity' in wage determination allows the authorities to respond to an exogenous disturbance before wages have had time to react.

Instead of taking the existing model and allowing the authorities to respond more quickly, we could alternatively, but with exactly the same result, have allowed wage and price adjustment to be stickier, extending over more than one period. A typical example of this in the literature is the multi-period wage contract (as in Chapter 14). Say some workers at least have committed their wage setting for at least two years; say, too, that there is a disturbance in the first year, so output increases. The authorities respond the next period but, although this is predictable, wages have been predetermined, and so the wage setting in the next period cannot take this development on board. Thus, policy will be effective.

Another assumption in the model is that governments do not have access to privileged information. Governments may have privileged (or superior) information allowing them to act in a stabilising capacity without being 'found out'.

We shall also see in the next chapter how much more complicated the analysis is when the model is extended to the open economy and the role of expectations is refined further.

It is evident that, once more realistic assumptions are made, there will be some scope for stabilisation policy. The strongest case will emerge if prices and wages are in reality very sticky, as in Keynesian economics (Chapter 9).

In a sense, the New Classical school have diverted attention from what may be potentially more fundamental difficulties with stabilisation policy: uncertainties about the structure of the economy, lags in adjustment (see Chapter 37).

Perhaps one can sum up the contribution of the New Classical school as follows. Provided wages and/or prices are flexible enough and provided they respond to expectations which are rationally formed, the distinction between anticipated and unanticipated policy is a very important one. This is not to say that the former is impotent; it simply means, in this context, that it is likely to be weaker than the latter. (See also on this the next chapter.)

An important implication of all this for policy is the following: suppose, in the face say of an ongoing excessive inflation rate the authorities announce a reduction in money growth. If it is credible and believed (anticipated), the real costs of disinflation will be reduced as we noted in Chapter 22. During the mid-1970s and again in the early 1980s, many governments announced disinflationary policies along these lines. It remains an open question how successful they were in these terms.

EMPIRICAL EVIDENCE ON THE NEW CLASSICAL PROPOSITIONS

The model presented above and the general New Classical framework yield predictions about the real effects of anticipated and unanticipated policies which, in principle at any rate, are empirically testable. From the late 1970s to this day there have been numerous studies attempting to test the New Classical ideas. Unfortunately, as we shall see, it has proved to be an extremely difficult task and the issues remain largely unresolved.

In this section, we focus primarily on the 'reduced form' tests, i.e. those studies which estimate a single or a very limited set of equations designed to test the New Classical hypotheses. However, a much more satisfactory attack on the question would be to simulate the effects of anticipated and unanticipated policies using a large-scale structural econometric model. Such studies are available. One such study will be reviewed in the next chapter while references to others will also be made.

A standard test would take the following form (see most recently Glick and Hutchison 1990):

$$yr_t = \pi_1 AF + \pi_2 UF + \pi_3 AM + \pi_4 UM \tag{13}$$

where yr is output, AF and UF are, respectively, anticipated and unanticipated fiscal policies and AM and UM are, respectively, anticipated and unanticipated monetary policies. Most of the testing has tended to focus on monetary policy. According to the 'pure' New Classical proposition $\pi_1 = \pi_3 = 0$, $\pi_2 > 0$ and $\pi_4 > 0$.

To undertake such a test we need an estimate of the *anticipated* component. The unanticipated component would then be the difference between the actual and the anticipated components.

How do we go about estimating the anticipated component? Because of its historical importance in this context and the influence that this seminal study exerted on the subsequent literature, we outline here briefly Barro's approach to this question.

Barro (1977) estimated an equation for the USA for the period 1941–73 which was intended to provide the best explanation for the money formation process:

$$\dot{DM}_t = 0.087 + 0.24DM_{t-1} + 0.35DM_{t-2} + 0.082FEDV_t + 0.027UN_{t-1} \qquad (14)$$

where $\dot{DM}_t$ is the predicted rate of growth of the money stock; DM_{t-1} and DM_{t-2} are the actual growth in the money stock in the two previous periods; $FEDV_t$ is a measure of the federal government expenditure relative to 'normal'; and UN_{t-1} is the unemployment rate in the previous period.

The inclusion of FEDV and UN as explanatory variables is justified as follows. Barro argues that if government expenditure follows a normal path it will tend to be financed by taxation. If, however, it is say abnormally high, the excess is likely to be financed by the creation of money. UN in the equation is justified as a counter-cyclical response of monetary policy.

If this equation is used as the 'rational predictor' for money (i.e. of anticipated money), we can then readily derive an unanticipated component and undertake tests along the lines represented by (13) above. Barro's own original statistical tests appeared to confirm the New Classical predictions.

Many studies have attempted to predict the money stock using a vector autoregressive (VAR) technique. This is a *non-theoretical statistical approach which uses any macro variables available to the public, which are thought to have a bearing on the formation of expectations about the future money stock*. This is to be distinguished from an analytical structural approach to the determination of the money stock.

Typical of this approach is the study by Glick and Hutchison (1990) who use the lagged values of the following set of variables to forecast monetary and fiscal policies: the money stock, the change in the real trend budget deficit as a percentage of potential GNP, the unemployment rate, the percentage change in the GNP deflator and the change in the three-month T-bill rate.

So what do the vast number of such studies show?

We are fortunate in that a study in 1987 prepared for the OECD by Clinton and Chouraqui (1987) carefully summarised the results of sixty-three such studies of monetary policy alone. They classified the results into three parts: studies which show that both anticipated and unanticipated policy are significant (any *difference* in significance is not reported); studies which find that anticipated policies are not significant but unanticipated policies are (this includes Barro's own studies); and studies which find neither anticipated nor unanticipated policies to be significant. In the first category were thirty-three studies, in the second seventeen and in the third thirteen.

Perhaps their own summary of the results tells it all:

Since the mid-1970s there has been a vast amount of research on the ... relative importance of anticipated and unanticipated monetary policy. The findings of this research need to be interpreted with caution as it is fraught with methodological problems.

In practice the results of the empirical work are quite varied .... Many of the

earlier studies found anticipated monetary policy to be neutral and the unanticipated component to have real effects ... but these results have not proved to be
robust; small changes in model specification overturn these results .... Results
tend to be sensitive especially to the specification of money growth equations ....
As things stand, a count of studies rejecting the hypothesis that only monetary 'surprises' influence real economic activity runs well ahead of those reporting empirical
support ... .

(1987: 37–8)

24

The effects of anticipated monetary and fiscal policies in a small economy with flexible exchange rates

INTRODUCTION

The model of the previous chapter is now extended to the open economy and refined in a number of ways. The model is then used to address the general question of the effects on a small economy of temporary or permanent anticipated/unanticipated macro policy changes at home. We focus particularly on effects of anticipated policies which occur before the events take place (so called announcement effects). Our central concern is with the dynamics of adjustment, starting from an anticipated change to the point where full equilibrium is restored. Throughout we assume expectations are rationally formed.

The question is of some importance in the real world. Financial markets, labour markets, but particularly the former, tend to be forward looking, anticipating changes in macro policies at home or abroad. At the same time markets form some idea of the effects of such policy changes on key variables in the economy; the anticipation of changes in these variables in the future will influence market behaviour even before the anticipated events take place. Instances of such behaviour abound. The daily newspapers regularly report behaviour in foreign exchange markets which are attributable to, for example, anticipated changes in monetary policy at home, e.g. the US dollar is reported to have risen today because of an anticipation that the Federal Reserve will in the future tighten policy.

Two excellent recent illustrations from the USA of the potential immediate effects of anticipated future changes in fiscal policy are the announcements of an easing of fiscal policy in early 1981 (to be phased over three years) and the subsequent Gramm–Rudman–Hollings legislation of a programmed fiscal tightening (see Branson *et al*. 1985; Johnson, R.A. 1986; McKibbin 1988a).

As we saw in the previous chapter the New Classical economists, using mostly models of closed economies, were the first to analyse in depth the implications of the distinction between a macro policy which is anticipated and one which is not. By the late 1970s the models had become more refined, the analysis had been extended to open economies and some attention came to be paid to potential announcement effects. These developments continued into the 1980s. (See Wilson 1979; Turnovsky 1981, 1986; Blanchard 1984; Marston 1985; Ahtiala 1987; Ambler 1988, 1989; Argy 1990a, 1992a). Some econometric analysis of the effects of anticipated monetary fiscal policies was also undertaken. (See Masson and Blundell-Wignall 1985; Haas and Masson 1986; McKibbin 1988a; Bryant *et al.* 1989).

Branson *et al.* (1985) and Johnson, R.A. (1986) use similar models of an open economy to analyse the effects of anticipated changes in the monetary–fiscal mix. In their model anticipations play no role in the labour market. Similar models are used in Ambler (1988, 1989). Wilson (1979) takes Dornbusch's 1976 model as a starting point (where expectations only appear in exchange markets) and analyses announcement and subsequent effects of a monetary expansion. (See Dornbusch 1976).

Blanchard (1984) analyses the effects of anticipated fiscal policies but in a closed economy. Likewise, Turnovsky and Miller (1984) analyse the effects of anticipated/ unanticipated fiscal policies in a closed economy variant of the Blinder–Solow model. Ahtiala (1987) uses a richer model of a small open economy (which incorporates wealth) to analyse the transmission of foreign policies under different assumptions about the formation of expectations and of wages.

Turnovsky (1981) comes closest to our own analysis, using a similar model and a similar conceptual framework, but he analyses only the effects of domestic monetary polices and of foreign price changes. Marston (1985) also presents a very similar model but undertakes very little actual analysis of announcement effects.

THE MODEL

The small economy

$$\text{yr} = \alpha_1(e + p^* - p_\text{d}) - \alpha_4[r_\text{d} - ({}_tE_{pt+1} - p_t)] + \alpha_3\text{gr} \tag{1}$$

$$r_\text{d} = r^* + {}_tE_{et+1} - e \tag{2}$$

$$\text{mo} - p_\text{d} = -\alpha_{10}r_\text{d} + \alpha_5\text{yr} \tag{3}$$

$$\text{yr} = \alpha_9(p_\text{d} - {}_{t-1}E_{pt}) \tag{4}$$

$$p = \alpha_{15}p_\text{d} + (1 - \alpha_{15})(e + p^*) \tag{5}$$

Notation

All variables are in logarithms except for the interest rates.

yr	output
gr	real government expenditure
r_d	interest rate at home
r^*	interest rate abroad
mo	money stock
p_d	prices
p^*	foreign price level
$_tE_{et+1}$	expected exchange rate formed in period t for $t + 1$
$_{t-1}E_{pt}$	expected price level formed in $t - 1$ for t
p	consumer price index at home
e	exchange rate
$_tE_{pdt+1}$	expectations about prices formed in period t for $t + 1$ (similar notation applies to all expectations formation)

The basic model is a familiar one so we can be brief in summarising it. In equation (1) the demand for goods is a positive function of the real exchange rate, of foreign output and of real government expenditure (the fiscal policy instrument) and a negative function of the real interest rate. Equation (2) captures the assumption of perfect asset substitution. Equation (3) is a conventional money demand equation. Equation (4) represents aggregate supply. The supply of output is a function of the real wage rate. In turn the nominal wage rate in period t is determined by the expected consumer price index formed during negotiations in period $t - 1$. Equation (5) is the definition of the consumer price index.

Expectations now appear in three places: in the calculation of the real interest rate (1), in the determination of asset substitution (2) and in the formation of wages (4).

FRAMEWORK AND QUESTIONS ADDRESSED

Basically we are interested in the time dynamics of adjustment to policy changes using, as in the model above, discrete time periods. Our time horizon encompasses four periods: the period prior to any change, when the economy is in steady state equilibrium $(t - 2)$, the period when a change may be anticipated $(t - 1)$ (our announcement effects), the period when an actual policy change may or may not occur (t) and the period $(t + 1)$ when the economy settles down into a new 'stationary' equilibrium, which may or may not be the same as $t - 2$ depending on whether a 'permanent' change in policy has occurred in t. During $t + 1$ all anticipations are fully realised, by definition.

The whole system can be reduced to an equation like

$$\text{ev} = f(_{t-1}E_{mpt},\ \text{mp},\ _{t-1}E_{mpt+1},\ _tE_{mpt+1}) \tag{6}$$

where ev stands for the endogenous variables in the home economy at time t and mp stands for macro policy. f indicates that ev is a function of actual and expected policies.

The endogenous variable (be it yr, e, p_d or r_d) is determined by actual macro policy undertaken at time t but as well by a set of expectations formed in the current or previous period about macro policy in t and $t+1$.

Inspection of (6) reveals that there are numerous variations on a basic theme. We take here deviations from a steady state:

a) an unanticipated macro policy change which is now expected to be permanent, $mp = {}_tE_{mpt+1} > 0$, ${}_{t-1}E_{mpt} = {}_{t-1}E_{mpt+1} = 0$;

b) an unanticipated macro policy change which is expected to be temporary, $mp > 0$, ${}_tE_{mpt+1} = {}_{t-1}E_{mpt} = {}_{t-1}E_{mpt+1} = 0$;

c) an anticipated, realised, temporary policy change, ${}_{t-1}E_{mpt} = mp > 0$, ${}_{t-1}E_{mpt+1} = {}_tE_{mpt+1} = 0$;

d) an anticipated, realised, permanent policy change, ${}_{t-1}E_{mpt} = mp = {}_{t-1}E_{mpt+1} = {}_tE_{mpt+1} > 0$;

e) an anticipated temporary but unrealised policy change (in t) now expected not to proceed (in $t+1$), ${}_{t-1}E_{mpt} > 0$, $mp = {}_{t-1}E_{mpt+1} = {}_tE_{mpt+1} = 0$;

f) an anticipated permanent, but unrealised, policy change (in t) now expected not to proceed (in $t+1$), ${}_{t-1}E_{mpt} = {}_{t-1}E_{mpt+1} > 0$, $mp = {}_tE_{mpt+1} = 0$;

g) an anticipated permanent, but unrealised, policy change (in t) now expected to proceed (in $t+1$), ${}_{t-1}E_{mpt} = {}_{t-1}E_{mpt+1} = {}_tE_{mpt+1}$, $mp = 0$.

In what follows we pay some attention to only four cases. Our case 1 corresponds to (d) above. Our case 2 corresponds to (c). Our case 3 corresponds to (b). Our case 4 corresponds to (f).

Model solutions are extremely cumbersome, so it was decided not to present them. These are available in Argy (1992a).

MONETARY POLICIES AT HOME

We now briefly discuss each of the four cases identified above.

Case 1 – an anticipated, realised, permanent monetary expansion

In period t we have New Classical results. Monetary expansion leaves output in period t unchanged (as in $t-2$); at the same time, the currency devalues and prices rise proportionately. This outcome is anticipated in $t-1$ when wages are set for period t.

What distinguishes this case from the New Classics is the dynamics of adjustment. Consider what will happen in $t-1$. Now ${}_{t-1}E_{pdt} = {}_{t-1}E_{et} = {}_{t-1}E_{mot} = {}_{t-1}E_{mot+1}$. Output, prices and the interest rate must all rise while the currency must devalue in real and nominal terms. Thus, importantly, output must first rise in $t-1$ and then fall equivalently in t.

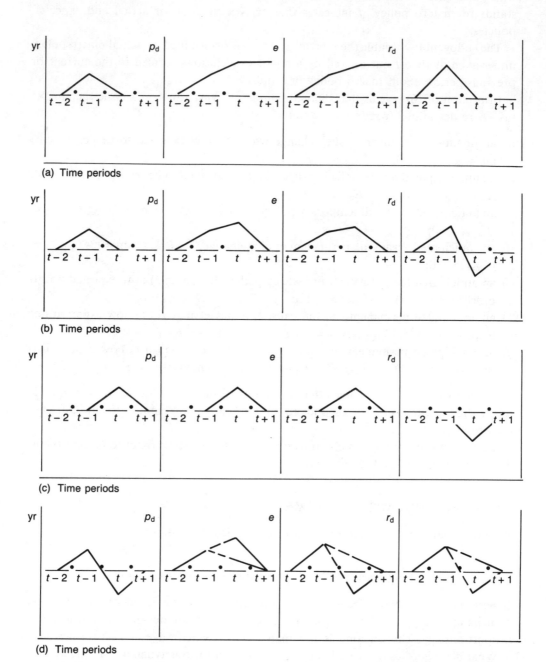

Figure 24.1 Monetary expansion at home: (a) case 1; (b) case 2; (c) case 3; (d) case 4. Broken lines represent uncertainties

The underlying economic reasoning is fairly straightforward. In $t-1$ wages are predetermined. At the same time there is an expectation of both inflation and a devaluation in the next period. On both counts (the first because the real interest rate falls) there will be some increase in output and home prices. With the money stock also fixed in $t-1$ the interest rate will rise.

It is readily shown that

$$\text{yr}_{-1} = k_5 \alpha_{1t-1} E_{et} + k_5 \alpha_4 \alpha_{15t-1} E_{pdt} \tag{7}$$

where

$$k_5 = \frac{\alpha_{10}\alpha_9}{\alpha_{10}\alpha_9 + (\alpha_1 + \alpha_4\alpha_{15})(1 + \alpha_5\alpha_9 + \alpha_{10})}$$

and, in this case, $_{t-1}E_{et} = {}_{t-1}E_{pdt}$.

Figure 24.1(a) illustrates this case. In $t-1$ output increases; there is also an increase in the price level and a nominal (and real) devaluation. At the same time the home interest rate rises (reflecting an expected devaluation). In t the nominal currency devalues further but there is now a real appreciation; output and the interest rate both fall.

Case 2 – an anticipated, realised, temporary monetary expansion

In t we again replicate New Classical results. The initial $(t-2)$, level of output is restored again but prices rise and the currency devalues, both now less than proportionately,[1] while restoring the original real exchange rate. At the same time the interest rate now falls below its initial level reflecting the fact that there is an anticipation that the currency will appreciate. In $t+1$ the price level and the currency return to their original levels.

What happens in $t-1$? Now $_{t-1}E_{pdt} = {}_{t-1}E_{et} < {}_{t-1}E_{mot}$ and so the increase in the level of output and prices will be less; the devaluation will also now be less but there will again be a real devaluation.

The dynamics of adjustment are illustrated in Figure 24.1(b).

Case 3 – an unanticipated expansion in money, expected to be temporary

This case is the most straightforward. There are no announcement effects; output increases in t and returns to its original level in $t+1$. In t there is a real devaluation (the currency devalues by more than inflation) while the home interest rate falls (reflecting an expected appreciation). All variables return to their original levels in $t+1$ (see Figure 24.1(c)).

Case 4 – an anticipated permanent but unrealised, monetary expansion now expected not to proceed

This case is of particular interest. In $t - 1$ wages are negotiated to rise in t in proportion to the anticipated monetary expansion, which in fact is now not realised. Period t thus inherits an exogenous wage shock, which will exercise a net deflationary effect on the level of output. Bearing in mind that in $t - 1$ the economy behaves exactly as it did in case 1, when the same anticipations were held, there is now a slump in output below the level in $t - 2$. The direction of change in the other three variables between $t - 1$ and t is ambiguous. (See Figure 24.1(d) where alternative paths are illustrated.)

In t, when the error is observed, there is now a new anticipation that the money stock will not change, an anticipation which we assume is realised in $t + 1$ when all variables now converge to their original levels.

FISCAL POLICIES AT HOME

What follows is a summary of the results for fiscal policies.

Case 1 – an anticipated, realised, permanent fiscal expansion

A (fully anticipated) 'permanent' fiscal expansion in t will increase output, appreciate the currency in real and nominal terms, lower home prices but leave the home interest rate unchanged. (See Chapter 8.)

More interesting is what happens in $t - 1$ (the announcement effect). With expectations in $t - 1$ rationally formed, there will be an anticipation that both e (the exchange rate) and p_d will fall but that e falls by more than p_d. (See also Chapter 8 on this.) So $_{t-1}E_{et} > _{t-1}E_{p_dt}$ (both negative). It is readily shown that on both counts output (and prices) in $t - 1$ must fall (see equation (7)). The combined effects of an anticipated appreciation and the fall in home prices act to depress activity. It is also easily shown that the currency appreciates while the interest rate falls (reflecting a further expected appreciation).

So, to sum up, in $t - 1$ output falls but it more than recovers in t (where it will stay at the higher level 'indefinitely'). The currency appreciates in $t - 1$, appreciates further in t and then stays at this new level. The interest rate falls and then returns to its original level. Home prices fall in $t - 1$, may rise or fall in t but settle in t 'indefinitely' at a lower level (see Figure 24.2(a)).

Class 2 – an anticipated, realised, temporary fiscal expansion

The outcomes in period t are different from the previous case. Output is above its initial ($t - 2$) level but below that of the previous case. The currency appreciates by less; at the same time the interest rate is above its initial position (now in anticipation of a devaluation) while the level of prices is now ambiguous (prices could rise or fall).

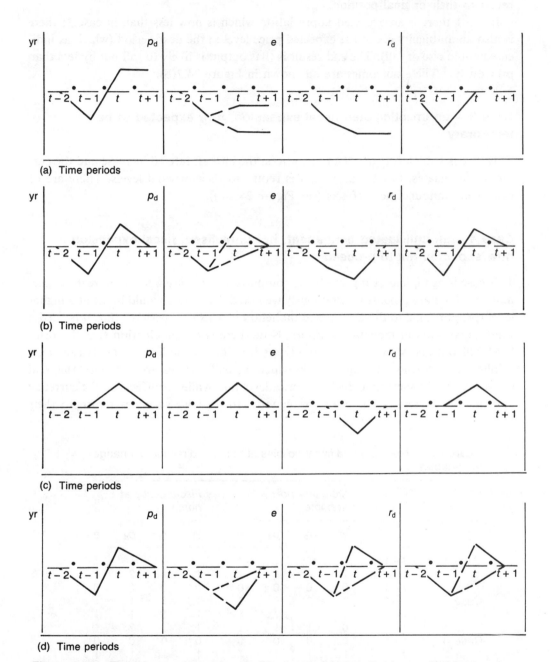

(a) Time periods

(b) Time periods

(c) Time periods

(d) Time periods

Figure 24.2   Fiscal expansion at home: (a) case 1; (b) case 2; (c) case 3; (d) case 4. Broken lines represent uncertainties

The real appreciation is also weaker than in the previous case. In $t + 1$ all variables revert to their original position.

In $t - 1$ there is an expected appreciation which is now less than in case 1; there is also an ambiguity about the expected price level in the next period (which as indicated could rise or fall). The end result is that output is likely to fall but by less than previously.[2] These outcomes are all shown in Figure 24.2(b).

Case 3 – an unanticipated fiscal expansion, now expected to be temporary

This case is straightforward. Output, prices, the interest rate all increase and the currency appreciates. In $t + 1$ all variables return to their original levels. There are of course no announcement effects (see Figure 24.2(c)).

Case 4 – an anticipated permanent, but unrealised, fiscal expansion now expected not to proceed

This case is again interesting and bears comparison with case 4 for an unrealised permanent monetary expansion. Previously we noted that wages would be set at a higher level (proportional to the anticipated monetary expansion); period t thus inherited a wage burst without monetary support. Now there is an anticipation that the price level will fall and so wages are actually set for t below the level of $t - 1$; thus now t inherits a downward wage shock which actually serves to stimulate the real economy. At the same time the home price level falls while the effects on the currency and on the interest rate in t are ambiguous. In $t + 1$ all variables return to their

Table 24.1 Monetary and fiscal policies at home – direction of change in variables

		Monetary policy at home				Fiscal policy at home			
		yr	r_d	p_d	e	yr	r_d	p_d	e
Case 1	$t - 1$	↑	↑	↑	↑	↓	↓	↓	↓
	t	↓	↓	↑	↑	↑	↑	?	↓
	$t + 1$	0	0	0	0	0	0	0	0
Case 2	$t - 1$	↑	↑	↑	↑	↓	↓	↓	↓
	t	↓	↓	↑	↑	↑	↑	↑	↓
	$t + 1$	0	↑	↓	↓	↓	↓	?	↑
Case 3	$t - 1$	0	0	0	0	0	0	0	0
	t	↑	↓	↑	↑	↑	↑	↑	↓
	$t + 1$	↓	↑	↓	↓	↓	↓	↓	↑
Case 4	$t - 1$	↑	↑	↑	↑	↓	↓	↓	↓
	t	↓	↓	?	↓	↑	↑	?	↑
	$t + 1$	↑	?	↓	?	↓	?	↑	?

$t - 2$ levels. Announcement effects are identical to those discussed in case 1 above. (The path of adjustment is shown in Figure 24.2(d).)

Table 24.1 summarises all these results for monetary and fiscal policy changes.

ECONOMIC VALIDATION, FOR AUSTRALIA, OF THEORETICAL OUTCOMES

We made some reference in the Introduction to econometric simulations of the effects of anticipated changes in macro policy, notably in the large countries. Of the smaller economies in the OECD (as at August 1992) only four now have a flexible rate regime: Australia, Canada, New Zealand and Switzerland. Australia is therefore one country to which one might expect some application of the results of the chapter.

It so happens that a recent paper by McKibbin (1988) carries out simulations, using the MSG2 model, of the effects of anticipated changes in monetary and fiscal policies in Australia. The simulations and results are so close to ours that they are worth reporting.

Consider, first, the case of an anticipated permanent monetary expansion in Australia 'believed in 1986 to occur in 1987'. The outcomes reported are that 'the exchange rate depreciates on the news, then further depreciates ... once the policy is implemented. Output rises before the implementation of the policy ... interest rates actually rise in anticipation of the shock ... .' Inspection of the detailed outcomes reveals that prices also rise. The simulation actually corresponds to our case 1. A careful comparison of our results with those reported by McKibbin completely validates our theoretical outcomes (see Table 24.1). The outcomes in the period when the anticipation is formed are identical. It is also worth noting that in McKibbin too output does in due course fall back, ultimately returning to its original level.

Consider, second, the case of an anticipated permanent fiscal expansion at home again 'anticipated in 1986 to occur in 1987'. The outcomes reported are that output and prices fall, the currency appreciates and the short-term interest rate falls. All these outcomes correspond exactly to those reported for case 1 earlier (Table 24.1). It is also well worth noting that output in the next period rises above its base level, eventually settling down at the new level. This again parallels our own results.

25

The equilibrium rate of inflation with discretion and some reputation

INTRODUCTION

This chapter reviews a large literature concerned with the potential implications, for the equilibrium inflation rate, of allowing governments complete discretion with respect to the use of monetary policy. The literature is relatively new and is, in fact, an extension of the New Classical framework, which assigns a key role to expectations, which in turn are assumed to be rationally formed.

The question we pose is the following. Suppose governments had complete discretion on monetary policy and suppose the private sector can anticipate potential strategies by the government. What is likely to be the ultimate outcome in terms of inflation and unemployment?

We know that it is only under completely flexible exchange rates that governments have full discretion on money stock policy. We know, too, that the more managed the exchange rate, the greater is the constraint imposed on governments. At the other end of the continuum, when exchange rates are fixed and asset substitution is perfect, governments lose all control over money stock policy and discretion is lost.

Since we want to develop the implications flowing from *discretion*, we shall assume, at least in our basic analysis, that exchange rates are flexible. The analysis draws on Kydland and Prescott (1977), Barro and Gordon (1983), Fischer (1988b), Persson (1988) and Rogoff (1987). Our own presentation owes much to Fischer.

THE EQUILIBRIUM RATE OF INFLATION UNDER FLEXIBLE RATES

We explain here in words the key elements of the New Classical analysis. An appendix presents the arguments more rigorously.

The starting point of the analysis is a simple sequential game between two parties: the trade unions and the authorities, with the authorities in the position of being able to play their cards last. Assume that in period $t - 1$ the authorities announce a money growth target for period t which is consistent with an inflation rate of zero; assume, too, that workers negotiate wages in $t - 1$ for t and that they believe the authorities. So for t they will set wages in line with the (zero) inflation rate anticipated. Assume further that the authorities have a welfare function which takes explicit account of deviations from a zero inflation rate and of deviations from an 'optimal' unemployment rate (which last is taken to be below the natural rate for reasons noted later), with weights attaching to each of those targets.

Period t starts with zero inflation and the natural rate of unemployment. If the authorities are very shortsighted (i.e. they will try to maximise the welfare function in period t only) they will have an incentive in the course of period t to renege on their announcement, adopt a more expansionary monetary policy, lower the real wage rate and drive the unemployment rate below the natural rate, albeit at a cost in terms of some inflation. Sooner or later, however, workers will anticipate the authorities' behaviour and adjust wages up accordingly. In time, the rate of inflation will settle above zero but the economy will revert to its natural rate of unemployment. Thus 'activism' will have produced an outcome where the inflation rate is non-optimal and there is no change in the unemployment rate.

The steady state inflation rate π with activism can be shown to be (see the Appendix)

$$\pi = \frac{b}{a}(k - 1)y^* \qquad k > 1 \tag{1}$$

where a is the weight attaching to the inflation objective, b is the real effect of an unanticipated change in money, $k > 1$ reflects the assumption that the target unemployment rate is below the natural rate and y^* is the level of output corresponding to the natural rate.

It is evident from the above that the less weight that attaches to inflation (the lower a), the larger k (the greater the divergence between the efficient and the natural rate) and the larger b, the larger will be the inflation rate (the excess over the optimal).

This base analysis could be modified or extended in several ways. We note here three potential criticisms and extensions.

First, the analysis assumed that in period t when the authorities sprang a monetary surprise on the public the wage rate was fixed, predetermined by the previous period's expectations. If, however, wages were automatically indexed *ex post* to the price level which eventuates in period t, the real wage rate could not fall, output could not increase and the monetary expansion would be completely absorbed in higher prices (Chapter 8). This is so even though the monetary expansion was unanticipated. In this case the problem posed by discretion disappears completely. Paradoxically, in this context at any rate, wage indexation reduces the equilibrium rate of inflation to its 'optimal' level of zero because the incentive to cheat now vanishes. In terms of equation (1) $b = 0$ and the expression becomes zero.

Second, a key assumption in the analysis is the notion that the 'efficient' rate of unemployment is below the natural rate of unemployment. Several reasons are sometimes advanced for this, e.g. the presence of household taxes, generous unemployment benefits, an excessive real wage rate.

The importance of the assumption is readily demonstrated. Suppose the efficient rate was also equal to the natural rate and suppose again that the economy starts in period t with a natural rate of unemployment and a zero rate of inflation. In these circumstances the authorities will have no incentive to push down the unemployment. Doing so would simply reduce welfare. In terms of equation (1) if $k = 1$ the expression would again be zero. Much therefore hinges on an underlying theory which, however, remains vague and controversial.

Third, our analysis also focused on a one-period horizon, assuming the authorities did not look beyond maximising a welfare function in one year. This is almost certainly unrealistic and we need at least to make a tentative stab at what might happen if governments had a longer horizon and were also concerned about their reputation.

At this point, the analysis can be very complicated, with numerous potential outcomes depending on how we represent private sector expectations and the behaviour of the government.

Here, we follow Fischer (1988b) in pursuing one particular possible outcome, noting again that it is just one of many conceivable results.

Suppose that once a government has cheated the private sector will come to expect the rate of inflation in (1). The government can get away with cheating *just one period*; that government (party) then faces an expected rate of inflation and hence a rate of growth of wages equal to (1) for *all* future periods. At this point, the government can follow one of two strategies. First, the authorities can revert to a zero-inflation money growth. In this case, real wages and unemployment would both rise. Second, the authorities can accommodate the new expected rate of inflation; in this case, inflation is stabilised at the higher rate while unemployment reverts to its natural rate. It is not difficult to see that, in the circumstances assumed, the authorities will opt for the second strategy; in other words, go for (1) on an indefinite basis.

If the authorities had a longer horizon they would need to set off all future losses discounted to the present against the one-period short-run gain. It is now no longer evident that they will pursue a short-run strategy. If the discount rate is not too high the authorities might well opt for a long-term strategy. Reputational considerations thus may serve to produce a more modest rate of inflation, closer to the optimal.

The framework we have used to analyse longer time horizons is admittedly far too simple. Party leaders, party commitments do change over time. The public is unlikely to hold it indefinitely against a party whose constituent has changed. In any event, 'punishment' is not likely to take the drastic form suggested in the example. If a government announces a new inflation strategy and for a while, at least, implements it, the public may well be prepared to give it the benefit of the doubt.

There are other questions one might ask about the above framework. Are workers, assumed to be rational and forward looking, able to predict the equilibrium rate of inflation, especially given the ideological shifts to which governments are subject? Is it true that governments, in targeting the unemployment rate, end up with more inflation? Experience, after the second oil price shock, suggests that most governments give a very high priority to inflation even at the cost of rising unemployment (Chapter 42).

INFLATION PERFORMANCE AND THE CONDUCT OF MONETARY POLICY

One general prediction thrown up by the theory is that governments with a strong medium-run orientation, who attach considerable importance to keeping inflation low, *are likely to end up with lower inflation rates without any higher unemployment rates*. How can we test this? One direct way is simply to see if countries with low inflation on average have performed any worse on unemployment. Countries with low inflation, by definition, would be those whose governments have given inflation a high priority in their macroeconomic management.

Figure 25.1 plots the relationship, for sixteen countries, over four different periods, between the rates of unemployment and the rates of inflation. The periods are long enough for one to be able to say, safely, that they represent medium-run adjustments. It is evident that there is little, if any, relationship between the two. Indeed, for the years 1974–81 there is a suggestion of a positive relationship.

The IMF in its World Economic Outlook for May 1991 carried out a similar analysis for fifteen countries for the one period 1971–90. They find a small positive relationship and conclude:

> the positive correlation over the medium term provides empirical support for the strategy of keeping monetary policy aimed at controlling inflation and achieving steady progress toward price stability.
>
> (1991: 107)

A different way to test this is the following. We take as a starting point the notion that governments who have greater control over monetary policy will be more likely to exploit these powers for short-run ends and are thus more likely to end up in the worst of all possible worlds. By contrast, countries which have relatively independent central banks, whose horizon would be more oriented towards the medium run, are more likely to perform better on inflation and no worse on unemployment.

Alesina and Summers (1990), in a recent study, attempt to test these hypotheses. Their finding is that in the years 1951–88, for seventeen industrial countries, on average those countries whose central banks were relatively more independent did tend to have lower inflation; at the same time, there is no evidence that their real economic performance is in any way inferior (real economic performance is here measured by the variance of economic growth).

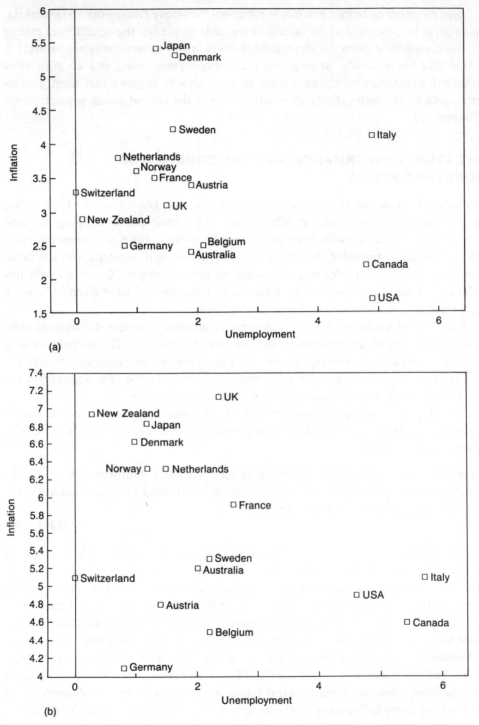

Figure 25.1 Inflation–unemployment: (a) 1960–7; (b) 1968–73; (c) 1974–81; (d) 1982–91

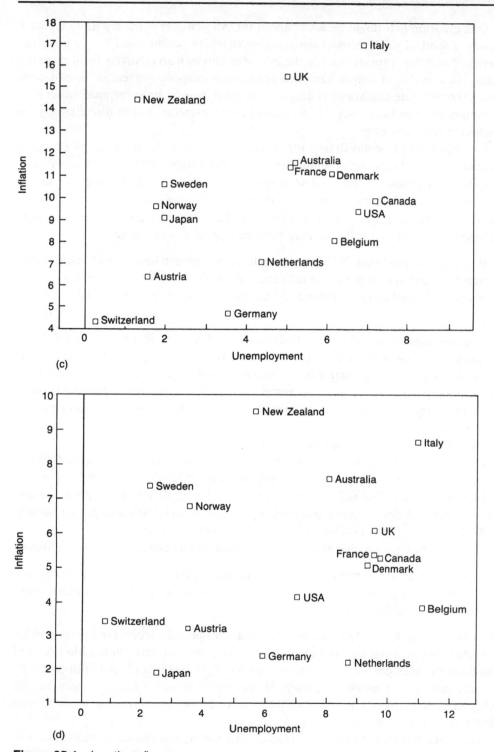

Figure 25.1 (*continued*)

One question that might be asked about the Alesina and Summers study is that it covers a span of some thirty-seven years, over which period many of the countries switched exchange rate regimes. In the case of countries with relatively fixed exchange rates, the question of central bank independence is only one element in the equation. The exchange rate constraint is another. In other words, however much discretion governments may have, they will be limited in the exercise of such discretion by the exchange rate constraint.

Swinburne and Castello-Branco review all empirical work in this area and find that, in general, it confirms these findings. However, the authors express legitimate doubts themselves over tests of this kind on at least two grounds. First, they rightly contend that there is a serious measurement problem in arriving at an indicator of independence. Second, they also note that there may be a *causality* problem: central bank independence and low inflation may both be due to a third factor.

> It might be argued that the German public's often quoted deep-seated fear of inflation has exerted a strong direct influence on the decisions of policy makers in that country, as well as being behind the creation of an independent Bundesbank.
>
> (1991: 15)

Assume governments do abuse their powers. How can we correct for this? The country can impose on itself a constitutional rule regarding monetary policy and inflation. Giving the central bank a much greater degree of independence from governments may achieve a similar result. As an alternative, a smaller country may be able to peg its currency to a large trading partner whose own inflation record is a good one.

How have the smaller countries coped with this question?

Of the OECD member countries outside the G3, only four – Australia, Canada, New Zealand and Switzerland – currently (August 1992) float their currencies.

In 1989 the New Zealand government passed new legislation which provided that the primary function of the central bank was to pursue an inflation target, set initially at 0–2 per cent, to be achieved by the end of 1993 (Chapter 48).

The Canadian case is also of interest. The Bank of Canada Act directs the Bank to

> regulate credit and currency in the best interests of the economic life of the nation ... and to mitigate by its influence fluctuations in the general level of production, trade, prices and employment.

This is a vague and wide mandate, allowing considerable scope for interpretation. The Act also provides that in the event of a disagreement between the Minister and the Bank the Minister may issue a formal directive, thus taking ultimate responsibility for the conduct of monetary policy. However, no directive has ever been issued; without such a directive, the bank is free to place its own interpretation on its responsibilities (Duguay and Poloz 1991).

The Governor of the Bank of Canada, John Crow, has chosen in recent years to take a fairly hard line on inflation. In his Hanson Memorial lecture, he articulated his conviction that 'monetary policy should be conducted so as to achieve a pace of monetary expansion that promotes stability in the value of money. This means pursuing a policy aimed at achieving and maintaining stable prices' (see Lucas 1989).

An interesting further development in Canada has been that in February 1991 the Governor, John Crow, announced an explicit downward target path for inflation: 3 per cent by the end of 1992, 2.5 per cent by the middle of 1994 and 2 per cent by the end of 1995.

The case of Switzerland is straightforward. Switzerland's central bank is very independent. The Swiss constitution is very vague about the objectives that the Swiss National Bank should pursue. It is directed to act 'in the interests of the country as a whole' and to 'combat unemployment and inflation'. In reality, the bank has interpreted its mandate even more narrowly, giving overriding priority to the achievement of price stability (Rich 1991).

The Reserve Bank Act of Australia gives the government ultimate responsibility for monetary policy. The Governing Board is required by the 1959 Reserve Bank Act to pursue a broad range of objectives (Chapter 48). The Opposition, however, is now committed to changing the Charter of the Bank to one that focuses on fighting inflation only, with formal targets in the range 0–2 per cent. At the moment, then, Australia is the odd one out in this group of four, being the 'least committed', formally at any rate, to inflation targets.

The UK is a particularly interesting case because it in fact switched over the last dozen years or so from inflation discipline 'at home' to external discipline (Miller and Sutherland 1990). Between 1980 and 1986 it followed a hard line monetarist strategy. The exchange rate was to find its own level; at the same time, monetary policy was to be directed at achieving medium-run inflation objectives. By 1986, the inflation objectives were largely attained but the monetarist strategy (primary emphasis on money growth policy) was downgraded. For a while after that the authorities began to give greater attention to the value of sterling in the setting of monetary policy. The policy of setting exchange rate targets was itself in turn also largely cast aside in the course of 1989 with some reversion to the earlier strategy. However, in October 1990, the UK accepted the exchange rate mechanism provisions of the European Monetary System (EMS). From then on, at least to September 1992, it shifted to a policy of achieving inflation objectives by pegging its currency to a low-inflation trading partner (Chapter 46).

Of the other countries virtually all are now either members of the EMS or likely to join soon; by pegging their currencies, these countries have opted for the external inflation discipline. France and Ireland provide a good illustration of countries with a past record of relatively high inflation now 'toeing the line' (Chapter 22).

This leaves the G3. Germany's central bank, the Bundesbank, has a high degree of independence and is committed to a policy of achieving price stability. Since 1985 the Bundesbank, in determining its money growth targets, has 'set an unchanged normative-price increase of at most 2%' (Schmid and Hermann 1991).

The Bank of Japan, which also enjoys a good deal of independence, has seen its task as one primarily of achieving price stability. This is confirmed by econometric analysis of Japanese monetary policy (Bryant 1991). (For details, see Chapter 47.)

In the USA monetary policy decisions are made by the Federal Reserve Board, composed of seven members appointed by the President for terms of fourteen years each. The Chairman is selected by the President from the Board members. Given the longevity of the terms the President has in general only limited capacity to appoint members of similar persuasion. However, the independence of the Board is circumscribed by the multiplicity of economic goals it is expected to pursue, including 'maximum employment, production and purchasing power' with no priorities prescribed. Moreover, despite the appearance of independence, the activities of the Federal Reserve are closely monitored by the government and Congress, making it in practice 'difficult, if not impossible, for the Federal Reserve to *sustain* a generally unpopular monetary policy course in the absence of substantial support from the President and the Congress' (Akhtar and Howe 1991).

In the USA too there have been proposals put forward by Congress at various times to reform the conduct of monetary policy so as to give a much higher priority to inflation. The most recent was the proposal in 1989 by the House Joint Resolutions 382 and 409 to establish a zero or near zero inflation objective to be achieved over a period of five years.

Proposals to fix exchange rates for the three major currencies also provide for price stability. McKinnon's prescriptions (McKinnon 1988) fall in this category (Chapter 36).

In the EMS too, the new central bank to be set up in the years to come is to be independent and to have responsibility for inflation in the region.

What are we to conclude on the question of central bank independence and inflation targeting?

Many subtle forces are at work in trying to resolve questions of central bank autonomy. First, governments have some limited capacity to bias central bank decisions in their favour by appointments they make to the governing boards. As a last resort, they can even sack Governors but this is an extremely rare event. Also, government nominees can make strong representations on behalf of the government. Second, there are subtle and non-subtle ways, which governments exercise, of drawing attention to differences of opinion and putting pressure on boards.

Third, government flexibility and discretion are very limited where the charter not only directs the central bank to achieve price stability, but also prescribes a low and narrow target range. This, however, is rare. There is more flexibility where the target range is to be negotiated with the government (e.g. as in New Zealand).

Fourth, many charters define a whole range of objectives, leaving Governors and managing boards considerable discretion in interpretation. Indeed, within the given constraints, Governors do often leave their personal imprint on the course of policy. For example, Paul Volker in the USA and Mieno in Japan both have had reputations as 'hardliners'.

Fifth, as we saw earlier, attitudes to inflation differ markedly across countries depending on a country's own cultural and economic history. This sometimes is more important than technical–legal questions bearing on relative discretionary powers. (See on some of these issues Swinburne and Castello-Branco (1991).)

QUESTIONS ASSOCIATED WITH A RIGID INFLATION TARGET

A first question is the price index to be targeted. Should it be the consumer price index, the GDP deflator, wholesale prices, the price of traded goods? For example, if the consumer price index is stabilised, this may require that the price of traded goods *fall* secularly. In both New Zealand and Canada, targets are defined in terms of the consumer price index.

A second question is: should it exclude transitory shocks to the price level? In both New Zealand and Canada, the effects of one-off changes in food and energy prices or in indirect taxes are discounted.

In this context, the p-star (p^*) approach to measuring underlying inflationary pressures has recently received a good deal of attention (Hoeller and Poret 1991). The price level predicted is calculated from the money stock per unit of *potential* output (mo $- y^*$) adjusted for trend velocity (v^*) as in

$$p^* = (\text{mo} - y^*) + v^*$$

A third question is: given the price index used, what should be its target rate of change? The notion of an 'optimal' rate of inflation is a complex and elusive concept (we review the issues in Chapter 34). There are two points worth making here. To begin, as we shall see, the literature does not support the idea that the target rate ought to be zero. A related point is that, whatever the optimal rate of inflation, it is bound to be different across different countries, a point, as noted above, which argues *against* imposing a *common* rate of inflation on a regional group (e.g. as in the EMS).

A fourth question has to do with how democratic an arrangement is which delegates responsibility in some circumstances for a vital element in macroeconomic policy to an independent institution. Governments can wash their hands of responsibility for outcomes which turn out to be unpleasant.

A fifth question has to do with the potential cost flowing from loss of monetary policy discretion associated with such policies. It is not difficult to demonstrate analytically that if we allow some discretion to respond within each period to observed real shocks (before wages have had time to adjust) there is some loss from the higher inflation but some potential gain from being able to respond flexibly (see the Appendix).

The basic point here, in words, is that, in the presence of say a supply shock, discretion allows the authorities to choose a combination of inflation and unemployment more consistent with society's preferences. For example, an adverse supply shock with a fixed money stock will normally generate some inflation and some unemployment. Monetary discretion, on the other hand, gives the authorities the capability of fine tuning the inflation–unemployment outcomes. (See also on this Flood and Isard (1989).)

Accommodating stochastic shocks introduces yet another possibility, first raised by Canzoneri (1985). Suppose there were a money demand shock (say a fall in money demand); there could then be a surprise 'inflation' for which the authorities were not responsible. A similar result could come from a lack of money stock control. The possibility may then arise that there may be a loss of credibility *which is undeserved*.

Finally, we need to address the question of short- and long-run trade-offs between inflation and unemployment. It is now widely agreed that in the short run at any rate there is a trade-off between inflation and unemployment. (For empirical evidence on this, see Kawasaki *et al.* (1990).) One important implication of the short-run trade-off is that, if the rate of inflation exceeds the target rate, monetary policy will have to be tightened and this will almost certainly create some short-run unemployment. In recent years (1989–92), there was an upsurge in unemployment in both Canada and New Zealand in the wake of tight monetary policies used to achieve target rates of inflation. The precise cost (the sacrifice ratio) will, of course, differ across different countries but few will be likely to escape such costs entirely (Chapter 22).

Moreover, if the natural (equilibrium) rate of unemployment is itself a function of the actual unemployment rate, as implied by theories of hysteresis in labour markets (Chapter 28), the unemployment costs of an anti-inflation policy may prove to be long-lasting. Thus, what is required here is a careful cost–benefit analysis which compares the short- and longer-run economic (and social) costs with the long-run benefits flowing from a permanently lower inflation rate. Such calculations are very difficult to make. (See Chapter 34.)

APPENDIX

One-period analysis

As in Barro and Gordon (1983), we begin with an analysis of the single-period case and then extend it to the multi-period case. We begin by writing a conventional loss function

$$L = a\pi^2 + (\mathrm{yr} - ky^*)^2 \qquad k > 1 \tag{A1}$$

Assuming that the optimal rate of inflation is zero, the loss in utility (L) is assumed to be positively related to the square of the inflation rate π and the square of the excess of output over the target level. The target level of output is, importantly, represented by ky^* where y^* is the level of output corresponding to the natural rate of unemployment; $k > 1$ reflects the assumption that the 'target' unemployment rate is below the natural rate. In equation (A1) a represents the weight that the authorities attach to inflation in their loss function.

Next assume that the deviation of actual output (yr) from its full employment (y^*)

is a function of the divergence between the actual and the expected rate of inflation (π^*).

$$\text{yr} = y^* + b(\pi - \pi^*) \tag{A2}$$

Equation (A2) is derived as follows. We start with a standard Cobb–Douglas production function in logarithmic form:

$$\text{yr} = \pi_1 l + (1 - \pi_1)k \tag{A3}$$

where l is labour and k is the fixed capital stock. π_1 and $1 - \pi_1$ are respectively the shares of wages and profits in production.

Assuming labour is employed to the point where the real wage rate is equal to the marginal product, we have with a fixed capital stock

$$\text{yr} = b(p_d - w) \tag{A4}$$

where b is the share of wages to profits $(\pi_1/(1 - \pi_1))$, p_d is the price of home produced goods and w is the nominal wage rate.

Assuming there is no formal indexation provision and workers set wages during negotiations to secure full employment at the natural rate, from equation (A4) we have the wage contract

$$w = -\frac{1}{b} y^* + {}_{t-1}E_{p_{dt}} \tag{A5}$$

where ${}_{t-1}E_{p_{dt}}$ is the home price level in t expected during negotiations in $t - 1$.

Inserting equation (A5) into (A4), we have

$$\text{yr} = y^* + b(p_d - {}_{t-1}E_{p_{dt}}) \tag{A6}$$

Remembering that $\pi = p_d - p_{dt-1}$ and $\pi^* = {}_{t-1}E_{p_{dt}} - p_{dt-1}$ allows us to arrive at equation (A2).

Money supply policy is used to minimise (A1). Underlying the unexpected inflation rate is an assumption about unanticipated monetary policy. Output can increase only if an increase in money is unanticipated.

The starting point is assumed to be one where there is a steady state inflation rate of zero and output is at its full employment level. Substituting equation (A2) into (A1), we have

$$L = a\pi^2 + [b(\pi - \pi^*) - (k - 1)y^*]^2 \tag{A7}$$

The authorities proceed to use money supply policy to minimise (A7), assuming expected inflation is given. Differentiating (A7) with respect to π and setting the expression equal to zero gives the 'optimising' discretionary rate of inflation for the one period:

$$\pi = \frac{b[(k - 1)y^* + b\pi^*]}{a + b^2} \tag{A8}$$

In due course, in steady state, $\pi = \pi^*$. From (A2), the economy returns to its full employment level of output. The equilibrium rate of inflation under discretion (π_d) will then be

$$\pi_d = \frac{b}{a}(k-1)y^* \tag{A9}$$

We want now to compare the loss implied by (A8) (Ls) and (A9) (Ld) with the loss for the case where the authorities followed a simple rule which aimed at a *zero* rate of inflation (Lr).

To arrive at Lr, we impose the condition that $\pi = 0$ in (A1). However, because the 'full employment' level of output is non-optimal, there will be some loss. This is readily shown to be (setting $yr = y^*$)

$$Lr = y^{*2}(k-1)^2 \tag{A10}$$

To arrive at Ls (the one-period loss), we substitute (A2) into (A1). This gives

$$Ls = \pi[(a+b^2)\pi - 2by^*(k-1)] + y^{*2}(k-1)^2 \tag{A11}$$

To arrive at the actual loss, we also need to substitute (A8) (with $\pi^* = 0$) into (A11) (which we do not do here).

To arrive at Ld, we have (with $yr = y^*$)

$$Ld = a\pi^2 + y^{*2}(k-1)^2 \tag{A12}$$

We now need to compare (A10), (A11) and (A12):

$$Ld - Lr = a\pi^2 > 0 \tag{A13}$$

Since ultimately there can be no improvement in welfare from increasing output (yr reverts back to y^*), the economy is left unambiguously worse off, having now a positive rate of inflation. Comparing steady states, a discretionary policy is clearly inferior to a zero-inflation rule.

We can also compare (A10) and (A11):

$$Lr - Ls = \pi[2by^*(k-1) - (a+b^2)\pi] > 0 \tag{A14}$$

Substituting (A8) for π in the bracketed expression would verify that the expression is greater than zero. There is, in other words, some advantage in pursuing a short-run discretionary policy.

The longer horizon

Our starting point for the analysis of a longer horizon is (A14) which defines the one-period short-run gain. This needs to be set off against all future losses defined by (A13) discounted to the present. The present loss L from following the short-period strategy is

$$L = -(Ls - Lr) + \left(\frac{Ld - Lr}{\delta}\right) \tag{A15}$$

where δ is the discount rate applying to all the given (infinite horizon) loss. This expression may be positive, in which case the zero-inflation rule will be followed, or negative, in which case the short-run strategy will be adopted. δ is crucial here. The higher the discount rate which the government applies to future losses, the more likely that the expression will be negative. At one extreme, when $\delta \to \infty$, we have the one-period result. As $\delta \to 0$, $L \to \infty$. So, in the end, in addition to the factors entering into (A9), we also have to accommodate a discount rate.

Discretion in the face of shocks

Following Fischer (1988b) and Rogoff (1985a), assume that we now add a stochastic term u_2 to our aggregate supply equation.

$$\text{yr} = y^* + b(\pi - \pi^*) + u_2 \tag{A16}$$

where u_2 is a disturbance term which has an expectation of zero and which is not serially correlated.

We can now again figure out losses under one-period discretion, long-run discretion and a simple rule which sets the money stock at a level which on average will yield price stability.

Following a procedure used previously we arrive at a one-period inflation rate of

$$\pi = b\,\frac{y^*(k-1) - u_2 + b\pi^*}{a + b^2} \tag{A17}$$

The loss can now readily be derived by inserting (A17) and (A16) into (A1). However, our interest is primarily in the other two losses (both corresponding to steady states).

To get the steady state inflation under discretion, we set $\pi^* = (b/a)(k-1)y^*$ which, it should be noted, is not equal to π because π is *also* affected by the shocks. We arrive at

$$\pi = \frac{b}{a}\,y^*(k-1) - \frac{b}{a + b^2}\,u_2 \tag{A18}$$

To arrive at the expected loss (noting that $u_2 = 0$ but the variance of u_2 $(= u_2{}^2)$ is not of course zero), we substitute (A18) and (A16) into (A1)

$$\text{Ld} = (1 + \theta)(k-1)^2 y^{*2} + \left|\frac{1}{1 + \theta}\right| u_2{}^2 \qquad \theta = \frac{b^2}{a} \tag{A19}$$

We turn now to the loss under the rule. $\pi^* = 0$ and π is the actual price level p.

Using the simple quantity theory equation

$$\text{mo} = y^* = p + \text{yr} \tag{A20}$$

the money stock is set at a level which will be exactly absorbed by the trend level of output. We have then

$$y^* - \text{yr} = p$$

and from (A16)

$$p = y^* - \text{yr} = -bp - u_2 \tag{A21}$$

or

$$p = -\left(\frac{1}{1+b}\right) u_2$$

Recalling again that $u_2 = 0$ but $u_2^2 \neq 0$, we can readily arrive at the expected loss

$$\text{Lr} = (k-1)^2 y^{*2} + \frac{1+a}{(1+b)^2} u_2^2 \tag{A22}$$

Comparing (A22) and (A19), it can be shown that the first expression is *larger* under discretion, as previously, but the second expression is larger under a rule.

26

The Ricardian equivalence hypothesis

INTRODUCTION

The Ricardian equivalence (RE) hypothesis, alternatively known as the tax discounting hypothesis, dates back to Ricardo, but in its modern guise was revived by Barro in a much cited article published in 1974 (Barro 1974).

It soon became the subject of a very lively and heated debate which centred around a number of key analytical questions. At the same time, as with the policy impotence hypothesis, it has also provoked, in the years since, a very large empirical literature.

The questions posed by RE are of great importance in any analysis of macro, and particularly fiscal, policy. RE overturns many Keynesian presumptions, which have become part of conventional wisdom. For example, in conventional macroeconomics, an income tax cut is (plausibly) assumed to increase disposable income and in turn to increase real household consumption expenditure. Barro's model, on the contrary, argues that the whole of the tax cut will be saved, leaving real consumption unchanged.

Barro is himself a major contributor to New Classical thinking. RE shares one important frame of reference with the New Classics. It assumes, as they do, that households behave *rationally* and are *forward looking*.

The formal integration of the hypothesis into a larger model is undertaken in Chapter 27. This chapter presents the analytics, the criticisms and the empirical evidence. It also presents a very simple model of the transmission of fiscal policies across large countries, with different assumptions made about RE.

THE HYPOTHESIS EXPLAINED

According to this hypothesis, households discount to the present all future taxes expected to be levied to meet interest payments on existing government debt.

Suppose at a given level of real government expenditure income taxes were cut and the deficit was financed by the issue of new bonds. Suppose, also, to take the simplest case first, that the bonds are to be repaid in one year's time. The interest rate on bonds is r_d. Households expect taxes in a year to be equal to the interest on the bond plus the face value of the bond, i.e.

$$r_d Bo + Bo = Bo(1 + r_d)$$

The present value of this expression is Bo. *Thus, the present value of future taxes is exactly equal to the tax cut.*

The results are unchanged if we extend the life of the bond. For example, over three years we would have a present value of

$$\frac{r_d Bo}{1 + r_d} + \frac{r_d Bo}{(1 + r_d)^2} + \frac{Bo(1 + r_d)}{(1 + r_d)^3} = Bo$$

So how will a rational forward-looking householder react to the tax cut? *He will save the whole of the increase in disposable income to meet future taxes.* The expansionary effect on real disposable income from the tax cut is exactly neutralised by the deflationary effect of the expected future taxes. This leaves real consumption unchanged. *It is thus a matter of indifference whether a given level of government expenditure is financed by present taxes or bonds* (= future taxes). Deficits in other words merely *postpone* taxes.

Implicit in this analysis too is the notion that the increased savings will be fully invested in government bonds, whose supply will now have increased.

The Barro model has been the subject of a good deal of criticism, which we now review.

THE CRITIQUE

Many analyses of the hypothesis have been fiercely critical of it. Typical, for example, of one reaction is that by Bernheim (1989) who says

> I dismiss the Ricardian paradigm on both theoretical and empirical grounds. While the Ricardian exercise is an interesting thought experiment, it is predicated upon extreme and unrealistic assumptions. Those who recommend this framework as a guide to actual policy formulation, offer a prescription for disaster.
>
> (1989: 56)

On the other hand, Barro (1989) has recently returned to the fray and, in a lucid presentation, has tried to defend himself point by point against his critics.

Critics have attacked what appear to be the key assumptions underlying RE. A failure to meet any one of the assumptions, it is argued, would be sufficient to produce a departure from RE.

So, what are these criticisms?

(a) People do not live forever and so pay little or no attention to taxes that may have to be paid after their death

This criticism derives from life-cycle models of saving, which focus attention on the saving-for-retirement motive. In these models bequests are unintended, flowing from premature death. Individuals will capitalise only those taxes expected to be paid over *their own* lifetime. There will thus only be a *partial* Ricardian effect.

Barro's riposte is that the criticism takes no account of the existence of a *bequest* motive which takes the form of altruistic intergenerational transfers; in this case 'people react to the government's imposed intergenerational transfers, implied by budget deficits . . . with a compensating increase in voluntary transfers' (Barro 1989), i.e. they will simply adjust their bequests or gifts to their children to accommodate the increased burden of taxes they will now have to bear. Although, in other words, individuals have finite lives, they act *as if* they were infinitely lived. Barro supports this argument with evidence of the importance of intergenerational transfers.[1]

Fine academic arguments to one side, *the real objection to Barro's contentions is that it presumes a degree of fine calculation and rationality that most of us know to be unreal*. On the other hand, one must concede that one might be attracted to the idea that households may in a very vague way be aware of future tax liabilities associated with debt finance; in other words, that a tax cut is not a 'free ride'. This, however, is saying something entirely different from Barro.

(b) Capital markets are imperfect

RE assumes that capital markets are perfect and that there are no limitations on borrowing by consumers. In the examples above, we used a discount rate which was equal to the interest rate paid by the government on its bonds. In reality, for reasons which are well known, the relevant discount rate for the private sector is likely to be higher than that for the government sector.[2] In this case, the present value of future taxes will tend to be less than the value of the bond issue. Moreover, borrowing constraints may make it difficult to *act* on one's perception of future taxes. For example, faced with an *increase* in taxes to repay current debt, some households may need to *borrow* to maintain consumption.

(c) Government debt may be monetised in the future

If there is an expectation that eventually some of the debt will be monetised (i.e. produce more inflation), future tax liabilities are correspondingly reduced and this may weaken the Ricardian effect. It is not so evident, however, that this reaction will be entirely rational. The reason is that inflation is itself a tax which imposes its own costs on the community; on the other hand, these costs are vague, imprecise and uncertain. (See Chapter 34.)

(d) Taxes are distortionary

If taxes are not lump sum it is possible to have departures from RE. As Barro himself concedes, the timing of, say, distortionary income taxes may affect people's incentives to work and produce in different periods.[3]

For example, if the current income tax rate falls while the expected rate in the future rises, the public may increase their work effort in the present and reduce it in the future. At the same time, since the tax also penalises saving, desired saving may rise in the present and fall in the future.

(e) Increased savings may not be absorbed into government bonds

The increased supply of bonds from the budget deficit is matched by an increase in the demand for total financial (and perhaps real) assets from the increase in savings. In Chapter 10 we analysed, in the context of a portfolio balance model, the effects of a budget deficit. We concluded that the increased supply of bonds threw the portfolio out of equilibrium; to restore equilibrium, a rise in the interest rate was required, but the effect on the currency was ambiguous although we did argue that if substitution effects dominated the currency would in fact appreciate.

Does this analysis hold in this case and, if so, does it invalidate RE?

The key criticism here is that the increased savings need not all be invested in government bonds. RE requires that the savings be placed in some asset that earns interest, presumably sufficient to meet future tax liabilities, but why should they all go into bonds? If some leak abroad there will be real effects; but in any event the structure of returns will change depending on where they are placed.

THE EVIDENCE

There is now also a vast empirical literature designed to test Ricardian propositions.

RE predicts that budget deficits should make no impact on interest rates; nor should they be associated with current account deficits. Tests of these two predictions, using somewhat crude reduced form regression analysis, turn out not surprisingly to be inconclusive. On the other hand, simulations with large-scale econometric models of changes in fiscal policy almost invariably go against RE (Chapter 15).

The most widely used method of testing RE is to estimate an extended consumption function (see Nicoletti (1988) for a detailed survey of the methods used).

We illustrate here with one widely used equation. Most others are refinements and variations on this theme

$$C = a_2 \text{We} + a_3 b + a_4 y_\text{d} + a_5 d$$

where C is real per capita private consumption, We is real private wealth net of government debt, b is real government debt, y_d is real disposable income and d is the real government deficit.

If RE held we would expect $a_3 = 0$, $a_4 = -a_5$. In other words, real government debt should not influence real consumption; at the same time, as we noted earlier, the *positive* effects of an increase in disposable income from a tax cut should be exactly offset by the negative effects of the real deficit.

Nicoletti (1988) has summarised the results of all these kinds of studies. Of the sixteen studies reviewed, RE in its extreme form is rejected by nine. Nicoletti's own multi-country study is particularly interesting. He, in fact, concludes:

> With the remarkable exceptions of Italy and Belgium the full tax-discounting hypothesis does not receive much support from the data. In the majority of the countries ... the Barro Model is strongly rejected ... moreover, most single country estimates of the tax discounting parameter are close to zero ....
>
> (1988: 39)

One particularly interesting result here is that he finds that in countries with large and unsustainable budget deficits RE is more likely to hold. This is strikingly so in Belgium and Italy (both of which have very high debt ratios) 'where it is impossible to reject the Barro Model'.

A SIMPLE TWO-COUNTRY MODEL WITH RICARDIAN EQUIVALENCE

In this section we present a very simple model which explicitly accommodates RE. The model is drawn from Masson and Knight (1986). The theoretical presentation focuses primarily on short-term adjustment. Later in their paper, however, they present empirical results of a much larger model.

Consider a two-country world. In each of the two countries the current account $X - M$ is determined by the excess of national savings over investments I. One country's excess saving over investment must exactly match the other country's excess of investment over saving. There is full employment in the two economies.

$$X - M = S - I - D \tag{1}$$

D stands for the public sector deficit and S is private savings. We also have

$$X - M = \alpha_2 E \tag{2}$$

where E is the exchange rate.

$$S = \alpha_4 r_d + (1 - \phi) D \tag{3}$$

Equation (3) says that private savings are a positive function of the interest rate (r_d).[4] At the same time, savings are allowed to adjust directly to D by a factor $1 - \phi$. If RE does not hold $\phi = 1$ and the last term drops out. If, at the other extreme, RE does hold (i.e. the private sector takes full account of future tax liabilities) $\phi = 0$ and an increase in the public sector deficit is exactly matched by an increase in private savings (as a cover against future tax liabilities). Also,

$$I = -\alpha_5 r_d \tag{4}$$

In the other country

$$X^* - M^* = -(X - M) \tag{5}$$

$$X^* - M^* = S^* - I^* \tag{6}$$

$$S^* - I^* = \alpha_6 r^* \tag{7}$$

$$r_d = r^* = r_w \tag{8}$$

where asterisks represent the other country. The public sector balance abroad is ignored.

These equations allow us to analyse the two-country effects of a deficit in the first country on the world interest rate r_w and the exchange rate. We have, using these equations,

$$(\alpha_4 + \alpha_5)r^* - \phi\, D = -\alpha_6 r^* \tag{9}$$

So,

$$\frac{r^*}{D} = \frac{\phi}{\alpha_4 + \alpha_5 + \alpha_6} \tag{10}$$

Given r^* we can solve for E and $X - M$:

$$\frac{X - M}{D} = -\frac{\alpha_6\phi}{\alpha_4 + \alpha_5 + \alpha_6} \tag{11}$$

$$\frac{E}{D} = -\frac{\alpha_6\phi}{\alpha_2(\alpha_4 + \alpha_5 + \alpha_6)} \tag{12}$$

This says that provided $\phi \neq 0$ (i.e. RE does not hold fully) an increase in the fiscal deficit in the first country will (a) raise the world interest rate, (b) appreciate the country's currency and (c) open up a current account deficit.

If, however, RE holds fully, $\phi = 0$, *there are absolutely no effects on any of these variables*. Quite simply, private saving increases to absorb the deficit, leaving all variables unchanged.

These results can easily be presented graphically for the case where RE does not hold fully. Figure 26.1 shows the world saving and investment. There is now a decline in world savings; the Sw schedule shifts to the left and this at once raises the world interest rate and reduces world savings and investment. Note that at the *global* level savings must equal investment.

Figure 26.2 shows the position in the two economies. The saving schedule shifts to the left in the first country. At the new world interest rate r_{w1} there is an excess of investment over savings in the first country (AB) and an equal excess of savings over investment in the other (CD). The decline in savings in the first country puts potential upward pressure on the interest rate; there is an appreciation and a capital inflow to match the current account deficit. The opposite occurs in the other country.

Masson and Knight find, in their empirical work, that RE holds only partially. They find, for example, a value for ϕ of 0.43 for the USA, Japan and Germany.

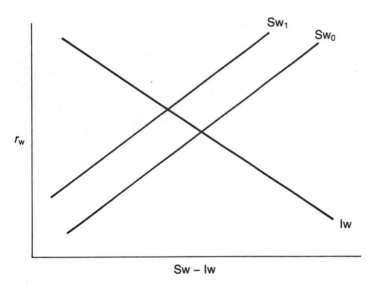

Figure 26.1 World savings and investment

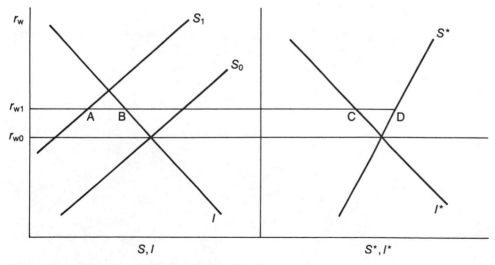

Figure 26.2 Effects of a fiscal deficit in the first country

A GENERAL FRAMEWORK

Chapters 27–30 are important. They represent the culmination of all the preceding chapters which each in turn introduced one new element into the analysis. The methodology was justified in terms of the need to explain in more detail the role of each new element introduced into the analysis in the adjustment process.

These chapters now not only bring together all the previous chapters incorporating each of these elements into a single larger model, but also add some new elements neglected, in whole or in part, in earlier chapters. The model is thus one of some complexity and indeed, because of its complexity, we shall not even attempt to solve it. A somewhat simpler version of the model, however, will be examined in more detail.

This part comprises four chapters. Chapter 27 provides an extended model of the goods and money markets. Chapter 28 reviews the large literature on how to model the production and labour markets. Chapter 29 returns to the important question of the kinds of constraints that need to be imposed to define long-run equilibrium. Finally, Chapter 30 takes a simpler version of the model of the previous chapters (but nevertheless a model which is much more complicated than anything attempted so far) and shows how it can be solved. This also serves to demonstrate how complex outcomes can be (and indeed sometimes counter-intuitive) when models are extensively refined.

A GENERAL FRAMEWORK

27

Modelling goods and money markets

INTRODUCTION

This is the first of three chapters which try to present a more general framework for modelling the (smaller) open economy. This chapter concentrates only on the goods and money market. The reader will readily recognise the earlier models as essentially special cases of the model presented in this chapter.

The goods market is refined in a number of ways. Ricardian equivalence is explicitly incorporated in the model; wealth and all interest payments are also explicitly modelled. Investment is introduced into the model; at the same time we accommodate the possibility that the public takes rational account of the perceived benefits flowing from government consumption expenditure.

The money market is modelled along portfolio balance lines. Perfect asset substitution falls out as a special case of this framework.

Exchange rate and price expectations explicitly appear in the model and so the chapter concludes with a review of theories of expectations formation and of the empirical literature.

THE DEMAND FOR GOODS

We begin with the base equation for the gross domestic product in real terms.

$$y = c + i + \text{gr} + x - m \tag{1}$$

where y is real gross domestic product, c is real consumption, i is real investment, gr is real government expenditure and $x - m$ is the trade balance in real terms.

$$c = a_1 y_d + a_2 \text{we} - a_3(r_d - \dot{p}_e) - \pi_{12}(1 - a_1)\text{gr} \tag{2}$$

Real consumption is assumed to depend on real disposable income (y_d), real wealth (we) and the real interest rate. The real interest rate is *assumed* to have a negative effect on real consumption, although strictly, as we noted in Chapter 11, the sign is ambiguous. p_e is the expected rate of inflation. As in Haas and Masson (1986), we also allow for the possibility that some portion of government expenditure (π_{12}) may be a direct substitute for private consumption (see later).

Real disposable income is defined as

$$y_d = \frac{yP_d}{P} + \frac{r_d B}{P} + \frac{r^* EFA}{P} - \frac{T}{P} - \frac{(1-\lambda)\,\Delta B}{P} \tag{3}$$

where P is the consumer price index. Real disposable income is composed of domestic output, interest on domestic bonds and on foreign bonds converted into domestic currency EFA, less taxes, less some adjustment for the change in bonds (to be explained below), all deflated by the consumer price index.

Real private sector wealth is defined as

$$we = \frac{Mo}{P} + \frac{EFA}{P} + \frac{\lambda B}{P} + k \tag{4}$$

where Mo is the money stock, E the exchange rate, FA the stock of foreign assets and k the real capital stock. The coefficient λ represents the component of bonds which is perceived as wealth and is intended to capture the degree to which Ricardian equivalence holds.

This hypothesis was examined in some detail in Chapter 26. We remind the reader that according to the hypothesis households discount all future taxes expected to be levied to meet service payments on existing government debt. In these special circumstances, we recall too that the substitution of debt for taxes will leave private sector wealth and real consumption unchanged.

If Ricardian equivalence holds completely, $\lambda = 0$. If it is totally rejected, $\lambda = 1$. Partial support would give a value between 0 and 1.

Consider again the simplest case where there is a tax cut today financed by the issue of bonds to be repaid in one year's time. Suppose Ricardian equivalence held and $\lambda = 0$. In (4) above, bonds are not perceived to be part of wealth, so bonds drop out of the equation altogether.

Consider now what happens in (3). T falls and ΔB increases equivalently (with $\lambda = 0$). The expansionary effect on real disposable income from the fall in T is exactly neutralised by the deflationary effect of the ΔB (= expected future taxes). With no wealth or disposable income effect real consumption is unchanged. So with taxes down and real consumption unchanged, savings will have gone up equivalently. *The public thus save the increase in disposable income to meet future taxes.*

What happens in the next period when the debt is repaid? Referring to (3) again, taxes now increase to repay the debt and the interest. At the same time ΔB now becomes negative; there is also interest accruing to households on the debt ($r_d B$).

These operations again leave real disposable income and hence real consumption unchanged. There is now a *drop* in savings equal to the debt repayment.

This conclusion that the real effects on consumption are independent of the form of financing of a given level of government expenditure *presupposes that there are no other indirect real effects on the economy*, e.g. through the interest rate or the exchange rate. This particular question is addressed in the next section where the monetary sector is modelled. *We show that this may or may not hold depending on how the assumed increase in savings is absorbed in the portfolio of financial assets.*

At the other extreme, if Ricardian equivalence did not hold at all ($\lambda = 1$), we have a more conventional result which we can again read off from (2), (3) and (4). There is, at once, a real wealth effect on consumption ((2) and (4)) and a real disposable income effect from the fall in taxes ((2) and (3)).

We turn now to the direct role of government consumption expenditure on private consumption. Most analyses of the effects of changes in government consumption totally ignore any benefits that may flow from such expenditure. The implicit assumption is that they have a value of zero (Clements 1979; Kormendi 1983). Taking rational account of the perceived benefits of government consumption expenditure can weaken the macro effectiveness of a fiscal expansion.

To investigate this important point, we now try to accommodate into the analysis of private consumption expenditure any perceived benefits flowing from government consumption expenditure.

We first redefine (2) in terms of *total* real consumption (ct).

$$\text{ct} = a_1 y_d + a_2 \text{we} - a_3 (r_d - \dot{p}_e) + a_1 \pi_{12} \text{gr} \tag{2a}$$

This says that *total* real consumption now also includes some *fraction* of government expenditure, where π_{12} represents the valuation placed on government consumption (which can vary between zero and unity). At the same time, we have

$$\text{ct} = c + \pi_{12} \text{gr} \tag{2b}$$

Equation (2b) says that total real consumption is also the sum of private consumption and *public* consumption. Combining (2a) and (2b) we have

$$c = a_1 y_d + a_2 \text{we} - a_3 (r_d - \dot{p}_e) - \pi_{12}(1 - a_1)\text{gr} \tag{2c}$$

which is (2) above.

Suppose we have an increase in government consumption expenditure. If Ricardian equivalence holds, as we have seen, the real effects will be independent of how it is financed (i.e. by taxes or debt). Suppose it is financed by taxes, so $\Delta \text{gr} = \Delta \text{tr}$ (tr, real taxes).

Using now (1), (2c) and (3) and disregarding irrelevant variables we have (for impact effects)

$$\Delta y = a_1 \, \Delta y - a_1 \, \Delta \text{gr} - \pi_{12}(1 - a_1) \, \Delta \text{gr} + \Delta \text{gr} \tag{2d}$$

$$\Delta y = \Delta \text{gr} - \pi_{12} \, \Delta \text{gr} = (1 - \pi_{12}) \, \Delta \text{gr} \tag{2e}$$

If the valuation is zero, $\pi_{12} = 0$, we have the textbook unit balanced budget multiplier. At the other extreme, if $\pi_{12} = 1$ there is perfect crowding out.

We turn now to the explanation of investment.

$$i = \pi_{16}(k^* - k_{-1}) \tag{5}$$

where the asterisk represents the desired level of the capital stock. Equation (5) says that real investment is some fraction of the gap between the desired and the lagged real capital stock.

$$k^* = \pi_{18} y - \pi_{20}(r_d - \dot{p}_e) \tag{6}$$

The desired real capital stock, in turn, is determined by the level of output and by the real interest rate.

Substituting (6) into (5) gives us our investment equation

$$i = \pi_{16}\pi_{18} y - \pi_{16}\pi_{20}(r_d - \dot{p}_e) - \pi_{16}k_{-1} \tag{7}$$

If there is a permanent change in output or in the real interest rate, investment will be undertaken until the desired capital stock is reached. At this point, in equilibrium, other things being equal and in the absence of real growth, net investment will be zero.

We turn, finally, to the determination of exports and imports.

$$x = \alpha_{15} \frac{P^* E}{P_d} + \alpha_{16} y^* \tag{8}$$

The volume of exports is determined by relative prices and by the level of output abroad (y^*).

We distinguish two types of imports: imported inputs for domestic production and imports of final private consumption goods. The demand for imported inputs is explained in the Appendix to the next chapter. It should be noted, however, that imported inputs do not enter into equation (1) which is a value added equation.

$$m = \pi_{10} c - \alpha_{18} \frac{P^* E}{P_d} \tag{9}$$

The volume of imports of final consumption goods is a proportion π_{10} of total real consumption expenditure, adjusted for changes in relative prices.[1]

This completes the formal presentation of the real demand for goods.

Combining terms yields the equation

$$y = \frac{a_1(1 - \pi_{10})}{1 - \pi_{16}\pi_{18}} y_d + \frac{a_2(1 - \pi_{10})}{1 - \pi_{16}\pi_{18}} \text{ we} - \frac{a_3(1 - \pi_{10}) + \pi_{16}\pi_{20}}{1 - \pi_{16}\pi_{18}}$$

$$\times (r_d - \dot{p}_e) + \frac{1 - (1 - \pi_{10})\pi_{12}(1 - a_1)}{1 - \pi_{16}\pi_{18}} \text{ gr} + \frac{\alpha_{15} + \alpha_{18}}{1 - \pi_{16}\pi_{18}} \frac{P^* E}{P_d}$$

$$+ \frac{\alpha_{16}}{1 - \pi_{16}\pi_{18}} y^* - \frac{\pi_{16}}{1 - \pi_{16}\pi_{18}} k_{-1} \tag{10}$$

The real demand for goods is a function of real disposable income, real wealth, the real interest rate, real government expenditure, relative prices at home and abroad,[2] the level of output abroad and the lagged real stock of capital.

This can be extended further by substituting (3) and (4) for yd and we respectively. Also, after these substitutions are made, the final equation can be converted into logarithmic form.

THE MONETARY SECTOR

Most of the work here was already covered in Chapter 10. All we need to do here, for convenience, is reproduce, with some variations, our earlier framework and summarise the key issues.

$$\frac{Mo}{P} = \alpha_8 y_d - \alpha_9 r_d - \alpha_{10}\left(r^* + \frac{E_e - E}{E}\right) + \alpha_{11}\frac{We}{P} \tag{11}$$

$$\frac{B}{P} = -\alpha_{12} y_d + \alpha_{13} r_d - \alpha_{14}\left(r^* + \frac{E_e - E}{E}\right) + \alpha_{25}\frac{We}{P} \tag{12}$$

$$\frac{EFA}{P} = -\alpha_{21} y_d - \alpha_{17} r_d + \alpha_{20}\left(r^* + \frac{E_e - E}{E}\right) + \alpha_{19}\frac{We}{P} \tag{13}$$

$$\alpha_8 = \alpha_{12} + \alpha_{21} \qquad \alpha_{13} = \alpha_9 + \alpha_{17}$$

$$\alpha_{20} = \alpha_{14} + \alpha_{10} \qquad \alpha_{11} + \alpha_{25} + \alpha_{19} = 1$$

$$We = Mo + B + EFA$$

If domestic and foreign bonds are perfect substitutes $\alpha_{13} = \alpha_{14} = \alpha_{17} = \alpha_{20} = \infty$ and the two asset demands merge into one consolidated demand for bonds.

$$\frac{B + EFA}{P} = \alpha_{22} y_d + \alpha_{23} r_d + \alpha_{24}\frac{We}{P} \tag{14}$$

and

$$r_d - r^* = \frac{E_e - E}{E}$$

How does Ricardian equivalence appear in the money market?

Suppose again that there is a fall in taxes financed by the issue of new bonds (ΔBo). We concluded in the previous section that, if Ricardian equivalence holds, there would be a matching increase in savings. This increase in savings is equivalent to an increase in the demand for assets in the portfolio. *Ricardian equivalence appears to presuppose that all the increase in savings is absorbed by domestic bonds.* The increase in the demand for domestic bonds is exactly matched by the increase in the supply, leaving the interest rate undisturbed. Why, however, should it *all* go into bonds?

The answer is that none of it can go into *money* because money does not earn interest and interest-earnings are necessary to meet the full tax liability eventually. But why not into some foreign assets or other domestic interest-earning assets? There is no simple answer to this. Perhaps it has to do with a potential exchange rate risk associated with foreign asset holdings. As already noted, if some of the savings went into other domestic assets, the structure of domestic interest rates would change, with potential implications for the real economy. We raise this issue here but do not try to resolve it.

To complete the monetary sector we need some explanation of the expected rate of devaluation. (A parallel analysis would hold for expected inflation which appears in the real demand for goods.)

MODELLING EXCHANGE RATE EXPECTATIONS

This section reviews the different approaches to the modelling of exchange rate expectations. It focuses on four major approaches to expectations: extrapolative, adaptive, regressive and rational. The section draws substantially on Takagi (1991).

Extrapolative expectations

Extrapolative expectations are represented as follows:

$$_tE_{+1} = E + h(E - E_{-1}) \tag{15}$$

or

$$_tE_{+1} = (1 + h)E - h(E_{-1})$$

The exchange rate expected in the next period is equal to the actual (observed) spot rate adjusted for some proportion of the recent change in the spot rate.

The advantage of this formulation is that it accommodates a variety of potential expectation patterns. The adjustment coefficient h could in principle be positive, negative or zero. If $h = 0$ we have the static expectations of the MF model. A value of $0 < h < 1$ implies that, when the currency has devalued, there is an expectation of a further fall in the future but by less than the recent fall. If $h \geqslant 1$ then the expected fall is equal to or larger than the recent fall. A value of $0 > h > -1$ implies that when the currency is falling there is an expectation that this fall will be partly reversed in the future. If $h = -1$ the expected exchange rate is stationary, insensitive to the recent change (i.e. the exchange rate will return to its pre-change level).

Adaptive expectations

In this case the expected change in the exchange rate is some proportion of the prediction error.

$$_tE_{+1} - E = g(t_{-1}E - E) \tag{16}$$

where $t_{-1}E - E$ represents the prediction error and g is the adjustment coefficient.

For example, if g were *positive* and if the currency devalued by more than antici-pated ($E > t_{-1}E$), there would be an expectation of a currency *appreciation*. For $g < 0$ we have the opposite tendencies.

Regressive expectations

In this formulation the expected change in the spot rate is some proportion of the gap between the equilibrium rate and the actual spot rate.

$$_tE_{+1} - E = k(\bar{E} - E) \tag{17}$$

We have already encountered this formulation in the Dornbusch model. A positive coefficient for k is indicative of *regressive* expectations.

Rational expectations

We have also encountered rational expectations, where it is assumed that all available information about the structure of the economy is exploited.

We note here again with reference to (17) that $\bar{E}$ might be rationally based in the sense that the long-run equilibrium rate is known and the speed of adjustment k may also reflect the known dynamic adjustment of the economy, as in the Dornbusch model. Or we may follow Mathieson (1977) and Kawai (1985) in supposing that, while the long-run rate is known, the speed of adjustment is not.

To anticipate Chapter 33 we note here that empirical work is not very supportive of the hypothesis that markets are efficient-rational.

Empirical evidence on expectations

The paper by Takagi (1991) reviews the empirical evidence which bears on the forma-tion of expectations, drawing on survey data of exchange expectations. We focus here particularly on the first three (deferring the discussion of rational expectations to Chapter 33).

On the extrapolative formulation, Takagi finds that the case of $h = 0$, static expec-tations, is rejected by the data. For short-run horizons of one week to one month the sign of h is positive (i.e. we have bandwagon effects); however, for longer-run horizons, extending from six to twelve months, h tends to be negative.

Reviewing the evidence on adaptive expectations, he again finds a difference, albeit less accentuated, for short- and medium- to long-run horizons. In general, for short horizons g tended to be negative and for longer horizons g tended to be positive.

Takagi also reviews evidence bearing on (17). To test (17), some calculation of the long-run equilibrium rate is needed. One of three procedures tend to be used here: purchasing power parity (into which most studies fall), a moving average of say the past six months or a constant. For short horizons, k tends to be negative; for longer horizons, k tends to be positive.

These reviews are very revealing and indeed a common pattern appears to emerge. All the studies indicate that in the short run we have 'bandwagon' expectations, whilst in the longer run we have stabilising-regressive expectations. Chapter 33 confirms these tendencies.

Econometric practice differs widely here in the treatment of expectations in financial markets. Some (e.g. the IMF MultiMod and the McKibbin–Sachs MSG2 models) assume rationality. Others (the US Federal Reserve MCM, Japan's EPA and the OECD models) assume that expectations are adaptively formed.

28

Modelling production and labour markets

INTRODUCTION

In this chapter we undertake a 'tour d'horizon' of the principal methods used in the theoretical literature to model these markets. At the same time, we try to review the empirical work in this area, which, understandably, is more sophisticated.

There are two approaches found in this theoretical literature. One approach draws on four key building blocks:

a) a production function;
b) a (derived) demand for labour function;
c) a supply of labour;
d) an equation which explains wages.

These can be combined to yield an aggregate supply equation and an equation which determines national unemployment.

A second approach draws primarily on a mark-up theory of pricing combined with some variant of an expectations-augmented Phillips curve.

We also discuss how the natural rate of unemployment is calculated and, as well, its determinants. Finally, theories of hysteresis (unemployment persistence) are reviewed.

THE DEMAND FOR AND SUPPLY OF LABOUR AND WAGE SETTING

This section first presents the basic theory underlying the demand for and the supply of labour. We then look at alternative wage equations and their implications for unemployment. Next we examine the role of the tax wedge (the sum of payroll, income and consumption taxes) in the generation of unemployment. Finally, we briefly summarise empirical work which bears on this general approach.

The demand for and supply of labour

We begin by writing a simple familiar Cobb–Douglas production function in logarithmic form:

$$y = \alpha k + (1 - \alpha)l + y_0 \tag{1}$$

where y is output, α and $1 - \alpha$ are respectively the shares of capital (k) and labour (l) in value added and y_0 stands for 'other' determinants, e.g. primarily technical progress. (The special case where there are imported inputs is dealt with briefly in an appendix.)

Assuming the marginal product of labour is equated to the real product wage, we can derive a demand for labour (l_d) of the form[1]

$$l_d = -\frac{1}{\alpha}(w - p_d) + \frac{1}{\alpha}\log(1 - \alpha) + \frac{1}{\alpha}y_0 + k \tag{2}$$

where w is the nominal wage rate and p_d is the price of home goods. In what follows, we ignore the expression $(1/\alpha)\log(1 - \alpha)$, treating it as a constant. Substituting (2) into (1) we have[2]

$$y = k - \frac{1 - \alpha}{\alpha}(w - p_d) + \frac{1}{\alpha}y_0 \tag{3}$$

We now write down a simple supply of labour (l_s) function:

$$l_s = a_2(w - t_y - p) + l_{s0} \tag{4}$$

where t_y is the rate of income tax. Equation (4) says that the supply of labour is a positive function of the real after-tax consumption wage rate. p (the consumer price index) is again

$$p = \alpha_{15}p_d + (1 - \alpha_{15})(e + p^*) \tag{5}$$

where e is the exchange rate and p^* the foreign price level.

We also allow for other exogenous influences on the supply of labour (l_{s0}), e.g. the real value of unemployment benefits.

Having defined a demand for labour and a supply of labour, we can represent a state of full employment by the condition $l_d = l_s$. (This abstracts from ongoing frictional–structural unemployment.) Equating (2) (in abbreviated form) and (4) yields a full employment wage rate w^*:

$$w^* = \frac{a_2}{a_2 + 1/\alpha}\, t_y + \frac{1}{\alpha a_2 + 1}\, p_d + \frac{a_2}{a_2 + 1/\alpha}\, p - \frac{1}{\alpha a_2 + 1}\, y_0$$

$$+ \frac{1}{a_2 + 1/\alpha}\, (k - l_{s0}) \tag{6}$$

If we substitute (6) into (3) we can arrive at a corresponding full employment level of output (y).

$$\bar{y} = \left(1 - \frac{1 - \alpha}{\alpha}\, \frac{1}{a_2 + 1/\alpha}\right)k - \frac{1 - \alpha}{\alpha}\, \frac{a_2}{a_2 + 1/\alpha}\, t_y$$

$$+ \frac{1 - \alpha}{\alpha}\left(1 - \frac{1}{\alpha a_2 + 1}\right) p_d - \frac{1 - \alpha}{\alpha}\, \frac{a_2}{a_2 + 1/\alpha}\, p$$

$$+ \frac{1 - \alpha}{\alpha}\, \frac{1}{a_2 + 1/\alpha}\, l_{s0} + \frac{1}{\alpha}\left(1 + \frac{1 - \alpha}{\alpha a_2 + 1}\right) y_0 \tag{7}$$

where of course p and p_d are related by (5).

This solution is an important one and we will use it in what follows as a reference point. Its economic rationale will be explained in due course.

Wage setting and unemployment

We turn now to actual wage setting drawing on some of the analysis of earlier chapters. We start with the simplest explanation, refining it a little as we progress.

We look first at one-period contracts.

$$w_t = {}_{t-1}E p_t + \pi_2(p_t - {}_{t-1}E p_t) \tag{8}$$

The contract has two components. First there is a wage negotiated the *previous* period based on the expected consumer price index in the *current* period (t). This reflects the forward-looking component of the contract. At the same time the contract allows for some retrospective adjustment to wages for the difference between the actual consumer price index and the one 'expected'. This is the 'backward-looking' component of the contract. π_2 is the degree of wage indexation. If $\pi_2 = 0$ wages are only 'forward' looking, i.e. based on expected *future* prices. If $\pi_2 = 1$, there is full wage indexation and (8) becomes

$$w = p_t \tag{9}$$

an equation we first used in Chapter 8.

An alternative, widely used, equation in the theoretical literature is one based on the work of Gray (1976) and Fischer (1977a) (Gray–Fischer henceforth).

Gray–Fischer assume that the wage contracted is the rate which is *expected* to clear the labour market. Using our own framework we can rewrite (6) as

$$w^* = \frac{a_2}{a_2 + 1/\alpha}\, t_y + \frac{1}{\alpha a_2 + 1}\, {}_{t-1}E_{p_{dt}} + \frac{a_2}{a_2 + 1/\alpha}\, {}_{t-1}E_{p_t}$$

$$- \frac{1}{\alpha a_2 + 1}\, y_0 + \frac{1}{a_2 + 1/\alpha}\, (k - l_{s0}) \tag{6a}$$

This replaces p_d and p by their expected values and assumes that all other variables are known.

We can now use equations (8) and (6a), the alternative wage equations, to arrive at a *full employment gap* equation, i.e. $y - \bar{y}$.

We already have our full employment output equation from (7) above. Substituting alternatively (8) and (6a) into (3) will give us our output gap equation.

Using first (8) we have

$$y - \bar{y} = \frac{1-\alpha}{\alpha}\, \frac{1}{a_2 + 1/\alpha}\, k + \frac{1-\alpha}{\alpha}\, \frac{a_2}{a_2 + 1/\alpha} t_y + \frac{1-\alpha}{\alpha}\, \frac{1}{\alpha a_2 + 1}\, p_d$$

$$- \frac{1-\alpha}{\alpha}\left(\pi_2 - \frac{a_2}{a_2 + 1/\alpha}\right) p - \frac{1-\alpha}{\alpha}\, (1 - \pi_2)_{t-1}E_{pt}$$

$$- \frac{1-\alpha}{\alpha}\, \frac{1}{\alpha a_2 + 1}\, y_0 - \frac{1-\alpha}{\alpha}\, \frac{1}{a_2 + 1/\alpha}\, l_{s0} \tag{10}$$

The expression is cumbersome. We can simplify this and come closer to the conventional literature by assuming $\pi_2 = 0$ and $a_2 = 0$, i.e. indexation is zero and the supply of labour is exogenous. This reduces the expression to

$$y - \bar{y} = (1-\alpha)k + \frac{1-\alpha}{\alpha}\, (p_d - {}_{t-1}E_{pt}) - \frac{1-\alpha}{\alpha}\, y_0 - (1-\alpha)l_{s0} \tag{11}$$

Given, in this context, the exogenous variables k, y_0 and l_{s0} this says that the output gap is determined by the excess of the *home* price level over the *expected consumer price index*.

Using now the Gray–Fischer equation (6a) and simplifying by setting $a_2 = 0$ (again in the spirit of this literature), we have

$$y - \bar{y} = \frac{1-\alpha}{\alpha}\, (p_d - {}_{t-1}E_{p_{dt}}) \tag{12}$$

In (11) if prices are correctly anticipated ${}_{t-1}E_{pt} = p_t$ and we have an equation which says that the deviation from full employment is a function of the real exchange rate (in addition to some exogenous variables) as in Chapter 8. In (12) if the price level is correctly anticipated the level of output cannot depart from full employment (because the wage rate will have been set at the actual price level). Despite the apparent unrealism of such an equation for most economies (with the possible exception of Japan, see Chapter 47), it is nevertheless very widely used (see for example Flood and Marion 1982).

Equation (12) captures the New Classical idea that only an error in forecasting the price level can produce unemployment. Abstracting from constants too in (11) it reduces to (12) in the special case where

$$p_d = p^* + e \qquad (13)$$

i.e. where the real exchange rate is unchanged (purchasing power parity (PPP) holds).

Milton Friedman (1968) provided an early theoretical foundation, for the closed economy, of a supply function identical in form to (12). A slight variation in our framework allows us to arrive at Friedman's result.

Assuming $p_d = p$, we can rewrite (4) in terms of the expected price level:

$$l_s = a_2(w - t_y - {}_{t-1}E_{p_{dt}}) + l_{s0} \qquad (4a)$$

We now again set (2) equal to (4a) and solve for the actual wage rate:

$$w = \frac{1}{a_2\alpha + 1} \, p_d + \frac{a_2}{a_2 + 1/\alpha} \, {}_{t-1}E_{p_{dt}} + \frac{a_2}{a_2 + 1/\alpha} \, t_y$$

$$+ \frac{1}{a_2 + 1/\alpha} \left(\frac{1}{\alpha} \, y_0 + k - l_{s0} \right) \qquad (14)$$

Full employment equilibrium is determined at the point where all expectations are realised, i.e. $p_d = {}_{t-1}E_{p_{dt}}$. So we have

$$w^* = p_d + \frac{a}{a_2 + 1/\alpha} \, t_y + \frac{1}{a_2 + 1/\alpha} \left(\frac{1}{\alpha} \, y_0 + k - l_{s0} \right) \qquad (15)$$

$$y - \bar{y} = -\frac{1 - \alpha}{\alpha} \, (w - w^*) = \frac{(1 - \alpha)a_2}{a_2\alpha + 1} \, (p_d - {}_{t-1}E_{p_{dt}}) \qquad (16)$$

What does this mean?

Friedman assumed labour markets were competitive and in equilibrium. At the same time deviations from full equilibrium can occur through 'misperceptions'. Producers are assumed to know their wage rate and the price they charge; workers know the wage rate being offered but cannot perceive the 'consumer price index'. Suppose now aggregate demand increases. Producers raise the wage rate to attract more labour but they raise their prices by even more, thus, to them, lowering the real wage rate. Workers observe the increase in the wage rate but they have to make some guess about the consumer price index; their information base is outdated, so they wrongly believe that the real wage rate, to them, has risen (when in reality it has fallen) and so they are willing to supply more voluntary labour. Production thus increases and the labour market remains in equilibrium. In due course, however, workers will realise the error of their way and withdraw their labour; eventually production will revert to its original level (as can readily be seen from (16)). In the equations above in the short run $w^* > w$ and $p_d > w$.

We turn now to the case where contracts are undertaken for longer periods, as in the USA, where typically contracts in large enterprises are for two to three years. We already encountered this case in Chapters 14 and 22 (Fischer 1977b).

We follow convention and previous chapters here in hypothesising that a proportion $1 - 2\lambda$ of contracts last one period while a proportion 2λ last two periods evenly distributed over these two periods. Allowing also for potential indexation, this gives a wage equation of the form

$$w = (1 - \lambda)[_{t-1}E_{pt} + \pi_2(p_t - {}_{t-1}E_{pt})] + \lambda[_{t-2}E_{pt} + \pi_2(p_t - {}_{t-2}E_{pt})] \qquad (17)$$

Contracts undertaken two years earlier are based on forward-looking expectations of the consumer price index two years later. In the special case where indexation is perfect, all expectations disappear and we are left with (9) above.

We recall that if all contracts are for one period $1 - 2\lambda = 1$, $\lambda = 0$, and we are left with an equation identical to (8). If all contracts are for two periods $1 - 2\lambda = 0$, $\lambda = 0.5$, i.e. each year half the contracts are renegotiated.

The tax wedge

In the literature on unemployment, particularly that based in Europe, considerable importance has been assigned to the so-called 'tax wedge' (see for example Layard *et al.* 1991; Andrews *et al.* 1985). We can use a simplified, but slightly extended, version of the model above to demonstrate how the so-called tax wedge impacts on the real demand for labour and hence, potentially, on unemployment.

We use first an abbreviated version of (2), extended to accommodate payroll taxes (t_p) (sometimes called taxes on employment). Equation (2) now becomes

$$l_d = -\frac{1}{\alpha}(w + t_p - p_d) \qquad (2a)$$

To simplify we again assume that $a_2 = 0$ and so the supply of labour is fixed.

We now modify (9) in two simple ways. Wages are assumed to be a function of the income tax rate t_y and of the consumer price index p_c on which we now also suppose that a consumption sales tax is imposed.

$$w = p_c + t_y \qquad (9a)$$

$$p_c = \alpha_{15}p_d + (1 - \alpha_{15})(e + p^*) + t_c \qquad (9b)$$

Substituting (9b) into (9a) and then into (2a) yields

$$l_d = -\frac{1 - \alpha_{15}}{\alpha}(e + p^* - p_d) - \frac{1}{\alpha}(t_c + t_y + t_p) \qquad (2b)$$

The tax wedge is the sum of the three taxes (the last bracketed expression).

Equation (2b) says that the real demand for labour is determined by the real exchange rate $(e + p^*) - p_d$, a now familiar result, but also by the three taxes. According to the equation, an increase in the tax wedge will reduce the demand for labour and so, given the supply of labour, increase unemployment.

Why is this? An increase in taxes on consumption (t_c) or an increase in income taxes (t_y) increases wage outcomes and in turn reduces the demand for labour. Also, an increase in payroll taxes increases the cost of employing labour and so reduces the demand for labour.

Before we conclude, however, that these last taxes have particularly adverse effects on unemployment, we need to note that the analysis ought to be placed in a general equilibrium context. If the underlying model is correct an increase in payroll taxes associated with a cut in income or sales taxes will not necessarily reduce employment. Or if payroll taxes increase without any reduction in other taxes we need to ask what happens to the public sector budget. If government expenditure increases or if bonds are retired there will be additional macro consequences which cannot be disregarded.

Empirical application of approach

To apply empirically the approach outlined above we need (with appropriate lags)

a) a production function;
b) a labour demand function;
c) a labour supply function;
d) a wage equation.

Item (d) is discussed in the next section. Work on (a) and (b) is reviewed by Adams *et al.* (1986). The latter provide detailed empirical estimates of labour demand equations. These studies all confirm the importance of real labour costs in labour demand. As expected, too, the sensitivity of labour demand to real labour costs depends on the time horizon, being higher for the longer horizon. There are also empirical estimations of labour supply equations but these in general tend to suggest, in our terms, a rather weak value for a_2 in equation (4) (Ball *et al.* 1988).

MARK-UP PRICING, THE EXPECTATIONS-AUGMENTED PHILLIPS CURVE AND THE NATURAL RATE OF UNEMPLOYMENT

This section has four objectives: first, to derive an equation, on the supply side, which explains inflation, drawing on the expectations-augmented Phillips curve; second, to show how the approach can be used to calculate a natural rate of unemployment (NRU) and to present some estimates of the NRU; third, to show how a simple version of the expectations-augmented Phillips curve can be used to derive the accelerationist hypothesis; fourth, to outline briefly the factors that enter into the determination of the NRU.

The expectations-augmented Phillips curve

We begin here with a simple mark-up pricing equation:

$$p_d = \pi_3(w - \bar{q}) + (1 - \pi_3)(p_{mi} + e) + \alpha_6(y - \bar{y}) \qquad (18)$$

The domestic price level is a mark-up over long-run unit labour costs, where $\dot{q}$ is the 'long-run' level of labour productivity, and the cost of imported materials ($p_{mi} + e$). The mark-up itself is also assumed to be influenced by the output gap.

We now add a conventional expectations-augmented Phillips curve (see, for example, Turnovsky 1977).

$$w - w_{-1} = (\bar{q} - \bar{q}_{-1}) + (t_{-1}E_{pt} - p_{t-1}) + \alpha_5(y - \bar{y}) \qquad (19)$$

The rate of change in wages is a function of long-run productivity growth, the expected rate of inflation and the output gap. The coefficient on the expected rate of inflation is constrained here to be unity.

Taking first differences of (18) and then substituting (19) gives us ($\bar{q}$ now drops out)

$$p_d - p_{d-1} = \pi_3[t_{-1}E_{pt} - p_{t-1} + \alpha_5(y - \bar{y})] + (1 - \pi_3)$$
$$\times \Delta(p_{mi} + e) + \alpha_6 \Delta(y - \bar{y}) \qquad (20)$$

Dornbusch's inflation equation (Chapter 18) resembles (20). The equation, it will be recalled, is

$$p_{d+1} - p_d = \pi_6(y - \bar{y}) \qquad (21)$$

This simply says that the rate of inflation responds to excess demand. π_6 reflects the speed of adjustment. Equation (21) is simple and intuitively appealing, explaining why it is so popular.

Can (21) be derived from (20)? The reader will note that if we set $\alpha_6 = 0$, assume that the expected rate of inflation is zero and that PPP holds (i.e. $p_d - p_{d-1} = \Delta(p_{mi} + e)$), (21) can be deduced from (20) (with $\alpha_5 = \pi_6$).

Calculating the natural rate of unemployment

The above framework can be modified to obtain an estimate of the NRU. We draw here on Coe and Gagliardi (1985). Rewriting and modifying (20) and (19) we have

$$w - w_{-1} = a_0 + a_1(t_{-1}E_{pt} - p_{t-1}) - a_2u + a_3x \qquad (22)$$

where a_1 is the degree to which wages adjust to expected inflation, the unemployment rate replaces the output gap and x captures all other influences on wages; also

$$p - p_{-1} = b_0 + b_1 \Delta(w + t_p - q) + (1 - b_1) \Delta(p_m + e) + b_3z \qquad (23)$$

where t_p represents, as previously, payroll taxes. p_m is now the price of *all* imports and z is all other influences on prices.

In long-run equilibrium we have

a) $\Delta(w + t_p - p) = \Delta(p_m + e)$ (the real exchange rate is fixed);
b) $a_1 = 1$ (there is full adjustment of wages to expected inflation);
c) $p - p_{-1} = {}_{t-1}E_{pt} - p_{t-1}$ (expectations are realised).

Imposing these conditions on the two equations and solving for Un (the NRU) yields

$$\text{Un} = \frac{1}{a_2} [a_0 + b_0 + (t_p - t_{p-1}) - (q - q_{-1}) + b_3 z + a_3 x] \tag{24}$$

The coefficients a_2, a_0, b_0, b_3 and a_3 can all be obtained from empirical estimates of (22) and (23), and so the NRU can be calculated in this way for a number of countries. This is what Coe and Gagliardi (1985) do. (In the latter study z is represented by the ratio of actual to potential real GDP, x is represented by productivity.)

Kawasaki et al. (1990) have recently updated the work of Coe and Gagliardi (1985), estimating equations similar to (22) and (23). Their most recent calculations, using the method outlined above, of the NRU for a number of OECD member countries are shown in Table 28.1.

Layard et al. (1991) estimate variants of the following two price and wage equations for nineteen OECD member countries.

$$p - w = \beta_0 - \beta_1 u - \beta_{11} \Delta u - \beta_2 \Delta^2 p - \beta_3 (k - 1) \tag{25}$$

$$w - p = \sigma_0 - \sigma_1 u - \sigma_{11} \Delta u - \sigma_2 \Delta^2 p + zw + \beta_3 (k - 1) \tag{26}$$

Table 28.1 Natural rate of unemployment

	1966–73[a]	1974–9[a]	1980–7[a]	1960–8[b]	1969–79[b]	1980–8[b]
Belgium	5.9	6.5	6.5	3.77	4.82	7.04
Denmark	4.3	6.0	6.9	2.19	4.64	7.30
France	–	–	–	1.76	3.88	7.81
Germany	–	–	–	0.47	1.87	4.04
Ireland	7.3	6.5	5.9	6.08	9.13	13.09
Italy	–	–	–	4.31	4.94	5.42
Netherlands	2.5	4.3	6.0	1.52	4.28	7.27
Spain	6.7	6.7	7.4	4.55	9.73	14.95
Greece	5.2	5.1	5.1	–	–	–
UK	–	–	–	2.55	5.15	7.92
Australia	2.8	3.2	5.1	2.35	4.01	6.10
New Zealand	1.6	1.5	1.6	0.43	1.96	3.91
Canada	–	–	–	5.46	7.01	8.14
USA	–	–	–	5.01	5.97	6.36
Japan	–	–	–	1.59	1.82	2.14
Austria	0.7	1.2	2.8	0.94	0.48	2.95
Finland	4.0	4.0	4.1	1.40	2.61	4.65
Norway	1.2	1.5	1.5	2.13	2.22	2.50
Sweden	2.6	2.6	2.8	1.64	1.93	2.36
Switzerland	0.5	1.3	0.8	0.09	0.83	1.44

Sources: [a] Kawasaki *et al.* 1990; [b] Layard *et al.* 1991)

where the variables are in logarithms and $k - 1$ is the capital–labour force ratio. σ_{11} captures hysteresis effects (the hypothesis, explained below, that the NRU is itself a function of the unemployment rate) and zw captures other influences on wages, e.g. trade union militancy.

Layard *et al.* justify the use of $\Delta^2 p$ as follows. Expectations about the rate of inflation assume that it follows a random walk, so:

$$\Delta p = \Delta p_{-1} + v \tag{27}$$

$$p_e = p_{-1} + \Delta p_{-1} \tag{28}$$

or equivalently

$$p - p_e = \Delta p - \Delta p_{-1} = \Delta^2 p \tag{29}$$

In equilibrium $\Delta u = \Delta^2 p = 0$ and $k - 1$ cancel out since they have equal and opposite effects. We then have

$$\text{Un} = \frac{1}{\sigma 1 + \beta_1} \left(\sigma_0 + zw + \beta_0 \right)$$

which again is readily calculated.

Their estimates for nineteen countries are also shown in Table 28.1. For the smaller countries these bear comparison with the calculations by Coe and Gagliardi. It is evident that whilst there are some parallels there are also some striking differences (for example in the case of Ireland, New Zealand, Spain), perhaps confirming the point made by Johnson and Layard (1986) that this method of calculating the NRU is 'subject to notorious difficulties', being very sensitive to the underlying equations used.

We note here an alternative method of calculating the NRU (Kurosaka 1991). The NRU is the point at which a $45°$ line intersects a vacancies–unemployment (VU) schedule. This is illustrated in Figure 28.1. P represents the natural unemployment which in turn is set equal to the vacancies (positions available). If VU shifts to the right, as it has tended to do in most industrial countries (see Chapter 44), the natural unemployment rate will rise.

The accelerationist hypothesis

This hypothesis has been important historically. It postulates that to keep the unemployment rate below the NRU the rate of inflation must continually accelerate. To see this, consider a simple three-equation system.

$$\dot{w} = \dot{p}_e - \pi_1 (U - \text{Un}) \tag{30}$$

$$\dot{p}_e = \dot{p}_{-1} \tag{31}$$

$$\dot{p} = \dot{w} \tag{32}$$

A dot represents a rate of change. $\dot{p}_e$ is the expected rate of inflation. The equations

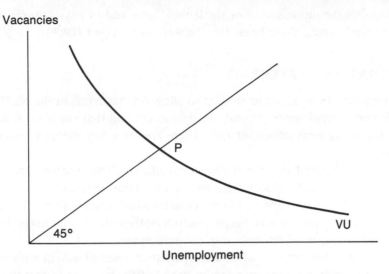

Figure 28.1 Calculating the natural rate of unemployment

are self-explanatory. Equation (32) is a simple price mark-up equation. These three equations yield

$$(\dot{p} - \dot{p}_{-1}) = -\pi_1(U - \text{Un}) \tag{33}$$

which is the accelerationist hypothesis. The *change* in the rate of inflation is a function of the gap between the actual and the natural unemployment rate.

The determinants of the natural rate of unemployment

We document here more explicitly the factors over time which can change the NRU. Hysteresis effects are held over to the next section.

A host of factors can explain a change in the NRU: first, the generosity of the unemployment insurance system (Chapter 44); second, the tax wedge as discussed above; third, a productivity slowdown or an adverse change in the terms of trade. An example of the latter is an upward oil price shock combined with real consumption wage rigidity (Chapter 42). Fourth, demographic changes: a change in the sex, age or ethnic composition of the work force can change the NRU (Chapter 44). Fifth, changes in the minimum wage legislation can also impact on the NRU by changing the demand for labour. Sixth, changes in the unionisation of the labour force can contribute to a change in the NRU (Chapter 44). Seventh, increasing labour market mismatches can also increase the NRU (Chapter 44).

There are several studies which attempt to explain increases in the NRU in terms of specific contributory factors. One such study is that of Coe (1990) who tries to identify the factors which contributed to increases in the NRU in Canada from 1971 to 1988. The principal influences were unemployment benefits and changes in the minimum wage, in the unionisation of the labour force and in payroll taxes. For a multi-country study along these lines, see Johnson and Layard (1986).

ACCOMMODATING HYSTERESIS

A further extension of the above analysis is to allow for *hysteresis* in the NRU. The hypothesis is that unemployment breeds unemployment and that the NRU is itself a function of the actual unemployment rate. There are three key theories underlying this hypothesis.

First, an adverse demand shock may reduce investment. The associated reduction in physical capital in turn reduces the amount of labour that can be employed. Second, there may be some erosion of human capital which comes from being unemployed. Third, the unemployed now become outsiders; they are thus no longer a party to wage determination, in which only insiders participate.

The first theory of hysteresis – associating persistent unemployment with capital shortages – has recently been investigated by Bean (1989). Bean notes that there are probably endogenous mechanisms at work that will tend *ultimately* to correct any capital shortage (say from an initial fall in demand); for example the relative price of labour will fall and induce more labour-intensive techniques, or a recovery in demand, increasing capacity utilisation, will induce firms to expand capacity. This, however, may take time; nor, indeed, is there any certainty that such endogenous mechanisms will work over time.

Some evidence in support of a capital shortage comes from the coincidence of high levels of capacity utilisation and historically high rates of unemployment. These tendencies have been striking in Europe (see also OECD 1989a).

The second theory of hysteresis – embodying the idea that human capital erodes with unemployment – has been tested in the literature. The theory predicts that the long-term unemployed exercise less negative effect on the growth of wages than the short-term unemployed. This prediction has been largely confirmed by econometric analysis (Cotis 1988; Blanchard and Summers 1989). In many countries in Europe the share of long-term unemployment in total unemployment has risen, thus weakening the potential adjustment mechanism.

.The third theory postulates that insiders (the employed) dominate over outsiders (the unemployed) in wage determination. According to the theory (as we saw in Chapter 9) insiders earn a rent over outsiders; the rent is based on

a) the costs of hiring and firing;
b) the cost of refusing cooperation with entrants; and
c) the adverse effect of labour turnover on work effort.

It is this rent which gives insiders a margin of advantage over outsiders and of control over the wage rate (Lindbeck and Snower 1985, 1989).

The insider–outsider theory is generally tested by trying to evaluate the relative importance of insider and outsider influences on wage determination. Insider variables include productivity gains, profitability, competitive position, and strength of unionism. Outsider variables are fundamentally the general state of the labour market. Not surprisingly, perhaps, a number of studies have found both sets of influences to be important, thus weakening the thesis in its pure form (see Blanchflower *et al.* 1988; Nickell and Wadhwani 1989).

To illustrate the workings of hysteresis effects in a more general framework consider a simple conventional Phillips curve relationship of the form

$$\dot{w} = \dot{p} - \pi_1(U - \text{Un}) \tag{34}$$

where $\dot{w}$ and $\dot{p}$ are the rates of increase in wages and prices respectively, U is the actual unemployment rate and Un is the natural unemployment rate.

Hysteresis postulates that Un is itself related in some way to the previous unemployment rate (U_{-1}) and so

$$\text{Un} = \pi_2 U_{-1} \tag{35}$$

Substituting this above and rearranging terms we have

$$w = p - \pi_1(1 - \pi_2)U - \pi_1\pi_2(U - U_{-1}) \tag{36}$$

Full hysteresis requires that $\pi_2 = 1$ in which case the rate of unemployment drops out of the last equation and the *change* in the unemployment rate dominates as the explanation. More generally, the higher π_2 the more important is the change in the unemployment rate relative to the level of the unemployment rate.

Hysteresis in its simplest form can be tested by estimating an equation such as (36) (see Cotis 1988; Gordon, R. 1989). Results are mixed depending on the country. Gordon finds no evidence of *full* hysteresis, the level of the unemployment rate retaining significance. Cotis finds strong evidence of near full hysteresis for the UK (with $\pi_2 \rightarrow 1$), support for some hysteresis in Germany but none in France. Layard *et al.* (1991) in a study of nineteen OECD countries find (partial) hysteresis to be a 'pervasive phenomenon, being absent only in Japan, the USA and Switzerland' (p. 408).

APPENDIX

This appendix shows how the production side of the economy is modelled when some imports are inputs in the production process (see Marston and Turnovsky 1985).

Notation (in logarithms)

yr   value added national produce
yg   gross output (including the value of imported inputs)
l   labour employed
n   volume of imported input

k capital stock
w wage rate
p_d price of gross output domestically produced
p_{mi} foreign price of imported inputs
e exchange rate

Model

$$\text{yr} = \alpha k + (1 - \alpha)l \tag{A1}$$

(the value-added Cobb–Douglas production function). α and $1 - \alpha$ are respective shares of capital and labour in value added as in the text.

$$\text{yg} = c_1 n + (1 - c_1)y \tag{A2}$$

(gross output function). c_1 and $1 - c_1$ are respective shares of inputs and value added in gross output.

The derived demands for labour l and imported inputs n are

$$l = -\frac{1}{\alpha}(w - p_d) - \frac{c_1}{\alpha(1 - c_1)}(p_{mi} + e - p_d) \tag{A3}$$

$$n = \frac{1 - \alpha}{\alpha}(w - p_d) - \frac{1}{1 - c_1}\left[\sigma + \frac{c_1(1 - \alpha)}{\alpha}\right](p_{mi} + e - p_d) \tag{A4}$$

where σ is the elasticity of substitution between domestic value added and imported inputs.

Substituting (A3) into (A1) we have (disregarding the fixed capital stock k)

$$y = \left|\frac{1 - \alpha}{\alpha}\right|(w - p_d) - \left|\frac{c_1}{1 - c_1}\frac{1 - \alpha}{\alpha}\right|(p_{mi} + e - p_d) \tag{A5}$$

Equation (3) in the text is a special case of this where $c_1 = 0$.

29

Imposing medium- to long-run constraints on the model

INTRODUCTION

The previous two chapters presented a fairly generalised model of a small economy. The question we address in this short chapter is the following: what sorts of constraints ought to be met in defining medium- to long-run equilibrium? We already touched on this question in Chapter 11; this chapter develops the analysis further. The concepts are applied in the next chapter to a simpler version of the model of the last two chapters.

THE CONSTRAINTS WITHOUT GROWTH

We have to this point modelled asset demands and the effects of changes in asset stocks (or their valuation) on the real economy. We also showed (in Chapters 10 and 11) how changes in these asset stocks, which drive the economy, are generated. To develop this further, we return to some of the constraints we drew on in Chapter 11.

In that chapter we arrived at

$$XP_d - \text{MPfE} + r^*\text{EFA} + G - T + r_dB = \Delta H + (\Delta \text{Bg} - \Delta \text{DA})$$
$$+ \Delta(EFA) \tag{1}$$

and

$$\text{Sp} = \Delta \text{We} = I + \Delta H + \Delta B + \Delta(EFA) \tag{2}$$

where $\Delta B = \Delta \text{Bg} - \Delta \text{DA}$. Substituting (2) into (1) we have

$$(XP_d - \text{MPfE} + r^*\text{EFA}) + (G - T + r_dB_0) + I = \Delta \text{We} \tag{3}$$

We are now ready to address a key question we touched on in Chapter 11. How is medium- to long-run equilibrium to be defined? What constraints ought one to impose on the model to define a steady state equilibrium? (See Branson and Buiter (1983), Kawai (1985) and Allen and Kenen (1980).)

Virtually all of this literature assumes that there is no growth in the economy, and so, to begin at least, we adopt this assumption. In these circumstances the economy will converge towards a stationary state where private savings and net investment are all zero.

From (3) with $\Delta We = I = 0$ the only question at issue is whether it is possible to have a steady state where the budget deficit (surplus) is equal to the current account deficit (surplus). Chapter 11 also addressed this question.

We can quickly rule out certain potential long-run outcomes. Suppose first we had fixed exchange rates. Sterilised intervention is not viable since it implies *continuous* changes in central bank international reserves.

What about unsterilised intervention? There are two questions to be asked here. First, whilst in *equilibrium* the overall balance of payments is zero, during the adjustment process there will have been a transitional stock movement in international reserves, which may need to be restored. Second, in equilibrium $CA = E \Delta FA$ (any current account surplus must be matched by an equivalent outflow of capital). This is also the condition for equilibrium for a float. How viable then is a solution where the two parts of the equation may be non-zero?

Suppose we have a current account deficit equal to $E \Delta FA$ which in turn is matched by a budget deficit. Can the budget deficit be financed in each period by an accumulation of *money*? If it were we would have in equilibrium some reduction in foreign asset holdings offset by an accumulation of money. This is clearly not a sustainable equilibrium since it will throw the portfolio out of balance; so we can rule this case out.

What if the budget deficit were financed by bonds? Now the private sector is unloading foreign bonds in exchange for domestic bonds. As we saw in Chapter 11, this cannot be a stable situation, *so long as the bonds are imperfect substitutes*, which for the long run is probably the more appropriate framework.

We are left, then, with a single possibility, that the bonds are perfect substitutes. Is this now viable? How are interest payments on bond accumulation and interest payments abroad on the accumulation of foreign debt (or decumulation of foreign assets) compatible with such an outcome?

It is now evident that a given primary budget deficit (i.e. non-interest component) will be associated with an ever larger stock of bonds and official interest bill and hence with an ever larger budget deficit, which now cannot remain static. Similarly, a primary current account deficit (excluding interest) means a worsening net foreign asset position, implying fewer interest earnings or more payments abroad to finance the borrowings. This means in turn an ever larger current account deficit as well.

But why is this a problem since if the real interest rate is the same the *twin deficits* will grow at the same rate? [1]

The problem is that the deficits as a proportion of the *stationary* GDP will become ever larger, converging ultimately to infinity. Such a result is unacceptable and explains why, given the assumptions that the literature has seen fit to impose as *conditions* of medium- to long-run equilibrium, *both* the current account and the budget balance must be zero in equilibrium.

This is reasonable and indeed inevitable given our reasoning. Note that interest payments also appear in the real demand for goods but this *in itself* is not a problem because what *you would have in equilibrium is more interest earnings on domestic bonds and equivalently, less interest earnings on foreign bonds.*

So we now have as long-run constraints

$$Sp = 0 \tag{4}$$

$$CA = 0 \tag{5}$$

$$G - T + r_d B = 0 \tag{6}$$

It is one thing, however, to impose such a constraint on the long-run result; it is quite another to show that the economy does in fact converge towards this result. This turns out to be extremely complex, depending as it does in the end on the dynamic stability of the model.

THE CONSTRAINTS WITH SOME REAL GROWTH

We now introduce the possibility of some real growth in the economy but continue to limit ourselves to the small-country case. We apply the *identical* framework both to domestic *bond* accumulation and to the growth in foreign indebtedness.

Suppose B stands for the stock of bonds or foreign debt, r is the interest rate on the debt and D stands for the *primary* deficit, i.e. before payment of interest. So we have

$$D + rB_{-1} = B - B_{-1} \tag{7}$$

Rearranging and dividing through by Y (the gross national product) we have

$$\frac{B}{Y} = \frac{D}{Y} + (1 + r) \frac{B_{-1}}{Y_{-1}} \frac{Y_{-1}}{Y} \tag{8}$$

$$\frac{Y_{-1}}{Y} = \frac{1}{1 + g}$$

where g is the growth of Y. We can now simplify further by rewriting (8) as

$$\frac{B}{Y} = \frac{D}{Y} + [1 + (r - g)] \frac{B_{-1}}{Y_{-1}} \tag{9}$$

This is a first-order difference equation. It defines what happens to the bond–GNP ratio B/Y when the primary deficit ratio D/Y increases. Provided that the coefficient on the lagged bond–GNP ratio is less than unity the bond–GNP ratio will ultimately converge to a new higher level. If the coefficient is greater than unity, however, the system is unstable, implying that the debt–GNP ratio will rise indefinitely.

The condition for stability is that $g > r$, i.e. the growth rate exceeds the interest rate. In terms of our previous analysis, if growth in GNP exceeds the interest rate a larger primary deficit is viable. If $g = 0$ as previously assumed the debt–GNP ratio effectively rises without limit. So, to conclude, with real growth in the economy, provided that $g > r$ a current account deficit combined with an equal budget deficit is strictly feasible. However, this is unlikely to provide us with a way out of our difficulties. First, the condition $g > r$ may not hold and indeed in the last twenty years or so in OECD countries has tended not to hold. Second, and more important, a further condition for sustainability is that the assets be perfect substitutes. This is extremely unlikely to hold for the longer run. (See Chapters 11, 32 and 33.)

30

The effects in the short and long run of a monetary and fiscal expansion under flexible exchange rates in a more general framework

INTRODUCTION

This chapter tries to provide a particular illustration of how one would go about analysing the effects of a monetary or a fiscal expansion, under flexible rates, using now a more extensive model than any used so far.

It will be recalled that we began with the simplest MF model, progressively extending that to accommodate (a) flexible wages and prices, (b) wealth and (c) dynamics.

This chapter presents a simplified version of the model presented in the immediately preceding chapters; the intention is to show how such a model can be solved and to draw attention to some of the difficulties which confront us in manipulating such a model.

Large models of the kind analysed in this chapter can be found in Allen and Kenen (1980), Branson and Buiter (1983), Turnovsky and Kingston (1977), Kawai (1985), Karakitsos (1989) and Genberg and Swoboda (1989). These models are all different from one another in some respects; it is therefore not possible to do full justice to all of them. To get the flavour of these models, we choose to focus on and reproduce just one, Kawai's.

Karakitsos (1989) uses a model which is even more extensive than Kawai's, incorporating more of the features found in the earlier chapters. The model is difficult to solve analytically, however, and so to carry out simulations the author takes plausible values, from the empirical literature, of the model coefficients. This is a useful device. The reader will find the study illuminating in this general context.

THE MODEL

The model presented here is reproduced with only slight modification from Kawai. There is some repetition with the preceding chapters but this is inevitable.

The entire model comprises essentially four equations: a goods market equation, a money market equation, a price adjustment equation and a current account equation (which in turn is equal to the rate of change of foreign assets in domestic currency). There is no investment in the economy. The model assumes that there is perfect asset substitution.

From our perspective we focus on the short- and longer-run effects of two policies: an open market purchase (with the budget assumed to be balanced) and a tax-financed increase in government expenditure.

Kawai defines a short run as one where prices are fixed and the stock of foreign assets (in foreign currency) is also given. The latter assumption excludes *stock* wealth but not *wealth valuation* effects due to a change in the exchange rate. The long run is defined as one where the current account is zero and prices have reached a new equilibrium. In this long run too, as we shall see, the economy returns to its full employment level of output.

Kawai thus distinguishes three phases of adjustment: a short run, a dynamic adjustment phase and a final long-run outcome. Dynamics in this context are defined by the rates of price inflation and of foreign asset accumulation. In the model expectations appear only in exchange markets but not in prices. Kawai adopts the Dornbusch device of assuming that exchange rate expectations are formed regressively. Unlike Dornbusch, however, he assumes expectations are only semi-rational (as in Mathieson 1977) in the sense that the public *know the long-run result but not the precise time path of adjustment.*

It turns out that the question of whether or not the system is dynamically stable, in the sense that the economy will ultimately converge towards its long-run results, is a very complicated exercise. The reader who is mathematically inclined can study the original source for the various tests of stability applied.

The goods market

$$y = a + g + x \tag{1}$$

where y is domestic output, a is real private sector spending (= consumption), g is real government spending and x is the real trade balance surplus.

$$a = a_1 y_d + a_2 we \qquad a_1 < 1 \tag{2}$$

y_d is real disposable income and we is real financial wealth.

$$y_d = y + r_d \frac{B}{P} + r^* \frac{\text{EFA}}{P} - t \tag{3}$$

r_d is the home interest rate, B is domestic bonds, r^* is the foreign interest rate, E the exchange rate, FA the stock of foreign-denominated bonds, t the real taxes and P the price of domestic output.

$$we = \frac{Mo + B + EFA}{P} \tag{4}$$

Equation (4) defines real wealth as in previous chapters.

Kawai also assumes, as already indicated, that the budget is always balanced, and so

$$t = g + r_d \frac{B}{P} \tag{5}$$

Substituting (5) into (3) yields

$$y_d = y + r^* \frac{EFA}{P} - g \tag{6}$$

Finally, we have (with the foreign price level given)

$$x = x_1 \frac{E}{P} - x_2 a \qquad x_2 < 1 \tag{7}$$

Net exports are a positive function of the real exchange rate E/P and a negative function of some proportion of real private absorption.

A number of substitutions allow us to write the equation for the goods market (the IS schedule) as

$$y = \frac{a_1(1 - x_2)}{k_2} r^* \frac{EFA}{P} + \frac{a_2(1 - x_2)}{k_2} \frac{Mo + B + EFA}{P}$$

$$+ \frac{x_1 E}{k_2 P} + \frac{1 - a_1(1 - x_2)}{k_2} g \tag{8}$$

$$k_2 = 1 - a_1(1 - x_2)$$

This only slightly modifies the equations for the goods market derived previously. Equation (8) is one of the four key equations of the system.

The money market

$$\frac{Mo}{P} = l_1 y - l_2 r_d + l_3 we \qquad l_3 < 1 \tag{9}$$

Real money balances are a function of output, the domestic interest rate and real wealth. At the same time, the assumption of perfect asset substitution implies that the excess of the home interest rate over the foreign interest rate is equal to the expected devaluation of the currency. In turn (as in Dornbusch), the expected devaluation is some function of the gap between the long-run and current spot rate. So we have

$$r_\mathrm{d} - r^* = \frac{{}_tF_{t+1} - E}{E} \tag{10}$$

and

$$\frac{{}_tF_{t+1} - E}{E} = \pi_4 \frac{\bar{E} - E}{E} \tag{11}$$

Substituting (11) into (10), (10) into (9) and (4) into (9) gives us our money market (LM) equation:

$$\frac{Mo}{P} = l_1 y - l_2 r^* - l_2 \pi_4 \frac{\bar{E} - E}{E} + l_3 \frac{Mo + B + EFA}{P} \tag{12}$$

where $\bar{E}$ is now our rationally formed expectation of the long-run exchange rate.

Price adjustment

$$\frac{P_{t+1} - P_t}{P_t} = \pi_5 (y - \bar{y}) \tag{13}$$

This is again an equation used previously and was a feature of Dornbusch's model (Chapter 18).

Rate of foreign asset accumulation (the current account)

$$\frac{E\,\Delta\mathrm{FA}}{P} = x_1 \frac{E}{P} - x_2 a_1 y - x_2 a_1 r^* \frac{EFA}{P} - x_2 a_1 g - x_2 a_2 \frac{Mo + B + EFA}{P}$$

$$+ r^* \frac{EFA}{P} \tag{14}$$

The real current account in domestic currency is the sum of the trade surplus x and the net investment account. In turn this current account surplus is equal to the net foreign asset accumulation abroad.

Equations (8) and (12)–(14) comprise the whole system.

Because this is a rational expectations model for the long run and because the long-run exchange rate has a bearing on the short-run solution (as in Dornbusch), we need to solve for the long run first.

From (13) in the long run $y = \bar{y}$ and so output is effectively exogenously given. At the same time, the current account is zero, and so $E\,\Delta\mathrm{FA}/P = 0$ in (14) and $\bar{E} = E$. This leaves us three equations – (8), (12) and (14) – to solve for E, P and FA. Having solved for E we can now use this solution to solve for the short run.

As already indicated, the short run is defined as one where P and FA are fixed.

After feeding in the solutions for $\bar{E}$, we can use equations (8) and (12) to solve for E and y (which in the short run is endogenous).

It should be noted that Mo and B are both exogenous. For an open market purchase we have $\Delta \text{Mo} = -\Delta B$. Recalling that the budget is always balanced there are no further changes in B. For a tax-financed increase in government expenditure $\Delta \text{Mo} = \Delta B = 0$.

AN OPEN MARKET PURCHASE

As indicated, an open market purchase is represented by $\Delta \text{Mo} = -\Delta B$; there is a one-off change in both bonds and money. We recall that to obtain the long-run solution for such a policy change, we hold output fixed and use (8), (12) and (14) (with the current account constrained to zero) to solve for P, E and FA.

The actual solutions are complicated and are not reported. These appear in an appendix in Kawai's paper. Here we only report the direction of the change.

In the long run a monetary expansion

a) increases the price level;
b) increases the net foreign asset position (so the cumulative current account is in surplus);
c) produces a real appreciation of the currency (as in Branson, Chapter 19);
d) has an *ambiguous* effect on the nominal exchange rate (a surprising outcome);
e) increases the real stock of foreign assets denominated in domestic currency;
f) has an ambiguous effect on the real stock of wealth (because, while the real stock of foreign assets increases, the *real* stock of money and bonds decreases).

What is worth highlighting in these results is the fact that, in a more sophisticated model such as this one, money is no longer neutral. We do not now replicate classical results.

To obtain a short-run result, we need to feed in the solution for the long-run exchange rate (which, as we noted above, is ambiguous). With FA and P fixed in the short run we can use (8) and (12) to solve for y and E given $\bar{E}$.

It so happens that the effects on y and E are both ambiguous. The ambiguity stems from the ambiguous result for the exchange rate in the long run. If the currency were to *appreciate* in the long run, output in the short run could fall for two reasons: the downward valuation of foreign asset holdings (a negative wealth effect) and a *current* appreciation.

If the currency in fact devalues in the long run (a likely outcome, as Kawai notes) we have more familiar results for the short run: output increases and the currency devalues.

A TAX-FINANCED INCREASE IN GOVERNMENT EXPENDITURE

Now, as already indicated, both Mo and B are unchanged. Using the same methodology as above, we find that in the long run

a) the price level will rise;
b) the currency will appreciate *in real terms*;
c) the effect on the net stock of foreign assets is ambiguous;
d) the effect on the currency is also ambiguous;
e) the real stock of foreign assets in domestic currency falls;
f) the real stock of wealth will fall (for two reasons: first, because the real value of money and bonds will fall and, second, because of item (e)).

In the short run, we again have ambiguous outcomes for both output and the currency. Again, this stems from the ambiguous long-run result for the exchange rate. Kawai concludes that such a fiscal expansion will have positive effects if it 'does not cause a large long run appreciation'.

MODELS OF EXCHANGE RATES

Part VI deals with exchange rate models. Two chapters review the models of exchange rates in the literature; a third examines the concepts of foreign exchange market efficiency and financial integration.

Chapter 31 focuses on three well-known models: purchasing power parity (PPP), a balance of payments model and the flexi-price monetarist model. Chapter 32 refines some of these models in a number of directions. The flexi-price model is extended to accommodate first sticky prices and next deviations from PPP and a risk premium. The chapter also presents a 'fundamentals' model of the real exchange rate. The role of 'news' in exchange rate determination is also introduced into the analysis. The importance of chartists and fundamentalists in exchange rate determination is also developed.

Chapter 33 tries to give the reader a feel for the literature on foreign exchange market efficiency. The literature is reviewed under two headings: tests of efficiency in the forward market and tests of efficiency in the spot market. The chapter also looks more closely at the concept of financial integration, now drawing on evidence and analysis to date.

31

Modelling exchange rates (1)

INTRODUCTION

This chapter and the next focus on one question: how exchange rates should be modelled for an economy whose currency is predominantly determined by market forces.

To some extent that question has already been answered. The theoretical models of flexible exchange rates we have presented and the econometric models to which we referred *all have exchange rate solutions*. The forces that drive exchange rates are already identified in those models, the more simple as well as the more complex ones. An example will suffice. If we were to take a small-country version of the two-country model of Chapter 13, focusing on the short-run fixed wage–price solutions with high capital mobility we would have

$$e = \pi_1 mo - \pi_2 gr - \pi_3 mo^* + \pi_4 gr^* \tag{1}$$

The country's exchange rate *vis-à-vis* the 'rest of the world' is determined by monetary and fiscal policies at home and abroad. These are the fundamental forces driving the exchange rate. The signs would be as shown: a monetary expansion at home (abroad) provokes a devaluation (an appreciation) while a fiscal expansion at home (abroad) provokes an appreciation (a devaluation) of the currency.

Needless to say this is too simple but (1) does serve to make the point that exchange rate solutions are already *implied* in some of our earlier analyses.

What we want to do in this chapter is extend the analysis, focusing particularly on how the literature has modelled the exchange rate and on some of the empirical work undertaken in this area.

Throughout the chapter we will find that the *expected* exchange rate plays a key role in determining the current spot rate. In Chapter 27, we outlined a variety of hypotheses underlying the formation of exchange rate expectations. These will need to be kept in mind in the course of this chapter.

RELATIVE PURCHASING POWER PARITY

Concept

PPP is one of the oldest theories. It says simply that, starting from a given base period, the exchange rate between any two currencies (or between one currency and a trade-weighted bundle of other currencies) will move in line with relative price levels in the two economies (or with prices at home relative to the trade-weighted inflation in the other currencies).

Put more formally we have

$$\Delta e = \Delta p - \Delta p^*$$

where e is the bilateral (or trade-weighted) exchange rate, p is the relevant price at home and p is the price in the foreign country (or the trade-weighted price abroad). All variables are in logarithms.

Some analytical questions

We need to address, briefly, a number of questions. What is the relevant price index? Over what time horizon would PPP be expected to hold? We need to define here not only a 'base' period, when the economy was roughly in fundamental equilibrium, but also a terminal point; in other words, we need to allow enough time for convergence to take place. In what circumstances would one expect divergences from PPP? How does causation run: is it from relative prices to exchange rates?

If there are no restrictions on trade and the relevant traded good is perfectly homogeneous, one should expect, as a matter of course, that the goods sell at the same price in a common currency (i.e. the 'law of one price', so called, would be expected to hold). This is manifestly so for certain types of agricultural and mineral products. In these cases PPP would hold *continuously*.

The case of differentiated manufactured traded goods is less obvious. Differences in prices expressed in a common currency, could well emerge and indeed persist over time. The difficulty with testing this proposition is to find differentiated products which are at the same time comparable in quality and service.

Finally, at the other extreme we have products, such as services, which do not enter into trade. Differences in real prices would be expected to be most apparent here. This does not, of course, exclude the possibility that internal adjustment mechanisms will ultimately bring these prices as well, in part at least, into line with the prices of traded goods.

To conclude here, a price index which comes closest to representing traded goods (e.g. export, wholesale prices) would be expected to conform most while a price index which includes many non-traded goods (e.g. the consumer price index) would be expected to conform less. (See also the model of Chapter 17.)

Some of the models presented in earlier chapters throw some light on some of the questions we addressed earlier. It will be recalled that in Dornbusch's model of Chapter 18 PPP is validated, in the wake of a monetary expansion, but only in the long run. Because money markets adjust more quickly than goods markets, it takes time for PPP to be restored. Moreover, in the Dornbusch model the exchange rate adjusts first and relative prices subsequently. Chapter 24 showed that when a monetary expansion is anticipated and prices are flexible PPP may be restored within one period.

On the other hand, in Branson's model of Chapter 19 (and, for that matter, in the more complicated model of Chapter 30) PPP does not hold in the longer run even for a monetary expansion. Moreover, fiscal policy will change the real exchange rate in the 'longer' run (Chapters 8, 20 and 30).

We can generalise some of these points. Any *protracted* real (or even monetary) change is likely to change the real exchange rate in the longer run. A real change can come from, say, an oil price shock, a fiscal change, a change in the degree of protection or a change in the demand for a country's exports. A change in the rate of inflow of capital over time would also be expected to produce a change in the real exchange rate.

To conclude this part of the discussion, then, there are strong theoretical reasons for not expecting PPP to hold in the shorter run; for the longer run the analytical issues are more complicated but even here there are circumstances where it might not hold.

PPP is sometimes presented as if causation logically runs from relative prices to exchange rates. The reality is much more complicated. We have seen that there are common underlying forces, e.g. monetary and fiscal, which drive both exchange rates and relative prices (but at different speeds). If differences in relative prices and in competitiveness persist and this manifests itself in persistent current account imbalances, corrective forces are likely to come into play, ultimately producing compensating changes in exchange rates. In an adjustable peg regime a policy change to the exchange rate may come after differences in inflation have persisted for a while.

Having said this, however, one can readily think of circumstances where causation might run from exchange rates to relative prices. A devaluation raises the price of imported goods; this, in turn, as we have seen in many of our models, may induce wage and further price adjustments. In the model of Chapter 8 we showed how an exogenous devaluation *might lead* to a proportionate increase in domestic prices, ultimately leaving the real exchange rate unchanged.

The evidence

What, finally, is the evidence? We can proceed in several ways.

The IMF, for some years, has published indices of real effective (essentially trade-weighted) exchange rates for a number of member countries. Series are published for unit labour costs and wholesale, export, value added and consumer prices. Inspection of these series reveals that there are very substantial fluctuations for periods extending over several years; there is some evidence of reversion, however: prolonged real appreciations (devaluations) tend to be followed by prolonged real devaluations (appreciations). Casual inspection of this kind cannot reveal whether there is long-run convergence to a *base* real rate; only more powerful statistical tests will throw light on this question.

PPP theory says that over time one should expect exchange rates to reflect, at least in a rough and ready way, differences in relative prices. Table 31.1 is intended to throw light on this.

It represents a crude way of testing PPP for the longer run for a sample of fourteen countries over the period 1973–89. It is readily seen that those countries which have performed better than the USA in terms of inflation (Austria, Germany, Japan and Switzerland) are also those whose currencies have appreciated relative to the US dollar. At the other end, countries with rates of inflation many times greater than that of the USA (Greece and Turkey) are also those which experienced very large devaluations. Finally, all the other countries had more inflation than the USA in varying degrees and they all devalued relative to the dollar. The point would be further reinforced if we were to compare the USA with countries, such as Brazil and Argentina, with very high rates of inflation. So there is at least evidence of adjustment in the right direction, even if PPP in its strict form is not necessarily upheld.

Table 31.1   Inflation and exchange rates *vis-à-vis* the USA, 1973–89

	Inflation[a]	Ratio to the USA[b]	Currency change vis-à-vis US$[c]
Australia	4.4	1.6	1.8
Austria	2.1	0.8	0.7
Canada	3.2	1.1	1.2
France	3.3	1.2	1.4
Germany	1.7	0.6	0.7
Greece	14.4	5.1	5.3
Italy	4.9	1.8	2.4
Japan	2.2	0.8	0.5
Korea	5.8	2.1	1.7
Sweden	3.7	1.3	1.5
Switzerland	1.7	0.6	0.5
Turkey	278.0	99.3	151.6
UK	4.9	1.8	1.5
USA	2.8	1.0	1.0

Source: IMF, *International Financial Statistics*
Notes: [a] Ratio of consumer price index 1989 divided by 1973.
         [b] Column 1 divided by US value.
         [c] Local currency per US$, 1973–89.

A recent paper by Giovannetti (1992) reviews some of the latest statistical–econometric work on PPP. He shows how most of the evidence rejects PPP even for the longer run. He does, however, raise the question of whether even a period of fifteen to twenty years over which the tests apply is 'long enough to detect the mean reverting behaviour of exchange rates implied by PPP' (p. 97).

To conclude, if what we are after is an explanation of movements in the exchange rate over the short to medium run we clearly need to go beyond PPP, particularly if inflation rates are relatively modest; however, for medium- to long-run analysis of exchange rate trends PPP can make a significant contribution.

CONVENTIONAL BALANCE OF PAYMENTS MODELS OF THE EXCHANGE RATE

A conventional balance of payments model is one of the best-known models of exchange rate determination. In essence it says that in a pure float the exchange rate will equilibrate the flow demand for foreign currency and the flow supply of foreign currency. Since the balance of payments must be zero in a pure float any current account surplus (flow supply of foreign currency) must be exactly offset by a capital account deficit (flow demand for foreign currency). Thus in this framework the exchange rate will be determined by the variables which explain the current and the capital accounts.[1]

It is evident that many variations are possible, depending on how the current and the capital accounts are modelled. By now the reader should be able to 'make up' his own exchange rate equation using this framework. There is thus no question of developing all the possibilities. We illustrate by reference to one formulation of the framework. The model below draws on a stock–flow framework.

We first write down the balance of payments equation:

$$\frac{B}{X_0} = \frac{CA}{X_0} + \frac{K}{X_0} \tag{2}$$

where B, CA and K are respectively the overall balance of payments, the current account and net capital inflows, all deflated by initial exports. The elements are all defined in domestic currency.

We now need to formulate equations explaining the current and capital accounts.

$$\frac{CA}{X_0} = \pi_1(e + p^* - p_d) + \pi_2(y^* - y) + CA_0 \tag{3}$$

This says, familiarly, that the current account (the flow) is explained by the real exchange rate $(e + p^* - p_d)$ and by the relative output levels $(y^* - y)$. (In earlier versions π_2 was set equal to 1 and π_1 was the Marshall–Lerner condition.) CA_0 represents all other 'exogenous' influences on the current account.

In the light of what was said in Chapter 21 about J curves and lags in adjustment (3) ought in principle to be extended to accommodate such lags. This can readily be done but since we are simply trying to illustrate this particular approach we simplify a little (or interpret (3) as an *annual* equation, assuming all the effects are manifest within one year).

Suppose now that we adopted a simple version of the portfolio approach to capital movements, omitting here prices and output but at the same time extending the analysis to a two-country framework.

We need now also to take account of the foreign country's purchases of domestic bonds (which represents inflows) (ΔBF) as well as home purchases of foreign bonds (representing outflows) (ΔEFA). So we have

$$K = \Delta BF - \Delta(EFA) \tag{4}$$

The stock demand by foreigners for domestic bonds is a function of foreign wealth (We^*) and relative returns. The stock demand by residents for foreign bonds is a function of home wealth (We) and relative returns. Drawing on this we can readily derive

$$\frac{K}{X} = \pi_3 \, \Delta we^* - \pi_4 \, \Delta we + \pi_5 \, \Delta(r_d - r^* - e_e + e) \tag{5}$$

where we is the logarithm of wealth and e_e is the expected exchange rate in logarithms.

If we combine (5) with (3), substituting into (2) we can arrive at an exchange rate equation

$$e = \frac{\pi_5}{\pi_1 + \pi_5} \, e_{-1} + \frac{1}{\pi_1 + \pi_5} \frac{B}{X_0} - \frac{\pi_1}{\pi_1 + \pi_5} \, (p^* - p_d)$$

$$+ \frac{\pi_2}{\pi_1 + \pi_5} \, (y - y^*) - \frac{\pi_3}{\pi_1 + \pi_5} \, \Delta we^* = \frac{\pi_4}{\pi_1 + \pi_5} \, \Delta we$$

$$- \frac{\pi_5}{\pi_1 + \pi_5} \, \Delta(r_d - r^* - e_e) - \frac{1}{\pi_1 + \pi_5} \, CA_0 \tag{6}$$

This equation says that (a) central bank intervention – represented by B/X_0 – in the form of *purchases* of foreign assets will depress the currency, (b) an increase in home prices relative to those abroad will depress the currency, (c) an increase in output at home relative to that abroad will also depress the currency, (d) an increase in wealth at home (abroad) will depress (appreciate) the currency, (e) an increase in returns favouring the home economy will appreciate the currency and (f) an exogenous improvement in the current account will appreciate the currency.

There are several empirical studies that use a framework compatible with the above. Examples of such studies are Hodgson (1972), Thomas (1973), Artus (1976), Haas and Alexander (1979) and Driskill (1981).

FLEXI-PRICE MONETARISM

This is the earliest version of monetarism and is generally associated with Frenkel (1976) and Bilson (1978). For a general overview, see Boughton (1988).

The model

There are four key assumptions underlying this model. There is, first, the assumption of perfect asset substitution, and so we have, familiarly,

$$r_d - r^* = e_e - e \tag{7}$$

Second, the assumption is made that PPP holds 'in the short run', effectively continuously, and so we have

$$e = p_d - p^* \tag{8}$$

Third, there are stable and simple money demand equations in the two relevant countries. In general, too, there are no lags in the adjustment of money demand to the exogenous variables. At the same time, the further assumption is frequently made that the structural coefficients are identical across countries, and so we can write

$$mo = p_d + \alpha_5 y - \alpha_{10} r_d \tag{9}$$

and

$$mo^* = p^* + \alpha_5 y^* - \alpha_{10} r^* \tag{10}$$

The fourth assumption made in these monetarist models is that expectations are 'rationally' formed, in the sense already explained in earlier chapters.

If we now subtract (10) from (9) and use (8) we can solve for the exchange rate as follows

$$e = (mo - mo^*) - \alpha_5(y - y^*) + \alpha_{10}(r_d - r^*) \tag{11}$$

We also have from (7) and (8)

$$r_d - r^* = (\bar{p}_d - p_d) - (\bar{p}^* - p^*) \tag{12}$$

i.e. the interest rate differential reflects the expected difference in inflation rates. (The bar here stands for expected values.)

We can also use (7) to obtain (from (11))

$$e = \frac{1}{1 + \alpha_{10}} (mo - mo^*) - \frac{\alpha_5}{1 + \alpha_{10}} (y - y^*) + \frac{\alpha_{10}}{1 + \alpha_{10}} e_e \tag{13}$$

Equation (13) says that the exchange rate is determined by the two fundamentals (relative money and relative output) and the expected exchange rate. Rational expectations could be applied to (13) (see below).

What does equation (11) tell us? Suppose there is a one-off increase in the domestic money supply by 10 per cent. The domestic interest will instantly fall. At the same time there is an expectation that the currency will devalue by 10 per cent. From equation (7) given r^* the fall in the home interest rate plus the expected devaluation would lead to instant potential outflows and a devaluation as in the now familiar Dornbusch model. Now in this model because of the assumption of PPP the devaluation will push up domestic prices in the same proportion. This also means, from the money demand equation, that the interest rate is pulled back up. Suppose that the actual devaluation is less than the expected devaluation; then prices increase by less than 10 per cent, real money balances also increase and the interest rate is lower than before the increase in the money supply. This, however, cannot be sustained; there is now an expected devaluation plus a lower relative domestic interest rate; hence potential capital outflows will persist and there will be a further devaluation. This devaluation continues until (a) domestic prices have increased in the same proportion as the increase in the money supply, (b) the devaluation is also in the same proportion, (c) real money balances are restored and (d) the interest rate returns to its original level. All of this is supposed to happen very quickly.

It is important to see that in this model there is no overshoot. Suppose the devaluation were greater than the expected devaluation. Prices would rise proportionately by more than the money supply; real money balances would fall and the interest rate would have to be above its level before the change in the money supply. At the same time, there is now an expected appreciation. On both counts (the higher interest rate and the expected appreciation) there would be potential inflows until the equilibrium exchange rate is achieved.

What about the relative output term? Suppose output at home increases relative to output abroad. Suppose the last term (the interest rate differential) is given. From (9) we can see that since r_d is given and so also the money stock, the price level must *fall* to equilibrate the money market. The incipient rise in the home interest rate appreciates the currency, lowering the price level correspondingly.

We have already explained the meaning of the interest rate differential (see (12) above). A higher expected rate of domestic inflation will depress the currency. This explains the positive coefficient.

It is worth highlighting the fact that when (6) is compared with (11) there appears to be different predictions about the signs of the coefficients. In a conventional balance of payments framework the coefficient on relative output is positive while in the monetarist framework it is negative. Also the coefficient on the interest rate differential is negative on the balance of payments approach but positive on the monetarist approach (because, to repeat, in this last case it reflects the difference in the expected rate of inflation).

Empirical evidence

Equations (11) and (13) correspond to alternative ways of estimating the simple monetarist model. Sometimes (11) is estimated exactly as is; sometimes $r_d - r^*$ is replaced by the difference in inflation rates (from (12)); sometimes it is replaced by the forward discount (see Chapter 33). To estimate (13) rational expectations are universally assumed.

A slightly more refined version of flexi-price monetarism would allow for lags in the money demand equation. Authors who have used lags in money demand equations in testing this approach are Bilson (1978) and Woo (1985). Also, it is not necessary to impose identical structural coefficients.

There has been an explosion of empirical tests of the monetarist model (see MacDonald and Taylor (1992) for a recent review). Some early studies seemed to be supportive; most later studies, however, were against the model. Three studies claim to be supportive: Hoffman and Schlagenhauf (1983), MacDonald (1984) and Woo (1985). All three assume rational expectations. Woo concludes that 'the monetary model is alive ...'. All authors agree, however, that there are serious econometric difficulties in testing these models.

We consider here briefly the paper by Hoffman and Schlagenhauf. The starting point for their analysis is our equation (13). Applying rational expectations to (13) yields

$$e = \frac{1}{1 + \alpha_{10}} (mo - mo^*) - \frac{\alpha_5}{1 + \alpha_{10}} (y - y^*) + \frac{\alpha_{10}}{(1 + \alpha_{10})^2} (\overline{mo} - \overline{mo}^*)$$

$$- \frac{\alpha_5 \alpha_{10}}{(1 + \alpha_{10})^2} (\bar{y} - \bar{y}^*) + \left(\frac{\alpha_{10}}{1 + \alpha_{10}} \right)^2 e_{e+1} \tag{14}$$

In this instance the fundamentals are relative money and relative output. The exchange rate is determined by current values of these variables and all future expected values (represented by bars) with declining weights. The last expression can be continuously expanded.

How do they go about explaining the expected values? For each of the (four) fundamentals they use an equation of the form

$$mo = mo_{-1} + p_m \Delta mo_{-1} + u \tag{15}$$

The forecast of the money supply is based on past movements in the money supply. In this instance the current percentage change in money is explained by the previous period's percentage change in money. u is the error term.

Hoffman and Schlagenhauf apply this framework to monthly data for the mark, French franc and pound rates all *vis-à-vis* the US dollar for the period 1974(1)–1979(12). The model appears to work well and they conclude that 'our study can be considered part of the increasing amount of evidence which concludes that the monetary model of the exchange rate does have empirical content'.

Critique of the model

Criticisms of the model turn on the model's four key assumptions. We take each in turn.

Perfect asset substitution might not hold for two distinct reasons: because of the existence of effective controls over capital movements or because of the existence of a risk premium (see the next two chapters). Putting aside the risk premium, what this implies is that it is inappropriate to test the model for currencies over periods when controls over capital movements were in place.

We also suggested that PPP might be more likely to hold over the longer run; the model is generally tested for much shorter periods, however, sometimes on monthly data, at best for annual data. How can a model which is so patently at odds with reality be empirically verified?

The third assumption, that the money demand functions are stable, is again at odds with the experience of the 1980s (Boughton 1988). It is now well known that deregulation of the domestic monetary system combined with a burst of financial innovations have destabilised money demand functions in many industrial countries (Chapter 43).

It is also too simplistic to suppose that money demand coefficients are identical across countries, although as noted, not all studies assume that (MacDonald and Taylor 1992).

The final assumption is that expectations are rationally formed. This may also be questioned (see Chapter 33); more importantly, rational expectations are applied to whatever model the author chooses to test, *including one which in fact may be patently wrong*, a point which may well hold for the monetarist model.

32

Modelling exchange rates (2)

INTRODUCTION

This chapter continues the discussion of exchange rate models.

Section 1 extends the flexi-price monetarist model to accommodate wage–price stickiness, a risk premium and deviations from PPP. In all other essentials the model is the same. Section 2 develops a simple fundamentals model of the real exchange rate where the fundamentals are the real interest rate differential and the cumulated current account imbalances. Section 3 looks at portfolio balance models of exchange rates.

Section 4 looks at the role of 'news' (unanticipated developments) in exchange rate determination. Section 5 reviews the out-of-sample performance of the models. Section 6 looks briefly at recent work on the roles of chartists and fundamentalists in exchange rates. In Section 7 we try to draw some tentative conclusions.

STICKY-PRICE MONETARISM

We have seen that the flexi-price monetarist model is too simple. The models in this section attempt to correct some at least of the deficiencies of this model. We present two such models which have had wide exposure in the literature: those of Frankel (1979) and of Hooper and Morton (1982).

Frankel makes one important modification to the flexi-price model. Drawing on Dornbusch's sticky-price model of 1976 (Chapter 18) he assumes that it takes time for PPP to be restored. The case where PPP holds continuously then falls into place as a special case.

Hooper and Morton extend Frankel's model in two further directions. First, they assume that asset substitution is imperfect, accommodating now a risk premium into the analysis. Second, they allow the real exchange rate to change in the long run; thus, they also relax the assumption that PPP necessarily holds even in the long run.

Frankel's model

Frankel begins with the equation:

$$r_d - r^* = \alpha_{30}(\bar{e} - e) + (\Delta \bar{p}_d - \Delta \bar{p}^*) \tag{1}$$

The first part of the right-hand side is the expression used by Dornbusch (1976) (Chapter 18); the second part extends Dornbusch's equation to accommodate differences in expected rates of inflation.

The equilibrium *long-run* exchange rate e is derived from the flexi-price monetarist model of the previous chapter (see equations (11) and (12)):

$$\bar{e} = (\overline{mo}^*) - \alpha_5(\bar{y} - \bar{y}^*) + \alpha_{10}(\Delta \bar{p}_d - \Delta \bar{p}^*) \tag{2}$$

If we substitute (2) into (1) we have

$$r_d - r^* = -\alpha_{30}\alpha_5(\bar{y} - \bar{y}^*) + \alpha_{10}\alpha_{30}(\Delta \bar{p}_d - \Delta \bar{p}^*) + \alpha_{30}(\overline{mo} - \overline{mo}^*)$$

$$- \alpha_{30}e + (\Delta \bar{p}_d - \Delta \bar{p}^*) \tag{3}$$

Solving now for e and assuming that $y = \bar{y}$, $y^* = \bar{y}^*$, $mo = \overline{mo}$ and $mo^* = \overline{mo}$, we have

$$e = -\frac{1}{\alpha_{30}}(r_d - r^*) - \alpha_5(y - y^*) + \frac{1 + \alpha_{10}\alpha_{30}}{\alpha_{30}}(\Delta \bar{p}_d - \Delta \bar{p}^*)$$

$$+ mo - mo^* \tag{4}$$

Note that an increase in the money stock at home will first lower the interest rate.

$$\Delta r_d = -\frac{1}{\alpha_{10}}\Delta mo$$

If we use this in (4) we have the *total* effects on e of a monetary expansion.

$$\frac{\Delta e}{\Delta mo} = \frac{1 + \alpha_{10}\alpha_{30}}{\alpha_{10}\alpha_{30}} \tag{5}$$

which is of course Dornbusch's overshoot result (Chapter 18).

An alternative way of writing (4) is

$$e = -\frac{1}{\alpha_{30}}[r_d - r^* - (\Delta \bar{p}_d - \Delta \bar{p}^*)] + \alpha_{10}(\Delta \bar{p}_d - \Delta \bar{p}^*) - \alpha_5(y - y^*)$$

$$+ (mo - mo^*) \tag{6}$$

where the first bracketed expression is the real interest rate differential.

Equation (4) is the equation that Frankel estimates for the deutschmark–dollar rate, with some success. The expected German–US inflation differential is proxied by the long-term bond differential.

The flexi-price model is a special case of the above where $\alpha_{30} \to \infty$ and $r_d - r^*$ replaces $\Delta p_d - \Delta p^*$. The reader can readily confirm that we can then arrive at equation (11) of the previous chapter.

The Hooper and Morton model

As already indicated, Hooper and Morton now make two further extensions. First, they allow for a risk premium ρ (see Chapter 20).

$$r_d - r^* = e_e - e + \rho \tag{7}$$

Second, they accommodate the possibility that the real exchange rate may change in the longer run.

$$\bar{e} = \bar{q} + (\bar{p}_d - \bar{p}^*) \tag{8}$$

where $\bar{q}$ is the expected real exchange rate. We also have

$$e_e - e = \alpha_{30}(\bar{e} - e) + (\Delta \bar{p}_d - \Delta \bar{p}^*) \tag{9}$$

Combining (9) and (10) from the previous chapter we also have for the long run

$$(\bar{p}_d - \bar{p}^*) = (\overline{mo} - \overline{mo}^*) - \alpha_5(\bar{y} - \bar{y}^*) + \alpha_{10}(\bar{r}_d - \bar{r}^*) \tag{10}$$

Equation (10) is substituted into (8). We also replace $\bar{r}_d - \bar{r}^*$ by $\Delta \bar{p}_d - \Delta \bar{p}^*$ and, using (7) and (9), arrive at

$$e = \bar{q} + (\overline{mo} - \overline{mo}^*) - \alpha_5(\bar{y} - \bar{y}^*) + \alpha_{10}(\Delta \bar{p}_d - \Delta \bar{p}^*) - \frac{1}{\alpha_{30}}$$

$$\times [(r_d - r^*) - (\Delta \bar{p}_d - \Delta \bar{p}^*)] + \frac{1}{\alpha_{30}} \rho \tag{11}$$

This equation is the same as Frankel's (equation (6)) except for the presence of ρ and $\bar{q}$.

Assuming as in the Frankel model that the long-run values can be approximated by current values we have an equation which can provide the basis for econometric work. This is what Hooper and Morton do. They explain the real long-run expected exchange rate by trends in the expected current account. The risk premium is a function of the sum of official intervention plus the current account balance which together represent 'the primary determinants of changes in the currency-composition of privately held assets'.

A 'FUNDAMENTALS' MODEL OF THE REAL EXCHANGE RATE

Another popular model of exchange rates focuses on the fundamental determinants of the *real* exchange rate. In this framework, the fundamentals are (a) the real interest rate differentials and (b) the cumulated current account imbalances. Variations on this theme are to be found in Hooper and Mann (1989) and Blundell-Wignall and Browne (1991). These studies find empirical support for the basic framework.

We have four equations here.

$$\bar{e} - e = b(r_d - r^*) \tag{12}$$

where $\bar{e}$ is now the expected value of e b years ahead and the interest rates are the annual rates with a term of b years.

Next we write the definition of the expected real exchange rate $\bar{q}$.

$$\bar{q} = \bar{e} + \bar{p}^* - \bar{p}_d \tag{13}$$

Rewriting (13) as expected annual rates of inflation at home ($\bar{\pi}$) and abroad ($\bar{\pi}^*$), we have, for the same time horizon,

$$\bar{q} = \bar{e} + b\bar{\pi}^* + p^* - b\bar{\pi} - p_d \tag{14}$$

where $(\bar{p}_d - p_d)/b = \bar{\pi}$ and $(\bar{p}^* - p^*)/b = \bar{\pi}^*$. Combining (14) and (12) allows us to arrive at

$$(e + p^* - p_d) = \bar{q} - b[(r_d - \bar{\pi}) - (r^* - \bar{\pi}^*)] \tag{15}$$

This says that the real exchange rate is determined by the expected real exchange rate and the real interest rate differential. In turn the expected real exchange rate could be explained in terms of cumulated current account imbalances.

An important finding in Blundell-Wignall and Browne (1991) is that in the more integrated markets of the 1980s real exchange rates responded more to real interest rates than to current account imbalances and that it took substantially longer for real exchange rates to reach their fundamental levels, as defined by equation (15).

PORTFOLIO BALANCE MODELS

The model

Much of this ground has already been covered in Chapter 10.

We reproduce here the two exchange rate equations derived from the portfolio balance model. The equations now are not in logarithms.

$$\Delta E = \pi_1(\Delta Mo) + \pi_2(\Delta r^* + \Delta E_e) + \pi_3(\Delta FA) + \pi_4(\Delta B) + \pi_5(\Delta Y) \tag{16}$$

where $\pi_1 > 0$, $\pi_2 > 0$, $\pi_3 < 0$, $\pi_4 \lessgtr 0$, $\pi_5 < 0$.

The alternative, it will be recalled, is to have a small model of the rest of the world, which allows us to solve for the foreign interest rate.

$$\Delta E = \pi_1(\Delta \text{Mo}) + \pi_3(\Delta \text{FA}) + \pi_4(\Delta B) + \pi_5(\Delta Y)$$

$$+ \pi_2 \Delta E_e + \pi_6(\Delta Y^*) + \pi_7(\Delta \text{Mo}^*) + \pi_8 \Delta B^*) \qquad (17)$$

where now $\pi_6 > 0$, $\pi_7 < 0$, $\pi_8 > 0$.

These two equations correspond to two alternative ways of testing the portfolio balance models.

Empirical work based on the model

An early attempt is by Branson *et al.* (1977). They try to explain the deutschmark–dollar rate for the period August 1971 to December 1976 in terms of the German and US money stocks and the German and US net private foreign asset stocks (defined as cumulations of current account balances on benchmark observations minus holdings of central banks), deliberately excluding home assets on the ground that their effects are ambiguous. The results are fairly good and consistent with expectations.

Murphy and Van Duyne (1980) estimate an equation based on (17) (but for levels of the variables). Exchange rate expectations are disregarded as are levels of output. As with Branson *et al.* they also drop domestic stocks of bonds. The results for the deutschmark–dollar rate (73.2–78.2) are mixed. Although the coefficients have the expected signs only the coefficient on US private foreign assets is significant.

Bisignano and Hoover (1982a,b) also estimate equations based on this model. In (1982b) they estimate an equation similar to (17) (again disregarding both expectations and output) for four bilateral rates: Canadian, German, Italian and Japanese *vis-à-vis* the US dollar. They conclude that the results are 'reasonably supportive of the portfolio balance approach'. In (1982a) they also estimate an equation for the US–Canadian rate similar to (16) with mixed results.

Backus (1984) estimates an equation virtually identical to (16) (dropping E_e however) for the Canadian–US dollar rate. He notes 'that all the signs are as predicted in theory for a positive FA. However, since FA has been negative (for Canada) over the entire period the signs are in fact the opposite of what we should see if the theory were true. The obvious inference is that the model is wrong' (p. 839).[1]

Comments on the model

What kinds of criticisms might be made of the model?

The first and most obvious criticism is that the model from which the exchange rate equation is drawn is much too simple. In reality there is a much wider range of assets available to residents, including domestic and foreign equities and foreign money. More important, the rest of the world does hold some of its wealth (albeit a tiny proportion, by definition) in domestic money, bonds and equities. If the model were refined to take all this into account it would be more complex; there is little doubt, however, that the solutions would look different from those derived from the simpler model.

A second criticism is that the so-called independent variables, as represented say in equation (16), are not all truly exogenous nor independent of one another. This last point is strikingly illustrated in the case of domestic output which is closely correlated both to the deficit and to the current account. Also, causation may run from the exchange rate to the current account and to output.

A third reservation one would have about the application of the model is the well-known data limitations associated with it. This is strikingly so (a) where the exchange rate concerned is a bilateral rate which requires bilateral current accounts and (b) where levels of stocks are required.

A final criticism is that it is more difficult to know how to handle exchange rate expectations in the context of this model. Rational expectations would be difficult to apply. A more complete model would be needed and the solutions would be complex. In practice, the assumption is frequently made that expectations are exogenous; alternatively, at times, it is assumed that PPP will be restored ultimately. (See on all these issues MacDonald and Taylor (1992).)

RATIONAL EXPECTATIONS AND 'NEWS'

To illustrate the approach here we take a simple structural model:

$$e = \alpha_{20}\text{mo} + \alpha_{22}\text{gr} + \alpha_{24}e_e \tag{18}$$

$$e_e = \alpha_{20}\text{mo}_e + \alpha_{22}\text{gr}_e + \alpha_{24}e_{e+1} \tag{19}$$

$$e_{+1} = \alpha_{20}\text{mo}_{+1} + \alpha_{22}\text{gr}_{+1} + \alpha_{24}e_{e+1} \tag{20}$$

$$e_{+1} - e_e = \alpha_{20}(\text{mo}_{+1} - \text{mo}_e) + \alpha_{22}(\text{gr}_{+1} - \text{gr}_e) \tag{21}$$

The error in forecasting the spot rate is attributable to 'news' (surprises), i.e. unanticipated developments in the variables which actually determine the exchange rate.

This can be extended further by assuming perfect asset substitution.

$$r_d - r^* = e_e - e \tag{22}$$

Solving for e_e and substituting above yields

$$(e_{+1} - e) - (r_d - r^*) = \alpha_{20}(\text{mo}_{+1} - \text{mo}_e) + \alpha_{22}(\text{gr}_{+1} - \text{gr}_e) \tag{23}$$

The first bracketed expression represents the percentage change in the spot rate. The second bracketed expression is the expected percentage change in the spot rate.

Alternatively, we have

$$(e_{+1} - e) = (r_d - r^*) = \text{NEWS (unanticipated change in spot rate)} \tag{24}$$

This can be used as a basis for deciding how much of the percentage change in the spot rate is anticipated and how much is unanticipated. It turns out that 'unanticipated changes constitute nearly all the actual variation in exchange rates' (Dornbusch 1980; see also Mussa 1979b).

Dornbusch (1980) estimates a 'variant' of (23) using the interest rate differential, the unanticipated current account and the cyclical positions. See also Edwards (1983) and Frenkel (1981).

THE OUT-OF-SAMPLE PERFORMANCE OF THE MODELS

One way of evaluating the models is to see how well they perform out of sample, i.e. in the periods beyond those used in the estimation.

A widely cited study here is one by Meese and Rogoff (1983). They compared the forecasting performance out of sample of three well-known structural models: the flexi-price monetarist model, the sticky-price version and Hooper and Morton's model (all presented above), with a random walk model (which says that the current spot rate is the best forecast of the future rate), the forward exchange rate, an autoregression of the spot rate and a vector autoregression. In forecasting with the structural models for all subsequent periods, the *actual* rather than forecast values of the exogenous variables were used.

Using various measures of forecast errors they reached the surprising conclusion that none of the structural models outperformed the random walk hypothesis.

Subsequent work by other researchers along similar lines produced mixed results, some confirming the Meese and Rogoff findings, others finding that some models can outperform a random walk. (For a summary of these studies, see MacDonald and Taylor (1992).)

CHARTISTS AND FUNDAMENTALISTS

A more promising recent approach to exchange rate determination is to take as a starting point the distinction between chartists who base their expectations predominantly on past movements in the exchange rate and fundamentalists who keep their eye on the fundamentals, so that when the exchange rate is driven away from fundamentals they form expectations that it will return in due course to levels projected by fundamentals. (See also Chapter 33.)

Froot and Frankel (1989) find that participants in the foreign exchange market rely predominantly on chartist analysis for short-term forecasts but on fundamental analysis for the longer run. They also find evidence of increasing dominance of chartists over fundamentalists and that chartist expectations are destabilising over the shorter run.

Taylor (1990) has studied this in great detail but his conclusion is different. He models chartist expectations, as reported in his studies, but finds their expectations to be essentially stabilising. (See also on this Miller and Weller (1991a).)

MacDonald and Taylor (1992) have argued, forcefully, that what is needed now in the analysis of market exchange rates is to combine 'a chartist view of exchange rate determination with an equilibrium or fundamentalist view ... (together with) a fresh approach to the underlying fundamentals'.

SOME TENTATIVE CONCLUSIONS

The survey of exchange rate models in this and the previous chapter reveals that, in general, models used to date have not been very satisfactory and have tended to perform poorly in sample and out of sample.

To illustrate this general point, we summarise briefly a paper by Leventakis. In his words:

> In this paper we have examined empirically five asset-market exchange rate models: the flexible price monetary model, the sticky-price model, the Hooper–Morton model, a stock–flow ... model and the portfolio balance model. Each of these models was estimated for the deutschemark/dollar exchange rate over the floating period. The empirical results suggest that none of the models is fully supported by the data. Our findings are similar to those of other studies .... .
>
> (1987: 373)

This conclusion should not surprise. The models reviewed are manifestly simplistic. They do not capture the dynamics of exchange rate markets; bandwaggons, bubbles tend to be neglected; lag structures tend to be too simplistic; fiscal policy and real disturbances are widely disregarded; rational expectations are frequently imposed on the analysis; all assume stable money demand functions; virtually all disregard the effects of official intervention. Moreover, it seems that there are serious econometric problems associated with the empirical studies.

There appears here to be a sharp division between the relatively simplistic reduced form equations of the type reviewed in this chapter and the structural econometric models, which are much more ambitious and which have embodied in them implicit but very complicated exchange rate models. Whatever the ultimate performance of the latter, it must be said that in terms of structural efficiency these are a big improvement over the simpler models presented in this chapter.

33

Foreign exchange market efficiency and financial integration – concepts and evidence

INTRODUCTION

This chapter first reviews the theory of foreign exchange market efficiency and the evidence bearing on it.

What is meant by market efficiency? An efficient foreign exchange market is generally taken to be one in which exchange rates (spot and forward) reflect all relevant available information. Tests of efficiency generally turn on the question of whether all existing information has been fully exploited to the point where systematic speculative profits are no longer available.

In broad terms there are two kinds of tests of efficiency that have been applied: first, tests of the efficiency of the forward market; second, tests of the efficiency of the spot market. (For recent surveys of some of this literature, see Takagi (1991), MacDonald and Taylor (1992) and Karfakis (1993). The reader is referred to these for detailed documentation on each issue raised.)

The chapter also reviews the conceptual literature on financial integration. It distinguishes three meanings of integration: first, the degree to which covered interest rate parity holds; second, the degree to which uncovered interest rate parity holds; third, the degree to which real interest rate parity holds.

TESTS OF THE EFFICIENCY OF THE FORWARD MARKET

How does one go about deciding whether speculation is efficient in the sense that it is based on the best available information at the time expectations were formed?

Suppose capital markets are completely free and that foreign exchange transaction costs are small enough to be disregarded. We would then expect the following to hold:

$$r_d - r^* = \frac{F - E}{E} \tag{1}$$

where r_d and r^* are respectively the short-term domestic interest rates at home and abroad, F is the forward rate, E is the spot rate and the last expression is the forward discount. Equation (1) says that arbitrage ensures that the covered interest rate differential will approach zero (i.e. that covered interest rate parity holds). This is also the condition for perfect capital mobility. This condition is invariably found to hold in economies which have abandoned controls over capital movements.

To illustrate, suppose the forward discount exceeds the interest rate differential. In this case earnings on a covered foreign investment $(F - E)/E + r^*$ exceed earnings on domestic investment (r_d). There will be outflows of capital which in turn will generate corrective forces which will restore parity: the domestic interest rate may rise, the forward rate may fall, the currency could fall (E would rise).

We can approximate (1) by

$$r_d - r^* = f - e \tag{2}$$

where f and e are respectively the logarithms of the forward and spot rates.

We now split the forward rate into its two components: an expected spot rate $({}_tE_{et+1})$ formed in period t for $t + 1$ and a risk premium ρ:

$$f = {}_tE_{et+1} + \rho \tag{3}$$

It is also widely held that if markets are rational and efficient we should expect

$$e_{+1} - {}_tE_{et+1} = \mu \tag{4}$$

Equation (4) says that the error in forecasting the spot rate is white noise and hence unbiased.

If $\rho = 0$, there is no risk premium, one should note that

$$e_{+1} = f_t + \mu \tag{5}$$

Using (5) one could estimate an equation of the form

$$e_{+1} = a + bf_t + \mu \tag{6}$$

Equation (6) says that the forward rate should be an unbiased predictor of the exchange rate. If the underlying theory is correct one should expect $a = 0$, $b = 1$ and that μ is a serially uncorrelated error. This in fact rarely holds. This may be because markets are not efficient ((4) does not hold)[1] or because of the existence of a risk premium ρ. There is other evidence, theoretical and empirical, to suggest that the risk premium is unlikely to account for the results. There is, moreover, plenty of suggestive evidence that speculators make persistent errors in their forecasts, as we shall see in a moment.

To avoid the problem of the risk premium one could get a direct measure of the expected exchange rate from survey data. One could then substitute this information for f_t in (6). Studies that do this confirm the presence of biases in the formation of expectations.

Another way to attack the problem is to use (2) and (3) and again assume that $\rho = 0$. We then have

$$r_d - r^* = {}_tE_{et+1} - e \tag{7}$$

This is the familiar condition of perfect asset substitution (open interest rate parity). Using now also (4) we can arrive again at an equation which, in principle, could be estimated:

$$e_{+1} - e = a + b(r_d - r^*) + \mu \tag{8}$$

We would again expect that $a = 0$, $b = 1$ and μ is a serially uncorrelated residual. Equation (8) says that the interest rate differential should give an unbiased forecast of the percentage change in the currency. Tests of (8) confirm that the conditions do not hold.

If all currently relevant information is embodied in the forward rate then the addition of some relevant information should not improve the forecast of the spot rate. If it did the market would be said to be inefficient in the sense that the information used to improve the forecast has been 'passed up'.

Here two kinds of tests are carried out. The first is simply to add information variables to (6) and see whether the variables are significant. So we have

$$e_{+1} = a + bf_t + cZ + \mu \tag{9}$$

where Z represents information variables, i.e. information available at the time that the forward rate is determined. If the market is efficient $c = 0$.

Equation (9) is frequently estimated with Z represented by $f_{t-1}f_{t-2}$, but in principle Z could be anything which influences the exchange rate. Illustrations of tests using a variation of (9) are given by Edwards (1983), Abraham (1985) and Sanderson (1984).

Edwards (1983) replaces Z by f_{t-1} and finds for the four currencies in his study that it does not add to the explanatory power of the equation.

Abraham (1985) uses the forward rate for f_{t-1} and f_{t-2} and also finds that these make no contribution. Sanderson (1984) replaces Z by lagged values of the ratio of (a) domestic to foreign price levels, (b) money supplies and (c) output. Again, none of these contributes to the explanation of e_{+1}.

Edwards (1983) also attempts to estimate an interesting variation of (9) where Z is now reinterpreted. Drawing on a structural model he replaces Z by unanticipated changes in monies, real incomes and real interest rates. If the underlying model is the correct one then those unanticipated changes ought to explain the failures of the forward rate to predict the future spot rate. In this case the coefficient c ought to be significant. The anticipated changes in the variables are obtained from a vector autoregressive process. In most cases the coefficients of the unanticipated changes do not have the expected sign.

A variation of (9) is

$$e - f_{t-1} = a + b_1(e_{-1} - f_{t-2}) + b_2(e_{-2} - f_{t-3}) + \mu \tag{9a}$$

where it would be expected, if markets were efficient, that b_1 and b_2 would not be significant. Hansen and Hodrick (1980) estimate this equation for seven currencies, finding that for three of the currencies b is significant. After experimenting with mixes of currencies and periods they conclude that the efficiency hypothesis is 'suspect for several currencies for the modern experience ... and for the experience in the 1920s'. Murfin and Ormerod (1984) estimate this equation with only one lagged forecast error ($b_2 = 0$) for sixteen currencies and find that b is significant for all currencies. Using this equation as a basis for forecasting the next period's spot rate they find that it performs better than the forward rate.

Takagi (1991) has recently summarised these kinds of studies, updated to 1990. His own conclusion is that 'the expected exchange rates as reported in the survey data did not fully incorporate all available information'.

One further extension of the above is to compare the predictive capacity of the forward rate against forecasts by professional services, without in this case knowing anything about the underlying model used by the professional forecasters. Levich (1985) reports that advisory service forecasts were not in general as accurate as the forward rate.

SPOT MARKET EFFICIENCY (TRADING-FILTER RULES)

This test is concerned with evaluating whether or not there are relatively simple rules which, had they been adopted as a basis for buying–selling currencies, would have yielded excess profits. One rule states that when a given currency appreciates (depreciates) x per cent from a previous low (high) switch funds into (out of) that currency. An alternative rule states that where the currency moves x per cent above (below) the moving average the speculator should move into (out of) the currency. The objective of these rules is to try and exploit market tendencies.

A study by Cornell and Dietrich (1978) applies these rules to six currencies. They find that three of the currencies were inefficient. Levich (1985) has reviewed more recent studies, notably those by Dooley and Shafer (1983) and Goodman (1981); the first finds that there were potential profits to be made from following simple trading rules, whereas the second finds that there are profits to be made from following buy–sell signals provided by professional services.

CONCLUSION ON EFFICIENCY

It is very difficult to summarise the findings. It is evident that some researchers find in favour of efficiency and many others find against it. Those with an inbuilt bias in favour of or against efficiency will read the results in ways which suit them best.

Having said this, however, the author does believe that it is difficult to come away from the vast literature here without more than a feeling that markets are inherently inefficient. This is also the conclusion of MacDonald and Taylor (1992), Krugman (1989) and Dornbusch (1989b).

FINANCIAL INTEGRATION

It is useful to distinguish three concepts of financial integration, corresponding to increasingly tighter conditions that need to be upheld (see Obstfeld 1986; Frankel 1991; Dooley *et al.* 1987).

The first is the degree to which covered parity holds. Suppose we rewrite (2) as

$$r_d - r^* - (f - e) = k \tag{10}$$

where k represents the deviation from covered parity (which we assume here goes beyond transactions costs). As already noted more than once, k would be significantly positive if capital controls are in place and are effective.

We can now use (3) and (10) to arrive at

$$r_d - r^* = (_t E_{et+1} - e) + \rho + k \tag{11}$$

The second concept of integration is one where open parity (perfect asset substitution) holds. It is readily seen from (11) that this will now hold when $\rho = k = 0$. The conditions required for this second concept of integration to be met are now tighter, requiring also that the risk premium be zero.

The third concept of integration is one where *real* interest rate parity holds.

$$(r_d - \Delta \bar{p}) - (r^* - \Delta \bar{p}^*) = 0 \tag{12}$$

Using (11) we can arrive at

$$(_t E_{et+1} - e) = (\Delta \bar{p} - \Delta \bar{p}^*) - (\rho + k) \tag{13}$$

Real interest parity requires that $\rho = k = 0$ but also now that *ex ante* PPP holds, i.e. that the expected change in the exchange rate be equal to the expected inflation rate differential.

To summarise the discussion to this point, the first concept will be met in economies without controls, the second requires that the risk premium be zero and the third also requires that PPP hold. It is therefore not surprising to find that, whilst the first two concepts are more or less met in the real world, the third is very unlikely to be met, except perhaps in the much longer run. So whilst financial integration is very high as defined by the first two concepts, it is 'low' as defined by the third concept.

We can now use our perspective to interpret the controversial findings in Feldstein and Horioka (1980). (See also Feldstein (1983) and Dooley *et al.* (1987).) The paper provoked a large literature, which continues to this day.

Feldstein and Horioka estimate an equation of the form

$$\frac{I}{Y} = a_0 + a_1 \left(\frac{S}{Y}\right) \tag{14}$$

where I/Y and S/Y are respectively national investment and savings ratios. They found a close correlation between these variables in cross-section studies for a large number of industrial countries. a_1 in the studies approached unity. This was largely confirmed in numerous subsequent studies.

What light does an equation such as (14) throw on the question of financial integration? Suppose we are dealing with a small country. How would we expect 'exogenous' shifts in S/Y to impact on I/Y?

Consider first the extreme case where real interest rates (rr) are equalised. This is illustrated in Figure 33.1 where the world real interest rate is rr_1 and the current account deficit will be AB.

A shift in S/Y to the left or to the right in these conditions will simply alter the level of the current account deficit, leaving both I/Y and the real interest rate unchanged. So in this case we would expect virtually no relationship between the two ratios; instead we would expect a close correspondence between shifts in S/Y (or for that matter in I/Y) and the current account ratio. This presupposes, importantly, that exogenous saving and exogenous investment are not correlated, i.e. that there are not common factors at work, such as cyclical influences or population and productivity growth. This is unlikely to be the case (Frankel 1991). Note too that if the world real interest rate rises (falls) there is now a negative relationship between the two ratios.

Suppose now financial integration in this third sense is very weak, allowing the small economy to have an independent real interest rate. It is readily seen that an upward (downward) shift in S/Y will be associated with an increase (decrease) in

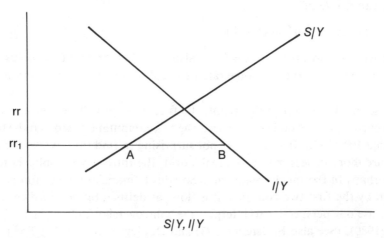

Figure 33.1 The impact of shifts in S/Y on I/Y

I/Y, replicating the findings of Feldstein and Horioka. The reason the finding evoked such controversy and astonishment is that it appeared to suggest that capital mobility was low and not very high, as widely thought. In the light of our earlier discussion, however, the 'puzzle' is now explained: capital mobility is indeed low in our third sense above.

Part VII

POLICY DESIGN

So far we have said very little about how policy ought to be designed. The previous chapters, however, were intended to provide the foundations for such an analysis. Evidently, before we can say anything about how the instruments of policy ought to be used, we need to know how these instruments impact on the economy. Armed now with some such background we are ready to address policy issues.

Chapter 34 addresses the question of what the appropriate macro targets of policy ought to be. Chapter 35 looks at constraints on policy imposed by the regulatory and institutional environment. It also looks at how instruments might be used to achieve policy targets. Finally, it presents a framework for comparing the macro performance of different economies.

Chapter 36 looks at the principles underlying the choice of exchange rate regime at the global as well as the small-country level. Chapter 37 reviews the historical evolution of the debate over rules and discretion. Chapter 38 summarises the most recent thinking on how to assign monetary and fiscal policy to internal and external balance.

Chapter 39 presents a broad two-country theoretical model which is used to evaluate a number of alternative simple policy regimes. Chapter 40 reviews the econometric evidence on policy regimes while Chapter 41 addresses specific issues raised by a strategy of targeting nominal income.

Chapter 42 reviews the evolution of the global economy between 1972 and 1991. Chapter 43 looks in a little more detail at the experience of money targeting in industrial countries. Chapter 44 tries to explain differences in unemployment performances in different industrial economies. Finally, Chapter 45 reviews the literature on macro policy coordination: its advantages and disadvantages and the recent experience with coordination.

34

Macro policy targets

INTRODUCTION

This chapter addresses the question of what the appropriate macro policy targets ought to be. Traditionally, four key targets have been highlighted in the literature: inflation, unemployment, the current account and the public sector balance.

The chapter looks more closely at how it is possible to rationalise these targets. It begins by looking at the costs of a steady state inflation; it also examines the costs and the benefits of a disinflationary policy which aims at reducing the steady state rate of inflation. Next, it asks what the target unemployment rate ought to be.

The chapter also critically examines the view that the current account reflects national decisions to save and invest and if these were made rationally the current account ought not to be a target of policy.

The chapter concludes with a discussion of the budget balance as a policy target. It argues that the public sector balance is both an instrument and a target. Sustained public sector imbalances can produce adverse long-run consequences.

THE MEDIUM-RUN TARGETS

It is appropriate that we begin a discussion of policy by asking what should be the principal targets of macro policy. These are usually taken for granted but we need to delve more closely into the underlying rationale.

We proceed as follows. First, we look at the medium-term objectives of policy, focusing primarily on the traditional targets of employment, inflation, the current account and the public sector deficit. Second, we look at the short-run targets, meaning here the stabilisation of macro variables of concern to policy-makers. Third, we draw an ideological line between those who are preoccupied solely with the medium-term outcomes and those who also attach considerable importance to short-run stabilisation.

As we have already noted, such targets are usually expressed in the form of *loss* functions (i.e. losses flowing from squared deviations of actual from perceived targets), so we can begin by writing down a very general and conventional loss function, to use as a basis for our subsequent discussion.

$$L = w_1(\dot{p} - \dot{p}^*)^2 + w_2(y - y^*)^2 + w_3(CA - CA^*)^2 + w_4(DEF - DEF^*)^2 \qquad (1)$$

where L is the 'national' loss in each period, $\dot{p}$ is the *rate* of inflation, y is the level of output, CA is the current account balance and DEF is the relevant public sector budget deficit. An asterisk represents the target value of the variable.

A slight variation on the above is to replace y by the rate of unemployment and y^* by the target unemployment rate. A more significant variation is to replace the p and y gaps by the gap between a target growth (or level) of nominal income and its actual growth (level). (This particular variation is analysed in Chapters 38–41.) Another significant variation would be to replace the *flow* variables CA and DEF by their corresponding *stocks*: the stock of net foreign assets as a percentage of GNP and the stock of net government indebtedness again as a percentage of GNP.

There are two further modifications that can be made. One is to drop both the current account and the budget deficit and replace them by the deviation of national wealth from target wealth. Another potential modification is to accommodate the deviation of the investment share of GNP from its target level in the loss function. Comments on these modifications will be made in due course.

How does one rationalise a loss function as in (1), and some of its potential variations, recalling that these are objectives to be tracked over the medium run, i.e. over a whole 'cycle'? We discuss each of the component parts in turn.

THE RATE OF INFLATION AS A TARGET

In addressing the question of the rate of inflation as a target, there are two issues to confront. The first is the cost of a *steady state anticipated* inflation; the second is the target rate of inflation ($\dot{p}^*$).

The costs of a fully anticipated inflation in the indexed economy

What are the costs of inflation in an economy where financial transactions (except money), wages and government transactions are all fully indexed and where the exchange rate is assumed to adjust over time to offset any inflation differential?

The transactions cost and the inflation tax

Easily the most widely cited and debated cost of inflation is the *transactions (shoe leather*) cost. For a while at least, this was also virtually the sole 'cost' identified in the literature.

Suppose, first, that no interest is paid on money, which we initially assume includes both currency in circulation and demand deposits. Any positive rate of inflation will now reduce the real rate of return on money relative to capital and other financial assets. There will thus be an incentive to reduce money balances and hold them in interest-earning investments. This is equivalent to a tax on money which distorts choices and hence is inefficient. The cost is sometimes referred to as 'shoe leather costs' because, having placed money deposits in an interest-bearing investment more time and effort will now be needed to access the money; in other words, there will be extra trips to the banks.

Friedman (1969a), drawing on this analysis, argued that efficiency demanded that the real return on money be equal to the real return on capital. If interest is not paid on money this requires that the rate of inflation ($\dot{p}_0$) be set equal to the negative of the real return on capital:

$$\dot{p}_0 = -(r_k - \dot{p})$$

where r_k is the return on capital. Money growth should then proceed to the point where the nominal return to capital is driven down to zero. This is Friedman's famous 'liquidity rule'. Without interest paid on money the optimal rate of inflation will thus normally be negative, as Friedman envisaged. Any rate of inflation above that (say zero) is inefficient in the sense that the real return on capital will exceed the real return on money.

To illustrate what Friedman has in mind suppose we start with a situation where the rate of inflation is zero and the return on capital is 3 per cent. The real return on money is zero but the real return on capital is 3 per cent. At this point a tighter monetary policy is needed to reduce the inflation rate to -3 per cent. At the same time the nominal return to capital will fall to zero. The real return is now 3 per cent on money and capital.

There are standard techniques drawn from welfare microeconomics which allow a rough measure of this excess burden. (In this case the estimate is equal to one-half of the product of the rise in money balances and the fall in the interest rate corresponding to the fall in the rate of inflation.) There are numerous estimates of these benefits in the literature. For money as defined above the benefit in national income for the USA amounts to anything between 0.3 and 0.45 per cent of GNP (Aiyagari 1990).

These benefits are generally assumed to be one-off. Feldstein (1979), however, has argued that the benefits grow at the same rate as the real economy. The difference is important.

Suppose the Phillips curve is vertical in the long run. Suppose, too, that the economy ultimately moves down from, say, a 10 per cent rate of inflation to a 2 per cent inflation. The unemployment costs, by definition, are only transitional (see later). The transactions benefits, however, are permanent but these come later and need to be discounted to the present. If the benefit is a fixed amount, albeit permanent, distant future benefits discounted to the present will be worth very little. In this case, the cost–benefit balance sheet – permanent but fixed gains against transitional costs – is a finite one, i.e. a finite benefit against some finite loss. If, however, the benefit has a real growth factor attached to it the calculation is more interesting. It is perhaps intuitive that if the real growth rate exceeds the discount rate the benefit from reducing inflation must exceed the transitional cost: indeed the discounted net benefit is now infinite. This last is Feldstein's result.

Several general comments are in order here. First, with deregulation and interest paid on demand deposits the excess burden will clearly fall substantially. The base for the calculation is now much narrower, being cash in circulation, on which interest cannot be paid. In one study for the USA, for example, the change from M1 to base money reduces the income gain from 0.3 to 0.08 per cent of GNP (Aiyagari 1990).

Second, inflation imposes a tax on money balances. This is distortionary. However, taxes are also imposed on other goods. Hence, the optimal rate of inflation is one that equalises at the margin the excess burden of the different taxes. There is now no reason why this optimal rate of inflation should not be positive. Phelps (1973) was the first to analyse in detail the revenue implications of a tax on money.

In even more general terms, if inflation is a form of tax, what is the optimal division of financing of government expenditure between revenue from inflation (seignorage), bonds and taxation? We do not pursue this very difficult but nevertheless interesting and important question. A few points are, however, in order.

How is revenue from seignorage calculated? As with any other tax it is equal to the rate of tax multiplied by the base of the tax. The rate of tax in this instance is the rate of growth of base money (H); the base is base money. In turn, the rate of growth of base money is equal to the real growth rate g plus the rate of inflation $\dot{p}$, and so revenue T_m as a proportion of GNP Y is

$$\frac{T_m}{Y_0} = \frac{\Delta H}{H_0} \frac{H_0}{Y_0} = (\dot{p} + g) \frac{H_0}{Y_0}$$

It is important to note that while the base for the calculation of *revenue* is base money the base for the calculation of the excess burden, as we have seen, in the case where interest is not paid on current deposits, is narrow money (cash in circulation plus current deposits). The revenue from the additional inflation tax on the broader base accrues either to the banking system (i.e. its owners) in the case of monopoly banking or to their clients in the case of competitive banking.

Seignorage is easily calculated for different economies. As a percentage of total revenue (including seignorage) it can vary widely, in part at least (but by no means exclusively) depending on the rate of inflation. What follows is important: any attempt to reduce seignorage as a source of revenue carries the implication that either other taxes will need to be raised or more interest-bearing public debt will need to be created. In countries where tax collection is inefficient or taxes are very distortionary or where the level of public debt is already very high there may be a case for some positive inflation tax. Since there are very important institutional differences across countries in these respects the 'optimal' rate of inflation has to be different across countries. We return to this question later.

Third, many would legitimately argue that shoe leather benefits are simply not comparable with unemployment costs. Translating excess burdens into national income terms does not establish a legitimate parallel.

Fourth, if much of the cash in hand is held to operate the underground economy (i.e. transactions to avoid tax) then a tax on those balances might well constitute a positive gain.

It is evident from the above discussion that, notwithstanding Feldstein's point, these inflation costs are not likely to be of great significance. Tobin sums up very well the reactions of many economists to this particular cost of inflation:

> According to economic theory, the ultimate social cost of anticipated inflation is the wasteful use of resources to economise holdings of currency and other noninterest-bearing means of payment. I suspect that intelligent laymen would be utterly astounded if they realised that this is the great evil economists are talking about. They have imagined a much more devastating cataclysm, with Vesuvius vengefully punishing the sinners below. Extra trips between savings banks and commercial banks? What an anti-climax!
>
> (1972: 15)

Other potential costs of inflation

We turn now to other potential costs (positive or negative) of inflation in an indexed economy.

A potential negative cost (i.e. a benefit) flowing from inflation has been suggested by Mundell (1963a) and Tobin (1965) (see Summers 1981). The higher return on capital may induce a substitution of capital for money, increasing capital intensity. If the capital stock is below optimal this might produce a benefit (assuming there is no other instrument to raise the suboptimal capital stock). Or the fall in the real value of base money produced by inflation, which reduces wealth, may induce more savings, which again may be beneficial. If these considerations were at all important they would need to be set against the transaction cost.

A positive cost frequently associated with inflation is the 'menu' costs, i.e. costs associated with more frequent price changes. These are not easily measurable but clearly would be larger when inflation is high.

So far it would appear that in an indexed economy the costs of inflation may not be very high and indeed from the analysis to this point some inflation may even on balance be beneficial (e.g. if the capital intensity saving effect dominates or revenue considerations are important). For some time now, however, in the analysis of inflation costs the emphasis has been on the *uncertainty* effects of inflation. We now explore these.

The argument here is that higher inflation is associated with more *uncertain* inflation. Why should this be so? The theory underlying this supposed association is still not well developed. Okun (1971) long ago suggested that the higher inflation is, the greater is the uncertainty about what government policy will be and therefore the harder it is to forecast inflation. This is not unreasonable, particularly if applied to inflation experiences outside the range actually observed in recent history. The perspective here is the macro aggregate rate of inflation.

But there may also be greater uncertainty about prices at the micro cross-section level. When there is any inflation the timing of sectoral price increases will inevitably not be synchronised. However, the higher the rate of inflation, given the lack of synchronisation, the greater is likely to be the dispersion of price levels for any given ongoing rate of inflation.

Theoretical rationale to one side, what is the evidence for this association and what are the costs of uncertainty, if any, bearing in mind that our economy is indexed?

The hypothesis can be tested at several levels. First, for a single country over a long historical run one might look for an association between periods of high inflation and the variability of that inflation. Second, one can undertake a cross-country study to see if the relationship holds. Third, one might undertake a parallel cross-sectoral study to see if the price dispersion is greater across sectors the higher the inflation rate.

One difficulty with this is that greater variability or dispersion does not necessarily go along with greater uncertainty, although there must be a presumption that this will be so. To take account of this some studies have tried to relate the unexplained component of inflation to its level, i.e. testing the notion that high rates of inflation are more difficult to predict.

There is now a very large empirical literature that attempts tests along the above lines. Much, but not all, of this literature is supportive, although some have claimed that any association found is or may be spurious. (See on this Katsimbris (1985), Holland (1984), Aiyagari (1990) and Carmichael (1990).)

Suppose that the association between rates of inflation and uncertainty holds. What are the welfare effects of such uncertainty? Here again we enter difficult terrain which is not too well understood.

We noted earlier that at higher rates of inflation there is likely to be greater sectoral dispersion of price levels. This creates distortions; the larger the distortions the larger the incentive to exploit these; such efforts to exploit them involves search activity which is itself costly.

Friedman (1977) and his followers have suggested another cost associated with uncertainty. To explain his important contribution consider the case where the macro rate of inflation is zero and is known to be so with certainty. Individual producers experiencing an increase in demand will then know that this is a sectoral increase, which calls for an increase in real supply. The same argument would hold for higher rates of inflation provided these were known with certainty and could thus be discounted by the producers. However, if with higher rates of inflation there is now greater uncertainty about the macro rate producers will be increasingly uncertain about how much of any increase in demand is real (sectoral) and how much is nominal (universal). This increased confusion generates progressively inefficient responses by producers. This is known as the signal extraction problem.

Friedman concludes that this cost, imposed on the economy, of inflation is likely, at least over the medium run, to raise the unemployment rate. So over the medium run there might actually be a positive association between rates of inflation and the rate of unemployment.

The existence of inflation uncertainty may impose more pervasive economic costs, e.g. on the allocation of effort,[1] on capital formation (see the review in Carmichael (1990) and Able (1980)).

Conclusions

So what can we conclude about the net benefits from reducing inflation? If indexation is in fact widespread and if inflation is not too high the positive costs are probably tolerable. They come down to costs associated with uncertainty (themselves very uncertain), menu costs and perhaps a small transaction cost. But even these need to be offset against potential revenue gains and gains in capital intensity saving.

In an indexed world, then, is inflation a case of 'much ado about nothing'? Is the answer to inflation universal indexation? This might be so if indexation could be readily implemented, at little administrative or social cost. This, however, is not so. Paradoxically, indexation is more prevalent in countries with three-digit or more inflation than in industrial countries with inflation between say 5 and 10 per cent. So the cost of inflation, in this sense, is less with very high than with low inflation.

The costs of a fully anticipated inflation with institutional rigidities

The most important of these institutional rigidities comes from the likelihood that taxes will not be fully indexed to inflation. The non-indexation of taxes creates potential distortions to saving–investment decisions, to labour markets, to the choice of financing and to government decisions about spending (Fischer and Modigliani 1978).

Suppose savings out of income were a positive function of the real after-tax interest rate (an assertion which may either not hold or hold weakly). The real after-tax interest rate is defined as

$$\mathrm{rr} = (1 - t)r_\mathrm{d} - \dot{p} \tag{2}$$

where rr is the real after-tax interest rate, t is the relevant marginal tax rate, r_d is the nominal interest rate and $\dot{p}$ is the rate of inflation.

Suppose now, too, that the nominal interest rate adjusts fully to any change in the rate of inflation (which might not happen). Then

$$r_\mathrm{d} = k + \dot{p} \tag{3}$$

where k is the positive (constant) component of the real pre-tax interest rate. We then have

$$rr = (1 - t)k - \dot{p}t \tag{4}$$

It is obvious from (4) that, given the marginal tax rate, an acceleration in inflation will lower the real after-tax return and thus reduce real savings.

There are also many ways in which investment may be distorted by inflation and the tax system but it is widely conceded here that the net effects are ambiguous. If *nominal* interest payments on corporate borrowings are allowable as a cost deduction the real cost of borrowing will be as in (2), t now being the tax on corporate profits, so inflation now reduces the real cost of borrowing. On the other hand, in so far as depreciation allowances are based on historical cost, inflation imposes an excessive tax on profits, which will be overstated. The first effect may encourage investment, the second discourage it.

Progressivity in the personal income tax scale means that 'bracket creep' will occur, potentially inflating tax revenue; such windfalls in turn may encourage governments to be less responsible in determining the scale of their expenditure.

Higher tax rates may make the holding of non-taxable assets (notably those with capital gains) more attractive. The higher taxes may also encourage a search for non-taxable sources of income (e.g. further develop the underground economy). Again, tax-deductible expenditures now become more attractive, distorting expenditure decisions. The real cost of debt also becomes cheaper, making debt financing relatively more attractive than equity; a high level of debt, in turn, makes borrowers more vulnerable in bad times. The uncertainty costs of inflation are also bound to be larger in a context where taxes are unindexed.

Outside of government institutions there may be rigidities in the financial system which will again create distortions to asset allocation. For example, institutions with relatively fixed interest rates (e.g. mortgages) will lose funds to other institutions.

In all these illustrative ways a positive rate of inflation, which is anticipated, will impose economic costs on the community. These costs are hardly negligible and indeed represent the more important costs of inflation.

What should be the target rate of inflation?

We turn now to the question of the rate of inflation to be targeted.

Friedman himself, as we saw, attacked this question and concluded that the optimal rate was negative. In subsequent years, however, he agonised further over the question and finally decided that a zero rate of inflation was as good as any. But is there anything sacrosanct about a zero rate of inflation?

Clearly if there exist institutional rigidities a zero rate of inflation avoids the distortions associated with some positive rate of inflation. But we have also seen that there are circumstances when a positive rate of inflation may be beneficial. Moreover, what index should be targeted? If the consumer price index is stabilised this may require that the price of traded goods falls secularly. This is because the consumer price index includes services whose productivity growth is less than that in traded goods, so with wages growth similar in the two sectors inflation in traded goods must be negative (see Chapter 47).

If we cannot determine what the optimal rate of inflation is our analysis does suggest that the 'optimal' rate of inflation is a function of a host of home-grown structural considerations. By way of illustration, we recall three of these: the extent to which interest is paid on transactions (deposit) balances, the importance of seignorage as a source of revenue and the degree to which the tax system is indexed.

If interest is paid on transactions balances the distortionary effect of the inflation tax on that component of money is eliminated. Thus the cost of inflation weakens with financial deregulation, and so, other things being equal, the optimal rate of inflation rises too.

We recall, too, that all other things being equal we argued that countries with inefficient and distortionary tax systems or with a large public debt ought to lean more heavily on seignorage as a source of revenue (Dornbusch 1988).

Finally, the more indexed the tax system is the weaker will be the distortions associated with the interaction of inflation on taxes; hence again the smaller the cost of inflation and the higher the optimal inflation.

What follows from this is that the optimal rate of inflation 'in the abstract' is almost certain to be different across countries, depending on these structural considerations, e.g. differences across countries in respect of financial deregulation, the efficiency of the tax system and public debt financing and the degree to which the tax system is indexed.

THE TARGET LEVEL OF OUTPUT

What level of output should the authorities target?

An important distinction here is between a level of output corresponding to the natural rate of unemployment (NRU) and a level of output corresponding to the 'efficient' unemployment rate. As we saw in Chapter 25, there may be reasons for believing that the NRU is not efficient and that the optimal efficient rate of unemployment is *below* the NRU.

Nevertheless, there are two good arguments for targeting the NRU rather than the efficient level of unemployment. First, as we have already noted, we know very little about the efficient rate of unemployment. We have some vague notions about the considerations that make for an inefficient NRU; these, however, do not allow a precise calculation to be made of what constitutes an efficient rate. Second, as we also saw, the 'efficient' rate is not an *equilibrium* rate (in the sense that ultimately the economy converges towards it), so any attempt to target a rate *below* the equilibrium NRU may expose the economy to an ever rising rate of inflation.

Deficient as the NRU may be, therefore, it is difficult to go beyond it as a target.

In principle, any gap between the actual rate of unemployment and the NRU is an indication of the room available for manoeuvre.

Having said this, however, we still have the problem of deciding what the NRU is. There are several serious difficulties here. First, we saw in Chapter 28 how difficult it is to calculate an NRU. Second, as we also saw in that chapter, the problem is compounded by the fact that the NRU may itself be a function of the actual unemployment.

Suppose now that 'in the abstract' there are benefits to be derived from moving from one steady state rate of inflation to another, lower one. A policy of disinflation will also, however, entail some output costs, so the appropriate analysis here is a cost–benefit framework.

What then are the costs? The most important are the unemployment costs and related output losses. What is the measure of this output cost?

The term sacrifice ratio is frequently used to denote the output cost. This sacrifice ratio, we recall from Chapter 22, is the ratio of the sum of the cumulative output loss as a percentage of annual GNP to the reduction in the inflation rate.

A parallel measure for unemployment is the point years of unemployment, defined as the cumulative excess of the actual unemployment rate over the full employment rate. So if the unemployment rate exceeds its full employment level by one point in each of three years the unemployment cost is three point years.

These costs need to be offset against the gains from reducing inflation. However, whilst on the one hand the costs are potentially calculable, the benefits are much more difficult to measure.

A critical question here is whether or not there is a long-run trade-off between inflation and unemployment. Without a trade-off the benefits from lower inflation are permanent whilst the costs are transitional. As already noted above, there is then a good chance that the benefits will exceed the costs, but even then much hinges on the discount rate applied to 'distant' gains. Unemployment costs are immediate; the benefits come later. If the discount rate is very high, the costs may exceed the benefits. Moreover, if there is hysteresis (a long-run negative trade-off) the unemployment costs persist well into the future, tilting the balance more against a policy of disinflation.

It would seem from what we have said that three policy strategies are conceivable when one is faced with an excessive rate of inflation. Strategy 1 is to reduce the rate of inflation. Strategy 2 is to stay with the excessive rate of inflation but live with certain institutional rigidities (which will be at least partially corrected in time). Strategy 3 is to live with the inflation and index (most notably the tax system).

Strategy 3 is superior to 2 if the cost of indexation is less than the marginal cost of inflation flowing from the institutional rigidities. This seems highly likely. So strategy 3 is almost certainly superior to 2.

Two important points need to be made in the general context of a formal indexation strategy. First, general indexation does have major implications for the way in which an economy responds to shocks and for a government's monetary strategy.

(On the former see Chapter 39 and Carmichael *et al.* (1985); on the latter see Chapter 25.)

Second, a government can move to index as from a point in time. However, there will be contractual financial arrangements inherited from the past which will not have been indexed and these will be associated with some redistributional effects. Non-indexed private pensions will also be affected. These technical questions are not unimportant in any decision to live with, say, a rate of inflation which is higher than one experienced in the past.

Is strategy 3 superior to 1? The key elements in the analysis have already been presented.

The importance of these comments is that if ultimately the costs of disinflation exceed the benefits, the *optimal rate of inflation itself becomes a function of the actual rate of inflation*.

TARGETING THE CURRENT ACCOUNT?

Here we enter into a more contentious domain. Whilst we know that governments do monitor the current account, not all economists agree that it ought, even in the medium run, to be a target of policy. We first present the 'new view' of some economists who argue that as a general principle it ought not to be a target of policy. Next, we review some criticisms of the new view.

The new view

These economists argue that (putting to one side the question of the optimal public sector balance, which we address shortly) over the medium run the current account will be a manifestation of private sector intertemporal decisions to save and invest, and assuming these decisions are 'optimally' made the current account will also turn out to be 'optimal'. This view of the current account starts with New Classical assumptions of full employment, frictionless adjustment, efficient resource allocation, liberalised financial markets and rational informed decision making. (See Pitchford (1990), Corden (1991), Sachs (1981), Svensson and Razin (1983) and Kehoe (1988).)

To illustrate this view, consider a simple two-country framework (A and B denoting the two countries) with savings and investment, as a share of GNP, determined in each economy by the real interest rate, which is shared by the two economies. The fundamentals of this model, and its graphical representation, were presented in Chapter 26.

$$\frac{CA}{Y_A} = \frac{Sp_A - Ip_A}{Y_A} + \frac{\overline{TA} - \overline{GA}}{Y_A} \tag{5}$$

Sp_A, Ip_A denote private savings and investment in A and $\overline{TA} - \overline{GA}$ denotes the exogenous public sector surplus, all as a proportion of A's full employment GNP (Y_A).

B's current account is the negative of A's, so we can write

$$-\frac{CA}{Y_A} = \frac{Sp_B - Ip_B}{Y_B} + \frac{\overline{TB} - \overline{GB}}{Y_B} \tag{6}$$

In turn we have

$$\frac{Sp_A - Ip_A}{Y_A} = s_A rr + \frac{\overline{Sp_A} - \overline{Ip_A}}{Y_A} \tag{7}$$

$$\frac{Sp_B - Ip_B}{Y_B} = s_B rr + \frac{\overline{Sp_B} - \overline{Ip_B}}{Y_B} \tag{8}$$

Each country's excess of private savings over investment is a positive function of the 'world' real interest rate (rr) and an exogenous component.

We now multiply (5) by s_B and (6) by s_A, substitute (7) and (8) and take (5) minus (6). Also to simplify we suppose $s_A = s_B$; we then have

$$\frac{CA}{Y_A} = \frac{1}{2}\left(\frac{\overline{Sp_A} - \overline{Ip_A}}{Y_A} - \frac{\overline{Sp_B} - \overline{Ip_B}}{Y_B} + \frac{\overline{TA} - \overline{GA}}{Y_A} - \frac{\overline{TB} - \overline{GB}}{T_B}\right) \tag{9}$$

We also have

$$rr = -\frac{1}{2s_A}\left(\frac{\overline{Sp_A} - \overline{Ip_A}}{y_A} + \frac{\overline{Sp_B} - \overline{Ip_B}}{y_B} + \frac{\overline{TA} - \overline{GA}}{y_A} + \frac{\overline{TB} - \overline{GB}}{y_B}\right) \tag{10}$$

Finally, to complete the model, we can write

$$\frac{CA}{Y_A} = \pi_6 er \tag{11}$$

where er is the real exchange rate (an increase denotes a real devaluation).

These elements can now be brought together.

Suppose the private savings ratio in A increased. This will lower the world real interest rate (10). At the same time, there will be an outflow of capital out of A, a real devaluation of A's currency (11) and a current account surplus in A. The current account surplus is less than the exogenous increase in savings because the fall in the world interest rate will itself reduce the savings ratio and lift the investment ratio. In B private savings fall and investment increases; this generates a current account deficit which in turn is consistent with the real appreciation of B's currency.

Similar analyses may be undertaken for a change, in A or B, in the investment ratio or in the public sector balance.

A current account, on this view, can act as a shock absorber, allowing consumption to be smoothed intertemporally. A typical example of this, frequently found in the literature, is the case of an economy exposed to temporary terms of trade shocks. Suppose there is a perceived temporary deterioration in the terms of trade (and hence in the real income of the community). Households may well react by spreading the loss over time, increasing their current consumption out of income. So now the fall in savings will be associated with a current account deficit. If consumption smoothing represents an optimal intertemporal behaviour such fluctuations in the current account must be regarded as making a positive contribution to the adjustment mechanism. (If capital flows were restricted such optimal behaviour would be, partially at least, frustrated.)

Critique of the new view

So how is one to react to this new view? Criticism of the view turns on the assumptions underlying the analysis. The question then is: as we relax the assumptions, can we make a case for targeting the current account?

Steady state distortions to saving and investment

Consider the possibility that economies A and B may not meet the first best conditions of efficiency, so there may be what we might call steady state distortions. In particular we note some, amongst many, potential distortions:

a) the presence of monopolies (product or trade unions);
b) distortions to saving and investment due to a tax system which is not fully indexed;
c) an inefficient level of output corresponding to the NRU;
d) a non-optimal inherited stock of foreign debt;
e) the presence of exchange controls.

The implications of (a) and (c) for saving and investment decisions are very difficult to analyse. Any such analysis is bound to be highly inconclusive, so we illustrate by confining our discussion to (b) and (d) which, in any event, have received the most attention. Also, as already noted above, the presence of (e) may prevent the current account from acting as a shock absorber and so introduces a potential inefficiency.

We have already noted above the distortions to saving and investment decisions stemming from the interaction of inflation and a tax system which is not fully indexed to inflation.

Consider by way of illustration in this context the case of savings. How does the distortion captured by equation (4) above impact on the current account? What matters here, as we can readily see from (9) above, is home savings relative to savings abroad. If the home country's inflation rate is higher in the steady state than that abroad or if, say, the inflation rate is the same (and greater than zero) but t is higher at home, there will be a bias, other things being equal, against savings at home and so its current account will worsen.

It is evident that the problem lies with the distortions which, ideally, ought to be removed; however, so long as they exist they manifest themselves in outcomes for the current account which are unsatisfactory.

The general point being made here is that tax/expenditure systems, inflation and their interaction all have implications for saving–investment decisions. But, as already noted, to establish that these have had an effect on the current account a comparative analysis is required.

We conclude, therefore, that whilst readily acknowledging that there are distortions that do impact on saving–investment decisions, at the theoretical level very little can be said about the current account implications.

At a given point in time an economy will have inherited a given external liability, which may or may not be optimal. Since the inherited stock is the cumulated sum of past deficits it will not be easy to evaluate the optimality or otherwise of the debt. There is one particular case, however, where such analysis might be undertaken with relative ease. Suppose public sector deficits in the past were excessive (relative to overseas) and this was partly responsible for the accumulation of foreign debt. In this case it is not sufficient to eliminate the 'excess' public sector deficit; it is necessary to run 'surpluses' to eliminate the excess debt. Of course it would be a fine calculation to determine the excess and how far back into the past one might need to go but the important point here is that one might need to correct for past errors in the public sector deficits.

Externalities

We next consider the possibility that current account deficits might impose *external* costs.

An obvious and widely discussed cost comes from the fact that foreign creditors may now exercise undue influence on decision making. This may tie the hands of governments in the sense of them being overtempted to adopt policies which will be more acceptable to foreigners.

Another potential externality is that a country with a large external debt may be more vulnerable to sudden shifts in confidence; this in turn may generate potential exchange rate instability. This is sometimes put in the form of hard versus soft landings, i.e. the ultimate correction needed may be brutal rather than gradual. (There was a widespread feeling that the USA was exposed to this in the mid-1980s.)

Governments too may ultimately decide to bail out large domestic borrowers, thus shifting the burden onto the taxpayer. This is a special case of the much more general case of government, *ex post*, assisting 'ailing' industries, be they domestic or external borrowers.

Also the cost of external borrowing may move against the economy as external debt accumulates. As Vinals put it:

> If investors systematically underestimate the true costs to society of borrowing in world markets private investment, the trade deficit ... may be too high. A particular case is when foreign banks use economy-wide information (such as a country's outstanding debt or current account prospects) ... in setting credit terms; the cost

of borrowing becomes higher as the amount of accumulated foreign debt increases and as the extent of current borrowing increases. Consequently . . . an externality is imposed on the country as whole . . . by the marginal borrower.

(1986: 714)

Another potential externality comes from the possibility that if persistent current account deficits are *perceived* as undesirable they may trigger protectionist tendencies, which in turn would impose a cost on the community. In the same spirit governments may react to current account deficits by adopting restrictive policies, the cost of which will fall on the community as a whole.

Myopia and irrationality in decisions to save and invest

It is frequently said that households suffer from myopia in making savings decisions, i.e. the discount rate they apply is too high. This may or may not be so but of course if all countries practise myopia, whilst there might be a case for compensating *public* savings, there are no current account implications.

Decisions about investment might also be based on poorly processed information or managerial incompetence. This certainly can and does happen and *ex post* such situations are often identifiable.[2]

What if, *ex post*, bad decisions were made? A bad investment decision is similar to a decision to consume more; future generations inherit a foreign liability without a productive resource. To meet the additional interest payment the trade balance needs to improve. It is true that the failed investors will have to meet their liabilities, if they can, but the community is not wholly protected from the mistakes made – the currency needs to devalue – and some strain is thus inflicted on everyone (a form of externality again).

It is difficult, however, to see how this could justify intervention *ex ante* (except, of course, in the broad sense of improving managerial skills, technical education etc.). This is not to say that governments should view with indifference *ex post* developments in foreign debt, which may need to be monitored.

Saving–investment decisions based on 'false' signals

Above we supposed that entrepreneurs might 'misread' signals because their competence might be called into question. A more subtle case is the one where the actual price signals provided in the market place are 'false' in the sense that they are a long way from their fundamentals. To the extent that saving–investment decisions are based on such signals they will be distorted. This does, of course, presuppose that entrepreneurs do not 'see through' the price signals.

Two examples (amongst many possible) will serve to illustrate this: one from episodes of excessive asset price inflation, the other from a real exchange rate misalignment.

Asset price inflation (in housing, in commercial property, in the share market) is an important and well-recognised feature of Western experience. Less appreciated is the fact that asset prices also have important implications for the real economy, e.g. the inflation of house prices above current reproduction costs will induce investment in housing; inflated share prices lower the yield on equities, again with implications for the cost of capital and investment. So on the one hand investment decisions will be upward biased; at the same time, soaring asset prices inflate household paper wealth, inducing a fall in household saving, which is now biased downward. Lending decisions by banks are also likely to be distorted by these signals.

So, in these cases, investment will be excessive while saving will be deficient. If asset price inflation in one economy exceeds that abroad this will open up a current account deficit, which will reflect distorted saving–investment decisions.

To conclude, then, if in one country asset price inflation is excessive and if households and enterprises act on the false signals the current account will certainly be distorted.

Miller and Weller provide a good example of distorted price signals coming from substantial real exchange rate misalignment. They are worth quoting in full.

Suppose that the exchange rate stands at 200 yen to the dollar, but that its true long run equilibrium value is 150. Then, at the margin, any investment project undertaken in the United States and financed by Japanese investors will displace a project in Japan whose true rate of return is one-third higher. In other words, when the exchange rate falls to 150, the welfare loss resulting from the diversion of resources from higher yielding investment projects in Japan is measured by the full amount of the drop in value of these investments. This loss is not simply a transfer from Japan to the United States, but rather represents the capitalised value of foregone profits stemming from the misallocation of investment resources. A rough estimate of the magnitude of these welfare losses can be obtained by calculating the net increase in the flow of portfolio investment from Japan to the United States during the period 1980–85, and multiplying this figure by the average overvaluation of the dollar for the same period. This gives a figure of close to $40 billion.

Exactly similar arguments apply too to the purchase of United States Government securities by the Japanese, to the extent that these purchases diverted United States private saving into low yielding domestic investment.

(1991a: 21)

These arguments suggest that the welfare costs of exchange rate misalignment are likely to be substantial.

The policy mix and the foreign debt

Suppose the authorities target the rate of inflation and unemployment using a mix of monetary and fiscal policies. Monetary policy is tightened, fiscal policy eased. In the new equilibrium the stock of foreign debt will be higher. The proponents of the new view accept inflation and unemployment as legitimate targets of policy but perhaps fail to see the implications for foreign debt of policy mixes aimed at achieving these targets.

Rigidities in the adjustment process

As already noted a disturbance to saving–investment at home or abroad requires an adjustment to the exchange rate and some convergence towards a new equilibrium. But the adjustment may be unduly slow for a number of reasons already reviewed in earlier chapters: the trade balance adjusts very sluggishly to exchange rate changes, wage price adjustments might neutralise real effects of nominal changes in exchange rates, domestic price rigidities will delay the adjustment. The ultimate stock of foreign debt to which the economy converges is not optimal because adjustment has not been frictionless. Hence some intervention might, in principle, be appropriate.

The sustainability of current account deficits

We turn finally to the question of the *sustainability* of current account deficits. Current account deficits may not be sustainable in the sense that, all other things remaining equal, the foreign debt in relation to GDP will explode. We showed in Chapter 29 that if the real growth rate exceeded the real interest rate, the debt to GDP ratio could explode. Questions pertaining to stability were also raised in the context of a larger economic model (Chapter 30).

Conclusions on the current account

What then should we conclude? We have to accept the fact that governments continue to target the current account but the more important question we addressed was: should they? We cannot entirely dismiss the case for targeting the current account or at least the stock of international debt. It is true that there are many circumstances when current account imbalances ought not to be a matter of concern but this is not to say that the stock of debt ought not to be monitored. Clearly a judgement will be needed in each case. This is as far as one can go at the theoretical level.

We have identified many circumstances when the stock of foreign debt which will emerge is quite clearly not optimal. In reality, however, it is extremely difficult to determine how much of the foreign debt is excessive. This is particularly so when account is taken of the framework presented in this chapter which has stressed *divergences* between conditions at home and abroad.

Despite all the reservations noted, many economists continue to argue that there is merit in targeting the current account; on this view the underlying full employment target current account should be equal to 'normal' net capital flows over say the next two or three years. Ideally, this should correspond to the medium-run current account which reflects autonomous private savings and investment decisions (amended for the 'optimal' public sector balance which we deal with next). (For calculations of the target current account, see Williamson (1990).)

TARGETING THE BUDGET DEFICIT

Is there an optimal budget balance? This is even more contentious and difficult than the case of the current account.

We are concerned here with the question of the medium- to longer-run implications of a sustained budget imbalance (i.e. over a whole cycle) (see on this Purvis 1985; Buiter and Kletzer 1992). The issues are complex and unresolved but we note here some of the considerations that enter into the analysis.

1 If Ricardian equivalence holds exactly a bond-financed budget deficit (as compared with the tax finance of a given level of government expenditure) will leave most real variables unchanged, as we saw in Chapter 26, including the current account, the interest rate and the level of output. In this case, there is no rationale for targeting the budget deficit. We did show, however, that Ricardian equivalence was very unlikely to hold in its extreme form.

2 Barro (1979) has argued that there is an efficiency case to be made for some planned deficit (bond) financing. Since taxes are not lump sum, fluctuations in tax rates over time impose an efficiency as well as an administrative cost. Hence, an important objective is to stabilise the planned tax rate.

Consider, by way of illustration, the case where there is some real growth in the economy. A long-run planned balanced budget means that the debt service ratio will fall progressively, requiring a continuing fall in the tax rate. This, however, is inefficient. A preferred policy is one of reducing the tax rate but running a deficit such that the original debt–output ratio is maintained.

3 If governments increase their expenditure on *investment* it is now widely agreed that it would be appropriate for this to be financed by the issue of bonds. If the investment is productive, the social return ought to meet the interest cost. The government's net indebtedness (i.e. the debt minus its capital stock) in this instance is unchanged. This highlights the importance, in calculating the government's indebtedness, of deducting from its gross debt any assets it owns.

4 Another important issue frequently raised in this context is the question of inter-generational transfers. Suppose there is an increase in the budget deficit caused by say an increase in government *consumption* expenditure and suppose exchange rates are flexible.

Putting to one side wealth effects, and drawing on models of earlier chapters, consider first the case where there is perfect asset substitution and the country is small. In the medium run with output and the real interest rate fixed, the budget deficit may manifest itself in an equivalent current account deficit (the twin deficit case). Suppose now we have imperfect asset substitution, because of, say, the presence of a risk premium. In this case we know that the current account will ultimately be zero. (See Chapter 20.) At the same time the domestic interest rate will have to rise; this in turn will increase domestic savings and reduce domestic investment sufficiently to absorb the deficit.

The analysis is only a little changed if the country is a large one. In this case the global real interest rate will be changed and there will be a mix of outcomes. There will be a current account deficit and a reduction in investment. (See equations (9) and (10) above.)

In these ways future generations inherit some combination of an external debt, which they will need to finance, and/or a lower stock of capital. They will thus be worse off.

5 There is also a large literature concerned with implications for *inflation* and *stability* of a persistent budget deficit. (See on this Sargent and Wallace (1981) and Brunner (1986).) The argument here is that there are close links between monetary and fiscal policies and that a persistent fiscal deficit, which is out of line with monetary policy, may in the longer run destabilise the debt to GNP ratio and force the monetary authorities to accommodate the fiscal deficit by inflation. This argument is demonstrated more formally below.

Notation

B nominal stock of government debt
b stock of debt (in real terms)
D nominal primary deficit (excluding interest on debt)
d deficit in real terms
H high-powered (base) money
r_d interest rate on bonds
rr real interest rate
P price level
n real growth rate
y real output
$\dot{p}$ rate of inflation

The model

$$D + r_d B_{-1} = (B - B_{-1}) + (H - H_{-1}) \tag{12}$$

$$\frac{b}{y} = (1 + rr - n) \frac{b_{-1}}{y_{-1}} + \frac{d}{y} - \frac{H_{-1}}{P_y} \frac{H - H_{-1}}{H_{-1}} \tag{13}$$

where $rr = r_d - \dot{p}$ and $1 + rr - n$ approximates $(1 + r_d)/(1 + \dot{p} + n)$

$$\frac{H - H_{-1}}{H_{-1}} = n + \dot{p} \tag{14}$$

Setting $b/y = b_{-1}/y_{-1}$ in (13) we have

$$\frac{b}{y} = \frac{1}{n - rr}\left[\frac{d}{y} - \frac{H}{Py}(n + \dot{p})\right] \tag{15}$$

where $n + \dot{p}$ is assumed to approximate $(n + \dot{p})/(1 + n + \dot{p})$. We can solve (15) for $\dot{p}$:

$$\dot{p} = \frac{Py}{H}(rr - n)\frac{b}{y} + \frac{Py}{H}\frac{d}{y} - n \tag{16}$$

Equation (12) says that the primary deficit (which excludes interest payments on the debt) plus interest on the existing stock of debt has to be financed by a combination of new bond issues $(B - B_{-1})$ and an increase in base money $(H - H_{-1})$. Deflating (12) by the price level and dividing through by real GNP converts (12) into (13). Equation (13) represents the dynamics of adjustment of the debt–output ratio. Equation (14) asserts that the rate of change in nominal income is equal to the rate of change in high-powered money. Equation (15) represents the stationary state counterpart of (13), i.e. where $b/y = b_{-1}/y_{-1}$. Equation (16) simply rearranges (15) to solve for the rate of inflation.

We can illustrate the argument as follows. Suppose $rr > n$ (the case almost universally assumed) and suppose now that there is some increase in the primary deficit. (At the same time suppose that the rate of growth of high-powered money is fixed.) Equation (13), which is a first-order difference equation, tells us that in these circumstances (because the coefficient $1 + rr - n$ is greater than 1) the debt–output ratio will ultimately explode. Interest payments on the debt rise at a faster rate than the real growth in the economy.

At this point there are two potential solutions: either the deficit ratio is brought down or money growth is allowed to accelerate to accommodate, so to speak, the fiscal deficit. This last solution produces more inflation, as shown in equation (16). Inflation solves the problem because it *reduces* the bond–output ratio and so acts to *neutralise* the effects on the bond-output ratio of the higher deficit. (This is readily seen in (13).) Thus a persistently higher deficit, assuming $rr > n$, will ultimately provoke an easier monetary policy and hence more inflation. It is also worth noting from (16) that, given the primary deficit ratio, the larger the equilibrium bond–output ratio is the higher will also be the equilibrium rate of inflation. The reason is that this will be associated with higher interest payments and hence a larger public sector deficit (including interest).

The framework developed above allows us also to derive an 'optimal' deficit ratio, in this context one that will be consistent with the independently determined rate of inflation. Such a deficit ratio is readily arrived at by now inverting (15) and solving for the endogenous deficit ratio. We have

$$\frac{d}{y} = \frac{H}{Py} \, n - (\mathrm{rr} - n) \, \frac{b}{y} + \frac{H}{Py} \, \dot{p} \tag{17}$$

Given $\dot{p}$ and given the bond–output ratio, we can solve for the deficit ratio.

6 Finally, there may also be externalities associated with a persistent public sector deficit but these are much harder to identify than in the case of the current account. The intergenerational effect was noted above. The one that comes most readily to mind is that persistent deficits might expose the economy to shifts in confidence which in turn might again generate exchange rate instability.

WEALTH AS A TARGET

We noted that a potential modification is to target national wealth (see on this McDonald 1989; Weale *et al.* 1989). The increase in national wealth comprises the sum of net investment and the current account surplus. The implications of targeting wealth in lieu of the current account are quite different. For example, a surge in investment matched by a current account deficit does not change wealth and hence does not need correcting.

Targeting wealth also raises questions about whether there is any remaining rationale for targeting the budget deficit. We have argued that the principal long-run consequences of a persistent budget deficit are

a) a legacy of an external debt and/or less capital stock, and
b) inflation.

Result (a) is already captured by a wealth target. Consequence (b) is in any event incorporated in the loss function.

One advantage of targeting wealth as such is that it enters directly into households' utility function. On the other hand, it would not be an easy task to define the target stock or growth in national wealth. Indeed all the difficulties encountered earlier in deciding whether the current account ought to be a target of policy reappear here. Additionally, some calculation of an optimal national investment ratio would also be required.

SHORT-RUN TARGETS

So far we have focused on medium-term targets. We turn now to the application of *short-run* criteria in the evaluation of macro strategies. What we are concerned with here is the *year-to-year* volatility in a number of macro variables as distinct from *persistent* deviations from targets.

Some of the variables that enter into the medium-run framework would not normally be a policy concern over the short run. The current account and the budget balance almost certainly fall into this category. Most (if not all) economists and policy-makers would not be very concerned over *cyclical* fluctuations in the current account or the budget deficit, so we can begin by discarding these two variables from consideration.

On the other hand, most economists would accept the view that there are costs associated with cyclical fluctuations (i.e. around trend levels) in *both* prices and output (employment). Some would also want to extend the list of variables to include the real (and perhaps nominal) interest rate and the real (and again perhaps nominal) exchange rate.

It could be argued that, the more volatile the real interest rate

a) the higher the *average* long-run real interest rate over the whole cycle (to compensate for risk); and
b) the greater the potential resource shifts.

These last may impose welfare costs and carry implications for structural unemployment.

What are the costs of real exchange rate volatility (as distinct from *misalignments* which are *sustained* deviations from long-run equilibrium rates)?

There are two identifiable potential costs. One parallels the costs of real interest rate volatility – the costs of resource shifts. At the same time, a greater amplitude of exchange rate movement increases the cost of forward cover. This cost of forward cover is measurable by the bid–ask spread, which itself increases with greater exchange rate uncertainty. The cost is very small, however: e.g. around $\frac{1}{10}$ per cent of the transaction price.

Does real exchange rate volatility also adversely affect trade and, if so, is there a welfare loss associated with this? On the first question, despite the general presumption that volatility impacts adversely on trade, theoretical analysis suggests that increased risk would have *ambiguous* effects on trade. De Grauwe (1988) addresses this question in the context of the effect of a change in risk on the supply of exports. He concludes that an increase in risk has a substitution effect which acts along conventional lines to lower the attractiveness of producing for exports, but, on the other hand, also has an income effect which works in the opposite direction: with higher risk the expected utility of export revenue declines, and if export producers are risk averse this may induce them to increase their export activity.

The question is thus an *empirical* one. Unfortunately, despite the numerous studies in this area, this is still an unresolved issue: some studies suggest some negative effects, others show weak or no effects.

If it is difficult to determine exactly how flexibility affects the volume of trade, it is even harder to evaluate how welfare is affected. Lanyi (1969) makes one or two telling points in this regard. Assuming that increased exchange rate flexibility reduces trade, why is the community necessarily worse off? Relatively fixed rates entail, in effect, a subsidy to trade but a subsidy leads to a misallocation of resources (subject to the usual second-best reservations) unless there are offsetting externalities. Hence, to argue that increased exchange rate flexibility actually misallocates resources because it reduces trade, one would need to make some case for externalities from subsidising trade. Lanyi gives two examples of potential externalities with relatively fixed rates: first, that the consumer will have a wider range of choice of products; second, that there may be increased foreign competition which, in turn, stimulates managerial efficiency as well as technical and product innovations.

On the strength of the above brief analysis, we could write a short-run (say annual) loss function (Ls) as follows:

$$Ls = w_1(\dot{p} - \dot{p}^*)^2 + w_2(y - y^*)^2 + w_3(rr - rr^*)^2 + w_4(er - er^*)^2 \qquad (18)$$

where rr and er are respectively the real interest rate and the real exchange rate and the asterisks represent target levels of the variables.

In a later chapter we shall actually use a function like (18).

SHORT- AND LONG-RUN TARGETS

Economists tend to be divided between those who attach overriding importance to getting the economy right *over the medium run* and who are opposed to directing policy instruments at stabilising the short-run economy and those who also attach considerable importance to short-run stabilisation.

Very loosely, those who are preoccupied with short-run stabilisation tend to be labelled Keynesians or New Keynesians while those who are oriented to the medium-run economy tend to be labelled monetarists, New Classical monetarists, rationalists or conservatives. The second group tend also to believe that *a preoccupation with short-run stabilisation can end up harming the economy in the medium run*. As a general rule, these tend to attach overriding importance to inflation and to fiscal rectitude.

There is little doubt that from about the mid-1970s we observe a decided shift towards more conservative policies. This escalated in the 1980s. The shift manifested itself in a variety of ways: the wave of liberalisation measures, domestic and external, the sharp shift towards fiscal rectitude manifest in the 1980s (with the exception of the USA), the determination to keep inflation within modest bounds, the neglect of unemployment.

A striking feature of the 1980s is the ascent to power of a number of conservative governments who actually tried to implement conservative-type policies. The two most prominent were Thatcher (1979–89) and Reagan (1980–8). Both, on paper, asserted their conservative leanings; both undoubtedly were strong protagonists of market-oriented policies and of reducing the role of the government (see Chapter 46).

The wave of 'rationalist' thinking engulfed not only conservative governments but also governments which were avowedly 'leftwing'. President Mitterand in France, after a brief flirtation with Keynesian-type policies in 1981–2, did an about-turn in 1983 and has hardly wavered since. The Australian and New Zealand Labour governments of the mid-1980s followed fairly conventional rationalist policies.

35

The regulatory–institutional environment, the policy regime and macro performance

INTRODUCTION

The previous chapter reviewed the macro targets of policy. This chapter tries to provide a framework for the evaluation of policy regimes. It begins by defining the regulatory and institutional environment within which policy operates. It then looks at alternative policy strategies, i.e. the policy regime.

The chapter also describes two methods of evaluating a policy regime: one drawing on theory, the other on empirical investigations. Next, we present a framework which allows us to compare macroeconomic performance across countries. Finally, we rank sixteen countries in terms of their performance on inflation and unemployment.

THE REGULATORY AND INSTITUTIONAL ENVIRONMENT

Policy operates within a particular regulatory and institutional environment. Such an environment defines the constraints or rules of the game, so to speak, under which policy will function.

What are these constraints? These appear in four important domains:

a) the exchange rate system;
b) the degree of regulation of external capital flows;
c) the degree of regulation of the domestic financial system;
d) production and labour markets.

The exchange rate system

We have already seen in Part II how the exchange rate regime plays a key role in determining the way in which a policy change impacts on the economy. Part I also reviewed the types of exchange rate regimes which have operated over the last 100–120 years. The next chapter also looks at a wider range of exchange rate policy options and addresses the question of how to evaluate alternative exchange rate regimes.

The regulation of capital movements

Part II also demonstrated the importance of capital mobility in an analysis of the effects of policy changes. Chapter 5 showed how the industrial world had become increasingly integrated financially in the 1970s and 1980s. By the end of the 1980s there were few remaining official barriers to the movement of capital.

The regulation of the domestic financial system

Most domestic financial systems in the industrial countries have been liberalised over the 1970s and 1980s. Extensive controls over interest rates and lending and prescriptions on the types and composition of asset holdings imposed on banks and other financial institutions have all been progressively dismantled. Interest rates are now freer to move, most restrictions on lending have been discarded while prescriptions on asset holdings have been made much less restrictive.

The domestic financial regulatory environment also plays a key role in determining how macro policy is going to function. This question is addressed in Chapter 48 when we review the Australian and New Zealand experience on this front.

Production and labour markets

The way in which wages are determined and the institutions which govern the working of the supply side of the economy also play a crucial role in determining how macro policy impacts on the economy. The question was raised in Chapters 14 and 22. Labour markets were modelled in Chapter 28. The question is an important one and will be addressed again in some of the chapters which follow, notably in Chapter 44 and in the three case studies of Part VIII.

At this point we simply describe how such institutions may differ across countries.

One way to classify wage determination systems is in terms of the level at which bargaining takes place. Such bargaining can be centralised or it can be at the industry (intermediate) level or at the enterprise (decentralised) level. A centralised economy is one where negotiations occur at the national level between a trade union body and employer bodies, with at the same time varying degrees of involvement by governments as the third party. Centralised economies include the Scandinavian countries, plus Austria. Intermediate economies include Germany, the Netherlands and Belgium. Decentralised economies include the UK, Italy, Switzerland, the USA, Canada and Japan (see Layard *et al.* 1991).

Some systems do not lend themselves quite so readily to this classification. Australia and New Zealand have in the past had systems of arbitration where a tribunal has tended to make national decisions about award wages for particular occupations and about minimum wages to be paid. These systems are described in Chapter 48. More recently, however, as we shall see, Australia and New Zealand have been converging towards an enterprise-based system.

Also, the minimum wage in force differs widely amongst OECD countries. In some a minimum wage is prescribed by law. This is the case, for example, in France, in the Netherlands, in Denmark and in the USA (but in the last it is low). In others it is established by collective bargaining.

Another relevant institutional characteristic which bears on wage outcomes, as we shall see, is union coverage, i.e. the proportion of the labour force which is unionised. Coverage is high in nearly all European countries and in Australia. Coverage is 'medium' in Canada, New Zealand, Japan and Switzerland; it is low in the USA. As we shall see in Chapter 44, the degree of trade union and employer *coordination* may also play a role in wage outcomes.

The industrial relations environment may be critical in moulding relations between unions and employers and in wage outcomes. Some countries have a long history of conflict and confrontation (e.g. the UK); others (e.g. Japan) have more harmonious relationships.

Unemployment benefits and their maximum duration are also important in determining search activity and in influencing wage negotiations. Conditions here tend to vary widely across OECD member countries. Typically, duration is generous in European Community countries and in Australia and New Zealand, moderately good in Sweden and Norway and low in the USA and Japan. Typically, too, the unemployment benefit is high in Europe and relatively low in the USA and Japan.

The tax wedge (as defined in Chapter 28) can also be important. This wedge is high in Europe and low in the USA and Japan.

Hiring and firing rules and work hours prescribed by legislation all have some potential implications for labour market flexibility (see Emerson (1988) for a general review of legislation in industrial countries). Suffice it to say that, in general terms, such legislation tends to be more oppressive in Europe than in the USA.

Increasing attention has been paid in the 1980s to supply side factors in macroeconomic performance. Many OECD member countries have tried to liberalise their labour markets and to remove some at least of the supply restrictions.

THE POLICY REGIME

Given the regulatory environment, a policy regime defines how instruments available to the authorities are actually used with an eye on the macro targets. Instruments include discount rates, open market operations, and the levels of government expenditure and of the tax rates. Many governments, too, have periodically chosen to intervene in the wage outcomes, sometimes providing broad guidelines, other times imposing mandatory wage orders. Examples of these will be provided in our case studies (Part VIII) and in Chapter 44. Active intervention of this sort has occurred in the past in the UK (Chapter 46), in Canada, Denmark and in Australia and New Zealand (Chapter 48).

This chapter focuses on broad principles which govern a policy regime.

Broad principles

How might instruments be set in relation to targets?

At one extreme, we can have a very simple rule for monetary and for fiscal policy which is set *without any regard to changes in the gap between actual and desired levels of the policy variables*. A regime of this kind is called a non-activist or more technically a non-state-contingent rule. An example of such a rule would be one which prescribes that the stock of money should grow at a fixed rate year in, year out, or a rule which prescribes that the public sector should be planned to be in balance, again year in, year out. (The case for rules is discussed in Chapter 37.)

At the other extreme we can have instruments being reset periodically in response to changes in target gaps or to disturbances. A regime of this kind is referred to as a discretionary or an activist regime or more technically one which is state contingent.

A middle position would be one where the authorities allow the instruments to respond *but only within certain bounds*. Such a regime is referred to as one of *constrained* discretion. An example would be the case where the monetary authorities announce money growth targets to be achieved within a certain band (see Chapter 43).

Feedback policies, i.e. policies which respond to target gaps or to disturbances, may take many different forms. At one level such policies may be applied in a very *ad hoc* fashion. An example of this is the so-called check-list approach: in determining monetary policy the authorities look at all major economic and financial variables, present and prospective, including the state of the economy, the balance of payments, prices, other policies, interest rates, the exchange rate, the money aggregates.

At another level the relationship between instruments and targets may be made more explicit. Three very influential approaches to policy-making in this general spirit are those of Tinbergen (1952), Theil (1961) and Mundell (1962).

Tinbergen advanced the important principle that if governments aimed at n independent targets of policy then they should also have n effective and unbounded instruments of policy if the targets are all to be met. Suppose, to illustrate Tinbergen's 'fixed-targets' approach, governments had three targets and only two instruments. Then clearly, except by coincidence, the three targets could not be met and some choice among the targets would need to be made. On the other hand, if governments had three targets and as many as four instruments, one instrument would be 'redundant' since only three need to be manipulated to achieve the targets.

To illustrate Tinbergen's approach with a very simple example, suppose we had two targets, income Y and the balance of payments BP, and two instruments, the money stock Mo and government expenditure G. We then have

$$Y = \alpha_1 Mo + \alpha_2 G + A_1 \tag{1}$$

$$BP = -\alpha_3 Mo - \alpha_4 G + A_2 \tag{2}$$

A_1 and A_2 are all other influences on Y and BP. If A_1 and A_2 are known, Mo and G can be solved for target values of Y and BP.

Theil's approach is different. He starts with the premise that governments have a welfare function, which includes both targets and instruments, with weights attaching to each component of the welfare function to reflect its relative importance. Thus, in this approach, there are no inherent limits to the number of targets accommodated. The welfare function would then be optimised subject to the constraints determined by the structure of the economy. An example of this was provided in Chapter 25. The approach will be taken up again in Chapter 39.

If governments were armed with detailed information about the structure of the economy (in the form, say, of a usable econometric model), Tinbergen's approach would be relatively simple to apply. As we noted above, but now in a more complex framework, it reduces, ultimately, to a mathematical exercise where the target values are plugged into the model, forecasts are made of the exogenous variables in the model (e.g. exports, foreign interest rates and prices), values are placed on the lagged variables and the model is then solved for the appropriate values of the instruments. Within this framework, if there were insufficient instruments then targets would have to be dropped to ensure the equality of targets and instruments.

Theil, on the other hand, offers the important insight that some instruments need to be included in the welfare function to allow for the possibility that there are costs incurred in changing instruments, possible diminishing returns in the use of instruments and constraints on the magnitude of changes in the instruments. Examples of instruments assuming a role similar to targets abound. Three obvious ones are interest rates, exchange rates and budget deficits.

Tinbergen's approach therefore is simpler than Theil's, which, though more realistic, is more difficult to apply. Tinbergen's approach would lead one to believe that there are sufficient instruments available to meet macro targets, while Theil's much broader approach suggests that there may be a problem of too many targets and an insufficient number of instruments. In practice Tinbergen's 'basic' approach has been much more widely used. However, it needs to be tempered by the awareness that there is no absolutely clear dividing line between instruments and targets and that frequently governments treat apparent instruments as targets.

Mundell's approach descends directly from Tinbergen. His major insight is that where the detailed structure of an economy is not known and/or where policy-making is decentralised, governments may be able to proceed, on the strength of only limited information, by assigning a policy instrument to that target for which it has a relative advantage. In other words, in a simple two-instrument two-target framework, one instrument would be assigned to one target and the other instrument to the other target. The instrument would be altered, whenever its target variable was outside the acceptable range, in a way that would bring the variable closer to its targeted value.

The assignment principle

On what basis would assignment be made? Formally, again in a two-target two-instrument context, we ask how the two instruments must be varied conceptually to achieve the same change in one of the targets. Then given the required changes in the instruments we need to determine how the other target responds to those same changes in the instruments. The instrument that produces the largest absolute change in the other target is the one that ought to be assigned to that target. It has been shown that this ensures stability in the sense that assignment in this way will tend to move the economy closer to its targets. However, the reverse assignment need not be unstable; indeed it may also be stable. So the Mundellian criterion for assignment ensures that the policy is stabilising while the reverse assignment may or may not be stabilising.

To understand Mundell's assignment principle, we now provide a simple example. Mundell's world was essentially a short-term fixed rate world where the exchange rate is either not available as a policy instrument or central banks do not choose to use it as an instrument over a short-term horizon. Governments are concerned over the level of employment (the internal balance target) and the state of the balance of payments (the external balance target) and have two instruments at their disposal: monetary and fiscal policies.

We assume fiscal policy takes the form of variations in government expenditure holding monetary policy neutral. Monetary policy can be defined in several alternative ways. The monetary authorities may manipulate the interest rate or the volume of money or finally their domestic assets. In what follows we will define the monetary instrument as the volume of money. Suppose we are in a simple Mundell–Fleming (MF) fixed price model. From our standpoint now we need to remind ourselves of three key assumptions: that capital flows are influenced only by relative interest rates, that the current account is determined only by the level of output (given prices and exchange rates) and that the country is small.

Recalling our assignment principle, suppose there is a monetary and fiscal expansion such that the increase in output is the same. The emerging deficit in the current account will by definition be the same; at the same time, if capital mobility is low, fiscal expansion and the associated higher interest rate will induce an inflow of capital that will serve partially to offset the deficit. Monetary expansion, on the other hand, and the associated lower interest rate will induce an outflow of capital that will come on top of the current account deficit. Hence, the absolute turnaround in the balance of payments will be larger for monetary than for fiscal expansion. It follows that in this case monetary policy should be assigned to the external target and fiscal policy to the internal target.

If capital mobility is high fiscal expansion will produce an overall surplus while monetary expansion will produce a deficit. In principle, the relative balance of payments outcome is indeterminate in this case and will depend on the extent of the drop in the interest rate for monetary expansion and the extent of the increase in the interest rate for fiscal expansion. If the surplus exceeds the deficit, the assignment principle dictates the reverse assignment: monetary policy to internal balance and fiscal policy to external balance.

More formally consider a simple structural model with two targets t_1 and t_2 and two instruments s_1 and s_2:

$$t_1 = \pi_1 s_1 + \pi_2 s_2 + \mu_1$$

$$t_2 = \pi_3 s_1 + \pi_4 s_2 + \mu_2$$

where π represents the impact of each instrument on the target and μ_1 and μ_2 are disturbance terms. The two equations are reduced forms from a structural model; π will be a complex expression derived from the model.

Comparative advantage is determined by the ratio

$$k_1 = \frac{\pi_1/\pi_3}{\pi_2/\pi_4}$$

If $k_1 > 1$, s_1 has a comparative advantage in controlling t_1; if $k_1 < 1$, s_2 has the comparative advantage in controlling t_1.

In this presentation determination of assignment appears deceptively simple. However, because the impact of particular policies on targets may be quite different over different time horizons, as we have seen, we need to distinguish short-, medium- and long-run assignment. These, as we shall see, do not always point in the same direction – hence the need to address assignment in a *dynamic* context. (These themes are developed further in Chapter 38.)

METHODS OF EVALUATING POLICY REGIMES

How does one go about evaluating policy regimes? There are basically three approaches to be found in the literature: one theoretical, two empirical. First, one can undertake an analytical evaluation of the policy proposals. The proposals are evaluated with reference to the targets spelt out in the previous chapter, using now an analytical framework or a theoretical model. This is the approach adopted in several of the chapters which follow. Second, one can undertake simulations, with econometric models, of policy proposals. The method is explained below; some results using this method are presented in Chapters 40 and 45. Third, one can undertake case studies of particular economies. The broad aim here is to address the question of why some economies perform well and others badly. Part VIII deals with a number of case studies. The general method is explained later in the chapter.

THE ECONOMETRIC METHOD

How does one proceed econometrically? There are several approaches.

Historical reruns

One way to attack the problem is to undertake, with an estimated econometric model, a rerun of history over a particular period of time, assuming that alternative policy strategies had been adopted. This, in principle, then allows us to compare the performance of the alternative strategies against one another *as well as* against the actual historical policies adopted. We illustrate with a very simple example.

$$Y = \alpha_1 G - \alpha_2 r_d + \alpha_3 A + \alpha_4 Y_{-1} + \varepsilon_1 \tag{3}$$

$$r_d = -\alpha_5 \text{Mo} + \alpha_6 Y + \varepsilon_2 \tag{4}$$

$$Y = \frac{\alpha_1}{1 + \alpha_2 \alpha_6} G + \frac{\alpha_2 \alpha_5}{1 + \alpha_2 \alpha_6} \text{Mo} - \frac{\alpha_3}{1 + \alpha_2 \alpha_6} A + \frac{\alpha_4}{1 + \alpha_2 \alpha_6} Y_{-1}$$

$$- \frac{\alpha_2}{1 + \alpha_2 \alpha_6} \varepsilon_2 + \frac{1}{1 + \alpha_2 \alpha_6} \varepsilon_1 \tag{5}$$

where Y is nominal income, Y_{-1} is lagged nominal income, G is 'fiscal' policy, r_d is the interest rate, A is an exogenous non-policy variable, Mo is the money stock, ε_1 and ε_2 are respectively goods and money market serially uncorrelated residual errors.

Equations (3) and (4) are goods and money market equations, and (5) is the reduced-form equation. The *historical* movement of Y can of course be *exactly* explained by the actual levels of the two policy instruments G and Mo, the non-policy variable A, lagged nominal income *and* importantly by the two error terms (ε_1 and ε_2). In principle it would be possible to undertake a simulation of Y with a different policy package for G and Mo. Thus the performance of actual policies, given the historical distribution of A, ε_1 and ε_2, can be compared with alternative policies.

Suppose we are interested in the behaviour of Y with a changed policy for Mo *only*. To evaluate the performance of an alternative Mo policy one may need to keep G neutral, since the actual behaviour of G may distort the evaluation of Mo. We can thus do a simulation with the same historical errors (ε) and A but with G held neutral, while at the same time Mo can be allowed to vary. This amounts to comparing pure alternative strategies for Mo (unadulterated by G) given the historical disturbances (A and ε).

ε was assumed to follow a particular historical evolution. A simulation could also be undertaken with a different distribution of disturbances (i.e. weights attaching to ε_1 and ε_2) and with a different value for A.

Different policy strategies in the face of individual disturbances

An econometric model can be simulated for different policy strategies in the face of individual disturbances, e.g. we might ask how Y behaves in the face of changes in ε_1 or ε_2 individually and given A for a particular policy strategy.

General comments on the econometric testing of policy strategies

a) Econometric models may and do differ substantially in structure and sophistication (see Frankel 1988a); hence, there may be wide divergences in the evaluation of policy strategies.

b) Estimated behavioural equations in the models are not the same; hence not only are the coefficients and lag structures different but so are the unexplained residuals. A historical package of residuals will thus convey something different in each model.

c) In the evaluation of a policy strategy it may not be appropriate to assume that the relevant distribution of disturbances is the *historical* one. What is clearly more relevant is the *expected* distribution in the future – hence the importance of undertaking alternative simulations, examples of which were given above.

d) An advantage of the piecemeal approach is that it allows a more careful analysis of how different policy strategies perform in the face of *particular* types of disturbances. It also conforms more with, and allows one to confirm or otherwise, *theoretical* analyses.

e) A typical econometric simulation of a policy strategy with some feedback from an economic variable requires some specification of a reaction coefficient. The coefficient ultimately used emerges only after considerable experimentation has been undertaken (notably with *ex post* data not available *ex ante*). This may inject some potential bias in favour of the policy strategy, at least for historical simulations (not, however, for post-sample simulations). Moreover, most econometric simulations of alternative strategies do not take account of information lags, data corrections, in defining a reaction function.

f) The treatment of expectations is always a troublesome feature of any simulation exercise. Frequently, rational expectations are assumed at least in financial markets; in reality this is not likely to hold, which means that 'errors' will appear in the equation residuals. Suppose, too, that a new policy rule was introduced; how much time should one allow the public to learn the new rule and incorporate it in its expectations structure?

It is thus readily seen that the econometric method does not necessarily provide the final answers to any evaluation of a policy strategy. This will be confirmed later in our reviews. (See McCallum (1992) for a general critique of the econometric tests.)

A FRAMEWORK FOR COMPARING MACRO PERFORMANCE

This section offers a methodological framework which, in principle at any rate, can be used to compare the macro performance across different countries.

Countries may differ in three very important respects:

a) the rules of the game, i.e. the regulatory–institutional environment as explained in Section 1;

b) the use to which instruments, including wage policies, are put, i.e. the particular macro policies implemented. Equation (2) defines how instruments are set in relation to targets, i.e. defines the policy regime as explained in Section 2.

c) the domestic and external shocks to which they are exposed and which, ultimately, represent the driving forces which produce potential instability in economies. These could take the form of oil price, monetary, productivity, real shocks.

Macro policy, in broad terms, comprises strategies with respect to *both* (a) and (b). Governments can change the regulatory environment and/or they can change the policy regime. When we look at the case studies in Chapters 46–48, we shall provide several illustrations of such changes.

Macro outcomes are the result of the interactions between these three important elements. Two countries, for example, can be identical with respect to (a) and (b) but different with respect to (c). In this case macro performance will reflect neither the regulatory environment nor the policy strategy but simply the fact that the shocks are different.

Or the shocks may be the same and indeed the policy response may be the same but because of differences in (a) the outcomes will be different. Finally, the shocks may be the same and the regulatory environment may be the same but the policy responses may be different, which in turn will produce different outcomes.

Although such a framework is a useful one in thinking about comparative macro policy, it is unfortunately not always easy to apply. Much is known about *differences* in the regulatory environment; less, however, is known about their implications for macro outcomes, particularly so *as a package*. It is also not easy to compare countries in terms of policy regimes although, in very broad terms, distinctive strategies are observable. Finally, the shocks are even harder to compare across countries.

INFLATION AND UNEMPLOYMENT IN INDUSTRIAL COUNTRIES

Table 35.1 ranks sixteen countries in terms of their performance on inflation and unemployment over four different time horizons: 1960–7, 1968–73, 1974–81 and 1982–91.

Consider first inflation performance. Some countries change their rankings over time. Japan was the worst performer in 1960–7 and the best in 1982–91 (see, however, Chapter 47). Australia performed well in the earlier years but very poorly in the later years. Germany is a consistently excellent performer. Switzerland and

Table 35.1 Inflation and unemployment in sixteen industrial countries, 1960–91

Country	Inflation								Unemployment							
	60–7	r	68–73	r	74–81	r	82–91	r	60–7	r	68–73	r	74–81	r	82–91	r
Australia	2.4	3	5.2	8	11.6	13	7.5	14	1.9	11	2.0	9	5.2	11	8.0	9
Austria	3.4	9	4.8	4	6.4	3	3.2	4	1.9	11	1.4	7	1.6	3	3.5	4
Belgium	2.5	4	4.5	2	8.1	5	3.8	6	2.1	13	2.2	10	6.2	13	11.1	16
Canada	2.2	2	4.6	3	9.9	9	5.2	9	4.8	14	5.4	15	7.2	16	9.7	14
Denmark	5.3	15	6.6	13	11.1	11	5.0	8	1.6	9	1.0	4	6.1	12	9.3	11
France	3.5	10	5.9	10	11.4	12	5.3	10	1.3	6	2.6	13	5.1	10	9.5	12
Germany	2.5	4	4.1	1	4.7	2	2.4	3	0.8	4	0.8	3	3.6	7	5.9	7
Italy	4.1	13	5.1	6	17.0	16	8.6	15	4.9	15	5.7	16	6.9	15	10.9	15
Japan	5.4	16	6.8	14	9.1	6	1.9	1	1.3	6	1.2	5	2.0	5	2.5	3
Netherlands	3.8	12	6.3	11	7.1	4	2.2	2	0.7	3	1.5	8	4.4	8	8.7	10
New Zealand	2.9	6	6.9	15	14.4	14	9.5	16	0.1	2	0.3	2	1.3	2	5.6	6
Norway	3.6	11	6.3	11	9.6	8	6.7	12	1.0	5	1.2	5	1.8	4	3.5	4
Sweden	4.2	14	5.3	9	10.6	10	7.3	13	1.6	9	2.2	9	2.0	5	2.2	2
Switzerland	3.3	8	5.1	6	4.3	1	3.4	5	0.0	1	0.0	1	0.3	1	0.8	1
UK	3.1	7	7.1	16	15.5	15	6.0	11	1.5	8	2.4	12	5.0	12	9.5	12
USA	1.7	1	4.9	5	9.4	7	4.1	7	4.9	15	4.6	14	6.8	14	7.0	8

Source: OECD, *Economic Outlooks*
Note: r, ranking.

Denmark improved their relative ranking while the USA and Canada worsened their relative positions. Austria has been a good performer since 1968. Norway and Sweden are both below-average performers.

We focus here on the most recent experience (1990–1). We classify a group of seventeen countries (now also including Ireland) into three groups: those with rates of inflation of 4 per cent and below, those with rates of inflation above 4 per cent but below 6 per cent, and those with rates of 6 per cent or above.

In the first category are Japan (2.6), Germany (3.1), France (3), Austria (3.2), Belgium (3.4), Denmark (2.3), Ireland (2.8), the Netherlands (2.8) and Norway (3.4). In the second category are the USA (4.6), Canada (4.5), Switzerland (5.6), Australia (4.8) and New Zealand (4.6). In the third category are Sweden (10), Italy (6.4) and the UK (6.5).

To simplify somewhat we can classify these countries into four basic groups.

In one group we have countries on flexible exchange rates whose central banks have followed an *eclectic* strategy, in the sense that inflation is one of a whole range of targets which have been monitored. In short, a good deal of discretion is exercised. In this group we have the USA and Australia.

In a second group we have countries again on flexible exchange rates whose central banks have tended to attach overriding, but not exclusive, importance to inflation. In this group belong Switzerland, Canada, New Zealand, Japan and Germany.

In a third group we have the European Monetary System (EMS) countries which, to simplify somewhat, have effectively been pegging to the deutschmark. Here we have Ireland, France, Denmark, the Netherlands, Belgium. The UK (who joined in 1990) and Italy (until 1991) have wider margins of exchange rate flexibility. Austria is not in the EMS but pegs to the deutschmark so it belongs in this group.

In a fourth group we have the Nordic countries, represented here by Norway and Sweden. These countries were pegging to the ECU but essentially continued to be on adjustable pegs.

On *a priori* grounds one would expect the best performers to be in the second and third groups. This is in fact largely confirmed. The UK and Italy had special treatment and so the external inflationary discipline was weaker. (In September 1992, under pressure, sterling and the lira withdrew from the exchange rate mechanism (ERM) and were floating independently.) New Zealand's rate of inflation in 1991 was down to 2.8 per cent.

The two 'surprises' in terms of this framework are Norway and Switzerland. Norway's rate of inflation is modest considering her situation, while Switzerland's crept up in 1990–1. The US performance is also perhaps better than expected.

Consider now the unemployment performance. The outstanding performers here are Switzerland, Japan, Norway and New Zealand (the latter until the second half of the 1980s). The US ranking improves significantly as does Sweden's and Austria's. The most consistently poor performers are Belgium, Canada and Italy. The UK is a little below average.

Chapter 44 tries to explain differences in unemployment performance.

36

Choosing the exchange rate regime

INTRODUCTION

Chapters 1–4 *described* the historical experiences of four types of exchange rate regimes: a gold standard, the IMF system, the managed float and the EMS.

What we want to do in this chapter is first to outline the options available to the world economy today and second to take a few tentative steps towards evaluating some of the regimes. Subsequent chapters will continue this task.

EXCHANGE RATE OPTIONS

We consider first the options for the *global* economy, which really comes down to the exchange rate regime operating amongst the big three economies (the G3) – the USA, Japan and Germany. Next, we review the small-country options.

The G3 options

Variations on the float

We note here three potential variations: the first is the pure float, the second is the float modified to 'penalise' capital flows (particularly at the short end of the market) and the third is the managed float.

The target zone proposal

The intention of the target zone proposal is to *formalise* guidelines for exchange rate management (Williamson 1983). The reforms proposed are as follows.

a) There would be a target zone which would comprise a central rate and a band of some 10 per cent on each side of the central rate.
b) The central rate would be defined in real terms, and would be *announced*. At the same time the central rate would move in line with real fundamentals.
c) There would be a firm *commitment* on all sides (in this context the G3) to defend the zones by interest rate policies. For example, if the exchange rate approached or reached the upper (lower) point of the zone the relevant monetary authorities would ease (tighten) interest rates.

There is now a very large literature on the target zone proposal (for a general reference see Frenkel and Goldstein 1986). This by itself is still widely regarded as a viable alternative. Williamson and Miller (1987), however, later extended the target zone proposal to accommodate now a role for fiscal policy as well. The more complete blueprint (as they call it) will be discussed in Chapter 38.

The adjustable peg

Kenen (1988a) and Krugman (1989) have recently advocated a return to an 'adjustable peg' type regime. Kenen proposes a return to a Bretton Woods type system but with wider bands than existed at the time of its demise. In effect he would like to see the G3 adopt a variation of the exchange rate arrangements in the EMS. Krugman has also argued that

> We should avoid a system in which massive exchange rate changes occur all the time for no very good reason, so that exchange rate changes will be effective when we need them, . . . I am now an advocate of an eventual return to a system of more or less fixed rates subject to discretionary adjustment.

> (1989: 99–100)

The differences between the target zone proposal and the adjustable peg may in the end be largely academic and perhaps just a matter of degree. One potential difference is that under the adjustable peg the permitted zone would probably be smaller, with the emphasis placed more squarely on fixing the rate rather than allowing a wide margin of flexibility. Another difference, in the same spirit, is that with an adjustable peg the central rate might change less frequently than envisaged under a target zone regime.

Proposals to fix exchange rates permanently

In recent years the two leading exponents of a return to a permanently fixed exchange rate regime, at least for the big three, are McKinnon (1984, 1988) and Cooper (1984, 1990). To be fair, the authors recognise that there may need to be a fairly long transitional period during which the 'world' economy would gradually converge towards this ultimate objective.

McKinnon's (most recent) proposals are fairly straightforward: permanently fixed exchange rates, symmetrical unsterilised intervention in the key participating countries and coordinated monetary policy directed at stabilising the world price of traded goods.

Cooper would go even further than McKinnon. He would like ultimately to see a common currency established for the major industrialised democracies.

A permanently fixed exchange rate regime would require resolution of the following key issues. First, what will be the initial set of equilibrium exchange rates that will be established? Second, who will have responsibility for setting the 'world' rate of inflation? Third, will there be restrictions on the reserve currencies/assets available under the system? Fourth, and related to the last point, how will the system provide for the secular growth in world reserves?

On the first question McKinnon would fix exchange rates on the basis of purchasing power parity based on a comparable basket of traded goods.

On the second question, both McKinnon and Cooper take the view that it would be a joint decision. Under fixed rates the rate of inflation would be determined by the 'world' money supply, which in turn is the sum of the domestic assets of the 'combined' central banks. Central banks would have responsibility for adjusting their domestic assets to achieve the inflation objectives.

Cooper is explicit about the institutional arrangements.

> The institutional aspects of a common currency are not so difficult to imagine: they could be constructed by adaptation of the US Federal Reserve System, which is an amalgam of twelve separate Reserve Banks, each of which issues its own currency. One could imagine an open market committee for all or any subset of the industrial democracies which would decide the basic thrust of monetary policy for the group as a whole. On it could sit representatives of all member countries, with votes proportional to GNP. At one extreme the representatives could be ministers of finance; at the other they could be outstanding citizens chosen by their governments for long terms solely for the purpose of managing the monetary system. An obvious interim (and possibly permanent) step would be to appoint the senior governors of existing central banks.
>
> (1990: 295)

Under both schemes adjustment would be 'symmetrical' in the sense that regional money supply would be regulated by its overall balance of payments. However, it is also possible to envisage a scheme which is asymmetrical in the sense that a single large key economy would determine the rate of inflation, sterilising its own balance of payments flows, while the other countries did not in fact sterilise. This approaches the Bretton Woods case, under which the USA played a similar role; it is also not unlike the role of Germany today in the EMS. As we have already seen (Chapter

13) the adjustment mechanism is quite different under a symmetrical and an asymmetrical system.

The last two issues were debated in great detail in the 1960s. It is possible to have a single reserve asset, e.g. the US dollar or the special drawing right (SDR), or to allow freedom of choice in the reserve asset. How the system provides for the secular growth in reserves depends on how the last issue is resolved. More precise control is possible only if the SDR were the only reserve asset; however, what is gained in terms of monitoring the growth of reserves is lost in terms of restricting the choice.

Small-country options

In Chapter 3, Section 4, we outlined the exchange rate regimes actually adopted by the smaller economies since the float. Here we review the potential *options* available to these in the current environment. (The options largely correspond to choices actually made at some point.)

First, a European economy can enter into a *collective* exchange rate arrangement such as the EMS (Chapter 4). Second, it can adopt a unilateral adjustable peg with a narrow band (*à la* IMF). The central rate could be pegged to a single currency or to a basket. Third, it can adopt a target zone with an adjustable central rate. Fourth, it can peg permanently to a basket or to a single currency.

What is the difference between the peg to a basket and the peg to the single currency? A basket peg, whilst it stabilises the weighted exchange rate, does not stabilise any *bilateral* rates; by contrast, a peg to a single currency creates at least one 'island of stability'.

Also the external inflation rate to which the country must ultimately conform is different. With a basket the home country's inflation rate must equal the trade-weighted inflation of the trading partners; with a peg it must equal that of the country to which it pegs.

Fifth, it can adopt a crawling peg. In contrast to the adjustable peg, exchange rate adjustments are now much smaller but they are made much more frequently.

Williamson (1981) distinguishes four basic variants:

a) a purchasing power parity (PPP) variant (where the exchange rate adjusts to offset inflation differentials);
b) a crawl based on past exchange rate movements;
c) a crawl based on reserve changes or reserve levels relative to some reserve 'norm';
d) a discretionary crawl (i.e. at the discretion of the monetary authorities).

New Zealand adopted the PPP variant between 1979 and 1982, Australia the discretionary variant between 1976 and 1983 (see Chapter 48).

Sixth, it could adopt a dual exchange rate regime. The authorities now regulate the exchange rate for commercial transactions but allow the rate for capital transactions to float more or less freely.

Belgium had a dual exchange rate regime between 1955 and 1990. France had one between August 1971 and March 1974 and Italy had one between January 1973 and March 1974.

Seventh, finally, it could float, with varying degrees of management.

A FRAMEWORK FOR THE EVALUATION OF EXCHANGE RATE REGIMES

Having outlined the options we now address the question of how such regimes might be evaluated. The chapter will be confined to a general application of principles to alternative regimes. More *formal* evaluation in terms of modelling and of econometric work undertaken is left for later chapters.

There are four key criteria one might apply in any general evaluation. (See on this Argy (1990b).)

The first is micro based and turns on *efficiency* considerations. To begin, an exchange rate regime may deliver efficiency gains from the removal of exchange rate uncertainty. Potential gains include the elimination of or the reduction in the costs of conversion, of portfolio revaluations, of forward cover and of speculation. An exchange rate regime may also, in principle, improve resource allocation in several ways: by mitigating distortions to trade and to capital flows, by maintaining the exchange rate closer to its longer-run 'equilibrium' path or by alleviating the costs of resource shifts.

A second criterion focuses on *inflation discipline*. In essence, we ask which exchange rate regime best succeeds in securing a steady state rate of inflation closest to its 'optimal' level. (The question of the optimal rate of inflation was addressed in Chapter 34.)

A third criterion focuses now on the insulation properties of exchange rate regimes. *Given the policy* stance, we ask here how each regime, in the short run, insulates the economy from disturbances of domestic and of foreign origin. A formal illustration of this approach, but in a broader context, will be provided in Chapters 39 and 40.

A fourth criterion has to do with *policy effectiveness*, i.e. the capacity of each regime to exploit the policy instruments available so as to achieve the key macro targets of policy.

We have, to sum up, four criteria to apply to a large number of potential exchange rate regimes. This is clearly a very tall order. Moreover, the criteria themselves are not always clearly defined or easy to apply. There is therefore no question of carrying out an exhaustive application of the principles to each exchange rate regime. The framework is intended to assist the reader in thinking about regimes. What we do in the sections which follow is provide a general discursive discussion of individual regimes, with closer attention paid to some than to others.

RESTRICTING CAPITAL MOVEMENTS

Several prominent economists (notably Tobin 1978; and Dornbusch 1982a) have expressed concern at the ease with which capital currently flows across frontiers and the magnitude of the amounts involved and have proposed that restrictions be placed on capital flows. The principal advantage these proponents see in limiting capital flows is that it will moderate exchange rate volatility.

The proposals have taken a variety of forms: the reintroduction of capital controls, a small tax on foreign transactions, a real interest rate equalisation tax. Tobin's proposal to impose a small tax on all foreign transactions (including trade transactions) has received the most attention.

Suppose a tax of the order t on foreign transactions is imposed on each trip. Suppose too that the amount invested is x in domestic currency and k is the time period of the transaction. k is expressed as a proportion of the year so if $k = \frac{1}{12}$ this represents an investment of one month; $k = 2$ represents an investment of two years. The amount which accrues in domestic currency for an investment abroad is

$$x(1 - t)^2 (1 + r^* k) \frac{E_e}{E}$$

If there is perfect asset substitution we have

$$x(1 - t)^2 (1 + r^* k) \frac{E_e}{E} = x(1 + r_d k) \tag{1}$$

where r_d and r^* are respectively the annualised interest rate at home and abroad; E_e and E are the expected and actual spot rates. Simplifying the mathematics we can arrive at

$$r_d = \frac{E_e - E}{E} + r^* - \frac{2t}{k} \tag{2}$$

If $t = 0$ we have the open interest rate parity condition.

Suppose now that $(E_e - E)/E = 0$, $t = 0.02$; then if $k = \frac{1}{12}$, $r^* - r_d = 0.48$, and if $k = 2$, $r^* - r_d = 0.02$. A monthly round trip requires that the foreign interest rate exceed the home interest rate by nearly 50 per cent; a two-year round trip requires a difference of only 2 percentage points. As $k \to \infty$ the interest rate parity condition will hold again.

A parallel analysis may be applied to the case where the home interest rate exceeds the foreign rate and there is a potential incentive to invest at home. A tax will now allow the home interest rate to be sustained above the foreign rate.

This serves to emphasise the important fact that a tax of this form will strongly discourage very-short-term capital movements while penalising long-term flows only slightly. If, in fact, it were true that the former are 'destabilising' while the latter are 'productive' the strategy serves to discourage short destabilising capital while 'letting off' more productive capital. At the same time the exchange rate will be stabilised while trade will only be marginally affected.

An almost universal reaction to the proposal is that, unless it were very widely implemented internationally, the tax could be evaded by shifting the transaction to a tax-free zone. Frankel (1988b) puts it as follows: 'If the United States were to impose a tax on foreign exchange transactions business would simply go to London and Tokyo. If G10 imposed the tax ... business would go to Singapore.' Not everyone, however, accepts this argument (see Cooper 1990).

Another common criticism of the proposal is that it would have adverse efficiency-allocation effects. Frenkel and Goldstein (1988), for example, cite a number of potential benefits from free markets: 'lower spreads between lending and deposit rates, increased returns to savers, a lower cost of capital to firms, and better hedging instruments against a variety of risks'.

The question should also be put in broader terms. The tax would effectively reduce the degree of capital mobility so we should also ask how reduced capital mobility affects (a) policy effectiveness and (b) the capacity of an economy to absorb shocks of domestic or foreign origin. Point (a) has already been addressed. The same model framework of Part II can also be used to address (b).

A final point to be made is that since the stock market is more volatile than the foreign exchange market and to avoid one potential 'distortion' a similar tax should also be imposed on stock market transactions (see, for example, Summers 1987). A parallel argument could be made about money market transactions at home.

UNILATERAL EXCHANGE RATE MANAGEMENT

As noted in Chapter 3 there is an important distinction to be made between unilateral exchange rate management and coordinated exchange rate management (involving several countries). The latter is dealt with in Chapter 45; here we deal only with the former.

We need to recall, too, the distinction made between two methods of intervening in foreign exchange markets to stabilise exchange rates: in the one case interest rates are used; in the other the authorities buy and sell foreign currency. Such purchases and sales in turn may or may not be sterilised. In our discussion in this section we focus entirely on the second method.

There are two questions to ask here. First, what are the channels by which intervention impacts on exchange rates? Second, given the potential impacts, were the effects favourable or unfavourable?

On the first question there is now a well-established literature (Edison 1990; Humpage 1991). This literature agrees that there are three potential channels of influence:

a) a direct portfolio balance effect from a sterilised intervention,
b) a direct money stock effect from an unsterilised intervention and
c) a signalling, expectations effect.

Consider first (a). Suppose the currency was falling and the authorities wanted to moderate the fall. They would buy the home currency and sell the foreign currency. Initially the public would hold less cash and more foreign currency. The authorities then undertake a sterilisation operation, buying bonds in exchange for cash. In the end the public will hold fewer bonds and more foreign currency assets. There is thus a change in the composition of the portfolio. Such changes were analysed in Chapter 10. The reader can readily confirm by inspection of the results in that chapter (Table 10.1) that the change in the composition will lead to an appreciation in the currency and a fall in the home interest rate. The results assumed that asset substitution was imperfect (e.g. because of the existence of a risk premium). If asset substitution had been perfect the swap operation would have left both the exchange rate and the interest rate unchanged. (See again the equations underlying the results.) So the success of the operation on the exchange rate hinges on the degree of asset substitution. Ultimately this is an empirical question; *a priori*, however, we should not expect the effect to be strong.

The effect of an unsterilised intervention on the exchange rate is straightforward. To pursue the example above the public will now end up holding less cash and more foreign currency. The currency appreciates and the interest rate rises.

Finally, a swap operation of this kind may also change expectations about the future exchange rate. For example, if the public become convinced that the currency will be *stronger* speculation will come into play and this will reinforce the stabilising effect. (Again, this is readily demonstrated in terms of the framework of Chapter 10.) The importance of the signalling effect is again an empirical matter.

What does the empirical evidence show?

A recent paper by Almekinders and Eijffinger (1991) reviews the empirical literature. It concludes that whilst sterilised intervention *as such* has only a limited capacity to influence the exchange rate the signalling effect could be more significant. This signalling effect operates, partly at least, by 'creating expectations of changes in monetary policy'. This general conclusion is confirmed in another study by Ghosh (1992) who, after controlling for the signalling effect, finds a 'weak, but statistically significant portfolio balance influence on the exchange rate' for sterilised intervention in the dollar–deutschmark market in the 1980s.

Having summarised the theory and the evidence, we can now address our second question: have the effects been favourable or unfavourable?

One avowed objective of exchange rate management is to stabilise the exchange rate around its long-run equilibrium rate. So, to begin, one might ask whether central banks achieved this.

Argy (1982) and Mayer and Taguchi (1983) try to evaluate the degree to which intervention stabilised exchange rates. Argy takes intervention to be stabilising if it 'pushed the exchange rate in the direction of its long-run level'. The 'long-run' level is defined, alternatively, as the PPP rate and as a moving average over six to eighteen months of actual rates. Variants of these tests are also carried out by Mayer and Taguchi. These two studies both find that, in this sense, intervention was on balance stabilising for the currencies studied.

Friedman attacks the question differently. He argues:

> it would do little harm for a government agency to speculate in the exchange market provided it held to the objective of smoothing out temporary fluctuations

and not interfering with fundamental adjustments. And there should be a simple criterion of success – whether the agency makes or loses money.

(1953a: 175)

Later, drawing heavily on a study by Taylor (1982) that found that in fact virtually all central banks had made losses on their foreign exchange operations, Friedman (1978) asserted that intervention had, if anything, destabilised exchange rates.

As it happens calculations of profitability are extremely hard to make. Moreover, there are theoretical objections to the test[1] (see Mayer and Taguchi 1983).

Numerous studies of the profitability of intervention have appeared since Taylor's. In general they do not confirm Taylor's results. Most studies find that on balance profits have been made (see Argy 1982; Bank of England 1983; Jacobson 1983; Jurgensen Report 1983 (especially para. 76); Mayer and Taguchi 1983; Murray *et al*. 1990).

Having said this there is a broader objection to all of these tests. They all assume that if intervention succeeds in stabilising the exchange rate around its equilibrium level *intervention will have been beneficial*. This, however, does not follow. Intervention may have had side-effects e.g. on output, inflation, interest rates, which were not necessarily favourable.

Ideally, what we want to know is the following. With the use of an econometric model we want to compare two scenarios, one with and one without intervention. We would then compare the two macro outcomes and, in principle, decide which is the more favourable. Unfortunately, there is no econometric model sufficiently refined nor are good enough data available on intervention to allow us to do this, so we have to fall back on a simpler way of attacking the question.

To take a concrete example, suppose we had random fluctuations in real private expenditure and these were recognised as such. We know that this will produce cyclical movements in the level of output and in the exchange rate. An upward expenditure shock will increase output and appreciate the currency. Suppose now that the authorities leaned against the wind with unsterilised intervention. This would mean pumping money into the economy in the upswing and reducing it in the downswing, which clearly is destabilising to output while stabilising the exchange rate. (The argument holds for *sterilised* intervention, if feasible, but in a weaker form.)

THE TARGET ZONE PROPOSAL AND THE EUROPEAN MONETARY SYSTEM

The EMS, as we saw in Chapter 4, is really a special case, with somewhat narrow margins, of a coordinated target zone regime (see on this Miller and Weller 1991b; Svensson 1992a; Alogoskoufis *et al*. 1991).

How would the target zone proposal, by itself, perform and what sorts of problems might one encounter in implementing it? (See also the Appendix to this chapter.)

A first problem one encounters is in the calculation of the equilibrium exchange rate. It is well known that there are huge differences in points of view about the fundamental equilibrium rate and how it should be calculated. Some economists lean on some version of relative PPP. According to this the central rate would be adjusted on the basis of relative price movements, e.g. the central rate would be allowed to devalue (appreciate) if inflation at home persistently exceeded (fell short of) that of the rest of the world. The limitations associated with such a PPP calculation are now well known and have been noted elsewhere (see Chapter 31).

Others again prefer to attack the problem directly by trying to calculate a rate which achieves a target current account. Ideally this ought also to correspond to the medium-run current account which reflects autonomous savings–investment decisions at full employment (Williamson 1990).

To illustrate the difficulties of measurement associated with the two approaches we note here that in the mid to late 1980s PPP calculations suggested an equilibrium yen–dollar rate of about 160 and a deutschmark–dollar rate of about 2.27. On the other hand a rate based on a current account target was around 100–110 and 1.41 respectively. At the time the yen rate was about 135 and the deutschmark rate was about 1.55. On PPP calculations both the yen and the deutschmark were substantially overvalued; on the second calculation both were undervalued.

Suppose now the focus is on short-term adjustment to temporary shocks. How will the target zone proposal perform?

1 Consider an upward money demand and a private expenditure disturbance. If the associated exchange rate movement occurs within the band the target zone proposal performs as in a flexible rate regime. If, however, the exchange rate is being pushed outside the zone then monetary policy will have to be brought into action. For a money demand shock the associated appreciation will call for an easier monetary policy which, in this case, is stabilising in all variables. However, for an expenditure disturbance the associated appreciation will again demand an easier monetary policy, now with destabilising effects, as we saw earlier.

Clearly then the target zone proposal may work favourably or unfavourably depending on the source of the shock.

2 We saw in Chapter 33 that exchange markets may not work very efficiently, and in particular that the exchange rate may run away so to speak from its fundamentals. In these cases exchange rate stabilisation may serve to keep markets closer to the fundamentals.

3 If the zone were perfectly credible exchange rate expectations at the upper and lower points of the zone might work to reinforce the zone and stabilise exchange rates. For example at the upper (lower) end the currency would be expected to devalue (appreciate); speculative capital flows would then serve to keep exchange rates within the zone, without the need for monetary intervention. (One obvious way to test for credibility is to see if the forward rate lies outside the bounds. If it does, that would be an indication of a lack of credibility (Chapter 33).)

4 The literature on target zones suggests that there may be a trade-off between exchange rate stability and interest rate stability. In other words it may be that exchange rate stability is achieved at the cost of destabilising interest rates. (See also Chapter 39 for a more formal treatment of this for the limited cases of fixed and flexible rates.) We deal with this now by looking at a number of contingencies that could arise and the light they throw on this potential trade-off.

The case of periodic speculative attacks

Suppose the currency is attacked on a periodic basis. Once it reaches the floor the currency will be defended by raising interest rates; at the same time, there will almost certainly be a loss of reserves.

Over time, then, what we would observe in these circumstances (compared with a flexible rate regime) is some exchange rate stabilisation but at the same time periodic interest rate instability, so in this case there is clearly a trade-off.

The case of external shocks which raise the foreign interest rate

We consider now the case where the foreign interest rate fluctuates. Suppose again we had perfect asset substitution. If the foreign interest rate rose (fell) significantly the domestic currency would fall (rise) to its lower (upper) target level, at which point the domestic interest rate would rise (fall). With a target zone some of the adjustment falls on the exchange rate, some on the interest rate. With flexible rates the adjustment falls on the exchange rate. There is thus again some trade-off between exchange rate and interest rate stabilisation.

Domestic real and monetary disturbances

We return again to the case of monetary and real disturbances. Recalling the underlying analysis, it will be evident that at the upper and lower points interest rate intervention will now stabilise *both* the exchange rate and the interest rate.

Conclusions on the potential trade-off

We have deliberately focused on particular cases to highlight the fact that the ultimate outcome can be very complex. In two instances above some trade-off emerges; however, where domestic shocks dominate there is no trade-off: there is now a reduction in both exchange rate and interest rate volatility.

5 How much monetary independence does a target zone allow? Can a target zone enhance the effectiveness of fiscal policy?

As we know, with perfect asset substitution and a zero target zone an independent monetary policy is not possible. What difference does a zone make? Focusing on the

EMS case, suppose, for argument's sake, that the rate was at its central level; a monetary expansion could push the exchange rate to its lower level. If the exchange rate in six months is expected to be the central rate, then the six-month interest rate annualised could diverge from the foreign rate by as much as $4\frac{1}{2}$ points, a very substantial margin. However, this needs to be qualified in several ways: the gain is temporary since it relies on the assumption of a reversal in the exchange rate; the gain is much weaker at the longer end of the interest rate maturity; expectations may not be as stabilising as represented.

A parallel argument can be made about fiscal policy. We recall that in the MF model with a float and perfect capital mobility, fiscal policy is completely ineffective (Chapter 6). With stabilising expectations a fiscal expansion can now raise the home interest rate relative to the foreign interest rate (reflecting an expected devaluation) and this allows some increase in domestic output.

The points made above, numbered 1–5, were concerned primarily with the short run. Over the medium run a different problem may present itself. Suppose there was a real shock which appreciated the currency in real terms and suppose too that, for a while at least, the central real rate was left unchanged. Monetary policy will be directed at keeping the *real* exchange rate within its bounds, but as we now know monetary policy cannot alter the real rate and so there is a risk that monetary policy will be overexpansionary, producing unnecessary inflation in the pursuit of an exchange rate target.

In summary, then, what case can be made for a target zone regime? First, as against a fixed rate, it does allow some, albeit small and temporary, monetary independence. Second, as against a float, the target zone regime may stabilise the exchange rate around its fundamentals. Moreover, fiscal policy may be more effective than in a float. Third, we note here that, as against an adjustable peg regime, the target zone regime allows the authorities to change the central peg without necessarily altering the actual value of the currency.

THE ADJUSTABLE PEG

Some general comments on the adjustable peg regime follow.

1 In the short run (i.e. between realignments) the adjustable peg regime operates similarly to a permanent peg. In both regimes if capital mobility is very high the authorities lose control over the money supply; on the other hand, if capital mobility is sufficiently restricted sterilisation is feasible and the authorities are able, in principle, to target both the money supply and the exchange rate.

2 It is difficult to operate an adjustable peg regime if the going rate of inflation is persistently and significantly different from that of the trading partners. Such differences would bring continuing pressures for exchange rate adjustment, creating

tensions and uncertainty. In such conditions a crawling peg or a float would be the more appropriate regime. (See item 4 below.)

One precondition, therefore, for the effective functioning of an adjustable peg regime is that the country maintain its rate of inflation within manageable reach of its trading partners. Exchange rate adjustments could then be used, in principle, to correct for *ex post* unanticipated price disturbances or for fundamental imbalances.

3 The fact that the exchange rate can be used periodically as a policy instrument can itself be very disruptive to the economy. In most cases such exchange rate changes are anticipated, provoking large outflows or inflows of capital.

Frequently therefore such movements of capital turn out to be one-way bets at the expense of central banks. A related point is that rumours of changes or suspicions of change may trigger large flows of capital, occasionally forcing the authorities into an unnecessary exchange rate adjustment.

These comments suggest that an adjustable peg regime is likely to function more efficiently if such flows of capital can be monitored – hence the perceived need to support the regime with some control over capital movements. Without restrictions over capital movements the authorities might at times lose control over the money supply or over the exchange rate. For example, an expected devaluation leading to huge outflows might place the authorities in a very serious dilemma: to sharply restrict the money supply and raise interest rates or to go along with market sentiment, which may be misguided, and devalue.

It is significant that, in general, in the countries where an AP has been in operation restrictions on the movement of capital have been in force (e.g. Sweden, Norway, Finland, Australia, New Zealand).

4 We can pursue 2 and 3 further here. We focus now on the implications, for interest rate behaviour, of a realignment of the central rate, anticipated some time in the future.

Suppose there is a build-up in imbalances (e.g. because of an excessive creation of credit) which is periodically neutralised by a realignment (devaluation).

Consider first the extreme case where the date and magnitude of the realignment is known with certainty and there is perfect asset substitution. Suppose the realignment occurs annually on a *particular* date. The interest rate maturity has to reflect the expected devaluation over that term. For example, three months before the event the nominal interest rate has to be set sufficiently above the foreign interest rate to compensate for the devaluation expected over the three months. A month earlier the interest rate differential on a one-month maturity has to be even higher. For example, if the devaluation is expected to be 5 per cent the annualised interest rate differential has to be roughly 60 per cent. As the date gets very close the interest rate on very short maturities (e.g. on overnight rates) will reach near-astronomical heights, a situation which is effectively untenable. (Note that, in principle at any rate, such interest rate changes avert the need to run down reserves.)

Suppose now, much more realistically, that there is *uncertainty* about the date or the magnitude of the realignment. Such uncertainty means that the interest rate margins are no longer as predictable, nor need they reach near-astronomical levels. Capital controls or the existence of a risk premium can also further relieve the situation.

We can compare these outcomes with the case of a smooth downward crawl, with the interest rate set on average above the foreign level to absorb the crawl. There is now a periodic (large) adjustment to the exchange rate against a smooth adjustment. At the same time, the interest rate movement will be more erratic. In one sense, both the exchange rate and the interest rate are destabilised by the adjustable peg.

5 If wages are fully indexed, a devaluation to correct a fundamental imbalance in the current account may be self-defeating, necessitating, ultimately, a new devaluation (Chapter 8). This creates the potential for a 'vicious' devaluation cycle. (To some extent this represents the earlier Swedish and Finnish experience.) This highlights the importance of accompanying a devaluation with a wages policy. The difficulty is that the exchange rate adjustment has to occur first, and so the authorities have to gamble that any subsequent wage negotiation will be successful. As a matter of fact, nearly all countries which have devalued have tried to implement a wages policy that will minimise the spillover of a devaluation into wages.

6 In the adjustable peg regime the authorities are required to make the very difficult judgement about when to adjust the currency and also by how much. If the market disagrees with their judgement on the size of the adjustment further uncertainty is created. Even if the market went along with the decision there is still a question of, say, whether the amount of the exchange rate adjustment will be adequate, taking account of relevant elasticities and spillovers into wages, to correct the imbalance in due course.

7 The role of real wage flexibility is critical.

Suppose we had *symmetrical* real wage flexibility in the sense that any change in the real wage rate (given unemployment) secured under, say, an adjustable peg regime can as readily and as speedily be secured under a peg.

It is evident that, in these circumstances at any rate, an adjustable peg regime offers no real advantage. The wage rate can now replace the exchange rate as a policy instrument. Indeed, since an exchange rate change is more disturbing than a wage change, this would count as a disadvantage of the adjustable peg.

Friedman (1953a), making his classic case for flexible rates, based one argument in favour of flexible rates on an asymmetry. Keynes also thought that real wages could be reduced by raising prices, but not so by lowering wages. Asymmetry could come from straight money illusion (particularly if a wage cut is required) or from the fact that wage policies are harder to negotiate and take longer than an adjustment to the exchange rate.

To sum up, if there is asymmetrical real wage flexibility and a fundamental imbalance in the current account emerges, the adjustable peg regime has a clear advantage over the peg. With a peg, output will have to be sacrificed to secure current account objectives.

THE CRAWLING PEG

We limit our comments here to the PPP crawl and the discretionary crawl. (For a discussion of the PPP crawl, see Dornbusch (1982b) and Adams and Gros (1986).) New Zealand's experience with the first and Australia's experience with the second will be briefly discussed in Chapter 48.

The PPP crawl

a) A PPP crawl, by definition, roughly maintains a country's competitive position. At the same time, exchange rate adjustments are relatively small and fairly predictable. These are the main advantages of a PPP crawl.

b) A PPP crawl may be giving the green light to a potentially high-inflation country to maintain its relatively high rate of inflation. From the standpoint of 'discipline' therefore the PPP crawl may be inferior to the adjustable peg.

c) As noted, with relative inflation rates largely known the crawl may be fairly predictable. If there are no restrictions on capital flows, the country crawling downwards (upwards) will have to maintain an interest rate advantage (disadvantage) which will exactly offset the anticipated exchange rate change. Thus, as Williamson (1981) notes, monetary policy could not be used for internal stabilisation (but, in principle, of course fiscal policy could be). In this respect, at any rate, the PPP crawl operates in a way which is similar to a peg with perfect asset substitution.

d) There will be occasions when a change in the real exchange rate will be needed. For example, whilst competitiveness may be maintained a current account imbalance may emerge, which may require a change in the real exchange rate. It is difficult, however, to accommodate periodic changes in real exchange rates within the system without exposing the economy to speculative bursts. At this point the system will resemble the adjustable peg.

e) Trying to maintain the real exchange rate in the face of a real shock may be destabilising at times. Suppose the model of Chapter 8 were the appropriate one and suppose too that we had full wage indexation, perfect capital mobility and a fixed exchange rate.

   An upward real disturbance (e.g. a fiscal expansion) will then lead to an expansion in both output and prices (see Chapter 8, Table 8.2). The authorities will now devalue to maintain the real exchange rate but, as Chapter 8 also showed, this will ultimately be self-defeating.

f) A relatively minor point is that there is a wide range of potential relative price indices that might be used as a basis for the PPP crawl: export prices, consumer prices, unit labour costs, wholesale prices.

The discretionary crawl

The principal difference between the discretionary crawl and the PPP crawl is that the basis of the crawl is now more flexible. This is both an advantage and a disadvantage. It is an advantage because, if necessary, the authorities can fine tune the small adjustments to the ongoing conditions. This also allows somewhat more scope for an independent monetary policy. It is a disadvantage because the crawl is now less *predictable* and so the system becomes more exposed to speculation, albeit on a modest scale.

In other respects it is similar to the PPP crawl. Inflation 'discipline' is lacking; at the same time if large changes in fundamentals occur the public will not believe that small changes are sustainable and the system will lose credibility.

We will illustrate some at least of the general points made above about the crawling peg by reference to the Australian and New Zealand experience.

DUAL EXCHANGE RATES

There has recently been a strong revival of interest in dual exchange rate regimes. Some very brief comments follow.

a) The dual exchange rate regime is a useful device for protecting commercial transactions as well as prices/wages from the vagaries of exchange rate movements. At the same time volatile capital flows can be absorbed by movements in the rate on capital transactions.
b) There are technical–administrative difficulties in managing a dual rate, however. The difficulties take two forms: how to define a capital and a commercial transaction and how to stop leakages between the two accounts if the rates diverge too significantly (Lanyi 1975).
c) There may well be a resource cost in applying different rates to different foreign exchange transactions. For example, in France tourism was treated as a capital expenditure/receipt and hence subject to the capital account rate which was different from the commercial rate.

For an analysis of the insulation properties of a dual rate regime, see Guidotti (1988) and Argy and Porter (1972).

COSTS AND BENEFITS OF JOINING AND PARTICIPATING IN A MONETARY UNION

We address now the question of the costs and benefits of joining a monetary union, such as that envisaged by the Maastricht agreement.

From the start we need to define the alternative with which this union is being compared. We will assume throughout that it is a flexible rate regime. In the two regimes we suppose that capital is free to move. Thus the question we address is: what are the benefits accruing from a single money and what are the *costs associated with the loss of the exchange rate instrument*?

We proceed in three steps. First, we try to spell out the *steady state* costs and benefits of membership compared with being on the outside (with flexible rates). Second, we try to say something about the *transitional* costs and benefits of joining. Third, we try to identify the country characteristics which determine what the costs of membership are likely to be. In essence, we ask here what constitutes an optimal currency zone (Mundell 1961; Ishiyama 1975).

Steady-state costs and benefits

There are, first, efficiency gains from joining a union. These were defined earlier. Emerson and Huhne (1991) report that the elimination of the present costs of converting one currency into another might produce gains of something of the order of 0.4 per cent of community output. Other efficiency gains however, are, much more difficult to estimate.

A related benefit is that capital will now flow even more freely in the union. This is because the absence of exchange rate changes eliminates any risk from capital movements.

A second benefit flows from the possibility that the union's common currency might serve as a reserve currency to the rest of the world. In this case the union would effectively be 'borrowing' on a permanent basis from the rest of the world, and using the funds to invest long term or to absorb resources from the rest of the world. (See on this Chapter 2.)

Third, it is frequently contended that there will also be a benefit flowing from the inflation discipline imposed on a member. However, this argument is more difficult to evaluate. Much depends on what the steady state rate of inflation would have been under flexible rates. This question was addressed in Chapter 25. The conclusion reached there was that, in principle at any rate, inflation discipline might be achieved under flexible rates if the central bank were made more independent, with inflation its dominant target. Moreover, in steady state in a union, there might be a permanent cost associated with adopting a *common* rate of inflation which may not be appropriate to the country.

We turn now to the *potential* costs of losing the exchange rate as an instrument and of accepting the rules governing the monetary union. We emphasise here potential costs because not all of the costs identified are necessarily costs, as we shall see.

A cost frequently identified is the loss of the monetary instrument (Feldstein 1992). This *presumes* that having the active use of a monetary instrument is a clear advantage, which of course begs the question. We have already raised this question in several places. It all depends on how wisely the monetary instrument will be used. (We return to this question below.)

A similar argument might be made about fiscal policy with one or two important differences. *In principle*, the short-term effectiveness of fiscal policy is enhanced in a fixed rate regime, so this *ought* to be a gain. However, the reality is that member countries in the union will be constrained in their use of fiscal policy, so this instrument may not be available.

Another potential cost flows from the fact that in the face of real disturbances the loss of the exchange rate adjustment may impose additional economic hardship. Suppose there is a real demand shift away from one member's product towards another member's product. Real adjustment requires that there be a real devaluation of the first member and a real appreciation of the second member. In the absence of any exchange rate adjustment prices and wages must fall in the first member and rise in the second member, but the end result may be harder to realise this way than with an exchange rate adjustment (as we have already noted in our discussion of the adjustable peg regime).

In the same spirit we can imagine, say, an oil price shock impacting differently on the different members and again requiring of union members wage–price adjustments which may prove costlier than exchange rate changes.

Yet another potential cost may come from the loss of seigniorage. Countries which have to reduce their inflation rates will suffer a loss of inflation revenue; this needs to be replaced by some combination of increasing taxes, increasing debt (which is in any event restricted) or reducing government expenditure.

Transitional costs and benefits

The benefits–costs outlined above are those that might *ultimately* accrue to member countries. In the meantime, however, there will be adjustment costs.

Suppose the country had a rate of inflation on entry which exceeded that which was common to the union or to the key country in the union (say Germany). Suppose too, for argument's sake, that the benefits from disinflating exceed the costs. The key question then reduces to comparing the costs of disinflating with flexible rates and those of disinflating with a peg. This question was also addressed in Chapter 22. We concluded then that the evidence on this was quite ambiguous, although at the theoretical level a presumptive case could be made that the costs will be less under a peg.

The optimal currency zone

All we have done so far is indicate the potential costs of joining a currency union. What we need to address now is the question of what determines the magnitude of such costs. In particular, what country characteristics serve to minimise such costs and hence make entry into a union an attractive proposition? Countries which meet these country characteristics are said to qualify for a currency zone. So we really want to know whether potential EMS member countries constitute an optimal currency zone. At the same time, whilst labouring on the EMS, we will also enquire how the EMS compares with the USA from the perspective of an optimal currency zone. The USA is made up of several distinct regions which, in principle, are comparable with the members of the EMS. Also, there is of course a single currency which is in use in the USA as in the currency union envisaged.

Openness (regional interdependence) is often advanced as a characteristic that serves to alleviate the costs of losing the exchange rate instrument. Why is this?

Put simply, the more open an economy is to trade, the smaller is likely to be the degree of money illusion; thus an exchange rate change will be less effective in securing an improvement in the real exchange rate. At the same time, in an open economy with fixed rates the use of demand management will be less effective and the leakages larger. The larger leakages also mean that adjustment in the current account can be achieved at less cost in terms of unemployment. Moreover, the more open the economy, the greater the potential cost of exchange rate volatility. At the same time the increased efficiency of money is itself a function of openness. One might therefore expect very open economies to opt for less exchange rate flexibility. On the other hand, openness may increase a country's exposure to external shocks under fixed rates.

Despite what appear to be ambiguities, openness has been widely perceived by academics and authorities as a strong element favouring exchange rate stability. For example, a study by the OECD of exchange rate practices in member countries notes, with reference to the Netherlands, that:

> The Netherlands has a very open economy, with exports and imports of goods and services each amounting to more than 50 per cent of national income. The immediate influence of the exchange rate on prices has led the authorities to attach a high priority to maintaining a stable exchange rate.
>
> (1985: 97)

Referring to Belgium, the study states that:

> Since Belgium has a very open economy, the stability of the Belgian franc's exchange rate against the currencies of its main trading partners has always been one of the monetary authorities' main preoccupations.
>
> (1985: 97)

How does the EMS compare with the USA in this regard? The degree of intra-regional trade is higher in Europe than it is in North America, so in this respect, at any rate, Europe qualifies better as a currency union.

A second important consideration is the degree of real wage flexibility. As we have seen, countries which have a high degree of real wage flexibility are better equipped to cope with real shocks and so will miss the loss of the exchange rate instrument less.

How do EMS countries and the USA compare in this respect? The widely held view that there is more real wage rigidity in Europe than in the USA is probably correct. This means that the USA comes closer to being an optimal currency zone than the EMS does.[2] On the other hand, with the widespread abandonment of wage indexation provisions in Europe there appears to be a trend towards increased flexibility in that region. Moreover, monetary unification is likely to enhance wage flexibility, given the loss of the exchange rate instrument.

A third consideration is the degree of labour mobility. Suppose again that we had a demand switch as above. Mundell (1961) argued that the emerging unemployment in the depressed area and the excess demand could be eased by migration from the first to the second country.

In this respect the USA has a substantial advantage over the EMS countries. Despite the geographical proximity there remains an important language and cultural barrier in the EMS absent from the USA. It is also noteworthy that factor mobility in the USA has not prevented wide differences in unemployment rates amongst the states (Eichengreen 1990).

A fourth very important consideration, implicit in the earlier discussion, is the degree to which members of a union are exposed to similar shocks. The significance of this is perhaps self-evident. If shocks are very similar, then

a) the loss of the macro policy instrument is less important (the union as a whole might choose to act in a cooperative away to combat the shock);
b) there is less need for real adjustment between members.

Shocks may be country specific or they may be common to all *but impact differently on the member states*. An obvious example of the latter is the case of an oil price shock. Sterling is a petro-currency and would be expected to respond quite differently from other members; Texas, too, in the USA, as the oil producer would also be affected differently.

Bayoumi and Eichengreen (1992) have analysed the importance of demand and supply shocks in Europe and the USA. The results are mixed and complicated, but in general point to shocks being more symmetric in type and response in the USA than in Europe.

Feldstein provides a good example of regional shocks and their importance within the USA:

During the 1980s the New England economy benefited from a strong national demand for the products and services in which it specialises, particularly computers, military equipment and financial services. The increased demand for these 'exports' from New England to the rest of the United States caused a rise in their prices and in the relative level of New England wages and salaries. During the decade of the 1980s, real incomes per head grew twice as fast in Massachusetts as in the rest of the country.

But now the demand for computers, for military equipment and for financial services has declined. Until there is a relative decline in New England wages and in the prices of New England's 'exports' to the rest of the country, the level of unemployment in New England will be abnormally high. Massachusetts has the second-highest unemployment rate among the industrial states, topped only by

Michigan. To shrink that unemployment, Massachusetts wages will have to decline relative to wages elsewhere in the nation.

Slowing the growth of wages is a painful process, accompanied by a high level of unemployment, declining property values and the widespread failure of New England banks. New England could deal with the transition in a much less painful way if there were a flexible 'New England dollar' that could be allowed to decline in value relative to the currencies of America's other regions.

(1992: 19–22)

Fifth, Kenen (1969) has argued that the more *diversified* the economy, the more insulated it will tend to be from micro shocks; it follows that the need for exchange rate flexibility, as a protection against such shocks, will be diminished. Hence, the case for a union is strengthened the more diversified internally the economies are. This consideration is probably of lesser importance; but in any event, whilst in general Europe does have a diversified production structure (Frenkel and Goldstein 1991) it is difficult to compare it with the USA in this respect.

To conclude then it seems that in most respects (labour mobility, wage flexibility, similarity of shocks) the USA is closer to an optimal currency zone; in other respects, however (openness), the EMS is closer to an optimal currency zone.

APPENDIX   TARGET ZONES – KRUGMAN'S MODEL, ITS LIMITATIONS AND EXTENSIONS

The technical literature on the subject is now very large. Svensson (1992b) has recently tried to summarise some of this literature in non-technical language. This Appendix draws on Svensson's paper. (See also Krugman (1991) and Krugman and Miller (1992).)

Much of the technical literature took off with a paper by Krugman which circulated for a while before it was published in 1991. The subsequent literature modified and extended Krugman's original model. Krugman's model was also the subject of numerous empirical tests applied primarily to the EMS and to Sweden.

Krugman's model

Krugman's model starts with the assumption that the exchange rate is determined by its fundamentals and as well by the expected value of the exchange rate. The fundamental in the simple model has two components: the velocity (of money) which is assumed to follow a random walk with zero mean; the money stock, which is fixed except when intervention to stabilise exchange rates is undertaken.

Krugman makes two key assumptions: first, intervention occurs only at the end points of the zone, i.e. there is no intra-marginal intervention; second, that the bands are perfectly credible, i.e. no realignment of the central rate is expected.

What will be the behaviour of the exchange rate under a pure float? We reproduce equation (13) of Chapter 31:

$$e = \frac{1}{1 + \alpha_6} \, \text{mo} \, \ldots \, \frac{\alpha_6}{1 + \alpha_6} \, e_e$$

If velocity in fact follows a simple random walk, then the best forecast of the exchange rate is the current value of the money stock. If we replace e_e by mo, then it is readily seen that the exchange rate will follow the path of the money stock. In Figure 36.1, the schedule FF which has a slope of unity represents this case.

Krugman shows that the target zone schedule will be S shaped. The reason is that, with perfect credibility as the upper (lower) zones are approached, there will be an increased probability that the exchange rate will reverse itself. At the edges speculators will face one way bets in the sense that the exchange rate can now only move in the one direction.

Empirical tests of the Krugman model

There are several empirical implications of the model which can be and have been tested.

One implication is that the larger the devaluation the lower the domestic interest rate relative to the foreign rate (because an appreciation will be expected). This is rejected by the data. Also, if one plots some measure of the fundamental against the exchange rate, we do not get the S shape of the Krugman model.

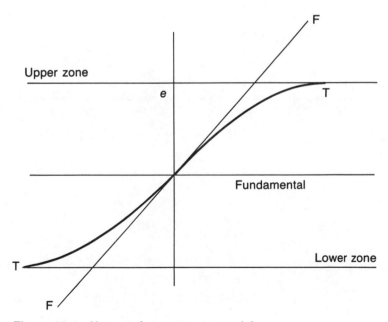

Figure 36.1 Krugman's target zone model

The empirical evidence is also against the assumption of perfect credibility. Periodic speculative attacks on EMS currencies (including those which occurred in the second half of 1992) provide striking evidence against this. Forward rate data confirm this. Finally, intra-marginal intervention within the EMS turns out to be more the rule than the exception.

Modifications and extensions

The Krugman model needs to be modified in three directions at least to make it conform more to reality. First, it must accommodate marginal intervention. Second, the fundamental does not necessarily follow a random walk with zero mean; this too needs to be modified. Third, and most important, the possibility of a realignment must also be accommodated. This can be done in a variety of ways, e.g. we can define a realignment rule which says that when the currency reaches the floor or the ceiling the central rate will be adjusted downwards or upwards.

Evidently these extensions make the models even more complex and technical. Such formal extensions take us far beyond the scope of this book. Suffice it to say that modifications of the kind noted can yield predictions which now conform much more to the observed data.

37

Rules versus discretion

INTRODUCTION

This chapter is in two parts. In Sections 1–5 we review the case made for simple rules. The approach is historical in the sense that we focus on the evolution of the case for rules (against discretion) made in the postwar years. Easily the most important person in this debate is Milton Friedman, so it is only appropriate to centre the discussion around some of his ideas. In describing the evolution of the debate we shall draw on some work developed in previous chapters.

In Sections 6 and 7 we summarise the more important kinds of monetary–fiscal rules which have been proposed. Our focal point is again Friedman; extensions are then made to Friedman's proposals.

THE KEYNESIAN FRAMEWORK FOR STABILISATION

Early Keynes

The early postwar short-run Keynesian framework was as follows.

a) Up to full employment nominal wages were 'rigid'. In the simple Keynesian text-book case so were prices; however, in more sophisticated Keynesian analysis the domestic price level would rise as full employment was approached so as to produce a fall in real wages. The problem of inflation (which was thought to come principally from excess demand) surfaced only after full employment was reached.

b) The private sector was very unstable; investment in particular was volatile and subject to 'animal spirits'. Some early Keynesians also believed that capitalist economies would be exposed to secular stagnation, i.e. there would be insufficient investment to absorb long-run savings.

c) An adverse demand shock could place the economy below its full employment level, where, in principle, it could remain for an indefinite period. With rigid wages there was no automatic mechanism by which full employment could be restored.[1]

These notions provided the analytical base for stabilisation policy. In the face of some involuntary unemployment, governments would increase aggregate demand, increase the price level, reduce real wages and thus restore full employment. Government intervention would also be needed to avert potential secular stagnation.

The choice between monetary and fiscal policies as instruments to achieve stabilisation objectives depended on the structural coefficients of the Keynesian system. The steeper (flatter) the IS schedule and the flatter (steeper) the LM schedule, the stronger the case for the use of fiscal (monetary) policy. In 'simplistic' Keynesianism LM would be represented as relatively flat (implying a high interest elasticity of money demand), while IS would be represented as relatively steep (implying a low interest sensitivity of investment), thus favouring the active use of fiscal rather than monetary policy.

The Phillips curve analysis and the open economy

During the late 1950s and early 1960s the Phillips curve dominated much of macroeconomic thinking. The Phillips curve identified a negative relationship between the rate of growth of wages or inflation and the rate of unemployment. This meant now that governments could not take the view that inflation could be disregarded until full employment was reached; nor was there a clearly defined point which could be taken to represent full employment.

The identification of a Phillips curve was also widely interpreted to mean that governments could now choose a particular combination of inflation and unemployment. In reality, however, in the Bretton Woods system which prevailed in those years the design of macro policy was more complicated. On the one hand, because the USA was able to finance its deficits by creating official dollar liabilities against itself (and hence did not have a balance of payments constraint), it was relatively free to choose its inflation–unemployment combination. On the other hand, other countries were subject to more severe constraints in designing their macro policies.

Consider a country which chose a combination which gave it a rate of inflation above that of say the rest of the world. It would then have to do one (or a combination) of three things: (a) devalue on a regular basis; (b) expose itself to intermittent external crises and be forced to adopt stop–go type policies; (c) try and improve its Phillips curve trade-off by the adoption of an appropriate incomes policy and/or manpower labour market policies. Failing (c), and given the IMF constraints on exchange rate adjustments, the country would sooner or later have to conform to the world rate of inflation and hence accept the corresponding unemployment rate.

By contrast a country which chose an inflation rate below world levels, given again the constraints on exchange rate adjustments, would be threatened with imported inflation.

In the fixed exchange rate world of the 1950s and 1960s the balance of payments loomed as an important constraint on policy. Thus governments became concerned over external as well as internal balance. Monetary policy came to be seen in those years as the appropriate instrument for external balance, and fiscal policy for employment. (Mundell (1962), as we saw in Chapter 35, provided the analytical rationale for this assignment.)

To sum up, then, macro policy could be seen as being conducted with three principal objectives in mind: high employment, low inflation and balance in the overseas accounts. The three instruments corresponding to these objectives were respectively fiscal, income and monetary policies. Stabilisation policy was still feasible but it now had to be put in a wider context and subject to a number of constraints.

FRIEDMAN'S ATTACK ON ACTIVISM

At the same time that the Keynesians were arguing the case for an activist policy Friedman, beginning in the early 1950s, launched a vigorous attack on such policies. Friedman's criticisms, which were multi-pronged, were based on political as well as economic considerations.

On the political front, Friedman took the view that governments do not necessarily act in the public interest and hence would be likely to adopt politically advantageous short-run policies which were against the longer-run public interest.

On the economic front, Friedman asserted that there were limitations in our 'ability to predict both the behaviour of the system in the absence of action and the effect of action'. As well there were long lags in the effects of (monetary) policy: these were 'the lag between the need for action and the recognition of this need, the lag between the recognition of the need for action and the taking of action and the lag between the action and its effects'. These (monetary policy) lags were not only long but also variable (Friedman 1969b).

Friedman also claimed that bond-financed fiscal policy would be likely to be ineffective, at least after a short time lapse. Precisely how fiscal expansion would crowd out the private sector remained just a little vague in Friedman's writings (Friedman 1970); he did offer several suggestions, however, many of which were developed in the subsequent literature.

To begin, he claimed that the IS schedule would tend to be relatively flat while the LM schedule would tend to be relatively steep. These are the conditions in which initial fiscal effects will tend to be weak. He also claimed that subsequent developments would weaken the real effects still further. There would be some reduction in private sector investment, reducing potential output in the future. There were also hints of direct substitutability between government and private expenditure.

At the same time continuing deficit financing (bond creation), by increasing money demand, would shift the LM schedule to the left; there would not be a significant off-setting wealth effect on expenditure, however (shifting the IS to the right), because the effect of additional bond holdings would be largely offset by an increase in expected future tax liabilities (Chapters 11 and 26).

Yet another attack on the effectiveness of fiscal policy flowed from one of Friedman's contributions: the permanent income hypothesis for consumption. Eisner (1969) showed that an income tax cut, say, which was thought to be temporary would produce very little increase in consumption and hence would be relatively ineffective.

Finally Friedman also contended that (a) with relatively stable monetary and fiscal policies in place the private sector will also be relatively stable; (b) in the face of pri-vate sector shocks the economy was, in any event, inherently resilient, absorbing these shocks with only minimal disruption.

At a more conceptual level, Friedman (1953b) tried to show that for government policies to be counter-cyclical the correlation coefficient between government actions and income (free of the effects of policies) would not only have to be negative but significantly negative.

Suppose we have

$$y_t = x_t + g_t$$

where y is the actual level of activity, x is the level of activity without the effects of policy and g is the addition to or the subtraction from the level of activity due to the effects of policy.

Taking variances of the above we have

$$\sigma^2{}_y = \sigma^2{}_g + \sigma^2{}_x + 2\rho_{xg}\sigma_x\sigma_g$$

where ρ stands for the correlation coefficient between x and g, σ^2 is the variance and σ is the standard deviation.

To demonstrate Friedman's case against discretion let us suppose for simplicity that $\sigma_x = \sigma_g$, i.e. the standard deviation of these two series is the same. We can then rewrite the second equation as

$$\frac{\sigma^2{}_y}{\sigma^2{}_x} = 2(1 + \rho_{xg})$$

The objective of stabilisation policy is to have $\sigma^2{}_y < \sigma^2{}_x$, i.e. the variance of activity after policy should be less than the variance of activity without policy. So we require that

$$\frac{\sigma^2{}_y}{\sigma^2{}_x} < 1$$

We can rewrite the previous equation as

$$\rho_{xg} < -\frac{1}{2}$$

The correlation coefficient has to be (negative) larger than 0.5 for policy to be stabilising. As an example, if

$$\frac{\sigma^2_y}{\sigma^2_x} = 0.7$$

(i.e. some 30 per cent of the initial variance of income is removed) we require that $\rho_{xg} = -0.65$.

Not content with simply making a presumptive case against discretion Friedman also tried to demonstrate that monetary policy had in fact tended to be destabilising (Friedman and Schwartz 1963; Bordo and Schwartz 1983).

For all these reasons then (theoretical, empirical and political) Friedman concluded that policy would be likely to be destabilising rather than stabilising. His own prescription (Friedman 1959) was to legislate to have money grow at a fixed rate – his famous constant money growth rule.

THE REACTION TO FRIEDMAN

Friedman's case against discretion directly or indirectly provoked a huge literature during the 1960s and early 1970s. This literature was at two levels: theoretical and empirical. The theoretical literature concerned itself with Friedman's theoretical case against discretion; on the other hand the empirical literature attempted to evaluate whether or not policy had or had not been stabilising.

The more important theoretical contributions came from Baumol (1961), who followed on the heels of Phillips (1957), Tucker (1966), Brainard (1967) and Fischer and Cooper (1973). A discussion and summary of the issues raised in this debate appear in Moore (1972), Okun (1972), Modigliani (1977), Turnovsky (1977), Gordon (1978), Tobin (1980) and Bryant (1980).

Phillips (1957) was one of the first to address the kinds of issues raised by Friedman. Phillips, using differential equations, evaluated the effectiveness of stabilisation policy in the context of a simple multiplier–accelerator type model. He distinguished three types of discretionary policies: first, a 'proportional' policy, where governments react to the gap between actual and full employment output; second, a 'derivative' policy where governments react to the preceding change in output; third, an 'integral' policy where governments react to the sum of past deviations in output from its full employment level. His principal contribution was to show that the effectiveness of policy depended on (a) the dynamics of the system, (b) the type of policy adopted and (c) the lags in policy adjustment.

Baumol (1961), using difference equations, took up this theme and reached similar conclusions. Allowing policy to respond with some lag and given the multiplier–

accelerator framework one ends up with a typical second-order difference equation, which may or may not be stable (Turnovsky 1977: 318–28).

Tucker (1966) addressed Friedman's point that monetary policy lags were long and hence policy was likely to be destabilising. Tucker showed that long lags in the product market did not necessarily translate into long lags in the effects of monetary policy. Suppose there is a long lag in the response of investment to an interest rate change and suppose too that the demand for money with respect to the interest rate is inelastic in the short run and much more elastic in the long run. Then a drop in the money supply will generate very strong increases in the interest rate, countering the weak initial effects on expenditure; later the interest rate drops back, neutralising, in part at least, the delayed effects on expenditure.

Howrey (1969) noted, too, that if monetary policy is used to counter disturbances, then the lags in the product and money markets will also determine the lags in the *effects* of such disturbances. If these disturbances have long lags it is appropriate for monetary policy to have long lags too.

Brainard (1967), in an important contribution, addressed himself to Friedman's contention that uncertainty about future developments as well as uncertainty about the size of the policy multiplier made discretionary policy hazardous to undertake.

Suppose we have the following reduced form equation: $Y = ax + u$ where Y stands for output, x is the policy instrument, a is the policy multiplier and u is a disturbance to output. Friedman had based his case against discretion on the uncertainty surrounding both a and u, so we want to evaluate the policy implications of these two types of uncertainties.

For policy purposes some expectation will be formed about the mean value of both a and u; at the same time there will be some error surrounding the expected mean value. For a this error (potential variation) will be larger the greater the deviation of x from its normal-historical level.

The following can readily be derived:[2]

$$x_0 = \frac{\bar{a}(Y_\mathrm{f} - \bar{u}) - \rho\sigma_a\sigma_u}{\bar{a}^2 + \sigma^2{}_a}$$

where x_0 represents the optimal setting of policy, Y_f is full employment output and ρ is the correlation coefficient between the two standard deviations. A bar over a coefficient indicates its mean value.

With complete certainty we have $\sigma_a = \sigma_u = 0$ and the result is the standard multiplier $(Y_\mathrm{f} - \bar{u})/\bar{a}$. If $\sigma_a = 0$ (there is no multiplier uncertainty) the result is unchanged. If, however, there is no uncertainty about u, $\sigma_u = 0$, the result is

$$x_0 = \frac{Y_\mathrm{f} - \bar{u}}{\bar{a} + \sigma^2{}_a/\bar{a}}$$

It is readily seen that the optimal setting of policy is now less than previously; how much less depends on the ratio of the standard deviation of a to the mean of a. This ratio increases the more 'vigorous' the policy.

The important result here is that multiplier uncertainty, but not so disturbance uncertainty, creates a case for more modest use of activist policy. At the same time this same argument offers a case for the use of more than one instrument even to achieve a single target.

The last conclusion can be further reinforced when account is taken of the fact that there are also costs associated with policy changes. These could be administrative, resource-allocation costs (notably in the case of fiscal policy), or they could be the result of side-effects (e.g. interest rate fluctuations flowing from the active use of monetary policy) (see Okun 1972). These costs also impose some constraint on activist policies.

Fischer and Cooper (1973) also made an important contribution to the debate over whether long monetary lags were likely to be destabilising to policy. It turns out, not surprisingly, that there is always some optimal feedback policy which will perform better than a simple money growth rule. A simple rule is therefore never a first-best policy. However, this in itself is not very helpful or very surprising. Suppose k represents the multiple of the optimal discretionary policy. Then they were able to demonstrate that within the range $0 < k < 2$ the variance of income under an activist policy is less than the variance of income under a rule. When $k = 0$ we have of course the rule. Thus from this analysis it appears that, provided policy is modest and not too aggressive, activism is superior to a rule. At the same time it also turns out that the longer the expenditure lag the stronger is the optimal monetary policy needed. The stronger the optimal policy the greater the range over which discretionary monetary policy outperforms a rule. Paradoxically, then, the longer the lag the greater the scope for stabilising monetary policy.

To sum up, then, much of the theoretical analysis in the end proved inconclusive. Everything depended on how dynamics were represented and how policy reacted. (See the Appendix for an example of an optimal monetary policy derived from an explicit model, albeit a simple one.)

As noted, there was, as well, a considerable empirical literature attempting to evaluate whether or not policy had been stabilising. The literature, which continues to this day, is reviewed in Chapter 40.

THE VERTICAL PHILLIPS CURVE

Although Friedman's early analysis implied the existence of an NRU, it was not in fact until the late 1960s that Friedman (1968) together with Phelps (1968) developed and highlighted the theory of the vertical Phillips curve and its associated NRU.

In this framework, a sharp distinction is made between the short-run and the long-run Phillips curve. In the long run the Phillips curve is vertical at the economy's NRU. In the short run, however, there is a negative trade-off between inflation and unemployment.

There were at least three macro policy implications flowing from this development. First, macro policy must ultimately be ineffective; moreover, any disturbances to which the economy is exposed will also be self-correcting. Second, if governments misjudged the true NRU, or if the NRU was very variable, there was a real risk that policy would push the economy into an ever-accelerating rate of inflation (or rate of deflation), and so policy would, so to speak, be 'walking a tight-rope' (Chapter 28).

Third, unemployment in much of the analyses was based on misperceptions; it was also 'voluntary' (Chapter 28). Such unemployment was not as serious or as urgently in need of attention as was involuntary unemployment. Hence the need for counter-active policies is lessened.

The counter arguments were at several levels. First, much depended on how rapidly the economy returned to its NRU. If expectations were formed adaptively or long-term contracts were in force or wages were institutionally tied to past inflation, wage and price adjustment would be very sluggish and hence the economy could take a long time to return to equilibrium, allowing considerable room for some potential counter-active policy in response to non-policy disturbances. All evidence in fact points to very sluggish adjustment. This is also the theme of the New Keynesians described in Chapter 9.

Second, the potential presence of hysteresis, explained in Chapter 28, adds a new dimension to the problem. If the NRU is itself a function of the unemployment rate, then a case could be made for a rapid policy response to the emergence of unemployment.

Third, the hypothesis that unemployment was voluntary was in conflict with all evidence as well as casual observation.

THE NEW CLASSICAL CONTRIBUTION TO THE DEBATE

The contributions of the New Classicists were discussed and evaluated in some detail in Chapters 23–26. It will be recalled that there are three key ideas associated with the school which have major implications for the debate about activist policies. The first is the claim that (a) anticipated policies have no real effects and (b) stabilisation rules will ultimately be anticipated and so will tend to be impotent.

The second is the Ricardian equivalence hypothesis which argues, in sharp contrast to conventional Keynesian economics, that a tax cut financed by debt creation will leave the real economy unaffected, the expansionary effect from the tax cut being exactly neutralised by the deflationary effect of expected future taxes (Chapter 26).

The third is the idea that discretion may ultimately lead to an excessive rate of inflation without any improvement in unemployment (Chapter 25).

SIMPLE RULES

A Friedmanite package

Friedman's macro policy package has four legs to it. First, keep base money growth on a fairly steady path so as to achieve an inflation rate of about zero. Second, let the exchange rate float without any management or capital controls. Third, balance the budget on an *ex ante* basis, i.e. projected annual receipts should be equal to projected expenditures. Fourth, keep domestic markets (including labour markets) free (Friedman 1953a, 1959, 1983).

The contention is that, with rates of inflation low and stable and budgets on average in balance, exchange rates should also be much more stable (this presumes at least that the rest of the world was equally stable). Current account imbalances will reflect only private sector decisions to save and invest and provided that these decisions are optimally made the current account will then also be optimal (see Chapter 34).

Variations on Friedman's monetary rule

To meet an obvious criticism of Friedman's rigid money rule, Meltzer (1988) has proposed a variation on the Friedman theme which allows base money growth to adjust in line with recent variations in base velocity, as follows:

$$b_t = \bar{y}_{t-1} - \bar{v}_{t-1}$$

where b is the current growth rate of base money, $\bar{y}$ is a moving average of the growth rate of domestic output and $\bar{v}$ is a moving average of the growth rate in base money velocity.

Variations on Friedman's fiscal rule

Friedman's fiscal rule appears extreme. First, it is likely to generate instability in the short run (a projected *downturn* has to be confronted by a *rise* in the tax rate).

In a widely discussed 1974 publication (Blinder and Solow) the Committee for Economic Development (CED) proposed that

> an appropriate way to maintain fiscal 'discipline' without destabilising the economy would be to determine the level of government spending on its own merits independent of the requirements of stabilisation policy, and set tax rates so as to produce a balance (or a small surplus) at full employment.
>
> (1974: 37–8)

Blinder and Solow add:

> Apparently the CED had confidence that the level of private investment would gravitate naturally toward the level of private saving out of full employment income . . . . One of the selling points of such a policy is presumably, that it replaces the rule of men with a 'rule of law'.
>
> (1974: 37–8)

In short the proposal here is to set the structural full employment (cyclically adjusted) budget balance at roughly zero, thus allowing built-in stabilisers to operate during cycles. A relatively minor extension to this is to balance the *current account* component of the budget whilst permitting the (productive) investment component of expenditures to be financed by borrowing.

Sargent and Wallace (1981) and Minford (see Minford and Peel 1983) have offered yet another rule for the conduct of fiscal policy, while accepting a monetary rule similar to Friedman's. These authors are predominantly concerned with the question of maintaining the long-run consistency of monetary and fiscal policy (see also Brunner 1986). This framework was developed in Chapter 34 and summarised in equation (17) in that chapter. This is reproduced here:

$$\frac{d}{y} = \frac{H}{P_y} n - (\text{rr} - n) \frac{b}{y} + \frac{H}{P_y} \dot{p}$$

The rate of inflation is set exogenously as in Friedman; the real growth rate is also given. If the real interest rate exceeds the real growth rate then, given the bond–output ratio b/y, this equation determines the optimal deficit–output ratio d/y.

POOLE'S SEMINAL CONTRIBUTION TO THE DEBATE

Poole (1970) wrote a seminal paper which has since been the inspiration for a particular approach to policy setting: the insulation properties of alternative policy regimes.

From our perspective Poole's model is very simple but its approach still stands and continues to be the basis for much current work on alternative policy regimes (see, for example, Chapter 39).

Poole's model is a Keynesian closed economy model. His loss function is one which focuses solely on minimising fluctuations to output. There are two types of shocks in his model: a money demand shock (a shift in LM) and an expenditure shock (a shift in IS). In the face of the two types of shocks and given his loss function, he proceeds to compare two polar monetary regimes: one which keeps the interest rate fixed, the other which keeps the money stock fixed.

Poole concluded that an interest rate target was superior to a money target for a money demand shock (because with the interest rate fixed the money demand shock would be fully accommodated by an increase in the money stock, thus suppressing all income effects) and that a money target was superior to an interest rate target for an expenditure shock (because in the latter case the effects on income would be reinforced by an increase in the money stock).

Less known is Poole's proposal that in the face of shocks originating from both sources, the more realistic situation, an optimal policy is a compromise which allows the money supply, in part at least, to respond positively to the interest rate. For recent analyses of such a rule see Benavie and Froyer (1983) and Dotsey and King (1983).

APPENDIX   OPTIMAL MONETARY POLICY IN THE FACE OF DISTURBANCES

Is it possible to design a monetary policy reaction function that will simultaneously attempt to neutralise disturbances from various sources? This is the question addressed by Turnovsky (1984, 1985) and Aizenman and Frenkel (1985). The approach raises important questions. I choose to illustrate this theme by using a simple model in Turnovsky (1984, 1985). The model in Aizenman and Frenkel is more elaborate but raises similar issues; its principal conclusions are summarised later.

The model comprises the following equations:

$$p = p^* + e \tag{A1}$$

$$\text{mo} - p = \alpha_1 y - \alpha_2 r_d + u_2 \tag{A2}$$

$$r_d = r^* + {}_t E_{et+1} - e \tag{A3}$$

$$y = \alpha_9 (p_t - {}_{t-1} E_{pt}) + u_3 \tag{A4}$$

$$\text{mo} = \pi_4 e + \pi_5 r^* + \pi_6 p^* \tag{A5}$$

Equation (A1) assumes that PPP holds (i.e. that the real exchange rate is fixed). Equations (A2)–(A4) have been used previously and require no explanation. We have disturbance terms to money demand (u_2) and aggregate supply (u_3). These disturbances are serially uncorrelated and have a mean of zero. Equation (A5) is the important novel feature of the model. It assumes a reaction function that allows the monetary authorities to respond, at once, to the exchange rate e (where π_4 is the coefficient of foreign exchange intervention), to the foreign interest rate r^* and to foreign prices p^*. Information on the exchange rate and the foreign interest rate is 'instantly' available but the assumption is also made that information on foreign prices is quickly available (from equation (A1), p must also be available).

There are four disturbances in the model: u_2, u_3, r^*, and p^*. Given the assumption about the disturbances, the rational expectations about the future exchange rate and price level are that they return to their initial levels. The model can readily be solved for output in terms of our four disturbances. The authorities cannot observe u_2 and u_3, but (as already noted) they can observe p^* and r^*.

$$y = \frac{\alpha_9 (\alpha_2 + \pi_6 - \pi_4)}{k_2} p^* + \frac{\alpha_9 (\pi_5 + \alpha_2)}{k_2} r^* - \frac{\alpha_9}{k_2} u_2 + \frac{1 + \alpha_2 - \pi_4}{k_2} u_3 \tag{A6}$$

$$k_2 = 1 + \alpha_2 + \alpha_9 \alpha_1 - \pi_4$$

We assume that the objective is to stabilise y. We have four coefficients in the solution corresponding to the four disturbances. We have only three coefficients in the monetary policy reaction function corresponding to the three indicators which are observable. If we drop one disturbance, we would have three coefficients in equation (A6) which could be set at zero (meaning that the disturbances have no effect on output). We could then solve for the optimal coefficients $(\pi_4^*, \pi_5^*, \pi_6^*)$ in the reaction function, which would yield perfect stabilisation.

By way of illustration of the method, suppose we drop u_2 from the system. We then have

$$\frac{\alpha_9(\alpha_2 + \pi_6 - \pi_4)}{k_2} = 0 \tag{A7}$$

$$\frac{\alpha_9(\pi_5 + \alpha_2)}{k_2} = 0 \tag{A8}$$

$$\frac{1 + \alpha_2 - \pi_4}{k_2} = 0 \tag{A9}$$

We can now solve this system of three equations for $\pi_4^*, \pi_5^*, \pi_6^*$. We have

$$\pi_4^* = 1 + \alpha_2 \qquad \pi_6^* = 1 \qquad \pi_5^* = -\alpha_2$$

If both u_3 and u_2 are relevant, we have an 'excess' of disturbances relative to indicators so that output cannot be completely stabilised.

Aizenman and Frenkel (1985) develop a similar theme. Again PPP is assumed, but the aggregate supply side is developed in considerable detail; in particular, a wage indexation coefficient is also accommodated. The monetary sector is conventional, and perfect asset substitution is assumed. There are three disturbances: to the foreign price level, to the foreign interest rate and to productivity. There are three independent indicators in the monetary policy reaction function: the exchange rate, the foreign interest rate and the foreign price level (as in Turnovsky). The authors assume that the goal of policy is to minimise the welfare loss associated with discrepancies 'between the realised levels of real wages and employment and the equilibrium levels obtained when labour markets clear continuously without friction'.

In their model there are four potential policy settings: the three coefficients in the monetary policy reaction function and the degree of wage indexation. Thus there are four policy settings but only three disturbances; one policy setting is redundant. Foreign exchange intervention can therefore be traded against wage indexation. So, in principle, there are enough instruments to eliminate the distortion to the real wage fully.

38

Assignment rules for internal and external balance

INTRODUCTION

This chapter looks at the question of how assignment ought to be undertaken when we have two instruments and two targets. Sections 1–3 focus on the case where the exchange rate is flexible, the two instruments are monetary and fiscal policy, and the two targets nominal income and the current account, corresponding to internal and external balance. (The question of whether nominal income is an appropriate target of policy is addressed in subsequent chapters.) Throughout we assume perfect asset substitution.

We begin with the small-country case; next we turn to the large-country case. In dealing with the large country we draw on two contributions in the literature: those of Boughton (1989) and Genberg and Swoboda (1991) on the one hand (henceforth BGS) and those of Williamson and Miller (1987) on the other (henceforth WM).

Section 4 deals with the adjustable peg regime. What distinguishes this regime from the previous one is that the exchange rate is now a potential policy instrument. We assume that the second available instrument is fiscal policy, with monetary policy held neutral. The two targets are again internal and external balance, as defined above. Section 5 deals very briefly with the fixed rate case. Finally, Section 6 tries to summarise the conclusions and to pave the way for a broader framework.

In our presentation of the underlying analysis, we lean heavily on models used in earlier chapters.

THE SMALL-COUNTRY CASE – SHORT- AND MEDIUM-RUN ASSIGNMENT WITH FLEXIBLE RATES

We assume that there are two targets of policy: nominal income and the current account. These correspond to internal and external balance. We also have two instruments: monetary and fiscal policies. The focus is on short- and medium-run assignment only. In the analysis which follows we also assume that exchange rates are flexible and that asset substitution is perfect.

The medium run

The model underlying the analysis here is the one presented in Chapter 8 (the MF model with flexible wages and prices and flexible exchange rates).

We want to know how the two instruments, monetary (mo) and fiscal (gr) policies, ought to be assigned to the two targets. We now go about applying the framework of Chapter 35. The solutions for nominal income (yr + p_d) and the current account (CA/X_0) were

$$yr + p_d = \pi_1 mo + \pi_2 gr \tag{1}$$

$$CA/X_0 = \pi_3 mo - \pi_4 gr \tag{2}$$

where $\pi_1 = 1$, $\pi_2 = \pi_3 = 0$, $\pi_4 > 0$.

Monetary policy impacts only on prices, leaving output and the current account unchanged. Fiscal expansion leaves nominal income unchanged (because the money stock and the interest rate are both fixed). It does, however, increase output and lower prices. At the same time, it worsens the current account.

We can readily calculate k_1 (Chapter 35) from (1) and (2):

$$\frac{\pi_1 \pi_4}{\pi_2 \pi_3} \to \infty \tag{3}$$

It follows that monetary policy has a comparative advantage in targeting income and fiscal policy has a comparative advantage in targeting the current account. This is intuitively obvious, in any event, since fiscal policy cannot impact on income and monetary policy cannot impact on the current account.

The short run

To evaluate short-run assignment within the same two-instrument two-target framework we now use the MF model of Chapter 6, with one important modification: we no longer assume that exchange rate expectations are static. Static expectations will emerge as a special case of a more general framework.

The equations underlying the model are

$$\text{yr} = \alpha_1 e - \alpha_4 r_d + \alpha_3 \text{gr} \tag{4}$$

$$\text{mo} = \alpha_5 \text{yr} - \alpha_{10} r_d \tag{5}$$

$$r_d = {}_t E_{et+1} - e \tag{6}$$

$${}_t E_{et+1} = \pi_8 e \tag{7}$$

$$\text{CA}/X_0 = \alpha_{13} e - \text{yr} \tag{8}$$

Equations (4), (5), (6) and (8) have been used previously and require no explanation. Equation (6) captures the assumption of perfect asset substitution. Equation (7) is the minor innovation. It says that the expected exchange rate is a positive function of the current spot rate. If $\pi_8 = 1$ we have the MF assumption of static expectations. If $\pi_8 = 0$ we have 'stationary' expectations with the expected spot rate insensitive to the movement in the spot rate (Chapter 27).

With domestic wages and prices fixed nominal income will reflect movements in the level of *output*, so we need to find solutions for output and the current account. These are

$$\text{yr} = \frac{\alpha_1 + \alpha_4(1 - \pi_8)}{k_2} \text{mo} + \frac{\alpha_3 \alpha_{10}(1 - \pi_8)}{k_2} \text{gr} \tag{9}$$

$$\frac{CA}{X_0} = \frac{\alpha_{13} - \alpha_1 - \alpha_4(1 - \pi_8)}{k_2} \text{mo} - \frac{\alpha_3 [\alpha_5 \alpha_{13} + \alpha_{10}(1 - \pi_8)]}{k_2} \text{gr} \tag{10}$$

where $k_2 = \alpha_{10}(1 - \pi_8) + \alpha_5 [\alpha_1 + \alpha_4(1 - \pi_8)]$ and $\alpha_{13} > \alpha_1$.

What this says now is that, in general, the two instruments impact on the two targets, so it is no longer intuitive which should be assigned to which target. We also note that the effect of a monetary expansion on the current account is ambiguous. If π_8 is sufficiently low a monetary expansion could produce a current account deficit. The reason is that the expected appreciation implied by the spot devaluation could offset the effect of the lower home interest rate and generate a net inflow of capital; this in turn requires a matching current account deficit.

We now proceed again to calculate k_1:

$$k_1 = \frac{[\alpha_1 + \alpha_4(1 - \pi_8)] \alpha_3 [\alpha_5 \alpha_{13} + \alpha_{10}(1 - \pi_8)]}{\alpha_3 \alpha_{10}(1 - \pi_8) [\alpha_{13} - \alpha_1 - \alpha_4(1 - \pi_8)]} \tag{11}$$

If we set $\pi_8 = 1$ (the MF case) $k_1 \to \infty$ and so monetary policy has to be assigned to output. We recall that in the MF model fiscal policy cannot impact on output and so it has to be assigned to the current account.

The general case, however, is ambiguous. How does one proceed here? First, one could try and find plausible values of the underlying coefficients from the empirical literature. (A variety of empirical counterparts can be found in Fischer (1988a). See also Chapters 6 and 12.) This procedure, however, is very hazardous since estimates do vary widely. Second, one could undertake an econometric simulation, over say one year, of a monetary and fiscal expansion with a roughly equivalent impact on output and then see what the outcomes will be for the current account. It is not difficult to apply this test from reported simulations. Unfortunately, no general conclusion could be reached. For example, for Australia and Canada it would seem that monetary policy ought to be assigned to output and fiscal policy to the current account. For the UK, however, with flexible rates it would seem that the reverse assignment is the appropriate one. The reason is that monetary policy has relatively weak effects on output and relatively strong effects on the current account. (For Canada and the UK see Masson *et al.* (1990); for Australia see Argy *et al.* (1989).)

A third approach is to experiment with assignment strategies using now a graphical presentation. This is also very hazardous because the slopes of the relevant schedules are not known. Nevertheless the general technique is a very helpful one and so is worth pursuing.

Figure 38.1 presents the analysis. The CA schedule shows the combinations of monetary and fiscal policies which will keep the current account on target (i.e. achieve external balance) (see equation (10)). In case 1 (the MF case with $\pi_8 = 1$) the slope is positive, implying that a monetary expansion will improve the current account and so a fiscal expansion, which worsens the current account, is needed to keep the current account on target. In case 2 we assume that a monetary expansion worsens the current account (i.e. in (10) the coefficient on mo is negative) and so the slope is negative.

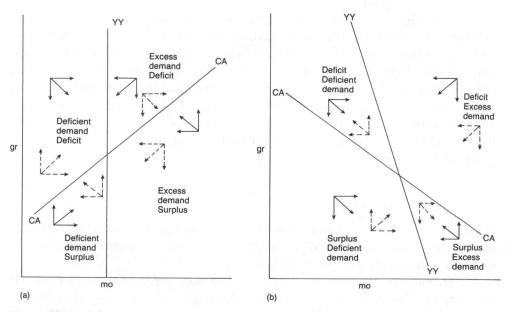

Figure 38.1 Assignment for internal and external balance
(---, mo → yr, gr → CA; - - -, mo → CA, gr → yr): (a) case 1 ($\pi_8 = 1$); (b) case 2 ($\pi_8 = 0$)

The YY schedule shows the combinations of monetary and fiscal policies which will keep nominal income on target (see equation (9)). The slope is infinite for case 1 (because only monetary policy influences income) and negative for case 2. It is also readily shown that the (negative) slope of CA is larger than the (negative) slope of YY.[1]

We now proceed as follows. We can identify on the figure various combinations of disequilibria. The area to the right (left) of YY must correspond to situations of excess (deficient) demand. For case 1 the area to the right (left) of CA corresponds to surpluses (deficits) while for case 2 the reverse is true. To see the last, for example, note that to the right we have an excessive level of government expenditure or an excessive money stock.

Two alternative assignment strategies are shown. Unbroken arrows represent the case where monetary policy is assigned to income and fiscal policy to the current account. Broken lines represent the reverse assignment. To illustrate what is going on, take for example the area in case 1 where there is excess demand and a surplus. On the first assignment monetary policy would be tightened and fiscal policy would be eased. On the second fiscal policy would be tightened (now to deal with the excess demand) and monetary policy would also be tightened (to reduce the surplus).

What do these reveal? In case 1 both appear, on the face of it, ultimately to converge towards equilibrium; there is a suggestion, however, of more rapid convergence for the first assignment. (This last, as we have seen, is in any event the appropriate one.) In case 2 the situation is even clearer. The first assignment does give you convergence; the second appears to be unstable. (To see this you need to follow through on the direction of change until a new area is reached and then move in the new direction and so on.)

The conclusion we appear to have reached is that assigning monetary policy to income and fiscal policy to the current account is the safer policy. This result is also quite intuitive and is confirmed by Genberg and Swoboda (1989, 1991) who show that this assignment is the appropriate one for both the short run and the long run for a variety of alternative model specifications.

THE LARGE-COUNTRY CASE – LONG-RUN ASSIGNMENT WITH FLEXIBLE RATES

In this section we focus on the contributions of BGS. Since we are here concerned with the long run we assume that there is full employment.

Consider a world comprising two countries. Each country targets its nominal income and its current account. Each country also has at its disposal a money stock policy instrument and a fiscal policy instrument (the level of government expenditure). Altogether there are four policy instruments but only *three* targets. The three targets are the two levels of nominal income and the *common* current account. Thus one policy instrument is redundant and, in principle, could be used to achieve a fourth target of policy. What could this target be?

BGS propose that the world real interest rate might be an appropriate fourth target. The world real interest rate would in turn determine the composition of output between consumption and investment. (We noted in passing in Chapter 34 that this might be an objective of policy.)

How would assignment be undertaken?

The foundation for the analysis was laid in Chapter 14. In effect, we take a special case of that model where now $\pi_3 = \pi_4 = \infty$ (i.e. that real wages are perfectly flexible in the medium to long run), allowing us to assume that output is fixed in the two economies.

With output fixed in A and B the medium- to long-run model (with all expectations realised) comprises four equations which we rewrite here as

$$\bar{y}_A = \alpha_1(e + p_{dB} - p_{dA}) - \alpha_4 r_w + \alpha_2 \bar{y}_B + \alpha_3 \mathrm{gr}_A \tag{12}$$

$$\bar{y}_B = -\alpha_1(e + p_{dB} - p_{dA}) - \alpha_4 r_w + \alpha_2 \bar{y}_A + \alpha_3 \mathrm{gr}_B \tag{13}$$

$$\mathrm{mo}_A = \bar{y}_A + p_{dA} - \alpha_{10} r_w \tag{14}$$

$$\mathrm{mo}_B = \bar{y}_B + p_{dB} - \alpha_{10} r_w \tag{15}$$

The bar over the levels of output indicates that these are given. For simplicity we have assumed that the coefficient on output in the money demand equation is unity (i.e. $\alpha_5 = 1$).

The model solves for e, r_w, p_{dA}, p_{dB} in terms of the two money stocks and the two levels of government expenditure. The model also solves for the current account which now is a function of the real exchange rate only.

The solution is straightforward. Substituting er for $e + p_{dB} - p_{dA}$ (the real exchange rate) we can solve directly for er and r_w from (12) and (13) in relation to gr_A and gr_B. An increase in gr_A will raise the world interest rate and appreciate A's currency in real terms (devalue B's currency). Monetary policy has no effects on either the real interest rate or the real exchange rate. It follows from (14) and (15) that monetary policy has only domestic price effects. Also, with real exchange rates unchanged nominal exchange rates adjust to neutralise the price effects as in the model of Chapter 14. Finally, fiscal policy has price effects but these are the same in the two economies. To see this, refer to (14) and (15). If fiscal expansion raises the world interest rate and if output and the money stock are both fixed, the price level must rise equally in the two economies. At the same time, with relative prices unchanged the fiscal expansion will appreciate the currency in nominal terms.

The model can be recast, for our purposes, as follows:

$$(y + p_d)_A = \pi_1 \mathrm{gr}_A + \pi_1 \mathrm{gr}_B + \pi_2 \mathrm{mo}_A + \pi_3 \mathrm{mo}_B \tag{16}$$

$$(y + p_d)_B = \pi_1 \mathrm{gr}_A + \pi_1 \mathrm{gr}_B + \pi_2 \mathrm{mo}_B + \pi_3 \mathrm{mo}_A \tag{17}$$

$$r_w = \pi_4 \mathrm{mo}_A + \pi_4 \mathrm{mo}_B + \pi_5 \mathrm{gr}_A + \pi_5 \mathrm{gr}_B \tag{18}$$

$$(CA/X_0)_A = -\pi_6 gr_A + \pi_6 gr_B + \pi_7 mo_A + \pi_7 mo_B \qquad (19)$$

where $y + p_d$ in logarithms represents the target nominal income.

We now know from the earlier discussion that the following holds:

$$\pi_2 = 1 \qquad \pi_3 = 0 \qquad \pi_1 > 0 \qquad \pi_4 = \pi_7 = 0 \qquad \pi_5 > 0 \qquad \pi_6 > 0$$

Equations (16)–(19) represent the underlying equations for the four target variables.

Each country will assign its monetary policy to nominal income (effectively the price level). This leaves fiscal policy to take care of, so to speak, the remaining two targets r_w and CA/X_0. One of the two countries will assign its fiscal policy to r_w, the other to the common current account.

Assuming that nominal income is taken care of as above, we can now represent the system graphically to show how it would work.

In Figure 38.2 the CA schedule represents the combinations of the two fiscal policies which will keep the current account at its target. This schedule represents (19) above; its slope will be unity. An increase in government expenditure in A requires a matching increase in government expenditure in B to keep the current account unchanged (on target). The r_w schedule represents the combinations of the two fiscal policies which will keep the world interest rate at its target level. If government

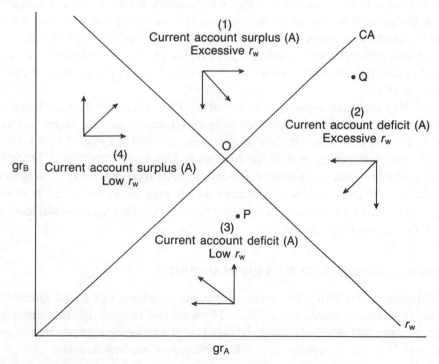

Figure 38.2 Fiscal policy coordination to achieve interest rate and current account objectives

expenditure increases in A the world interest rate will rise, and so to restore the world interest rate to its target level the level of government expenditure must fall in B by the same amount. The schedule is represented by (18) above and the slope is (minus) unity.

In quadrants (2) and (3) A has a current account deficit (B a surplus). This is readily seen by extending a horizontal line from the gr_B axis; beyond CA, given gr_B, A's government expenditure is excessive relative to target. Similar reasoning would show that to the left of the CA schedule A has a current account surplus. Again, to the right (left) of the r_w schedule the world interest rate is too high (too low).

We assume below that A has the task of securing the current account target, B the task of securing the real interest rate target. The question of who ought to do what is not addressed here (see, however, Genberg and Swoboda 1991).

If A represented the USA and B say Japan and Germany in 1989, then clearly we would have to place the world economy in the late 1980s in quadrant (2) where A has a current account deficit (B a surplus) and r_w is 'too high' (Chapter 42). If the world economy were at Q where the CA deficit is relatively small but the real interest rate is very high both A and B must adopt tight fiscal policies (A's being the tighter) to reach O. If the economy were at P, where the deficit is the overriding problem (but less so the real interest rate), A must tighten and B must ease its fiscal policy (A tightening by more than B eases).

Arrows point in the direction in which each country would proceed if assignment were undertaken. Suppose we were in region (2) where there is a current account deficit in A and an excessive world interest rate. A would tighten its fiscal policy while B would also tighten its own fiscal policy. In region (4) where the interest rate is too low and A now has a current account surplus, easier fiscal policies would be put into place in A and B.

In the BGS approach some agreement will need to be reached over the target current account; in addition there will need to be an agreement over the target real world interest rate and also over who has responsibility for which target. These tasks are difficult enough but made even more difficult in a multi-country world. Moreover, it is not evident that the real interest rate ought to be a target of policy; if the objective is to change the consumption–investment mix it may be better to do it through changes in the tax structure (e.g. investment incentives). This again would leave one fiscal policy instrument unused.

THE WILLIAMSON AND MILLER BLUEPRINT

The Williamson and Miller blueprint extends the target zone proposal discussed in Chapter 36 to accommodate fiscal policy. There are two targets: the full employment current account and nominal income.[2] There is also a real exchange rate intermediate target which is set to achieve the full employment current account; this is the equilibrium real rate which is the centre of a target zone. The *immediate* target is thus the real exchange rate.

The key elements of their proposal are as follows.

a) As previously, each central bank would defend the upper and lower points of the target zone by adjusting its interest rate.
b) National fiscal policies would also be adjusted so as to achieve target rates of growth of nominal income. If, however, fiscal deficits are already too high or the public adebt to GDP ratio is excessive the rule that fiscal policy should be expansionary when nominal income growth has stalled would be suspended.
c) The average level of the world interest rate, as distinct from its distribution, should be adjusted so as to achieve the target growth of nominal income for the participating countries.

We have already addressed some issues which bear on the target zone proposal in Chapter 36. Also in Chapters 39–41 we look more closely at the proposal to target nominal income. Here we limit ourselves to some general comments on the proposals.

Suppose again a two-country framework and suppose too that in A (B) there is an excessive real devaluation (appreciation). A will implement a tighter monetary policy, raising its interest rate, while B will implement a symmetrical easy monetary policy, lowering its own interest rate. All other things being equal the world interest rate need not change.

Suppose now in both A and B nominal income growth is excessive. Fiscal policy will tighten in both A and B. According to (c), however, since world income is excessive the average world interest rate will also be allowed to rise. Thus, in dealing with nominal income both national fiscal policies and the *average* world interest rate are to be used. Presumably this serves to spread the adjustment between the two instruments (see our discussion of Brainard in Chapter 37).

To simplify a little, WM propose that monetary policy be directed at the real exchange rate (and thus indirectly at the current account) and fiscal policy at the level of income.[3] This is the reverse of the assignment that we found in the previous section to be the more plausible.

THE ADJUSTABLE PEG

We consider here the case where the exchange rate is a policy instrument, in the sense that it can be changed by the authorities occasionally.

Suppose we are in a Keynesian short-run world with fixed domestic wages and prices and that, in the spirit of the adjustable peg regime (as we noted in Chapter 36), there is now imperfect asset substitution. We retain the same two targets of internal and external balance as defined previously, but we now have the exchange rate as one policy instrument and fiscal policy as the other. We assume throughout that the money stock is fixed. The analysis draws on Swan (1955).

We can use equations (4), (5) and (8) above to arrive at solutions for output (nominal income) and the current account in terms of the exogenous exchange rate

$\bar{e}$ and government expenditure (fiscal policy). The solutions are

$$yr = \frac{\alpha_1\alpha_{10}}{k_3} \bar{e} + \frac{\alpha_3\alpha_{10}}{k_3} gr \tag{20}$$

$$\frac{CA}{X_0} = \frac{\alpha_{10}(\alpha_{13} - \alpha_1) + \alpha_{13}\alpha_4\alpha_5}{k_3} \bar{e} - \frac{\alpha_3\alpha_{10}}{k_3} gr \tag{21}$$

where $k_3 = \alpha_{10} + \alpha_4\alpha_5$.

Both policy instruments act on the two targets. A devaluation increases output and improves the current account; a fiscal expansion increases output and worsens the current account. It is therefore not intuitive which instrument should be assigned to which target.

We can calculate k_1:

$$k_1 = \frac{\alpha_1\alpha_{10}}{\alpha_{10}(\alpha_{13} - \alpha_1) + \alpha_{13}\alpha_4\alpha_5}$$

If $k_1 < 1$ the exchange rate should be assigned to external balance. A closer look at the coefficients suggests that this is in fact likely to hold. This would then give us the 'conventional' assignment of the exchange rate to the current account and fiscal

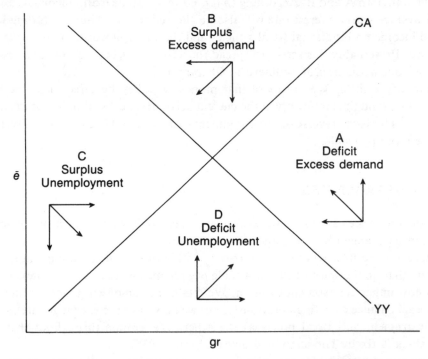

Figure 38.3 Conventional assignment of exchange rate and fiscal policy to external–internal balance

policy to output. In broad terms this is also how countries which have had adjustable peg regimes have tended to assign responsibility for the two instruments.

The conventional case is illustrated graphically in Figure 38.3. YY represents the combinations of $\bar{e}$ and gr which yield internal balance (see equation (20)). A devaluation increases output and so a tight fiscal policy is needed to re-establish internal balance. CA represents the combinations of $\bar{e}$ and gr which yield current account (external) balance. A devaluation improves the current account and so a fiscal expansion is needed to restore balance to the current account.

The conventional assignment is also represented by arrows in each of the four zones. Zone A represents a deficit plus excess demand, so it calls for a devaluation (to correct the deficit) and a fiscal contraction (to correct the excess demand).

The reader can also readily figure out that if the analysis is now extended to the medium run, with flexible wages and prices, the conclusions are even less clear-cut. It should be evident by now that if capital mobility were perfect or if, alternatively, we assumed that the authorities targeted the interest rate, an exogenous devaluation would only influence prices, leaving all real variables unchanged. In this case, the exchange rate would have to be assigned to the price level (nominal income) and fiscal policy to the current account.

THE FIXED RATE CASE

How would assignment be undertaken if we had a small country which pegged its currency to a larger economy?

Inflation and monetary policy are now predetermined. This leaves us with only fiscal policy to manipulate. With exchange rates fixed, fiscal policy impacts on both the current account and on the level of output. So, in principle at any rate, fiscal policy could be used for current account or output objectives. This, however, is subject to some of the reservations noted in Chapter 34.

SOME CONCLUSIONS AND A BROADER FRAMEWORK

What conclusions can we draw from our analysis in this chapter?

A number of conclusions stand out. First, we noted in Chapter 35 that Mundell thought that assignment could be determined on the strength of rather *limited* information. This chapter has shown that, often, knowledge of structural coefficients is needed to determine assignment, which can then turn out to be a more complex matter.

Second, we have demonstrated that assignment in the short run can be quite different from assignment in the medium to long run. In the end, which assignment is appropriate in the real world will depend on the structural model, the nature and persistence of the disturbances to which the economy is exposed and the form and strength of the two reaction functions. (On the last, see the discussion of Phillips and

Baumol in Chapter 37.) This is difficult to do *analytically*; it is more sensible to evaluate assignment strategies by econometric simulations (see on this Chapter 40).

Third, it is not intuitive that assignment requires that each instrument be assigned to only *one* target. A more flexible strategy is one which allows the two instruments to act on the two targets (see Chapter 40).

Finally, we note a major limitation of the analysis of this chapter. Its entire focus has been on two instruments and two targets, but as we saw in Chapters 34 and 35 policy setting is broader and more complex. The number of targets could be extended and so could the number of instruments. As an illustration (only) of a broader framework, suppose we had inflation, unemployment and, more controversially, the current account as targets and we had monetary, fiscal and wage policies as instruments. Monetary policy could be assigned to inflation, fiscal policy to the current account (so far as in BGS) and now wage policy could be assigned to unemployment (see on this last Chapter 44).

39

Theoretical evaluation of alternative simple policy regimes

INTRODUCTION

This chapter uses a two-country model framework, largely familiar from earlier chapters, to evaluate alternative simple policy regimes in terms of one criterion only: the degree to which each regime insulates the economy from a variety of unanticipated 'shocks'.

We assume shocks come from three sources: expenditure, money demand and supply (productivity). We also make one further limiting assumption and that is that each shock is temporary (more technically the shocks are serially uncorrelated, with an expected mean value of zero).

Since this is a short-term analysis we adopt the most general short-run loss function presented in Chapter 34. It will be recalled that the loss function takes account of deviations from optimal levels of prices, output, the real exchange rate and the real interest rate.

The policy regimes we compare are the following. Regime 1 is one where the money stock is assumed to be fixed and exchange rates are flexible. Regime 2 is also a flexible rate regime but we now allow monetary policy to be used to target nominal income. More explicitly, we assume that when nominal income exceeds (falls short of) its target level monetary policy is tightened (eased); to simplify, too, we assume the monetary authorities are able to achieve their nominal income target exactly. (This key assumption is questioned in Chapter 41).

The proposal to target nominal income was first advocated by Meade (1978), Tobin (1980) and Corden (1981). Among the earliest of the analytical studies was Bean (1983) whose work became very influential in the later treatment of the subject. Subsequently, formal analysis was also undertaken by Aizenman and Frenkel (1986),

Taylor (1985a), Alogoskoufis (1989), Frankel and Chinn (1991) and most recently by Argy (1991a). McCallum (1987) has proposed a rule of this kind for the USA, contending that it would have performed better than other simple rules.

Regime 3 is again one with flexible rates but now we assume that the *wage rate is linked to nominal income*. For example, if nominal income should fall (rise) the wage rate would be allowed to fall (rise) proportionately. It will readily be seen that this makes the wage rate respond to the level of activity and is a form of profit-sharing arrangement. It should be noted that there are no formal advocates of such a rule but it is one that has surfaced in the literature (see Aizenman and Frenkel 1986; Wagner 1989).

Regime 4 is our *symmetrical* fixed exchange rate regime, while regime 5 is an *asymmetrical* fixed rate regime. These regimes were described in Chapter 13. It will be recalled that a symmetrical regime is one where *neither* country sterilises while an asymmetrical regime is one where one country sterilises, the other does not.

There are no serious current advocates of an asymmetrical system; however, we noted in Chapter 13 that such a scheme was effectively in operation in the Bretton Woods years and more recently within the EMS. Cooper (1990) and McKinnon (1988) advocate a symmetrical fixed rate regime (as we saw in Chapter 36).

THE MODEL

The two-country model is a straightforward extension of the models presented in Chapters 13 and 14. The two countries are assumed to be identical in size and to share identical behavioural characteristics. The model now allows for shocks in each economy to expenditure, to money demand and to productivity. The labour market is also modified to accommodate some of the proposed policy regimes.

The model has been solved by a computer program. The results, being extremely complex, are not reproduced here. (See Argy (1991a) for details on how the model is solved). See also the Appendix for the technical derivation of the solutions in one regime.

Goods markets

$$y_A = \alpha_1(e + p_{dB} - p_{dA}) - \alpha_4[r_A - (_tE_{p_{At+1}} - p_A)] + \alpha_2 y_B + \alpha_3 u_{1A} \tag{1}$$

$$y_B = -\alpha_1(e + p_{dB} - p_{dA}) - \alpha_4[r_B - (tE_{p_{Bt+1}} - p_B] + \alpha_2 y_A + \alpha_3 u_{1B} \tag{2}$$

Money markets

$$m_A = y_A + p_{dA} - \alpha_{10}r_A + u_{2A} \tag{3}$$

$$m_{As} = \bar{m}_A - \pi_7(e - \bar{e}) \tag{4}$$

$$m_B = y_B + p_{dB} - \alpha_{10}r_B + u_{2B} \tag{5}$$

$$m_{Bs} = \bar{m}_B + \pi_8(e - \bar{e}) \tag{6}$$

$$r_A - r_B = {}_tE_{et+1} - e \tag{7}$$

$$m_A = m_{As} \tag{8}$$

$$m_B = m_{Bs} \tag{9}$$

Labour markets/production

$$y_A = -\alpha_6(w_A - p_{dA}) + \alpha_6/k_1 u_{3A} \tag{10}$$

$$y_B = -\alpha_6(w_B - p_{dB}) + \alpha_6/k_1 u_{3B} \tag{11}$$

$$w_A = \pi_2[{}_{t-1}E_{p_At} + \pi_1(p_A - {}_{t-1}E_{p_At})] + \pi_3(y_A + p_{dA}) \tag{12}$$

$$w_B = \pi_4[{}_{t-1}E_{p_Bt} + \pi_5(p_B - {}_{t-1}E_{p_Bt})] + \pi_6(y_B + p_{dB}) \tag{13}$$

$$p_A = \alpha_{15}p_{dA} + (1 - \alpha_{15})(e + p_{dB}) \tag{14}$$

$$p_B = \alpha_{15}p_{dB} - (1 - \alpha_{15})(e - p_{dA}) \tag{15}$$

Loss function

$$L_A = \pi_{10}(p_{dA} - \bar{p}_{dA})^2 + \pi_{11}(y_A - \bar{y}_A)^2 + \pi_{12}(er - \bar{e}r)^2 + \pi_{13}(rr_A - \bar{rr}_A)^2 \tag{16}$$

$$L_B = \pi_{14}(p_{dB} - \bar{p}_{dB})^2 + \pi_{15}(y_B - \bar{y}_B)^2 + \pi_{16}(er - \bar{e}r)^2 + \pi_{17}(rr_B - \bar{rr}_B)^2 \tag{17}$$

Notation

Subscripts A and B stand for countries A and B respectively. A bar over a variable indicates its target level. All variables should be seen as deviations from a base path.

y	output
r	interest rate
P_d	home price
p	consumer price
e	exchange rate (units of A's currency per unit of B's currency)
m	money stock
w	wage rate
u_1	serially uncorrelated expenditure disturbance
u_2	serially uncorrelated money demand disturbance
u_3	serially uncorrelated productivity disturbance
${}_tE_{xt+1}$	expectations about x formed in period t for $t + 1$
er	real exchange rate ($e + p_{dB} - p_{dA}$)
rr	real interest rate ($r - ({}_tE_{pt+1} - p)$)
α_6	share of wages to profits in private sector
k_1	share of wages in private sector production
L	welfare loss

Equations (1) and (2) represent the real demand for goods in A and B. Real demand is a function of the real exchange rate, the real interest rate, the other country's level of output and an expenditure disturbance.

Equations (3)–(9) describe the money markets. Equations (3) and (5) are the money demand equations (the coefficient on output is constrained to be unity) with a disturbance term u_2. Equations (4) and (6) are equations which explain the money stock in A and B. π_7 and π_8 again represent the degree to which the monetary authorities 'lean against the wind' to stabilise exchange rates. If exchange rates are flexible $\pi_7 = \pi_8 = 0$; if exchange rates are symmetrically managed $\pi_7 = \pi_8$ and, when $\bar{m}_A = \bar{m}_B = 0$, $m_{As} = -m_{Bs}$; if exchange rates are asymmetrically managed with A fully sterilising, $\pi_7 = 0$ and $\pi_8 \to \infty$. Equation (7) embodies the assumption of perfect asset substitution.

Equations (10) and (11) describe the production side of the economy. Output in A and B is a negative function of the real wage rate; u_3 represents a productivity disturbance. Equations (12) and (13) are generalised wage equations which accommodate a number of possibilities. Contracts are negotiated one period in advance. If these contracts are unindexed and are based solely on the expected consumer price index $\pi_1 = \pi_5 = 0$, $\pi_2 = \pi_4 = 1$ and $\pi_3 = \pi_6 = 0$. If contracts are fully indexed $\pi_3 = \pi_6 = 0$, $\pi_2 = \pi_4 = 1$ and $\pi_1 = \pi_5 = 1$. If wages adjust in line with nominal income $\pi_2 = \pi_4 = 0$; $\pi_3 = \pi_6 = 1$. The equations also accommodate potential asymmetries in wage determination in the two economies: e.g. if A has indexed contracts but B does not then $\pi_3 = \pi_6 = 0$; $\pi_1 = 1$; $\pi_5 = 0$; $\pi_2 = \pi_4 = 1$ (see Chapter 14). Equations (14) and (15) define the consumer price index, which is a weighted average of home and imported prices.

Finally, equations (16) and (17) describe the loss functions for the two economies. There are welfare losses from deviations of actual from 'desired' levels of output, home prices, the real exchange rate and the real interest rate. Since the weights attaching to each of these variables may be different in A and B the equations allow us to accommodate potential asymmetries in loss functions.

BASE REGIMES TO BE COMPARED

Our first task is to define the alternative strategies. These have already been summarised in the introduction:

Regime 1 Flexible rates with a target money stock
Regime 2 Flexible rates with a monetary rule which targets nominal income (in one or both countries)
Regime 3 Flexible rates with a wage rule linked to nominal income (in one or both countries)
Regime 4 A symmetrical fixed exchange rate regime
Regime 5 An asymmetrical fixed exchange rate regime (with A sterilising)

We have, then, a structural model, a loss function for each economy and five base alternative policy strategies. The question we address is: in the face of expenditure, monetary and supply disturbances and given the structural model, which regime performs best in terms of the defined loss function? Each country will have its own ranking of the regimes; these rankings, as we shall see, need not be the same.

The disturbances take five forms:

a) a unilateral expenditure disturbance (u, $a > 0$ or u, $b > 0$);
b) an expenditure switch ($u_{1A} = -u_{1B}$);
c) a unilateral money demand disturbance ($u_{2A} > 0$ or $u_{2B} > 0$);
d) a money demand switch ($u_{2A} = -u_{2B}$);
e) a unilateral productivity disturbance ($u_{3A} > 0$ or $u_{3B} > 0$).

All disturbances, which are unanticipated, are assumed to be temporary and correctly perceived as such. This means that, with expectations rationally formed, $_tE_{p_At+1} = {}_tE_{p_Bt+1} = {}_tE_{et+1} = 0$. Also with disturbances unanticipated $_{t-1}E_{p_At} = {}_{t-1}E_{p_Bt} = 0$.

To anticipate, the final rankings of the regimes in each country will be shown to depend on

a) the type of disturbance (expenditure, monetary, productivity);
b) the country origin of the disturbance (whether it originates in A or in B);
c) the country loss function (the importance each country attaches to the target variables);
d) the particular structural model used (notably in this context the coefficients in the behavioural equations);
e) institutional conditions (notably in this context whether contracts are indexed or otherwise).

SOME RESULTS FOR THE FIVE BASE REGIMES

In this section we present results for the five base regimes described above. Where possible, in summarising, we try to present an intuitive explanation for some at least of the results.

One way to understand how the adjustment mechanism works in each regime is to take regime 1 outcomes as our starting point and then to show how each of the other regimes entails some additional policy adjustment which in turn will modify the initial outcomes.

Two variables in the initial solution for regime 1 are critical in an assessment of the further adjustments required to obtain solutions for the other regimes: the level of nominal income and the exchange rate. Starting with regime 1, then, suppose that a disturbance occurs in A which (a) raises nominal income in both A and B ($y_A + p_{dA} > 0$; $y_B + p_{dB} > 0$) and (b) appreciates A's currency (devalues B's). To move from regime 1 to regime 2 we note that A and B have now targeted nominal income (at its original level), so monetary policy will initially at least be tighter in both A and

B. Since world nominal income cannot change, the world money stock must fall in equilibrium. In the end adjustment will generate a new set of outcomes for regime 2.

To move from regime 1 to regime 3 we note that with nominal income up in A and B the wage rate will rise, initially at least, in the two economies. Again the wage rate in the world economy will need to rise; this will provoke adjustments and generate a new set of outcomes for regime 3.

To move from regime 1 to regime 4 it must be recalled that we now require symmetrical monetary adjustment to restore the original exchange rate. Since the exchange rate has appreciated this requires that A increase its money stock and B reduce its money stock equivalently. This generates a new set of outcomes which now represents the solution for regime 4.

Finally, to move from regime 1 to regime 5 (with asymmetrical adjustment), as in regime 4 the exchange rate must be restored to its original level but now the full burden of monetary adjustment falls on B, which means that B will now have to reduce its money stock by twice as much to achieve the same result. So whereas in regime 4 the world money stock is fixed, in an asymmetrical regime such as 5 the world money stock will change, depending on the exchange rate outcome in the country which has responsibility for adjustment.

In our presentation below we intend to proceed as above, always taking the first regime as the base for the analysis of all other regimes. Initially, we assume that contracts are unindexed, except for regime 3 where indexation takes a special form.

A unilateral money demand disturbance

Suppose the disturbance occurs in A. Consider what happens in regime 1 (Table 39.1). Output and home prices in A fall but the impact on output and home prices in B is ambiguous. A's currency appreciates in nominal and real terms; A's real interest rate rises while in B the outcome is again ambiguous. Given the net disturbance to the world economy, world output and prices, on balance, must fall while the real interest rate, on average, must rise.

What happens in regime 2? Nominal income unambiguously falls in A. If monetary policy targets nominal income the money stock will rise in A; on balance the world money stock must rise. Nominal income is restored in both A and B and so in equilibrium neither output nor prices will change in the two economies. The real exchange rate as well as the real interest rates will also be unchanged (see equations (1) and (2)). In the end then all variables return to their original levels. Nominal income targeting in A and B thus acts as a perfect stabiliser on all counts. It is readily seen that to equilibrate all markets the money stock must rise in A to absorb the money demand disturbance while the money stock in B will in the end be unchanged (see the Appendix).

Consider now what happens in regime 3. Whereas in regime 2 with world nominal income down the money stock was allowed to rise, now the money stock in both A and B is fixed but the wage rate is allowed to adjust. This acts as a perfect stabiliser

Table 39.1 Direction of change in key target variables: two-country model, temporary disturbances[a]

	y_A	y_B	p_{dA}	p_{dB}	er	rr_A	rr_B
Regime 1							
u_{2A}	↓	?	↓	?	↓	↑	?
$u_{2A} + u_{2B} = 0$	↓	↑	↓	↑	↓	↑	↓
u_{1A}	↑	↑	↑	↑	↓	↑	?
$u_{1A} + u_{1B} = 0$	↑	↓	↑	↓	↓	↑	↓
u_{3A}	↑	?	↓	?	?	?	?
Regime 2							
u_{2A}	0	0	0	0	0	0	0
$u_{2A} + u_{2B} = 0$	0	0	0	0	0	0	0
u_{1A}	0	0	0	0	↓	↑	↑
$u_{1A} + u_{1B} = 0$	0	0	0	0	↓	↑	↓
u_{3A}	↑	0	↓	0	↑	↓	?
Regime 2a[b]							
u_{2A}	0	0	0	0	0	0	0
u_{2B}	0	↓	0	↓	↑	?	↑
u_{1A}	0	↑	0	↑	↓	↑	↑
u_{1B}	0	↑	0	↑	↓	↑	↑
u_{3A}	↑	?	↓	?	↑	↓	?
u_{3B}	0	↑	0	↓	↓	?	↓
Regime 3							
u_{2A}	0	0	↓	0	0	0	0
$u_{2A} + u_{2B} = 0$	0	0	↓	↑	0	0	0
u_{1A}	0	0	↑	↑	↓	↑	↑
$u_{1A} + u_{1B} = 0$	0	0	↑	↓	↓	↑	↓
u_{3A}	↑	0	↓	?	↑	↓	?
Regime 3a[c]							
u_{2A}	0	0	↓	0	0	0	0
u_{2B}	0	↓	?	↓	↑	?	↑
u_{1A}	0	↑	↑	↑	↓	↑	↑
u_{1B}	0	↑	↑	↑	?	↑	↑
u_{3A}	↑	↑	↓	?	↑	↓	?
u_{3B}	0	↑	↓	↓	↓	?	↓
Regime 4							
u_{2A}	↓	↓	↓	↓	0	↑	↑
$u_{2A} + u_{2B} = 0$	0	0	0	0	0	0	0
u_{1A}	↑	?	↑	?	↓	↑	↑
$u_{1A} + u_{1B} = 0$	↑	↓	↑	↓	↓	↑	↓
u_{3A}	↑	?	↓	?	↑	↓	?
Regime 5							
u_{2A}	↓	↓	↓	↓	0	↑	↑
$u_{2A} + u_{2B} = 0$	↓	↓	↓	↓	0	↑	↑
u_{1A}	↑	?	↑	?	↓	↑	↑
$u_{1A} + u_{1B} = 0$	↑	↓	↑	↓	↓	↑	?
u_{3A}	↑	?	↓	?	↑	↓[d]	?
Regime 5							
u_{2B}	0	0	0	0	0	0	0
u_{1B}	↑	↑	↑	↑	↑	↑	↑
u_{3B}	?	↑	?	↓	↓	↓[d]	↓

Notes: [a] Results assume $\alpha_1 > \alpha_4(1 - \alpha_{15})$ and $2\alpha_{15} > 1$. Unindexed contracts except for regime 3 (see text). A rise in er indicates a real devaluation.
[b] In regime 2a, A targets nominal income using monetary policy. B targets the money stock (see text).
[c] A adopts a wage rule, B does not.
[d] Very likely.

to output in A and B.[1] It is readily shown that A's currency appreciates in nominal terms (but the real exchange rate is unchanged), its home prices fall and its real interest rate is unchanged. The nominal interest rate in A falls in the same degree as the appreciation. In B, however, prices and real and nominal interest rates are unchanged. Interestingly, B is completely sheltered in real terms from the money disturbance in A.

Now consider regime 4. Taking regime 1 as the starting point A will increase its money stock and B will decrease it equally, sufficiently to restore the original exchange rate. As a result, output will partially reverse itself in A and fall back in B. In the end output will fall equally in A and B and there will be parallel falls in home prices. The real exchange rate will be unchanged (since home prices in A and B fall equally) while the real interest rate rises equally in A and B.

Finally, consider regime 5. There is now an asymmetrical monetary adjustment which is set in motion. Intuitively, it is readily seen that to restore the original exchange rate, with A's money stock fixed, the drop in B's money stock must be twice that in regime 4, so the world money stock falls, injecting a further deflationary bias to the world economy. Output and home prices again fall equally in A and B but now by more than in regime 4. The nominal and real interest rate will rise equally in A and B again by more than previously. It is also readily seen from equations (3) and (5) that with $y_A = y_B$, $p_{dA} = p_{dB}$, $r_A = r_B$, $m_B = -u_{2A}$. Finally the real exchange rate is also unchanged.

With asymmetry assumed, it now matters greatly which country experiences a money demand disturbance. Suppose it originated in B and A held its money stock fixed. Now B would pump sufficient money into its economy to restore the exchange rate and this will stabilise all variables, not only in B, but also in A (see Table 39.1, regime 5, for u_{2B}). So, if the money demand disturbance originates in the economy which sterilises, the two economies are disturbed, while if the disturbance originated in the other country, the two economies are perfectly stabilised. (See also Chapter 13.)

A money demand switch

Suppose money demand increases in A and falls equally in B. We can now superimpose on the previous results a fall in money demand in B.

In regime 1, output and prices fall in A and rise equally in B while the nominal and real exchange rate appreciates in A. The real interest rises in A and falls equally in B.

What happens in regime 2? A implements an easy monetary policy, B an equally tight monetary policy. This serves to neutralise the money demand shifts, stabilising all key variables in the two economies.

In regime 3 the changes in nominal income will set in motion wage adjustments in A and B: in the end output is perfectly stabilised in A and B, prices (and wages) fall in A and rise equally in B. There is a nominal appreciation in A but this is exactly neutralised by the relative price change, so there is no change in the real exchange rate. The real interest rate is also unchanged in A and B (this is readily seen from equations (1) and (2)). So, interestingly, in this regime all real variables are stabilised; the money demand shifts are exactly absorbed by price changes.

In regime 4 the money stock will rise in A and fall equally in B to stabilise the exchange rate. This acts as a perfect stabiliser (unlike the case of a unilateral money demand shift).

Technically, as we have shown, a nominal income target regime performs identically to a symmetrical fixed rate regime. In reality, however, the fixed rate regime is likely to perform better because exchange rate data are available instantly whereas nominal income data are only available with some lag. We return to this question in Chapter 41.

Finally, consider regime 5. The money stock will now fall in B to stabilise the exchange rate. This injects a deflationary bias to the world economy. Output falls equally in A and B, as do prices. (This result exactly parallels the result of a unilateral money demand disturbance in A.) The real exchange rate is unchanged but the real interest rate rises equally in A and B.

A unilateral expenditure disturbance

In regime 1 output and prices increase in A and B but by more in A than in B.[2] A's currency appreciates in nominal and in real terms. The real interest rate rises in A but the outcome is ambiguous in B.

What happens when monetary policy is used to target nominal income? Again in the two economies output and prices are stabilised. An important result here is that tight monetary policies (more stringent in A than in B) will now reinforce A's real appreciation and as well the rise in the real interest rate.

What happens when the wage rate is linked to nominal income? The wage rate rises in the two economies, output is stabilised while prices rise in A and B, in A by more than in B. At the same time there is a real appreciation while the real interest rate rises in A and B.

In regime 4 A will now implement an expansionary monetary policy, B an equally restrictive policy. The increase in output and prices will be reinforced in A but in B the outcome is ambiguous. There will be a real appreciation while real interest rates will rise, in A by more than in B.

Finally what happens in regime 5? The money stock in B falls by more than in regime 4. Output and prices increase in A but the impact on B is ambiguous. There is now a real appreciation while the real interest rate rises in A and B.

What if the expenditure disturbance had originated in B instead of A? Now B's currency would (potentially) appreciate, so B would now inject money into its economy to stabilise its currency. In sharp contrast to the previous case the world money stock increases, so output and prices increase in B as well as in A. In effect, real world expansion is reinforced by monetary expansion. There is a real devaluation of A's currency while the real interest rate rises in A and B.

An expenditure switch

In regime 1 an expenditure switch (A increasing, B decreasing) increases output and prices in A and decreases them equally in B. A's currency appreciates in nominal and real terms; also the real interest rate rises in A and falls equally in B.

If the monetary authorities targeted nominal income the money stock would fall in A and rise equally in B. This stabilises output and prices in the two economies. However, the relative change in the money stock destabilises both the real exchange rate and the real interest rate.

If wages are linked to nominal income wages will rise in A and fall equally in B. This again stabilises output in A and B but, in the end, the home price level rises in A and falls equally in B. A's currency appreciates in real terms while the real interest rate again rises in A and falls equally in B.

With exchange rates fixed and adjustment symmetrical A will now increase the money stock, B decrease it equally, to stabilise the currency (so the direction of change in monetary policy is exactly the opposite to that in regime 2). Output and prices are thus destabilised in both A and B. The currency appreciates in real terms while the real interest rate will increase in A and fall equally in B.

What will happen in regime 5? Now the money stock falls in B to stabilise the currency. B's output and prices are further destabilised downwards, while output and prices will rise in A. At the same time the real exchange rate appreciates while the real interest rate rises in A, but in B the outcome is ambiguous (the downward push being reversed by the fall in the money stock).

Had the switch been the reverse, expenditure rising in B and falling in A, B's money stock would have increased, not fallen, with of course quite different consequences for aggregate outcomes.

A unilateral productivity disturbance

Suppose there is an upward productivity disturbance in A. In regime 1, in A output unambiguously rises while home prices fall, but the outcome for nominal income is ambiguous; so is the impact on A's currency and on A's interest rate. At the same time, in B output and prices move together but again the outcome for nominal income is ambiguous.

It is these ambiguous initial outcomes for regime 1 that make it so difficult to compare performance across regimes. Nevertheless, a few general comments can be made.

Suppose in A and B the monetary authorities targeted nominal income. Because in B output and prices move in the same direction, the monetary authorities will take steps to adjust monetary policy (one way or the other) and this will again stabilise both output and prices. So B's output and prices are completely protected from a productivity disturbance in A. In A, however, the situation is more complicated. If nominal income increases (decreases) in A money will be tightened (eased), stabilising (destabilising) output but destabilising (stabilising) prices. Output in A must ultimately increase and prices fall exactly in proportion to the productivity disturbance.

We also have an interesting result for regime 3. The wage rate will again adjust in B (in either direction) in such a way that output (but not prices) is completely stabilised. B's output is again fully protected from A's productivity disturbance. In A, output will also increase exactly in proportion to productivity (as in the previous regime). (These results are easily confirmed by appropriate substitutions in the aggregate supply equations).

Because of ambiguous effects on the exchange rate in regime 1 it is difficult to determine the direction of change in monetary policies in A and B for regimes 4 and 5. The performance of these regimes in relation to the others is thus difficult to evaluate.

Asymmetrical nominal income targeting

Suppose again contracts are unindexed and exchange rates are flexible, but suppose now that only one country (the monetary authority in A) targets nominal income while the other (B), for one reason or another, does not (it targets the money stock).

We now pose the following question. Is B actually better off from the fact that A targets nominal income? In other words, we compare B's welfare under regime 1 and an asymmetrical version of regime 2 (regime 2a, see Table 39.1).

In some ways the analysis of this case is straightforward. The only difference between regime 1 and regime 2a is A's monetary strategy and the impact this has on B's welfare.

Consider a money demand disturbance in A. A implements an expansionary monetary policy which exactly neutralises all effects on both A and B. In this case B is clearly advantaged by A's strategy.

Suppose the money demand disturbance had originated in B. Nominal income falls in B but the impact on nominal income in A, as we have seen, is ambiguous. A now takes steps to neutralise the change in nominal income, which could mean an easier or a tighter monetary policy. This in turn has ambiguous effects on output and price in B. All in all the change in B's welfare is indeterminate.

Suppose there is an expenditure disturbance in A. Monetary policy is unambiguously tightened in A; this stabilises output and prices in A. In turn this has ambiguous effects on B's output, prices and the real interest rate. (See solutions for u_{2A} in regime 1.) However, the real exchange rate appreciation is unambiguously reinforced, as we have seen, so on this front B is clearly worse off.

Suppose the expenditure disturbance had originated in B. The spillover of nominal income into A is positive in the model, so A will tighten monetary policy. This again has ambiguous feedback effects on B's output, prices and the real interest rate.

Finally, suppose we have a productivity disturbance in A. Because the effect on nominal income in A is ambiguous, A's monetary policy is also ambiguous, as is the impact on B.

If the productivity disturbance had originated in B, outcomes would continue to be ambiguous.

To sum up, then, it is difficult to reach conclusions about the impact on B's welfare of A's adopting a nominal income monetary rule.

An asymmetrical wage rule

Instead of an asymmetrical nominal income monetary rule we can visualise an asymmetrical wage rule and we can again ask a parallel question: how is B's welfare affected by A's adoption of the wage rule? We now compare regime 1 with the asymmetrical variant of regime 3 (see Table 39.1, regime 3a).

We can proceed in a similar way, except that now when A's nominal income alters in regime 1 a change in the wage rate is brought into play, so instead of analysing the effects on B of any change in monetary policy in A we need to analyse effects on B of a change in the wage rate in A.

If there is a money demand disturbance in A, B will again be better off by A's adoption of a wage rule. Indeed B will be totally sheltered from this disturbance.

If the money demand disturbance had originated in B the effects of A's adoption of a wage rule on B are indeterminate.

An expenditure disturbance in A raises income in A and B. If A adopted a wage rule the effects on B are again indeterminate. B, however, is not insulated from the disturbance in A.

An expenditure disturbance in B also raises income in A, where now the wage rate will adjust upwards, but this has mostly ambiguous feedback effects on B.

Finally, for productivity disturbances in A or B we have parallel difficulties in evaluating impacts on B.

We can conclude, as in the case of an asymmetrical nominal income rule, that, except for a money demand disturbance in A, it is difficult to determine how B's welfare is affected by A's adopting a wage rule.

The case of indexed contracts

A key to understanding the results here is first to evaluate the effects of a monetary change in regime 1. As we have already seen this is going to determine how the other regimes compare. The monetary change will be triggered in regime 2 by any potential change in nominal income and in regimes 4 and 5 by any potential change in the currency.

We now have the familiar result that a monetary change leaves all real variables (output, the real exchange rate, the real interest rate) unchanged. Only nominal variables change. This means that a change in monetary policy initiated in regimes 2, 4 or 5 will not change the base real outcomes (as we have already seen in Chapter 14).

CONCLUSIONS

The framework presented above now allows us to rank in A and B the five base regimes for each disturbance in terms of the four key variables in our loss function. The details are not shown here (see, however, Argy 1991a).

We now demonstrate how rankings in A and B are sensitive to: (1) the type of disturbance; (2) the country of origin of the disturbance; (3) the loss function used in A and B; (4) the structural coefficients in the model; and (5) institutional considerations.

The type of disturbance

Other things being equal, it is readily seen that if we focus on output–price volatility in A a symmetrical fixed rate regime (4) is superior to a money stock–flexible rate regime (1) for a money demand disturbance but inferior for an expenditure disturbance all originating in A. This result is now commonplace in the literature.

The country of origin of the disturbance

We can demonstrate the importance of the country of origin with two illustrations. For a given expenditure disturbance originating in A, A will rank regime 1 unambiguously above regime 4, while B, in all probability, will reverse the ranking. If the expenditure disturbance had originated in B the rankings would be reversed.

A more powerful illustration, already noted, is the case of a monetary disturbance in regime 5. The regime has a very low rating if the disturbance originates in A (the country which sterilises); it has the highest rating if the disturbance originates in B.

The loss function

The role of the loss function is easily illustrated. For an expenditure disturbance in A, ultimate rankings will depend on weights attaching to output–price on the one hand and real exchange rate–real interest rate on the other. A and B will both rank regime 2 ahead of regime 1 if price–output considerations dominate; by contrast, regime 1 will rank ahead of regime 2 if real exchange rate–interest rate considerations dominate. These differences also imply that if the country loss functions were different the rankings for the two regimes would also diverge.

A striking illustration of the importance of the loss function is evident in the case of a productivity disturbance in A. Suppose in regime 1 that a (negative) productivity disturbance in A increases nominal income (lowering output but increasing prices), appreciates the currency in real terms and raises the real interest rate. In regime 2 money will tighten; this reduces output further but stabilises prices; at the same time the real exchange rate and the real interest rate are both destabilised. If, on the other hand, nominal income had fallen the associated monetary expansion in regime 2 would have stabilised all the real variables.

The structural coefficients in the model

There are question marks attached to some of the signs of the solutions; in turn, the ambiguities here are inevitably reflected in ambiguities in the rankings. The case of the productivity disturbance discussed above provides a good illustration of the ambiguities flowing from uncertainty about the model coefficients.

Institutional considerations

Finally, we recall that labour market assumptions, and hence institutional considerations, were critical in determining the choice of regime. We were able to demonstrate that, in terms of our own analysis, if wage contracts were perfectly indexed and if the loss function took account only of the three real variables (output, the real exchange rate and the real interest rate) A and B would both be indifferent between the regimes.

APPENDIX   NOMINAL INCOME TARGETING (REGIME 2)

In this Appendix we try to demonstrate the mechanics of how the solutions can be obtained for the case where both countries successfully target nominal income, using monetary policy. We focus on the case where indexation is zero, so $\pi_1 = \pi_5 = 0$, $\pi_3 = \pi_6 = 0$ and $\pi_2 = \pi_4 = 1$, and the money demand shock originates in A.

We have equations (1), (2), (3), (5), (7), (10), (11) (w_A, w_B are both now fixed by definition). We add two more equations:

$$y_A + p_{dA} = 0 \tag{A1}$$

$$y_B + p_{dB} = 0 \tag{A2}$$

This gives us a total of nine equations which solve for y_A, y_B, p_{dA}, p_{dB}, r_A, r_B, e, m_A, m_B.

Substituting (A1) and (A2) into (10) and (11) respectively, it is readily seen that output and prices will be unchanged in A and B. This leaves (1), (2), (3), (5), and (7) to solve for r_A, r_B, e, m_A, m_B. We can eliminate e using (7). Equations (1) and (2) then become

$$0 = \alpha_1(r_B - r_A) - \alpha_4 r_A - \alpha_4(1 - \alpha_{15})(r_B - r_A) \tag{1}$$

$$0 = -\alpha_1(r_B - r_A) - \alpha_4 r_B + \alpha_4(1 - \alpha_{15})(r_B - r_A) \tag{2}$$

Equations (1) and (2) show that neither interest rate can change. It is then easily shown that $\Delta m_A = \Delta u_{2A}$ and $\Delta m_B = 0$.

40

Econometric evaluation of policy regimes

INTRODUCTION

This chapter introduces the reader to econometric work undertaken to evaluate policy proposals and regimes. The work to be reviewed represents applications of the methodology summarised in Chapter 35.

It is convenient to divide the studies into five categories. First, we consider those that compare the performance of alternative *monetary* policy regimes. Typically in this group are studies which compare five types of policy regimes:

a) the actual monetary policy implemented;
b) a monetary policy which targets nominal income or inflation;
c) a constant money growth rule with flexible rates (*à la* Friedman);
d) the Meltzer variation on the Friedman rule (see Chapter 37);
e) an econometrically derived feedback monetary rule.

Second, we review studies which compare a wider range of policy regimes including now monetary rules and exchange rate regimes.

Third, we consider studies which look at the performance of alternative assignment strategies for both monetary and fiscal policies (as reviewed in Chapter 38).

Fourth, we review one study which looks at the econometric effects of stabilising policy variables.

After the econometric review we try to summarise the findings.

ALTERNATIVE MONETARY POLICY STRATEGIES

McCallum (1987) provides a perfect application of the methodology reviewed in Chapter 35. He first estimates a structural equation for the USA (1954 (I)–1985(IV)) of the form

$$\Delta y = 0.00749 + 0.257 \Delta y_{-1} + 0.487 \Delta b_t + \varepsilon \tag{1}$$

where the variables are in logarithms, y is nominal income and b stands for base money.

Next he uses a policy reaction function for base money of the form

$$\Delta b_t = 0.00739 - \tfrac{1}{16}[(y_{t-1} - y_{t-17}) - (b_{t-1} - b_{t-17})]$$
$$+ \lambda_2(y_{t-1}^* - y_{t-1})$$

where the first bracketed expression represents the four-year average change in base velocity while the last expression represents the deviation of nominal income from its target path. 0.00739 reflects the 3 per cent annual growth rate. λ_2 is the reaction coefficient.

McCallum evaluates several alternative monetary rules, applying the criterion of the root mean square error of nominal income from its target path of 3 per cent growth. The strategies are: actual monetary policy (in (1) the actual percentage change in base money growth is used), a Friedman-type zero base money growth, the case where $\lambda_2 = 0$ and (his preferred rule) the case where $\lambda_2 = 0.25$. He finds his rule performs best (he does, however, introduce numerous provisos). (For an application to Germany of McCallum's rule see Scheide (1989) and for a commentary see Loef (1989); see also McCallum (1988).)

Taylor (1985a) estimates a two-equation system for the USA which he interprets as dynamic aggregate supply and demand functions. The data are annual and the period covered, 1954–83, is very similar to McCallum's. He then simulates the effects of a variety of nominal income rules. Importantly, he concludes that 'nominal GNP rules that focus solely on the growth rate could worsen business-cycle fluctuations by always causing the economy to overshoot its equilibrium after shocks'.

Cooper and Fischer (1972) compare the historical performance of alternative monetary rules using the FRB–MIT–Penn (FMP) econometric model. The criteria they use to evaluate the rules is the minimisation of the standard deviation of inflation and unemployment. They conclude that a monetary rule which systematically leans against the wind would have reduced the variability of the rates of inflation and unemployment over the period 1956–1968 as compared with a constant growth rate rule.

Craine et al. (1978) use the MPS model to arrive at an optimal feedback monetary rule based on the best available forecasts of its exogenous variables (which number 136). They compare the historical performances of this rule and a number of other rules, including that of Cooper and Fischer, Friedman's constant money growth rule, the actual policy. The criteria they apply are more complicated than those of Cooper and Fischer. They penalise unemployment rates in excess of 4.8 per cent, inflation rates in excess of 2.5 per cent, changes in the T-bill rate of more than 150 basis points and deviations in M1 from a 5.1 per cent growth path.

To their surprise, the optimal feedback rule (and Cooper and Fischer's rule) performed relatively badly, outperformed by both the constant money growth rule and actual policy. They conclude: 'Normally feedback policies can be expected to give better results than fixed rules ... however given uncertainty about the structure of the economy and future events there is no guarantee that performance will be improved as the two feedback policies demonstrate' (Craine *et al.* 1978: 775–6).

Taylor (1981) uses a small econometric model of the US economy to arrive at a general monetary policy reaction rule which has as arguments past output, changes in output, real money balances, inflation and an inflation shock. This outperforms a monetarist rule as well as actual policy.

Pauly and Peterson (1990) use the National Institute Global Econometric Model to compare two monetary strategies in the face of two types of shocks. The two strategies are the model responses to the shocks (effectively an inflation targeting rule using the interest rate as the instrument) and an optimal nominal income feedback rule. The shocks are an oil price shock and a US reduction in defence spending. The results are mixed and difficult to summarise in a few words, depending as they do on both the loss function and the individual disturbance.

BROADER COMPARISONS OF POLICY REGIMES

Frenkel *et al.* (1989) carry out simulations of alternative policy strategies using the IMF Multimod. From our perspective two simulations are of particular interest. They report root mean square deviations for a number of key target variables for three simple rules: a money target, a nominal income target monetary rule (where the interest rate is allowed to respond contemporaneously to the gap between the target *level* of income and the actual level of income) and an *asymmetrical* fixed rate regime (where the USA is assumed to sterilise). In a first simulation they use historical shocks (1974–85) while holding fiscal policy neutral.

They report results for the USA, Japan and Germany. Nominal GNP targeting is unambiguously superior in all three countries to money stock targeting (although the difference is not in general very large) in relation to variations in real GNP, in inflation and in the real effective exchange rate. Its performance, however, is mixed in comparison with fixed rates.

In a second simulation they generate shocks from a much longer historical base (now forty years rather than the twelve years above). The results are substantially less favourable to the nominal income strategy. They are very mixed; in the USA, at any rate, the strategy is in general inferior on most counts to both a money stock strategy and a fixed rate strategy.

In the Frenkel *et al.* approach how does a fixed rate regime compare with a money target flexible rate regime? Interestingly, for the two simulations they report there is essentially very little difference between the regimes, at least in so far as outcomes for output and prices are concerned.

McKibbin and Sachs (1989), using the McKibbin–Sachs Global Model (MSG), evaluate three simple rules for the G3 countries: a fixed money growth rule, a monetary policy rule which targets nominal income in each country and a *symmetrical* fixed exchange rate rule. They report results for individual disturbances, thus facilitating comparison with our own theoretical analysis. Through these simulations fiscal policy is held neutral. The three disturbances are an oil price shock, a money demand shock (originating in one of the G3 countries) and a real demand shock (again originating in one of the G3 countries). They also report standard deviations of a number of key variables (of which output, inflation and the real exchange rate are of primary interest to us).

Consider a money demand shock originating in the USA. Output, inflation and real exchange rate standard deviations are easily the lowest for nominal income targeting in all three countries. The worst performer on these fronts is the fixed money growth rule.

Consider now a real demand shock in the USA.

In terms of output and inflation standard deviations the nominal income strategy in general is again the best performer in all three countries. In the USA the fixed rate regime is now the worst performer. Abroad, the fixed money growth rule is the worst performer. Finally, in terms of real exchange rate standard deviations the nominal income regime performs relatively poorly.

Finally, for an oil price shock (the closest to our productivity shock) a nominal income strategy has mixed results.

Are the Frenkel *et al.* results, only marginally if at all in favour of nominal income targeting, inconsistent with the McKibbin and Sachs results which are substantially more supportive? The apparent differences could be due to any number of factors: the differences in the way the reaction functions are formulated (superficially similar 'strategies' are in fact represented a little differently), differences in the underlying model, differences in the distribution of disturbances (a strong weight attaching to oil productivity disturbances in the McKibbin and Sachs approach would generate a less favourable outcome).

In the McKibbin and Sachs approach how does the symmetrical fixed rate regime compare with the money target flexible rate regime? The results conform to theoretical expectations. Focusing on output and inflation, a fixed rate is on balance better for a money disturbance, a flexible rate better for an expenditure disturbance. The outcomes are similar for an oil price shock.

Taylor (1989a), using his own multi-country model, evaluates alternative simple monetary strategies. Briefly, his basic comparison is between, on the one hand, a flexible rate regime where central banks use interest rate policy to stabilise the price level and, on the other hand, a fixed rate regime where central banks adjust the 'world' interest rate, again to stabilise the price level. He finds that flexible rates work better 'according to almost all measures of internal economic stability'.

Jonson (1987), using the Reserve Bank of Australia econometric model (RB11), estimates a monetary policy function that responds in a systematic way to deviations in a whole range of variables from their desired levels. He compares this with a simple money rule with flexible rates (*à la* Friedman) and a fixed exchange rate rule, in the face of three disturbances: money demand, terms of trade and capital flow shocks. On balance over all the shocks he finds that the estimated equation performs well. Focusing on inflation and output outcomes he also finds that a fixed rate regime is better than a flexible rate regime for a money demand shock but inferior for a terms of trade shock.

ALTERNATIVE ASSIGNMENT STRATEGIES

The basic comparisons here are between the Williamson and Miller blueprint, the Boughton, Genberg and Swoboda reverse assignment and the 'historical' performance. There are four econometric studies that bear on this: Frenkel *et al*. (1989), Currie and Wren-Lewis (1989, 1990), McKibbin and Sachs (1989) and Edison *et al*. (1987). These are briefly reviewed below.

The study of Frenkel *et al*. (1989)

These exercises are extensions of those reported above for 'historical' and 'generated' shocks (drawn from a longer sample). They compare the blueprint with the reverse assignment. In the blueprint they have the difference between the short interest rate and the base rate responding to competitiveness and also to the gap between world income and its target value. At the same time they have government expenditure, relative to base, responding to domestic absorption relative to its base. In the reverse assignment the interest rate is allowed to react to absorption while government expenditure responds to the current account, all relative to base.

The results are very similar for historical and generated shocks. *In general*, on the key variables (output, inflation and the real effective exchange rate) the blueprint outperforms the reverse assignment.

The study of Currie and Wren-Lewis (1989, 1990)

The Currie and Wren-Lewis strategy is closest to that of Frenkel *et al*. Econometric simulations are undertaken for the G3 with the National Institute Global Econometric Model over the years 1975–86.

The target growth of nominal domestic demand depends on the inflation rate gap (the difference between actual and target inflation), a 'constant' productivity growth, capacity utilisation and the deviation of the current account from its target. The blueprint is represented as follows. The real interest rate is allowed to respond to the deviation of actual growth from the target growth of 'world' nominal demand and to the difference between the actual and target real exchange rates (competitiveness). Government expenditure responds to the *national* deviations between actual growth and the target growth of nominal demand. The reverse assignment has government expenditure responding to the deviation of the current account from its target and to the deviation of the growth of nominal *income* from its target (where the target growth in nominal income is defined as in the target growth in domestic demand (with the last term − the current account deviation − dropped). At the same time the real interest rate is now set to respond to nominal income deviations from its target path. These representations are the closest in spirit to the Williamson and Miller blueprint.

There are some innovative features in this study worth highlighting. First, the policy reaction functions are expressed in *both* proportional and integral form (e.g. the change in the real interest rate responds to the *level* of the nominal income gap as well as to the change in the nominal income gap) (see Chapter 37). Second, they use an explicit loss function, assigning welfare losses to deviations of capacity utilisation, inflation, government expenditure and, most importantly, the real exchange rate from their desired paths. They choose particular weights for each of the targets but they experiment with different weights for the real exchange rate target. Third, the reaction coefficients are 'chosen so as to minimise the objective function'.

The simulations are designed to evaluate the relative performance of the blueprint, the reverse assignment and history. Their conclusions are easily summarised: 'Both schemes improved welfare compared to history over this period but the gains associated with . . . (the blueprint) . . . were generally larger and more substantial,' and 'our model suggested that fiscal policy had a comparative advantage over monetary policy in directly controlling demand at a national level'.

Thus, although the model is different, the methodology used is different and the design of policies is different, this study in essence agrees with Frenkel *et al*. that the blueprint outperforms the reverse assignment.

The study of McKibbin and Sachs (1989)

McKibbin and Sachs try to evaluate one proposal which they label the blueprint; however, they have difficulties simulating the blueprint as conceived by Williamson and Miller. They allow the computer to figure out the most appropriate assignment; it turns out that the best results are obtained when fiscal policy is primarily linked to the real exchange rate and monetary policy primarily linked to nominal income, especially so for US money demand and real demand shocks. So this study, if anything, appears to be critical of the Williamson and Miller blueprint and appears to endorse the reverse assignment.

The study of Edison *et al*. (1987)

Edison *et al*. use the multi-country model of the Federal Reserve Board to undertake a number of simulations for the period 1976(I)−1985(IV). They evaluate variations of a target zone proposal against history. In one simulation the short-term interest rate in the large countries responds to real exchange rate deviations, while at the same time fiscal policy is used to hold 'real GNP at its baseline level'. The results for the blueprint are mixed, but on the whole satisfactory.

Flexible assignment rules

To conclude this section we report some econometric work which attempts to arrive at monetary and fiscal policy reaction functions.

Suppose, by way of illustration, that our two instruments are the real interest rate (rr) and government expenditure (gr) and the two targets are the current account (CA^*) and nominal income (y^*). Then we can write out two reaction functions in general form as

$$\Delta rr = \pi_1(y - y^*) + \pi_2 \Delta(y - y^*) - \pi_3(CA - CA^*) - \pi_4 \Delta(CA - CA^*)$$

and

$$\Delta gr = -\pi_5(y - y^*) - \pi_6 \Delta(y - y^*) + \pi_7(CA - CA^*) + \pi_8 \Delta(CA - CA^*)$$

The two instruments are directed at the two targets (there is in this case no simple assignment). Policy reaction is expressed in both derivative form (the change in the target gap variable) and integral form (the level of the target gap). (In principle we could also add some lagged values of the gaps.)

These equations assert that when income is above its target level, the real interest rate will be raised and fiscal policy will be tightened. At the same time if the current account is better than its target level the real interest rate will be lowered and fiscal policy will be eased.

The coefficients π can be estimated by historical simulations to maximise a particular welfare function. For examples of such estimated policy reaction functions for monetary and fiscal policies see Currie and Wren-Lewis (1990), Christodoulakis *et al.* (1991), and Weale *et al.* (1989).

THE EFFECTS OF STABILISING POLICY VARIABLES

Frenkel *et al.* pose the following question: suppose the policy stance, represented by money growth, tax rates and the level of government spending, were 'smoothed' (i.e. replaced by their five-year moving average); what would that do to macro performance? As they note by way of summary:

Interestingly enough, smoothing of policy variables is nowhere near sufficient to produce smooth values for major macroeconomic variables. On the contrary, such a *simple* smoothing rule tends to accentuate some of the fluctuations in the historical data. For example, though the average growth of real gross domestic product is about the same as in the historical data, its standard deviation is higher in the policy smoothing simulation. Real effective exchange rates are somewhat less variable with smoothing, but real short-term interest rates are considerably more variable.

(1988: 176)

CONCLUSIONS

The results in general are very disappointing. If we had hoped to resolve a number of disagreements over the optimal stance of policy by reference to econometric work we would find ourselves somewhat frustrated. Theory tends to be too simple-minded, inevitably neglecting real-world refinements (see Chapter 41), and so considerable weight ought to attach to empirical findings but this turns out to be a little illusory.

Consider four key issues raised in the literature:

a) a money growth rule versus a feedback policy;
b) fixed versus flexible rates;
c) a nominal income strategy versus other money strategies;
d) assignment strategies.

On (a) the studies perhaps marginally support a feedback policy. On (b) Taylor's work contradicts the work of Frenkel *et al.* (1989). Frenkel *et al.* are in principle, however, in agreement with McKibbin and Sachs. With disturbances coming from all sources, it is not surprising to find that, in the end, there is little to choose between fixed and flexible rates. This also confirms our theoretical findings.

On (c) we reviewed numerous studies but unfortunately these do not agree with one another. Some (those of McKibbin and Sachs and McCallum) are very supportive; others (Frenkel *et al.* 1989; Pauly and Peterson 1990) are less so.

Finally, on (d) again there are differences. Frenkel *et al.* (1989) and Currie and Wren-Lewis (1989, 90) find the blueprint outperforms the reverse assignment but McKibbin and Sachs (1989) are less supportive.

41

Issues raised by nominal income targeting

INTRODUCTION

Chapters 39 and 40 evaluated a strategy of targeting nominal income as one amongst a number of alternative policy regimes. Because the idea of targeting nominal income has been so influential in recent years, it is appropriate that we now spend a little more time on the proposal. This chapter aims at clarifying a number of issues raised by nominal income targeting. In particular,

a) it asks some questions about how it might be implemented in practice and
b) it draws attention to a number of analytical problems associated with the strategy.

We show that the *theoretical* models underlying the conventional evaluation of a nominal income strategy are too simple. At this point, there are two ways to proceed: one is to *refine* the models; another is to put the proposal in the hands of econometricians and have them evaluate it by appropriate simulations. Unfortunately, neither solution turns out to be very satisfactory. As we now know a detailed structural model is very difficult to manipulate and, as we have seen, econometric analysis turns out to be somewhat unhelpful.

We begin this chapter by representing the conventional case for nominal income targeting, now highlighting its key underlying assumptions graphically and at the same time simplifying further by taking the small-country case. This allows us to capture the essential *spirit* of the proposal.

TARGETING NOMINAL INCOME – A SIMPLE GRAPHICAL REPRESENTATION

We consider here the proposal to target nominal income using monetary policy. The proposal is compared with a money stock target policy and with a monetary policy which targets inflation. In the analysis of this section we disregard lags in obtaining information, in responding to information and in policy impacts.

In Figure 41.1 AD and AS represent, respectively, the aggregate demand and aggregate supply schedules for a hypothetical small economy. If nominal income is the target the AD schedule will have a slope (in logarithms) of -1 (any reduction in inflation has to be exactly offset by an equivalent increase in output to maintain nominal income). This is represented by AD_1 which embodies in it reactions by the monetary authorities aimed at keeping the economy along that schedule. This schedule by construction does not shift. ADM_1 and ADM_2 represent alternative hypothetical AD schedules, one of which is steeper than AD_1 and the other flatter than AD_1. These represent conventional aggregate demand schedules with a money stock target.

Suppose we now have AD and AS disturbances. An AD disturbance to the right could come from a fall in money demand or an increase in real expenditure. ADM_1 or ADM_2 will now shift to the right but by definition AD_1 will not shift. So whereas price and output will be disturbed when a money target is in place neither price nor output will be disturbed by an income target. This is because any increase in income away from the target will provoke a tight monetary policy which in turn will restore the income to its target level (as indeed we saw more formally in Chapter 39).

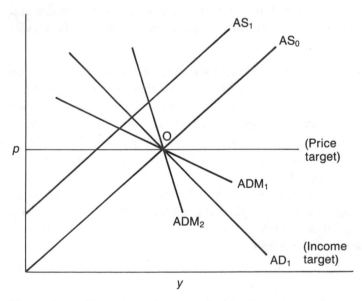

Figure 41.1 Targeting prices, nominal income and money

Suppose now an AS disturbance displaces the AS schedule to the left, and suppose too that the government's objective is to minimise fluctuations in output. Then it is easy to see that if ADM is flatter than AD_1 (as in ADM_1) a policy of targeting nominal income will minimise the reduction in output; if, however, ADM is steeper (as in ADM_2) a money target is the preferred policy.

Why is this? A downward shift in aggregate supply increases prices and lowers output. The effect on nominal income is ambiguous. If income rises (the price effect dominates – the case of ADM_2) a tight monetary policy will be set in motion and this will destabilise output. If income falls (the case of ADM_1) monetary policy will be eased, thus stabilising output.

If the authorities targeted prices they would maintain the economy on the horizontal line. For an exogenous shift in demand the analysis is unchanged; the economy would be equally stabilised by a nominal income or price target. Any action taken to restore prices would return the economy to point O.

For a supply shock, however, the outcomes are different. If the authorities stabilised prices aggregate demand would have to be reduced further to achieve the price target. Thus, in the face of an adverse supply shock a price target carries the risk that the authorities will be obliged to reinforce adverse unemployment effects.

SOME PRACTICAL QUESTIONS

We review here a number of practical questions associated with a nominal income strategy.

Political feasibility

Are there political constraints on nominal income targeting?

It is sometimes contended that governments do not like to announce nominal income targets because nominal income cannot be directly controlled and so errors will entail a loss of credibility. To support this argument reference is made to the disappointing experience with money stock targeting (see Chapter 43). If, the argument runs, money targets have been frequently missed, even in cases where generous bands were allowed, how much more difficult would it be to achieve nominal income targets?

Definition of the target

A key question is how the target is to be defined. There are several proposals here. Meade (1978) and Tobin (1980) propose a GNP target, Williamson and Miller (1987) propose a gross domestic expenditure target and Gordon (1985) proposes a 'final sales' target. It is the first two alternatives that have in fact received the most attention, yet surprisingly there has been no serious analytical treatment of the differences between these two.[1]

A related question is the following: assume a failure to achieve a target income — should 'bygones be bygones' in setting the next period target or should a correction be undertaken? The difference is crucial. Suppose that the target income is expected to grow by 5 per cent each year. This can be converted into a GNP level in each of a succession of years or, alternatively, it can be revised each year to achieve a target growth. To take a concrete illustration, suppose income is targeted to grow at 5 per cent in the next year but, in fact, because of a major unanticipated disturbance it grows by 10 per cent. In the next period the new 'excessive' level of income can be taken as a base and a new target growth of income of 5 per cent can be prescribed. Alternatively, a correction is undertaken to restore the target level of income; the new target growth of income may be 2.5 per cent in each of the next two years (or zero if adjustment is over one year).

Assume a target growth rate is adopted. How is this target growth rate to be determined? In particular, if the inflation rate is 'above' the target rate of inflation, should the target growth of nominal income be brought down gradually or sharply?

Which instrument should be used to achieve a nominal income target?

There are two questions here. First, which *monetary* instrument is appropriate, assuming monetary policy is used? Second, should monetary or fiscal policy be used?

The bulk of the theoretical literature assumes that the money stock is used to achieve a nominal income target. The bulk of the econometric literature assumes that the interest rate (sometimes nominal, sometimes real) is the appropriate instrument. Taylor (1985a) emphasises that the instrument should be the 'real after-tax interest rate'.

We have already addressed the assignment question. We recall here that some would assign monetary policy, and some fiscal policy, to nominal income (Chapter 38).

A related question is the frequency with which the monetary instrument should be allowed to adjust in line with the gaps between actual–forecast and target income. Is the strategy a short-run or medium-run one?

Alternative strategies

In the theoretical literature the alternatives analysed are a money stock target, fixed exchange rates, an 'optimal' monetary policy (Bean 1983; Aizenman and Frenkel 1986), a discretionary monetary policy (Frankel and Chinn 1991) and price or interest rate targeting (Aizenman and Frenkel 1986).

The theoretical literature aside, what monetary policy strategies have the industrial countries adopted?

In reviewing experience, a useful division is between those countries whose currencies are largely determined by market forces and which are able, in principle, to conduct an independent monetary policy and those who have entered into some exchange rate arrangement or commitment and whose capacity to control monetary policy, and hence nominal income, is restricted to a greater or lesser degree. In the first category are the big three and some smaller OECD economies (Australia, Canada, New Zealand and Switzerland) whose currencies float.

In turn the countries in the first category fall roughly into two groups: those which adopt a very eclectic policy (the USA and Australia) and those which make it the primary business of the central bank to target inflation (Japan, Germany, Canada, New Zealand and Switzerland). None actually targets nominal income as such. The analytical differences between targeting nominal income and inflation were noted in the first section of this chapter.

SOME ANALYTICAL QUESTIONS

A number of analytical questions also need to be raised.

Potential instrument instability

A question that needs to be addressed in any evaluation of nominal income targeting is what it implies about instrument instability. We have already noted that for certain types of disturbances (e.g. domestic expenditure disturbances) stabilising nominal income may entail greater interest rate instability; more serious is the possibility that the interest rate may, in principle, explode.

A more formal presentation of this is given in Frenkel *et al.* (1989). We now allow for the fact (but, however, absent from our theoretical models) that there is a lag in the adjustment of nominal income to a change in the interest rate.

$$y = -ar_d - br_{d-1} + u \tag{1}$$

where y is nominal income, r_d is the interest rate and u is a disturbance to y; a and b represent first- and second-period effects.

Suppose the authorities are determined to stabilise $\bar{y}$ in the face of a disturbance. What path for the interest rate does this entail?

Rearranging (1),

$$r_d = -\frac{b}{a} r_{d-1} + \frac{1}{a} (u - \bar{y}) \tag{2}$$

This is a simple first-order difference equation. The system could be unstable and oscillatory if $b/a > 1$. In any event even with $b/a < 1$ cycles and overshoots are almost certain to occur.

The intuitive reason is straightforward. Suppose a disturbance raises nominal income. The interest rate is raised sufficiently to stabilise nominal income; however, in the next period nominal income falls, requiring a fall in the interest rate, and so on.

Realism of theoretical models

Theoretical models cannot capture the subtleties of the real world. In particular, lags in adjustment in goods and money markets and the time pattern of disturbances are all much more complex in reality than in simple models.

From our perspective, in this context, an important question that needs to be addressed concerns information lags and lags in the implementation and impacts of monetary policy. Suppose it takes some two to three months for information on nominal income to be available[2] (such information will be subsequently revised, but we put that point to one side). Suppose, too, that it takes a month or two for a decision on a change in the direction of monetary policy to be made. Suppose, finally, that there is a mean lag of some six months from the change in the direction of policy to the impact on nominal income. Monetary policy then impacts on nominal income some nine to eleven months 'after the event' so to speak. The potential for destabilising nominal income remains a distinct possibility.

To have perhaps a better chance of stabilising nominal income, it seems that monetary policy must react to the gap between the *forecast* nominal income (in, say, six months) and the target nominal income. The success or otherwise of monetary policy then hinges on the success or otherwise of nominal income forecasts (see McNees 1987; Artis 1988; Kahn 1988; Kenen 1988b). Such forecast errors can be very large and persistent (Argy 1991a).

42

Global macro performance – 1972–91

INTRODUCTION

This chapter describes the evolution of the global macroeconomy between 1967 and 1991–2. Its focus is on the principal developments in industrial countries as a group rather than on individual performances. Comparisons of individual performances are made in the next two chapters and in Part VIII.

We begin by summarising the cycles in economic activity in the industrial countries as a whole. We then try to present a simple framework to interpret the business cycle experience.

Next, we review the macro performance of the industrial countries. In our review we have found it convenient to divide the period into four distinct sub-periods: the years between 1967 and 1975, the years between 1976 and 1983 and the years between 1984 and 1991–2.

We conclude with a summary of the ways in which the international environment has changed since the late 1960s.

A FRAMEWORK FOR INTERPRETING THE REAL BUSINESS-CYCLE EXPERIENCE

Table 42.1 summarises the business-cycle experience of the industrial countries since 1972. There were three recessions in the period (1974–5, 1980–3 and 1990–2 (the last incomplete)) and three recovery phases (1972–3, 1976–9 and 1984–9).

The framework we try to apply in interpreting these real developments is one which assigns importance to a number of key variables. The key variables are the growth in real money balances, the fiscal policies of the G7, the increase in the real price of

Table 42.1   Real cycles, industrial countries, 1972–91

	Years	Real growth rates (OECD)	Unemployment (OECD)
Recovery	72–3	5.6	3.3
Recession	74–5	0.4	5.3
Recovery	76–9	4.3	5.1
Recession	80–3	1.4	8.6
Recovery	84–9	3.6	6.4
Recession	90–2	1.7 (90–1)	7.1 (1991)

Source: OECD, *Economic Outlooks*

oil, real interest rates and some measure of the real wage gap (the real product wage adjusted by some measure of productivity). (On the last, see the Appendix.)

Table 42.2 presents these variables (where available) for the years 1972–91.

We shall argue in the text that there are deflationary (expansionary) forces at work if the growth in real money balances declines (increases), if the real interest rate rises (falls), if fiscal policy tightens (eases), if the real price of oil rises (falls) and if the real wage gap increases (declines).

THE POSTWAR YEARS TO THE MID TO LATE 1960s

If we take a long historical perspective it is evident now that the world economy in those years performed exceptionally well. Real growth rates were high, unemployment rates low, inflation rates low and current account and fiscal imbalances relatively modest.

Why were real growth rates high and unemployment rates low? Amongst the more important factors were the following: postwar reconstruction, technological advances, high rates of investment, convergence of productivity levels towards those of the USA, trade liberalisation, economies of scale, structural change (notably the shift from agriculture to manufacturing), the absence of major shocks to the world economy and, perhaps, stabilising demand management policies (see Maddison 1986).

Why were inflation rates low? Under the Bretton Woods system, an essentially fixed exchange rate regime as it operated then, the USA played a key role as the inflation setter for the world economy. Not only was the USA the dominant economy, but the US dollar was the world's reserve currency. Thus, by keeping its own rate of inflation at very modest levels the USA acted as a stabilizing force in the world economy.

Current account imbalances were modest, at least to the early to mid-1960s, because (a) there were no major shocks to the world economy, (b) inflation differentials were small, (c) cyclical fluctuations were moderate and (d) financial policies were directed at correcting emerging imbalances (e.g. as in the UK and Japan).

Table 42.2 Key impulses driving the real economy (industrial countries)

	Real price of oil[a] (% inc.)	Increase in real base money[b] (%)	Increase in real broad money[b] (%)	Fiscal impact, G7[c]		USA, real interest rates[d]	Japan, real interest rates[d]	Germany, real interest rates[d]	Europe, real wage gap[a,e]	Europe, real wage gap[b,f]
1972	9.6	6.9	10.4	−0.5	(−1.4)	2.9	1.8	2.4	100.3	100.94
1973	30.0	6.2	5.8	0.0	(−0.1)	0.6	−4.3	2.3	100.7	102.34
1974	220.7	−2.0	−2.2	0.1	(0.2)	−3.4	−13.9	3.4	102.8	107.53
1975	−13.3	−5.5	0.8	−2.5	(−2.4)	−1.1	−2.6	2.6	105.9	116.08
1976	−0.4	−1.0	6.3	0.5	(0.0)	1.8	−0.7	3.5	104.9	114.93
1977	−0.2	0.2	4.1	0.3	(0.1)	0.9	−0.9	2.5	104.4	114.62
1978	−7.2	2.8	5.0	−0.9	(−1.7)	0.8	1.9	3.1	103.0	112.99
1979	37.6	1.6	1.5	0.0	(0.0)	−1.9	4.0	3.3	103.0	113.64
1980	52.2	−4.1	−3.8	0.1	(0.6)	−2.0	1.5	3.1	104.1	117.34
1981	6.0	−5.2	−1.9	0.4	(0.2)	3.6	3.8	4.1	104.3	119.77
1982	−13.6	−0.2	1.3	0.0	(0.6)	6.8	5.4	3.7	102.8	117.78
1983	−16.6	3.5	7.0	−0.1	(0.5)	7.9	5.5	4.6	101.1	115.60
1984	−8.5	1.7	3.7	0.3	(0.5)	8.2	4.5	5.4	98.8	111.85
1985	−9.4	3.9	4.9	0.0	(0.4)	7.0	4.3	4.7	98.2	110.94
1986	−47.7	6.0	6.3	0.0	(0.3)	5.8	4.3	6.1	97.1	108.80
1987	16.4	6.4	5.2	0.8	(0.8)	4.6	4.2	5.5	97.1	109.37
1988	−20.7	4.4	3.9	0.0	(−0.1)	4.8	3.6	4.8	96.3	107.81
1989	13.1	1.8	6.1	0.5	(0.6)	3.7	2.8	4.3	96.1	107.52
1990	22.6	1.5	−	−0.7	(−0.9)	3.2	4.3	6.2	NA	NA
1991	−17.4	−	−	−0.3	(−0.3)	3.6	3.2	5.1	NA	NA

Notes: [a] Calculated from the price of oil and inflation (OECD, *Economic Outlooks*).
[b] IMF financial statistics – weighted data for industrial countries.
[c] Change in general government cyclically adjusted financial balance as a percentage of trend GDP (OECD calculations). The figures in parentheses are the G7 less the USA (+, expansionary; −, restrictive).
[d] Real interest rates are calculated from the long-term bond yield less the ongoing rate of inflation.
[e] Compensation per employee in real terms divided by labour productivity (OECD calculations). 1970–3 = 100.
[f] Compensation per employee in real terms divided by total factor productivity (TFP). TFP is a weighted average of labour and capital productivity, with 1985 shares used as weights (OECD calculations). 1970–3 = 100.
NA, not available.

THE LATE 1960s TO 1975

By the late 1960s performance had begun to deteriorate on a number of fronts.

First, beginning in the late 1960s, many industrial countries (notably Germany, France, Japan, Italy, Canada and the UK) experienced a sharp acceleration in the growth of wages (the so-called wage explosion). This could not be fully accounted for in conventional economic terms. Many economists, bewildered by the phenomenon, sought explanations outside of economics, notably in the area of sociology (OECD 1977; Argy 1981). The importance of this development is that it represented a new kind of shock to the industrial economy (a supply shock), which is more difficult to deal with by traditional macroeconomic tools.

Second, as we saw in Chapter 2, the failure to adjust exchange rates, within the IMF rules, in the face of emerging evidence of fundamental external imbalances had become a major source of friction by the late 1960s. A succession of crises culminated in the Smithsonian Agreement of December 1971, under which there was a major realignment of exchange rates.

Third, as a result of the Vietnam War and the social programmes of the Johnson presidency, public expenditure rose sharply in the USA; this fiscal expansion was financed by money growth, fuelling an acceleration in inflation in the USA by the late 1960s, early 1970s. The stabilising role which the USA had provided until then was now being compromised.

Fourth, as we also saw in Chapter 2, between 1968 and 1971 sharp fluctuations in US monetary policy became a very disruptive force in the world economy. Other industrial countries resorted to a number of devices to insulate their own economies in those years from these changes in US policies. They tried to limit the flows of capital; at the same time they tried to sterilise the effects of capital flows on their cash base. In general, however, such policies failed, and so these countries found it increasingly difficult to maintain an independent monetary policy more suited to their own needs.

Stressful as these years had been, by the early 1970s conditions had deteriorated sharply. Between 1971 and 1973 the world economy was exposed to three major shocks.

First, with the world economy overheated, severe pressures were placed on capacity as well as on food and commodity prices. The upward pressures on commodity prices were reinforced by supply shortfalls. At the same time, during this three-year period money growth in industrial countries accelerated sharply (Table 42.3). Some of this acceleration originated in the USA and, in part at least, transmitted to the rest of the industrial world; but some of the acceleration in other countries was also home grown, partly to accommodate wage–price pressures, partly to implement a 'go for growth' policy, partly to resist upward pressures on the currency (as in Japan's case).

The acceleration of some 5 percentage points in money growth in industrial countries would, *in itself*, have been expected to lift inflation in the industrial countries in due course to the same degree.

Table 42.3 Key economic indicators – OECD industrial countries (1967–91)

	Inflation[a]	Price of oil[b]	Increase in base money[a] (%)	Increase in broad money[a] (%)	OECD unemployment[b]	OECD growth in GDP[b]	General government financial balance		Average current account as percentage of GDP unsigned	
							G7	Other	G3	G7
1967	2.9	1.73	6.0	9.2	3.0	3.8			0.9	0.9
1968	3.9	1.73	7.4	10.9	3.0	5.4			1.1	1.2
1969	4.7	1.73	7.9	9.7	2.9	5.3			1.0	1.2
1970	5.6	1.73	7.3	7.5	3.1	3.3	−0.1	0.1	0.7	0.8
1971	5.2	2.14	11.5	13.7	3.5	3.7	−0.8	−0.5	1.0	1.0
1972	4.6	2.45	11.5	15.0	3.6	5.3	−0.7	−0.6	1.0	0.8
1973	7.6	3.37	13.8	13.4	3.3	6.0	−0.2	0.0	0.7	0.8
1974	13.1	11.25	11.1	10.9	3.6	0.7	−0.9	−0.7	1.3	2.1
1975	11.1	11.02	5.6	11.9	5.2	0.1	−4.4	−4.0	0.7	1.1
1976	8.3	11.89	7.3	14.6	5.3	4.6	−3.2	−2.9	0.6	1.0
1977	8.5	12.88	8.7	12.6	5.2	3.7	−2.4	−2.3	1.0	0.9
1978	7.2	12.88	10.0	11.2	5.1	4.1	−2.7	−2.7	1.3	1.4
1979	9.2	18.91	10.8	10.7	5.2	3.6	−2.2	−2.3	0.5	0.8
1980	11.9	31.03	7.8	8.1	5.9	1.2	−2.7	−2.7	0.9	1.0
1981	10.1	36.3	4.9	8.2	6.7	1.6	−2.8	−3.0	0.4	1.2
1982	7.5	33.9	7.3	8.8	8.0	0.1	−4.0	−4.1	0.5	1.1
1983	5.1	30.0	8.6	12.1	8.6	2.7	−4.3	−4.4	1.3	1.1
1984	4.8	28.9	6.5	8.5	8.1	4.4	−3.4	−3.5	2.3	1.0
1985	4.2	27.4	8.1	9.1	8.0	3.4	−3.2	−3.3	3.1	1.3
1986	2.4	15.0	8.4	8.7	7.9	2.8	−3.2	−3.2	4.1	1.7
1987	2.9	17.9	9.3	8.1	7.4	3.2	−2.3	−2.3	3.7	2.1
1988	3.4	14.8	7.8	7.3	6.9	4.4	−1.6	−1.7	3.1	2.2
1989	4.5	17.4	6.3	5.6	6.4	3.3	−0.9	−1.0	2.8	2.5
1990	5.0	22.2	6.5		6.2	2.5	−1.6	−1.7	2.0	2.1
1991	4.3	19.3			7.1	1.0	−2.3	−3.6	1.2	1.5

Sources: [a] IMF, *International Financial Statistics*; [b] OECD, *Economic Outlooks*

Second, by March 1973 the IMF system had collapsed and key currencies began to float *vis-à-vis* one another. In retrospect, this breakdown had become inevitable following the succession of exchange crises beginning in 1967 and the failures, as it turned out, of the Smithsonian Agreement (Chapter 2).

The shift to flexible rates meant that the world economy was now operating under a new set of rules. Despite some academic literature and some experience in the 1920s, these new rules were not well understood (see Chapter 3).

The third major disturbance to the world economy was the first oil price shock at the end of 1973. The price of oil quadrupled (Table 42.3). Oil revenue increased by some $70 billion in 1974, leaving large current account deficits in the oil-importing countries. The OECD share represented a transfer of income of some 2 per cent of OECD GNP. Also, the financing of such large current account deficits placed tremendous stress on the international financial system.

At the same time, with unchanged macro policy the oil price shock would of itself have been expected to raise OECD prices directly by some 2 percentage points (on top of that due to the acceleration in money growth). Indirect wage adjustments would have added more to the inflationary effect. The direct deflationary effect − flowing from the increased oil import bill − was also some 2 per cent of GDP. The deflationary effect of itself would have acted to reduce government revenue and hence to increase budget deficits. The oil price shock also provoked substantial and disruptive structural change within the economies, e.g. away from energy-intensive industries.

Faced with stagflationary forces of this order of magnitude, how did the authorities react in 1974–5? The stance of monetary policy was ambiguous, depending on the measure used. Nominal money growth slowed while real money growth fell even more sharply. On the other hand, real interest rates became negative. Fiscal policy, as we note shortly, did unambiguously ease.

How do we explain the developments in the real economy in 1974–5? Table 42.2 shows that there were several deflationary forces at work: the sharp increase in the real price of oil, the excessive real wage adjustments (the mirror image of which was the sharp fall in the share of profits), the very pronounced decline in real money balances. On the other hand, notably in 1975, fiscal policy was expansionary to the extent of nearly 2 per cent of the combined GNP of the G7. Moreover, real interest rates were mostly negative in those years.

On balance, however, the deflationary forces dominated and real growth declined sharply while the unemployment rate rose on average by some 2 points. At the same time, the earlier money growth combined with the oil price shock produced a sharp acceleration in inflation in 1974–5. Inflation jumped from less than 5 per cent in 1972 to over 12 per cent in 1974–5. The fiscal expansion combined with the decline in activity also led to a large jump in public sector deficits (Table 42.3) (see Llewellyn 1983; Black 1985).

THE YEARS 1976–83

In the years 1976–9 the industrial economies grew at an average of some 4 per cent. Despite this, however, the unemployment rate fell only marginally by some 0.2 points. Inflation dropped to an average of some 8.3 per cent, still high by postwar standards.

How do we explain the recovery in real growth? At least until late 1979 the real price of oil fell. At the same time, the growth of real money balances recovered sharply. Fiscal policy, however, was on balance marginally restrictive. Also, the real interest rate rose but on average continued to be relatively low. Finally, the real wage gap improved marginally but was still high in relation to the levels achieved in the 1960s and early 1970s. On balance, the expansionary influences dominated.

The world economy was still precariously placed in 1979 when it was shaken by a second oil price shock. Measured in terms of GNP the income transfer from OECD countries was of the same order of magnitude as before; so were the direct and indirect impacts on inflation.

Unemployment rose sharply between 1981 and 1983, while the real growth rate fell substantially in the four years 1980–3. The immediate effect of the oil price shock also pushed up inflation in 1980–1. So the industrial economies experienced now a second major round of stagflation.

The deflationary forces at work were more powerful than they had been during the first oil price shock. In the setting of macro policy, overall priority was now assigned to fighting inflation. Policies tightened, reinforcing the direct deflationary effects of the oil shock. Between 1980 and 1982 monetary policies tightened sharply. The growth in real money balances fell dramatically in 1980–1. Real interest rates also rose to historically high levels (a sharp contrast to the first oil price shock when real interest rates were negative). At the same time concern over the persistently high budget deficits led the authorities in a number of the large industrial countries to adopt tight fiscal policies. Excluding the USA, fiscal policy in 1980–2 tightened in the six largest industrial countries by over 2 per cent of GNP (Table 42.2). Including the USA reduces this to 0.7 per cent. The sharp fall in activity, however, led to increases in public sector deficits in those years, despite the fiscal tightening. Finally, the real wage gap rose again, but only slightly, in the wake of the second oil shock.

The next major shock to the world economy between 1981 and 1983 was the implementation of Reagan's supply-side policies. Beginning in August 1981 the US administration put into place three successive annual cuts in personal income tax rates as well as some tax relief to business (Chapter 46).

Those years were particularly dramatic because they also saw a substantial change in the US monetary–fiscal policy mix. Monetary policy began to tighten in late 1979; at the same time fiscal policy eased, leaving in its wake large budget deficits in the USA. Easy fiscal policies and tighter monetary policies combined to put severe upward pressures on real interest rates in the USA.

There were three other important developments in the years between 1976 and 1983. Current account imbalances widened in 1977–8 (Table 42.3). This largely reflected the shift to a current account deficit in the USA, after years of surpluses, and the switch in Japan from a current account deficit to a large surplus. These imbalances created new trade frictions between the two largest economies; they also triggered a real devaluation of the US dollar and a real appreciation of the yen.

The second important development in the second half of the 1970s was the adoption by all the large industrial countries of 'monetarist-type' policies. These countries, from 1974 to 1975, began to announce money growth targets in advance with the avowed aim of containing and gradually reducing money growth. (The experience with money targeting is reviewed in Chapter 43.)

The third important development which dates from the end of this period is the Third World debt crisis. The origins of this crisis can readily be traced to

a) the second oil price shock (which escalated oil payments),
b) the reduction in the real growth in industrial countries (which cut back the demand for the exports of the Third World countries),
c) the sharp rise in real interest rates (which increased the payments to service the debt) and
d) the domestic mismanagement in many debtor countries, which also played a contributory role.

In its wake the debt crisis left many banks in industrial countries vulnerable, over-exposed as they were with bad debts, and, for some years at least, there were grave concerns over the possibility of a crisis. However, by the late 1980s these concerns had abated.

THE YEARS 1984 TO 1991–2

Beginning in 1983 economic activity began to recover. This was the start of a protracted period of economic growth which was to last some six years. Although on average real growth was more subdued than in the recovery phase of 1976–9, it did last longer. The other major difference between the two post oil shock recovery phases is that, whereas unemployment barely improved in 1976–9, in 1984–9 the unemployment rate fell, ultimately, by over 2 points.

The tight monetary–fiscal policies, combined with the sharp fall in the price of oil, also led to substantial falls in the rate of inflation. By the second half of the 1980s the rate of inflation had reached levels comparable with those of the second half of the 1960s. Interestingly, the second half of the 1980s saw substantial declines in *both* inflation and unemployment.

What were the underlying forces acting on the real economy in 1984–9? The growth in real money balances accelerated substantially. At the same time, real interest rates declined over the period, while remaining high by historical standards. Also, importantly, the real wage gap fell significantly, by 1988–9 reaching levels, on one measure at any rate, comparable with those of the late 1960s. At least until 1988 and into 1989, too, the real price of oil fell sharply. On the other hand, fiscal policies continued to be tight: the cumulative restriction was nearly 1.5 per cent of GNP.

By 1989 the industrial economies were beginning to show signs of weakness. For a while weaknesses were primarily located in the USA and the UK, with Japan and Germany continuing to grow strongly. However, by 1991 Germany and Japan had also weakened. By 1992 it is fair to say that the industrial economies were in the throes of a recession. Growth slowed down significantly while the unemployment rate climbed again. The fall in activity also led to a resurgence of public sector deficits, despite fiscal stances which continued to be fairly conservative.

What forces were at work in generating the recession? Again, we can draw on our framework but we will need, now, to add one further element which served to reinforce and sustain the downturn: the 'financial fragility' apparent in a number of the larger economies.

We can almost certainly rule out real wage gaps as a factor contributing to the downturn. It is apparent from Table 42.2 that, whatever the measure used, the real wage gap continued to decline in the second half of the 1980s.

In part because of the earlier easier monetary policies and the now rising price of oil, inflation had begun to accelerate in 1989–90. With the economies overheated and inflation rising monetary policy became tighter by 1989. The real price of oil also rose sharply in 1989–90. In 1988–9, too, fiscal policies continued to be tight.

All three of the largest international organisations (the IMF, the OECD and the Bank for International Settlements) agree that there were some additional financial factors at work by 1990–2 (IMF 1991, 1992; Bank for International Settlements 1992; OECD 1992). Two developments in particular have received a good deal of attention.

The first is the deteriorating financial balances of the corporate and household sectors. The second is the unfavourable balance sheet positions of financial institutions in some industrial countries.

In a number of countries, it seems, household financial positions deteriorated. This manifested itself in a number of ways: falling net worth to income positions (e.g. because of excessive borrowing combined with declining asset values), rising ratios of debt to disposable income and rising gross interest payments relative to disposable income. Falling net worth positions may induce households to increase their saving to restore net worth; rising debt or interest payments in relation to income increase household commitments in the form of interest and amortization payments, inducing some reduction in consumption spending.

Debt–income ratios rose sharply in the second half of the 1980s in Japan, Germany, the USA, France and the UK. Gross interest payments in relation to income also rose sharply in the USA, Japan and the UK. Finally, household net wealth as a proportion of disposable income fell sharply at the end of the 1980s in Japan and the UK.

In the corporate sector manifestations of financial vulnerability would take the form of rising interest payments in relation to income, of rising debt–equity ratios or of falling business net worth. Financial vulnerability could lead to bankruptcies, declining investment and reduced employment. Attention has focused here primarily on the USA and the UK. In the other large countries the problem was either less evident or non-existent.

In the USA business net interest payments as a ratio of output rose very sharply in the 1970s and again in the 1980s. As well, net worth declined in the second half of the 1980s but debt—equity ratios actually declined slightly in the second half of the 1980s. In the UK both debt—equity ratios and the interest burden rose sharply in the second half of the 1980s.

We turn now to the balance sheet positions of the financial institutions, particularly the banks. Here it is contended that a number of factors, including bad loans, asset deflation, and the imposition of Bank for International Settlements capital adequacy rules, have all combined to place the banks in a more vulnerable financial position and this has made them increasingly reluctant to make loans (the so-called 'credit crunch'). In 1992 this continued to be the subject of a lively debate, unfortunately without any real resolution. However, a very recent study by the OECD (O'Brien and Browne) concluded:

> It would appear that an increase in the cost of bank intermediation, resulting from loan losses and higher capital costs, has caused the supply of bank credit to contract so that borrowers must pay more for the same quantity of bank credit. This increase in cost is likely larger than in past cycles because of the current marked deterioration in banks' asset quality and the costs of complying with the BIS capital standards.
>
> (1992: 12)

To conclude, it would appear that there were almost certainly some financial factors at work in 1990–2 which may have acted as a further constraint on spending and may thus have served to prolong the recession, all other things being equal.

Another important development beginning in 1983 and into the second half of the 1980s was the persistent large current account deficit in the USA and the large current account surpluses in Japan and Germany (the latter at least to 1990). As Table 42.3 shows, current account imbalances widened substantially beginning in 1983. As in 1977–8 this again provoked growing tensions between the USA and Japan.

How can we account for this escalation in the imbalances?

Most of the variations in the US current account can be explained in terms of two key variables: the real effective exchange rate (appropriately lagged) and the relative growth in total real domestic demand (Dean and Koromzay 1987; Corker 1991). In the USA real domestic demand grew between 1983 and 1985 by an average of 5.9 per cent; in Japan it was only 3.2 per cent and in Germany it was 1.7 per cent. At the same time, there was a very sharp real appreciation of the US dollar. Econometric tests suggest that at least two-thirds of the deterioration in the US current account between 1982 and 1985 can be accounted for by these two factors alone (Krugman and Baldwin 1987).

The same framework can also go some way to explaining the substantial reversal in the current account imbalances in the years between 1988 and 1990. First, differentials in domestic demand growth now worked in favour of reversing the imbalances. Real demand growth stalled in the USA while it continued to be vigorous in both Germany and Japan. Second, there was a substantial real effective devaluation of the US dollar and a real effective appreciation of the yen. This served to reinforce the effects of divergent real growth rates.

It is worth noting that the two driving forces identified – the real exchange rate and relative spending – can themselves be reduced to underlying monetary and fiscal policies at home and abroad. So ultimately the current accounts will be explained predominantly by monetary and fiscal forces.

However, relative monetary and fiscal policies will impact quite differently on the current account through these two variables. A relative monetary contraction leads to a real appreciation but also lowers spending. On average these two effects tend to neutralise each other, so relative monetary policies account for little of the movement in the current account. In sharp contrast, fiscal expansion leads to a real appreciation and an increase in relative spending; thus the two effects reinforce one another. It is therefore not surprising to find that fiscal expansion in the USA combined with fiscal tightening abroad will account for roughly some three-quarters of the US current account deficit between 1982 and 1985.

Another development in the period worthy of mention was the worldwide collapse of the stock market in October 1987. This was seen then as a much needed correction to the growing gap between yields on bonds and equity yields. Its timing, however, was not unrelated to the failures on the part of the leading countries to resolve the fundamental imbalances (Institute for International Economics 1987). The stock market collapse provoked many governments into easing monetary policy to neutralise its anticipated deflationary effects.

As it happens, the stock market recovered fairly quickly from the 1987 collapse. Indeed by 1989–90 much of the ground had been regained in many of the large industrial countries. In retrospect it appears that there may have been unnecessary panic at the time. However, Japan which had survived the original collapse, did experience its own dramatic collapse in the course of 1990–2 (Chapter 47).

SOME GENERAL COMMENTS ON THE GLOBAL EXPERIENCE

A striking feature of the global macro performance is the fact that real cycles have tended in general to be synchronised across industrial countries. Why is this? There are four potential explanations. First, business-cycle theory suggests that there will be purely endogenous forces at work (e.g. an unsustainable rate of investment) which will produce business cycles. Second, as we saw in Chapter 13, business cycles can be transmitted, even under flexible rates. Third, policy reactions could also be common to many industrial countries. Fourth, there may be common external factors at work, the most important of which are the oil price shocks.

THE CHANGED INTERNATIONAL MACRO ENVIRONMENT

Our review of the principal developments in the world economy in the 1970s and 1980s has revealed how the world economy has been transformed in a number of respects since the late 1960s. It is worthwhile at this point to summarise the principal differences between the policy environment today and that of the early 1970s.

a) We now have a managed float for the key currencies. Also, and most important, we have the EMS, an important aim of which is to stabilise exchange rates amongst its member countries.

b) Domestic and international financial markets are now freer and there is greater economic interdependence amongst Western economies (Chapter 5). These developments have major implications for the transmission of disturbances across nations, the way in which monetary and fiscal policies work, and real exchange rate volatility.

c) There is now greater exposure to supply (e.g. notably oil price) shocks than in the 1950s and 1960s.

d) Despite recent attempts to rein in the role of government, the public sector now absorbs a much larger share of GNP than it did in the late 1960s. For the OECD as a whole, total outlays of general government represented some 32.3 per cent of GDP in 1970; by 1989, this had increased to some 40 per cent.

e) Persistent large budget deficits in the 1970s and the early years of the 1980s have left a legacy of much larger debt to GDP ratios and much larger interest payments to total government outlays. For example, for an average of fourteen OECD countries, in 1973 net government debt was some 16 per cent of GNP; in 1990 it was 31 per cent. The much larger burden of debt and interest payments currently acts as a major constraint on governments' use of fiscal policy.

f) Average unemployment rates are now much higher. For the OECD as a whole, the average unemployment rate at the start of the 1970s was about 3.5 per cent; in 1991 it was over 7 per cent. With inflation rates now reverting to late 1960s levels the trade-off between inflation and unemployment has clearly dramatically deteriorated.

g) The USA's economic dominance is receding while Japan's is in the ascendancy. Large and persistent current account deficits in the USA have now transformed it from a position of a large net creditor *vis-à-vis* the rest of the world to a large net debtor (see Fieleke 1990). On the other hand, Japan is a very large net creditor.

In 1982 the US net external asset position as a percentage of GNP was about 4 per cent. By 1990 its net debt position was some 16 per cent of GNP, a deterioration of the order of 20 per cent. Japan in 1982 had a creditor position close to the USA's (about 2–3 per cent); in 1990 it was around 10 per cent of GNP.

h) There is a real possibility that the world economy is converging towards a situation where three large economic blocs will dominate the economic scene. We have seen how Europe is rapidly moving towards one unified bloc with Germany at its centre. The USA and Canada, in the wake of the free trade agreement, have merged into one unified market. It is expected that Mexico will soon join this market. Japan dominates the Asian region and may in time dominate a new regional bloc. Other countries will have to decide which of the three blocs they will choose to join.

APPENDIX   THE REAL WAGE GAP

In this appendix we try to explain briefly the concept of the real wage gap and its limitations.

Given a base period a real wage gap is said to emerge if the real wage rate (i.e. the wage rate divided by the price of value added) increases faster than labour productivity. In index form we can write

$$\frac{W/\mathrm{Pv}}{Y/L} = \frac{WL}{Y\mathrm{Pv}} = \frac{W/Y/L}{\mathrm{Pv}}$$

where W is the wage rate, Pv is the price of value added, L is the labour force and Y is real output. These are three equivalent indices of the real wage gap. The first is the ratio of the real product wage to productivity, the second is the share of wages in national product and the third is real unit labour costs (i.e. unit labour costs deflated by the value added price).

Calculations of the real wage gap in index form based on the above principle can be, and have been, made. If the real wage gap is positive over time the presumption is that there are 'classical' factors at work which would be expected to have an adverse effect on employment.

Calculations of this kind are now widely recognised to be subject to many limitations (see Adams *et al.* 1986; Helliwell 1988). First, the base year chosen can sometimes be critical. Second, cyclical factors at work may give a wrong reading of the situation; a fall in demand may be associated with a fall in productivity which in turn increases the wage gap. Third, if real wages are excessive there may be a substitution of capital for labour; this, in turn, increases labour productivity, implying a fall in the real wage gap at a time when unemployment is actually rising. Fourth, Japan, surprisingly, had a comparatively large real wage gap as measured, at least to the late 1970s, yet Japan's unemployment performance was excellent. To explain this apparent contradiction one has to invoke special explanations, e.g. that Japan's profit share was initially too high or that the wage share rose because labour was scarce or that the unemployment rate in Japan simply does not respond to the gap.

Table 42.3 showed calculations of the real wage gap for Europe arrived at as above. A striking feature of the series is that the wage gap virtually disappeared by the late 1980s, although unemployment in 1989 was substantially higher than in the late 1960s.

OECD (1987) notes that, although the profit share (the mirror image of the wage share) returned to levels of the late 1960s, the profit rate (i.e. the return to capital) had not recovered and, indeed, in some countries continued to deteriorate. The

OECD makes the point that

> this is because the increase in capital–labour ratios, which has tended to improve labour productivity, has been accompanied by falling capital productivity. Because part of the increase in the average labour productivity is due to the increase in capital intensity, labour productivity may be an inappropriate measure of the warranted increase in real wages. In these circumstances a restoration of the profit rate to its level in the 1970s requires that the profit share be above, rather than equal to, its previous level.
>
> (1987: 53, 57)

Calculations of the adjusted real wage gap (Table 42.3) (i.e. adjusted for total factor productivity) demonstrate that although the adjusted real wage gap has fallen substantially in the second half of the 1980s it is still higher than in the late 1960s, early 1970s.

Bruno (1986) and Bruno and Sachs (1985) have also tried to refine the real wage gap concept further. To eliminate cyclical influences they try and calculate a real wage rate (equal to the average product of labour) at *full employment*; any excess of the real wage rate over the calculated full employment real wage rate represents a 'real wage gap'.

43

The rise and fall of monetarism

INTRODUCTION

Beginning in the mid to late 1970s all the large, and a few small, countries began to announce targets in the growth of one or more money aggregates. This was widely hailed at the time as a triumph for monetarist thinking. By the 1980s, however, there was some disenchantment with the policy and with monetarism. Some countries abandoned the policy altogether; others continued to use it but in a much less doctrinaire fashion.

This chapter reviews in some detail country experiences with money targeting. The chapter looks at the background to targeting and at the implementation strategies adopted. It then tries to evaluate the experience.

BACKGROUND TO THE ADOPTION OF MONETARY TARGETING

Beginning in the mid-1970s a number of industrial countries adopted a policy of targeting the growth in money aggregates. By the late 1970s all of the seven largest Western economies (the USA, Japan,[1] Germany, the UK, France, Italy and Canada) and two smaller economies[2] (Australia and Switzerland) had monetary targets of one form or another in place.

Why did so few smaller countries adopt money targeting? Two reasons are sometimes offered for this. The first is that many smaller economies are and have been on fixed exchange rates, so they do not have or have not had control over the money stock. The argument, in part at least, explains why countries like Belgium, Austria, Ireland and Denmark have not announced money growth targets. It also explains why

Switzerland, which has a flexible rate regime, is able to target. On the other hand, it does not explain why Australia, on a crawling peg regime after 1976 (to 1983), chose to adopt a form of money growth targeting, while the other Scandinavian countries, with adjustable peg regimes, chose not to. New Zealand has never announced money growth targets, even after it floated in 1985.

The second reason is that many smaller economies have the perception that their money demand is relatively unstable, thus rendering money growth targeting inappropriate. The judgement may be correct (indeed their relative openness may argue for this) but, as it happens, there is no available empirical support for the proposition.

From our perspective there are three distinctive ideas which to a greater or lesser degree are associated with a strategy of money growth targeting, as originally conceived. First, money growth would be closely monitored and would be directed principally at reducing, or holding, the rate of inflation to a modest level. Second, money growth would be stable, avoiding excessive fluctuations which were seen as disruptive to the economy. A corollary of this was that in the fight against excessive inflation money growth would be brought down gradually until it reached acceptable levels.

Third, the targets would be publicly announced in advance. The objective here was one of favourably influencing expectations by making a credible commitment to policies which would contribute to a reduction in inflation.

What motivated many industrial countries to adopt monetary targeting when they did? First, there was the determination to avoid a repetition of the years 1971–3; in those years, as we saw, money growth exploded and this was followed soon afterwards by a sharp acceleration in inflation. Second, there was the disappointing performance of discretionary monetary management, with the growing conviction that steadier monetary growth might improve an economy's performance. As we saw too there was some theoretical support for this.

Third, with large and growing public sector deficits in the mid-1970s monetary targeting was seen as a means of constraining the potential for excessive money creation. Fourth, influenced by New Classical thinking there was the idea that an announcement that money growth would be gradually reduced would help to minimise the real costs of disinflation. Fifth, the switch to flexible rates had now also given the central banks the *capability* of controlling the money stock, making the policy more feasible.

IMPLEMENTATION STRATEGIES

There are important differences in the way in which the policy has been implemented in the countries. (See Table 43.1 for details.)

Many changed the aggregate they targeted as institutional conditions changed. Switzerland switched in 1980 from M1 to M0 (base money). West Germany switched from central bank money (see note e to the table) to a broad M3 aggregate. France switched from M2 to M3 in 1991. The UK abandoned sterling M3 as a target after 1986.

Many announced targets in more than one aggregate. The UK did this for some years. In 1982–3 she announced targets in three aggregates. The USA has always announced targets in several aggregates, with M2 the 'preferred' aggregate in more recent years (but now becoming discredited).

Some adopted wide bands of up to 4 points (i.e. 2 points on each side of a central rate); others preferred much narrower or zero bands. Some again changed their bands over time. Canada and the UK opted for very wide bands of 4 points; the USA has had bands of between 2 and 4 points. Switzerland has opted for a zero band;

Table 43.1 Monetary targeting – select countries (key features to 1991)

Country	Money aggregate targeted (period)	Band	Special characteristics
Australia	M3 (77–85)	2 points (except for 1980)	Targeting abandoned in early 1985
Canada	M1 (76–82)	4 points	Targeting abandoned in November 1982
France	M2 (77–90) M3 (91)	0–2 points (band increasing over time)	–
Italy	Total domestic credit (75–85) M2 credit to private sector (85–91)	0–4 points	–
Japan	M2 + CDs (75–91)	0–1 point	Forecast not strictly target[a]
Switzerland	M1 (75–8) M0[b] (80–91)	Zero range	No target was announced in 1979
UK	M3 (sterling) (76–86) M1 (82–3), M0 (84–91) PSL$_2$[c] (82–3)	4 points	–
USA	M1 (75–86), M2 (75–91) M3 (75–91), TOND[d] (83–91)	2–4 points	–
West Germany	Central bank money[e] (75–87) M3 (88–91)	0 (to 78) 2–3 (79–91)	–

Notes: [a] Forecasts are announced in the first month of each quarter and refer to the growth of M2 + CDs between the current quarter and the same quarter of the previous year. This means that, while the forecasts are of annual growth in the money stock, they are announced after three quarters of the year have passed. Events in the final two months of the fourth quarter will have a relatively small weight in determining the outcome. Consequently, the outcomes have invariably been very close to the forecasts.
[b] Base money.
[c] Private sector liquidity 2 (PSL$_2$) includes sterling assets of up to one year to maturity as well as currency and short-term bank deposits.
[d] Total domestic debt of non-financial sectors.
[e] Currency and required minimum reserves on domestic bank liabilities at constant reserve ratios (January 1974 as base).
CDs, certificates of deposit.

Australia and more recently Germany had bands of about 2–3 points. Germany and France switched from a zero band to a wider band.

A target range which is too wide begins to lose credibility. If governments have too wide a margin in which to manoeuvre it will be difficult to underpin firm expectations about outcomes. On the other hand, a target range which is too narrow leaves little or no room for discretion; moreover, it may be harder to achieve.

Many countries which targeted announced their target once a year for a year forward. In Canada targets were set for unspecified periods into the future. Japan announces a target each quarter (see note a to Table 43.1). The UK occasionally varied the period over which the target applied.

How would a central rate be set and how would the margin of flexibility provided by a band be used?

Germany is the most articulate about how its central rate is set and how it uses its band. The required money growth depends on assumptions made about the rate of inflation, the growth of output and the change in velocity. On inflation, they have some notion of an 'unavoidable' increase in prices. In general, this is related to the rate of inflation in the year immediately preceding, though if that is seen as excessively high a downward adjustment is made.

The assumption about the growth of output comprised two parts: capacity growth and the growth due to a change in the utilisation of capacity. The determination of the first was fairly straightforward; a projection was also made of the latter, based on the state of the business cycle. Finally, the change in velocity had a long-term component and a cyclical component which, it was argued, was itself related to the degree of capacity utilisation.

This determines the central rate. In turn Germany allows a band of some 2–3 points (i.e. $1-1\frac{1}{2}$ points on each side of the central rate). So how does she decide on the appropriate point within the range in the course of the year?

The emphasis here is on unanticipated developments on three fronts: inflation, pressures on the (real) value of the deutschmark and economic activity. In principle, there is a strong disposition to counter unexpected inflationary tendencies. In practice a distinction is made between, on the one hand, first-round effects of externally induced inflation (an oil price shock, rising commodity prices) and of a devaluation and, on the other hand, second-round effects flowing from wage adjustments to external shocks or devaluations. In the last case, not only is the inflation not accommodated, but it is actively countered, even at the expense of lower activity. In the first case the authorities will exercise discretion over the appropriate policy.

As for pressures on the currency, a distinction needs to be made between the associated inflationary effects, which are already taken care of, as above, and the effects on the traded goods sector of large changes in the real value of the currency. If there is what is perceived to be an excessive real devaluation (appreciation), the money target tends to be set in the lower (upper) range.

Finally, unexpected changes in economic activity are also taken into account in the setting of policy. Here again the authorities will exercise discretion. If the economy is unexpectedly overheated the authorities will set monetary policy in the lower point of the band. On the other hand, if the economy is unexpectedly sluggish the monetary policy will ease and money growth will be closer to the upper point of the band.

THE CHOICE OF MONEY AGGREGATE

How do the authorities go about deciding which money aggregate to target?

It is now generally accepted that there are two criteria which govern the choice of the money (or credit) aggregate. First, how effectively it is controlled, and second, how closely it is associated with the final target of policy (e.g. nominal income or inflation).

On the first question of 'controllability', there are two issues. One is the question of which potential money aggregate can be most effectively controlled. Another concerns the 'optimal' operational strategy to achieve control over any given money aggregate.

Consider, as an illustration, the choice of three aggregates: base money, M1 and M2 (which includes all deposits of the banking system). Most economists would probably concede that, of the three, base money is the easiest to control (provided exchange rates are allowed to move freely) with M2 next and M1 the most difficult to control. The reason for the last ranking is that M1 is largely demand determined while M2 is largely supply determined (i.e. determined predominantly by the amount of base money in the system).

As one reviews the academic literature one finds two broad approaches to money stock control: one based on a reserve asset control (e.g. base money, bank reserves) and another based on interest rate control.

The issue of reserve asset control versus interest rate control has provoked a huge literature (Sivesind and Hurley 1980; Axilrod and Lindsay 1981). The basic conclusion of this literature is that base money control will be superior if money demand disturbances and errors in forecasting income are dominant. If, however, money supply disturbances are dominant the interest rate is the preferred method of control. (See the Appendix for a formal demonstration.)

To illustrate, suppose data on interest rates and a reserve asset (base money) are available more frequently than data for the money stock (which is targeted). Suppose now that there is a supply shock (e.g. an unanticipated shift in the demand for currency or in the demand for banks' excess reserves). If the interest rate is targeted, immediate action will be taken to restore the money target. If, however, base money is targeted the excess supply will be allowed (at least until it manifests itself in a change in the money stock). By contrast, if there is a money demand shock the excess demand for money would be accommodated with an interest rate target but not so with a base money target. Thus, the error will now be larger with an interest rate target than with a base money target.[3]

We turn now to the second criterion in the choice of a money aggregate: the closeness of the association with income.

The task of selecting the most appropriate money aggregate is difficult enough in a closed economy; it is made much more difficult in economies which are closely integrated financially with the rest of the world. Consider the possibilities in the open economy. Suppose we start with a broad money definition which is limited to non-bank resident holdings of currency and deposits in the home currency. Potential additions to this definition would include the following:

a) resident holdings of foreign currency deposits abroad;
b) resident holdings of foreign currency deposits at home;
c) resident holdings of home currency deposits abroad;
d) non-resident holdings of home currency deposits at home;
e) non-resident holdings of foreign currency deposits at home;
f) non-resident holdings of home currency deposits abroad.

It is evident that the issues are now much more complex.

It is possible to proceed at two levels: at the empirical level and at the theoretical level.

At the empirical level, one possibility is to regress income (or inflation) against the alternative money aggregates to see which definition provides the 'best' explanation for the movement in income. The classic study of this kind is by Friedman and Meiselman (1963), emulated since by many others. Or more powerful statistical tools could be used to try and establish the closeness of a relationship between a money aggregate and income or inflation. Still another possibility is to estimate money demand equations using different definitions of money as the dependent variables; the 'best' definition is now the one that gives the most stable money demand equation (see for example Boughton 1979).

The theoretical approach takes as a starting point the fact that an economy is exposed to unanticipated disturbances over a given period; it then asks, in the face of such disturbances, which money aggregate is the most closely associated with nominal income. Again, using this approach it is difficult to reach any definitive conclusion. In the end everything turns on the sources of disturbances. Indeed, because the optimal money aggregate depends on the sources of disturbances it is possible to rationalise the adoption of targets in more than one aggregate (see Argy 1983).

EVALUATING THE EXPERIENCE WITH MONETARY TARGETING

How does one go about evaluating the experience?

One simple way is to see to what extent targets were actually achieved. This is a test so to speak of how *credible* the targets have been.

Argy *et al.* (1990) find that from 1975 to 1988 out of some 140 individual annual targets (including more than once for countries with multiple targets such as the USA) less than half were actually achieved. (The experience since 1988 appears to be on a par.) Moreover, misses above targets were far more numerous than those on the low side.

We said that the original intention was to bring money growth down gradually. Did they at least succeed in this objective? It is not always easy to judge because sometimes apparent trends are reversed. Canada and Switzerland clearly did succeed; the others were far more ambiguous.

Why the failures here? Four reasons come to mind. First, there could have been technical difficulties in *controlling* the money stock. Second, some countries used monetary policy to try and stabilise what were perceived as excessive exchange rate movements. Germany, Australia, Switzerland and the UK provide strong illustrations of this.

In Germany when there has been excessive upward pressure on the deutschmark, as in 1976-8 or 1986-7 the monetary authorities have allowed the money growth targets to be overshot, sometimes substantially. On the other hand when the deutschmark has been weak, as in 1980-1, money growth has settled just below the lower end of the band.

In Switzerland, up to 1975 exchange rates were determined freely by market forces, with very little management on the part of the monetary authorities. From 1975 concern over the loss of competitiveness from a substantial, then, real appreciation provoked the authorities into intervening on a larger scale. This peaked in 1978 when there was massive intervention in support of the dollar. In those years too attempts were made to restrict the inflow of capital. The aim here was to monitor money growth as well as the real appreciation. These attempts failed, however. The growth in M1 in 1978 was 16.2 per cent against a target growth of 6 per cent.

In the UK when sterling was strong in 1977 the authorities eased monetary policy to moderate the appreciation; as a consequence the monetary target was overshot by a large margin.

The Australian experience with exchange rate management is summarised in Chapter 48. We note here, anticipating, that in 1980-1 when there were large inflows of capital the authorities tried to mitigate the appreciation of the Australian dollar by undertaking large official purchases of US dollars. The authorities found it difficult to sterilise these purchases, however, and money supply grew rapidly, exceeding its target.

Third, targeting the money stock effectively means allowing the interest rate to find its own market level. Governments are sometimes reluctant to let this happen, however. This may have been the case in Australia in 1979, for example, when the money growth target was overshot.

Fourth and most importantly in many industrial countries, as we have already noted, there has been a trend towards the deregulation of both domestic and international financial markets. At the same time, remaining regulations, budget deficits, high and volatile interest rates, inflation and technological advances combined to provoke a variety of innovations in the financial sector. These developments had extremely important implications for the way in which monetary policy worked. In many countries the combination of deregulation and innovation made it more difficult to interpret a money aggregate; at the same time, it weakened the relationship between a money aggregate and income. Uncertainty about the relationship between particular money aggregates and income rendered a policy of announcing money growth targets less efficacious and reliable.

Many countries experienced difficulties of this kind, particularly so in the 1980s. Some of these experiences will be described later in the chapter.

At this point we provide a very simple illustration of how deregulation can distort the significance of a money aggregate. Suppose interest rates are deregulated, leaving banks now free to set their own interest rates on their deposits and on their loans. Typically, banks will now be better placed to compete with non-bank institutions. As a consequence, their deposits become more attractive. If the stock of money is fixed the increase in the demand for deposits (a shift to the left in the LM schedule) will of itself have a deflationary impact on the economy. Other things being equal, income drops; the same money stock now does less work (velocity falls) and the relationship between the given stock of money and income breaks down. To maintain the original level of income the money stock needs to rise to accommodate the increase in demand. If the money target was originally set without regard to the deregulation the appropriate strategy is now to allow the money stock to *overshoot* its target. More than anything else it is the financial deregulation, with its distorting effects on the money aggregates, that has led to the disenchantment with monetarist-type policies.

The effects of deregulation combined with the exchange rate experience described earlier, in combination, also help to explain why it is that overshoots tended to dominate over undershoots.

There are several other tests one might apply to the experience with monetary targeting. One is to see if money growth had become *steadier*. The variability (measured as the standard deviation of the quarterly percentage change) of money did decline in the targeting period to 1988 compared with the period from 1971 to the commencement of targeting in five of the eight countries for which data are available for a long enough period to make a comparison. Of the three exceptions, the USA saw an increase in the variability of M1, though this was affected by the big shifts in M1 in the 1980s. Variability of M3 did decline in the targeting period. The remaining exceptions were Switzerland and Canada, which perhaps paradoxically were the most successful in achieving targets (Argy *et al.* 1990).

Another test is to see if targeting saw an improvement in inflation. The real difficulty with this test is that one does not know what performance would have been like without monetary targeting (the same difficulty applies to the test of money growth reduction and to its variability).

For what the evidence is worth most countries which targeted saw inflation fall during the targeting period. The two exceptions, Italy and Canada, make an interesting pair. Italy saw inflation higher, on average, during the targeting period. Canada, on the other hand, was able to achieve its target range on almost every occasion (and the only 'misses' were when monetary growth was lower than targeted), but had no success in reducing inflation. In fact, Canada only achieved a significant decline in inflation after targeting had been abandoned. Australia is also an interesting case in that inflation has been lower on average after monetary projections were discontinued than in either the targeting or the immediate pre-targeting periods.

Finally, one might ask whether disinflation was credible enough to reduce the output costs. The evidence (reviewed in Chapter 46) is that the costs of the disinflation implemented by Thatcher and Reagan were probably no less than in previous disinflation episodes.

DEREGULATION, INNOVATION AND THE DISTORTION TO THE MONEY AGGREGATES

This section describes in somewhat more detail some select experiences with deregulation and innovation. The focus is on the experiences in Canada, the UK and the USA; we describe particular episodes rather than attempt to provide a continuing and comprehensive review of these country experiences (see on this Bank for International Settlements 1984; Suzuki and Yumo 1986). (The Australian and New Zealand experiences are described in Chapter 48.)

The Canadian monetary authorities began announcing targets in M1 growth from 1976. Not long after, a succession of financial innovations began to distort the signals that M1 growth was providing. From the late 1970s, cash management packages became available to larger enterprises; this reduced their demand for working balances. In 1979 banks began to offer savings accounts with interest computed daily; this provoked some (modest) flight out of M1. In 1981 the banks began to offer checkable savings accounts which paid daily interest. This led to a large flight out of M1, sharply reducing the growth of M1 below its target levels from mid-1981 to late 1982. M1 became less appropriate as an intermediate target because, although M1 had fallen sharply, it could not be inferred that monetary policy had tightened and thus had to be eased. In November 1982, the Bank of Canada decided that financial innovations had made it difficult to interpret M1 and so money growth targeting was abandoned. This was replaced by a more flexible approach based on trends in a variety of economic and financial indicators.

In the UK deregulation and innovations have also produced serious distortions to the money aggregates. At the end of 1973 the 'corset' was introduced;[4] it was removed in early 1975, reintroduced at the end of 1976, then removed in mid-1977 until mid-1978, when it was reintroduced. It was then finally abolished in June 1980. Until 1979, too, exchange controls, principally directed at discouraging resident outflows, were in operation. In October 1979 these controls were completely abolished.

We consider here only the distortions to the money aggregates created by the corset, its removal and the abandonment of exchange controls, focusing primarily on the years 1979–80 when the effects were most in evidence.

The imposition of the corset generated a variety of reactions by the banking system and their customers aimed at offsetting or relieving the effects of the new legislation.

First, the corset induced some 'onshore' disintermediation. One important form this took became known as the 'bill leak'. Banks would accept bills issued by customers and then sell these to non-bank holders. The bills, which did not appear as liabilities on the books of the banks, were similar to the certificates of deposit whose growth was being restricted by the legislation. During the third corset period (mid-1978 to June 1980) the bills rose from a base of some £150 million to some £2,700 million.

Second, after the abolition of exchange controls in November 1979, the corset also induced some 'offshore' disintermediation. UK residents were now able to place sterling deposits in banks overseas. These then lent them on to UK residents who had been denied loans by the operation of the corset. What happens here is that the ownership of a sterling deposit shifts from one UK resident to another, so although sterling M3 is unaffected additional lending is generated.

Third, the corset, again after the abolition of exchange controls, induced some offshore 'pure intermediation' by the banking system. Now banks could borrow and lend in foreign currency to UK residents who in the absence of exchange controls could switch into sterling by selling the foreign currency to other UK residents. Thus the ownership of a sterling deposit would change hands from one UK resident to another. So sterling M3 would be unchanged but there would be more lending in sterling.

For these three reasons then the significance of sterling M3 would have been understated.

Because from mid-1979 the corset was producing substantial distortions to banking behaviour and the money aggregates, its removal produced equally dramatic reversals. In the (banking) month of July alone sterling M3 grew by $5\frac{1}{4}$ per cent while interest-bearing liabilities rose some 14 per cent; at the same time the bill leak fell dramatically. The growth of sterling M3 accelerated significantly.

We concluded earlier that, while the corset was on, because of the disintermediation process sterling M3 tended to understate the thrust of the monetary sector. The removal of the corset reversed this. As a result of the reintermediation process, sterling M3 now tended to overstate the thrust of the monetary sector. This view was in fact widely held and indeed allowed for at the time the corset was removed. Not surprisingly, the growth of sterling M3 in 1980 substantially overshot its target.

The US experience is also rich in the areas of financial deregulation and the pace of financial innovation. Deregulation and innovation have all at various times distorted the signals coming from the money aggregates. This has led the authorities to downgrade some aggregates; at the same time money aggregates have been redefined to accommodate the changing financial scene. The experience is too detailed and complex to be summarised here. We therefore limit ourselves to a brief description of the years beginning in the late 1970s and particularly the early 1980s.

From 1975 the Federal Reserve began to announce targets in the growth of several money aggregates. However, from the late 1970s, a number of innovations in the financial sector were making it difficult to interpret the signals coming from, in particular, the M1 and M2 aggregates.

The most important of these financial innovations have been conveniently summarised in the OECD Annual Survey of the US economy published in December 1983 (OECD 1983):

- the growth of money market funds (MMMFs) since the late 1970s, offering the investor unregulated rates of interest and checking facilities for withdrawals of over $500;
- the January 1981 introduction of Negotiable Order of Withdrawal (NOW) (checkable, interest-bearing) accounts with a $5\frac{1}{2}$ per cent interest ceiling;
- the December 1982 introduction of the money market deposit account (MMDA), allowing banks and thrifts to offer services which compete with the MMMFs;
- the January 1983 introduction of super-NOW accounts with no interest ceilings;
- the spread of cash management services offered by banks and brokers, including services such as 'deposit sweeping' (automatic – often daily – transfers between transactions and investment accounts), which maximise clients' investment returns while meeting their immediate liquidity requirements.

To understand how these developments might affect the demand for the money aggregates, particularly M1 and M2, we need to note that NOW accounts and ATS (Automatic Transfers) were included in M1 but MMMFs and MMDAs were not. The last two were included in the M2 aggregate which also included, principally, savings and time deposits.

Consider the innovations which occurred from end-1980. NOW accounts could attract funds from non-interest transactions deposits and/or from other interest-earning assets (e.g. savings deposits) included in M2. To the extent that they came from the former, the demand for M1 in the aggregate would be unaffected. Thus, in targeting M1 growth virtually no adjustment would have been needed. However, to the extent that they came from the latter, the demand for the M1 aggregate would have been bloated and an 'easier' M1 growth target would have been appropriate. The 'easier' money growth target would not have reflected an easier monetary policy – it would have simply accommodated the increased demand for the M1 aggregate. It was thus difficult for the authorities to judge *ex ante* how the M1 growth target should be set. In the event what may have happened is that any increase in the demand for M1 which came from shifts out of savings accounts may have been exactly neutralised by the reduction in the demand for M1 which came from continuing financial innovation (cash management, MMMFs). (See on this Pierce (1984).)

Similar issues arose with the introduction of MMMFs and subsequently MMDAs, both included in M2. Funds could have come from M1 deposits, from other interest-bearing assets included in M2 (e.g. large time deposits) or from assets outside M2.

In the first case, M1 would be distorted; in the second, neither M1 nor M2 would be distorted; in the third, M2 would be distorted.

The introduction of super-NOW accounts in January 1983 raised questions similar to those arising out of NOW accounts.

These difficulties led the Federal Reserve by late 1982 to de-emphasise M1 as a target.

APPENDIX   MONEY STOCK CONTROL

Consider a very simple money demand equation which takes the following form:

$$\text{Mo} = -\alpha_4 r_\text{d} + \alpha_5 Y + m \tag{A1}$$

where Mo is the volume of money, r_d is the interest rate, Y is income and m is a random error term with zero mean.

$$Y = Y_\text{F} + Y_\text{E} \tag{A2}$$

where Y_F is the forecast value of income and Y_E is the error in forecasting income.

Now consider a simple money supply equation of the form

$$\text{Mo} = \alpha_1 r_\text{d} + \alpha_3 B + v \tag{A3}$$

where B is now base money and v is a random error term with zero mean.

The money supply function asserts that (a) if the interest rate rises, other things being equal, the money supply will increase (because the banks will want to reduce their holdings of excess reserves) and (b) if base money increases, the money supply increases, along familiar lines.

Solving (A1) for r_d, substituting the solution in (A3) and then using (A2) gives the equation for base money control.

$$\text{Mo} = b_1 Y_\text{F} + b_1 Y_\text{E} + b_2 B + b_3 v + b_5 m \tag{A4}$$

where

$$b_1 = \frac{\alpha_1 \alpha_5}{\alpha_1 + \alpha_4} \qquad b_2 = \frac{\alpha_3 \alpha_4}{\alpha_1 + \alpha_4} \qquad b_3 = \frac{\alpha_4}{\alpha_1 + \alpha_4} \qquad b_5 = \frac{\alpha_1}{\alpha_1 + \alpha_4}$$

If we now substitute (A2) into (A1) we have

$$\text{Mo} = -\alpha_4 r_\text{d} + \alpha_5 Y_\text{F} + \alpha_5 Y_\text{E} + m \tag{A5}$$

which is the equation for interest rate control.

For base money control we need to forecast Y, v and m, the last two set at zero mean. This gives the volume of base money needed. For interest rate control we need to forecast Y and m (at zero); given the money target we then set r_d at the required level.

Assuming that B and r_d are exactly controlled and assuming no errors in coefficients, the question is which method of control minimises the variances of the money stock. If we deliberately disregard covariances we have for base money

$$\text{Mo}_{\text{var}} = b_1{}^2 Y_{E\,\text{var}} + b_3{}^2 v_{\text{var}} + b_5{}^2 m_{\text{var}} \tag{A6}$$

and for the interest rate

$$\text{Mo}_{\text{var}} = \alpha_5{}^2 Y_{E\,\text{var}} + m_{\text{var}} \tag{A7}$$

where $\alpha_5 > b_1$ and $1 > b_5$.

Base money will be superior if money demand disturbances m and errors in forecasting income are dominant. If, however, money supply disturbances v are dominant the interest rate is the preferred method of control.

44

Unemployment performance and policy

INTRODUCTION

Chapter 35 presented data on the unemployment performance of some sixteen OECD member countries. We showed how some countries performed better than others on this front; moreover, individual countries' rankings changed over time.

This chapter tries to explain these unemployment differences, drawing on a framework proposed in Chapter 35. Later in the chapter we shall also say something about unemployment policy.

It is perhaps disappointing that, given the vast literature and extensive treatment of the topic, there still exist acute divisions within the economics profession about the best strategy to deal with unemployment. At one extreme are those who have a strong conviction that the answer lies in labour market reforms and nothing more. On this view, the way to attack unemployment is simply to make labour markets much more competitive. With labour markets competitive any emerging excess supply of labour would quickly drive real wages down and clear the market. At the other extreme are those who argue that labour markets are somehow different and that they cannot be expected to behave like other competitive markets (see Chapter 9). Whilst not excluding labour market reforms they would advocate a much more activist role for governments, e.g. labour market programmes, incomes policies and a *judicious* use of Keynesian-type policies.

Why is it that some countries perform better than others? We will demonstrate that no single hypothesis can account for these differences. Our approach will be eclectic in the sense that we will draw on several strands of thought.

We have found it convenient to classify explanations in terms of six broad categories:

a) real wage flexibility, the real wage gap and hysteresis;
b) the level of bargaining, trade union power and corporatism;
c) 'social welfare' policies;
d) structural–demographic factors;
e) incomes policies, labour market programmes and profit-sharing arrangements;
f) classical and Keynesian contributions to unemployment.

REAL WAGE FLEXIBILITY, THE REAL WAGE GAP AND HYSTERESIS

Consider the simplest Phillips curve relationship.

$$\Delta w = \Delta p + \pi_{12}(\text{yr} - \text{yr}^*) \tag{1}$$

where Δw and Δp are respectively the rate of change in wages and prices and yr, yr* are respectively the actual and full employment levels of output.

π_{12} is a measure of the degree of real wage flexibility. It is perhaps evident that, other things being equal, countries which have a high degree of real flexibility will tend to perform better on unemployment than those with relatively rigid real wages. Variants of (1) can be estimated for different countries and so we can actually get an empirical measure of comparative real wage flexibility. Such estimates are subject to wide margins of error and to different interpretations; nevertheless they may provide a rough indication of where countries stand on this front.

Andersen (1989) has 'averaged' estimates for fourteen countries drawn from several studies of real wage flexibility. These estimates are shown in Table 44.1 alongside the unemployment rankings. It is evident that those countries with the lowest unemployment rates are also those with the highest degree of real wage flexibility. Beyond the top four, however, the estimates are bunched together, so it is not surprising that the relationship is less clear-cut. Moreover, US labour markets are almost certainly more flexible than is suggested by the relatively low measure of flexibility (see OECD 1989a; Eberts and Groshen 1992).

We have already encountered the concept of the real wage gap in Chapter 42 and noted then some of the difficulties of measurement. The real wage gap was almost certainly an element in the increase in unemployment in the second half of the 1970s in the UK, Belgium, Denmark, Germany, France, Italy and Australia (see Bruno 1986; Coen and Hickman 1987). As we already noted, if the real wage gap is calculated along conventional lines, it disappears in nearly all countries some time in the second half of the 1980s. Some of the drop in unemployment in the second half may be associated with the drop in the real wage gap but the rate of unemployment was still substantially higher at the end of the 1980s than at the end of the 1960s (when the wage share was about the same) and so the level of the real wage gap as

Table 44.1 Real wage flexibility and unemployment outcomes[a]

| | Real wage flexibility | | Unemployment rate (1982–91) |
	Level	Rank	Rank
Australia	− 0.81	6	7
Austria	− 2.61	3	4
Belgium	− 0.74	7	15
Canada	− 0.46	11	12
Denmark	− 0.45	12	9
France	− 0.65	10	10
Germany	− 0.68	9	5
Italy	− 0.70	8	13
Japan	− 7.02	2	3
Netherlands	− 0.92	5	8
Sweden	− 2.35	4	2
Switzerland	− 7.83	1	1
UK	− 0.42	13	10
USA	− 0.34	14	6

Source: Andersen 1989 (average of studies); OECD, *Economic Outlook*
Note: [a] The unemployment rate does not correspond to exactly the same period as
the studies of real wage flexibility which in any event cover different
periods. It is readily verified that the unemployment rankings have not
changed much between 1974 and 1991. See Table 35.1.

conventionally measured cannot explain the level of unemployment of the 1980s (see, however, the Appendix to Chapter 42).

One would expect, on *a priori* grounds, that countries which experienced high real wage gaps would have a low degree of real wage flexibility. This again holds for the second half of the 1970s. (The exception is Japan which appeared to have a substantial real wage gap at the same time that its unemployment rate remained low. See again the Appendix to Chapter 42.)

The concept of hysteresis in labour markets was discussed in Chapter 28 and the evidence for it was reviewed then. Again, this evidence is very mixed. Hysteresis was widely invoked to explain unemployment persistence in the second half of the 1970s and again in the 1980s. As we saw in Chapter 42 unemployment surged in the mid-1970s and then persisted at the new higher level for some years; in the early 1980s it surged again and now, for a while at least, persisted at the new higher level. By the late 1980s, however, it began to drop again at least to the end of the 1980s.

Other things being equal, one would also expect countries that suffer from hysteresis to have a relatively low degree of real wage flexibility. This makes intuitive sense. Because the empirical evidence on hysteresis is ambiguous and hard to come by, however, this particular hypothesis is difficult to confirm.

THE LEVEL OF BARGAINING, CORPORATISM AND TRADE UNION POWER

In a recent careful paper Calmfors and Driffill (1988) rank industrial countries in terms of centralisation (defined as 'the extent of inter-union and inter-employer cooperation in wage bargaining with the other side') and successfully relate this measure to macro performance (defined as the rate of unemployment plus the current account in percentage of GNP) and to indicators of real wage flexibility.

As we noted in Chapter 35, centralised economies include the Scandinavian countries plus Austria; intermediate economies include Germany, the Netherlands, Belgium and New Zealand; decentralised economies include France, the UK, Italy, Switzerland, the USA, Canada and Japan. They find evidence of a hump-shaped relationship: the best performers are to be found among the centralised and decentralised economies while the worst performers are among the intermediate economies.

What is the theoretical rationale for this? At the enterprise level a wage push will have the strongest unemployment effects but also the strongest effect on the real consumption wage; at the same time employer resistance will be strong. At the intermediate level employer resistance will be weaker but now both the direct unemployment effect and the real consumption wage effect will be weaker. At the central level the price effect is strongest and the real consumption wage effect weak: the overall unemployment effect now depends on the exchange rate adjustment, the stance of the monetary authorities and the price adjustment mechanism. If the monetary authorities are accommodating and the currency devalues, wage increases can readily be passed on with minimal unemployment effects. Also centralised wage bargaining is likely to generate more disciplined and responsible behaviour with a greater sensitivity towards national unemployment and inflation outcomes.

So, to sum up, with enterprise bargaining the immediate unemployment outcome combined with strong employer resistance will tend to weaken the capacity of unions or employees to make excessive wage demands. However, with weaker employer resistance and more modest unemployment outcomes unions are likely to be more aggressively successful in wage negotiations when bargaining is at the intermediate level. Finally, as Layard *et al.* (1991) put it (p. 483) where 'there is a single national bargain ... this reduces the pressure for fruitless increases in nominal wages'.

Whilst there is some theoretical and empirical support for the hypothesis a closer look at the evidence reveals that, at best, it provides only a partial explanation of the differences in unemployment. First, Denmark and Finland, for example, are as centralised as Sweden and Norway but their unemployment rates have been relatively high. Second, the internal dynamics and stability of regimes may be important. Calmfors and Forslund note, on Sweden:

> The traditional Swedish model of centralised wage setting, with private sector employers and blue-collar workers playing the dominating role, has recently begun to crumble, partly because of the emergence of new strong collectives of wage

earners, and partly because of a tendency to shift the emphasis in negotiations from the central to lower levels.

(1989: 1)

Third, France, the UK and Italy all have enterprise bargaining. Germany, by contrast, has an intermediate system, yet its unemployment performance is superior to the others.

Fourth, the performance of all those countries which are decentralised varies very widely. Switzerland and Japan perform very well in this group but France, the UK, Italy and Canada are poor performers. The USA stands somewhere in the middle.

The term corporatism has also been widely used in this broad context. It embraces more than the level of bargaining, however. An economy is said to be more corporatist the more centralised the bargaining, the greater the degree of government involvement in wage negotiations and the greater the 'consensus' between labour and firms with shared perspectives on the goals of economic activity (Calmfors and Driffill 1988). Many economists have tried to construct rankings in terms of corporatism and to show that more corporatist economies perform better (Bruno and Sachs 1985; Newell and Symons 1987; OECD 1988).

Minford (1988) notes that there are positive as well as negative aspects of corporatism, more broadly defined. Centralised bargaining is associated with strong unionisation; this in turn tends to be associated with political leverage which in turn encourages 'welfare state' characteristics which may be unfavourable to employment (see later).

Finally, what is the link between trade union 'power' and unemployment? We have seen that a strong nationally coordinated trade union movement combined with coordinated employer groups can actually be favourable to unemployment. A high union 'coverage' can thus be good or bad depending on how the power is exercised. Norway and Sweden have a very high union coverage but their outcomes are good. Belgium, the UK and Australia also have high union coverage but it is less coordinated so their outcomes are less satisfactory.

How is trade union power measured? The empirical literature uses three types of measures. The first is trade union coverage. The second is strike activity. The third is the mark-up of union over non-union wages. If what we are trying to capture here is *militancy*, in the adverse sense, then, as we have seen, the first measure is unsatisfactory but the last two are appropriate.

It is not difficult to find theoretical support for the view that the exercise/ exploitation of trade union power can reduce economy-wide employment (Blanchflower and Milward 1989). Lindbeck and Snower (1989) also show how trade union power can increase unemployment in an insider–outsider framework. There is as well some empirical support for this (Minford 1988; Blanchflower and Milward 1989).

SOCIAL WELFARE POLICIES

The two most eminent proponents of the view that the welfare state and the regulatory environment, in combination, have tended to stifle and inhibit economic adjustment, with adverse effects on employment, are Giersch (1987) and Lindbeck (1988; 1990). (For a careful analysis of the impact of the size of government on unemployment and growth see also Tullio (1987).)

The level of unemployment benefits and their duration, minimum wage legislation, the tax wedge, employment protection laws, regulations imposed to foster social justice, all have some potential implications for labour market flexibility. These have received wide attention in the literature. (For an application to Germany see Soltwedel (1988); see also Emerson (1988) for a general review of industrial countries.)

What appears appealing at first sight about this explanation is that it does allow us to differentiate the Economic Community (EC) countries and Australia and New Zealand, on the one hand, from Japan and the USA, on the other. Non-EC Europe, however, which has performed well despite having an advanced welfare state, does not quite fit the pattern. Of course, as we shall see, there may be other factors common to non-EC European countries which have tended to neutralise such tendencies.

Not only is the level of government expenditure (and the associated tax wedge) considerably higher in the EC (at around 48 per cent of GNP) than in the USA (around 36 per cent) and Japan (around 32 per cent) but the regulatory framework is much more onerous. Also, the rate of increase in government has been greater in the 1970s and 1980s in the EC than in the USA and Japan.

Hiring and firing rules are much more oppressive in the EC than in the USA. (In Japan there are cultural and institutional factors, rather than legal, which inhibit firing.) The effects of such rules on employment, however, are strictly ambiguous. For example, generous redundancy payments encourage employers to hold on to their staff but on the other hand discourage the acquisition of new staff. Lindbeck (1988) has argued that in the face of symmetrical fluctuations in activity the regulations may serve to stabilise employment over the cycle. He contends, however, that in the conditions prevailing in the second half of the 1970s and the 1980s the regulations may on balance have discouraged the employment of labour. So it is possible that unemployment was actually reinforced by the regulations.

In evaluating the role of unemployment benefits, attention needs to be paid to at least three aspects: their levels, the monitoring procedures (eligibility, vetting) and their duration. (For details across countries, see Layard et al. (1991: Table A1, pp. 514–16).) Because unemployment benefits have so many different dimensions, however, inter-country comparisons are not always easy to make.

In general, on a priori grounds, one would expect that countries with the least generous benefits, where the payment is the most tightly monitored and where the duration is the most restricted, have lower unemployment (other things being equal). This is because such benefits tend to reduce the relative return to work, to increase search time and hence the duration of unemployment; they also increase the bargaining strength of unions. In general, one would expect benefits to reduce the degree of real wage flexibility.

Minford (1988) highlights the differences in unemployment benefits and eligibility conditions in accounting for differences in unemployment performance between continental Europe, the USA, Switzerland and Sweden. The last two offer generous unemployment benefits but monitoring is strict and the duration of the benefit is limited in time (after which, in Sweden, the unemployed are automatically absorbed in community work) (see also Burda 1988). Layard (1990) highlights the importance of the duration of unemployment benefits (see later).

The issues here are all complex. Moreover, our treatment has inevitably been not only superficial but also selective. Nevertheless, one has to conclude that the hypothesis that social welfare policies may contribute to unemployment cannot be dismissed out of hand.

STRUCTURAL–DEMOGRAPHIC INFLUENCES

One frequently mentioned potential cause of growing unemployment is the possibility of increasing labour market 'mismatches'. A mismatch occurs when the level of skill available is mismatched with the level of skill demanded. This can happen at the regional level (e.g. if there is a regional redistribution of demand), at the sectoral level (e.g. if there is a redistribution of demand across different sectors) or at the occupational level (e.g. if there is a change in the distribution of demand across different occupations).

One way in which a mismatch manifests itself is through an outward shift in the so-called Beveridge curve, a curve which traces an inverse relation between vacancies, plotted on the vertical axis, and unemployment, plotted on the horizontal axis. An outward shift to the right over time means that at given vacancy rates the unemployment rate rises. It is easy to see how this would occur with a mismatch, e.g. a regional redistribution of demand means that now a given total of vacancies is likely to be associated with more aggregate unemployment (particularly so if the level of employment is initially quite high).

Many countries did indeed experience such shifts and it is quite manifest for OECD countries as a whole. One problem, however, with using this as evidence for a mismatch is that the curve can shift to the right for other reasons (e.g. increases in unemployment benefits, improved eligibility conditions, employment protection legislation) so a shift in itself is not necessarily proof of a mismatch.

A more direct test involves computing indices of industrial, regional and occupational imbalances. There is extensive testing along these lines in the literature. At most, however, it would seem that mismatching might have made only a marginal contribution to the unemployment in some countries (Flanagan 1987; Gordon 1988).

Demographic changes can also change the rate of unemployment over time. For example, since unemployment rates differ across the sexes, age and ethnic groups, a change in the composition of the labour force does carry implications for the overall rate of unemployment. There is no detailed cross-country study of the demographics underlying changes in unemployment but it is most unlikely that these would be of any significance.

Yet another structural source of unemployment is discussed in Krugman (1987), who refers to a view popularly held that a combination of new labour-substituting technology and increased competition from the new industrialised countries (NICs) might have played some role in the rising unemployment. There is little academic support for this, however, although Krugman himself concludes 'whether the automation–competition view makes sense or not it is influential and a force to be reckoned with'.

INCOMES POLICIES, LABOUR MARKET PROGRAMMES AND PROFIT-SHARING SCHEMES

Over the years, and in several industrial countries, governments have resorted to some form of direct control over prices and incomes, with the principal aim of securing an improved relationship between unemployment and inflation. Other objectives of a prices and incomes policy have included an improved distribution of factor incomes, an improved allocation of resources and an improved productivity performance.

In the most general terms a prices and incomes policy sets out criteria for both wage and price changes. These policies are either statutory (enforceable by law) or voluntary. A less conventional type of incomes policy is the wage–tax trade-off or the social contract. In the first case, governments will offer tax cuts in return for wage restraint. (The Nordic experience with the wage–tax trade-off is reviewed in Calmfors and Nymoen (1990).) In the second case governments will trade wage restraint for a broader set of undertakings (e.g. social welfare provisions). (See Chapters 46 and 48 and Flanagan (1992).)

How successful have conventional incomes policies been? Here it is worth citing Layard *et al.* in full:

There are two main problems with fully centralized governmental incomes policies. First, they infringe the principle of free bargaining between workers and employers. Thus, many individual groups have a strong incentive to breach the norm. This is also the case, of course, where a norm has been bargained centrally between confederations of employers and unions; but individual groups are more inclined to accept a deal to which they are, at least, an indirect party. For this reason governmental incomes policies that have the support of the confederations of employers and unions are themselves more likely to last than those that are imposed. But history suggests that nearly all such policies are eventually breached. A permanent centralized incomes policy is probably infeasible.

The second problem is that a centralized incomes policy is inherently inflexible. It is bound to impose rigidity on the structure of relative wages. But the reallocation of labour may be much easier if relative wages rise where labour is scarce and vice versa. Without this, structural unemployment is likely to become worse, unless major efforts are made, as in Sweden, to promote movement of labour between industries and regions. Incomes policies sometimes try to incorporate committee mechanisms for adjusting relativities, but these cannot work as effectively as the market.

The result is that incomes policies of this kind have always been short-lived.

(1991: 485)

Labour market programmes can take a variety of forms including, importantly, wage subsidies for the unemployed, retraining schemes for the unemployed, and direct job creation schemes (OECD 1990). (See Table 44.2 for the comparative experience here.)

Broadly, there are two types of profit-sharing schemes: one relates basic pay directly to profits; in the other, employees acquire an equity (through share ownership) in their firm. Numerous illustrations of the two variants can be found in industrial countries (see Estrin *et al.* 1987). The most celebrated and most widely discussed application of the first is the case of Japan where a bonus payment is made twice a year as a supplement to the base wage (Chapter 47). On a lesser scale, in the USA, too, in recent years schemes of this kind have become increasingly popular (Bell 1989).

The recent debate over the merits of profit sharing has focused primarily on the first type to which we also briefly limit ourselves.

There are three claims made for profit sharing. The first is that it will improve morale, the industrial relations environment and productivity. The second is that it represents a form of wage flexibility, with actual earnings depending on the state of

Table 44.2 Public expenditure on labour market programmes as a percentage of gross domestic product, 1987–9

Australia	1.29	Luxembourg	1.57
Austria	1.24	Netherlands	3.77
Belgium	4.23	New Zealand	1.71
Canada	2.09	Norway	1.96
Denmark	5.71	Portugal	0.91
Finland	2.26	Spain	3.14
France	2.87	Sweden	2.38
Germany	2.32	Switzerland	0.36
Greece	0.93	Turkey	0.16
Ireland	4.88	UK	1.62
Italy	1.52	USA	0.62
Japan	0.52		

Source: OECD 1990

the economy. This is probably the strongest case that can be made for profit sharing (see Chapter 39). The third is that, if it were widely introduced, under certain circumstances it would have the effect of pushing the economy permanently towards full employment; indeed there would be a constant excess demand for labour. This is the principal argument made by Weitzman (1984, 1985).

Not every one, however, has been convinced by the theoretical arguments, particularly the last one. Moreover, empirical work, both on Japan and on countries where some firms have experimented with profit-sharing schemes, is not very supportive of the claims made (Blanchflower and Oswald 1986; Estrin *et al.* 1987; Wadhwani and Wall 1990).

CLASSICAL AND KEYNESIAN CONTRIBUTIONS TO UNEMPLOYMENT – AN INTEGRATED APPROACH

Consider the following framework for a particular country:

$$U = \pi_1 MP + \pi_2 FP + \pi_3 OPS + \pi_4 Yw + \pi_5 RWG \tag{2}$$

where U is the unemployment rate, MP and FP are measures respectively of monetary and fiscal policies, OPS is an oil price shock, Yw is the level of output abroad and RWG is the real wage gap.

The rate of unemployment over time in any particular country could be explained in terms of policy stances (MP, FP), shocks from abroad (OPS, Yw) (the influences on the demand side) and the real wage gap (RWG) (the 'classical influences'). Other potential influences could be added or variations on this basic theme could be used. Equations like this could serve to explain differences across countries in unemployment performance. (The reader is alerted to the fact, however, that whilst the equation is attractive, allowing us as it does to combine Keynesian and classical influences, it is not easily derived directly from structural models of the kind we have manipulated to date.)

Bruno (1986) regresses unemployment rates against his measure of the wage gap and indicators of 'demand' factors. The latter are real money balances, the inflation-corrected structural budget deficit and deviations from the trend in world trade. The framework is applied to several OECD member countries. The wage gap plays virtually no role in the USA and Canada, most of the variation being associated with demand. Focusing on EC countries the findings are mixed. In Germany and France, demand factors dominate in the later period. In the UK, on the other hand, the wage gap remains important throughout but there is a substantial contribution, additionally, from demand. In Belgium the wage gap dominates throughout. In Denmark the wage gap plays a lesser role in the later period but nevertheless continues to be important. Tootell (1990) updating Bruno confirms even more strongly the importance of Keynesian influences.

Bean *et al.* (1987) construct a model which explains unemployment in terms of a total tax wedge (which is the sum of the employment, income and consumption tax rates), real import prices, a variable labelled 'search' (intended to capture mismatches and unemployment benefits), which is measured by the outward shift in the unemployment—vacancy relationship, and a demand variable, measured by the level of government spending, the tax wedge and GDP in the rest of the OECD. The results vary significantly across countries. The tax wedge makes a significant contribution in most countries as does the search variable; the role of demand varies widely in the sample of countries.

CONCLUSIONS ON UNEMPLOYMENT DIFFERENCES

An interesting recent paper by Layard (1990) allows us to summarise some of our own explorations and provides a good basis for thinking about some of these issues. Layard tries to explain, by econometric analysis, cross-section differences in unemployment rates (1983—8) in twenty OECD countries in terms of two broad sets of factors: wage bargaining arrangements and unemployment policies. He has three key variables to represent the first: unionisation, *trade union* coordination and *employer* coordination. He has four key variables to represent the second: the level of the unemployment benefit, the duration of the unemployment benefit, the level of active labour market spending and the change in the inflation rate between 1982 and 1988 (a measure of demand pull).

Layard argues on *a priori* grounds that high unionisation (in itself) ought to increase unemployment but high coordination ought to reduce unemployment (as we saw earlier); at the same time a high replacement ratio or a long duration of unemployment benefit ought to increase unemployment while active labour market spending should reduce unemployment; finally a fall (rise) in the inflation rate should increase (reduce) unemployment. All these expectations are perfectly realised; the signs are all right, the seven variables combined explaining over 90 per cent of the cross-section variation in unemployment. Roughly half is explained in terms of wage bargaining arrangements and the other half in terms of unemployment policies.

Jackman *et al.* (1990) reach rather similar conclusions, using now an unemployment—vacancy framework. Unemployment is explained by the vacancy rate and additionally by the benefit duration, replacement ratio, corporatism, labour market policies and lagged unemployment.

UNEMPLOYMENT POLICIES

It is convenient to divide unemployment policies into two broad types: demand- and supply-side policies.

Policies acting on demand

The difficulties of fine-tuning have already been noted in other chapters. The advantage of using monetary policy is that it can be changed quickly and flexibly; the disadvantages are that it acts with a substantial lag and that if applied injudiciously can lead to more inflation without ultimately changing unemployment. Having a target growth of nominal income or a medium-run inflation target can help protect the economy from this last risk.

We have already noted the adverse consequences of persistent public sector deficits (Chapter 34). Too liberal use of easy fiscal policy in the past, which leave a legacy of a high debt to GNP ratio, can tie the hands of governments later should unemployment re-emerge. We saw how governments back-tracked on fiscal policy in the first half of the 1980s (Chapter 42). In mid-1992 when the US economy was in recession the US government felt severely constrained by the ongoing budget deficits in its use of fiscal policy. By contrast, Japan, also in recession, was better placed then to resort to fiscal policy. Fiscal policy is less flexible than monetary policy but, on the other hand, acts more quickly.

It is difficult to prescribe rules or define the circumstances in which it is appropriate to use monetary–fiscal instruments. The strongest case for the implementation of stabilisation policies arises when hysteresis threatens. If they are to be used it is probably also wiser to use them *together* to avoid adverse side-effects than to resort to one instrument alone. For example, to combat unemployment, a modest expansion in both monetary and fiscal policy can mitigate effects on interest rates, exchange rates or budget deficits.

This last point can be made more explicit. A monetary expansion increases employment, lowers interest rates, devalues the currency and improves the budget balance. On the other hand, a fiscal expansion reinforces the effect on employment but reverses the effects on interest rates, on the exchange rate and on the budget balance. A fiscal expansion may also in some circumstances reverse the current account effects of a monetary expansion.

Policies acting on supply

These have already been reviewed and need only be summarised. The limitations of some of the policies have also been noted.

If intermediate bargaining has adverse consequences and if there is now some disenchantment with centralised bargaining, there is a case for encouraging decentralised enterprise bargaining.

Incomes policies could be used *temporarily* in a crisis or to minimise disinflation costs. A case for a tax-based wage policy has been made over many years now by Layard and his colleagues at the London School of Economics. To quote Jackman and Layard:

> The solution is to have a fixed norm for the growth of average earnings in each firm (without regard to grade structure), and to tax heavily any excess earnings growth – while not making it unlawful. This would exert a strong downward pressure on excess wage growth, while leaving much of the needed flexibility intact.
>
> (1987: 8)

Labour market policies, work-sharing as well as profit-sharing schemes, may help a little too. Unemployment benefits arrangements could be reformed too, e.g. by tightening eligibility conditions and restricting their duration.

We have noted the importance of avoiding hysteresis effects on unemployment. If hysteresis comes from the erosion of human skills the case for preserving skills by job creation and retraining is correspondingly stronger. If hysteresis comes from a *capital* shortage a strong case could be made for offering investment incentives. If hysteresis comes from insider–outsider forces and if insider strength comes from the exercise of monopoly power by unions, there is a case for restricting such power by legislation (see Chapters 46 and 48).

45

Macro policy coordination

INTRODUCTION

It is fair to say that until around the mid-1980s the literature on policy coordination was slight and spasmodic. There were a few contributions which addressed the topic but interest until then was generally very subdued. Amongst the more important early contributions were those by Niehans (1968), Cooper (1968, 1969) and Hamada (1974, 1976, 1979). In retrospect now Hamada's contributions are perceived as seminal, laying the foundations for the literature a decade or so later.

A paper by Oudiz and Sachs (1984) reopened the debate on policy coordination. Subsequently, there was an explosion of literature on the topic; indeed so much was published in the second half of the 1980s that by the end of the decade the topic had almost exhausted itself and already by the early 1990s we observe a sharp decline in interest.

Why this explosion of literature in the space of some five years or so? We can explain this at several levels.

First, the paper by Oudiz and Sachs opened up a lot of questions which were new and which had not been dealt with properly in the literature to that point. Economists who were more mathematically inclined saw possibilities for applying game theory to this new unexplored terrain. Econometricians saw some scope for econometric applications, notably in the area of the measurement of the potential gains from cooperation. Economists interested in applied policy were also given fertile new ground to develop.

Second, the increasing interdependence among nations, manifestly in trade and capital markets, may also have increased the need for coordination.

Third, the failures of macroeconomic policies and the disappointing macro performance, especially from the second half of the 1970s, raised new questions about the potential contribution that coordination might make to improved performance. From 1982, too, the huge fiscal policy asymmetry that opened up between the USA on the one hand and Europe and Japan on the other, and the stresses and adverse economic effects associated with it, all looked like a manifest *failure* of policy coordination, at least on the fiscal front.

Fourth, we also observe from the mid-1970s increased efforts at consultation and, moreover, from the mid-1980s a new burst of coordination, particularly on the exchange rate front but also on other fronts, as we shall detail later.

LEVELS OF POLICY COORDINATION

It is convenient to distinguish four potential levels of coordination.

At the lowest rung we have periodic intergovernmental exchanges of information, consultations and declarations of policy intent. *At a second-order level* we have what Wallich has called 'a significant modification of national policies in recognition of international economic interdependence' (Wallich 1984). In this case particular policies are agreed to on an *intermittent* (*ad hoc*) basis.

At a third-order level we have the voluntary adoption by a group of countries of particular policy rules to which they now commit themselves. Examples of such rules are the gold standard exchange rate regime, the trade rules associated with membership of GATT and the monetary rules associated with the IMF system (which collapsed in 1973). An even more recent example is the coordination rules adopted by members of the ERM in the EMS. In all these cases there is an original major act of coordination after which countries are expected independently to live by the rules without a need for renegotiation.

Third-order level *reform* proposals were also reviewed in Chapters 36 and 38. These include a variety of policy recommendations including changes to the exchange rate regime and global policy assignment rules. In each case the claim is made that the adoption of such global cooperative policy rules would improve performance over a situation where each country acted independently. Third-order cooperative reform proposals also represent *competing* forms of coordination.

At a fourth-order level we have full-fledged coordination in the sense of the cooperative maximisation of some joint welfare function.

Few would quarrel with coordination of the first order. Coordination of the second and third orders remains a matter of some controversy. Few, however, would be venturesome enough, in the present state of knowledge, to seriously contemplate moving in the direction of coordination of the fourth order.

THE CASE MADE FOR COORDINATION – SOME ILLUSTRATIONS

The best way to proceed in dealing with policy coordination is to take specific illustrations from the literature and historical experience and to show how, in particular circumstances, coordination may improve the joint welfare of the countries concerned. The discussion in this section will be entirely literary and discursive. Needless to say, the examples cited are merely illustrative and far from exhaustive. *The next section deals more rigorously with one particular case widely analysed in the literature: the case where countries are exposed to a common exogenous price shock*. This particular case is not treated at all in this section but is deferred to the next.

It should be noted that although many of the instances discussed here would appear to constitute what, on the surface, is a strong case for coordination, not all economists would agree that even in those instances the case for coordination is irrefutable.

Coordination and convergence towards global objectives

Cooper (1969) made an early case for coordination on these grounds. Using a short-run fixed exchange rate multi-country model he compares two types of coordination. The first is *internal* coordination which he defines as the case where 'the fiscal and monetary authorities in each country are concerned with the simultaneous determination of national income and interest rates, ... but they are not concerned with the values of these variables in the *other* country' (p. 22).

The second is full coordination in which policy-makers take account of interdependences in using their policy instruments. In this case each instrument is related to 'all the target variables on which it has an impact'.

Cooper undertakes a number of numerical simulations for each type of coordination for two types of disturbances: an expenditure disturbance and a shift in asset preferences. He concludes that a lack of coordination amongst policy-makers

a) *delays* achievement of national objectives such as full employment and a targeted rate of growth (via the interest rate objective);
b) *increases* the requirements for international reserves ... when the balance of payments is simply allowed to adjust passively to policy changes directed at other objectives.

(1969: 22)

At the same time, he also finds that the delays in reaching targets and the need for reserves both increase as the degree of interdependence increases.

Incompatible reserve objectives

In what proved to be a seminal paper on policy coordination, Hamada (1974) analysed a short-term two-country model under fixed rates where each country had two targets: output and international reserves. Domestic credit is the single policy instrument employed by the two countries to pursue the two targets. The 'disturbance' is one where, other things being equal, the two countries wish to increase their individual reserve levels. Global reserve levels, however, are fixed and so the objectives are not achievable. Each country proceeds to restrict its domestic credit with an eye on improving its own reserve position, but such restrictive policies end up reducing the two countries' levels of output. In the end, not surprisingly, equilibrium is reached at the point where output levels in the two countries fall below their original levels *without any gain in reserves to either country*. At this point, each country is prepared to trade off some loss of output against its original level of reserves.

This sort of problem lends itself to three types of solutions. The two countries can coordinate, recognise the futility of pursuing independent policies and agree to maintain their original positions, where both economies would unambiguously be better off (with higher output and the same reserve levels). The two countries can coordinate in a different sense and agree to create additional international reserves as, for example, the IMF did in 1968 with SDRs to meet what looked then like an international shortage of reserves which threatened precisely the sorts of outcomes envisaged in Hamada's paper (Argy 1981). Finally, the countries could agree to a regime change. A switch to a pure float, for example (or to a more flexible rate regime), does away with the need for international reserves (or it may reduce reserve needs).

Competitive devaluations to reduce unemployment

This case has frequently been taken as one which describes, in a rough and ready way, what happened in the 1930s (Canzoneri and Gray 1985). Independent attempts by individual countries to reduce their own unemployment by devaluing their own currencies will ultimately leave the individual country's (and global) unemployment unchanged. Meanwhile, damage is inflicted on the international monetary system in the form of transitory shifts in resources, additional exchange rate uncertainty and intensified global tensions. One reason for the creation of the Bretton Woods (IMF) system was to avert precisely such situations, avoid competitive devaluations to achieve more employment, stabilise the exchange rate system and harmonise international economic relations.

As Devereaux and Wilson (1989) note, faced with just such a situation of global unemployment, a better policy than one of competitive devaluations is probably one of coordinated fiscal expansion.

Current account constraint on unilateral expansion

The starting point here is again one of say global unemployment. Each country, acting individually, will hesitate to implement expansionary (fiscal) policies out of fear that such policies will worsen the current account. In principle, the global economy might find itself stuck at an excessively high level of unemployment because of individual anxieties. However, a policy of coordinated fiscal expansion overcomes this problem, allowing countries to reduce their levels of unemployment without adverse effects on individual current accounts (Fischer 1987a).

Negative spillovers from fiscal expansion under flexible rates

In Chapter 14 we presented a model of flexible rates with fixed real wages in two economies, where fiscal expansion in one country had positive real effects at home but a *negative* real effect abroad.

The example used in that chapter is worth repeating here. If A had excess unemployment while B's unemployment rate was about right, A might undertake a fiscal expansion which now has the effect of increasing B's unemployment. B retaliates with its own fiscal expansion. Ultimately, in that model there may be no individual or global gains to employment but the world price level is higher. Thus again, here, a lack of coordination could make all countries worse off.

AN EXTERNAL PRICE SHOCK – A DETAILED ANALYSIS

In this section we analyse in some detail one special case, widely cited in the literature, to illustrate more rigorously the potential gains that might accrue from coordination. This will also allow us to identify the key factors that underlie the potential gains. The two-country model used is one which is already familiar from Chapters 13 and 14. The section draws on McKibbin (1988b), Oliva and Sinn (1988) and Oliva (1987).

The world again is assumed to comprise two countries A and B. A flexible rate regime is in operation; at the same time, there is perfect asset substitution between the two economies which we define here to mean that interest rates are equalised in the two economies. To simplify the analysis further, we assume that the two economies are identical in size and structure. Finally, initially at any rate, we also assume that wages and domestic prices are fixed in the two economies.

We focus on the case where there is a *common* external price shock which is imposed on the two economies. The two economies are assumed to have recourse to only a *single* money stock policy instrument but each tries to minimise a common loss function which is determined by a weighted average of squared deviations of output and inflation from their target levels.

The model

$$y_A = \alpha_1 e + \alpha_2 y_B - \alpha_4 r \qquad \alpha_2 < 1 \tag{1}$$

$$y_B = -\alpha_1 e + \alpha_2 y_A - \alpha_4 r \tag{2}$$

$$mo_A = \alpha_5 y_A - \alpha_{10} r \tag{3}$$

$$mo_B = \alpha_5 y_B - \alpha_{10} r \tag{4}$$

$$p_A = p_0 + (1 - \alpha_{15}) e \tag{5}$$

$$p_B = p_0 - (1 - \alpha_{15}) e \tag{6}$$

$$L_A = \pi_1(y_A - y_A{}^*)^2 + (1 - \pi_1)(p_A - p_A{}^*)^2 \tag{7}$$

$$L_B = \pi_1(y_B - y_B{}^*)^2 + (1 - \pi_1)(p_B - p_B{}^*)^2 \tag{8}$$

$$L_A + L_B = L_W = \pi_1[(y_A - y_A{}^*)^2 + (y_B - y_B{}^*)^2] + (1 - \pi_1)[(p_A - p_A{}^*)^2 \tag{9}$$
$$+ (p_B - p_B{}^*)^2]$$

Equations (1)–(4) are now very familiar. These four equations solve for r (the common interest rate), y_A, y_B and e in terms of the money stock in A and B. Equations (5) and (6) define the consumer price index in each economy. With domestic prices fixed in A and B the consumer price index is determined by the common exogenous shock (p_0) and by the exchange rate. Note that a devaluation of A's currency increases A's price level but decreases B's proportionately.

Equations (7)–(9) are the loss functions. Equations (7) and (8) describe the identical loss functions in A and B while (9) describes the combined loss function (L_W).

We are now ready to put this model to work for an assumed external price shock. Two particular types of solutions will be analysed. The first is the so-called *Nash–Cournot* solution; this is the non-cooperative case in which each country acts independently to minimise its own loss function while taking as given the other country's monetary policy. The second is the *cooperative* solution which we define here as one where the authorities attempt to minimise the *combined* welfare function, as in (9).[1] All solutions are *deviations* from original levels.

The Nash–Cournot equilibrium

We can readily obtain solutions for output and the consumer price index in each country in terms of the monetary policies in the two economies.

$$y_A = k_1 mo_A - k_2 mo_B \tag{10}$$

$$y_B = k_1 mo_B - k_2 mo_A \tag{11}$$

$$p_A = p_0 + k_3(mo_A - mo_B) \tag{12}$$

$$p_B = p_0 - k_3(mo_B - mo_A) \tag{13}$$

We also have

$$e = k_4(mo_A - mo_B) \tag{14}$$

where

$$k_1 = \frac{\alpha_{10}(1 - \alpha_2) + 2\alpha_4\alpha_5}{\alpha_5[2\alpha_{10}(1 - \alpha_2) + 2\alpha_4\alpha_5]}$$

$$k_2 = \frac{\alpha_{10}(1 - \alpha_2)}{\alpha_5[2\alpha_{10}(1 - \alpha_2) + 2\alpha_4\alpha_5]}$$

$$k_3 = (1 - \alpha_{15})k_4$$

$$k_4 = \frac{1 + \alpha_2}{2\alpha_5\alpha_1}$$

Note that $k_1 > k_2$ and that there is here, as in Chapter 13, a 'negative' spillover of monetary policy from one economy to the other.

The next step is for each country independently of the other to use its monetary policy to minimise its individual loss function.

$$\frac{dL_A}{dMo_A} = 0 = \frac{dL_A}{dy_A}\frac{dy_A}{dMo_A} + \frac{dL_A}{dp_A}\frac{dp_A}{dMo_A} \tag{15}$$

$$\frac{dL_B}{dMo_B} = 0 = \frac{dL_B}{dy_B}\frac{dy_B}{dMo_B} + \frac{dL_B}{dp_B}\frac{dp_B}{dMo_B} \tag{16}$$

where now, from (7)

$$\frac{dL_A}{dy_A} = 2\pi_1 y_A$$

from (10)

$$\frac{dy_A}{dMo_A} = k_1$$

from (7)

$$\frac{dL_A}{dp_A} = 2(1 - \pi_1)p_A$$

and from (12)

$$\frac{dp_A}{dMo_A} = k_3$$

Combining terms and using a similar procedure for B we have

$$0 = 2\pi_1 y_A k_1 + 2(1 - \pi_1)p_A k_3 \tag{17}$$

$$0 = 2\pi_1 y_B k_1 + 2(1 - \pi_1)p_B k_3 \tag{18}$$

We can now substitute the solutions for y_A, p_A, y_B and p_B from (10), (12), (11) and (13). This allows us to arrive at a monetary policy reaction function for each economy, given the other country's monetary policy and the exogenous price shock. We can readily arrive at the following:

$$mo_A[2\pi_1 k_1^2 + 2(1 - \pi_1)k_3^2] = mo_B[2\pi_1 k_1 k_2 + 2(1 - \pi_1)k_3^2] \tag{19}$$
$$- 2(1 - \pi_1)k_3 p_0$$

$$mo_B[2\pi_1 k_1^2 + 2(1 - \pi_1)k_3^2] = mo_A[2\pi_1 k_1 k_2 + 2(1 - \pi_1)k_3^2] \tag{20}$$
$$- 2(1 - \pi_1)k_3 p_0$$

Initially, each country will be at its full employment level. Each country is subject to a price shock. To improve 'welfare' each will implement a tight monetary policy aimed at dampening the price effect and restoring a better balance between the output–inflation trade-off. With wages–prices fixed in this model a tight monetary policy acts on the price level only through the exchange rate; however, as already noted, one country's gain on the inflation front exactly matches the other country's loss. So, as we shall see, at the global level there is no improvement in inflation. At the same time, a tight monetary policy does *reduce* output in each economy. Briefly, what happens is that output is reduced sufficiently to trade off against the exogenous shock to inflation.

It is intuitive that since the two countries are identical in every respect and both are exposed to the same external price shock, the *equilibrium* money stock in the two economies must be the same. So to find that equilibrium money stock we set $mo_A = mo_B$. Alternatively, we simply solve (19) and (20) for mo_A and mo_B. This yields

$$mo_A = -\frac{(1 - \pi_1)k_3}{\pi_1 k_1 (k_1 - k_2)} \, p_0 \tag{21}$$

$$mo_B = -\frac{(1 - \pi_1)k_3}{\pi_1 k_1 (k_1 - k_2)} \, p_0 \tag{22}$$

We can also readily solve for the equilibrium levels of y_A, y_B, e, p_A, p_B. Recalling that $mo_A = mo_B$ we have

$$y_A = y_B = -\frac{(1 - \pi_1)k_3}{\pi_1 k_1} \, p_0 \tag{23}$$

$$p_A = p_B = p_0 \tag{24}$$

$$e = 0 \tag{25}$$

These results are important. They tell us that output will fall equally in the two economies; the price level will be higher by the exogenous shock and will ultimately not change. The end result of the *individual* attempts to neutralise the price shock is a lower level of output and no net improvement to the price level.

Equation (23) defines the loss in output corresponding to the equilibrium stock of money. In this simple model the loss in output, which, as we shall show shortly, is also the loss of welfare from a policy of non-coordination, is dependent on the structural coefficients of the underlying model (k_3, k_1) and, most importantly, also on the relative weights attaching to output and inflation in the loss function. It is evident that if $\pi_1 = 1$ (inflation is not in the loss function) the loss will be zero. At the other extreme if $\pi_1 = 0$ the loss approaches infinity (in other words there is a 'continual' competitive appreciation which continues to reduce the level of output indefinitely).

The cooperative solution

The cooperative solution is one where the two countries together attempt to minimise their *joint* loss function. So we now have for one of the two money stocks (which will be equal to the other)

$$\frac{dL_A + dL_B}{dMo_A} = 0 = \frac{dL_A}{dy_A}\frac{dy_A}{dmo_A} + \frac{dL_A}{dp_A}\frac{dp_A}{dmo_A} + \frac{dL_B}{dy_B}\frac{dy_B}{dmo_A} + \frac{dL_B}{dp_B}\frac{dp_B}{dmo_A} \tag{26}$$

We can now readily arrive at

$$0 = 2\pi_1 y_A k_1 + 2(1 - \pi_1)p_A k_3 - 2\pi_1 y_B k_2 - 2(1 - \pi_1)p_B k_3 \tag{27}$$

Substituting again for y_A, y_B, p_A and p_B we have (recalling that $mo_A = mo_B$)

$$0 = 2\pi_1 k_1 mo_A (k_1 - k_2) - 2\pi_1 k_2 mo_A (k_1 - k_2) \tag{28}$$

The equilibrium stock of money is

$$mo_A = mo_B = 0 \tag{29}$$

This makes intuitive sense. The optimal monetary policy in the circumstances is to keep the money stock unchanged. This unambiguously improves welfare relative to the Nash–Cournot solution since it retains the same higher price level (p_0) *without now the loss in output*. Thus, to conclude, in the non-cooperative solution the money stock *is excessively restricted*.

The formal welfare loss is (from (23))

$$\frac{2(1 - \pi_1)k_3}{\pi_1 k_1} p_0$$

i.e. the sum of the two output losses.

Some extensions and further reflections

All we have been able to establish is that, *in terms of the very simple model used here*, the cooperative solution is to be preferred over the non-cooperative solution. We also showed that in the model the gain from cooperation depended on the weights in the loss function and the structural coefficients. It is also readily appreciated that if the economies had *different* structural coefficients (as we saw in Chapter 13) and if they had different *loss* functions the solutions would be more complicated. Evidently the games one can play are almost endless. These games assume massive complexity when, as in the real world, we have more than two countries.

In the analysis above we assumed that, faced with a common price shock, the countries in question had resort to a single monetary instrument. An extension by McKibbin and Sachs (1986) allows countries use of both monetary and fiscal policies now to maximise a welfare function which takes account of inflation, the GDP gap and the current account and budget deficits. They show that in response to a common price shock and assuming non-cooperation

> suddenly everybody tries to maintain a strong currency in order to help fight off the inflationary shock. Each country therefore has more expansionary fiscal policy than in the cooperative solution ... and has more contractionary monetary policy than in the cooperative case. The result is that non-cooperation under floating leads to very high world interest rates, since the whole world is tilted toward fiscal expansion and monetary contraction.
>
> (1986: 95)

The model above adopted the MF assumption that wages and prices were fixed and this gave us the well-known *negative* spillover effect from monetary policy. It is convenient to extend the model at least to take account of potential wage and price adjustment. (See also here Oliva (1987) and Oudiz and Sachs (1984).)

We turn now to the case where there is *full* wage indexation in the two economies as in the model presented in Chapter 14. We know from previous analysis that coordinated monetary contraction would now reduce each home price level *proportionately* while leaving the exchange rate unchanged. *What this means is that each country can now succeed in achieving its inflation objective without any cost in terms of output loss.*

OBJECTIONS TO COORDINATION

Not all economists agree that coordination, as a general principle, is necessarily a good thing. In this section we review the kinds of objections that have been raised in the literature to coordination. The objections raise matters of principle or are directed at particular efforts at coordination.

Vaubel (1985) has argued that policy-makers in combination with bureaucrats do not necessarily act to maximise a country's welfare, but rather to enhance their own personal power and profit. Coordination efforts may not, therefore, be in the best interests of the public. This view is perhaps over-cynical.

In a different vein but still at the level of politics, Feldstein (1988) has argued that, for the USA at least, there are constitutional and legal restrictions on international policy agreements.

> The separation of powers in the American form of government means that the Secretary of the Treasury cannot promise to reduce or expand the budget deficit or to change tax rules. This power does not rest with the President or the administration but depends on a legislative agreement between the President and the Congress.
>
> (1988: 216)

Horne and Masson (1988) also note that coordination may be 'costly in terms of the negotiating process and time lags in reaching agreement'. These costs are at several levels. Economic summits and negotiations are time consuming, taking attention away from domestic issues. When agreements are reached there are costs associated with their monitoring and implementation. These costs may also increase with the number of participants involved. To this one should add the fact that there will be circumstances when participants will find it in their own interest to renege on any agreement reached, raising questions about its sustainability. However, this risk is exaggerated when account is taken of the damage this may inflict on a country's reputation.

Although not an objection, as such, to coordination we also have to face up to the 'real politics' of the negotiating process. Pressures to achieve particular outcomes can in reality be very much a function of economic power and standing. The USA will often suggest a policy stance that it would like to see other countries adopt which it perceives to be in its own interest but is not necessarily in the interest of others. It is arguable that Japan some time after 1986, under international pressure, eased its monetary policy by too much (Chapter 47).

Economic concessions may be made in the interests of political harmonisation or in exchange for non-economic concessions. Negotiated outcomes are sometimes the result of conflicts *at home* over appropriate policies. Proponents of particular views may use the international forum as a means of tilting policy in their preferred direction. It is argued, for example, that Germany's Chancellor Schmidt in 1978 leaned towards domestic fiscal expansion and used the Bonn Summit in that year to achieve his end (Fischer 1987a; see also the next section).

Rogoff (1985b) produced a model in which coordination might actually increase the rate of inflation. The underlying idea is straightforward. As we saw in Chapter 25, short-sighted discretionary monetary policy aimed at reducing the unemployment rate may *ultimately* produce more inflation without delivering any improvement in unemployment. *Individual* attempts by monetary authorities to expand the money stock will run up against the fact that this will be associated with a weaker currency and hence with more inflation. Thus devaluation will itself act as a constraint on the pursuit of expansionary monetary policies. However, if the monetary authorities coordinated and expanded jointly the adverse inflationary exchange rate side-effects would be absent. Coordination thus removes the constraint, allowing an overexpansionary monetary policy with ultimately more inflation and the same unemployment.

Feldstein (1988) also addresses his criticisms at particular acts of coordination in the second half of the 1980s. He finds the pursuit of exchange rate goals to be both futile and economically harmful. At the same time he finds that agreements reached on the monetary–fiscal fronts were either too vague or in fact required countries to do what they would have done anyway. Feldstein also believes that, given the fact that the US economy is relatively closed, with only a small share of GNP absorbed by imports and exports, the USA has in any event little to gain from coordination.

The strongest criticisms of policy coordination have come from Frankel and Rockett (1988) and Frankel (1988a). Frankel's (1988a) principal contribution to the debate is to introduce uncertainty into the analysis. Frankel incorporates uncertainty at three levels.

There is first uncertainty about what he calls the initial values of the variables which the authorities may be targeting, such as output, inflation and the current account. This uncertainty, in turn, can be broken down into three distinct uncertainties:

a) regarding the *current* values of the target variables;
b) regarding their likely values in the near future (assuming no policy change);
c) regarding the *optimum* levels of the target variables.

He shows how there could be wide margins of error on each of these counts and hence how coordinated policies based on misguided calculations can move the economy in the wrong direction.

There is second uncertainty about the weights that one ought to attach to the target variables. As he notes, the preferences of different actors will vary widely.

There is third uncertainty regarding the policy multipliers, i.e. the effects of policy changes originating in a particular large country on itself and on other large countries. To evaluate this question he presents some second-year simulation results for a monetary and fiscal expansion in twelve widely used econometric models. As he demonstrates, there are substantial differences in outcomes; by definition the models cannot all be true.

Frankel and Rockett (1988) drawing on the results of eight of these econometric models pose the question: what if the 'wrong' model is used as a basis for coordinated policies? They then proceed to demonstrate that if the true model is not known there is a good chance that economies will stand to lose from coordination.

Ghosh and Masson (1988), however, taking uncertainty about the model as a starting point, are able to reach diametrically opposite conclusions to Frankel. They, in fact, try to demonstrate that when policy-makers take explicit rational account of model uncertainty the gains from coordination can be quite substantial. Indeed, these gains are more substantial than in the case where certainty about the model is assumed. Put differently, when the *transmission* effects are unknown, the greater the uncertainty the larger will tend to be the gains from coordination.

EMPIRICAL STUDIES OF THE GAINS FROM COORDINATION

In earlier sections we reviewed the potential gains to be had from coordination, at least in some circumstances. In the last section, however, we also noted that some economists, at any rate, felt that the idea of macro policy coordination had perhaps been oversold. One way to resolve these differences of opinion is to try to undertake empirical studies to see whether, retrospectively or prospectively, there might have been (be) gains made (to be made) from coordination.

There are two kinds of empirical studies of the effects of coordination. The first uses econometric models to compare independently implemented policies with cooperative type macro policies that aim at maximising some joint welfare function.

There are a few studies that fall in this category and, as we shall see, they turn out to be very confusing.

A second is concerned with evaluating alternative global macro rules (e.g. a change in exchange rate regime, a universally adopted assignment rule). There is a good deal of empirical work here as well but this has already been reviewed in Chapter 40. Again, we found the results to be mixed.

One of the first of the empirical studies is that by Oudiz and Sachs (1984). Using two econometric models (Japan's Economic Planning Agency (EPA) model and the US Federal Reserve model (MCM)) they compare two scenarios for the G3, one where monetary and fiscal policies are used in disregard of the other countries, and another where there is coordination amongst the three countries in the use of macro policies. Each country is assumed to have two instruments: the money stock and government expenditure, and a welfare function which takes account of inflation, the output gap and the current account. They first use the econometric models to project the evolution of the three targets in each of the economies in 1984–6, given policies actually implemented, which they assumed were used to maximise individual utility functions. They are also able to calculate weights for the three targets in the three countries. Given these welfare functions, they are then able to simulate a set of joint cooperative monetary–fiscal policies to maximise the 'global' utility function. They are thus able to calculate welfare gains for each of the three countries from coordination, just as we did at the theoretical level. These welfare gains turn out to be small (at most $\frac{1}{2}$ per cent of GNP for the USA and Germany, but a little more for Japan).

We have already reported the empirical finding in Frankel and Rockett (1988) that in the face of uncertainty there is a risk that cooperation might reduce welfare and the opposite claim by Ghosh and Masson (1988).

The results of empirical studies subsequent to that of Oudiz and Sachs have been mixed, although if a general conclusion is to be drawn it is that they tend to confirm Oudiz and Sachs. Taylor (1985b) and McKibbin and Sachs (1986) also found small gains; Hughes-Hallet (1987) had virtually no gains for the EC but, surprisingly, some for the USA. On the other hand, Ishii et al. (1985) did find significant gains. (These studies are all briefly summarised in McKibbin (1988b). See also Kenen (1987).) Finally, Canzoneri and Minford (1986) are also able to find substantial gains.

This is, to say the least, confusing. As in so much econometric work each new study employs a different methodology, claiming it is an improvement on earlier work. Only a very careful examination of each of these studies and their underlying framework will reveal which are the more reliable. This is well beyond our task in this chapter.

COORDINATION IN PRACTICE – SOME ILLUSTRATIONS

Economic coordination and consultation amongst the major industrial countries dates back at least to the early nineteenth century (Fischer 1987a). As we saw, the gold standard rules of the game in the nineteenth century provided a good instance of a coordinated policy. A good example of a *breakdown* in coordination and the adverse consequences flowing from that occurred in the course of the 1930s with the competitive devaluations and the escalation in protectionism that came in the wake of the collapse of the gold standard.

In the postwar years joint consultation and coordination have appeared in a variety of forms: international forums for the sharing of information and discussions of policy, the setting of exchange rate policies and targets, some commitment on the setting of monetary and fiscal policies, and the use of indicators to determine target compatibility and the appropriateness of policy in relation to set targets (see Dobson 1991).

International forums

These have taken a variety of forms. There is regular consultation within the IMF on policy issues and stances. The OECD's Economic Policy Committee and the Working Party 3 meet several times a year with similar objectives. The Bank for International Settlements holds regular consultation meetings with member central banks. Beginning in 1975 too regular 'summits' have been held at which the largest countries meet to discuss matters of policy and to 'negotiate' policy stances.

Exchange rate policies

We have already mentioned the creation of the Bretton Woods (IMF) system in 1946 which in retrospect was a big step forward in the coordination of exchange rate policies with its own implications for the conduct of macro policy. The IMF system emerged as a compromise between, on the one hand, the rigidities associated with the permanently fixed exchange rate regime of the interwar gold standard and, on the other hand, the breakdown of exchange rate stability that came after the collapse of the gold standard.

After a succession of crises the IMF system broke down in early 1973 when the major currencies began to float *vis-à-vis* one another. Between 1972 and 1978 there were attempts amongst a number of European economies to stabilise their currencies *vis-à-vis* one another (the so-called Snake agreements). A giant step forward in European exchange rate stabilisation occurred in 1979 with the establishment of the EMS (Chapters 2 and 4).

Although the major currencies were nominally floating from 1973, both Japan and Germany and other large economies outside the USA continued to engage in some unilateral exchange rate management. There were sporadic acts of coordinated exchange rate management, however (with the USA now as an active intervener in agreement with other major countries).

The Reagan administration, during its first four years of office, took the strong view that exchange rates should not be interfered with and should be left alone to be determined by market forces. However, by late 1984, early 1985, with large and continued current account imbalances, protectionist stirrings in Congress and the continuing very strong US dollar, the US administration did an about-turn and decided there was now a case for a more activist approach.

Since 1985, acting on this change of heart by the USA, there have been periodic bursts of coordinated intervention as well as intermittent official announcements signalling the appropriateness or otherwise of market exchange rates. By way of illustration, three particular phases will be briefly reviewed.

A first phase came after the long upward movement in the US dollar starting in mid-1980. In September 1985, the G5 Plaza meeting agreed that 'some further orderly appreciation of the main non-dollar currencies against the dollar is desirable and that the G5 governments would stand ready to cooperate more closely to encourage this when to do so would be helpful'. (Funabashi 1988; Obstfeld 1988). It was agreed to sell up to $18 billion to bring the dollar down by some 10–12 per cent over a short period of six weeks. (This would have corresponded roughly to short-term targets of 215 yen and 2.55 DM to the dollar at a time when the actual rates were 240 and 2.85.)

These short-term objectives were realised but the dollar continued to fall. In the course of 1986 the fall in the dollar had begun to acquire a momentum of its own.

A second phase came in early 1987. The G7 Ministers and Governors, meeting in Louvre in February 1987, now issued a strong statement that currencies were now 'within ranges broadly consistent with underlying economic fundamentals' (given the policy commitments undertaken).

It is widely reported that the G7 ministers agreed to stabilise the deutschmark and the yen within ±5 per cent ranges of 1.825 DM (1.734–1.916) and 153.5 yen (145.8–161.2). As exchange rates approached those limits intervention would be 'expected to intensify'. At the 5 per cent limit there would be mandatory 'consultation on policy adjustment'. None of this was publicly announced, however (Obstfeld 1988).

The Louvre resolutions were soon put to the test. In the months that followed sentiment continued strongly against the dollar, particularly *vis-à-vis* the yen. There was now massive coordinated intervention (including a US contribution in the order of $4 billion of foreign currency sales), a large interest rate realignment favouring US investment and strong official supportive statements.

Despite these efforts the dollar continued to fall (Table 45.1) and indeed by late 1987 had substantially breached the Louvre Agreement, particularly with respect to the yen rate. According to Funabashi (1988) the yen–dollar rate was then rebased, the new 5 per cent range being 139.04–153.3.

A third phase came with the strong upward thrust of the US dollar, beginning at the end of 1988 and lasting to mid-1990. At each meeting of the G7 during this period some statement was made about the need to coordinate on exchange rates, to keep these in line with 'fundamentals'. Typical of such statements was one in September 1989 asserting that the rise in the dollar to then had been 'inconsistent with longer-run economic fundamentals' and that further appreciation or an excessive decline 'would

Table 45.1   Deutschmark–US dollar and yen–US dollar rates

	1985	1986	1987	1988	1989	1990
	(averages of month)					
Germany						
January	3.17	2.44	1.86	1.165	1.83	1.69
February	3.29	2.33	1.83	1.70	1.85	1.68
March	3.31	2.26	1.83	1.63	1.87	1.70
April	3.08	2.27	1.81	1.67	1.87	1.69
May	3.11	2.23	1.79	1.69	1.95	1.66
June	3.06	2.24	1.82	1.76	1.98	1.68
July	2.92	2.15	1.85	1.84	1.89	1.64
August	2.79	2.06	1.86	1.89	1.93	1.57
September	2.84	2.04	1.81	1.87	1.95	1.57
October	2.64	2.00	1.80	1.82	1.87	1.52
November	2.59	2.03	1.68	1.75	1.83	–
December	2.51	1.99	1.63	1.76	1.74	–
Japan						
January	254.2	200.1	154.5	127.6	127.2	145.1
February	260.2	184.6	153.5	129.2	127.8	145.5
March	258.6	178.9	151.5	127.3	130.4	153.1
April	251.7	175.6	143.0	124.9	132.1	158.5
May	251.5	166.8	140.5	124.8	138.4	153.5
June	249.0	168.0	144.5	127.1	143.8	153.8
July	241.8	158.6	150.2	133.1	140.7	149.3
August	237.2	154.0	147.6	133.6	141.1	147.4
September	237.0	154.7	143.0	134.4	145.1	139.0
October	214.7	156.0	143.5	129.0	141.9	129.7
November	203.7	162.6	135.3	123.2	143.5	–
December	202.8	162.3	128.6	123.6	143.7	–

Source: IMF, *International Financial Statistics*

adversely affect prospects for the world economy'. At several points substantial coordinated sales of US dollars occurred.

By mid–1990, however, there were signs emerging that the G3 had themselves become a little disenchanted with coordinated intervention.

Monetary–fiscal policy coordination

Probably the most widely discussed act of policy coordination post war occurred at the Bonn Summit of 1978. The deal struck then was that Germany would increase its government spending by 1 per cent of GNP (acting as a potential locomotive for world recovery) while the USA in its turn would (a) adopt a programme aimed at reducing its oil imports and (b) agree to implement anti-inflationary policies, which included a reduction in a tax cut planned for 1979. Japan also agreed at the time to stabilise its own exports.

At the Plaza meeting the United States indicated that it was 'firmly committed to reducing the budget deficit'. Other participant countries also produced some, but very vague, statements about their policy intentions.

It was not until the Louvre meeting, however, that somewhat firmer commitments were made on the fiscal front. Germany and Japan undertook to ease their fiscal policy stance while the USA pledged to cut its Federal deficit to 2.3 per cent of GNP in 1988. Similar commitments were repeated at the April 1988 meeting of the G7.

There was one well advertised instance of monetary coordination: in March–April 1986 the central banks of several major countries lowered their discount rates in synchronisation, the aim being to encourage growth without altering exchange rate relationships.

The 'indicators' approach

The 'indicators' approach to coordination was first given public exposure at the Tokyo Summit of May 1986. At that meeting a new group of G7 Finance Ministers was formed to work more closely and to meet more frequently between summit meetings. One of the tasks assigned to this new G7 was to 'review their individual economic objectives and forecasts, using a wide range of indicators, with a particular view to examining their mutual compatibility'. The particular indicators chosen were GNP growth rates, inflation rates, interest rates, unemployment rates, fiscal deficit ratios, current account and trade balance, money growth targets, reserves and exchange rates. This multilateral surveillance was to be undertaken in close collaboration with the IMF.

Frenkel and Goldstein (1988) justify the use of indicators as a means of assisting the process of coordination as follows:

> These indicators are employed to help gauge the international implications of domestic policy changes, to spot likely inconsistencies among policy objectives, both within and across countries; to monitor whether short term developments are 'on track' in terms of longer term objectives; and as early-warning signals of emerging global inflationary trends.

At the Venice Summit in June 1987, the list of indicators was reduced to six: growth, inflation, trade balances, government budgets, monetary conditions and exchange rates. At the Toronto Summit in June 1988, the G7 added a commodity price indicator to the list.

Boughton (1991) argues that if indicators are to be useful in the process of cooperative policy-making, they must be extensive and should fall into three groups: indicators of economic performance, of the stance of macroeconomic policies and of the economic processes linking policies to performance (in this last category would fall market interest rates, exchange rates and the growth rate of domestic demand).

A brief evaluation

It is difficult to be too enthusiastic about the achievements of policy coordination on any of the fronts noted above.

Argy (1991b), drawing on the evidence available, tries to evaluate the episodes of coordinated exchange rate management. He asks three broad questions. First, did the authorities succeed in moving the currencies by coordinated intervention? Second, did they move them closer to the official targets? Third, were these targets correct to begin with?

Argy summarises the literature finding that most of the intervention undertaken was sterilised but that, nevertheless, it probably had a significant 'signalling' effect in the market, particularly when the intervention was public rather than secret. However, the signalling effect was generally not lasting (unless supported by changes in fundamentals like monetary policy) and, in any event, appeared to be wearing off by 1990. Moreover, the signalling effect at times was blurred by conflicting signals given by officials about the proper course of the currencies.

Nor did the signalling effect always work as desired. At most, the Plaza Agreement helped to nudge the US dollar downwards. In due course, however, the fall acquired a life of its own, possibly overshooting the mark from the authorities' perspective. At the Louvre meeting the authorities tried to stabilise the currencies with some (modest) success in the first six months; after that the dollar resumed its fall. The target yen–dollar rate, faced with the continuing appreciation of the yen, was apparently eventually revised. Was this a concession to the 'wisdom' of the market forces? When the US dollar finally rose it acquired a new momentum against which coordinated intervention seemed powerless.

Finally, the whole exercise assumes that the authorities have a good idea of the level of the fundamental equilibrium exchange rate, but this is a highly contentious issue.

In the light of the above comments, Argy concluded that 'the record is hardly a good one'.

If exchange rate management had small but uncertain impacts, 'agreements' on fiscal policies reflected either policies that would have been undertaken anyway (Feldstein 1988; Shinkai 1990) or policies with impacts which not everyone agrees were necessarily good (e.g. as in the case of Germany's commitment at the Bonn Summit or in Japan in the second half of the 1980s). Moreover, the recent US undertakings to reduce their budget deficit were never really taken too seriously by the USA.

Finally, on the indicators approach the strongest case that could be made for it is that it contributes to a better understanding of how countries are likely to interact on one another and that it may avoid the pursuit of inconsistent external targets.

Part VIII

CASE STUDIES OF MACRO POLICY

There are three chapters in Part VIII which review country experiences.

Chapter 46 looks at Thatcher's macroeconomic policy reforms in the UK. It also reviews the background to her reforms and the problems that the UK had encountered in the previous fifteen years or so. The chapter concludes with a summary of the principal features of Reaganomics, comparing the achievements and failures of the latter with Thatcherism.

Chapter 47 is a study of Japan's macroeconomic performance on three fronts: inflation, unemployment and the current account. It tries to explain why Japan has managed to have both a low rate of inflation and a low rate of unemployment. At the same time, it looks at the principal elements underlying Japan's persistent current account surplus.

Chapter 48 looks at Australia's and New Zealand's experience with financial and labour market deregulation. In the space of less than a decade the two economies deregulated on four fronts: they floated their currencies, removed all controls over capital flows, deregulated their domestic financial system and, as well, deregulated their labour markets.

CASE STUDIES OF MACRO POLICY

46

A decade of Thatcherism: 1979–89 – Thatcherism and Reaganomics compared

---

INTRODUCTION

This chapter tries to evaluate Thatcher's macroeconomic performance in the decade or so when she was Britain's Prime Minister. Thatcher was first elected in May 1979 and then re-elected twice more in 1983 and in 1987. She retired from government in November 1990 before completing a full third term in office.

The chapter begins with a fairly detailed account of the years prior to Thatcher. This is particularly important because it gives us a better perspective on what Thatcher was trying to achieve and what was supposed to be wrong with the UK economy.

Next we summarise the Thatcher ideology. We then proceed to a review of the policies implemented and to an evaluation of those policies. We conclude with a summary of Reaganomics and its parallels and differences with Thatcherism.

THE BACKGROUND TO THATCHERISM

Tables 46.1 and 46.2 try to sum up the earlier record. Britain's performance was inferior in respect of inflation and output growth but about average on unemployment. The growth in productivity in the business sector also tended on average to be inferior, particularly so in relation to OECD Europe (Table 46.2). There had also been recurring problems with current account deficits as well as large and persistent public sector deficits. The latter left a legacy, by 1980, of a gross and net public debt to GNP ratio above the average of Europe and the G7 (Table 46.1).

We proceed to summarise the experience under three broad headings: monetary–

Table 46.1   Inflation, output growth and unemployment

	Inflation (1972–9)	Unemployment (1972–9)	Growth in GNP (1972–9)	Public debt as percentage of GNP (1980) Gross	Net
UK	13.6	4.6	2.4	54.6	47.5
EC	10.5	4.3	3.2	42.5	26.3[a]
OECD	8.9	4.6	3.3	42.4	22.0[b]

Source: OECD, Economic Outlooks
Notes: [a] Europe.
       [b] G7.

Table 46.2   Productivity in the business sector (percentage changes at annual rate)

	Total factor productivity[a] 1960–3	1973–9	1979–90	Labour productivity[b] 1960–73	1973–9	1979–90
USA	1.6	−0.4	0.2	2.2	0	0.5
Japan	5.8	1.4	2.0	8.6	2.9	3.0
Germany	2.6	1.8	0.8	4.5	3.1	1.6
France	4.0	1.7	1.8	5.4	3.0	2.7
Italy	4.4	2.1	1.4	6.3	3.0	2.0
UK	2.3	0.6	1.6	3.6	1.6	2.1
Canada	2.0	0.8	0	2.8	1.5	1.2
OECD Europe	3.2	1.4	1.3	5.0	2.7	2.1
OECD	2.8	0.5	0.8	4.1	1.4	1.5

Source: OECD, Economic Outlooks
Notes: [a] Total factor productivity growth is equal to a weighted average of the growth in labour and capital productivity. The sample-period averages for capital and labour shares are used as weights.
       [b] Output per employed person.

fiscal policies and exchange rate management, prices and incomes policies, the regulatory environment.

Monetary–fiscal policies and exchange rate management

The UK entered the float in June 1972 with considerable under-utilised capacity and unemployment. At the same time, inflation was steady or slightly accelerating at some 8 per cent. The policy strategy (the 'go-for-growth' policy) that the authorities adopted during 1972–3 had three key elements. First, expansionary monetary and fiscal policies were implemented in coordination to counter the unemployment. Second, the exchange rate was to be allowed to find its own level and so free policy from the external constraint. Third, to ensure that excess demand created became absorbed in real growth and did not flow over significantly into prices, an incomes policy was adopted. In effect, then, monetary–fiscal policies were being assigned to the real economy, the exchange rate to external balance, and incomes policies to containing inflation.

It is clear in retrospect now that monetary policy was much too expansionary in 1972–3 and that this did contribute to the subsequent acceleration in inflation. It is also clear now that the policy was inconsistent with the incomes policy then in operation (see below).

In the years that followed macro policy reversed itself. By mid-1973 it became evident that money growth had to be restrained but it is arguable that it was restrained far too sharply in 1974–5. Even allowing for distortions to the money aggregates, the slowdown was substantial, coming at a time, too, when the oil price and wage shocks were placing substantial independent pressures on prices. The result was a very vicious turnaround in the growth of real money balances. At the same time fiscal policy also tightened in the years 1974–7.

The combination of a real wage gap and tight macro policies produced an upsurge in unemployment. Over the years 1974–7 inflation also remained very high, averaging some 18 per cent.

With unemployment persisting high monetary policy began to ease from 1976; by mid-1978, however, it had tightened significantly again. Fiscal policy did not ease until 1978, despite the unfavourable conditions in the labour market.

From the late 1960s increasing emphasis was placed on the control of money aggregates. From late 1973 money growth targets became an internal aim of the authorities. It was not until July 1976, however, that money targets were announced. At first the target was in terms of M3, but from late 1976 the target was expressed in terms of sterling M3. From this point on a money target band of 4 percentage points was adopted. The record of monetary targeting to 1979 was not encouraging. In 1976–7 money growth undershot its target; in 1977–8 there was a large overshoot. However, before losing government to the Conservatives money growth was settling within the band (Table 46.3).

From June 1972 to late 1976 sterling was weak. On an effective basis sterling fell by some 45 per cent; however, after adjusting for relative prices, the fall in the effective rate was of the order of 20 per cent. At the same time, the UK's current account was consistently in deficit. By contrast, from end-1976 to early 1979 sterling became strong, the real effective rate now rising substantially over this period. By 1977–8 too the current account had moved into surplus.

The initial professed aim of the float had been to let the rate find its own level and not to oppose any well-defined trend. In reality, between 1972 and 1976 there was considerable exchange rate management. Foreign exchange intervention in support of sterling increased over the period, reaching massive heights during 1976. Moreover, monetary policy was not independent of exchange rate pressures. In 1975–6 when sterling was very weak monetary policy tightened in part at least to ease the pressures on sterling. After sterling recovered, from late 1976, the authorities took advantage of the situation to stabilise the exchange rate, build up reserves and minimise the loss of competitiveness. This, however, came into conflict with the money targets for

Table 46.3 UK key economic indicators, 1979–90

	1979	1980	1981	1982	1983	1984	1985	1986	1987	1988	1989	1990
Inflation	13.5	18.0	11.9	8.6	4.6	5.0	6.1	3.4	4.1	4.9	7.8	9.5
GDP growth	2.6	−1.7	−1.0	1.5	3.5	2.2	3.6	3.9	4.8	4.3	2.3	1.0
Unemployment (standard)	5.0	6.4	9.8	11.3	12.4	11.7	11.2	11.2	10.3	8.6	7.1	6.8
Current account as percentage of GDP	−0.2	1.2	2.6	1.7	1.2	0.6	0.8	0	−1.0	−3.3	−4.0	−2.8
General government financial balance	−3.2	−3.3	−2.6	−2.4	−3.3	−3.9	−2.7	−2.3	−1.2	+1.2	+1.2	−0.7
Real effective exchange rate index[a] (1985 = 100)	960	115.4	121.8	114.4	105.4	101.0	100.0	94.2	94.0	99.9	98.7	99.2
Fiscal impulse[b]	0.9	−2.6	−2.4	−1.4	0.8	0.2	−0.4	0.2	−0.1	−1.4	−0.2	1.1
Money targeting[c]	8–12	7–11	6–10	8–12	7–11	6–12	5–9	11–15	–	–	–	–
M3	(10.3)	(20.0)	(14.6)	(9.8)	(10.0)	(12.3)	(13.6)	(20.7)	–	–	–	–
M1	–	–	–	8–12 (10.8)	7–11 (14.1)	–	–	–	–	–	–	–
PSL_2	–	–	–	8–12 (8.9)	7–11 (12.6)	–	–	–	–	–	–	–
M0	–	–	–	–	–	4–8 (5.6)	3–7 (4.2)	2–6 (5.8)	2–6 (5.8)	1–5 (6.2)	1–5 (6.3)	1–5 (2.7)
Real interest rate[d]	−0.5	−4.2	+2.8	+4.3	+6.2	+5.7	+4.5	+6.5	+5.4	+4.5	+1.8	+2.6

Source: OECD, *Economic Outlooks* IMF, *International Financial Statistics, World Economic Outlooks*

Notes: [a] IMF calculations relative to normalised unit labour costs.
[b] IMF calculations − central government (+, expansionary; −, contractionary).
[c] Targets and outcomes (shown in parentheses) for varying periods not identified in the table. (See also Chapter 43.)
[d] Long-term bond yield less the rate of inflation.

1977–8. As a result of massive foreign exchange intervention, in support of foreign currencies, money growth substantially overshot its target.

Prices and incomes policies

We focus particularly on the prices and incomes policies (PIPs) in the thirteen years or so before Thatcher.

The UK's experience between 1965 and 1978 has been rich and wide ranging and serves well to demonstrate many of the inherent problems associated with a PIP. The UK in the postwar years has felt a continuing need to implement a PIP because of her relatively militant trade unions, her relatively high inflation and her persistent balance of payments deficits.

It is possible to identify three cycles in the use of a PIP in those years, corresponding to the experience of, first, a Labour government (1964–70), then a Conservative government (1970–4) and then a Labour government (1974–8). As we note shortly, there are certain common patterns in each of these cycles.

The Labour Party came into power at the end of 1964. Its first serious effort at a PIP was to create, in April 1965, a National Board for Prices and Incomes. This Board had the task of examining claims for increases in wages and prices referred to it by the government and making recommendations using various norms. Initially, the Board had no statutory powers and hence there was no obligation to accept its recommendations.

The first 'norm' for wage increases applicable over the period May 1965 to June 1966 was 3–3.5 per cent, corresponding roughly to the expected national growth of productivity, but several exceptions were allowed.

In mid-1966 with inflation continuing high and the balance of payments in deficit the government switched to a statutory policy. Between July 1966 and January 1967 a general statutory freeze was enforced, followed by a six-month period of severe restraint during which the norm was zero, while exceptions were now defined more tightly. From the end of June 1967, the norm effectively continued to be zero but the exceptions were looser and defined as in 1965. The last phase ran from April 1968 to the end of 1969 when the norm was again zero but now, for the exceptional cases, the maximum allowable increase was 3.5 per cent. All these provisions were embodied in a succession of Acts in 1966, 1967 and 1968, which gave the Board delaying powers ranging from six to twelve months. By the end of 1969, the PIP had effectively collapsed, as reflected in the wage explosions of 1969–70. The powers given to the government under the 1968 Act were not then renewed.

The Conservative Party, which was in power between 1970 and 1974, first tried to implement a voluntary PIP; when that failed it enforced a statutory freeze on wages and prices from the end of November 1972 to the end of April 1973. Between April and November 1973 the government assumed new statutory powers to regulate wages and prices and established two new agencies, a Price Commission and a Pay Board, to operate the new rules. The price and wage norms were to be administered by the

Price Commission and the Pay Board respectively. Detailed norms were prescribed for price and wage increases.

The next phase, from November 1973, was more flexible and relaxed but it continued to be compulsory. Pay increases were limited to £2.25 a week or 7 per cent whichever was higher; in addition there were complicated 'threshold' clauses permitting a pay increase for increases in prices in excess of 7 per cent and an exception relating to productivity agreements was also allowed. But, with mounting trade union opposition, an explosion in commodity prices, a rapidly growing money supply and severe problems in interpreting the new regulations, this phase of the PIP broke down completely and a new wage explosion followed. In March 1974 the Conservatives were voted out of office.

After attempts by the two previous administrations to implement a statutory PIP, the Labour government abandoned all statutory controls on wages, relying now entirely on voluntary controls. At the same time, it retained control over prices.

It began by experimenting with a Social Contract, trading wage restraint by the unions for a number of undertakings, including continuing price and rent control, public transport and housing subsidies, improvements in social welfare provisions, the fostering of industrial democracy and the repeal of the Tories' Industrial Relations Act. Wage restraint was understood to mean that wage deals would aim at maintaining real incomes and no more, while all major increases would be twelve months apart. There were numerous exclusions, however, including again for productivity deals, for lower paid workers and to improve the status of women.

This experiment by the Labour Party failed for a number of reasons. The Trade Union Congress did not have the power to vet agreements, the guidelines were not observed, while the loopholes – exceptions – proved, in the end, too generous and loose.

After its initial failure, the Labour Party, in August 1975, proposed that wage increases for the succeeding year be voluntarily restricted to £6 a week (with those earning over £8,500 receiving no rise at all). The only exception allowed was for equal pay. An increasing feature here was that wage increases that exceeded the norm were not allowable in entirety as cost increases. In phase II, which ran from August 1976 to July 1977, a 5 per cent increase in basic pay was allowed subject to a minimum of £2.50 and a maximum of £4, with no exceptions this time. Also the Price Code was relaxed to assist investment and the cash position of enterprises. Phase III, which ran from July 1977 to July 1978, proposed a 10 per cent ceiling on pay increases while phase IV, beginning in July 1978, proclaimed a 5 per cent limit on pay increases. But already during phase III there was considerable unrest and opposition to the policies; the situation deteriorated further later in 1978 when there was a new upsurge in wage claims, during which the PIP effectively collapsed. In May 1979 the Labour government was ousted.

Several features of the UK experience are especially worth noting. First, both the Labour and the Conservative parties have felt a need, when in power, to institute some form of control over wages. Second, in two of the three cycles summarised above there was some resort, after an attempt at voluntary controls, to a statutory freeze, followed by looser and more flexible rules. Third, each of the three cycles ended in increasing restlessness and a wage explosion, which, as it happened, contributed to the downfall of the government in power at the time.

There is a vast econometric literature for the UK that attempts to evaluate the degree to which an incomes policy served independently to reduce the rate of inflation or the rate of growth in wages. For the UK there now appears to be a growing consensus which is best summarised in one econometric study.

> Our results indicate that whilst some incomes policies have reduced the rate of wage inflation during the period in which they operated this reduction has only been temporary. Wage increases in the period immediately following the ending of the policies were higher than they would otherwise have been, and these increases match losses incurred during the operation of the incomes policy.
>
> (Henry and Ormerod 1978: 39)

The conclusion for the UK is a most important one. It suggests that in the longer run any short-term gains are lost or reversed when the PIP is relaxed or abandoned. (See Chapter 44.)

The regulatory environment

We deal first with external controls. The UK, until October 1979, had 'outward' exchange controls. These were tightened a little at the time of the float in June 1972 and again in the crisis of 1976.

If these outward controls were, in fact, effective, one would expect the following. When, say, as a result of adverse expectations about sterling or a change in the foreign interest rate there is a net incentive to move capital out, this incentive will not be completely arbitraged away. When, however, for opposite reasons, there is a net incentive to move capital in, this incentive will be removed by inward arbitrage. Finally, when exchange controls are entirely removed, one would expect the covered differential to be close to zero, whatever the initial incentives (Chapter 33).

These potential implications are largely confirmed by the data. In the period to 1979 there were several months when the covered interest rate differential favoured outward investment by a significant margin. Clearly, if the data are correct these were not arbitraged away because outward exchange controls were 'biting'. There are no instances, however, where there is a significant net incentive for inward arbitrage.

It does appear, therefore, on the surface that outward exchange controls may have been effective. In this case, a reasonable hypothesis is that until 1979 sterilised intervention was feasible for potential outflows but possibly not for potential inflows. In other words there may have been an asymmetry in the scope for sterilisation (Chapter 36).

It is interesting that, until 1976, intervention was in support of sterling, and so in principle, according to our hypothesis, sterilised intervention was to a point feasible.

During 1977 intervention was in support of foreign currencies; the strong inflows then, as it turned out, proved difficult to sterilise.

Turning now to domestic financial regulation, in the years 1971–9 several changes were made to banking legislation in the UK. In September 1971 the banking system was deregulated (the so-called Competition and Credit Control Legislation – CCC). The principal changes introduced by CCC were the following: controls over bank interest rates were lifted; lending ceilings, which had been the principal method of monetary control up to then, were discontinued; the 8 per cent minimum cash ratio and the 28 per cent minimum liquid asset ratio were replaced by a 1.5 per cent cash ratio and a 12.5 per cent minimum reserve asset ratio, respectively.

In December 1973 the 'corset' was introduced. Its principal aim was to contain the growth of sterling M3 which, as we have seen, had been growing very rapidly in the previous two years. It laid down certain penalties for banks whose interest-bearing eligible liabilities grew at a faster-than-prescribed rate. The penalty, which took the form of lodgement of non-interest-bearing deposits with the Bank of England, was progressive, ranging from 5 per cent to 50 per cent depending on the degree of infringement.

The corset was removed in early 1975, reintroduced at the end of 1976, and then removed again in mid-1977 until mid-1978 when it was reintroduced.

THE THATCHER IDEOLOGY

We have seen that, while Thatcher inherited an economy which had been substantially interventionist, moves had already been made to shift towards more conservative policies and a more liberalised financial environment. We note particularly the adoption of money growth targets, the tighter fiscal policies in 1974–7 and the financial deregulation of 1971 (the first two by a Labour government).

The essentials of Thatcher's policies can be summed up under four broad headings; the role of government, the monetary–fiscal and exchange rate policies, the policies towards the unions and the supply-side policies.

The role of government

What was stressed primarily was that there was to be more freedom of individual choice and a reduction in the role of government (Johnson 1991: 6). This would manifest itself in a number of ways: a fall in the ratio of government expenditure to GNP; the adoption of a hands-off policy with respect to wages (the abandonment of all forms of incomes policies); a programme of privatisation, the removal of financial regulations and of intervention in foreign exchange markets.

Monetary, fiscal, incomes and exchange rate policies

The policies were intended to be distinctive in a number of ways. To begin, the stability of growth was stressed; this called 'for the provision of a more stable economic climate *with as few sudden changes as possible*' (Johnson 1991: 5). Also conventional fine-tuning was to be abandoned. As Sir Geoffrey Howe, the new Chancellor of the Exchequer, said in his first Budget Speech: 'the notions of demand management, expanding public spending and fine tuning of the economy have now been tested almost to destruction'.

Inflation was now to be the 'enemy number one'. In the attack on inflation both monetary and fiscal policy would be used to bear down on prices. The policy was expected to carry credibility and thus to reduce the disinflation costs. Considerable stress was also to be placed on reducing public sector deficits.

Macro policy as such would not target unemployment. This, however, did not exclude resort to micro measures aimed at improving employment. Moreover, it was contended that there would be a spontaneous improvement in growth and employment after the right macro–micro policies had been put into place.

The original intention was also to let exchange rates find their own levels without any management. Finally, there was to be no control over prices and wages. Wages and prices would also find their own levels, driven by market forces now in an environment which was itself to be remoulded by the Thatcherites.

Policies towards the unions

The government was to take measures which would aim at reducing the power and the privileged position of the unions. Restrictive work practices would be more difficult to enforce and this in turn would promote greater productivity. Unions, within the new constraints, would be left free to bargain with employers over wages. Monetary policy would be set with an eye on inflation and so if wage settlements were 'excessive' in relation to the monetary stance adopted unions would have to take the consequences, i.e. endure higher unemployment.

To summarise, the ultimate aim of the reforms was to promote greater flexibility of wages and of working practices.

Supply-side policies

The burden of taxes was to be switched from direct to indirect. There was to be a cut in income taxes; at the same time, indirect taxes (VAT) would be allowed to rise. Also, corporate taxation would be reformed to improve incentives for short-term profits and capital expenditure. With the cuts in government expenditure and the elimination of the public sector deficit envisaged, it is not clear what that would have implied for the *overall* burden of taxes.

The combined tax reforms were intended to increase work effort, encourage more saving and investment and restore business profitability.[1]

THE IMPLEMENTATION OF POLICY

A programme of financial deregulation was put into place. In October 1979 all exchange controls were abandoned; by June 1980 the corset was abolished. Reforms were introduced and some deregulation of the banks and the building societies. Control over hire purchase terms were abolished in July 1982.

The monetary and fiscal policy programme announced had two innovative features. First, it required that monetary and fiscal policies be coordinated, both being, as noted above, jointly directed at inflation. In this respect Thatcher had been strongly influenced by Professor Patrick Minford who, in turn, had ideas which paralleled those propagated by Sargent and Wallace (1981) (see Chapter 34). Second, it was to be a medium-term plan of monetary and fiscal restriction *which would be announced years ahead*.

In the *initial* plan money growth was to be brought down gradually from a range of 7–11 in 1980–1 to 4–8 by 1983–4. At the same time the public sector borrowing requirement (PSBR) would be brought down from $3\frac{3}{4}$ per cent in 1980–1 to $1\frac{1}{2}$ per cent by 1983–4. These targets were revised each subsequent year in the light of actual outcomes and unanticipated developments in the economy.

In the years to 1986 exchange rate management was limited and indeed never reached the scales of intervention of the years 1973 to mid-1978. The emphasis was on money targeting and inflation and on letting the exchange rate more or less find its own level. By 1986, however, there was evidence of a shift in policy towards what Miller and Sutherland (1990) called 'shadowing the DM'. This shift in policy was officially confirmed by Lawson, the Chancellor of the Exchequer, who in a speech in September 1987 said that 'our objectives should be clear: to maintain the maximum stability of the key exchange rates and to manage any changes that may be necessary in an orderly way'. Some time in 1988, however, this policy was again put to one side, now to allow monetary policy to be redirected at domestic objectives.

The promised tax cuts were implemented over time. The top rate on earned income fell from 83 per cent to 60 per cent in 1979 and in 1988 all rates of income tax above 40 per cent were abolished. There was also a progressive reduction in the basic rate of income tax from 33 per cent to 25 per cent. Also, the VAT rate was raised from 8 per cent to 15 per cent.

Reforms aimed at reducing the power of the unions were implemented in a succession of changes to the law, passed in 1980, 1982, 1988 and 1989.

McConnell and Takla (1990) note that many changes in the legislation were aimed at reducing strikes. First, there were new restrictions imposed on the extent to which workers were immune from liability and prosecution; a trade union no longer had immunity if the striker's employer was 'not a party' to the dispute. This was intended to reduce secondary or sympathy strikes. There were as well restrictions introduced on picketing. For striking workers, too, to have immunity it was necessary for a strike to be preceded by a secret ballot. There was also a loss of immunity for the trade union as an organisation. This left the unions exposed in certain circumstances to substantial claims for damages.

Second, there was also some reduction in the benefit that a worker could claim while on strike. Third, the legislation made it easier for employers to dismiss workers on strike.

There was as well legislation aimed at limiting the closed shop. All action to enforce a closed shop became illegal by 1988.

AN EVALUATION OF THATCHERISM

Framework

Having summarised the background to Thatcherism, its basic ideology and the policies it tried to implement, we are now ready to evaluate the outcomes and performance.

To begin, however, we need to ask: how does one evaluate Thatcherism? What principles can one apply in this task?

There are several ways one can attack the question. First, one can, after the event so to speak, think up alternative policy strategies that could have been adopted (presumably from amongst those put forward by critics) and see whether, *given the particular shocks to which the economy was exposed*, the outcomes might have been better. Ideally, what would be needed here would be econometric simulations of alternative policy paths.

Second, one can evaluate Thatcherism *in terms of the objectives it actually set for itself*. This may be too easy or unfair depending on whether unforeseen shocks went against it or were in its favour.

Third, one could compare, using conventional criteria, the pre-Thatcher with the post-Thatcher years to see if there had in fact been any marked improvement. There are two difficulties here. One is again that the exogenous shocks might be different in the two periods and this could bias outcomes. Another is that one also needs to look at what other countries have been doing. If, for example, other countries also recorded big improvements in macro performance, this might take some of the lustre off Thatcherism.

Fourth, one can focus on Thatcher's economic performance *relative to other countries*, to see if her *relative* performance had improved. This, however, also presupposes that shocks are about the same abroad.

It is evident that any balanced assessment of Thatcherism needs at least to take account of the 'shocks' to which the economy was exposed. So what were the principal shocks?

In the early 1980s Thatcherism was confronted by a recession abroad. However, as we saw, from 1983 until 1989–90 the industrial economies grew at a rapid rate. Other countries also faced such fluctuations, so relative to other countries Britain would not have been significantly advantaged or disadvantaged. The recession of 1974–5 also meant that the early Thatcher years were not noticeably disadvantaged relative to the previous four to five years.

An important development in the Thatcher years was the North Sea oil production, which now began to make very positive contributions to the current account. Britain became thenceforth a petro-currency. One important implication was that at least until the late 1980s sterling became, in part at least, sensitive to the movement in the price of oil, rising (falling) as the price rose (fell). Not everyone, however, saw this as a plus for Britain. Other things being equal, an improvement in the oil balance would be expected to strengthen sterling and this in turn would provoke a decline in net (manufacturing) exports, which some saw as undesirable.

Macro management

We begin by addressing two questions. First, we might ask whether the targets for money growth and the PSBR were met. Second, we can look beyond that and see if the broader objective of reducing inflation was achieved.

Consider first the record of money targeting (Table 46.3). In general the record is not a good one. There were several misses, all in fact overshoots. There was a little more success in meeting M0-growth targets than sterling M3 targets. In any event the policy was taken less and less seriously as time went by with progressively less credibility attaching to it. An important reason for the failure of this monetarist experiment was that financial deregulation had distorted the money aggregates (see Chapter 43).

There was more success in meeting the PSBR targets; again the misses were overshoots but the cumulative overshoot was nowhere near that of the money targets (Johnson 1991). *More important, however, is that Thatcher did succeed in turning the PSBR around*: whereas in 1978–80 the average PSBR as a percentage of GNP was over 5 per cent, by 1988–90 this had been converted into a *surplus* of over 2 per cent. (A similar trend is observable in the general government financial balance in Table 46.3.) So there was clearly some 'success' on this front. Public expenditure as a percentage of GNP fell from some 43 per cent to 38 per cent but the revenue share rose marginally.

Impressive as the performance on the PSBR appears, it does need to be qualified in an important way. The public sector *current* surplus (i.e. excluding investment) actually *fell* from 2.2 per cent of GDP in 1973–9 to 1.9 per cent in 1980–90. What really happened was that the adjustment fell particularly heavily on *public investment*.

What about performance on inflation? Thatcher inherited an inflation rate of the order of nearly 14 per cent. This got worse in Thatcher's first year for two reasons: the 'one-off' effects of the imposition of the additional VAT and the rise in public sector pay to which the government was committed.

Inflation fell steadily after that for some years, reaching a low point of some

4 per cent by 1987; the fall in commodity prices and the strength of sterling were particularly helpful in the first few years. However, subsequently it rose steadily again, reaching some 7 per cent by 1991. So there was clearly some improvement in performance on this front; we return to this question later.

If there was some success on the inflation front the unemployment record was very poor. Unemployment went up from some 5 per cent in 1979 to over 12 per cent in 1983 before gradually coming down to under 7 per cent in 1990 (but rising again in 1991). Nor was the record on the current account much better. The account benefited from the North Sea oil sales and indeed until 1986 was in surplus, albeit progressively dwindling; after 1986, however, the deficit ballooned, reaching some 4 per cent in 1989 (Table 46.3).

It is now generally agreed that in retrospect at least the early Thatcher years were turbulent on several fronts. To begin with, by 1982 the real exchange rate had risen by some 20 per cent. Several influences were at work here: the North Sea oil, the early 'Thatcher factor' and the progressively higher real interest rates.

Also, despite what looked like a relatively lax monetary policy, measured in terms of money growth, there is now universal agreement that monetary policy in the early 1980s was in fact very tight. This is readily confirmed if attention focuses on the real interest rate which rose very sharply in those years.

Again, if we use the change in the cyclically adjusted central government balance, as calculated by the IMF, as the measure of the fiscal stance, we find that the cumulative net *deflationary* impact in the three years 1980–2 was of the order of 6.4 per cent (Table 46.3) which is very large and certainly easily the largest of the G7.

The combination of very tight monetary and fiscal policies, a very strong currency and a recession abroad proved destructive to economic activity and employment and to the manufacturing sector in particular. On the other hand, it did contribute to the sharp fall in inflation after 1980 (Table 46.3).

To quote a recent commentator on Thatcherism:

The last 13 years of Thatcherism are strewn with costly examples of woolly-headed thinking born of complacency. The most outstanding was the destruction of 25 per cent of manufacturing capacity in the early 1980s. Admittedly this happened partly through not realising in time the disastrous effects of an overblown exchange rate and record interest rates. The demise was, however, hailed as the entry into the age of the post-industrial society.

(Claasen 1992)

In the years that followed to 1988 nominal interest rates eased, while fiscal policy remained roughly neutral. At the same time, sterling, in real terms, fell quite sharply from the heights reached in 1981–2. Also, the real wage gap fell. Britain's economy was aided in those years by the fact that industrial economies were growing rapidly. Between 1983 and 1988 Britain's economy grew, on average, by some 3.7 per cent a year and the unemployment rate almost halved (Table 46.3). However, in the later years the economy became overheated and there was an upsurge in asset prices which itself, in turn, would have encouraged further spending.

The Thatcherites were also true to their word in refusing to use macro policy to target unemployment. They were not, however, averse to adopting some special job creation measures, albeit on a very modest scale. The 'Restart' programme introduced in 1986 offered training courses to the long-term unemployed, in the process removing these from the ranks of the official unemployed. There was for a while a Community Programme offering some limited work, an Employment Training Scheme and a Youth Training Scheme. (For details and some evaluation, see Johnson (1991).)

How did Thatcher's performance compare with that of other OECD countries? Much depends on what the starting and end points are and what base is used for other countries. If we start with 1979 and take our end point as 1990, the inflation rate came down by some 8 points. In OECD Europe inflation was down by over 5 points; in the EC it was down by 6 points. Of the big G7, France and Italy experienced a comparable disinflation.

On the unemployment front using the same base and terminal points her performance was about average but this *overstates* the performance because in the earlier years it grew much more rapidly than elsewhere, however the calculations are made. So on a *cumulative* basis the performance remains poor.

Did other countries reduce their PSBR by comparable amounts? Of the G7 only Japan's turnaround was superior. The others either recorded a smaller improvement (Germany) or got worse (USA, Canada, France) or recorded no change (Italy). On a weighted average basis for the OECD the fall was only of the order of some 1 per cent.

Attacking her macro performance from a different angle, it is not difficult to fault particular policies at particular times. All the evidence suggests that a large proportion of the early upsurge in unemployment came from demand factors (Bean and Symons 1990). In retrospect now it is possible to argue that the deflationary forces at work were too powerful in the early 1980s and that some relief was probably called for.

Another perspective on this is to argue, as some have, that, had a 'corporatist' approach been adopted, the costs of disinflation would have been mitigated. But it is difficult to see how one could have corporatist policies (which in the past had not worked) and simultaneously confront the unions with reforms which they found indigestible.

On the exchange rate front there were too many U turns, as we saw. Thatcher refused to join the European Monetary System exchange rate mechanism (ERM) arrangements despite opportunities offered to her in 1979 and again in 1985. Britain did join the ERM scheme in October 1990 just before Thatcher actually resigned.[2] As we saw too after 1986 there was some shift towards exchange rate targeting, which itself was an admission that earlier policies had failed.

Also, Johnson (1991: 258) notes that during its third term 'the government threw away its achievements by allowing domestic demand to expand too quickly, letting inflation rise again to the double-figure level it had inherited'. The mistake may have been made in early 1988 when the government lowered income taxes, fuelling consumption at a time when consumer spending was overheating the economy.

In 1988–9 with the economy overheated, some asset inflation and growing financial imbalances (Chapter 42), inflation accelerating, a stronger currency and interest rates rising abroad, the UK authorities began to tighten monetary policy. Nominal interest rates rose sharply in 1989–90. It is arguable that monetary policy was now too tight for too long; by 1990–1 the economy had fallen into a severe recession. It will be recalled that one aim of Thatcherism was to put the economy on an even keel and to avoid stop–go.

Finally, some would accuse the Thatcherites of being 'obsessive' about public sector deficits and that a less doctrinaire approach and a more judicious use of fiscal policy might have improved the macroeconomy.

To sum up the macro management, the record is quite good on inflation and (with the reservations noted) the PSBR but less satisfactory on the unemployment and current account fronts. What must also be counted a serious failure is that her disinflation strategy lacked, it seemed, credibility and so the costs of the disinflation were very substantial, indeed as substantial as in previous disinflations (Layard and Nickell 1989).

Supply-side policies

The Thatcherites have claimed notable successes on the productivity front, so much so that it has been dubbed by some a miracle. There was a significant improvement over the earlier period (1973–9) however productivity is measured (Table 46.2). Moreover, in 1979–83 her performance was about twice as good as that of the EC and the OECD. Indeed, whereas productivity growth almost *halved* in Europe, it *doubled* in Britain. However, this relative performance was not *sustained* in the later years (1983–8) when Britain once again fell behind Europe (Layard and Nickell 1989).

We can go a little beyond that. Over the whole period her performance was slightly better than the G7 average when in the previous fifteen years it had been below. However, this understates the improvement. If we focus on manufacturing productivity her relative performance is even more striking (Vane 1992). So we can fairly conclude that there was some success here. Why the productivity gains?

We lean here on Layard and Nickell (1989). They begin as others do by ruling out gains due to exceptional investment or expenditure on research and development. In fact, on both these fronts there was if anything some deterioration. They end up showing that the two most important influences were the decline in union power (the weakening of unions enabled managers to introduce productivity-improving measures more readily) and the collapse of output and employment (the increase in closures and bankruptcies combined with the fall in competitiveness providing the jolt). Such views are also widely held by others. (See also Metcalf 1988; Bean and Symons 1990).

Will these gains persist into the future? It seems unlikely and indeed there is evidence that this is tailing off. The gains from reforms to work practices will exhaust themselves and the shock effect from unemployment is not lasting.

What about the effects of Thatcherism on investment and private sector savings? Public infrastructure investment was badly neglected, as we noted earlier (Hirst 1989: 119). Over the 1980s as a whole investment was actually weaker than in the previous decade. Worse still, investment was extremely erratic, falling very sharply in 1980–1 and rising very sharply in 1987–8. Investment in human capital also proved disappointing. As Healey and Strobel note:

> The proportion of manufacturing workers in training slumped sharply during the 80s . . . . Britain has the lowest proportion of 16–25 years old in further education of any advanced country and the least qualified managerial class.
>
> (1990: 422–3)

In addition the ratio of research and development to GNP also fell in the 1980s (Healey and Strobel 1990), as did the private saving ratio.

On the other side of the ledger, we note that (as in many other industrial countries) there was a recovery in the share of profits and that, after years of decline, the rate of return on capital did increase sharply in the 1980s.

To sum up, the results are a mixed bag. There was some success on the productivity front but much less so on investment and on private savings.

The impacts of the trade union reforms

There are two studies that address this question directly: Brown and Wadhwani (1990) and McConnell and Takla (1990).

We have already noted the improvement in productivity, some of which it is now widely agreed is attributable to the industrial relations legislation.

Productivity to one side, what other potential gains could one expect from the legislation? Two in particular were in fact additional primary objectives: the reduction in industrial strikes and the increased flexibility of wages in response to market forces. Have these been realised?

On the first Brown and Wadhwani (1990) conclude that 'British strike activity has diminished substantially from the levels of the 1970s, but since this is in line with a world-wide decline in strikes it would be wrong to link it too closely to the legislation'. They go on to concede, however, as we noted earlier, that to resort to strikes is now more costly for unions. McConnell and Takla (1990) in a more detailed study reach broadly similar conclusions, but with some refinements. They are worth quoting in full.

> The results in this paper show that the dramatic fall in the number of strikes in the 1980s was due more to changing economic conditions than to changes in Trade

Union legislation. We find that after taking into account changes in industrial composition and unemployment, there was actually an increase in the number of strikes after the legislation was introduced. The number of strikes only began to fall after 1984 when the requirement for compulsory secret ballot was introduced.

Although there was no fall in the number of stoppages or the number of workers involved in stoppages, the legislation did reduce the number of working days lost through stoppages. Thus although strikes have become more frequent, they have also become shorter .... If we judge the legislation by the extent it has reduced the loss of output caused by strikes then the legislation has been a success.

(1990: 25)

It is now universally agreed that Thatcher did break the power of the unions. As casual evidence of this, we can cite the fact that the proportion of the work force unionised fell dramatically. Between 1984 and 1990 it dropped from 58 to 48 per cent. But have wages become more flexible? It appears not but it is difficult to judge and on *a priori* grounds one might have expected this to happen. Layard and Nickell note that:

despite high unemployment the growth of average hourly earnings was almost constant at $7\frac{1}{2}$ per cent a year from 1982–87 and with the fall in unemployment rose to over 9 per cent in 1988.

(1989: 17)

A similar conclusion appears in Brown and Wadhwani (1990).

REAGANOMICS

Reagan also inherited an economy which at the time, by conventional criteria, had not been performing too well. Inflation had been rising steadily in the three to four years before Reagan, reaching some 10 per cent in 1980. At the same time the unemployment rate had also risen to some 7 per cent in 1980 while the public sector deficit stood at just over 1 per cent of GNP, a deterioration in relation to the three previous years but not exceptionally highly by historical standards (in 1975–6 it had stood at over 3 per cent). On the other hand, the current account was roughly in balance.

The newly elected president railed against what he chose to represent as 'runaway deficits', 'the very high double digit rate of inflation', 'the high taxes' and the 'seven million unemployed'.

His broad prescriptions for putting the economy back on its feet were not unlike Thatcher's. First, considerable importance was attached to reducing the role of government. Government expenditure as a percentage of GNP was to be brought down. At the same time, deregulatory measures on a variety of fronts were to be put into place. Second, as the 1982 Annual Report of the Council of Economic Advisors put it, one of the 'key elements of the Administration program is support for a policy of continued gradual reductions in the rate of monetary growth to bring down inflation'. As in Thatcher's case the policy was expected to carry credibility and thus to minimise disinflation costs. Already by the end of 1979 the Federal Reserve, under the chairmanship of Paul Volker, had begun to implement a tight monetary policy with an eye on inflation. This now received the strong endorsement of the new administration.

Third, another key element in the programme was the supply-side policies, notably the progressive cuts in income taxes and the 'incentive' reductions in taxation to be offered to business. These were implemented but the tax breaks for investment were subsequently removed.

There were a number of important differences with Thatcherism. First, labour market reform was never pushed as vigorously as in the UK. Unions in the USA had never been as militant or 'obstructive' as in the UK. Second, the supply-side policies were elevated as the centrepiece of the programme, even more so than with Thatcher. Supply-side policies were intended to achieve increased private savings, investment and work effort. Moreover, whilst Thatcher did try to offset the loss of revenue from the cut in income tax by increasing sales taxes, Reagan was ambiguous about how the tax cuts were to be financed.

The biggest ambiguities appear on the budget deficits. There is still some debate about what the administration really intended. One view is that so much real growth would be generated that revenue would increase sufficiently to offset the cut in tax rates. A second view is that the administration believed it would achieve sufficient expenditure cuts to offset the tax cuts. According to this argument they were subsequently frustrated by Congress.

A third, related, view is that Reagan was prepared to 'play chicken' with Congress, present them with *ex post* budget deficits and force Congress's hand, ultimately, to make the expenditure cuts. (On this scenario Congress would take fright and play ball.)

A fourth view is that despite the rhetoric the administration really did not worry too much about the consequences of budget deficits. In his rhetoric Reagan had stressed that 'inflation results from deficit spending' (Modigliani 1988). As we shall see, inflation did come down while budget deficits persisted at a high level, making the link questionable and at the same time the policy more politically acceptable (see Auerbach 1989).

We can now summarise the principal outcomes of Reaganomics.

1 As with Thatcherism there is no denying the success on the inflation front. Inflation fell to some 4 per cent by 1984 and remained within that range from then on. However, this was achieved at substantial cost in terms of unemployment, which shot up from 7 to 9.5 per cent in 1982 and 1983 before receding gradually after that. Modigliani (1988), after a careful review of the evidence, concludes that the disinflation cost was about on a par with previous disinflations. So in these respects, at any rate, there is almost a perfect parallel with Thatcherism.

2 In the wake of the tax cuts the budget deficit ballooned from just over 1 per cent

of GNP to some 4 per cent in 1983, falling after that to around 2 per cent.[3] Despite numerous efforts at reducing the deficit, including the Gramm–Rudman–Hollings initiatives of 1985 and again in 1990, there has not been much progress on that front. It is here that we find the sharpest contrast with Thatcherism.

At the end of the day the net public debt as a percentage of GDP rose in the USA between 1980 and 1989 from nearly 20 per cent to nearly 30 per cent. Over the same period in the UK it fell from some 48 per cent to 35 per cent.

3 What happened on the expenditure front is that defence outlays escalated while non-defence expenditure and public capital expenditures fell as proportions of GNP. There was also some slowdown in public expenditure on research and development. Total outlays of government as a percentage of GNP rose significantly from about 34 per cent to over 36 per cent while the tax take increased marginally. In this respect the policy was a failure, unlike Thatcher's who had in fact succeeded in cutting back the share of government expenditure (if not in taxes).

4 The tax cuts did help launch an upsurge in the growth in output. Between 1984 and 1989 output grew on average by some 3.7 per cent. The boom was sustained over some six years (it collapsed in 1990–1). What is sometimes attributed to the 'supply-side' policies can just as readily be represented as a 'Keynesian' success story. Interestingly, throughout the six years when the economy was booming inflation remained at around the 4–5 per cent range.

5 There was some further deregulation of the domestic financial system but, in one notorious instance, the case of the Savings and Loans collapse, this proved disastrous.

Interest rates on deposits were deregulated; at the same time insurance coverage for deposits was extended. On both counts this attracted a large volume of deposits into the institutions which, given the high interest rates they had to pay, were looking for high yielding investments. The authorities then obliged by substantially relaxing the kinds of loans-investments they were allowed to make. Very poor as well as dishonest management compounded the problems. The banks made huge losses on their investments.

At the end of the day the government was forced into a massive bail-out of the banks. This was going to continue to be a drain on the federal deficit for years to come.

6 Easily the most unfavourable side-effect of Reaganomics has been the persistent current account imbalances, explained in large part by the persistent fiscal deficits, which were occurring at a time when many other industrial countries were moving in the other direction. In turn these cumulative current account deficits and their associated 'borrowings' from abroad converted the USA by 1985 from the position of being a large net creditor to being the largest net debtor. This dramatic turnaround in the US position has been variously described as Après Reagan, le Déluge? (After Reagan – chaos?) (Auerbach 1989), 'We are selling off America and living on the

proceeds' (Friedman 1988) and 'the party will soon be over' (Weidenbaum 1988). In short this is saying that the burden will fall on future generations. Friedman (1988) has also contended that the trade deficits were largely responsible for converting the USA into a 'hamburger' economy with the share of employment in services growing at the expense of manufacturing.

The claim, however, that the USA has now become the largest net debtor is being questioned on two grounds. First, US assets abroad are more undervalued than foreigners' claims on the USA. Second, the USA is a net *creditor* in so far as investment income is concerned (Roberts 1991).[4]

7 One of the aspects of Reaganomics most widely commented on was the change in the policy mix (the tight monetary policy associated with the easy fiscal policy). This policy had important side-effects (apart from the effects on the current account) on the dollar (the real appreciation) and on real interest rates. The global consequences have already been noted (Chapter 42).

8 Were the original claims made for supply-side economics realised in the end? It will be recalled that positive gains were expected on the savings, productivity, investment and work fronts.

Private saving actually *fell* at the same time as public saving fell (an outcome which, on the surface at least, appears to contradict the Ricardian equivalence hypothesis). But private savings also fell in other countries and so it is difficult to hold Reaganomics responsible for this. Moreover, it has been argued that part, at least, of the decline in national savings might be explained in terms of the expectations created by Reaganomics. As Auerbach (1989) put it: 'consumers anticipating the dawn of a new age of profits and productivity growth would have found their ability to consume increased'.

The growth in output per worker did improve significantly after 1983 but the US performance on this front continued to be relatively poor. There was here no dramatic upsurge that one observes with Thatcher (Table 46.2).

What happened to investment? A careful recent study by Akhtar and Harris concludes:

> On the whole developments in US fiscal policy during the 1980s were unfavourable for the long run performance of the economy .... Large and persistent deficits have already lowered the level of potential output by roughly $2\frac{1}{2}$ to $3\frac{1}{2}$ per cent ... the reduced share of (public) capital spending ... put further downward pressures on the capital stock ... changes in tax policy in the 1980s appear to have made no significant net contribution to capital formation for the decade as a whole.
>
> (1992: 16)

Finally, Akhtar and Harris (1992) review the studies of the impacts of tax cuts on labour supply, concluding that there was probably some positive effect here but the magnitude of this effect is still the subject of some debate.

9 There is some evidence that inequality increased with Reaganomics (Blanchard 1987, but see also Roberts 1991). This is also very much what happened under Thatcherism. Reviewing the evidence on this in Britain, Layard and Nickell (1989) concluded 'on inequality, the record is clear, it has increased hugely'.

THATCHERISM AND REAGANOMICS

So how do we evaluate the two experiments?

The parallels were many. Both succeeded in bringing inflation down, although here they were in good company. Neither may have succeeded in reducing the disinflation costs. Both failed on key supply-side tests: neither improved private sector savings or investment. Both neglected the public infrastructure. Both almost certainly made income more unequal. Both 'fought' the unions, although Thatcher more so than Reagan.

The USA was successful in maintaining unemployment within relatively modest levels. With both countries in recession in 1992 the US unemployment rate was just over 7 per cent; in the UK it had surged to over 10 per cent. In the USA, particularly in the later Reagan years, labour markets did, it seems, become more flexible (Eberts and Groshen 1992); there is less evidence of that for the UK.

Both succeeded in 'freeing' up the economies in some degree but here again they were in very good company. Most other industrial countries did too but with far less fanfare.

The only major difference already noted was the outcome for the public sector balances. However, by 1993 in the UK with a severe recession the public sector deficit was approaching some 6–7 per cent of GDP.

47

Japan's macroeconomic performance (1960–90)

INTRODUCTION

This chapter addresses two key questions about Japan's macro performance. First, it is concerned, importantly, with trying to explain Japan's performance on inflation and unemployment, focusing primarily although not exclusively on the role of monetary policy and labour markets in that performance. Second, it looks at the reasons for Japan's persistent current account surpluses since the second half of the 1960s.

Section 1 summarises Japan's macroeconomic performance in the years 1960–90. Section 2 defines the framework to be used in the evaluation of Japan's performance on inflation and unemployment. Sections 3–5 examine the evolution of the macro economy over three distinctive periods: 1960–72, 1973–9 and 1980–91.

Section 6 tries to reach some conclusions about Japan's macro policy performance. Finally, Section 7 looks at the fundamentals underlying Japan's current account performance.

JAPAN'S GENERAL RECORD

Table 47.1 sets out Japan's record on inflation, GNP growth, unemployment and the current account balance.

Japan's ranking on inflation depends on how inflation is measured. Measured by the consumer price index Japan's inflation was *above* the OECD average for the whole period 1960–76. On the other hand, measured by the wholesale price index Japan's performance in those years is on average, about on a par with industrial countries. It is only from 1977 that Japan's inflation performance is significantly superior on all counts to the OECD average.

Table 47.1 Japan: key economic indicators, 1960–90

Year	Unemployment rate[a]		Growth of real GNP		Inflation, consumer prices		Inflation, wholesale prices		Current account balance as percentage of GNP
	Japan	OECD	Japan	OECD	Japan	OECD	Japan	Industrial countries	
1960	1.6	3.2	13.1	7.1	3.6	1.9	1.1	0.7	0.3
1961	1.3	2.9	14.6	4.1	5.3	1.8	0.9	0.5	−1.8
1962	1.3	2.7	7.1	5.3	6.8	2.4	−1.6	0.7	−0.1
1963	1.2	2.7	10.5	4.7	8.5	2.6	1.9	0.8	−1.1
1964	1.2	2.4	13.2	6.0	3.9	2.4	0	1.2	−0.5
1965	1.2	2.2	5.1	5.3	6.6	3.0	0.9	2.1	1.1
1966	1.3	2.3	9.8	5.5	5.1	3.4	2.3	2.9	1.3
1967	1.3	2.8	12.9	3.8	4.0	3.1	1.8	0.2	0
1968	1.2	3.0	13.5	5.5	5.3	4.0	0.9	1.8	0.8
1969	1.1	2.9	10.7	4.7	5.2	4.8	2.2	3.9	1.3
1970	1.2	3.3	10.9	3.1	7.7	5.6	3.6	4.4	1.0
1971	1.2	3.5	4.3	3.5	6.8	5.8	−0.7	3.4	2.5
1972	1.4	3.5	8.4	5.4	5.8	5.4	0.8	4.0	2.2
1973	1.3	3.2	7.6	6.0	10.8	8.3	15.9	12.2	0
1974	1.4	3.5	−0.8	0.7	21.0	14.1	31.4	21.0	−1.0
1975	1.9	5.1	2.9	−0.1	11.2	10.9	3.0	8.5	−0.1
1976	2.0	5.2	4.2	4.6	9.6	8.8	5.1	7.1	0.7
1977	2.0	5.2	4.8	3.8	7.4	8.5	1.9	7.1	1.6
1978	2.2	5.1	5.0	4.3	4.4	7.4	−2.5	5.6	1.7
1979	2.1	5.2	5.6	3.6	3.6	8.7	7.3	10.5	−0.9
1980	2.0	5.9	3.5	1.3	7.5	11.4	17.8	13.7	−1.0
1981	2.2	6.7	3.4	1.7	4.5	9.5	1.4	9.1	0.4
1982	2.3	8.0	3.4	−0.1	2.7	7.2	1.8	5.5	0.6
1983	2.7	8.6	2.8	2.6	2.0	5.5	−2.2	3.3	1.8
1984	2.7	8.1	4.3	4.6	2.5	5.0	−0.3	3.7	2.8
1985	2.6	8.0	5.2	3.4	2.2	4.3	−1.1	1.5	3.6
1986	2.8	7.9	2.6	2.7	0.4	2.6	−9.1	−3.1	4.3
1987	2.9	7.4	4.3	3.3	0.2	3.4	−3.8	0.9	3.6
1988	2.5	6.9	6.2	4.5	−0.1	3.4	−1.0	3.0	2.7
1989	2.3	6.4	4.7	3.3	1.8	4.4	2.6	4.5	2.0
1990	2.1	6.2	5.6	2.6	2.4	4.6	2.1	2.7	1.2

Sources: OECD, *Economic Outlook*; IMF, *International Financial Statistics*
Note: [a] 1960–7 average of thirteen OECD member countries.

It is on the unemployment front that Japan's macro performance really stands out. Between 1960 and 1990 the unemployment rate fluctuated by less than 2 points (the maximum range being from 1.1 in 1989 to 2.9 in 1987); at the same time it jumped to a higher average level from about 1975. Not only has the variability been very slight but the level has been remarkably low. Her average unemployment rate in the 1960s was something like half the OECD average; in the 1970s, however, the gap widened significantly, being on average about a third of that in the OECD. Even countries which until recently had had unemployment rates close to Japan's (New Zealand, Austria, Sweden and Switzerland), by the late 1980s, early 1990s, had fallen well behind.

Standardising unemployment measures makes very little difference to Japan's standing. This is readily verified by inspection of the corrected unemployment rates as published in the biannual OECD *Economic Outlooks* (see also Vollmer 1988). As we note later, however, the labour force participation rate may be more cyclically variable in Japan than in other OECD countries, so revising unemployment rates to take account of such cyclical movements would give Japan a somewhat greater degree of *variability* in the unemployment rate.

Japan's growth of real GNP has also been outstanding. In the years 1960–73, the so-called high growth years, Japan's real growth rate was on average over twice the OECD average. However, after 1973 when Japan's real growth rate fell her margin of advantage dropped.

Japan's performance in terms of output volatility has been mixed (Table 47.2). Measured by the standard deviation of the annual rate of growth of output Japan's performance is poor in 1960–73 but much better in 1974–90. Measured by the coefficient of variation, however, perhaps a more appropriate measure, its performance is relatively good. (The better Japanese performance on this front is also confirmed in Taylor, J. (1989b).)

Japan's recent current account performance has been 'the envy' of many OECD

Table 47.2 Volatility of annual real gross national product growth, 1960–73 and 1974–90 (G7)

	1960–73			1974–90		
	Mean	Standard deviation	Coefficient of variation[a]	Mean	Standard deviation	Coefficient of variation[a]
USA	3.9	1.9	0.49	2.5	2.5	1.0
Japan	10.5	2.8	0.27	4.0	1.6	0.4
Germany	5.0	2.4	0.48	2.2	1.9	0.86
France	5.8	1.2	0.21	2.5	1.3	0.52
UK	3.1	1.6	0.52	1.9	2.1	1.11
Canada	5.3	1.7	0.32	3.4	2.3	0.68
Italy	5.2	1.9	0.37	2.9	2.2	0.76

Note: [a] Standard deviation divided by the mean.

countries. Until the mid-1960s the current account tended to reflect fluctuations in activity, going into deficit when the economy was overheated and into a surplus when the economy was stalling. From about the mid-1960s, however, there was a structural change in Japan's current account performance. Between 1965 and 1990 Japan recorded a current account surplus, or a balance, in each year, with notable exceptions in 1974–5 and 1979–80, corresponding to the first and second oil price shocks respectively. The surpluses peaked, and generated the most international stress, in the years 1969–72, 1977–8 and 1983–91.

THE FRAMEWORK FOR THE EVALUATION OF JAPAN'S PERFORMANCE ON INFLATION AND UNEMPLOYMENT

In this section we try and use the framework developed in Chapter 35. In that chapter we argued that three considerations were of crucial importance in evaluating macro performance: the regulatory–institutional environment, the policy regime and the domestic and external shocks to which the economy is exposed. We therefore proceed to examine each of these in turn in the context of Japan.

The regulatory–institutional environment

Between 1960 and 1973 Japan's exchange rate regime was dictated by its membership of the IMF. From early 1973 the yen floated with, as we shall see, some management of the exchange rate.

Until 1980 the Bank of Japan closely regulated the movement of international capital. During the fixed rate years the principal objective of the controls was to secure an independent monetary policy. Between 1973 and 1980 controls continued to be used, but now their objective was partially to stabilise the currency. From 1980 controls were largely abandoned.

Until the late 1970s there were also very rigid controls over the domestic banking and financial sectors. After that, controls were progressively relaxed but at a much slower pace than for external controls. (For details of the deregulation measures on the two fronts, see Takeda and Turner (1992).)

In Japan the tax burden is one of the lowest in the OECD; the government in general also tends to be less intrusive-regulatory than in Europe.

There are several key institutional features of labour markets in Japan. First, bargaining is at the enterprise level. Such bargaining, however, is synchronised across Japan and occurs during the Spring (known as the Spring Offensive or in Japanese the Shunto). It is then that annual wage increases are determined, with contracts typically running for one year.

Second, bonuses are an important component of 'earnings' in Japan. These bonuses are paid twice a year as a supplement to the base wage and represent about a quarter of the base rate.

Third, and importantly, enterprise unions tend to identify strongly with, and are loyal to, the enterprise. At the same time unions appear to be more concerned with employment than with real wage objectives (Tachibanaki 1987).

The industrial relations environment is also, in general, marked by cooperation rather than confrontation; consistent with this, Japan has one of the best records on industrial strikes in the OECD (Nester 1990).

Fourth, the rate of unionisation is low in Japan, particularly so compared with Europe. One reason is that small enterprises, which are not unionised, absorb a larger proportion of production in Japan than in most other OECD countries.

Fifth, in large companies a system of lifetime employment is in place. To quote Vollmer on job security:

> The actual importance of such job attachments in Japan relative to other countries is indicated by the average duration of employment spells on a given job and by the variability of the overall number of jobs: the average employed Japanese worker has a job tenure of nearly 12 years compared to only 7 years in the USA and to 8.5 years in West Germany. Moreover about 50 per cent of the Japanese workforce have been in their current job for more than 10 years, while in both other countries the majority of workers have a job tenure of less than 5 years.
>
> (1988: 298–9)

Two points need to be emphasised about the system of lifetime employment. First it applies strictly to only about one-third of the work force (Van Wolferen 1989). Second, salaried men are beginning to be more mobile than in the past and so the institution itself is undergoing change.

Sixth, although there is a minimum wage law which varies by prefecture it is 'not obeyed strictly . . . by employers and the penalty is non existent . . . it is hard to believe that the minimum wage law has been an obstacle to hire new employees. This is contrary to European or American experiences in which some adverse effects are often mentioned' (Tachibanaki 1987: 663).

Seventh, unemployment benefits tend to be less generous than in Europe.

The policy regime

We distinguish four 'arms' of policy: monetary, fiscal, foreign exchange management and wages.

In Japan monetary policy decisions are made by the Policy Board of the Bank of Japan. The Policy Board comprises the Governor (appointed for a term of five years), four other members drawn from the banking and industrial sector (appointed for four years) and two government appointees. The last two, however, have no voting rights, but provide an important means of liaising with government policy (Nakao and Horii 1991). On a scale of relative independence, the Bank of Japan tends to get a high rating, although not as high as either the Swiss or the German central banks (see Haan and Sturm 1992).

The Bank of Japan has seen its task, particularly from 1973–4, as one primarily of achieving price stability. Bryant (1991) undertook an econometric study of Japan's monetary policy reaction function. He found that easily the largest weight attaches to the inflation target with much smaller weights attaching to output, the exchange rate and the balance of payments. Bryant summarises:

> The status of inflation as a goal variable for Japanese monetary policy is unambiguous. A great variety of statements from the Bank of Japan and other parts of the government forthrightly assert that control of inflation is a central if not paramount objective.
>
> (1991: 21)

If monetary policy was primarily directed at inflation, foreign exchange management was directed at moderating exchange rate movements.

Fiscal policy is a little harder to represent. In broad terms it is possible to distinguish three developments on the fiscal policy front: a first phase when classical–conservative principles dominated; a second phase after 1973–5 when the principles were abandoned and fiscal policy became much looser (in an important sense these were years when, perhaps half-heartedly, Keynesianism was 'embraced'); a third phase in the 1980s marked by a return to more conservative policies, although now less strict than in the first phase (Ishi 1986; OECD 1989b; Asako and Ito 1991). (1992 marked a return to Keynesian policies.)

The first phase continued to about 1973–5, although a distinct break occurred in 1965.

Up to 1965 the fiscal rule implemented was to balance the central budget. Public expenditure was to be contained within some 20 per cent of GNP; if taxes exceeded that level tax schedules would be realigned to bring tax revenue in line with expenditure. The issue of public bonds to finance current expenditure was prohibited; the issue of bonds, within limits, were permitted, however, for expenditure on construction.

In 1965 in the wake of the recession a special statute was passed which allowed the central government to issue bonds to finance current expenditures but this only happened on a small scale. Indeed, until 1973 the central government's financial balance was roughly zero over the business cycle.

The second phase began in earnest in 1975 when fiscal deficits began to escalate. General government financial deficits were large and persistent to 1984. Indeed, between 1976 and 1982 Japan's performance on this front was actually inferior to that of the G7 (Table 47.3). These cumulative deficits led to a very sharp rise in the public debt to GNP ratio (Table 47.3). Whereas Japan had been well below the OECD average (for gross debt) to 1977 it overtook the OECD from 1978. However, in terms of net debt, while the relative position sharply deteriorated, Japan remained below the OECD average.

The third phase dates from the early 1980s when the central government decided that the debt burden was too large and that deficits had to be brought under control.

Table 47.3 Japan: monetary and fiscal policies, 1971–90

Year	Real interest rate (long term), Japan	Change in money growth, end of year (M2 and CDs), Japan (%)	Change in real money balances (%) Japan	General government financial balances Japan	OECD (G7)	General government gross public debt as percentage of GDP Japan	OECD (G7)	General government net public debt as percentage of GDP Japan	OECD (G7)	Change in cyclic adjusted budget balance,[a] Japan
1971	1.0	20.5	13.7	+1.2	-0.8	13.5	40.1	-7.3	20.6	-0.1
1972	1.8	26.5	20.7	-0.1	-0.8	17.5	39.7	-6.5	19.6	-2.0
1973	-4.3	22.7	11.9	+0.5	-0.2	17.0	36.8	-6.1	17.2	0.1
1974	-13.9	11.9	-9.1	+0.4	-0.9	18.0	36.3	-5.4	16.8	1.8
1975	-2.6	13.1	1.9	-2.8	-4.4	22.4	39.2	-2.1	20.1	-2.9
1976	-0.7	15.1	5.5	-3.7	-3.2	28.0	39.9	1.9	21.0	-1.1
1977	-0.9	11.4	4.0	-3.8	-2.5	33.4	40.2	5.5	21.2	-0.5
1978	1.9	11.7	7.3	-5.5	-2.8	41.9	41.2	11.3	21.6	-2.1
1979	4.0	11.9	8.3	-4.7	-2.2	46.9	40.7	14.9	21.2	0.0
1980	1.5	9.2	1.7	-4.4	-2.7	52.0	41.7	17.3	21.8	0.5
1981	3.8	8.9	4.4	-3.8	-2.8	57.0	42.9	20.7	22.5	0.8
1982	5.4	9.2	6.5	-3.6	-4.0	60.9	48.0	23.1	25.8	0.7
1983	5.5	7.3	5.3	-3.6	-4.1	66.5	51.6	26.0	28.8	0.6
1984	4.5	7.8	5.3	-2.1	-3.4	67.8	53.6	27.0	30.4	1.6
1985	4.3	8.7	6.5	-0.8	-3.2	68.5	55.9	26.6	32.2	1.0
1986	4.3	9.2	8.8	-0.9	-3.2	72.1	58.3	26.3	33.7	0.5
1987	4.2	10.8	10.6	+0.5	-2.2	74.4	59.4	21.4	33.5	1.5
1988	3.6	10.2	10.3	+1.5	-1.7	72.4	59.1	17.7	32.7	0.2
1989	2.8	12.0	10.2	+2.5	-1.0	70.2	58.3	14.6	31.4	0.8
1990	4.3	7.9	5.5	+2.7	-1.7	66.5	57.9	10.9	31.0	0.0

Sources: OECD, Economic Outlook; IMF, International Financial Statistics.
Note: [a] −, expansionary; +, contractionary; OECD calculations.

Particularly after 1983 thc deficits fell sharply; by 1990 the general government budget was in substantial surplus.

Finally, on the wages policy front, although there is no formal wages policy as such the Japanese government does not detach itself entirely from the annual wage negotiating process (see Wagner 1989).

The shocks

We define a shock as a significant disturbance external to the policy stance. As we shall see, this can be triggered by a policy act but then assumes a lifc of its own.

The more significant shocks to which Japan was exposed were, in chronological order, the Nixon yen shocks (1971–2), the first oil price shock (1973–4), the second oil price shock (1979–81), Reaganomics (1982–5), a succession of smaller oil price shocks (1986–90), the second yen shock (1986–8) and the asset price inflation– deflation (1986–91).

PHASE 1 – 1960–72

What characterises this period is fixed exchange rates and extensive controls over the domestic financial system and over external capital flows.

The environment for monetary policy

In those years, all capital movements were forbidden unless specifically authorised. Non-resident acquisition of real estate, bonds and equities was tightly monitored. At the same time, non-bank resident investments abroad were subject to approval. There were also tight controls over leads and lags for trade-related financing. A variety of instruments were also in use to monitor the flow of capital through the banking system, including direct controls over their net foreign positions and (varying) special reserve requirements over their free yen (non-resident) deposits. There were severe limitations on the activities of foreign banks.

At least until 1970 these capital controls did succeed, in the main, in giving Japan a relatively independent monetary policy, sheltered from developments abroad. In other words the conduct of monetary policy in the years to 1970 was not unduly frus- trated by offsetting capital flows. Evidence for this comes from findings that (a) the interest rate effect on capital flows was 'weak' (OECD 1972) and (b) the offset coeffi- cient (i.e. the degree to which monetary restriction in the form of a reduction in the domestic assets of the central bank was offset by an inflow of capital) was relatively low (see for example Miller (1980) who finds a first quarter offset coefficient of 0.3).

On the domestic front the key features of the conduct of monetary policy in those years were the following.

a) Bank credit to the corporate sector was the primary intermediate target of the monetary authorities.

b) Banks were at the centre of the system, commercial banks accounting in 1970 for nearly 40 per cent of all lending by financial institutions.

c) Commercial banks and bank credit were subject to rigid controls. Interest rates on their deposits and on their prime lending were regulated. They were also subject to varying reserve requirements and to quantitative control over (a ceiling on) their lending to the private sector. Such lending was also indirectly controlled by the Bank of Japan (BOJ) in part by changes in reserve requirements but primarily through its own lending policies: the discount rate at which it lent and the volume it was prepared to lend at that rate. The efficacy of such lending policies was reinforced, moreover, by the fact that the banks, as a group, tended to be 'overloaned' in the sense that their reserve position (cash less borrowings from the Bank of Japan or deposits less loans) was negative.

Thus the combination of tight exchange controls and the policy instruments available allowed the Bank of Japan, certainly until at least 1970, to monitor the volume of bank lending closely.

d) The household sector tended to have a substantial financial surplus (an excess of own saving over investment). At the same time household financial assets were mostly held with the banking system. The corporate sector, by contrast, was in substantial deficit, financing the excess of its own investment over its savings by borrowing heavily from the banking system.

e) There was no active secondary securities market to speak of. This reflected three institutional facts: Japan's financial isolation from the rest of the world, the predominance of indirect financing by the corporate sector (i.e. through the banking system) and the small public sector deficit. Because of the lack of a securities market, too, open market operations were not an important instrument of policy.

f) The lack of an active capital market and of alternative sources of short-term credit outside the banks also meant that, at the given bank lending rate, there was an excess demand for credit which went largely unsatisfied. Credit rationing was thus an important feature of the financial system.

Given the institutional environment described above, the implementation of monetary policy was a relatively straightforward affair. The ultimate objective of policy was to stabilise aggregate demand and in particular to remove overheating in the economy, which tended to spill over into inflation and, at least until the late 1960s, also into trade deficits.

The economy was 'driven' by fluctuations in business investment, which was the most destabilising component of demand. A boom (collapse) in investment activity would provoke restrictive (easier) bank credit policies; given, in turn, the importance of bank credit to the corporate sector this would serve to restrain (encourage) investment and to stabilise the real economy.

Summing up the conduct of monetary policy, there were two key features of the way it operated until 1970. First, there was a tight control over bank credit. Second, there was a close and predictable relationship between bank credit on the one hand and prices, investment activity and the trade balance on the other.

The years 1970–2 and the Nixon yen shock

In the years to 1970, when the yen rate was expected to be maintained, small differences in interest rates brought about by differences in monetary policy did not provoke big movements of capital, protected as the economy was by the exchange controls. The years 1971–2, however, were watershed years when the Bretton Woods system was under considerable stress. Fuelled by the persistent surpluses on the current account and the exchange crises and realignments abroad there was considerable speculation in favour of the yen. Now in the face of potentially very large rewards from the purchase of yen-denominated assets, exchange controls failed to protect the economy; the result was huge inflows, particularly in the course of 1971. These inflows added to the monetary base and the foreign exchange reserves.

Fukao notes that

> these capital flows are believed to have arisen mostly from the activities of Japanese companies abroad. The subsidiaries of Japanese firms borrowed large amounts in dollars, and used them to remit prepayments for exports to parent companies or to purchase yen-denominated securities. At this time, there were controls on the receipt of advances for contracted exports, but when huge profits over a very short period could be foreseen, the effectiveness of such controls was limited.
>
> (1990)

In the second half of 1971 came the Nixon yen shock. Facing renewed attacks on the dollar the US President, Nixon, announced on 15 August 1971 a number of measures to try and relieve a situation which had become critical. From Japan's perspective three measures were particularly important: the imposition of a 10 per cent surcharge on imports into the USA; the exclusion from a proposed investment tax credit of imported capital equipment; the tax advantages extended to exports through domestic sales corporations.

These measures were a bargaining ploy intended to force Europe and Japan to remove certain trade barriers and revalue their currencies. The strategy largely worked and in December 1971 under the Smithsonian Agreement there was a general currency realignment. The yen officially appreciated by nearly 17 per cent *vis-à-vis* the dollar, although on an effective basis the appreciation was nearer 11 per cent.

Speculation in favour of the yen, however, persisted into 1972, and so in the course of the year additional measures were taken now to encourage outflows and discourage inflows as a means of stabilising the yen. (For details see Komiya and Suda (1991).)

There was, at the time, a fear that the appreciation might force the economy into recession, so fiscal policy became easier and money growth accelerated sharply

(Table 47.3). There are two interpretations to be placed on the very easy monetary policy of 1971–2. One is that it was *intended*. Another, perhaps much more plausible, is that, given the way in which the money base was bloated by speculative inflows, the authorities effectively lost control over the money supply and bank credit and thus policy was easier than intended.

If it had in fact been intended then in retrospect it was clearly a major policy error. The relevant (M2 + CDs) money growth accelerated from an average of nearly 17 per cent in 1968–70 to an average of some 23 per cent in 1971–3. (In this respect Japan was in very good company as money growth also accelerated sharply in most OECD countries.) As we shall see, the timing could not have been worse. When the lagged effects of the easier monetary policy on inflation began to surface the inflation was compounded by the commodity price boom, the oil price shock and the associated devaluation.

As the OECD survey of Japanese monetary policy noted:

> Thus, in the course of 1971, the combined effect of a huge current account surplus and a shift in leads and lags due mainly to the strength of the yen *vis-à-vis* the dollar was so large as to enable the city banks to repay their massive borrowing to the Bank of Japan, thereby wiping one of the major structural characteristics of the 1960's [the overborrowing of the commercial banks].

(1972: 69)

PHASE 2 – 1973–9

The three major developments in this period were the first oil price shock of 1973–4, the dramatic fall in the real growth rate[1] and the switch, from February 1973, to a flexible rate regime. The shift to flexible rates allowed the Bank of Japan to regain control over its monetary policy which, as we have argued, it had probably lost in 1971–2.

The new environment for monetary policy

From about 1975 there was a succession of substantial public sector deficits financed by the issue of government bonds (Table 47.3). The accumulation of government bonds in the hands of the private sector helped promote the development of open financial markets. For example, whereas in 1970 trade in government bonds (including local government) represented some 16 per cent of all transactions in secondary markets in bonds, by 1980 this had risen to some 73 per cent (Suzuki 1984). This gave monetary policy a wider impact; at the same time the gradual evolution of the open market meant that open market operations, as a technique of monetary control, became increasingly feasible.

Meanwhile, the corporate sector came to rely less and less on bank credit for financing. At the same time it came to rely more on internal finance and on non-bank credit as a source of external finance. The commercial bank share of lending to the private sector correspondingly fell.

These last developments also meant that changes in bank credit now had a weaker impact on corporate investment. Reinforcing this was the fact that corporate investment as a share of aggregate demand also declined. On the other hand, as Suzuki (1984) notes, the fact that an open market was evolving, that corporations were beginning to invest in these open markets and that interest rates in the open market reflected changes in monetary policy also meant that the opportunity cost of investment fluctuated with market interest rates; in this sense monetary policy was making a bigger impact on investment.

In the course of the period, too, there was a gradual shift in the choice of intermediate target of policy from bank credit towards the money stock (eventually M2 + CDs). One reason for this was that with the decline in bank credit in the bank balance sheet (and the correspondingly increased importance of public bonds) there was now a weaker relationship between bank credit and the money stock. Another was that with some open markets now in place the direct 'credit rationing' effect of changes in bank credit was weakening.

From July 1978, this shift became formalised when the Bank of Japan began announcing quarterly forecasts for a range in the growth of M2 + CDs.

As we noted in Chapter 43, the 'forecasts' of the Bank of Japan show some differences with the targets generally set in other countries. Forecasts are announced in the first month of each quarter and refer to the growth of M2 + CDs between the current quarter and the same quarter of the previous year. This means that, while the forecasts are of annual growth in the money stock, they are announced after three quarters of the year have passed. Consequently, the outcomes have invariably been very close to the forecasts (see Table 47.4).

Shigehara has argued that

> by announcing the projected course of the money supply and commenting on its possible implications for the central bank's ultimate objectives (with due caution about the possibility of short-run instability in the relationship between money on the one hand and real income and prices on the other) the Bank hoped that it could obtain valuable assistance in expediting anti-inflationary monetary policy.
>
> (1990)

M2 + CDs has been the focus of monetary control because of empirical evidence that suggests that it has the closest relationship with future income and expenditure. Work by the Bank of Japan suggests that between 1972 and 1979 there was a close relationship between the growth of M2 + CDs and the subsequent movement in the growth of the GNP deflator. Indeed, the correlation coefficient was as high as 0.91 for a six-quarters lag (Shigehara 1990).

At the same time we note, too, in this context, that after 1975 the accumulation of government bonds by the banks and the gradual shift towards indirect methods of control now made it harder to *control* the money stock.

Table 47.4   Japan: monetary 'forecasts' and outcomes (M2 + CDs)[a]

Year	Forecast	Outcomes
1978	12–13	12.6
1979	11	10.3
1980	8	7.6
1981	10	10.4
1982	8	8.3
1983	7	6.8
1984	8	7.9
1985	8	9.0
1986	8–9	8.3
1987	11–12	11.8
1988	10–11	10.6
1989	9–10	10.6
1990	11	10.0
1991	2–3	2.2

Source: Bank for International Settlements, *Annual Reports*
Note: [a] Fourth quarter to fourth quarter.

Foreign exchange management

With flexible rates in place in this period one objective of the Bank of Japan was to mitigate movements in the yen rate. Two principal methods were used. One was to vary the capital controls in place (Argy 1987; Fukao 1990; Komiya and Suda 1991). When the yen was strong (weak) net capital outflows (inflows) were encouraged. One can here identify three distinct periods (Table 47.5): first, in 1974–5 when in the wake of the first oil price shock the yen was weak and the intent was, on balance, to encourage inflows; second, from mid-1977 to the end of 1978 when the yen was strong and policy reverted to encouraging net outflows; third, the period from 1979 to December 1980 when the yen was again weak and there was yet another policy reversal, with net inflows now being encouraged. On balance it would seem that these variations in capital controls succeeded in reversing capital movements and this went some way towards stabilising the currency.

The Bank of Japan also engaged in sterilised foreign exchange intervention to stabilise the yen rate (Argy 1982; Haynes *et al.* 1986; Komiya and Suda 1991). When the yen was strong (weak) the Bank of Japan tended to buy (sell) US dollars in the open market (thus leaning against the wind), at the same time sterilising the effects of the purchases (sales) on the money base. Finally, there is some evidence that on one occasion at least, notably in early 1978, the monetary policy was partly directed at exerting downward pressure on the yen (Argy 1982; Nakao and Horii 1991).

Adjustment to the first oil price shock and its aftermath

We now examine more closely how the Japanese authorities coped with the first oil

Table 47.5   Japan: real effective exchange rate

1971	94.6
1972	101.9
1973	112.3
1974	114.6
1975	104.2
1976	102.9
1977	110.8
1978	127.9
1979	110.9
1980	100.1
1981	109.0
1982	97.1
1983	101.7
1984	102.7
1985	100.0
1986	121.0
1987	124.2
1988	133.2
1989	127.2
1990	116.1
1991	125.6

Source: IMF, *International Financial Statistics*
Note: 1985 = 100 (normalised unit labour cost).

price shock. (See on this Komiya and Yasui (1984), Shigehara (1982) and Onitsuka (1990).)

In the wake of the first oil price shock, Japan suffered its worst recession since the early 1950s. The growth of output was negative in 1974, one of the worst performances in the OECD (Table 47.1). The recession lasted some five quarters from the first quarter of 1974 to the first quarter of 1975. Altogether in that period real GNP fell by 2.2 per cent. However, by mid-1975 the economy was already recovering and 1975 recorded some positive growth; by 1976 growth was again substantial. The unemployment rate, however, rose only marginally by less than 1 percentage point (in sharp contrast to the OECD as a whole where the unemployment rate on average rose by nearly 2 points).

At the same time the oil price shock left in its wake a substantial deficit in the current account (equal to 1 per cent of GNP in 1974); however, by 1975 the current account had virtually returned to balance (Table 47.1). The yen had already been weakening before the first oil price shock but in the wake of the current account deficit the decline in the yen accelerated (Table 47.5).

The economy was already overheated before the first oil shock; the excess demand combined with the commodity price inflation of 1972–3 had produced an acceleration in the rate of inflation. As already noted, money growth had accelerated sharply in 1971–3 and fiscal policy, notably in 1972, had been expansionary.

Confronted with the overall conditions prevailing in the economy in 1973 the monetary authorities had begun to tighten monetary policy some six months before the shock. In 1974 money growth was half that recorded in 1973. More importantly, real money balances turned around by more than 20 points (Table 47.3). In the same year, too, fiscal policy also tightened.

An important development is that wage settlements in 1974 were very high, even in relation to the ongoing rate of inflation. Real product wages rose faster than productivity; the real wage gap rose and corporate profitability fell. By 1975, however, wage inflation fell sharply, thus paving the way for a recovery. Whereas in 1974 base wages rose by 33 per cent, in 1975 they rose by only a third of that.

In 1974, then, many adverse inflationary influences were coming to a head. There were the lagged effects of the 5–6 point acceleration in money growth, the commodity price inflation of 1972–3, the oil price shock which took its full toll in 1974, the devaluation, and the wage Shunto agreement of 1974 which, in the event, proved quite unhelpful. Inflation in fact more than doubled from what was already a high base in 1973 (see Table 47.1).

In the wake of much more favourable wage adjustments in 1975, the restrictive monetary policy and the unwinding of the one-off direct effect of the oil price shock, inflation halved in 1975. This allowed monetary policy to ease in 1975–6 (Table 47.3).

What happened to fiscal policy? Table 47.3 shows that fiscal policy (measured by the cyclically adjusted deficit), was very expansionary in the three years 1976–8. Fiscal expansion was officially justified first in terms of the recession and later in terms of the growing current account surpluses.

In the four years 1976–9, real growth averaged nearly 5 per cent while in the same period OECD real growth was nearly 4 per cent. In less than two years the economy had recovered from the first oil shock.

PHASE 3 – 1980–91

The major developments in this period are the measures to deregulate the financial system, the second oil price shock and a succession of rather 'smaller' shocks between 1982 and 1991.

Deregulation and the changed environment for monetary policy

Until 1980 it is difficult to detect a clear trend in respect of international liberalisation, although there was probably some net intent to liberalise. From December 1980, with the passing of the Foreign Exchange and Foreign Trade Control Law, a decisive step forward was taken towards liberalisation. After 1980, additional measures to liberalise were adopted but the pace is to some extent still regulated with one eye on the strength of the yen.

The 1980 legislation provided that, in principle, most capital flows were free unless specifically disallowed. Thus the earlier principle that flows were prohibited unless specifically allowed was reversed.

On the domestic front financial deregulation proceeded at a slower pace and tended to be spread over the whole decade (see Takeda and Turner (1992) and Shigehara (1990) for details). The slow pace of interest rate decontrol meant that through the period a dual structure of interest rates was in place, with some interest rates liberalised, others remaining under control.

The domestic deregulation also brought with it some distortion to the money aggregates (see Bank of Japan 1988; Yoshida and Rasche 1990). On the one hand many banking decontrol measures enhanced the attractiveness of the broader money aggregate (M2 + CDs). On the other hand, some liberalisation measures made non-bank financial assets, such as postal savings and securities offered by trust and insurance fund accounts, also more attractive. The result was to make money demand somewhat unstable. On balance, however, money demand rose, as manifested in the steady decline in the 1980s in the velocity of M2 + CDs.

Three illustrations of this distortion produced by deregulation are provided.

Amongst the deregulation measures in the late 1980s that made M2 + CDs more attractive were the introduction of money market certificates and the progressive liberalisation of the terms of issue and of interest rates on CDs and time deposits (all included in the broader aggregate). This made it difficult to judge after 1987 how much of the growth in the money aggregate was being distorted by the upward shift in demand.

A second example comes from the effects of deregulation on the banks' competitiveness and their deposit and lending rates. In the late 1980s interest rates on some deposits were higher than lending rates of comparable maturity. This provoked some arbitrage: firms borrowed from the banks and placed their borrowings on deposit. The result was that the growth of M2 ballooned, but this had no apparent implication for the real side of the economy (Okina and Ui 1992).

In 1991–2 the opposite problem occurred. There was a large shift out of M2 + CDs into postal savings which had now become more attractive. By 1991–2 there was a sharp decline in the growth of the money aggregate; if we take an even broader measure of liquidity, however, which now includes postal savings, the decline is nowhere near as severe. So it seems that the sharp decline in the growth of M2 + CDs can at least in part be explained by the decline in its demand.

These distortions weakened (but did not destroy) the relationship between the growth in the money aggregate and the rate of inflation. Shigehara notes that

> The close correlation between quarterly developments in M2 & CD and the behaviour of the GNP deflator in the subsequent quarters, which had been observed in the 1970s, somewhat loosened in the 1980s and the lead period for money shortened.... For the period from the third quarter of 1979 to the fourth quarter of 1987 the highest coefficient obtained was 0.61 and this was when the GNP deflators lagged two quarters.
>
> (1990: 1)

(This is in contrast to 1970, when the correlation coefficient was 0.91 with the GNP deflator lagged six quarters, as already noted earlier.) While the loosening in the relationship is to be expected the substantial shortening of the lag is much harder to explain.

Not surprisingly, by 1991–2 the Bank of Japan was agonising over the significance of the money aggregates. In any event, by then M2 + CDs had been de-emphasised and the Bank of Japan was monitoring more than one money aggregate, including a much broader measure of liquidity.

The second oil price shock – adjustment and aftermath

The second oil price shock was about as large as the first, but by then Japan's direct macroeconomic exposure had declined somewhat (Hutchison 1991). Also, as we will note shortly the background, the policy orientation and the wage settlements were now all different.

This time the economy was less heated than at the time of the first shock. There was no lagged accelerated money growth or a commodity price inflation to contend with. Consumer prices had also been rising modestly in 1978–9. Monetary restraint was again applied but it was far less abrupt, falling now by some 3 points on average. Moreover, in terms of real money balances there was a fall of some 6–7 points but this was nowhere near the 20 point turnaround after the first shock. Finally, and importantly, fiscal policy actually tightened after the second shock (Table 47.3).

The most dramatic development occurred on the wages front. Wages rose very modestly at 6–7 per cent in 1979–81. Inflation did accelerate in 1980 but only by four points (a little more than the OECD average) and it fell to a modest 4–5 per cent by 1981 (a better performance than the OECD average). Most remarkably there was virtually no movement in the unemployment rate (a much better performance than the OECD) while real growth fell by only some 2 points in 1980.

As in the first oil price shock the current account deteriorated sharply in 1979–80 but by 1981 was again in surplus. In the wake of the current account deficit the yen again fell sharply but by 1981 had begun to recover (Table 47.5).

To sum up, then, Japan's recovery from the second oil price shock was particularly commendable. It is true that circumstances were much less unfavourable at the time of the second shock but in general monetary policy was applied more judiciously (less brutally) and, most important of all, wage outcomes were much more modest and were in fact the key to the smooth transition. As Fischer (1987b) put it: 'The great success of Japan's macro policy was the avoidance of a recession in the second oil shock'. This is what made Japan's experience so unique compared with European countries.

Monetary policy continued to be modestly restrained while fiscal policy tightened significantly to the mid-1980s (Table 47.3).

The lesser shocks and their impacts

In order of their appearance we have Reaganomics (1982–5), the oil price shocks (1986–90), the second yen shock (1986–8) and the asset price inflation-deflation (1986–91). We note here that the asset price inflation was *triggered* by the easier monetary policies after 1986 and the deregulation but then *assumed a life of its own*. The sharp asset deflation after 1990 was again triggered by the tight monetary policies and then again acquired a momentum of its own.

Reaganomics

We focus here primarily on the fiscal impacts of Reaganomics. OECD calculations of the cyclically adjusted fiscal impact suggest that the cumulative positive impact of the easier policies was close to 3 per cent of GNP. The econometric evidence suggests that each 1 per cent fiscal expansion in the USA very roughly adds a little over 0.1 per cent to GNP and a bit to inflation (see Chapter 15, Table 15.3, MultiMod and MSG2). The 3 per cent US fiscal expansion would have added some three times to that but spread over several years.

The 'minor' oil price shocks (1989, 1990)

In 1986 alone the price of oil fell by some 45 per cent. The price stayed relatively low until 1990 when it jumped by an average of some 27 per cent. Econometric evidence confirms that an oil price rise (fall) has negative (positive) effects on output and positive (negative) effects on domestic inflation (Hutchison 1991).

The yen shock (1986–8)

Between 1986 and 1988 the nominal effective appreciation of the yen took on the elements of a 'bubble', appreciating over the period by some 35 per cent. This compares with an appreciation of some 20 per cent during the first Nixon yen shock (1971–3) and some 25 per cent over 1977–8, when the yen was also strong.

How would an 'excessive' appreciation impact on the economy? Simulations of the OECD InterLink model suggest that, after one year, a 10 per cent effective appreciation will lower GNP by something like 0.2 per cent and lower the GNP deflator by a little over 1 per cent. There is also a small deterioration in the current account (of some $0.6 billion). By the end of the second year, however, these overall effects (on output, prices and the current account) become much more pronounced. On the other hand, in the first six months J curves are in evidence (simulations undertaken for the author by the OECD).

Asset price inflation–deflation

An important development in the years 1986–9 was the asset price inflation, which saw huge increases in the prices of stocks and real estate. Table 47.6 summarises the facts on the asset price inflation in those years. The increase in property prices is largely concentrated in the years 1986–7. Real rents for office space also rose substantially over the whole period. Share prices rose by a factor of $2\frac{1}{2}$ between 1985 and 1989. The table also shows various measures of household wealth. All show substantial increases, but this is strikingly so for real assets.

Why the asset inflation? There were some fundamental monetary forces at work: the easier monetary policy and the domestic financial deregulation which spurred additional lending by the banks. In the case of property prices there were, additionally, some real factors present. Internationalisation of the Japanese economy created an acute shortage of office space; this was reinforced by the population movement from rural areas to cities. All this manifested itself in sharp increases in rent.

Nevertheless, it seems now to be generally agreed that a speculative bubble also came into play, substantially exacerbating the asset inflation. (On equity prices, see Hardouvelis (1988); on property prices, see Bank of Japan (1990).)

What consequences could be expected from a 'bubble' of this sort? There would be a positive household wealth effect on expenditure; also with the yield on equities down and the price of the existing stock of property up, investment would be stimulated; the balance sheets of the banks and financial institutions would improve,

Table 47.6   Japan: asset price inflation, 1986–9

	1985	1986	1987	1988	1989
Property prices (% increase)					
Japan (commercial)	1.3	48	61	3	5
Tokyo (residential)	3	22	69	0	7
Inflation-adjusted					
office rents	6.0	18.2	22.8	5.4	20.9
housing prices (Tokyo)	1.5	22.8	67.1	–0.7	3.4
Share prices					
Index average	100	132.9	196.4	213.9	257.8
Wealth[a]					
Net financial wealth	1.71	1.76	1.75	1.80	1.84
Financial assets	1.88	1.92	1.91	1.97	2.02
Corporate equities	0.30	0.42	0.52	0.70	0.90
Real assets	3.96	4.51	5.53	5.73	6.21

Sources: Bank for International Settlements, *Annual Reports*; IMF, *International Financial Statistics*; OECD, *Economic Outlooks*
Note: [a] As ratio of household nominal disposable income.

inducing more lending. On the other hand, with the increase in the value of wealth the demand for money would increase and this in itself would have a deflationary effect.

On balance, one would expect the positive effects to dominate. The wealth effects on money demand are now well documented for Japan (see Bank of Japan 1992), but the other effects are less so, although there is little doubt that they have also been significant.

By 1990 we begin to observe the opposite phenomenon of asset deflation. Between 1990 and the end of 1992 stock prices fell by some 50 per cent; in 1991 alone, property prices in Tokyo fell by nearly 10 per cent and the fall continued into 1992. Again, there were some fundamental forces at work (the tighter monetary policy in 1990) but the fall acquired a momentum of its own. The asset deflation was now having opposite effects on the economy.

The monetary–fiscal mix 1986–91

Beginning in January 1986 the Bank of Japan initiated a succession of discount rate cuts. From January 1986 to February 1987 when the last cut occurred the discount rate was halved from 5 to 2.5 per cent. Money growth (M2 + CDs) accelerated substantially between 1986 and 1989 (Table 47.3). Whereas the growth of M2 + CDs had been of the order of 7.9 per cent in the three years 1983–5, in the four years 1986–9 it was some 10.6 per cent.

Why did this happen? First, external political pressure was placed on Japan to weaken the yen. Second, by 1986 the economy was beginning to stall; the real growth rate fell whilst unemployment had begun to rise slightly. Third, the consumer price index barely rose in 1986–7. Thus, the combination of a stalling economy, negligible inflation and a strong yen looked like an attractive recipe for an easier monetary policy.

At the same time that monetary policy eased between 1986 and 1989, fiscal policy continued to tighten substantially (Table 47.3). Such a mix in itself produces opposing effects on activity, at least initially, but the downward effects on the currency are reinforced (Tables 15.2 and 15.3).

Real GNP growth began to accelerate in 1987; in the three years 1987–9, growth averaged some 5.1 per cent. After 1987 too the unemployment rate began to drop significantly (by Japanese standards). Inflation, however, continued to be very modest; in the three years 1986–8 it averaged some 0.3 per cent.

An important reason for the modest inflation, despite the easier monetary policy, was the strength of the yen and the drop in oil prices, both of which served to dampen inflationary impulses.

In 1989 the economy was still overheated; inflation by now had accelerated to 1.8 per cent while asset price inflation continued to be a major concern to the monetary authorities. In May 1989 monetary policy began to tighten. In retrospect now the Japanese authorities will readily concede (at least in private) that monetary policy should have been tightened perhaps a year or so earlier and that the delay was a serious error of judgement.

By 1991–2 there was a sharp decline in real growth. Four factors were primarily responsible for the downturn: the tight monetary policy, the asset deflation, the recession abroad and the fact that there had been an excessive rate of investment in the previous years which now needed correcting. Faced with a deteriorating domestic economy, monetary policy began to ease in September 1991. Subsequently, the discount rate was reduced on several occasions in small steps. By the second half of 1992 fiscal policy had also eased.

Through the 1980s exchange rates continued to be managed unilaterally by the Bank of Japan. From 1985, however, there was some coordinated intervention with the US authorities aimed at stabilising the dollar–yen rate (Chapter 45).

CONCLUSIONS ON JAPAN'S MACRO PERFORMANCE

We proceed here as follows. We first try to explain Japan's performance on the unemployment front. Next, we try and identify the main reasons for the inflation performance. We then say a few words about fiscal policy and exchange rate management.

The unemployment performance

As we have already noted, an important factor in Japan's macro performance is its very low and stable unemployment rate. This unemployment rate has crept upwards in the last twenty years but only by something like 1 percentage point on average.

There are thus two phenomena to explain: the stability of the unemployment rate and the fact that on average it is relatively low.

Why is the unemployment rate stable?

We set out what appear to be the principal factors underlying this performance.

1 One widely held view is that real wages, in general, appear to be more flexible in response to fluctuations in real demand than in most, if not all, industrial countries (Taylor, J. 1989b). Virtually all studies of real wage flexibility place Japan far ahead of all other industrial countries, with the possible exception of Switzerland (Chapter 44).

Suzuki has contended:

the Japanese economy behaves quite like the Classical model of a labour market. The critical point by which the Classical world and the Keynesian world differ is that in the Keynesian system nominal wages are sticky, while in the Classical world, real wages are flexible. The Keynesian assumption that nominal wages are sticky stresses such institutional factors as long-term wage contracts or a high cost of wage adjustments. I would argue that Japan is far from this assumption and is closer to the Classical world than the Keynesian world.

(1985: 3–4)

Suzuki also argues, as an implication of the above contention, that Japan can move down a vertical Phillips curve to a lower rate of inflation without much disruption to the unemployment rate. In other words the unemployment cost of a disinflation policy is much lower in Japan than elsewhere. This is confirmed by simple observation of the unemployment rate and the fact that there have been numerous examples of monetary disinflation (see later).

Hamada extends the argument as follows:

If real wages are perfectly flexible in response to excess demand, all the observed unemployment should be frictional and not involuntary. However, even in Japan the labour market is not that efficient. The Spring Labour Offensive determines wages on the basis of the information available at the time of negotiation, and the wages thus determined are effective for approximately one year.

(1985: 194)

Why are hourly real wages so flexible? According to conventional wisdom, the principal reasons are the following. First, unions identify with the enterprise and try to aim at maintaining employment. Second, the bonus system probably does inject an automatic degree of real wage flexibility. (How much, however, is still a matter of debate. See Tachibanaki (1987), Brunello (1989b) and Peck (1986).) Third, although there is no formal incomes policy as such in Japan the Japanese government does not detach itself entirely from the annual Shunto bargaining; indeed, when it deems necessary it does participate directly, using a kind of 'informative incomes policy' (see Wagner (1989) on the last).

Despite the eminence of the two Japanese economists cited above, the views expressed are almost certainly too extreme (see Yoshikawa and Takeuchi 1989). Whilst there is almost certainly a substantial degree of real wage flexibility in Japan, it is hard to believe that real wage flexibility is anywhere near perfect even after allowing for a lag in adjustment. If real wages were indeed that flexible, we would expect to see a fairly rapid convergence towards full employment output. Such rapid convergence, however, is not in evidence (notably so, for example, in 1992–3).

Brunello and Wadhwani (1989) also question the notion that unions in large enterprises set wages so as to re-establish full employment. Comparing wage behaviour in Japan and the UK in large firms they conclude that

There is no substantial difference in the responsiveness of wages to unemployment. Further, in *both* countries, wages in *small* firms are *more* responsive to unemployment than wages in *large* firms.

On the basis of these findings, it is argued that it is unlikely that the oft-observed flexibility of aggregate wages in Japan arises from different labour market institutions or policies, but more plausibly derives from the fact that the proportion of

Japanese employees who work in small firms is substantially higher than other OECD countries.

(1989: Abstract)

2 Employment demand, given the real wage rate, is also very inflexible. Although the rate of change in production does fluctuate substantially in response to variations in demand this does not manifest itself in corresponding fluctuations in employment.

There are several reasons for this. First, as noted above, there is the institutional feature of lifetime employment. Second, *working hours* are very flexible, providing an important element of adjustment. Tachibanaki notes:

> Japan shows the highest standard deviation in working hours and the lowest in employment among the major industrial nations despite very high fluctuations in output. When we use the total man-hours, the story is considerably different since Japan shows the lowest fluctuation. In sum, a very high adjustment by working hours and a low adjustment by employment are the Japanese ways of labour adjustment. The US is the other extreme, namely a high adjustment by employment and a low adjustment by working hours. Europe stays between the two extremes.
>
> (1987: 656)

Third, labour tends to be particularly mobile within the enterprise. Training tends to be more generalised, so transfers within the organisation provide an element of adjustment.

3 Labour *supply* is also highly flexible. There is a good deal of part-time work, primarily female, which is cyclically sensitive. Moreover, the participation rate is very cyclically sensitive, many workers, for example, dropping out of the labour force in bad times.

Tachibanaki (1987) notes that because of the existence of discouraged workers the rate of unemployment is 'considerably underestimated'.

Why is the unemployment rate low?

One can only speculate here about the social and cultural reasons underlying the low average unemployment rate (see on this Weiner 1987).

a) Both the agricultural and the self-employed sectors are relatively large in Japan. There may be considerable disguised unemployment in these sectors which do not get counted in the statistics.
b) In Japan, as in most OECD member countries, teenage unemployment is relatively high compared with other age groups, but in Japan the teenage participation rate is relatively low.
c) The education system in Japan may be more efficient in matching the supply and demand for different skills.
d) Japan's labour force is relatively homogeneous. This may give it an advantage compared with a labour force composed of many different ethnic groups.

e) The relatively strict unemployment benefits system may also have helped keep unemployment rates low (Hamada and Kurosaka 1987).

f) Whilst on average very low, there is evidence that the natural rate of unemployment has been creeping upwards since about the mid-1970s (Brunello 1989a; Kurosaka 1991).

The inflation performance

We need to distinguish the fixed exchange rate years from the years after the float, particularly after the first oil shock.

Wholesale and consumer prices in the fixed rate years in Japan

Why do we have this large discrepancy between the behaviour of the wholesale and the consumer price index in the earlier fixed exchange rate period? The explanation lies in the gap between productivity growth in the traded and non-traded goods sectors.

Suppose that the growth in wages is the same in the traded and non-traded goods sectors and suppose too that the growth in wages in the traded goods sector is set equal to productivity growth in that sector *plus* the rate of inflation in traded goods abroad. Unit labour costs and prices of traded goods will thus rise at the same rate as the inflation abroad. This is indeed what one would expect in a fixed rate regime. If, however, productivity growth is much smaller in the non-traded sectors unit labour costs and hence prices of non-traded goods will rise faster than in traded goods. The consumer price index is a weighted average of the price of traded and non-traded goods. *So, if the gap in productivity growth is much wider in Japan than in other industrial countries the discrepancy in performances is readily explained*. The gap in the two rates of inflation will be wider in Japan than abroad.

There is substantial evidence that this is essentially what was happening in Japan, which had an exceptional rate of productivity growth in the traded sector. Price measures which better reflect traded goods (export, wholesale) tend to give Japan if anything a competitive edge (McKinnon 1971).

The argument can be put more formally as follows:

$$p_T = w_T - q_T \tag{1}$$

$$p_N = w_N - q_N \tag{2}$$

$$w_T = q_T + p_{Tw} \tag{3}$$

$$w_N = w_T \tag{4}$$

$$p = \pi_1 p_T + (1 - \pi_1) p_N \tag{5}$$

$$p = (1 - \pi_1)(q_T - q_N) + p_{Tw} \tag{6}$$

where p_T, p_N are respectively the price of the traded and the non-traded goods; w_T, w_N are respectively the wage rate in the traded and non-traded goods sectors; q_T, q_N are respectively productivity in the two sectors; p is the overall price index and p_{Tw} is the price of traded goods abroad. (All variables are in logarithms.)

In both sectors prices reflect unit labour costs (i.e. wages less productivity). The wage rate in the traded sector is set equal to productivity in that sector plus the inflation abroad. Wages are the same in the two sectors. The overall price index p is a weighted average of traded and non-traded prices.

We can then readily reach (6) which is the key equation. It says that two countries may be perfectly competitive in the sense that the change in unit labour costs in traded goods may be the same, yet one country may have more overall inflation if there is a larger gap between the productivity growth in the two sectors at home than abroad.

Inflation from the mid-1970s

One element in the explanation of the inflation performance from about the mid-1970s can be sought in the relative independence of the central bank, which allows it to pursue primarily, but not exclusively, inflation objectives.

Until the late 1970s, as well, the Bank of Japan had relatively good control over the intermediate money aggregate it targeted. From the late 1970s, however, there was some slippage in money stock control, as we noted (Kasman and Rodrigues 1991).

There has also been a fairly close relationship between the intermediate target chosen and the rate of inflation. This relationship has been weakened and modified but not totally disrupted by domestic deregulation, at least until the late 1980s.

While money growth has typically been a good advance indicator of the rate of inflation, the rate of inflation has additionally been influenced by wage outcomes, fluctuations in the yen rate, commodity and energy price inflation and taxes on commodities.

Finally, flexible labour markets have also played an important role. The fact of flexible labour markets allows the Bank of Japan to pursue its disinflation policies without major adverse effect on unemployment. In 1974 the disinflation did produce a serious recession in activity but within a year wage outcomes were more responsible and economic growth resumed.

None of this is to say that there were no 'mistakes' made in the conduct of monetary policy. The 1971–2 overexpansion in the money supply might, in principle, have been avoided had the yen appreciated sooner. Monetary policy was too easy in 1987–8 and this was in part responsible for the asset inflation of those years. But it must be recalled that international pressure was placed on Japan to ease policy so perhaps this is more a commentary on politics and international coordination than on any misjudgement on the part of the Bank of Japan (although there was almost certainly some bad judgement here too).

In summary, it appears that, in broad terms, monetary policy has been managed judiciously and competently. This much also appears to be confirmed in a recent econometric study by Meredith (1992) who finds that, over the period 1980–91, had the Bank of Japan resorted to other monetary policy strategies (such as nominal income targeting, broad money targeting, a pure inflation targeting), the macro outcomes (as measured by fluctuations in output, inflation, short-term interest rates and exchange rates) would have been, on balance, inferior to those actually observed (i.e. reflecting actual monetary policies).

Fiscal policy and exchange rate management

Fiscal policy is harder to evaluate. The Japanese authorities would probably argue that fiscal policy was too loose in the second half of the 1970s and that this had to be reversed. If we accept the econometric evidence that Keynesian fiscal policy changes do have real effects, at least for a while, then one could argue that in 1975–6, when the economy was still weak, and in the later 1980s, when the economy was growing strongly, fiscal policy was stabilising, but that in 1977–8, 1980–3 and perhaps in 1986 it may have been destabilising.

In Japan's case most intervention to stabilise the currency was sterilised. In general, the authorities tended to follow a policy of leaning against the wind. A broad range of studies finds that the policy was modestly successful in achieving its immediate objectives. A very recent study of coordinated intervention also finds that in most cases of concerted intervention the authorities involved did succeed in countering the trend in the dollar (Catte *et al*. 1992).

Conclusions

Recalling the macro framework we used, we can conclude that it is unlikely that Japan was advantaged by the shocks to which she was exposed (if anything the opposite could be argued). On the other hand, we have argued that her monetary policy was judicious and, more importantly, she was advantaged by a regulatory–institutional environment (notably in relation to labour markets) which allowed her to absorb shocks relatively painlessly.

JAPAN'S PERSISTENT CURRENT ACCOUNT SURPLUS

With few exceptions Japan has recorded a current account surplus in each year since the second half of the 1960s. Why is this? What are the *fundamental* forces at work which underlie this result?

Savings–investment analysis

It will be recalled that in Chapter 34 we showed that in a two-country world one country's current account was determined by the *difference* between the two countries' exogenous components of savings and investment. The result is reproduced here. For country A

$$\frac{CA}{Y_A} = \frac{1}{2}\left(\frac{\overline{Sp}_A - \overline{Ip}_A}{Y_A} - \frac{\overline{Sp}_B - \overline{Ip}_B}{Y_B} + \frac{\overline{T}_A - \overline{G}_A}{Y_A} - \frac{\overline{T}_B - \overline{G}_B}{Y_B}\right) \tag{7}$$

If we want to apply this framework to Japan we need to modify it slightly. Equation (7) assumes that the two countries are identical with respect to size and structural coefficients. If we now assume, to simplify greatly, that the other country is the USA we need to accommodate the fact that the US economy is larger than Japan's. Suppose we write $Y_B = \pi Y_A$ where Y_B refers to the US economy. Then if we carry out exactly the same analysis and continue to assume that the structural coefficients are the same we can readily show that $\pi/(1 + \pi)$ will replace $\frac{1}{2}$ in (7). The larger π, the larger will be the ratio. If A were a very small country $\pi \to \infty$ and the coefficient would be unity. Very roughly we can set $\pi = 1.5$ which corresponds to the size of the US economy relative to the Japanese economy, so the coefficient 0.6 replaces 0.5.

How can we use this framework to identify the underlying fundamentals driving the Japanese current account? Table 47.7 provides the data which we can use as a basis for our analysis.

We focus only on the USA and Japan. We have data for four periods for Japan's current account balance, as a percentage of GDP, and the US and Japanese public sector balances, again as a percentage of GDP. We treat these public sector balances as exogenous over the medium run. We also know Japan's current account balance. Using (1), we can derive an expression which represents the differences in exogenous private sector savings and investment. The exercise can be carried out to explain *levels* of the current account in each period or *changes* in the levels.

The results of the exercise are shown in Table 47.7. Consider first the level of the

Table 47.7 Explaining Japan's current account *vis-à-vis* the USA in terms of fundamentals

Public sector balance as percentage of GDP	1970–4	1975–9	1980–5	1986–91
1 USA	− 0.6	−1.4	− 3.0	− 2.6
2 Japan	+ 0.8	− 4.1	− 2.5	+1.7
3 Japan–USA (× 0.6)	+ 0.8	−1.6	+ 0.3	+ 2.6
4 Change in 3	–	− 2.4	+1.9	+ 2.3
Current account				
5 As percentage of GNP (Japan)	+1.0	+ 0.6	+1.4	+ 2.7
6 Change in 5	–	− 0.4	+ 0.8	+1.3
7 Unexplained current account balance (5 − 3)	+ 0.2	+ 2.2	+1.1	+ 0.1
8 Unexplained change in current account (6 − 4)	–	+ 2.0	+1.1	−1.0

Source: OECD, *Economic Outlooks*

current account. Row 3 shows how much of the current account can be accounted for in terms of differences in public sector balances (adjusted as above). For example, in 1975–9 the current account was in surplus by 0.6 per cent; the difference in public sector balance in itself would have generated a current account balance of the order of −1.6. This leaves an unexplained residual of 2.2 per cent that can be attributed to private sector positions (row 7). In 1986–91 the difference in the public sector balance would in itself have produced a surplus of 2.6 per cent. This corresponds to the actual surplus, leaving little to be explained by private sector differences (row 7). Thus, in 1986–91 the large US public sector deficit and the substantial Japanese surplus can almost completely account for the surplus.

The same exercise is carried out in terms of changes. In 1986–91, for example, the current account surplus increased by 1.3 percentage points (row 6). The change in the public sector difference would have improved the current account by 2.3 per cent. Therefore the private sector account would have worsened the current account by some 1 per cent. (For an econometric analysis of the Japanese–US current account in terms of autonomous savings and investment, see Glick (1988).)

Table 47.8 also allows us to make comparisons between Japan and other industrial countries in respect of savings and investment. Japan's high *household* saving ratio has attracted a good deal of attention in the literature. Why have households in Japan been such big savers? Horioka (1990) has published a very useful survey of this literature. He reviews some thirty hypotheses advanced to account for the phenomenon. His conclusion, however, is that there are four primary factors which can account for Japan's high saving ratio. The first is differences and deficiencies in the measurement of savings in Japan and other countries, notably in the treatment of consumer durables and depreciation allowances. This biases Japan's saving ratio upwards. A

Table 47.8 Savings and investment rates, 1990

	Gross national saving as percentage of GNP	Gross investment as percentage of GNP	Net household saving as percentage of disposable income
USA	14.4	17.0	4.5
Japan	34.6	32.6	14.1
Germany	24.6	21.4	12.4
France	21.2	22.1	12.2
Italy	19.3	20.7	16.1
UK	15.6	19.2	8.3
Canada	16.7	21.5	10.3
Austria	26.1	25.6	13.3
Belgium	21.8	20.4	15.1
Denmark	18.0	17.5	15.5
Netherlands	25.4	21.2	6.5
Norway	24.1	20.6	0.3
Sweden	17.1	20.6	−1.2
Switzerland	33.1	29.1	12.0
Australia	17.7	22.9	7.7

second factor is the age structure of the population (in particular the low proportion of the aged). Third, the bonus system encourages savings. Fourth is Japan's rapid rate of economic growth. These four factors combined go a long way towards accounting for Japan's performance. It is worth noting that with the fall in Japan's growth rate and the demographic changes under way Japan's advantage on this front will probably decline.

The table also reveals that Japan's investment ratio is very high. The ratio, however, declined sharply from the second half of the 1970s, reflecting the declining real growth rate. Japan has therefore both a high national savings ratio and a high investment ratio with ambiguous implications for the current account.

Institutional factors

A quite different view of the determinants of Japan's structural current account balance places particular emphasis on Japan's alleged export practices and her *informal* barriers to imports.

On the export side the USA has frequently charged Japan with export aggressiveness, export dumping (offering a substantially lower yen price abroad than at home) and an obsessive determination to make markets in new products and to maintain existing established export market shares (even at the expense of sustaining unprofitable trading over substantial periods) (see Cohen 1991). A typical reaction to 'export aggression' has been to enter into a bilateral deal (voluntary export restraint) that will limit the volume of Japanese exports in the US market (as in steel, automobiles and colour televisions).

The so-called invisible informal barriers to imports can be direct or indirect (Lincoln 1990). The direct barriers are said to take several forms: product standards, testing and certification processes all defined in ways which tend to exclude foreign imports; delays and arbitrary procedures by customs; delays in patent approvals which benefit Japanese competitors; government procurement practices which favour domestic suppliers; administrative guidance to importers or users to inhibit imports; explicit industry collusion to deter imports; official defence of depressed industries.

Indirect barriers are also said to take a variety of forms. First the retail system, dominated by small stores, is said to discriminate against imports. Small stores are more beholden to local manufacturers who practise exclusive dealing. Second, business practices, including legal cartels, close ties amongst certain business groups, and long-standing relationships all act to reduce imports. Consumer preference for local products works in the same direction. Finally, longer working and commuting hours all act as a restraint on spending and importing.

Such factors are extremely unlikely to account for current account trends. These barriers have been progressively coming down as Japan has opened up her economy at the same time that the current account has actually improved. In any event, to explain the persistent *level* of the surplus in these terms, we need to relate the barriers to 'autonomous' savings and investment. It would have to be shown that removing these barriers would reduce the excess of private saving over investment, a task which is not easy. Moreover, what makes the task particularly difficult is that in a flexible rate world, other things being equal, one would expect the exchange rate to absorb the potential removal of barriers. It may well be, for example, that the end result will be a devaluation of the yen, reducing some imports while increasing exports, and so the trade balance may not change.

48

Macroeconomic policy and the regulatory environment: the Australian and New Zealand experience 1973–91

INTRODUCTION

The chapter begins by presenting some broad facts about the two economies.

The next section deals with the regulatory environment, and the evolution in that environment, in the two economies. This is addressed under several broad headings:

a) domestic financial regulation;
b) controls over capital movements;
c) the exchange rate regime;
d) the regulation of labour markets;
e) the status of the central banks.

Section 3 addresses the question of how Australia and New Zealand would go about choosing the exchange rate regime most tailored to their own conditions. This draws on principles developed in Chapter 36.

Sections 4 and 5 review the experience of Australia and New Zealand in the years prior to the float. Section 6 reviews the more recent experience with floating exchange rates.

Section 7 looks briefly at the theory of domestic financial deregulation and applies the framework to Australia.

In the last decade or so, the two economies have undergone radical change. They have both liberalised their financial systems and both are moving towards deregulating their labour markets (New Zealand having moved further in this direction). New Zealand has also changed its central bank constitution, now making inflation the sole objective of its monetary policy. Australia has not yet moved in this direction.

For a general discussion of the Australian experience, see OECD, *Annual Surveys*, and Argy (1992b) (see also an extensive bibliography on Australia in the last reference). For New Zealand, see Reserve Bank of New Zealand (1986, 1992), OECD Annual Surveys, and Wells (1990) and Reserve Bank of New Zealand Quarterly Bulletins.

SOME BROAD FACTS ABOUT THE TWO ECONOMIES

On the inflation front, from about 1975, the two countries started performing worse than the OECD average but Australia's performance has been relatively superior to New Zealand's. It is only in recent years that New Zealand's inflation started converging towards Australia's and in 1991 their performance was better than that of the smaller OECD countries and the OECD as a whole (Table 48.1).

Australia's unemployment has tracked fairly closely the OECD average (but it has been below that of the smaller OECD countries); in the last two years, however, its relative position has deteriorated dramatically (the unemployment rate in mid-1992 was about 11 per cent). New Zealand's performance on unemployment was excellent, at least until the early 1980s. There has been a steady increase in the rate since, reaching now over 10 per cent of the labour force by mid-1992 (Table 48.1).

Both countries have agonised over the years over large current account deficits (Table 48.1); New Zealand's has been brought down most dramatically in recent years. The persistently large current account deficits in the two economies have left a legacy of a relatively large foreign debt. In both countries the foreign debt to GDP ratio has accelerated sharply in the 1980s, reaching some 42 per cent in Australia and some 70 per cent in New Zealand by 1990–1 (all in gross terms).

Australia managed to convert years of persistent public sector deficits into surpluses by the second half of the 1980s (at least to 1991). New Zealand also adopted a policy of fiscal consolidation from the mid-1980s and succeeded in sharply reducing the deficits by the end of the 1980s (Table 48.1). The gross public debt as a percentage of GDP is currently only some 16 per cent in Australia while in New Zealand it is around 55 per cent. On this front, Australia compares very favourably with the average OECD performance while New Zealand is somewhat worse.

Real interest rates have tended over the long haul to follow the pattern of other industrial countries; real interest rates were negative in the middle to late 1970s but became substantially positive in the 1980s (Table 48.2).

Of the two economies New Zealand's is the more open. Average exports–imports as a percentage of GNP is some 30 per cent in New Zealand but only 23 per cent in Australia. As small industrial economies neither, however, could be described as being very open. The proportion of rural exports as a percentage of total exports is higher in New Zealand, being over half. In this respect, Australia's export commodity structure is more diversified, with exports roughly divided into three equal parts: rural, minerals and manufactures. Australia is also two-thirds self-contained in oil but New Zealand has to import all her oil.

Table 48.1 Macroeconomic performance, Australia (A) and New Zealand (NZ) (1972–91)

	Inflation				Unemployment				Growth of real GDP				Current account as percentage of GDP		Government financial balance, financial years	
	A	NZ	OECD	Smaller OECD	A	NZ	OECD	Smaller OECD	A	NZ	OECD	Smaller OECD	A	NZ	A	NZ central government
1972	6.0	7.6	5.4	7.4	2.6	0.5	3.6	3.3	3.4	1.5	5.2	5.3	1.9	0.7	+0.9	–
1973	8.4	4.9	8.1	9.8	2.3	0.2	3.3	3.2	5.6	9.0	5.5	6.0	1.6	1.5	+2.0	–
1974	16.2	6.0	13.9	14.5	2.7	0.1	3.6	3.4	1.9	11.2	3.4	0.7	-3.3	-11.4	-0.8	+1.0
1975	17.9	14.9	10.9	12.9	4.9	0.3	5.1	4.4	1.8	-5.1	0.3	0.1	-1.1	-10.1	-3.1	+0.4
1976	14.6	18.5	8.8	11.1	4.7	0.4	5.2	4.6	4.0	3.2	3.7	4.6	-1.9	-7.0	-0.3	-1.5
1977	10.3	16.2	8.6	11.6	5.6	0.6	5.2	4.9	0.9	-1.2	2.0	3.7	-3.1	-5.7	-1.6	+0.8
1978	8.4	12.2	7.5	10.9	6.3	1.7	5.1	5.6	3.5	-6.1	2.1	4.1	-3.8	-2.9	-4.2	0.0
1979	9.7	14.0	8.6	11.8	6.2	1.9	5.2	6.3	3.6	1.6	2.8	3.6	-2.0	-3.6	-2.1	-4.1
1980	10.5	17.8	11.3	15.3	6.0	2.7	5.9	7.2	2.3	0.5	2.2	1.2	-2.8	-4.4	-0.2	-2.1
1981	9.3	14.7	9.4	12.6	5.7	3.5	6.7	8.2	3.7	4.4	0.7	1.6	-4.9	-5.0	+0.1	-3.9
1982	10.4	15.2	7.3	11.0	7.1	3.7	8.0	9.4	-0.2	2.9	0.9	0.1	-5.0	-7.4	-1.0	-3.7
1983	9.3	7.1	5.8	9.4	9.9	5.4	8.6	10.5	0.6	1.3	1.6	2.7	-3.7	-4.5	-3.0	-4.6
1984	6.4	6.6	5.1	8.9	8.9	4.6	8.1	10.7	7.4	8.6	3.4	4.4	-4.8	-8.7	-2.9	-6.6
1985	7.1	16.5	4.5	8.0	8.2	3.6	8.0	10.5	4.8	1.2	3.1	3.4	-5.6	-7.5	-2.9	-5.2
1986	8.7	12.2	2.9	5.7	8.0	4.0	7.9	10.1	2.3	1.0	2.8	2.8	-5.6	-6.4	-1.8	-2.6
1987	8.0	13.4	3.3	5.7	8.0	4.1	7.4	9.7	4.4	-2.4	2.9	3.2	-4.1	-5.5	-0.2	-3.5
1988	7.0	8.1	3.5	6.6	7.1	5.6	6.9	9.4	3.5	2.9	3.4	4.4	-4.1	-1.4	+1.5	-2.2
1989	6.7	6.4	4.5	7.5	6.1	7.2	6.4	8.8	4.4	-0.7	3.6	3.3	-6.1	-3.1	+1.6	-1.5
1990	6.2	6.4	4.7	7.8	6.9	7.8	6.2	8.6	1.7	0.5	2.9	2.5	-4.8	-3.2	+1.4	-1.4
1991	3.5	2.8	4.5	7.7	9.6	10.3	7.1	9.6	-1.9	-2.1	0.6	1.0	-3.5	-1.1	+0.3	-1.7

Table 48.2 Real interest rates[a] Australia and New Zealand

	1972	1973	1974	1975	1976	1977	1978	1979	1980	1981	1982	1983	1984	1985	1986	1987	1988	1989	1990	1991
Aust.	−0.1	−2.3	−6.0	−5.3	−3.2	−2.0	1.2	0.7	1.6	4.3	4.3	4.2	9.8	7.4	4.5	5.0	5.1	6.0	5.9	7.5
NZ	−1.4	−2.4	−5.0	−8.3	−9.3	−5.1	−2.0	−1.7	−3.8	−2.5	−3.3	4.8	6.4	2.3	3.3	0	6.7	7.1	6.4	7.2

Source: IMF, *International Financial Statistics*
Note: [a]The government bond yield less the percentage change in the consumer price index.

Table 48.3 Percentage change in terms of trade, Australia and New Zealand

	1972	1973	1974	1975	1976	1977	1978	1979	1980	1981	1982	1983	1984	1985	1986	1987	1988	1989	1990
Aust.	10.0	28.6	−15.9	−17.0	−0.5	−7.2	−2.7	−0.1	−9.5	−0.1	−2.1	−1.0	−2.1	−5.3	−7.4	−1.9	14.5	6.5	−3.0
NZ	15.7	22.0	−22.8	−25.3	7.1	4.5	2.6	7.6	−10.9	−0.6	−1.1	−2.5	−0.2	−1.8	−	11.0	6.8	4.9	−1.2

Source: IMF, *International Financial Statistics*

In both economies the principal trading partner is Japan. In Australia, the USA and the UK are next in that order. In New Zealand, Australia is the second trading partner with the USA and the UK next in that order.

As major producers of rural products and commodities, both countries are exposed to large swings in their terms of trade, more so than in most industrial countries (Table 48.3). The fluctuations are roughly similar but not identical. The differences reflect primarily the differences in the export commodity base and the sensitivity of the prices of the exports to fluctuations in the level of world activity.

THE REGULATORY ENVIRONMENT

Domestic financial regulation

In both economies until the early 1980s there were extensive interest rate controls and prescribed asset ratios on banks and other financial institutions. There were also lending guidelines for the banks. Entry into the banking system was limited. In both economies some steps towards liberalisation had been taken in the middle to second half of the 1970s. In New Zealand progress was very slow and by the early 1980s remained more heavily regulated than in Australia. In Australia, by mid-1982 quantitative lending guidelines to banks were abandoned; by 1984–5 all significant controls had been removed. In New Zealand controls were removed between the middle and end of 1984.

External financial regulation

In both economies capital movements were regulated, in principle, until December 1983 in Australia and December 1984 in New Zealand. The evolution of controls, however, was different in the two economies. In New Zealand capital flows were strictly monitored to the end, with only minor variations in the regulations.

Australia's experience is richer in this respect. Australia varied the regulations depending on the state of the balance of payments.

Until late 1971 the general principle was that capital flows were prohibited unless specifically authorised. In reality most capital inflows were allowed entry and indeed encouraged. In sharp contrast, capital outflows were rigidly controlled. Between 1971 and 1978 capital flows were monitored as a method of managing the Australian dollar. When the dollar was strong, as in 1972–3, and from December 1976 to June 1977, capital inflows were discouraged. Two methods were used here: embargoes on borrowings of a certain maturity, and a cost penalty on certain types of borrowing (the variable deposit requirement). In sharp contrast, when the dollar was weak, as in 1974–6, these regulations were reversed, with inflows now encouraged. By June 1978, although technically controls over inflows were still in place, these were not enforced and so inflows had by then become largely free. When the dollar was very strong again in 1980–1 and in March–December 1983, controls over inflows were not reimposed.

The exchange rate regime

The evolution of exchange rate policy is similar in the two economies.

The Australian dollar was pegged (but adjustable) to the US dollar between 1973 and September 1974. Between September 1974 and November 1976 the Australian dollar was pegged (but adjustable) to a currency basket. In the years to November 1976 there were several discrete exchange rate adjustments: February 1973 (11 per cent +); July 1973 (25 per cent tariff cut, 5 per cent +); September 1984 (12 per cent −); November 1976 (17.5 per cent −). Between November 1976 and March–December 1983, Australia adopted a discretionary version of the crawling peg. A small committee of four adjusted the Australian dollar daily. The basis for the crawl varied. To early 1981 the principal determinant was the overall balance of payments; after that increased attention came to be paid to the current account. In December 1983 the Australian dollar floated. It has never been a completely clean float, however.

The New Zealand dollar was pegged (but adjustable) to the US dollar to July 1973. Between July 1973 and June 1979 it was pegged (but adjustable) against a basket. Between June 1979 and June 1982, New Zealand adopted a purchasing power parity (real exchange rate) variant of the crawling peg. The exchange rate was adjusted to offset differences in inflation rates between New Zealand and her trading partners. New Zealand operated an *ex ante* scheme based on consumer prices. If the realised inflation rates were different from the anticipated rates some correction would be made. In June 1982 New Zealand reverted to an adjustable peg against a basket.

As in Australia, there were several discrete exchange rate adjustments: September 1974 (6.2 per cent −); August 1975 (15 per cent −); November 1976 (2.7 per cent −); June 1979 (5 per cent −); March 1983 (6 per cent −); July 1984 (20 per cent −). In the three years of the crawl the New Zealand dollar devalued by some 6 per cent each year. In March 1989 the New Zealand dollar floated, again not cleanly.

Regulation of labour markets

The New Zealand experience

To simplify slightly, we can say that until 1987 the system of wage determination was three-tiered.

a) Unions and employers negotiated national award wages for particular occupations.

b) In the event the parties did not agree reference would be made first to conciliation and then to arbitration.

c) There was periodic intervention by the government in the determination of national wage outcomes. Intervention took several forms: guidelines, direct controls, the imposition of minimum periods of currency for new agreements and constraints on the renegotiating of old agreements, wage pauses and freezes, partial indexation directives.

A new phase began in 1987. Legislation was passed in 1987 and again in 1991. The legislation aimed ultimately at decentralising wage bargaining, weakening the unions and increasing labour market flexibility. The 1987 Act had only limited objectives. Unions but not employers were allowed to opt out of the award system. At the same time it sought to reduce the fragmentation of the union movement by prescribing a minimum size of 1,000 members. Compulsory unionism was retained. The 1991 legislation went much further down the road. To summarise from Kerr (1991) its principal features are as follows:

1. compulsory unionism is abolished and replaced with freedom of association;
2. unions will become incorporated societies, with no special rights and no minimum size;
3. unions lose the exclusive right to negotiate on behalf of workers – workers may negotiate for themselves, or use the services of any bargaining agent (including unions, if so desired by the workers);
4. awards and agreements disappear and are replaced with employment contracts;
5. parties are free to negotiate the type of contract they want in the way they choose.

(1991: 12–13)

The Australian experience

The Australian wage determination environment has also undergone radical change. When the Liberal Party was elected to government in the 1993 election they adopted something like the New Zealand 1991 legislation which goes beyond anything accomplished to date.

The traditional Australian model of wage setting is one in which an independent Arbitration Commission periodically hears submissions from interested parties, including, most importantly, the government, employer groups and the Australian Confederation of Trade Unions. The government's input into the proceedings is very important but is not necessarily decisive. After hearing all the evidence the Commission makes a ruling on national wages. In this sense it is a highly centralised system (but unlike the corporatist systems in, say, Austria, Sweden and Norway). At times, however, collective bargaining between unions and employers has been encouraged and has assumed some importance in wage outcomes. In turn such collective bargaining agreements will be registered as awards by the Commission.

The Labour government which took over in early 1983 negotiated an 'Accord' with the unions. The Accord has passed through three stages. In the first stage full wage indexation was endorsed. In the second stage this was modified to discount for the effects of the devaluation of 1985–6. In the third stage the Accord became less centralised, with increased emphasis being placed on enterprise agreements, within certain ground rules. An important feature of the Accord was the wage-tax trade-off: the government would offer tax concessions in return for wage moderation. (For an evaluation of the Accord see Argy (1992b).)

Conclusions on Australia and New Zealand

Would enterprise bargaining in the two economies improve labour market adjustment?

We recall that there is a large literature that tries to rank countries in terms of the degree of centralisation in wage setting and macro performance (primarily, unemployment and real wage flexibility). It turns out that the best performers are the centralised and the decentralised economies (i.e. those with enterprise bargaining), while the worst performers are the intermediate economies (with industry bargaining) (Chapter 44). Assuming that Australia and New Zealand are both 'centralist' (a question which could be debated) and assuming that we took this framework seriously, it is not evident that the switch to enterprise bargaining will improve macro performance.

Central bank status

As we saw in Chapter 25, there is a large literature concerned with the potential implications, for the equilibrium inflation rate, of allowing governments complete discretion with respect to the use of monetary policy.

Who has had responsibility for monetary policy in Australia and New Zealand?

The Reserve Bank Act of Australia gives the government ultimate responsibility for monetary policy. The Governing Board is required by the 1959 Reserve Bank Act to conduct its monetary policy in a way which 'will best contribute to the stability of the currency . . . the maintenance of full employment . . . and the economic prosperity and welfare of . . . Australia'. The current government's position is that the Reserve Bank should 'have a broad range of objectives . . . . It is not there to pursue one objective (inflation) singlemindedly' (Dawkins, the Treasurer, reported in *The Australian*, 27 March, p. 3). The Liberal Party, however, changed the Charter of the Bank to one that focuses on fighting inflation only, with formal targets in the range of 0–2 per cent.

Under the earlier New Zealand Act the Reserve Bank was required to carry out 'the monetary policy of the Government, which shall be directed to the maintenance and promotion of economic and social welfare in New Zealand having regard to the desirability of promoting the highest degree of production, trade and employment and of maintaining a stable internal price level'.

The Act was changed in 1989 by a Labour government. Section 8 now states:

The primary function of the Bank is to formulate and implement monetary policy directed to the economic objective of achieving and maintaining stability in the general level of prices.

Section 9 states that

The Minister shall before appointing or reappointing any person as Governor fix in agreement with that person policy targets for the carrying out by the Bank of its primary function during that person's term of office.

In accordance with this last section the then Minister of Finance and the Governor agreed on an inflation target in the range 0–2 per cent to be achieved by end-1992. The new Conservative government extended the deadline to end-1993.

THE CHOICE OF EXCHANGE RATE REGIME FOR AUSTRALIA AND NEW ZEALAND

Dealing as we are with small economies with similar economic structures and experience, it seems reasonable to apply a common framework in addressing the question of the choice of exchange rate regime.

We have seen that most of the smaller industrial countries have chosen to either peg or float. Norway, Finland and perhaps Sweden are still caught in a halfway house between a permanent and an adjustable basket peg (but their hearts are set on a peg).

Drawing on these tendencies and experiences the serious choices for Australia and New Zealand come down to a peg or a continuation of the float. They can peg to a single country or to a basket. Japan is the biggest trading partner. It also has a good inflation record. Both Australia and New Zealand also now (mid-1992) have an inflation rate (below 2 per cent) which parallels Japan's. Would pegging to the yen make sense? In our discussion of this question we draw in part on the optimal currency literature (Chapter 36).

To begin, there will be some efficiency gains (reduction in uncertainty and in the costs of conversion) but these will not be large.

The argument that turns on inflation discipline is weak since as we have seen that Australia and New Zealand can achieve that on their own.

Any loss of the exchange rate as an adjustment tool between Australia–New Zealand and Japan could in principle be counteracted, in part at least, if labour were very mobile across the regions. There is virtually no labour mobility, however, between Australia–New Zealand on the one hand and Japan on the other.

Another relevant consideration is the structure of disturbances. If disturbances are common to the region the case for the union is strengthened. As it happens, on this criterion the case against such a union is strong. Given that Australia and New Zealand are predominantly commodity exporters and Japan is a commodity importer, their terms of trade will often move in opposite directions, which means that at a time when commodity prices are depressed and the yen is strong Australian and New Zealand currencies will be appreciating in trade-weighted terms, reinforcing any adverse effects on the current account.

Yet another relevant consideration is the degree of real wage flexibility. As we saw, countries with a high degree of real wage flexibility are better equipped to cope with real shocks and so will miss the loss of the exchange rate instrument less. At least until recently Australia and New Zealand did not have a high degree of real wage flexibility but as we have seen the two governments are working hard at this. If real wage flexibility could, in principle, be achieved as well by wage adjustment as by an exchange rate change the case for a union is much stronger.

We note too the loss of the monetary instrument and the potential enhanced effectiveness in the short run of the fiscal instrument.

To conclude, the case for pegging to the yen appears on the face of it to be weak (but, on the other hand, many of the above considerations would argue for a monetary union between Australia and New Zealand).

Argy *et al.* (1989) use a three-country model to evaluate the insulation properties of alternative exchange rate regimes, for different assumptions about wage indexation. The three-country world comprises two large countries and one small one (Chapter 16). The small country can peg to either of the larger countries or to a basket or it can float. Real or monetary disturbances can originate in either of the larger economies or in the small economy.

Using the MSG2 model and applying this framework to Australia (the small country) and Japan and the USA (the two large countries), the final conclusion reached was that 'the floating rate regime for Australia performs well . . . except for a shock to money demand in Australia . . . of the fixed exchange rate regimes it is better to peg to a basket of currencies, especially for foreign shocks in a world of globally floating exchange rates'.

Blundell-Wignall and Gregory (1990) also undertake an analysis for Australia and New Zealand of the insulating properties of fixed and flexible rate regimes. They take as a starting point that the two dominant disturbances in economies such as Australia and New Zealand have come from money demand and terms of trade shocks. The terms of trade appear to dominate, so their conclusion is that 'a floating exchange rate regime is essential in a commodity-exporting country subject to terms of trade shocks if an inflation target is to be achieved'.

Jonson (1987) using the Australian Reserve Bank model (RB11) explores the insulating properties of a fixed and flexible rate regime faced with a money demand and a terms of trade shock. He focuses on output, employment and inflation outcomes. A fixed rate regime is better on all counts for a money demand shock but worse on all counts for a terms of trade shock. So again if shocks to terms of trade dominate there is a case for adopting flexible rates.

To conclude, it does appear that, on balance, taking all these considerations and empirical studies into account, Australia and New Zealand are probably better off with flexible rates than with fixed rates.

MONETARY AND EXCHANGE RATE POLICIES – THE AUSTRALIAN EXPERIENCE (1973–83)

We try to summarise the experience with fixed and crawling rates by addressing three key questions. First, was there monetary independence (i.e. did the monetary authorities have control over their chosen money aggregate or the domestic interest rates)? Second, how effective were the exchange controls? (Evidently, if they were ineffective

Table 48.4   Australia: index of competitiveness

Mar 72	98.9	Dec 81	112.1
Sep 72	96.3	Mar 82	113.9
Dec 72	96.0	Jun 82	116.0
Mar 73	104.8	Sep 82	115.7
Jun 73	109.4	Dec 82	113.3
Sep 73	108.3	Mar 83	109.0
Dec 73	114.7	Jun 83	100.0
Mar 74	123.1	Sep 83	102.9
Jun 74	120.6	Dec 83	106.8
Sep 74	131.1	Mar 84	108.7
Dec 74	117.8	Jun 84	108.3
Mar 75	118.6	Sep 84	105.2
Jun 75	117.6	Dec 84	107.7
Sep 75	119.8	Mar 85	100.5
Dec 75	123.3	Jun 85	86.2
Mar 76	121.8	Sep 85	86.4
Jun 76	122.3	Dec 85	82.5
Sep 76	123.4	Mar 86	81.5
Dec 76	116.2	Jun 86	79.9
Mar 77	109.7	Sep 86	68.7
Jun 77	109.1	Dec 86	71.8
Sep 77	108.7	Mar 87	72.3
Dec 77	108.0	Jun 87	74.1
Mar 78	105.2	Sep 87	76.6
Jun 78	101.0	Dec 87	72.4
Sep 78	96.4	Mar 88	73.4
Dec 78	93.7	Jun 88	79.4
Mar 79	93.5	Sep 88	86.0
Jun 79	94.4	Dec 88	88.5
Sep 79	95.0	Mar 89	91.1
Dec 79	95.3	Jun 89	88.5
Mar 80	97.1	Sep 89	88.6
Jun 80	96.9	Dec 89	92.2
Sep 80	99.3	Mar 90	90.4
Dec 80	98.8	Jun 90	93.9
Mar 81	102.5	Sep 90	95.8
Jun 81	106.6		
Sep 81	113.1		

Source: (Australian) Economic Planning and Advisory Council
Notes: An increase means a loss in competitiveness.
    Unit labour costs 1984–5 = 100.

the money stock could not be independent.) Third, assuming there was some monetary independence, how appropriate was the policy?

The Labour government (1973–5)

Money growth had been substantial prior to the change in government at the end of 1972. The terms of trade were favouring Australia, the Australian dollar was undervalued and there were large inflows *which had proved difficult to sterilise* (Porter 1974). The controls over inflows which finally came in September–December 1972 had come too late.

One of the first tasks of the new government was to rein in money growth; this was achieved by tight monetary policies and by a succession of appreciations and a 25 per cent cut in tariffs. In the event money growth (particularly *real* money balances) fell too sharply, creating financial panic at the time.

By mid-1974 in the wake of the appreciations, tariff cuts and the recession abroad the Australian dollar started to weaken and steps were taken to reverse the stance of capital controls. On 25 September after strong speculative outflows the Australian dollar was devalued. (See Table 48.4 for the trends in the real effective exchange rate.)

The Conservative government (1976–82)

The new government opted for a 'monetarist' strategy, which was now becoming fashionable abroad.

Beginning in the financial year 1976–7 money growth targets (officially called projections) were announced. A policy of gradually reducing money growth was adopted with the objective of gradually bringing inflation down. In the Budget Speech for 1978–9 we find the contention that 'within this monetary projection the outlook for employment will be affected by the outcome of the wage determination process both inside the arbitral tribunals and outside them'.

The authorities did succeed in the first two years in reducing money growth (indeed money growth fell from some 15 per cent in 1974–5 to 11 per cent in 1975–6 and then to 8 per cent in 1976–7) (Table 48.5). In turn this reduced the rate of inflation: by 1978 the rate of inflation had more than halved from its heights of nearly 18 per cent in 1975 (Table 48.1).

In the subsequent three years, however, money growth significantly overshot its target (projected) rate. Although in the two years that followed (1981–2 and 1982–3) money growth was close to target the policy had in the meantime lost some credibility. Despite the failures here it is worth noting that, although the objectives of the policy failed, money growth over a period of six years was remarkably stable (in sharp contrast to the volatility under the previous government).

On the external front in the course of 1976 the Australian dollar was again weak and by the third quarter there were large speculative outflows. In November there was another devaluation after which the authorities switched to a crawling peg.

Table 48.5   Australia: money growth targets and outcomes

Financial year	M3 money growth target	M3 outcome
1975–6		(13.3)
1976–7	10–12	11.0
1977–8	8–10	8.0
1978–9	6–8	11.8
1979–80	max 10	12.3
1980–1	9–11	12.7
1981–2	10–11	11.3
1982–3	9–11	11.1
1983–4	9–11[a]	11.4
1984–5	8–10[b]	(17.5)

Source: *Reserve Bank Bulletin*
Notes: [a] Revised to 10–12 at mid-year.
[b] Suspended January 1985.

Late in 1977 and 1978 the current account took a further turn for the worse (Table 48.1). The authorities responded in two ways. First, they reversed the stance of capital controls, progressively dismantling all restrictions on inflows. Second, they began to adjust the effective rate downwards on a gradual basis.

The distinctive feature of the period from mid-1980 to 1981 was the short-lived (but nevertheless important in terms of its impacts) resources boom which came in the wake of the second oil price shock. Australia suddenly became the recipient of huge amounts of capital seeking to take advantage of what looked like very attractive investment prospects, particularly in coal, mineral resources and allied industries.

Capital inflows, some of which were also speculative, more than offset the current account deficit which now again deteriorated sharply. This led to a potentially very large overall surplus. The authorities responded in part by allowing the currency to appreciate; by about August 1981 the real effective rate had risen by some 12 per cent (Table 48.4). At the same time there were large official purchases of US dollars, notably in the first half of 1981. The authorities, however, found it difficult to steri-lise these purchases and money supply grew rapidly, again exceeding its target for the year 1980–1. Thus the authorities tried to moderate the appreciation but at the cost of some loss of control over monetary policy.

It is interesting to note that this time the authorities did not try to reimpose controls over inflows, although on the face of it this might have helped in part to resolve the dilemmas. On the other hand, some modest measures were taken at the time to encourage more outflows.

With the price of oil beginning to fall back by 1982 and the resources boom exhausting itself, increased attention came to be placed on the current account, which in 1982 continued to deteriorate rapidly. Capital inflows, however, continued to be large, more than offsetting the current account deficit. Nevertheless, now the authori-ties, with an eye on the current account, chose gradually to lower the Australian dollar and buy US dollars in the foreign exchange market. From late 1982 to mid-1983 the dollar in real terms had fallen by roughly as much as the gains made in 1980–1 (Table 48.4).

The Labour government – March 1983 on

In February 1983 with an election campaign under way fears that the Labour Party might win government led initially to some cautionary outflows of capital. Those out-flows gathered momentum and, from late February, reached massive proportions. On 8 March, with the new Labour government installed, the dollar was devalued by 10 per cent. With this devaluation the 'crawling peg' system, under which only small daily adjustments would be made, had broken down.

The current account was beginning to show some improvement in 1983; at the same time, the interest rate differential moved more in favour of Australia; moreover, some confidence in the new government was beginning to surface. These forces com-bined to produce a dramatic reversal in capital flows. In the months that followed inflows became massive; indeed, for a while they were almost double the current account deficit. As in 1980–1 the authorities responded, partly by allowing the dollar to appreciate and partly by intervening in the foreign exchange market. As in 1980–1 they found it impossible to sterilise the inflow. During those months money growth was overshooting its projected range (revised upward by 1 point in December). Finally, on 12 December the Australian dollar was allowed to float; at the same time most exchange controls were removed. The float enabled the authorities to regain control over money growth in the second half of the year and this allowed money growth over the whole financial year 1983–4 to remain close to its target range.

The Australian experience summarised

We return to our three original questions (for details see Argy 1987).

There was clearly no monetary independence in 1972, in 1980–1 and again in the course of 1983. These were all periods of intense speculation in favour of the Aus-tralian dollar. It needs to be emphasised, importantly, that on all these occasions there were no effective controls over inflows and so the economy was left exposed.

It is more difficult to judge whether there was monetary independence in other years. Undoubtedly the domestic interest rate could not diverge too sharply from for-eign interest rates, so in this respect there was some constraint. Nevertheless, with the help of discrete devaluations and in less turbulent periods one judges that there was probably some degree of monetary independence.

Were the capital controls effective *either in stemming inflows when the restrictions were applied or in mitigating the outflows*? Argy (1987) reviews all the evidence from several quarters, and concludes that there was probably some effectiveness; however, their effectiveness weakened in the longer run or by continued application. Testimony to the fact that the controls over outflows were not completely effective comes from the fact that there were large *and increasing* speculative bouts (in 1974, in 1976 and in early 1983). Leakages came primarily in the form of the activities of the multi-nationals and of the traders (leads and lags); in due course the authorities did move to regulate the timing of payments and to increase surveillance over multinational accounts but, at best, these would have only had a marginal impact.

Argy also suggests that if the controls were effective in some degree the timing of their imposition, removal or reimposition did leave something to be desired. In short, they were not applied judiciously. We saw that in 1972 the controls came too late. The reversal in 1974 was again late in coming. The embargo on borrowings over six months was retained from November 1974 to January 1977, during which period the currency was weak. Nor was any attempt made to reintroduce controls over inflows either in 1980 or in 1983 when those inflows assumed massive proportions. Again at a time when net outflows ought to have been encouraged there was very little attempt, except for a weak one in 1980, to ease up on controls over outflows.

The third question addressed was the aptness of the policies. This is very difficult to answer. We just indicated that more judicious use could have been made of capital controls. We also indicated that there were times when monetary policy was too volatile. Discrete devaluations in an environment where wages are predominantly indexed are ultimately self-defeating and they probably were so in Australia.

Assuming some monetary discretion the only way to judge the policy is to compare it with an alternative feasible strategy which could potentially include a float or a different monetary policy rule. Only econometric simulations of alternative strategies over the period 1972–82 would throw light on this question and there are none. Crudely, too, judging the monetary policy in terms of inflationary outcomes, we have already seen that Australia's relative performance was a mixed one: it was worse than the OECD's in nearly every year between 1972 and 1982 (but at least between 1979 and 1983 better than that of the smaller countries).

MONETARY AND EXCHANGE RATE POLICIES – THE NEW ZEALAND EXPERIENCE (1972–84)

The New Zealand experience with fixed and crawling rates is much simpler to summarise and can be described in very broad terms. The consensus view appears to be that there was in general *more* monetary independence in New Zealand *but that this independence was being increasingly threatened with time.*

Money growth in New Zealand also fluctuated wildly at least until 1976, after which until 1982 the fluctuations were more moderate but the average growth rate was probably excessive, which in turn explains New Zealand's particularly poor performance on the inflation front. New Zealand never did adopt a policy of announcing money growth targets (Spencer 1980).

In the course of the three years 1979–82 when the crawl was in operation the current account steadily deteriorated. In principle, the adoption of the crawl did not rule out changes in the *real* exchange rate but these would have had to be implemented in small doses (a policy which might not have been credible). In the event in 1982, confronted with such an imbalance, the authorities reverted to the adjustable peg. In one sense the timing of the adoption of the crawling peg was perhaps unfortunate. The terms of trade in those years moved significantly against New Zealand (Table 48.3).

The breakdown parallels the Australian experience in 1983 when the huge outflows were no longer consistent with small changes in the currency. Also in Australia in 1980–1 during the resources boom when the imbalances were very large, this placed great strains on the operation of the crawling peg.

Exchange controls were probably more effective in New Zealand (Nicholl 1977) but became increasingly less effective (Carey and Duggan 1986). It is now widely conceded that by 1984 the exchange controls were no longer functioning well. Capital flows in that year were responding massively to perceived arbitrage or speculative gains. To cite Carey and Duggan, 'with wide scope for currency flows within the current account it made little sense to focus control on the capital account. Apart from the relative ineffectiveness in controlling foreign exchange flows, the regulations imposed inordinately heavy costs on compliance and enforcement of the rules.'

THE FLOAT IN AUSTRALIA AND NEW ZEALAND

Australia

Soon after the Labour government took over in March 1983 the policy of announcing money growth targets was abandoned. The principal reason was that the domestic financial deregulation was severely distorting the money aggregates (see later). A secondary reason was that the policy had also lost some credibility in Australia and, by then, overseas.

The authorities then adopted a 'check-list' approach to monetary policy. In determining the setting of monetary policy the authorities looked at all major economic and financial factors, present and prospective. These included the state of the economy, the balance of payments, prices, other policies, interest rates, the exchange rate and the money aggregates. These were periodically reviewed and a judgement was then made about the appropriate monetary policy.

In retrospect it is possible to be critical of the conduct of monetary policy. One view widely held was that policy was too easy in 1986–8 and then too tight for too long in the face of an overheated economy. The tight monetary policy was primarily responsible for the sharp downturn in the economy in 1990.

New Zealand

As in Australia's case an important aim of the float in New Zealand was to regain and secure control over monetary aggregates and policy. Spencer notes:

> Following the float of the New Zealand dollar in March 1985, the Reserve Bank achieved discretionary control over the monetary base of the New Zealand financial system. The Bank was therefore in a position, for the first time, to effectively pursue targets for the money and/or credit aggregates; a strategy which had been continually frustrated under the 'adjustable-peg' exchange rate regime.
>
> (1992: 122)

New Zealand's monetary policy during the float followed a course roughly similar to Australia's. Policy eased in 1985–7 and then became very tight. *The principal difference is that New Zealand in due course adopted an inflation target and its policies were intended while in Australia the outcomes were unintended.*

As in the Australian case, too, the money aggregates became seriously distorted after domestic deregulation (Spencer 1992).

New Zealand adopted its own version of the check-list. Australia used a whole range of variables to determine the stance of its monetary policy. New Zealand has an inflation target; it also monitors the settlement cash balances held by banks at the Reserve Bank to achieve its monetary stance. In determining this stance it has been guided since 1985 by a set of indicators which include the exchange rate, the level and structure of interest rates, the growth of money and credit, inflation expectations and trends in the real economy (Spencer 1990).

The unemployment cost of the recent disinflations in Australia and New Zealand

In Australia between 1988 and 1991–2 the inflation rate fell by some 7 points. At the same time the unemployment rate rose by some 5 points over approximately three years, a *cumulative* excess over the 1988–9 figure of 9.5 points. In New Zealand inflation fell by some 12 points between 1987 and 1992 while the unemployment rate rose by 6.5 points. The cumulative excess unemployment is approximately 14 points. On these very crude calculations the *cumulative* disinflation cost is slightly less in New Zealand.

The Australian experience reported above appears to be a little higher than that of disinflation costs reported for previous episodes of disinflation (see Carmichael 1990). For more sophisticated measures of the disinflation costs using econometric simulations see Murphy (1991) and Andersen (1992).

If one accepted the view that labour market deregulation reduces the costs of disinflation the argument can be made that both governments *put the cart before the horse*, in the sense that they should have deregulated the labour markets before embarking on a disinflation policy.

DOMESTIC FINANCIAL DEREGULATION – THEORY AND APPLICATION TO AUSTRALIA

This section reviews briefly the theory of domestic financial deregulation and tries to apply the framework to Australia (there is almost no comparable documentation for New Zealand). For the application to Australia, we draw on MacFarlane (1991), Harper (1991), Valentine (1992), Hawtrey *et al*. (1991) and Twrdy (1992).

Theory

The case for domestic financial deregulation is usually put in terms of the micro efficiency gains that will accrue. These can take many forms: the greater variety of financial services; the removal of discriminations stemming from a regulated system of credit rationing; the removal of interest rate distortions (allowing financial flows to move into the most efficient sectors); welfare-augmenting switches from the payment of implicit interest (e.g. subsiding transactions and deposit accounts and offering an extended system of branches) to the payment of explicit interest; greater competitiveness amongst financial institutions with benefits to consumers in terms of reduced profit margins.

There is another side to the ledger, however. One other important aspect of deregulation is its potential for creating 'financial fragility' by exposing the financial sector to greater risk (see Blundell-Wignall and Browne 1991).

There are several potential links between deregulation and financial fragility. First, greater competition amongst financial institutions may encourage greater risk-taking, in an effort to earn a larger return on assets. Second, the relaxation of asset controls may free institutions to make riskier loans. Third, the liberalised environment may generate excessive speculation, driven by institutional borrowing, which drives up asset prices to unsustainable levels. Fourth, we shall also see that deregulation might be associated with greater interest rate volatility. At times when interest rates are rising institutions with relatively inflexible loan rates may become particularly vulnerable.

What about the macro implications of domestic deregulation? Here it is important to distinguish steady state from transitional effects. (For a fuller discussion, see Argy (1992a).)

First, what does domestic deregulation do in steady state to (a) policy effectiveness and (b) the capacity of the economy to absorb shocks, i.e. is deregulation a good or a bad insulator?

If banks are now free to adjust the interest rates on their deposits in response to changes in market interest rates the interest sensitivity of money demand is likely to fall. Suppose the market interest rate rose; without deregulation there would be a shift out of deposits into 'bonds'; with deregulation the interest rate on deposits increases, thus limiting the shift out of deposits. At the limit, if interest is earned on bank cash the interest sensitivity approaches zero.

There are several important implications flowing from this. First, monetary policy becomes more effective,[1] but on the other hand the effect on income of a money demand shock is *amplified*. Second, it may become harder to control the money aggregates. At the limit, when the interest elasticity of money approaches zero, open market operations are no longer viable (but on the other hand interest rate policy is still feasible). In any event, to achieve a given interest rate outcome, *more* pressure will now need to be placed on the money stock. Third, fiscal policy is weakened but on the other hand the economy is better insulated from real shocks. Fourth, for any given disturbance the interest rate will now become more *volatile*. More volatile interest rates in turn may also mean higher average interest rates (Argy 1983).

What happens in the transition phases? A most important initial effect is the reintermediation process, as we saw in Chapter 43. Deregulation of interest rates allows banks to offer more competitive interest rates on their deposits, provoking an upward shift in money demand. In principle the cash base could be expanded to absorb the increase in money demand but there will be a good deal of uncertainty about the magnitude of the money demand shift, so accommodation will be difficult in practice.

During the transition stages the effects of monetary policy will be very uncertain and thus for a while at least it will be more difficult to conduct a monetary policy. Money aggregates will become distorted as signals of monetary policy. However, when the economy has fully adjusted to the deregulation, money aggregates will come into their own again.

The initial stages of deregulation will also be associated with substantial changes to the whole financial scene. Competition amongst financial institutions will be fiercer. Non-banks will respond to greater competition from the banks by providing new services, perhaps trimming their profit margins and competing more aggressively on interest rates. They may also compete by offering checkable deposits. Thus one undoubted consequence of deregulation is that banks and non-banks become more alike. Portfolio restrictions on banks and non-banks are also likely to be relaxed or abandoned with financial deregulation, creating additional ripples on the financial scene.

As is well known, financial regulation tends to breed innovations which aim at sidestepping the regulations; so deregulation may set in motion some reversal of previous innovations (although here ratchet effects may be at work) while creating new opportunities and challenges for innovation in the liberalised environment.

Application to Australia

We deal with the issues under the following headings: efficiency, risk (financial fragility) and macro consequences.

Have there been micro efficiency gains, as claimed by the proponents of deregulation? What at first sight appears a relatively straightforward question turns out to be immensely complicated and indeed is still the subject of a very heated debate. It is impossible to do full justice to all the issues here but we can try and summarise the spirit of the debate.

It is universally agreed that the *range* of financial services offered is now much more comprehensive and this is perceived to be a net benefit. One other expectation was that with the entry of new banks and with the lowering of barriers between banks and non-banks, competition would become fiercer. This is almost certainly true at the wholesale level (for large business customers) but less evident at the retail level, where four major banks continue to dominate the scene.

Deregulation was also expected to reduce the profitability of the banks; in general, this has probably happened. There is some evidence, however, that the profitability of retail banking may have increased slightly while that of wholesale banking may have fallen, reflecting perhaps the differences in the level of competition experienced in the two sectors.

Much attention has focused on the impacts of deregulation on banks' interest rate margins (i.e. the difference between their borrowing and their lending rates). The original expectation was that deregulation would reduce margins because (a) prior to deregulation the interest rates were set by the Reserve Bank at levels which were highly profitable (compared with other OECD countries); (b) banks would become more competitive and this would reduce their operating costs; (c) banks would switch from 'non-interest' to interest methods of pricing (i.e. there would be a replacement of implicit interest with explicit interest).

Here the signals are very conflicting and indeed confusing. Hawtrey *et al.* (1991) argue that there has not been a fall in the average net interest margin earned by the established banks. Moreover, they try to demonstrate that there is a disparate sectoral impact of deregulation on margins and charges: interest margins applying to small to medium businesses and households (i.e. the difference between the housing mortgage rate and the return on saving–investment accounts) may have widened while that for larger firms may have narrowed slightly. This again may reflect the differences in competition on those two fronts.

Hawtrey *et al.* (1991) also argue that there were special structural changes in 1988 (the reduction in the prime asset ratio and the removal of the obligatory reserve requirement) which should have acted to reduce the interest margin. Valentine (1992), however, also argues that there were factors (e.g. the Bank for International Settlements capital adequacy controls and the high interest rates which prevailed) working in the opposite direction. To complicate matters further, Twrdy (1992) has recalculated margins and finds that they may actually have fallen in the last part of the 1980s.

Finally, we note that there is evidence to suggest that operating costs as a proportion of total assets may have been reduced (Twrdy 1992).

Earlier we listed the potential links between deregulation and financial fragility. Some of these were clearly manifest in Australia between 1983 and 1988. Bank credit and credit in general grew excessively in those years (on average by some 23 per cent a year at a time when broad money grew on average by half as much). The deregulatory environment contributed in a variety of ways to these developments (Argy

1992b). The excess credit in turn went not into spending but into asset purchases which then unleashed the asset inflation in those years. Almost certainly, too, there was some reduction in credit standards. Coinciding with the asset inflation was an overheated economy; it was in fact this combination which prompted the Reserve Bank to tighten monetary policy in the course of 1988. The 'bubble' has since burst leaving some banks exposed to bad loans and lower property prices.

Finally, we noted that there were several potential macro consequences of domestic deregulation. These, however, are difficult to verify directly. It is almost self-evident that the interest elasticity of money demand has fallen (Swamy and Tavlas 1989). Although difficult to verify the hypothesis that interest rates have been destabilised by deregulation, this too is highly likely to have occurred. Many of the transitional 'stresses' noted (the distortion to the money aggregates, the difficulties with monetary policy) were clearly also manifest in Australia (and as well in New Zealand) as we have seen.

Perhaps one of the most important revelations from any analysis of the impacts of deregulation is that *it appears to take considerably longer for its effects to be absorbed into the system than had been suspected.*

Notes

2 THE INTERNATIONAL MONETARY FUND SYSTEM

1 By the end of 1971 the USA had accumulated official liabilities which were more than $4\frac{1}{2}$ times her holdings of gold.

4 THE EUROPEAN MONETARY SYSTEM

1 In July 1963 the Interest Equalisation Tax, designed to discourage portfolio investment by US residents abroad, became effective. Then in March 1965 the US authorities introduced a balance of payments programme (the Voluntary Foreign Credit Restraint Program and the Foreign Direct Investment Program) designed to restrict credit to non-residents and US overseas affiliates.

6 THE MUNDELL–FLEMING MODEL

1 In MF models the trade balance is equal to the current account balance and so these terms can be used interchangeably. This is because the net investment income account is assumed to be unchanged.
2 For purposes of modelling the term money stock is used interchangeably with the cash base (high-powered money). This implicitly assumes a money multiplier of unity.

8 THE MUNDELL–FLEMING MODEL WITH WAGE AND PRICE ADJUSTMENT

1 $Sl = \pi_1(w - p) = \pi_1(w - p_d) - \pi_1(1 - \alpha_{15})(e - p_d)$. A real devaluation will shift the supply of labour function to the left for any given real wage rate $w - p_d$.

9 DISEQUILIBRIUM MODELS OF PRODUCT AND LABOUR MARKETS

1 We note here the 'academic' possibility in an intertemporal context that producers will produce at B and *store* the good.

10 THE PORTFOLIO BALANCE MODEL OF THE MONETARY SECTOR

1 A given percentage change in real wealth will lead to an equal percentage change in the demand for each asset. So, to illustrate for money, we have

$$\frac{\Delta(\text{Mo}/P)}{\text{Mo}/P} = \frac{\Delta(\text{We}/P)}{\text{We}/P}$$

It follows that

$$\frac{\Delta \text{Mo}}{\text{Mo}} = \frac{\Delta \text{We}}{\text{We}}$$

and similarly for the other two assets. In semi-logarithmic form we have

$$\text{mo} - p = a_1 \text{yr} - a_2 r_{\text{d}} - a_3 [r^* - (E_{\text{e}} - E)] + a_4 (\text{we} - p)$$

If $a_4 = 1$, p drops out of the equation.

2 A budget deficit increases wealth and the interest rate. The increase in wealth provokes an outflow while the increase in the interest rate induces an inflow.

11 THE MUNDELL–FLEMING MODEL WITH WEALTH

1 For a refinement on this to take account of Ricardian equivalence, see Chapter 26.

2 α_3 is the direct effect of wealth on expenditure. α_6/α_5 is the effect of wealth on the interest rate; α_2 is the effect of the interest rate on expenditure. Stability requires that the direct positive effect of an increase in wealth on expenditure exceeds the indirect negative effect of an increase in wealth on expenditure (via the interest rate); i.e. that $\alpha_3 > \alpha_2 \alpha_6/\alpha_5$. This parallels the stability condition of the closed economy case (Blinder and Solow 1973). See also the graphical representation later.

3 There will, however, be *transitional* capital flows which have implications for the one-off accumulation of net foreign assets and wealth.

4 In the MF model without wealth the increase in taxes will be

$$\frac{\alpha_5 t}{\alpha_5 [1 - \alpha_1 (1 - t)] + \alpha_2 \alpha_4}$$

and so the budget deficit will be

$$\Delta G - \frac{\alpha_5 t}{\alpha_5 [1 - \alpha_1 (1 - t)] + \alpha_2 \alpha_4} > 0$$

12 THE CLASSICAL ELASTICITIES APPROACH TO A DEVALUATION

1 Initial values of all prices are conveniently set at 1.

2 The solution is slightly different for the balance of trade in foreign currency.

3 If the balance of trade is initially in deficit the condition for an improvement is different depending on whether the balance of trade is measured in domestic or in foreign currency. In foreign currency it can be shown that the condition is

$$(edm - 1) + (M/X)edx$$

This last determines what will happen to reserves in foreign currency and it shows that if $M/X > 1$ the sum of the two demand elasticities may be less than 1 and yet the balance of trade may improve. In domestic currency the sum may need to be greater than 1 for some improvement to occur.

4 It is worth noting that the export supply elasticity has two components to it: a domestic *demand* response and a *production* response (Kreinin 1975). The domestic demand response occurs when the domestic price of the exportable increases and this reduces domestic demand, releasing more of a *given production* to be sold overseas. This is likely to occur fairly quickly whereas the production response takes more time.

13   A TWO-COUNTRY MUNDELL–FLEMING TYPE MODEL

1 How do we generalise the model for regime 2 so as to be able to reach the small country as a special case?

We note first that in each country the change in the money stock is the sum of the domestic assets and its balance of payments, and so

$$\Delta Mo_A = \Delta D_A + B_A$$

$$\Delta Mo_B = \Delta D_B + B_B$$

with $B_A = - B_B$ and

$$\Delta Mo_A + \Delta Mo_B = \Delta D_A + \Delta D_B$$

Dividing though by Mo_{A0} and dropping ΔD_B we can rewrite the last equation as

$$mo_A + \pi mo_B = \overline{mo}_A$$

where π is Mo_B/Mo_A. The small country is then the case where $\pi \to \infty$ and, as well, $b_2 = 0$.

2 See note 1.

18   DYNAMIC EFFECTS OF A MONETARY EXPANSION UNDER FLEXIBLE RATES – THE DORNBUSCH 1976 MODEL

1 Setting

$$\alpha_{30} = k_1 = \frac{\alpha_4 \pi_{12}}{\alpha_{10}} + \alpha_1 \pi_{12} + \frac{\alpha_1 \pi_{12}}{\alpha_{10}\alpha_{30}}$$

yields a quadratic equation in α_{30}.

2 Frenkel and Rodriguez actually drop the interest rate in (19).

19   BRANSON'S PORTFOLIO BALANCE MODEL – MONETARY EXPANSION UNDER FLEXIBLE RATES

1 These can be rewritten as

$$\frac{b_7}{(B/We)(FA/We)} \quad \text{and} \quad \frac{b_{12}}{(FA/We)(B/We + Mo/We)} \qquad b_7 > b_{12}$$

and the denominator is smaller in the former case. To see why this is so, suppose the home interest rate fell by a given amount; the devaluation required to restore equilibrium has to be larger in the bond than in the foreign asset market.

21   AN EXTENDED MUNDELL–FLEMING MODEL WITH J CURVES

1 For simplicity we assume that the *same* coefficient α_1 applies to the short and the long run. α_1 simply switches sign in the long run.
2 It needs to be noted that if the exchange rate did not influence money demand $(1 - \alpha_{15} \to 0)$ a devaluation would unambiguously worsen the trade balance (given that $\alpha_{13} > \alpha_1$). In this model, despite the J curve, a devaluation could conceivably *improve* the trade effects through the 'real balance' effect.

23   MACRO POLICY IMPOTENCE AND THE NEW CLASSICAL PARADIGM

1
$$yr_d = -b_1r_d + b_2gr + b_3u_1$$

$$mo - p_d = b_4yr - b_5r_d$$

$$r_d = \frac{b_4}{b_5}\,yr - \frac{1}{b_5}\,mo + \frac{1}{b_5}\,p_d$$

$$yr_d = -\frac{b_1b_4}{b_5}\,yr + \frac{b_1}{b_5}\,mo - \frac{b_1}{b_5}\,p_d + b_2gr + b_2u_1$$

where α_1 in (1) is $b_1/(b_5 + b_1b_4)$, $\alpha_3 = b_2b_5/(b_5 + b_1b_4)$ and r_d is the interest rate.

24   THE EFFECTS OF ANTICIPATED MONETARY AND FISCAL POLICIES IN A SMALL ECONOMY WITH FLEXIBLE EXCHANGE RATES

1
$$\frac{\Delta e}{\Delta mo} = \frac{\Delta p_d}{\Delta mo} = \frac{1}{1 + \alpha_4}$$

2 The result is strictly ambiguous: output may rise but this appears unlikely.

26   THE RICARDIAN EQUIVALENCE HYPOTHESIS

1 Many of the criticisms levelled at Barro on these issues have been shown in one way or another to be of secondary importance, simply wrong or somewhat unpersuasive. Typical of such criticisms are the following:

a) people are uncertain about the timing of their death;
b) some persons have no children;
c) transfers could be in *either* direction (parents to children or children to parents);
d) future generations might be expected to have higher real incomes and this might weaken the bequest motive.

One criticism, universally conceded to be valid in principle, is the so-called 'corner solution', where 'zero transfers' occur and where parents would have opted, if they could, for making *negative* transfers. Barro dismisses this case as unimportant but Bernheim (1989) contends that there are good reasons for believing that 'a very large number of individuals would in equilibrium ordinarily find themselves at corner solutions ... neither making transfers, nor receiving gifts'.

2 Leiderman and Blejer (1988) mention the default risk, the higher costs of verifying solvency and the higher administrative and transaction costs of administering a loan to the private sector.

3 A related but more contentious criticism is that *uncertainty* about future taxes will be associated with a higher rate of discount applicable to future liabilities (Barro 1989).

4 This is strictly ambiguous but we simplify here.

27 MODELLING GOODS AND MONEY MARKETS

1 The extension to imported investment goods is not made here but can be treated in a parallel fashion.

2 How do J curves appear here? If all components of GNP are deflated by the deflator for national value added (p_d), then the *real* trade balance is

$$X - \frac{MEP^*}{P_d}$$

where $MEP^*/P_d = m$ in (1).

   Given P^* and P_d, it is obvious that with M given a devaluation will *by itself* increase the *value* of imports in domestic currency. However, there is also a *substitution* effect in operation on the *volume* of imports and exports which may offset the valuation effect. See Chapter 12.

28 MODELLING PRODUCTION AND LABOUR MARKETS

1 From (1) we have

$$\frac{\Delta Y}{Y_0} = (1 - \alpha) \frac{\Delta L}{L_0}$$

or

$$\frac{\Delta Y}{\Delta L} = (1 - \alpha) \frac{Y_0}{L_0}$$

The marginal product of labour ($\Delta Y/\Delta L$) is set equal to the real wage rate and so we have

$$\frac{W}{P_d} = (1 - \alpha) \frac{Y}{L}$$

Taking logarithms yields

$$w - p_d = y - 1 + \log(1 - \alpha)$$

We can then solve for y and substitute in (1) to arrive at (2).

2 This is the equation most widely used in the literature. However, it can be shown that in an imperfectly competitive world the real demand for labour will *also* be a positive function of the real aggregate demand for goods. See Attanasio and van der Ploeg (1987) and Bean *et al.* (1987).

29 IMPOSING MEDIUM- TO LONG-RUN CONSTRAINTS ON THE MODEL

1 More precisely, in steady state one country may have a higher rate of inflation than the rest of the world. Its own currency will thus devalue periodically by the excess. The

foreign interest rate will be correspondingly lower but when converted into domestic currency it will equal the home rate.

31 MODELLING EXCHANGE RATES (1)

1 For a description of this balance of payments model see Mussa (1979a), Dornbusch (1980), Argy (1981), Krueger (1983), Frenkel and Mussa (1985).

32 MODELLING EXCHANGE RATES (2)

1 See also Blundell-Wignall (1984) for a more elaborate test of the portfolio balance model.

33 FOREIGN EXCHANGE MARKET EFFICIENCY AND FINANCIAL INTEGRATION – CONCEPTS AND EVIDENCE

1 Equation (4) may not hold because of the existence of a so-called peso problem. Markets could be persistently proved wrong and yet maintain their 'forecasts'. Indeed in some way the longer they are proved wrong the more convinced they will be that the event forecast will eventuate. Gruen and Menzies (1991) have also suggested that costs of changing portfolio shares may also create the appearance of inefficiency.

34 MACRO POLICY TARGETS

1 Inflation uncertainty may divert more effort and resources into forecasting and hence away from 'production'.
2 A variation on this is to say that decision making is made under *uncertainty*. The role of uncertainty in investment decisions and hence on the current account is still an area relatively unexplored. (See on this Molho (1990).)

36 CHOOSING THE EXCHANGE RATE REGIME

1 The absence of profits (or even the making of losses) is in principle consistent with stabilisation of the exchange rate.

Consider the (simplest) case where, in the absence of any speculation, the exchange rate would fluctuate around a constant level. Suppose, too, that information about these fluctuations is available with certainty. We also assume away all transaction costs and assume that interest rate differentials are zero.

In these conditions what would happen without central bank intervention? The answer depends on whether private speculation is competitive or monopolistic. A monopolist would take account of the effects of his own purchases and sales on the price of the currency and would maximise profits at some point between complete exchange rate stability and the original fluctuation. By contrast, competitive speculators would eliminate all profits and produce a fixed exchange rate.

Would there now be any role for central bank intervention? First, if private speculation were competitive central bank intervention to stabilise the exchange rate would be unnecessary. Stabilisation of the exchange rate would have been achieved by private speculators. Second, if private speculation is monopolistic the exchange rate is not completely stabilised, presumably falling short of its optimal level. Now central bank intervention could be justified on the ground that more aggressive intervention by the

central bank could secure the (preferred) perfectly competitive outcome. In this case, however, the central bank would not be making profits even though it was stabilising the exchange rate. An (admittedly unrealistic) extension of this case would have the central bank undertake marginally excessive intervention but in the right direction, generating some losses at the same time that the currency is, nevertheless, stabilised.
2 There is something paradoxical about this consideration. If Europe has very weak real wage flexibility, *neither* exchange rate regime will work. On the other hand, if the USA has substantial real wage flexibility then, at this level at any rate, *either* regime will work. Nonetheless, in this last case, all other things being equal, the fixed rate regime is to be preferred.

37   RULES VERSUS DISCRETION

1 Keynesians, however, also contended that because of the presence of a 'liquidity trap' downward flexible wages would not necessarily restore full employment; but Patinkin (1965) showed that in the presence of a real balance effect this argument was incorrect.
2 For the technical derivation see Turnovsky (1977: 310–11).

38   ASSIGNMENT RULES FOR INTERNAL AND EXTERNAL BALANCE

1 The slope of CA is

$$- \frac{(\alpha_1 + \alpha_4) - \alpha_{13}}{\alpha_3\alpha_5\alpha_{13} + \alpha_3\alpha_{10}}$$

($\pi_8 = 0$; see equation (10)). The slope of YY is

$$- \frac{\alpha_1 + \alpha_4}{\alpha_3\alpha_{10}}$$

($\pi_8 = 0$; see equation (9)).
2 Strictly in the WM approach the target is *domestic demand* which is nominal income less the external balance, but we simplify slightly here in the interest of maintaining a parallel with the BGS approach.
3 It is difficult to see how fiscal policy can control the *growth* of nominal income. It seems more appropriate to suppose that there is a long-run money growth setting which governs the long-run growth in nominal income and the policies proposed would then represent deviations from these long-run paths.

39   THEORETICAL EVALUATION OF ALTERNATIVE SIMPLE POLICY REGIMES

1 Again this is readily seen from equations (10) and (11). If we substitute (12) and (13) and set $\pi_2 = \pi_4 = 0$ and $\pi_3 = \pi_6 = 1$ we have $y_A = y_B = 0$. With y_A and y_B fixed, equations (1), (2), (3), (5) and (7) then solve for p_{dA}, p_{dB}, e, r_A and r_B.
2 Strictly the impact on B is ambiguous but positive transmission is almost certain. A sufficient condition is $\alpha_1 > \alpha_4(1 - \alpha_{15})$.

41   ISSUES RAISED BY NOMINAL INCOME TARGETING

1 Since nominal income equals gross domestic expenditure (absorption) plus the current account, stabilising absorption implies that nominal income will reflect movements in

the current account. For an empirical evaluation of the difference see Pauly and Petersen (1990). See also Argy (1991a).

2 A review of the industrial countries for quarterly GNP data reveals large divergences in information lags. At one end we have Japan and the USA where the delay is about one month in reporting the quarter. In Germany, Italy, Australia and Norway the delay is two to three months; in Austria, Sweden, the UK and France, the delay is five to seven months.

43 THE RISE AND FALL OF MONETARISM

1 Japan's case is somewhat special (see Chapter 47 and later).

2 The Netherlands also adopted money (credit) growth targets but its case is also special and is disregarded here.

3 We note here, however, that in this instance the money demand shock ought to be accommodated to avoid spillovers into interest rates and activity. (See the discussion of Poole's analysis in Chapter 37.) The point here of course is that, if money demand shocks dominate, the money stock ought not to be targeted.

4 Its principal aim was to contain the growth of sterling M3. It laid down certain penalties for banks whose interest-bearing eligible liabilities grew at a rate faster than prescribed. The penalty, which took the form of lodgement of non-interest-bearing deposits with the Bank of England, was progressive, ranging from 5 per cent to 50 per cent depending on the degree of infringement.

45 MACRO POLICY COORDINATION

1 Yet another possibility which we do not explore is the Stackelberg equilibrium, in which one country acts as a leader, setting its own policy in full knowledge of the other country's reaction function.

46 A DECADE OF THATCHERISM: 1979–89 – THATCHERISM AND REAGANOMICS COMPARED

1 The privatisation programme which was also implemented is not analysed here, being outside the scope of this chapter. See on this Johnson (1991: ch. 5).

2 It would be possible to argue that conditions (e.g. inflation convergence) were more favourable to joining the ERM in 1990 than much earlier. (This would not hold for the mid-1980s (1985) when Britain's inflation was within reach of Europe and Britain could have had the 6 per cent margin of flexibility.)

3 The big jump by 1983 was largely accounted for by the recession. Nonetheless, the structural deficit did also increase substantially.

4 In this general context Roberts also makes the intriguing point that in the early stages of Reaganomics there was no significant change in *foreign* capital inflow; what happened was that there was a big fall in US capital outflows, which stayed at home to take advantage of the higher real after-tax returns in the USA.

47 JAPAN'S MACROECONOMIC PERFORMANCE (1960–90)

1 In part because of the oil price shock and in part because of some exhaustion of technological possibilities.

48   MACROECONOMIC POLICY AND THE REGULATORY ENVIRONMENT: THE AUSTRALIAN AND NEW ZEALAND EXPERIENCE 1973–91

1 If the original financial system is relatively primitive (in the sense that there are few sources of funds outside the banking system) and credit rationing is in place, deregulation will weaken rather than strengthen monetary policy. This argument may have had some force in the New Zealand case but much less so in Australia.

References

Able, Stephen L. (1980) 'Inflation uncertainty, investment spending and fiscal policy', *Economic Review, Federal Reserve Bank of Kansas City*, February, 3–13.

Abraham, F. (1985) 'Efficiency, predictability and news on the foreign exchange markets: floating exchange rates versus adjustable E.M.S. rates', *Weltwirtschaftliches Archiv*, 232, 1.

Adams, Charles and Gros, Daniel (1986) 'The consequences of real exchange rate rules for inflation: some illustrative examples', *IMF Staff Papers*, 33, 3, September, 439–76.

Adams, C., Fenton, P.R. and Larsen, F. (1986) 'Differences in employment behavior among industrial countries', *IMF Staff Studies for the World Economic Outlook*, July, 439–76.

Ahtiala, Pekka (1987) 'The effects of foreign disturbances under flexible exchange rates', *Journal of International Money and Finance*, 6, 387–400.

Aiyagari, S. Rao (1990) 'Deflating the case for zero inflation', *Federal Reserve Bank of Minneapolis Quarterly Review*, Summer, 2–11.

Aizenman, Joshua and Frenkel, Jacob A. (1985) 'Optimal wage indexation, foreign exchange intervention and monetary policy', *American Economic Review*, 15, 3, June, 402–23.

—— and —— (1986) 'Supply shocks, wage indexation and monetary accommodation', *Journal of Money Credit and Banking*, 18, 3, August, 304–22.

Akhtar, M.A. and Harris, Ethan S. (1992) 'The supply-side consequences of US fiscal policy in the 1980s', *Federal Reserve Bank of New York Quarterly Review*, Spring, 1–20.

Akhtar, M.A. and Howe, H. (1991) 'The political and institutional independence of US monetary policy', *Banca Nazionale Del Lavoro Quarterly Review*, 178, September, 343–89.

Alesina, Alberto and Summers, Lawrence H. (1990) *Central Bank Independence and Macroeconomic Performance: Some Comparative Evidence*, manuscript, Harvard University, Cambridge, Mass., June.

Allen, P.R. and Kenen, P.B. (1980) *Asset Markets, Exchange Rates, and Economic Integration*, Cambridge: Cambridge University Press.

—— and —— (1983) *Asset Markets and Exchange Rates: Modeling an Open Economy*, New York: Cambridge University Press.

Almekinders, G.J. and Eijffinger, S.C.W. (1991) 'Empirical evidence on foreign exchange market intervention: where do we stand?' *Weltwirtschaftliches Archiv*, 127, 645–77.

Alogoskoufis, George S. (1989) 'Monetary, nominal income and exchange rate targets in a small open economy', *European Economic Review*, 33, 687–705.

Alogoskoufis, George, Papademos, Lucas and Portes, Richard (eds) (1991) *The External Constraint on Macroeconomic Policy: The European Experience*, Cambridge: Cambridge University Press.

Ambler, Steve (1988) 'Fiscal and monetary policy in an open economy with staggered wages', *Weltwirtschaftliches Archiv*, 124, 1, 58–72.

—— (1989) 'The international transmission of policy announcement effects', *Journal of International Money and Finance*, 8, 219–32.

Andersen, P.S. (1989) 'Inflation and output: a review of the wage price mechanism', *Bank for International Settlements (BIS) Economic Papers*, 24, January.

—— (1992) 'OECD country experiences with disinflation', in Adrian Blundell-Wignall (ed.) *Inflation Disinflation and Monetary Policy*, Sydney: Reserve Bank of Australia.

Andrews, M.J., Bell, D.N.F., Fisher, P.G., Wallis, K.F. and Whitley, J.D. (1985) 'Models of the UK economy and the real wage-employment debate', *National Institute Economic Review*, 112, May, 41–52.

Argy, Victor (1981) *The Postwar International Money Crisis: An Analysis*, London: Allen & Unwin.

—— (1982) 'Exchange-rate management in theory and practice', *Princeton Studies in International Finance*, 50, Princeton University, New Jersey, October.

—— (1983) 'Choice of intermediate money target in a deregulated and an integrated economy with flexible exchange rates', *IMF Staff Papers*, 30, 4, December, 727–54.

—— (1987) 'International financial liberalisation – the Australian and Japanese experience compared', *Bank of Japan Monetary and Economic Studies*, 5, 1, May, 105–67.

—— (1990a) 'The transmission of foreign disturbances under different exchange rate regimes', *Journal of Banking and Finance*, 14, 5, November, 929–46.

—— (1990b) 'Choice of exchange rate regime for a smaller economy: a survey of some key issues', in V. Argy and P. de Grauwe (eds) *Choosing an Exchange Rate Regime: The Challenge for Smaller Industrial Countries*, Washington, D.C.: IMF.

—— (1991a) 'Nominal income targeting: a critical evaluation', *IMF Working Paper 91/92*, Washington, D.C.

—— (1991b) 'The design of macro policy in the world economy: proposals for reform', in J.A. Frenkel and M. Goldstein (eds) *International Financial Policy: Essays in Honor of Jacques J. Polak*, Washington, D.C.: IMF.

—— (1992a) 'Announcement effects of anticipated monetary fiscal policies at home and abroad', *Australian Economic Papers*, 31, 58, June, 20–46.

—— (1992b) *Australian Macroeconomic Policy in a Changing World Environment*, Sydney: George Allen & Unwin.

Argy, V. and Kouri, P.J.K. (1974) 'Sterilisation policies and the volatility in international reserves', in R.Z. Aliber (ed.) *National Monetary Policies and the International Financial System*, Chicago, Ill.: University of Chicago Press.

Argy, V. and Murray, G.L. (1985) 'Effects of Sterilising a Balance of Payments Surplus on Domestic Yields – a Formal Analysis', *Journal of International Money and Finance*, 4, 2, June, 223–36.

Argy, V. and Porter, M.G. (1972) 'The forward exchange market and the effects of domestic and external disturbances under alternative exchange rate systems', *IMF Staff Papers*, XIX, November, 503–32.

Argy, V. and Salop, Joan (1979) 'Price and output effects of monetary and fiscal policy under flexible exchange rates', *IMF Staff Papers*, XXVI, 2, June, 224–56.

—— and —— (1983) 'Price and output effects of monetary and fiscal expansion in a two-country world under flexible exchange rates', *Oxford Economic Papers*, 35, 228–46.

Argy, Victor, Brennan, Anthony and Stevens, Glenn (1990) 'Monetary targeting: the international experience', *The Economic Record*, 66, 192, March, 37–62.

Argy, Victor, McKibbin, Warwick and Siefloff, Eric (1989) 'Exchange rate regimes for a small economy in a multi-country world', *Princeton Studies in International Finance*, 67, December.

Artis, Michael J. (1984) *Macroeconomics*, Oxford: Clarendon, ch. 9.

—— (1987) 'The European monetary system: an evaluation', *Journal of Policy Modeling*, 9, 1, Spring, 175–98.

—— (1988) 'How accurate is the World Economics Outlook? A post mortem on short-term forecasting at the IMF', in *IMF Staff Studies for the World Economic Outlook*, Washington, D.C.: IMF, July.

Artus, J.R. (1976) 'Exchange rate stability and managed floating: the experience of the Federal Republic of Germany', *IMF Staff Papers*, 23, July, 312–33.

Artus J.R. and Knight, M.D. (1984) 'Issues in the assessment of the exchange rates of industrial countries', *International Monetary Fund Occasional Paper*, 29, IMF, Washington, D.C.

Asako, Kazumi and Ito, Takatoshi (1991) 'The rise and fall of deficit in Japan (1965–1990)', *Journal of the Japanese and International Economies*, 5, 451–72.

Attanasio, O. and van der Ploeg, F. (1987) 'Real effects of demand- and supply- side policies in interdependent economies', Discussion Paper 282, Centre for Labour Economics, London School of Economics, May.

Attfield, C.L., Demery, D. and Duck, N.W. (1985) *Rational Expectations in Macroeconomics – An Introduction to Theory and Evidence*, Oxford: Basil Blackwell.

Auerbach, Alan J. (1989) 'Après Reagan, le déluge? A review article', *Journal of Monetary Economics*, 24, 2, September, 299–312.

Axilrod, S. and Lindsay, D. (1981) 'Federal Reserve System: Implementation of monetary policy – analytical foundations of the new approach', *American Economic Review*, 71, May, 246–52.

Azariadis, C. (1975) 'Implicit contracts and underemployment equilibria', *Journal of Political Economy*, 83, 6, December, 1183–202.

Backus, D. (1984) 'Empirical models of the exchange rate: separating the wheat from the chaff', *Canadian Journal of Economics*, XVII, 4.

Ball, Laurence, Mankiw, N. Gregory and Romer, David (1988) 'The new Keynesian economics and the output-inflation trade off', *Brookings Papers on Economic Activity*, 1, 1, 65.

Bank for International Settlements (BIS) (1984) *Financial Innovation and Monetary Policy*, CB383 Basle, March.

—— (1986) *Recent Innovations in International Banking*, prepared by a Study Group established by the Central Banks of the G10 countries.

—— (1992) *62nd Annual Report*, June.

Bank of England (1983) 'Intervention stabilisation and profits', *Quarterly Bulletin*, September, 384–90.

Bank of Japan (1988) 'Recent growth of money stock', Research and Statistics Department, Special Paper 161, February.

—— (1990) 'The recent rise in Japan's land prices: its background and implications', Research and Statistics Department, Special Paper 193, December.

—— (1992) 'Recent developments in monetary aggregates', Research and Statistics Department, Special Paper 221, September.

Barro, Robert J. (1974) 'Are government bonds net wealth?', *Journal of Political Economy*, 82, 1095–117.

—— (1977) 'Unanticipated money growth and unemployment', *The US American Economic Review*, 67, 101–15.

—— (1979) 'On the determination of the public debt', *Journal of Political Economy*, 87, 940–71.

—— (1989) 'The Ricardian approach to budget deficits', *Journal of Economic Perspectives*, 3, 2, Spring, 37–54.

Barro, R.J. and Gordon, D.B. (1983) 'Rules discretion and reputation in a model of monetary policy', *Journal of Monetary Economics*, 12, 101–21.

Barro, Robert J. and Grossman, Herschel (1971) 'A general disequilibrium model of income and employment', *American Economic Review*, 61, 1, March, 82–93.

Baumgartner, U. (1977) *Capital Controls in Three European Countries*, Washington, D.C.: IMF, February.

Baumol, W.J. (1961) 'Pitfalls in contracyclical policies: some tools and results', *Review of Economics and Statistics*, 43, 21–6.

Bayoumi, Tamim and Eichengreen, Barry (1992) 'Shocking aspects of European monetary unification', in F. Giavazzi and F. Torres (eds) *The Transition to Economic and Monetary Union in Europe*, Cambridge: Cambridge University Press.

Bean, C.R. (1983) 'Targeting nominal income: an appraisal', *Economic Journal*, 93, 806–19.

—— (1989) 'Capital shortages and persistent unemployment', *Economic Policy*, 8, April, 12–53.

Bean, C.R. and Symons, J. (1990) 'Ten years of Mrs T.', Discussion Paper 370, Centre for Labour Economics, London School of Economics, January.

Bean, C.R., Layard, P.R.G. and Nickell, S.J. (1987) 'The rise in unemployment: a multi-country study', in Charles Bean *et al.* (eds) *The Rise In Unemployment*, Oxford: Basil Blackwell (reprinted from *Economica*, 53 (1986)).

Begg, D.K. (1982) *The Rational Expectations Revolution in Macroeconomics – Theories and Evidence*, (Baltimore, Md:) Johns Hopkins University Press.

Bell, Linda A. (1989) 'Union concessions in the 1980s', *Reserve Bank of New York Quarterly Review*, 14, 2, Summer, 44–58.

Benavie, A. and Froyer, R. (1983) 'Combination monetary policies to stabilise price and output under rational expectations', *Journal of Money, Credit and Banking*, 15, 186–98.

Bergstrand, J.H. (1983) 'Is exchange rate volatility "excessive"?', *New England Economic Review*, September/October, 5–14.

Bernheim, B. Douglas (1989) 'A neoclassical perspective on budget deficits', *Journal of Economic Perspectives*, 3, 2, Spring, 55–72.

Bhagwati, Jagdish (1989) 'The rise of protectionism', *Economic Impact*, 2, 6–12.

Bhandari, Jagdeep S. (1981) 'A theory of exchange rate determination and adjustment', *Weltwirtschaftliches Archiv*, 605–21.

—— (1983) 'Aggregate dynamics in an open economy', *Manchester School of Economic and Social Studies*, 2, June, 129–51.

Bilson, J. (1978) 'The monetary approach to the exchange rate: some empirical evidence', *IMF Staff Papers*, 25, 48–75.

Bisignano, J. and Hoover, K. (1982a) 'Some suggested improvements to a simple portfolio balance model of exchange rate determination with special reference to the US dollar/Canadian dollar rate', *Weltwirtschaftliches Archiv*, 118, 1, 19–38.

—— and —— (1982b) 'Monetary and fiscal impacts on exchange rates', *Federal Reserve Bank of San Francisco Economic Review*, winter.

Black, S.W. (1985) 'Learning from adversity: policy responses to two oil shocks', *Essays in International Finance*, 160, Princeton University, New Jersey, December.

Blanchard, Olivier Jean (1984) 'Current and anticipated deficits, interest rates and economic activity', *European Economic Review*, 25, 7–27.

—— (1987) 'Reaganomics', *Economic Policy: A European Forum*, 5, October, 15–56.

Blanchard, O.J. and Summers, L.H. (1989) 'Hysteresis and the European unemployment problem', in S. Fischer (ed.) *National Bureau of Economic Research (NBER) Macroeconomic Annual*.

Blanchflower, D.G. and Milward, N. (1989) 'Unionization and employment behaviour', Discussion Paper 339, Centre for Labour Economics, London School of Economics, March.

Blanchflower, D.G. and Oswald, A.J. (1986) 'Profit-sharing – can it work?', Discussion Paper 255, Centre for Labour Economics, London School of Economics, October.

Blanchflower, D.G., Oswald, A. and Garrett, M. (1988) 'Insider power in wage determination', Discussion Paper 319, Centre for Labour Economics, London School of Economics, August.

Blinder, A.S. and Solow, R.M. (1973) 'Does fiscal policy matter?' *Journal of Public Economics*, 2, November, 318–37.

—— (1974) *Analytical Foundations of Fiscal Policy in the Economics of Public Finance*, Washington, D.C.: Brookings Institution.

Bloomfield, A. (1959) *Monetary Policy under the International Gold Standard 1880–1914*, Federal Reserve Bank of New York.

Blundell-Wignall, Adrian (1984) 'Exchange rate modelling and the role of asset supplies: the case of the deutschemark effective rate 1973–1981', *The Manchester School of Economic and Social Studies*, 1, March, 14–27.

Blundell-Wignall, Adrian and Browne, Frank (1991) 'Increasing financial market integration, real exchange rates and macro economic adjustment', *OECD Working Paper*, 96, February.

Blundell-Wignall, Adrian and Gregory, Robert G. (1990) 'Exchange rate policy in advanced commodity-exporting countries: Australia and New Zealand', in V. Argy and Paul De Grauwe (eds) *Choosing an Exchange Rate Regime: The Challenge for Smaller Industrial Countries*, Washington, D.C.: IMF.

Bordo, M.D. and Schwartz, A.J. (1983) 'The importance of stable money: theory and evidence', *CATO Journal*, 3, 1, Spring, 63–82.

Boughton, James M. (1979) 'Demand for money in major OECD countries', *OECD Economic Outlook: Occasional Studies*, Paris, January, 35–7.

—— (1988) 'The monetary approach to exchange rates: what now remains?' *Essays in International Finance*, 171, Princeton University, New Jersey, October.

—— (1989) 'Policy assignment strategies with somewhat flexible exchange rates', in Marcus Miller, Barry Eichengreen, Richard Portes (eds) *Blueprints for Exchange Rate Management*, London: Academic Press.

—— (1991) 'The role of policy assignment and cooperation in intermediate exchange rate regimes', in H.J. Blommestein (ed.) *The Reality of International Economic Policy Coordination*, Paris: OECD, ch. 9, 199–220.

Bovenberg, A.L., Kremers, J.J.M. and Masson, P.R. (1991) 'Economic and monetary union in Europe and constraints on national budgetary policies', *IMF Staff Papers*, 38, 2, June, 374–98.

Boyer, R.S. (1977) 'Devaluation and portfolio balance', *American Economic Review*, 67, 54–63.

Brainard, W. (1967) 'Uncertainty and the effectiveness of policy', *American Economic Review*, Proceedings 57, 411–25.

Branson, William H. (1977) 'Asset markets and relative prices in exchange rate determination', *Sozialwissenschaftliche Annalen des Instituts für Höhere Studien*, Reihe A, 1, 69–89 (reprinted in *Princeton University International Finance* 20 (1980)).

—— (1985) 'Causes of appreciation and volatility of the dollar', Reprint 785, NBER (National Bureau of Economic Research), in *The US $ – Recent Developments Outlook and Policy Options*, Federal Reserve Bank of Kansas City.

—— (1988) 'International adjustment and the dollar: Policy illusions and economic constraints, proceedings of an international seminar held in Hamburg', *Economic Policy Coordination*, IMF, Hamburg Institut für Wirtschaftsforschung.

Branson, William H. and Buiter, Willem H. (1983) 'Monetary and Fiscal Policy with Flexible Exchange Rates', in J.S. Bhandari and B.H. Putman (eds) *Economic Interdependence and Flexible Exchange Rates*, Cambridge, Mass.: MIT Press.

Branson, W.H. and Henderson, D.W. (1985) 'The specification and influence of asset markets', in R.W. Jones and P.B. Kenen (eds) *Handbook of International Economics*, II, Amsterdam: North-Holland.

Branson, W.H. and Hill, R. (1971) 'Capital movements in the OECD area: an econometric analysis', *OECD Occasional Studies*, December.

Branson, W. and Rotemberg, J. (1980) 'International adjustment with wage rigidity', *European Economic Review*, 13, 309–32.

Branson, W.H., Halttunen, H. and Masson, P. (1977) 'Exchange rates in the short run: the dollar deutsche mark rate', *European Economic Review*, 10, 303–24.

Branson, William H., Fraga, Arminio and Johnson, Robert A. (1985) 'Expected fiscal policy and the recession of 1982', *International Finance Discussion Papers*, 272, December.

Brittan, Samuel (1992) 'Economic viewpoint', *Financial Times*, January 23.

Brown, W.A. (1940) *The International Gold Standard Reinterpreted: 1914–1934*, 2 vols, Washington, D.C.: National Bureau of Economic Research.

Brown, W. and Wadhwani, S (1990) 'The economic effects of industrial relations legislation since 1979', Discussion Paper 376, Centre for Labour Economics, London School of Economics, March.

Brunello, G. (1989a) 'Hysteresis and "The Japanese unemployment problem": a preliminary investigation', Discussion Paper 330, Centre for Labour Economics, London School of Economics, January.

—— (1989b) 'Bonuses, wages and performance in Japan: evidence from micro data', Discussion Paper 359, Centre for Labour Economics, London School of Economics, September.

Brunello, G. and Wadhwani, S. (1989) 'The determinants of wage flexibility in Japan: some lessons from a comparison with the UK using micro-data', Discussion Paper 362, Centre for Labour Economics, London School of Economics, October.

Brunner, Karl (1986) 'Fiscal policy in macro theory: a survey and evaluation', in R.W. Hafer (ed.) *The Monetary vs Fiscal Policy Debate*, Rowan and Allanheld.

Bruno, Michael (1986) 'Aggregate supply and demand factors in OECD unemployment: an update', in Bean *et al.* (eds) *The Rise in Unemployment*, Oxford: Basil Blackwell (reprinted from *Economica* Supplement (1986)).

Bruno, Michael and Sachs, Jeffrey (1985) *The Economics of Worldwide Stagflation*, Oxford: Basil Blackwell.

Bryant, Ralph C. (1980) *Money and Monetary Policy in Interdependent Nations*, Washington, D.C.: Brookings Institution.

—— (1987) *International Financial Intermediation: Issues for Analysis and Public Policy*, (Washington, D.C.:) Brookings Institution.

—— (1988) 'Macroeconomic interactions between the United States and Japan: an interim report on the empirical evidence', *Brookings Discussion Papers in International Economics*, 67, Brookings Institution, Washington, D.C., December, 67.

—— (1991) 'Model representations of Japanese monetary policy', *Bank of Japan Monetary and Economic Studies*, 9, 2, September.

Bryant, Ralph C., Helliwell, John and Hooper, Peter (1989) 'Domestic and cross-border consequences of US macroeconomic policies', *Brookings Discussion Papers in International Economics*, 68, Brookings Institution, Washington, D.C., January.

Buiter, Willem H. (1986) 'Macroeconomic policy design in an interdependent world economy: an analysis of three contingencies', *IMF Staff Papers*, 33, September, 541–82.

Buiter, Willem H. and Kletzer, Kenneth (1992) 'Who's afraid of the public debt?', *The American Economic Review*, 82, 2, May, 290–4.

Burda, Michael (1988) 'Wait unemployment', *Economic Policy*, 7, October, 391–426.

Calmfors, Lars and Driffill, John (1988) 'Bargaining structure, corporatism and macroeconomic performance', *Economic Policy*, 6, April, 13–62.

Calmfors, Lars and Forslund, Anders (1989) 'Wage setting in Sweden', *Institute for International Economic Studies*, Seminar Paper No. 430, January.

Calmfors, Lars and Nymoen, Ragnar (1990) 'Real wage adjustment and employment policies in the nordic countries', *Economic Policy*, 11, October, 398–447.

Canzoneri, Matthew B. (1985) 'Monetary policy games and the role of private information', *American Economic Review*, 75, 1056–70.

Canzoneri, Matthew B. and Gray, J. (1985) 'Monetary policy games and the consequences of non-cooperative behavior', *International Economic Review*, 26, 3, 547–64.

Canzoneri, Matthew B. and Minford, Patrick (1986) 'When international policy coordination matters: an empirical analysis', *CEPR Working Papers*, 119, London.

Carey, D.A. and Duggan, K.G. (1986) 'The abolition of exchange controls: financial policy reform', *Reserve Bank of New Zealand*, New Zealand.

Carmichael, Jeffrey (1990) 'Inflation: performance and policy', in S. Grenville (ed.) *The Australian Macro-Economy in the 1980s*, Sydney: Reserve Bank of Australia.

Carmichael, Jeffrey, Fahrer, Jerome and Hawkins, John (1985) 'Macroeconomic implications of wage indexation: a survey', in V. Argy and J. Nevile (eds) *Inflation and Unemployment*, London: Allen & Unwin.

Casas, Francisco R. (1977) 'Capital mobility and stabilization policy under flexible exchange rates: a revised analysis', *Southern Economic Journal*, 43, April, 1528–37.

Catte, Pietro, Galli, Giamparlo and Rebecchini, Salvatore (1992) 'Exchange rates can be managed', *International Economic Insights*, September/October, 17–21.

Chadha, Bankim, Masson, Paul and Meredith, Guy (1991) 'Models of inflation and the costs of disinflation', *IMF Working Paper*, 91/97.

Christodoulakis, Nicos M., Gaines, Jessica and Levine, Paul (1991) 'Macroeconomic policy using large econometric rational expectations models: methodology and application', *Oxford Economic Papers*, 43, 1, January, 25–58.

Claasen, S.Z.D. (1992) 'The woolly-headed thinking born of complacency', *Guardian Weekly*, 27 September.

Clements, K. W. (1979) 'Commentaries and discussion', in W.E. Norton and I.W. Little (eds) *Conference in Applied Economic Research*, Sydney: Reserve Bank of Australia, December, 164–6.

Clinton, Kevin and Chouraqui, Jean-Claude (1987) 'Monetary policy in the second half of the 1980s: How much room for manoeuvre?', *Department of Economics and Statistics Working Papers*, 39, OECD, Paris, February.

Coe, D.T. (1990) 'Structural determinants of the natural rate of unemployment in Canada', *IMF Staff Papers*, 37, 1, March, 94–115.

Coe, D. T. and Gagliardi, F. (1985) 'Nominal wage determination in ten OECD countries', *OECD Economics and Statistics Department Working Papers*, 19, OECD, Paris.

Coen, R.M. and Hickman, B.G. (1987) 'Keynesian and classical unemployment in four countries', *Brookings Papers on Economic Activity*, 1, 123–93.

Cohen, Stephen D. (1991) *Cowboys and Samurai*, New York: Harper Business.

Collins, Susan M. (1988) 'Inflation and the European Monetary System', in F. Giavazzi, S. Micossi and M. Miller (eds) *The European Monetary System*, Cambridge: Cambridge University Press.

Cooper, J.P. and Fischer, S. (1972) 'Simulation of monetary rules in the FRB-MIT-Penn model', *Journal of Money, Credit and Banking*, 4, May, 384–96.

Cooper, R. (1968) *The Economics of Interdependence*, New York: McGraw-Hill.

—— (1969) 'Macroeconomic policy adjustment in interdependent economies', *Quarterly Journal of Economics*, 83, 1–24.

—— (1984) 'A monetary system for the future', in *Foreign Affairs*, (reprinted in *The International Monetary System* (1987), Cambridge: MIT Press).

—— (1990) 'What future for the International Monetary System', in Y. Suzuki, J. Mayake and M. Okabe (eds) *The Evolution of the International Monetary System – How Can Efficiency and Stability be Attained*, Tokyo: University of Tokyo Press.

Corden, Max (1977) *Inflation, Exchange Rates and the World Economy*, Oxford: Oxford University Press, ch. 1–3.

—— (1981) 'Comments on monetary targets', in Brian Griffiths and Geoffrey Wood (eds) *Monetary Targets*, London: Macmillan.

—— (1991) 'Does the current account matter? The old and the new view', in J.A. Frenkel and M. Goldstein (eds) *International Financial Policy: Essays in Honor of Jacques J. Polak*, Washington, D.C.: IMF.

Corker, Robert (1991) 'The changing nature of Japanese trade', *Finance and Development*, 28, 2, June, 6–9.

Cornell, W.B. and Dietrich, J.K. (1978) 'The efficiency of the market for foreign exchange under floating exchange rate', *Review of Economics and Statistics*, 60, 111–20.

Cotis, Jean-Philippe (1988) 'Fund staff study finds evidence of "Hysteresis" in Europe', *IMF Survey*, August.

Craine, R., Havenner, A. and Berry, J. (1978) 'Fixed rules vs activism in the conduct of monetary policy', *The American Economic Review*, 68, 5, December, 769–83.

Cuddington, J.T. (1980) 'Fiscal and exchange rate policies in a fix-price trade model with export rationing', *Journal of International Economics*, 10, 319–40.

Cuddington, J.T., Johansson, P. and Lofgren, K. (1984) *Disequilibrium Macroeconomics in Open Economies*, Oxford: Basil Blackwell.

Currie, David and Wren-Lewis, Simon (1989) 'Evaluating blueprints for the conduct of international macro policy', *American Economic Association Papers and Proceedings*, 79, 2, May, 264–69.

—— and —— (1990) 'Evaluating the extended target zone proposal for the G3', *Economic Journal*, 100, 399, March, 105–23.

Dean, Andrew and Koromzay, Val (1987) 'Current account imbalances and adjustment mechanisms', *OECD Economic Studies*, 8, Spring, 7–34.

De Grauwe, Paul (1988) 'Exchange rate variability and the slowdown in growth of international trade', *IMF Staff Papers*, 35, 1, March, 63–84.

Devereaux, M. and Wilson, T.A. (1989) 'International co-ordination of macroeconomic policies: a review', *Canadian Public Analyse de Policy Politiques*, XV, February, 20–33.

Dobson, Wendy (1991) 'Economic policy coordination: requiem or prologue?', *Institute for International Economics*, 30, April.

Dooley, M.P. and Shafer, J.R. (1983) 'Analysis of short-run exchange rate behavior: March 1973 to November 1931', in D. Bigman and T. Taya (eds) *Exchange Rate and Trade Instability*, Cambridge, Mass.: Ballinger.

Dooley, M.P., Frankel, J. and Mathieson, D.J. (1987) 'International capital mobility: what do saving-investment correlations tell us?', *IMF Staff Papers*, 34, 3, September, 503–30.

Dornbusch, Rudiger (1975) 'Alternative price stabilisation rules and the effects of exchange rate changes, *Manchester School of Economic and Social Studies*, September, 275–92.

—— (1976) 'Expectations and exchange rate dynamics', *Journal of Political Economy*, 84, 6, 1161–76.

—— (1980) 'Exchange rate economics: where do we stand?', *Brookings Papers on Economic Activity*, 1, 145–85.

—— (1982a) 'Equilibrium and disequilibrium exchange rates', *Zeitschrift Fur Wirtschafts – Und Sozialwissenschaften*, 102, 573–99.

—— (1982b) 'PPP Exchange-rate rules and macroeconomic stability', *Journal of Political Economy*, 90, 1, February, 158–65.

—— (1983) 'Flexible exchange rates and interdependence', *IMF Staff Papers*, 30, 3–30.

—— (1988) 'The European monetary system, the dollar and the yen', in F. Giavazzi and S. Micossi (eds) *The European Monetary System*, Cambridge: Cambridge University Press.

—— (1989a) 'Credibility, debt and unemployment: Ireland's failed stabilization', *Economic Policy*, 8, April, 173–210.

—— (1989b) 'International payments imbalances in the 1980s', *Federal Reserve Bank of Boston Conference Series*, 32.

Dornbusch, R. and Fischer, S. (1980) 'Exchange rates and the current account', *The American Economic Review*, 70, 5, December, 960–71.

—— (1990) *Macroeconomics*, New York: McGraw-Hill.

Dornbusch, R. and Krugman, P. (1976) 'Flexible exchange rates in the short run', *Brookings Papers on Economic Activity*, 3rd quarter, 537–75.

Dotsey, M. and King, R. (1983) 'Monetary instruments and policy rules in a rational expectations environment', *Journal of Monetary Economics*, 12, 357–82.

Driskill, R.A. (1981) 'Exchange rate dynamics: an empirical investigation', *Journal of Political Economy*, 89, 2, 357–71.

Duguay, P. and Poloz, S. (1991) 'The orientation of monetary policy and the monetary policy decision-making process in Switzerland', *The Orientation of Monetary Policy and the Monetary Policy Decision-Making Process*, Bank for International Settlements (BIS), Basle, 390, April, 191–200.

Dunn, R.M. (1983) 'The many disappointments of flexible exchange rates', *Essays in International Finance*, 154, New Jersey: Princeton University Press.

Eberts, Randall W. and Groshen, Erica L. (1992) 'The causes and consequences of structural changes in US labor markets: a review', *Economic Review*, 28, 1, quarter 1.

Edison, Hali J. (1990) 'Foreign currency operations: an annotated bibliography', *International Finance Discussion Papers*, 380, May.

Edison, H.J., Marquez, J.R. and Tryon, R.W. (1986) 'The structure and properties of the FRB multicountry model; part 1: model description and simulation results', *International Finance Discussion Papers*, October, 293.

Edison, H.J., Miller, M.H. and Williamson, J. (1987) 'On evaluating and extending the target zone proposal', *Journal of Policy Modelling*, 9, Spring, 199–224.

Edwards, S. (1983) 'Floating exchange rates, expectations and new information', *Journal of monetary economics*, 11, 321–36.

Egebo, Thomas and Englander, A. Steven (1992) 'Institutional commitments and policy credibility: a critical survey and empirical evidence from the ERM', *OECD Economic Studies*, 18, Spring, 46–82.

Eichengreen, Barry (1990) 'One money for Europe? Lessons from the US Currency Union', *Economic Policy – A European Forum*, 10, April, 118–66.

Eisner, R. (1969) 'Fiscal and monetary policy reconsidered', *American Economic Review*, 59, 897–905.

Emerson, Michael (with Andre Dramais) (1988) *What model for Europe*? Boston, Mass.: MIT Press.

Emerson, Michael and Huhne, Christopher (1991) *The ECU Report – The Single Currency and What It Means to You*, London: Pan Books.

Estrin, Saul, Grout, Paul and Wadhwani, Sushil (1987) 'Profit-sharing and employee share ownership', *Economic Policy*, 4, April, 14–62.

Feldstein, Martin S. (1979) 'The welfare cost of permanent inflation and optimal short-run economic policy', *Journal of Political Economy*, 87, 4, August, 749–67.

—— (1983) 'Domestic saving and international capital movements in the long run and the short run', *European Economic Review* (Amsterdam), 21, March–April, 129–51.

—— (1988) 'Rethinking international economic coordination', *Oxford Economic Papers*, 40, 205–19.

—— (1992) 'The case against EMU', *The Economist*, 13 June.

Feldstein, Martin and Horioka, Charles (1980) 'Domestic saving and international capital flows', *Economic Journal* (London), 90, June, 314–29.

Fieleke, Norman S. (1990) 'The United States in debt', *New England Economic Review*, September–October, 34–54.

Fischer, Stanley F. (1977a) 'Wage indexation and macroeconomic stability', in K. Brunner and A. Meltzer (eds) *Stabilization of the Domestic and International Economy*, 5, Carnegie-Rochester Conference Series on Public Policy, Amsterdam: North-Holland.

—— (1977b) 'Long term contracts, rational expectations and the optimal money supply rule', *Journal of Political Economy*, 85, 191–205.

—— (1986) 'Exchange rate versus money targets in disinflation', in S. Fisher (ed.) *Indexing, Inflation and Economic Policy*, Cambridge: MIT Press.

—— (1987a) 'International macroeconomic policy coordination', *NBER Working Paper Series*, 2244.

—— (1987b) 'Monetary policy and performance in the U.S., Japan, and Europe, 1973–86', in Y. Suzuki and M. Okabe, (eds) *Toward a World Economic Stability*, Tokyo: University of Tokyo Press.

—— (1988a) 'Real balances, the exchange rate and indexation: real variables in disinflation', *The Quarterly Journal of Economics*, February, 27–49.

—— (1988b) 'Rules versus discretion in monetary policy', *National Bureau of Economic Research Working Paper Series*, 2418, Cambridge, Mass.: NBER, February.

Fischer, S. and Cooper, J.P. (1973) 'Stabilization policy and lags', *Journal of Political Economy*, 81, 847–77.

Fischer, Stanley F. and Modigliani, Franco (1978) 'Towards an understanding of the real effects and costs of inflation', *Weltwirtschaftliches Archiv*, 114, 811–33.

Flanagan, Robert J. (1987) 'Labour market behavior and European economic growth', in Robert Z. Lawrence and Charles L. Schultze (eds) *Barriers to European Growth: A Transatlantic View*, Washington, D.C.: Brookings Institute.

—— (1992) 'Wages and wage policies in market economies: lessons for Central and Eastern Europe', *OECD Economic Studies*, 18, Spring, 106–31.

Fleming, J.M. (1962) 'Domestic financial policies under fixed and under flexible exchange rates', *IMF Staff Papers*, IX, November, 369–80.

Flood, Robert P. and Isard, Peter (1989) 'The impact of macroeconomic policies on the level of taxation and the fiscal balance in developing countries', *IMF Staff Papers*, 36, 3, September, 612–32.

Flood, Robert P. and Marion, N.P. (1982) 'The transmission of disturbances under alternative exchange-rate regimes with optimal indexing', *Quarterly Journal of Economics*, February, 43–66.

Ford, A.G. (1962) *The Gold Standard 1880–1914 – Britain and Argentina*, Oxford: Oxford University Press.

Frankel, Jeffrey A. (1979) 'On the mark: a theory of floating exchange rates based on real interest differentials', *The American Economic Review*, 69, September, 610–22.

—— (1984) 'The yen/dollar agreement: liberalizing Japanese capital markets', *Policy Analyses in International Economics*, 9, Institute for International Economics, Washington, D.C., December.

—— (1988a) 'Obstacles to international macroeconomic policy coordination', *Princeton Studies in International Finance*, 64, Princeton University, December.

—— (1988b) 'International capital mobility and exchange rate volatility', in Norman S. Fieleke (ed.) *International Payments Imbalances in the 1980s*, Conference Series No. 32, Boston: Federal Reserve Bank of Boston.

—— (1989) 'An analysis of the proposal for international nominal income targeting', manuscript.

—— (1991) 'Quantifying international capital mobility in the 1980s', in B.D. Bernheim and J.B. Shoven (eds) *National Saving and Economic Performance*, Chicago, Il: University of Chicago Press.

Frankel, J.A. and Chinn, M. (1991) 'The stabilizing properties of a nominal GNP rule in an open economy', manuscript, Department of Economics, University of California, Berkeley.

Frankel, Jeffrey A. and Rockett, Katharine E. (1988) 'International macroeconomic policy coordination when policymakers do not agree on the true model', *American Economic Review*, 78, June, 318–40.

Frenkel, Jacob A. (1976) 'A monetary approach to the exchange rate: doctrinal aspects and empirical evidence', *Scandinavian Journal of Economics*, 78, 200–24.

—— (1981) 'Flexible exchange rates, prices, and the role of news: lessons from the 1970s', *Journal of Political Economy*, 89, 4, August, 665–705.

Frenkel, Jacob A. and Goldstein, Morris (1986) 'A guide to target zones', *IMF Staff Papers*, 33, December, 633–70.

—— and —— (1988) 'Exchange rate volatility and misalignment: evaluating some proposals for reform', in *Financial Market Volatility*, Kansas City: Federal Reserve Bank of Kansas City.

—— and —— (1991) 'Monetary policy in an emerging European economic and monetary union', *IMF Staff Papers*, 28, 2, June, 356–73.

Frenkel, J.A. and Mussa, M.L. (1985) 'Asset markets, exchange rates and the balance of payments', in R. Jones and P. Kenen (eds) *Handbook of International Economics*, Amsterdam: North-Holland.

Frenkel, Jacob A. and Razin, Assaf (1987) 'The Mundell Fleming model; a quarter century later: a unified exposition', *IMF Staff Papers*, 34, December, 567–620.

Frenkel, J.A. and Rodriguez, C.A. (1982) 'Exchange rate dynamics and the overshooting hypothesis', *IMF Staff Papers*, 29, 1, March, 1–30.

Frenkel, Jacob A., Goldstein, Morris and Masson, Paul R. (1988) 'International coordination of economic policies: scope, methods and effects', in Wilfried Guth (ed.) *Economic Policy Coordination*, Washington, D.C.: IMF.

—— and —— (1989) 'Simulating the effects of some simple coordinated versus uncoordinated policy', in R.C. Bryant, D.A. Currie, J.A. Frenkel, P.R. Masson and R. Portes (eds) *Macroeconomic Policies in an Interdependent World*, Washington, D.C.: Brookings Institution; London: Centre for Economic Policy Research; Washington, D.C.: IMF.

Friedman, Benjamin M. (1988) *Day of Reckoning*, New York: Random House.

Friedman, Milton (1953a) 'The case for flexible exchange rates', in *Essays in Positive Economics*, Chicago, Ill.: University of Chicago Press.

—— (1953b) 'The effects of a full-employment policy on economic stability: a formal analysis', in *Essays in Positive Economics*, Chicago, Ill.: University of Chicago Press.

—— (1959) 'A program for monetary stability', *The Millar Lectures*, New York: Fordham University Press.

—— (1968) 'The role of monetary policy', *American Economic Review*, 58, 1–17.

—— (1969a) 'The optimal supply of money' in *The Optimal Supply of Money and Other Essays*, Chicago, Ill.: Aldine Publishing.

—— (1969b) 'The lag in effect of monetary policy' in *The Optimal Supply of Money and Other Essays*, Chicago, Ill.: Aldine Publishing.

—— (1970) 'Comments on the critics: a theoretical framework for monetary analysis', *Journal of Political Economy*, 78, March–April, 193–238.

—— (1977) 'Nobel lecture, inflation and unemployment', *Journal of Political Economy*, 85, 3, June, 451–72.

—— (1978) 'Back to the gaming table', *Newsweek*, 30 January.

—— (1983) 'Less red ink', *The Atlantic*, February.

Friedman, M. and Meiselman, D. (1963) 'The relative stability of monetary velocity and the investment multiplier in the US, 1897–1958', *Stabilization Policies* – a series of studies prepared for the commission on money and credit, Englewood Cliffs, N.J.: Prentice Hall.

Friedman, M. and Schwartz, A.J. (1963) *A Monetary History of the United States 1867–1960*, Princeton, N.J.: Princeton University Press.

Froot, K.A. and Frankel, J.A. (1989) 'Forward discount bias: is it an exchange risk premium?', *Quarterly Journal of Economics*, CIV, February, 139–61.

Fukao, Mitsuhiro (1990) 'Liberalization of Japan's foreign exchange controls and structural changes in the balance of payments', *Bank of Japan, Monetary and Economic Studies*, 8, 2, September, 101–65.

Funabashi, Y. (1988) 'Managing the dollar: from the Plaza to the Louvre', *Institute for International Economics*, Washington, D.C.

Gardner, R. (1975) 'Bretton Woods', in M. Keynes (ed.) *Essays on J. M. Keynes*, Cambridge: Cambridge University Press.

Genberg, Hans and Swoboda, Alexander K. (1989) 'Policy and current account determination under floating exchange rates', *IMF Staff Papers*, 36, 1, March, 1–30.

—— and —— (1991) 'The current account and the policy mix under flexible exchange rates', in Jacob A. Frenkel and M. Goldstein (eds) *International Financial Policy: Essays in Honor of Jacques J. Polak*, Washington, D.C.: IMF.

Ghosh, Atish R. (1992) 'Is it signalling? Exchange intervention and the dollar–Deutschemark rate', *Journal of International Economics*, 32, 201–20.

Ghosh, Atish R. and Masson, Paul R. (1988) 'International policy coordination in a world with model uncertainty', *IMF Staff Papers*, 35, 2, June, 230–58.

Giersch, Herbert (1987) 'Eurosclerosis – what is the cure?', *European Affairs*, 4, winter, 33–43.

Giovannetti, Giorgia (1992) 'A survey of recent empirical tests of the purchasing power parity hypothesis', *Banca Nazionale de Lavoro Quarterly Review*, 180, March, 81–101.

Giovannini, Alberto (1990) 'The Transition to European Monetary Union', *Essays in International Finance*, 178, Princeton, N.J.: Princeton University, November.

Glick, Reuven (1988) 'Saving-investment determinants of Japan's external balance', *Economic Review Federal Reserve Bank of San Francisco*, 3, Summer, 3–14.

Glick, Reuven and Hutchison, Michael (1990) 'New results in support of the fiscal policy ineffectiveness proposition', *Journal of Money, Credit and Banking*, 22, 3, 288–304.

Goodhart, Charles, (1990) 'Economists' perspectives on the EMS', *Journal of Monetary Economics*, 26, 3, December, 471–87.

Goodman, S. (1981) 'Technical analysis still beats econometrics', *Euromoney*, August, 48–60.

Gordon, Jenny (1991) 'Depreciation: an analysis', in G. Hooke and R. Reilly (eds) *Macroeconomic Policy*, Sydney: Allen & Unwin.

Gordon, Robert J. (1978) 'What can stabilization policy achieve?', *American Economic Review*, American Economic Association Papers and Proceedings, 68, 2, May, 335–41.

—— (1985) 'The conduct of domestic monetary policy', in A. Ando *et al.* (eds) *Monetary Policy in our times*, Cambridge Mass.: MIT Press.

—— (1988) 'Back to the future: European unemployment today viewed from America in 1939', *Brookings Papers on Economic Activity*, 1, 271–304.

—— (1989) 'Hysteresis in history: was there ever a Phillips Curve?', *The American Economic Review*, 79, 2, May, 220–5.

—— (1990) 'What is New-Keynesian economics?', *Journal of Economic Literature*, XXVIII, September, 1115–71.

Gray, J.A. (1976) 'Wage-indexation: a macroeconomic approach', *Journal of Monetary Economics*, 2, 221–35.

Gros, Daniel, and Thygesen, Niels (1988) 'The EMS – achievements, current issues and directions for the future,' *Centre for European Policy Studies (CEPS) Paper*, 35, March.

Gruen, David and Menzies, Gordon (1991) 'The failure of uncovered interest parity: is it near-rationality in the foreign exchange market?', Research Discussion Paper RDP9103, Reserve Bank of Australia.

Guidotti, Pablo E. (1988) 'Insulation properties under dual exchange rates', *Canadian Journal of Economics*, 21, 4, November, 799–813.

Guitian, Manuel (1988) 'The European Monetary System: a balance between rules and discretion', in *Policy Coordination in the European Monetary System*, IMF Occasional Paper 61, September.

Haan, Jacob de and Sturm, Jan Edbert (1992) 'The case for central bank independence', *Banca Nazionale del Lavoro Quarterly Review*, 182, September, 305–24.

Haas, R.D. and Alexander, W.E. (1979) 'A model of exchange rates and capital flows: the Canadian floating rate experience', *Journal of money, credit and banking*, XI, November, 467–82.

Haas, Richard D. and Masson, Paul (1986) 'Minimod: specification and simulation results', *IMF Staff Papers*, 33, 4, December, 722–67.

Hamada, K. (1974) 'Alternative exchange rate systems and the interdependence of monetary policies', in R. Aliber (ed.) *National Monetary Policies and the International System*, Chicago, Ill: University of Chicago Press.

—— (1976) 'A strategic analysis of monetary interdependence', *Journal of Political Economy*, 84, August, 677–700.

—— (1979) 'Macroeconomic strategy and coordination under alternative exchange rates', in Dornbusch and Frenkel (eds) *International Economic Policy: Theory and Evidence*, 292–324.

—— (1985) 'Lessons from the macroeconomic performance of the Japanese economy', in Victor Argy and John Nevile (eds) *Inflation and Unemployment Theory, Experience and Policy Making*, London: Allen & Unwin.

Hamada, K. and Kurosaka, Y. (1987) 'Trends in unemployment, wages and productivity: the case of Japan', in C. Bean, R. Layard and S. Nickell (eds) *The Rise in Unemployment*, Oxford: Basil Blackwell.

Hansen, Bent (1951) *A Study in the Theory of Inflation*, London: Allen & Unwin.

Hansen, L.P. and Hodrick, R.J. (1980) 'Forward exchange rates as optimal predictors of future spot rates: an econometric analysis', *Journal of Political Economy*, 88, 5, October, 829–53.

Hardouvelis, Gikas (1988) 'Evidence on stock market speculative bubbles: Japan, the US and Great Britain', *Reserve Bank of N.Y. Quarterly Review*, summer, 4–16.

Harper, Ian R. (1991) 'Bank deregulation in Australia: choice and diversity, gainers and losers', prepared for the Reserve Bank of Australia Conference on Deregulation of Financial Intermediaries, Sydney, May.

Hawtrey, Kim, Favotto, Ivo and Gilchrist, David (1991) 'The impact of bank deregulation on Australian manufacturers', *Economic Papers*, Economic Society of Australia, 10, 4, December, 10–29.

Hawtrey, R.G. (1931) *The Gold Standard in Theory and Practice*, London: Longman.

Haynes, Stephen, Hutchison, Michael and Mikesell, Raymond (1986) 'Japanese Financial Policies and the U.S. Trade Deficit', *Essays in International Finance*, Princeton University, New Jersey, April.

Healey, Nigel and Strobel, Frederick (1990) 'The "productivity miracle" of the Reagan–Thatcher years in perspective', *Banca Nazionale del Lavoro Quarterly Review*, 175, December, 413–30.

Heller, Peter S., Haas, Richard D. and Mansur, Ahsan S. (1986) 'A review of the fiscal impulse measure', IMF Occasional Paper 44, May.

Helliwell, John F. (1969) 'Monetary and fiscal policies for an open economy', *Oxford Economic Papers*, XXI, March, 35–55.

—— (1988) 'Comparative macroeconomics of stagflation', *Journal of Economic Literature*, XXVI, March, 1–28.

Henry, S.G.B. and Ormerod, P.A. (1978) 'Incomes policy and wage inflation: empirical evidence for the U.K. 1961–1977', *National Institute Economic Review*, 85, August, 31–9.

Hildebrandt, Paula (1991) 'The Path to European Monetary Union', *Economic Review Federal Reserve Bank of Kansas City*, March–April, 35–48.

Hirst, Paul (1989) *After Thatcher*, London: Collins.

Hodgson, J. (1972) 'An analysis of floating exchange rates: the dollar–sterling rate 1919–1925', *Southern Economic Journal*, 39, October, 249–57.

Hodjera, Z. (1973) 'International short-term capital movements: a survey of theory and empirical analysis', *International Monetary Fund Staff Papers*, XX, November, 683–740.

Hoeller, P. and Poret, P. (1991) 'Is P-star a good indicator of inflationary pressure in OECD countries?' *OECD Economic Studies*, 17, Autumn.

Hoffman, D.L. and Schlagenhauf, D.E. (1983) 'Rational expectations and monetary models of exchange rate determination', *Journal of Monetary Economics*, 11, March, 247–60.

Holland, A. Steven (1984) 'Does higher inflation lead to more uncertain inflation?', *Review*, The Federal Reserve Bank of St Louis, 66, 2, 15–26.

Hooper, Peter and Mann, Catherine L. (1989) 'The emergence and persistence of the U.S. external imbalance, 1980–87', *Princeton Studies in International Finance*, Princeton University, New Jersey, 65, October.

Hooper, Peter and Morton, J. (1982) 'Fluctuations in the dollar: a model of nominal and real exchange rate determination', *Journal of International Money and Finance*, April, 1, 39–56.

Horioka, C.Y. (1990) 'Why is Japan's household saving rate so high? A literature survey', *Journal of the Japanese and International Economics*, 4, 49–92.

Horne, Jocelyn and Masson, Paul R. (1988) 'Scope and limits of international economic cooperation and policy coordination', *IMF Staff Papers*, 35, 2, June, 259–96.

Horngren, L. and Viotti, S. (1985) 'Foreign exchange movements and monetary policy – an analysis of the outflow of foreign currency from Sweden in the Spring of 1985', *Skandinaviska Enskilda Banken Quarterly Review*, 2, 46–55.

Horsefield, J.K. (ed.) (1969) *The I.M.F. 1945–1965: Twenty Years of International Monetary Co-operation*, vols 1–3, Washington, D.C.: IMF.

Howrey, E.P. (1969) 'Distributed lags and the effectiveness of monetary policy: notes', *American Economic Review*, 59, December, 997–1001.

Hughes-Hallet, A. (1987) 'Optimal policy design in interdependent economies', in C. Carraro and D. Sartore (eds) *Developments of Control Theory for Economic Analysis*, Dordrecht: Kluwer Academic Publishers.

Humpage, Owen F. (1991) 'Central-Bank intervention: recent literature, continuing controversy', *Economic Review*, 27, 2, 12–26.

Hutchison, Michael (1991) 'Aggregate demand, uncertainty and oil prices: the 1990 oil shock in comparative perspective', *Bank for International Settlements (BIS) Economic Papers*, 31, August.

IMF (1980) IMF Survey 9, 24 November.

—— (1991) 'World Economic Outlook', *World Economic and Financial Surveys*, May.

—— (1992) 'World Economic Outlook', *World Economic and Financial Surveys*, May.

—— (1993) *World Economic Outlook Interim Assessment*, January.

Institute for International Economics (1987) 'Resolving the global economic crisis: after Wall Street', Special Report 6, December.

Ishi, Hironitsu (1986) 'An overview of fiscal deficits in Japan with special reference to the fiscal policy debate', Discussion Paper 7, Institute of Fiscal and Monetary Policy, Ministry of Finance, Japan, April.

Ishii, N., McKibbin, W. and Sachs, J. (1985) 'The economic policy mix, policy cooperation and protectionism: some aspects of macroeconomic interdependence among the United States, Japan and other OECD countries', *Journal of Policy Modelling*, 7, 14, 533–72.

Ishiyama, Y. (1975) 'The theory of optimum currency areas: a survey', *International Monetary Fund Staff Papers*, XXII, 2, July, 344–83.

Jackman, R. and Layard, R. (1987) 'Innovative supply-side policies to reduce unemployment', Discussion Paper 281, London School of Economics, May.

Jackman, R., Pissarides, Christopher and Savouri, Savvas (1990) 'Unemployment policies', *Economic Policy*, October, 449–90.

Jacobson, L.R. (1983) 'Calculations of profitability for US dollar, deutsche mark intervention', *Staff Studies*, 131, Board of Governors of the Federal Reserve System.

Johnson, Christopher (1991) *The Economy under Mrs Thatcher 1979–1990*, London: Penguin Books.

Johnson, G.E. and Layard, P.R.G. (1986) 'The natural rate of unemployment: explanation and policy', in O. Ashenfelter and R. Layard (eds), *Handbook of Labor Economics*, II.

Johnson, Robert A. (1986) 'Anticipated fiscal contraction: the economic consequences of the announcement of Gramm-Rudman-Hollings', *International Finance Discussion Papers*, 291, US Federal Reserve System, July.

Jonson, Peter D. (1987) 'Monetary indicators and the economy', *Reserve Bank Bulletin of Australia*, December.

Journal of Money, Credit and Banking, Special Issue on Rational Expectations, (1980) 2, XII, May.

Jurgensen Report (1983) *Report of the Working Group on Exchange Market Intervention*, Washington, D.C.: United States Treasury.

Kahn, George A. (1988) 'Nominal GNP: an anchor for monetary policy?', *Economic Review*, Federal Reserve Bank of Kansas City, November, 18–35.

Karakitsos, E. (1989) 'Monetary policy exchange rate dynamics and the labour market', *Oxford Economic Papers*, 41, 2, April, 408–33.

Karfakis, Costas (1993) 'Foreign exchange market efficiency: what have we learnt?', unpublished manuscript, Sydney, May.

Kasman, Bruce and Rodrigues, Anthony (1991) 'Financial liberalisation and monetary control in Japan', *Federal Reserve Bank of N.Y. Quarterly Review*, Autumn, 28–46.

Katsimbris, George M. (1985) 'The relationship between the inflation rate, its variability and output growth variability', *Journal of Money, Credit and Banking*, 17, 2, May, 179–88.

Kawai, Masahiro (1985) 'Exchange rates, the current account and monetary fiscal policies in the short run, and in the long run', *Oxford Economic Papers*, 37, 3, September, 391–425.

Kawasaki, Kenichi, Hoeller, Peter and Poret, Pierre (1990) 'Modelling wages and prices for the smaller OECD countries', *OECD Department of Economics and Statistics Working Papers*, 86, October.

Kehoe, Patrick J. (1988) 'Comment on the roles of international financial markets and their relevance for economic policy', *Journal of Money Credit and Banking*, 20, 3, part 2, August, 550–4.

Kenen, Peter B. (1969) 'The theory of optimum currency areas: an eclectic view', in R.A. Mundell and A.K. Swoboda (eds) *Monetary Problems of the International Economy*, Chicago, Ill.: University of Chicago Press.

—— (1987) 'Exchange rates and policy coordination', *Brookings Discussion Papers in International Economics*, 61, October.

—— (1988a) *Managing Exchange Rates*, London: Routledge.

—— (1988b) 'International money and macroeconomics', in Kimberley Ann Elliott and John Williamson (eds) *World Economic Problems*, Institute for International Economics, Special Report No. 7, April.

Kerr, Roger (1991) 'Freedom of contract – NZ's answer to industrial constriction', *Institute of Public Affairs (IPA) Review*, Autumn, 11–13.

Khan, M.S. and Montiel, P.J. (1987) 'Real exchange rate dynamics in a small, primary-producing country', *IMF Staff Papers*, 34, 4, December, 681–710.

Kindleberger, C.P. (1973) *The World in Depression 1929–1939*, Berkeley, Ca.: University of California Press.

Komiya, Ryutaro and Suda, Miyako (1991) *Japan's Foreign Exchange Policy 1971–82*, London: Allen & Unwin.

Komiya, Ryutaro and Yasui, Kazuo (1984) 'Japan's macroeconomic performance since the First Oil Crisis: Review and appraisal', *Carnegie Rochester Conference Series on Public Policy*, 20, 69–114.

Kormendi, R.C. (1983) 'Government debt, Government spending and private sector behavior', *The American Economic Review*, 73, 5, December, 994–1010.

Kouri, P.J.K. (1976) 'The exchange rate and the balance of payments in the short run and in the long run: a monetary approach', *Scandinavian Journal Economics*, 2, 78, 280–304.

Kouri, P.J.K. and Porter, M.G. (1974) 'International capital flows and portfolio equilibrium', *Journal of Political Economy*, 82, 443–67.

Kreinin, Mordechai (1975) *International Economics: A Policy Approach*, 2nd ed, Harcourt Brace Jovanovich, Inc., USA.

Kremers, Jeroen J.M. (1990) 'Gaining policy credibility for a disinflation', *IMF Staff Papers*, 37, 1, March, 116–45.

Krueger, A.O. (1983) *Exchange Rate Determination*, Cambridge: Cambridge University Press.

Krugman, Paul (1987) 'Slow growth in Europe: conceptual issues,' in Robert Z. Lawrence and Charles L. Schultze (eds) *Barriers to European Growth: A Transatlantic View*, Washington, D.C.: Brookings Institute.

—— (1989) *Exchange-Rate Instability*, Cambridge, Mass.: MIT Press.

—— (1991) 'Target zones and exchange rate dynamics', *Quarterly Journal of Economics*, 106, August, 669–82.

Krugman, P. and Baldwin, R.E. (1987) 'The persistence of the US trade deficit', *Brookings Papers on Economic Activity*, 1, 1–56.

Krugman, Paul and Miller, Marcus (eds) (1992) *Exchange Rate Targets and Currency Bands*, Cambridge: Cambridge University Press.

Kurosaka, Y. (1991) 'A simple estimation of the Nairu in the Japanese economy: 1953–85', Discussion Paper 45, Centre for Economic Performance, London School of Economics, August.

Kydland, F.E. and Prescott, E.C. (1977) 'Rules rather than discretion: The inconsistency of optimal plans', *Journal of Political Economy*, 85, 3, June, 473–91.

Lanyi, A. (1969) 'The case for floating exchange rates reconsidered', *Essays in International Finance* 72, Princeton University, Princeton, N.J.

—— (1975) 'Separate exchange markets for capital and current transactions', *International Monetary Fund Staff Papers*, XXII, November, 714–49.

Layard, Richard (1990) 'Wage bargaining and incomes policy: possible lessons for Eastern Europe', *Centre for Economic Performance Discussion Paper*, 2, May.

Layard, R. and Nickell, S. (1989) 'The Thatcher miracle?' Discussion Paper 343, Centre for Labour Economics, London School of Economics, March.

Layard, Richard, Nickell, Stephen and Jackman, Richard (1991) *Unemployment, Macroeconomic Performance and the Labour Market*, Oxford: Oxford University Press.

Leiderman, Leonardo and Blejer, Mario I. (1988) 'Modeling and testing Ricardian equivalence', *IMF Staff Papers*, 35, 1, March, 1–35.

Leventakis, John A. (1987) 'Exchange rate models: do they work?' *Weltwirtschaftliches Archiv*, 123, 2, 363–76.

Levich, R.M. (1985) 'Empirical studies of exchange rates: price behavior, rate determination and market efficiency', in R. Jones and P. Kenen, (eds) *Handbook of International Economics*, 2, Amsterdam: North Holland.

Lincoln, E. (1990) *Japan's Unequal Trade*, Washington, D.C.: Brookings Institution.

Lindbeck, Assar (1988) 'Consequences of the advanced welfare state', *The World Economy*, 11, March, 19–38.

—— (1990) 'The Swedish experience', Seminar Paper 482, Institute for International Economic Studies.

—— (1991) 'Microfoundations of unemployment theory', Seminar Paper 503, Institute for International Economic Studies, Stockholm University, October.

Lindbeck, Assar and Snower, Dennis (1985) 'Explanations of unemployment', *Oxford Review of Economic Policy*, 1, 2, 34–59.

—— and —— (1987) 'Efficiency wages versus insiders and outsiders', *European Economic Review* 31, February–March 407–16.

—— (1989) 'Demand and supply-side policies and unemployment: policy implications of the insider-outsider approach', *Institute for International Economic Studies Seminar Paper*, 439, April.

Lindert, P. (1969) 'Key currencies and gold: 1900–1913', *Princeton Studies in International Finance*, Princeton University, Princeton, N.J.

Llewellyn, J. (1983) 'Resource prices and macro economic policies: lessons from two oil price shocks', *OECD Economic Studies*, 1, Autumn, 197–212.

Loef, Hans E. (1989) 'The case for rules in the conduct of monetary policy: a critique on a paper by B.T. McCallum', *Weltwirtschaftliches Archiv*, 125, 1, 168–82.

Lucas, R.F. (1989) 'The Bank of Canada and zero inflation: a new cross of gold?' *Canadian Public Policy*, XV, 1, 84–93.

McCallum, Bennett T. (1987) 'The case for rules in the conduct of monetary policy: a concrete example', *Economic Review Federal Reserve Bank of Richmond*, 73–5, September–October, 10–18.

—— (1988) 'Robustness properties of a rule for monetary policy', *Carnegie-Rochester Conference Series on Public Policy*, 29, Amsterdam: North-Holland, 173–204.

—— (1992)'Specification of policy rules and performance measures in multicountry simulation studies', National Bureau of Economic Research, Working Paper 4233, December.

McConnell, S. and Takla, L. (1990) 'Mrs Thatcher's trade union legislation: has it reduced strikes? Discussion Paper 374, Centre for Labour Economics, London School of Economics, January.

McDonald, Ian M. (1989) 'How far should Mr. Keating go?', *The Australian Economic Review*, 2nd quarter, 25–8.

MacDonald, R. (1984) 'The monetary approach to the exchange rate revisited', *Applied Economics*, 16, 5, October, 771–82.

MacDonald, Ronald and Taylor, Mark P. (1992) 'Exchange rate economics: a survey', *IMF Staff Papers*, 39, 1, March, 1–57.

MacFarlane, I.J. (1991) 'The lessons for monetary policy, prepared for the Reserve Bank of Australia', *Proceedings of the Conference on Deregulation of Financial Intermediaries*, Sydney: Reserve Bank of Australia, June.

McKibbin, Warwick J. (1988a) Policy analysis with the MSG2 model', *Australian Economic Papers*, supplement, 27 June, 126–150.

—— (1988b) 'Time-consistent policies: a survey of the issues', Research Discussion Paper 8801, Reserve Bank of Australia.

—— (1989) 'The world economy from 1979 to 1988: results from the MSG2 model', *Brookings Discussion Papers in International Economics*, 72, Brookings Institution, April.

McKibbin, Warwick and Sachs, Jeffrey (1986) 'Coordination of monetary and fiscal policies in the OECD', National Bureau of Economic Research Working Paper 1800, in Jacob Frenkel (ed.) *International Aspects of Fiscal Policy*, Chicago, Ill.: University of Chicago Press.

—— and —— (1989) 'Implications of policy rules for the world economy', in R. Bryant *et al.* (eds) *Macroeconomic Policies in an Interdependent World*, Washington, D.C.: Brookings Institution; London: Centre for Economic Policy Research; Washington, D.C.: IMF.

—— and —— (1991) *Global Linkages: Macroeconomic Interdependence and Cooperation in the World Economy*, Washington, D.C.: Brookings Institute.

McKinnon, Ronald I. (1969) 'Portfolio balance and international payments', in R.A. Mundell and A.K. Swoboda (eds), *Monetary Problems of the International Economy*, Chicago, Ill.: University of Chicago Press, 199–235.

—— (1971) 'Monetary theory and controlled flexibility in the foreign exchanges', *Essays in International Finance*, Princeton University, New Jersey.

—— (1984) *An International Standard for Monetary Stabilisation*, Washington, D.C.: Institute for International Economics.

—— (1988) 'Monetary and exchange rate policies for international financial stability: a proposal', *Journal of Economic Perspectives*, 2, 83–103.

McKinnon, Ronald I. and Oates, Wallace R. (1966) 'The implications of international economic integration for monetary, fiscal, and exchange rate policy', *Princeton Studies in International Finance*, 16, Princeton University, New Jersey.

McNees, Stephen K. (1987) 'Prospective nominal GNP targeting: an alternative framework for monetary policy', *New England Economic Review*, Federal Reserve Bank of Boston, September–October, 3–9.

Maddison, A. (1986) 'Growth and slowdown in advanced capitalist economies', *Journal of Economic Literature*, XXV, June, 649–98.

Malinvaud, E. (1977) *The Theory of Unemployment Reconsidered*, Oxford: Basil Blackwell.

Marston, R.C. (1982) 'Wages, relative prices and the choice between fixed and flexible exchange rates', *The Canadian Journal of Economics*, XV, 1, February, 87–103.

—— (1985) 'Stabilization policies in open economies', in R.W. Jones and P.B. Kenen (eds) *Handbook of International Economics*, 2, Amsterdam: North Holland.

Marston, Richard C. and Turnovsky, Stephen (1985) 'Imported materials, prices, wage policy and macro-economic stabilization', *Canadian Journal of Economics*, XVIII, 2, May, 273–84.

Martin, W.J., Murphy C.W. and Nguyen, D.T. (1987) 'Influences on the Australian real exchange rate: an analysis using the amps model, Discussion Paper 177, The ANU Centre for Economic Policy Research, August.

Masson, Paul and Blundell-Wignall, Adrian (1985) 'Fiscal policy and the exchange rate in the big seven', *European Economic Review*, 28, 11–42.

Masson, P.R. and Knight, M. (1986) 'International transmission of fiscal policies in major industrial countries', *International Monetary Fund Staff Papers*, 33, 3, September, 387–438.

Masson, P.R. and Taylor, M.P. (1992) 'Issues in the operation of monetary unions and common currency areas' in *Policy Issues in the Evolving International Monetary System*, IMF Occasional Paper 96, June.

Masson, Paul, Symansky, Steven and Meredith, Guy (1990) *MultiMod Mark II*: *A revised and Extended Model*, Washington, D.C.: IMF, July.

Mathieson, Donald J. (1977) 'The impact of monetary and fiscal policy under flexible exchange rates and alternative expectations structures', *IMF Staff Papers*, XXIV, 3, November, 535–568.

Mayer, H. and Taguchi, H. (1983) 'Official intervention in the exchange markets: stabilising or destabilising?' *Bank for International Settlements (BIS) Economics Papers*, 6, March.

Meade, J.E. (1951) *The Balance of Payments*: *The Theory of International Economic Policy*, 1, Oxford: Oxford University Press.

—— (1978) 'The meaning of internal balance', *Economic Journal*, 88, 423–35.

Meese, R. and Rogoff, K. (1983) 'Empirical exchange rate models of the seventies: do they fit out of sample', *Journal of International Economics*, 14, February, 3–24.

Meltzer, A.H. (1987) 'Limits of short-run stabilization policy', *Economic Inquiry*, XXV, January, 1–14.

—— (1988) 'On monetary stability and monetary reform', in Y. Suzuki and M. Okabe (eds) *Toward a World of Economic Stability*, Tokyo: University of Tokyo Press.

Meredith, Guy (1992) 'Discretionary monetary policy versus rules: the Japanese experience during 1986–91', IMF Working Paper 92/63, August.

Metcalf, D. (1988) 'Trade unions and economic performance: the British evidence', Discussion Paper 320, Centre for Labour Economics, London School of Economics.

Metzler, L.A. (1951) 'Wealth, saving, and the rate of interest', *Journal of Political Economy*, 59: 93–116.

Miller, Marcus and Sutherland, Alan (1990) 'Monetary and exchange rate targets, and after: a stochastic "hard landing" for sterling?', in V. Argy and P. De Grauwe (eds) *Choosing an Exchange Rate Regime*: *The challenge for smaller industrial countries*, Washington, D.C.: IMF.

—— and —— (1991) The 'Walters Critique' of the EMS – a case of inconsistent expectations?, *The Manchester School*, LIX supplement, June, 23–37.

—— and —— (1992) 'Britain's return to gold and entry into the EMS: joining conditions and credibility', in P. Krugman and M. Miller (eds) *Exchange Rate Targets and Currency Bands*, Cambridge: Cambridge University Press.

Miller, Marcus and Weller, Paul (1991a) 'Financial Liberalisation, Asset Prices and Exchange Rates', OECD Working Paper 95, February.

—— and —— (1991b) 'Currency bands, target zones, and price flexibility', *IMF Staff Papers*, 38, 1, March, 184–215.

Miller, N.C. (1980) 'Offset and growth coefficient for 5 industrial countries 1960–70', *Review of Economics and Statistics*, 3, LXII, 329–38.

Minford, Patrick (1988) 'Wages and unemployment half a century on', Discussion Paper 262, Centre for Economic Policy Research, August.

Minford, P. and Peel, D. (1983) *Rational Expectations and the New Macro-economics*, Oxford: Martin Robertson.

Modigliani, Franco (1977) 'The monetarist controversy or should we forsake stabilization policies', *American Economic Review*, 67, 2, March, 1–19.

—— (1988) 'Reagan's economic policies: a critique', *Oxford Economic Papers*, 40, 397–426.

Moggridge, D.E. (1972) *British Monetary Policy 1924–1931*: *The Norman Conquest of $4.86*, Cambridge: Cambridge University Press.

Molho, Lalzaros (1990) 'The significance of the current account: implications of European financial integration', IMF Working Paper 90/30.

Montiel, P.J. (1987) 'Output and unanticipated money in the dependent economy model', *IMF Staff Papers*, 34, 2, June, 228–59.

Moore, B.J. (1972) 'Optimal monetary policy', *Economic Journal*, 82, 116–29.

Muellbauer, J.M.J. and Portes, R.D. (1978) 'Macroeconomic Models with Quantity Rationing', *Economic Journal*, 88, 788–821.

Mundell, Robert A. (1961) 'A theory of optimum currency areas', *The American Economic Review*, 51, September, 657–65.

—— (1962) 'The appropriate use of monetary and fiscal policy for internal and external stability', *International Monetary Fund Staff Papers*, IX, March, 70–9.

—— (1963a) 'Capital mobility and stabilisation policy under fixed and flexible exchange rates', *Canadian Journal of Economics and Political Science*, XXIX, November, 475–85.

—— (1963b) 'Inflation and real interest', *Journal of Political Economy*, 71, 3, 280–3.

—— (1964) 'A reply: capital mobility and size', *Canadian Journal of Economics and Political Science*, 30, August, 421–31.

Murfin, A. and Ormerod, P. (1984) 'The forward rate for the U.S. Dollar and the efficient markets hypothesis, 1978–1983', *The Manchester School*, 3, September, 292–9.

Murphy, Chris W. (1991) 'The transitional costs of reducing inflation using monetary policy, in Australia's inflation problem', *Economic Planning Advisory Council Background Paper*, 11, April.

Murphy, R.G. and Van Duyne, C. (1980) 'Asset market approaches to exchange rate determination: a comparative analysis', *Weltwirtschaftliches Archiv*, 4, 116, 627–55.

Murray, John, Williamson, Shane and Zelmer, Mark (1990) 'Measuring the profitability and effectiveness of foreign exchange market intervention: some Canadian evidence', *Bank of Canada Technical Report*, 53, March.

Mussa, M. (1979a) 'Macroeconomic interdependence and the exchange rate regime', in R. Dornbusch and J.A. Frenkel (eds) *International Economic Policy: Theory and Evidence*, Baltimore, Md: Johns Hopkins University Press.

—— (1979b) 'Empirical regularities in the behavior of exchange rates and theories of the foreign exchange market in Carnegie Rochester conference series', in *Policies for Employment, Prices, and Exchange Rates*, Amsterdam: North-Holland.

Nakao, Masaaki and Horii, Akinari (1991) 'The process of decision-making and implementation of monetary policy in Japan', Bank of Japan, Special Paper 198, March.

Nester, William (1990) *The Foundation of Japanese Power*, London: Macmillan.

Newell, A. and Symons, J.S.V. (1987) 'Corporatism, the laissez-faire and the rise in unemployment', *European Economic Review*, 31, 3, 567–601.

Nicholl, P.W.E. (1977) 'New Zealand monetary policy in the 1970s: analysis and perspective', Reserve Bank of New Zealand, Research Paper 23, December, 7–19.

Nickell, S. and Wadhwani, S. (1989) 'Insider forces and wage determination', Discussion Paper 334, Centre for Labour Economics, London School of Economics, January.

Nicoletti, Giuseppe (1988) 'Private consumption, inflation and the "debt neutrality hypothesis": the case of eight OECD countries', *Department of Economics and Statistics Working Papers*, 50, OECD, Paris, January.

Niehans, Jürg (1968) 'Monetary and fiscal policies in open economies under fixed exchange rates: an optimizing approach', *Journal of Political Economy*, 76, 893–920.

—— (1975) 'Some doubts about the efficacy of monetary policy under flexible exchange rates', *Journal of International Economics*, 5, 275–81.

Oates, W.E. (1966) 'Budget balance and equilibrium income: a comment on the efficacy of fiscal and monetary policy in an open economy', *Journal of Finance*, 21, 489–98.

O'Brien, Paul Francis and Browne, Frank (1992) 'A "Credit crunch"? The recent slowdown in bank lending and its implications for monetary policy', OECD Economics and Statistics Department Working Papers, 107.

Obstfeld, Maurice (1986) 'Capital mobility in the world economy: theory and measurement', *Carnegie-Rochester Conference Series on Public Policy*, 24, Amsterdam, Spring, 105–14.

—— (1988) 'The effectiveness of foreign-exchange intervention: recent experience', NBER Working Paper 2796, National Bureau of Economic Research, Cambridge, Mass., December.

OECD (1972) *Monetary Policy in Japan Monetary Studies Series*, OECD, December.

—— (1977) *Towards Full Employment and Price Stability*, The McCracken Report, Paris, June.

—— (1983) *Annual Survey of the United States – Paris*.

—— (1985) *Exchange Rate Management and the Conduct of Monetary Policy*, Monetary Studies Series, Paris.

—— (1987) *Economic Outlook*, Paris: OECD, December.

—— (1988) *Economic Outlook*, Paris: OECD, June.

—— (1989a) *Economies in Transition*, Paris: OECD.

—— (1989b) *Economic Survey of Japan*, 1988–1989, Paris: OECD.

—— (1990) *Labour Market Policies for the 1990s*, Paris: OECD.

—— (1992) *Economic Outlook*, Paris: OECD, June.

—— Annual Surveys of Australia and New Zealand.

Okina, Kunio and Ui, T. (1992) 'Puzzling movements of M2CDs since the mid-1980s: is it still useful?', Macquarie University Centre for Japanese Economic Studies Working Paper 92–4.

Okun, Arthur M. (1971) 'The mirage of steady inflation', *Brookings Papers on Economic Activity*, 2, 485–98.

—— (1972) 'Fiscal-monetary activism: some analytical issues', *Brookings Papers on Economic Activity*, 1, 123–63.

—— (1975) 'Inflation: its mechanics and welfare cost', *Brookings Papers on Economic Activity*, 2, 351–401.

Oliva, di Juan Carlos Martinez (1987) 'Macroeconomic policy coordination of interdependent economies: the game-theory approach in a static framework', *Banca D'Italia Discussion Paper*, 96, October.

Oliva, di Juan Carlos Martinez and Sinn, Stefan (1988) 'The game-theoretic approach to international policy coordination: assessing the role of targets', *Weltwirtschaftliches Archiv*, 124, 2, 252–67.

Onitsuka, Yusuke (1990) 'The Oil Crises and Japan's internal-external adjustment', University of Tokyo, Working Paper 15, March.

Oudiz, G. and Sachs, J. (1984) 'Macroeconomic policy coordination among the industrial economies', *Brookings Papers on Economic Activity*, 1.

Patinkin, Don (1965) *Money, Interest, and Prices*, 2nd edn, London: Harper and Row.

Pauly, Peter and Peterson, Christian E. (1990) 'Feedback rules for nominal income targeting', prepared for Brookings Conference on Empirical Evaluation of Alternative Policy Regimes, Washington, D.C., 8–9 March.

Peck, Merton J. (1986) 'Is Japan really a share economy?', *Journal of Comparative Economics*, 10, 427–32.

Penati, Alessandro (1983) 'Expansionary fiscal policy and the exchange rate', *IMF Staff Papers*, 30, 3, September, 542–69.

Persson, Torsten (1988) 'Credibility of macroeconomic policy: an introduction and a broad survey', *European Economic Review*, 32, 519–532.

Phelps, Edmund S. (1968) 'Money-wage dynamics and labour market equilibrium', *Journal of Political Economy*, 76, August, 678–711.

—— (1973) 'Inflation in the theory of public finance', *The Swedish Journal of Economics*, 75, 67–82.

Phillips, A.W. (1957) 'Stabilization policy and the time form of lagged responses', *Economic Journal*, 67, 265–77.

Pierce, J.L. (1984) 'Did financial innovation hurt the great monetarist experiment?' *The American Economic Review*, Papers and Proceedings, 74, 2, May, 372–6.

Pitchford, John (1990) *Australia's Foreign Debt – Myths and Realities*, Sydney: Allen & Unwin.

Poole, William (1970) 'Optimal choice of monetary policy instruments in a simple stochastic macro-model', *Quarterly Journal of Economics*, LXXXIV, May, 197–216.

Porter, M.G. (1974) 'The interdependence of monetary policy and capital flows in Australia', *Economic Record*, 50, 1–20.

Prachowny, M.F.J. (1984) *Macroeconomic Analysis for Small Open Economies*, Oxford: Clarendon Press.

Purvis, Douglas D. (1985) 'Innis lecture: public sector deficits, international capital movements, and the domestic economy: the medium term is the message', *Canadian Journal of Economics*, XVIII, 4, November, 723–42.

Reserve Bank of New Zealand (1986) *Financial Policy Reform*, Wellington.

—— (1992) *Monetary Policy and the New Zealand Financial System*, 3rd edn.

Reserve Bank of New Zealand Quarterly Bulletins.

Rich, Georg (1991) 'The orientation of monetary policy and the monetary policy decision-making process in Switzerland', *The Orientation of Monetary Policy and the Monetary Policy Decision-Making Process*, Bank for International Settlements (BIS), Basle, 390, April, 191–200.

Roberts, Paul Craig (1991) 'What everyone "knows" about Reaganomics', *Commentary*, 91, 2, February, 25–30.

Rodriguez, C.A. (1979) 'Short and long-run effects of monetary and fiscal policies under flexible exchange rates and perfect capital mobility', *American Economic Review*, 69, 176–82.

Rogoff, Kenneth (1985a) 'The optimal degree of commitment to an intermediate monetary target', *Quarterly Journal of Economics*, 100, 4, November, 1169–90.

—— (1985b) 'Can international monetary policy cooperation be counterproductive?', *Journal of International Economics*, 18, February, 199–217.

—— (1987) 'Reputational constraints on monetary policy', *Carnegie-Rochester Conference Series on Public Policy*, 26, Amsterdam: North-Holland, 141–182.

Rowan, D. (1976) 'Godley's law, Godley's rule and the "New Cambridge Macroeconomics"', *Banca Nazionale del Lavoro Quarterly Review*, 117, 151–74.

Russo, Massimo and Tullio, Giuseppe (1988) 'The European monetary system: a balance between rules and discretion', IMF Occasional Paper 61, September, 3–37.

Sachs, Jeffrey D. (1980) 'Wages, flexible rates and macroeconomic policy', *Quarterly Journal of Economics*, 94, June, 731–47.

—— (1981) 'The current account and macroeconomic adjustment in the 1970s', *Brookings Papers on Economic Activity*, 1, 201–82.

Sachs, Jeffrey and Wyplosz, Charles (1984) 'Real exchange rate effects of fiscal policy', Discussion Paper 1050, Harvard Institute of Economic Research, April.

Sanderson, P. (1984) 'Rational expectations and forward exchange market efficiency', *Applied Economics*, 16, 1, February, 99–109.

Sargent, T.J. and Wallace, N. (1976) 'Rational expectations and the theory of economic policy', *Journal of Monetary Economics*, 2, 169–83.

—— and —— (1981) 'Some unpleasant monetarist arithmetic', *Federal Reserve Bank of Minneapolis Quarterly Review*, Fall, 1–17.

Scarth, W.M. (1975) 'Fiscal policy and the government budget constraint under alternative exchange rate systems', *Oxford Economic Papers*, 27, 1, March, 10–20.

Scheide, Joachim (1989) 'A K-percent rule for monetary policy in West Germany', *Weltwirtschaftliches Archiv*, 125, 2, 326–35.

Schinasi, Garry J. (1989) 'European integration, exchange rate management, and monetary reform; a review of the major issues', *US Federal Reserve System – International Finance Discussion Papers*, 364, October.

Schmid, P. and Hermann, H. (1991) 'The orientation of monetary policy and the monetary policy decision-making process in Switzerland', *The Orientation of Monetary Policy and the Monetary Policy Decision-Making Process*, Bank for International Settlements (BIS), Basle, 390, April, 191–200.

Shigehara, Kumiharu (1982) 'Absorption of the two oil shocks, the Japanese case', *European Economic Review*, 18, 249–61.

—— (1990) 'Some reflections on monetary policy issues in Japan', *Monetary and Economic Studies*, Bank of Japan, 8, 2, September, 1–8.

Shinkai, Yoichi (1990) 'Evaluation of the Bretton Woods regime and the floating exchange rate system', in Y. Suzuki, J. Miyake and M. Okabe (eds) *The Evolution of the International Monetary System – How can Efficiency and Stability be Attained?*, Tokyo: University of Tokyo Press.

Simes, Richard (1991) 'The monetary transmission mechanism in macroeconometric models of the Australian economy', in Colm Kearney and Ronald MacDonald (eds) *Developments in Australian Monetary Economics*, Cheshire: Longman.

Sinclair, Peter (1987) *Unemployment: Economic Theory and Evidence*, Oxford: Basil Blackwell.

Sivesind, C. and Hurley, K. (1980) 'Choosing an operation target for monetary policy', *Quarterly Journal of Economics*, XCIV, February, 199–203.

Soltwedel, R. (1988) 'Employment problems in West Germany – the role of institutions, labor law, and government intervention, in stabilization policies and labor markets', *Carnegie-Rochester Conference Series on Public Policy*, 28, Spring, 153–220.

Spencer, G.H. (1980) 'Monetary targets: comparison of some alternative aggregates', Research Paper 30, Reserve Bank of New Zealand, May, 16–23.

—— (1990) 'Monetary policy: the New Zealand experience 1985–1990', *Reserve Bank Bulletin*, 53, 3, 252–66.

—— (1992) 'Monetary policy: the New Zealand experience 1985–1990', *Monetary Policy and the New Zealand Financial System*, Reserve Bank of New Zealand, 3rd edn.

Summers, Lawrence H. (1981) 'Optimal inflation policy', *Journal of Monetary Economics*, 7, 2, March, 175–194

—— (1987) 'A few good taxes', *New Republic* (Washington), 30 November, 14–15.

Suzuki, Yoshio (1984) 'Monetary policy in Japan: transmission mechanism and effectiveness', *Bank of Japan Monetary and Economic Studies*, 2, 2, December, 1–22.

—— (1985) 'Japan's monetary policy over the past ten years', *Bank of Japan Monetary and Economic Studies*, 3, 3, September, 1–10.

Suzuki, Y. and Yomo, H. (eds) (1986) *Financial Innovation and Monetary Policy: Asia and the West*, Tokyo: University of Tokyo Press.

Svensson, Lars E.O. (1992a) 'Why exchange rate bands? Monetary independence in spite of fixed exchange rates', Working Paper 4207, National Bureau of Economic Research, November.

—— (1992b) 'An interpretation of recent research on exchange rate target zones', *Journal of Economic Perspectives*, 6, 4, Fall, 119–44.

Svensson, Lars and Razin, A. (1983) 'The terms of trade, spending and the current account: the Harberger–Laursen–Metzler effect', *Journal of Political Economy*, 97–125.

Swamy, P.A.V.B. and Tavlas, George S. (1989) 'Financial deregulation, the demand for money, and monetary policy in Australia, *IMF Staff Papers*, 36, 1, March, 63–101.

Swan, T.W. (1955) 'Longer run problems of the balance of payments', in H.W. Arndt and W.M. Corden (eds) *The Australian Economy: A Volume of Readings*, Melbourne: Cheshire Press.

Swinburne, M. and Castello-Branco, M. (1991) 'Central bank independence: issues and experience 1', IMF Working Paper 91/58, June.

Swoboda, A.K. (1978) 'Gold, euro-dollars and the world money stock under fixed exchange rates', *The American Economic Review*, 68, September, 625–42.

Swoboda, A.K. and Dornbusch, R. (1973) 'Adjustment, policy and monetary equilibrium in a two-country model', in M.B. Connolly and A.K. Swoboda (eds), *International Trade and Money*, London: Allen & Unwin.

Tachibanaki, Toshiaki (1987) 'Labour market flexibility in Japan in comparison with Europe and the US', *European Economic Review*, 31, 647–84.

Takagi, Shinji (1991) 'Exchange rate expectations', *IMF Staff Papers*, 38, 1, March, 156–83.

Takeda, Masahiko and Turner, Philip (1992) 'The liberalisation of Japan's financial markets: some major themes', *Bank for International Settlements (BIS) Economic Papers*, 34, November.

Taylor, D. (1982) 'Official intervention in the foreign exchange market or bet against the central bank', *Journal of Political Economy*, 90, 2, 356–68.

Taylor, John B. (1980) 'Aggregate dynamics and staggered contracts', *Journal of Political Economy*, 88, 1, February, 1–24.

—— (1981) 'Stabilization, accommodation and monetary rules', *The American Economic Review, Papers and Proceedings*, 71, May, 145–9.

—— (1985a) 'What would nominal GNP targeting do to the business cycle?', in *Understanding Monetary Regimes, Carnegie-Rochester Conference Series on Public Policy*, 22, 61–84.

—— (1985b) 'International coordination and design of macroeconomic policy rules', *European Economic Review*, 28, 53–81.

—— (1989a) 'Analysis with a multi-country model', in R. Bryant *et al.* (eds) *Macroeconomic Policies in an Interdependent World*, Washington, D.C.: Brookings Institution; London: Centre for Economic Policy Research; Washington, D.C.: IMF.

—— (1989b) 'Differences in economic fluctuations in Japan and the United States: the role of nominal rigidities', *Journal of the Japanese and International Economies*, 3, 127–44.

Taylor, Mark (1990) 'Charts, noise and fundamentals: a study of the London foreign exchange market', Discussion Paper 341, Centre for Economic Policy Research, London, October.

Theil, H.C. (1961) *Economic Forecasts and Policy*, 2nd revised edn, Amsterdam: North-Holland.

Thomas, L.B. (1973) 'Behavior of flexible exchange rates: additional tests from the post World War 1 episode', *Southern Economic Journal*, 40, October, 167–82.

Tinbergen, J. (1952) *On the Theory on Economic Policy*, Amsterdam: North-Holland.

Tobin, James (1965) 'Money and economic growth', *Econometrica*, 33, 4, 671–84.

—— (1969) 'A general equilibrium approach to monetary theory', *Journal of Money, Credit and Banking*, 1, 15–29.

—— (1972) 'Inflation and unemployment', *The American Economic Review*, 62, March, 1–18.

—— (1978) 'A proposal for international monetary reform', Discussion Paper 506, Cowles Foundation for Research Economics, New Haven: Yale University.

—— (1980) 'Stabilization policy ten years after', *Brookings Papers on Economic Activity*, 1, 19–78.

Tobin, J. and Buiter, W.H. (1976) 'Long-run effects of fiscal and monetary policy on aggregate demand', in J.L. Stein (ed.) *Monetarism*, Amsterdam: North-Holland, 273–309.

Tootell, Geoffrey M.B. (1990) 'How natural is the natural rate of unemployment in Europe?', *New England Economic Review, Federal Reserve Bank of Boston*, January–February, 23–36.

Triffin, R. (1960) *Gold and the Dollar Crisis*, New Haven, Conn.: Yale University Press.

—— (1964) 'The evolution of the international monetary system: historical reappraisal and future perspectives', *Princeton Studies in International Finance*, 12, Princeton University, Princeton, N.J.

Tucker, D.P. (1966) 'Dynamic income adjustment to money supply changes', *American Economic Review*, 56, 433–49.

Tullio, Giuseppe (1987) 'Long run implications of the increase in taxation and public debt for employment and economic growth in Europe', *European Economic Review*, 31, 741–80.

Turnovsky, Stephen J. (1976) 'The dynamics of fiscal policy in an open economy', *Journal of International Economics*, 6, May, 115–42.

—— (1977) *Macroeconomic Analysis and Stabilization Policies*, Cambridge: Cambridge University Press.

—— (1981) 'Monetary policy and foreign price disturbances under flexible exchange rates: a stochastic approach', *Journal of Money, Credit and Banking*, 13, 2, May, 156–76.

—— (1984) 'Exchange market intervention under alternative forms of exogenous disturbances', *Journal of International Economics*, 17, 279–97.

—— (1985) 'Optimal exchange market intervention: two alternative classes of rules', in J.S. Bhandari (ed.) *Exchange Rate Management Under Uncertainty*, Cambridge, Mass.: MIT Press.

—— (1986) 'Monetary and fiscal policy under perfect foresight: a symmetric two country analysis, *Economica*, 53, May, 139–57.

Turnovsky, S. J. and Kingston, G.H. (1977) 'Monetary and fiscal policies under flexible exchange rates and perfect myopic foresight in an inflationary world', *Scandinavian Journal of Economics*, 79, 424–41.

Turnovsky, S.J. and Miller, M.H. (1984) 'The effects of government expenditure on the term structure of interest rates', *Journal of Money, Credit and Banking*, 16, 1, February, 16–33.

Twrdy, Karen (1992) 'Has financial deregulation improved the efficiency and competitiveness of the banking sector?' Honours thesis, Macquarie University, Sydney, June.

Ueda, Kazuo (1983) 'Permanent and temporary changes in the exchange rate and trade balance dynamics', *Journal of International Economics*, 15, 1/2, August 27–44.

Ungerer, Horst, Hauvonen, Jouko J., Lopez-Claros, Augusto and Mayer, Thomas (1990) 'The European Monetary System: developments and perspectives', IMF Occasional Paper 73, November.

Valentine, Tom J. (1992) 'The impact of banking deregulation: further thoughts', *Economic Papers*, Economic Society of Australia, 11, 2, 87–93.

Vane, Howard (1992) 'The Thatcher years: macroeconomic policy and performance of the UK economy, 1979–1988', *National Westminster Bank Quarterly Review*, May, 26–43.

Van Wolferen, Karel (1989) *The Enigma of Japanese Power*, London: Macmillan.

Vaubel, Roland (1985) 'International collusion or competition for macroeconomic policy coordination? a restatement', *Recherches Economiques de Louvain*, 51, 223–40.

Vinals, Jose (1986) 'Fiscal policy and the current account', *Economic Policy*, 3, October, 711–31.

Vollmer, Uwe (1988) 'Reasons for Japan's low unemployment rate', *Intereconomics*, 23, November–December, 297–300.

Wadhwani, S. and Wall, M. (1990) 'The effects of profit-sharing on employment wages, stock returns and productivity: evidence from UK micro-data', *Economic Journal*, 100, March, 1–17.

Wagner, Helmut M. (1989) 'Alternatives of disinflation and stability policy – cost, efficiency and implementability: a comparison between Japan and West Germany', *Bank of Japan Monetary and Economic Studies*, 7, 1, April, 41–97.

Wallich, Henry C. (1984) 'Institutional cooperation in the world economy', in Jacob A. Frenkel and Michael L. Mussa (eds) *The World Economic System: Performance and Prospects*, Dover, Mass.: Auburn House.

Walters, Alan (1990) *Sterling in Danger*, London: Fontana.

Weale, Martin, Blake, Andrew, Christodoulakis, Nicos, Meade, James and Vines, David (1989) *Macroeconomic Policy: Inflation, Wealth and the Exchange Rate*, London: Allen & Unwin.

Weidenbaum, Murray (1988) *Rendezvous with Reality*, New York: Basic Books.

Weiner, Stuart E. (1987) 'Why is Japan's unemployment rate so low and so stable?', *Economic Review Federal Reserve Bank of Kansas City*, April, 3–18.

Weitzman, M.L. (1984) *The Share Economy*, Cambridge: Harvard University Press.

—— (1985) 'The simple macroeconomics of profit-sharing', *American Economic Review*, 75, 3, December, 937–53.

Wells, Graeme (1990) 'Economic reform and macroeconomic policy in New Zealand, *The Australian Economic Review*, 4th Quarter, 45–60.

Whitman, Von Neumann Marina (1970) 'Policies for internal and external balance', *Special Papers in International Economics*, 9, Princeton University, New Jersey, December.

Williamson, John (ed.) (1981) *Exchange Rate Rules*, London: Macmillan.

—— (1983) 'The exchange rate system', *Institute for International Economics*, 5, Washington, D.C., September.

—— (1990) 'Equilibrium exchange rates: an update', October, manuscript, Washington, D.C.: Institute for International Economics.

Williamson, John and Miller, M.H. (1987) 'Targets and indicators: a blueprint for the international coordination of economic policy', *Institute for International Economics*, 22, September.

Wilson, Charles A. (1979) 'Anticipated shocks and exchange rate dynamics', *Journal of Political Economy*, 87, 3, 639–47.

Woo, W.T. (1985) 'The monetary approach to exchange rate determination under rational expectations: the dollar–deutsch mark rate', *Journal of International Economics*, 18, February, 1–16.

Yeager, L.B. (1976) *International Monetary Relations: Theory, History and Policy*, 2nd edn, New York: Harper & Row.

Yoshida, Tomoo and Rasche, Robert H. (1990) 'The M2 demand in Japan: shifted and unstable?' *Monetary and Economic Studies*, Bank of Japan, 8, 2, September, 9–30.

Yoshikawa, Hiroshi and Yoshiyuki, Takeuchi (1989) 'Real wages and the Japanese economy', *Bank of Japan Monetary and Economic Studies*, 7, 1, April, 1–40.

Index